STUDY GUIDE AND STUDENT'S SOLUTIONS MANUAL

GAIL ILLICH
McLennan Community College

PAUL ILLICH
Southeast Community College

STATISTICS FOR MANAGERS USING MICROSOFT® EXCEL®

NINTH EDITION

David Levine
Baruch College, City University of New York

David Stephan
Two Bridges Instructional Technology

Kathryn Szabat
La Salle University

Pearson

Reproduced by Pearson from electronic files supplied by the author.

ScoutAutomatedPrintCode

Pearson

ISBN-13: 978-0-13-597002-7
ISBN-10: 0-13-597002-4

ScoutAutomatedPrintCode

Table of Contents

Preface

The ***Student's Solutions Manual*** consists of three major sections. The ***Objective*** section summarizes what is expected of a student after reading a chapter. The ***Overview and Key Concepts*** section provides an overview of the major topics covered in a chapter and lists the important key concepts. The overview and listing of the key concepts are meant not to replace but to supplement the textbook and to reinforce understanding. The ***Solutions to End of Section and Chapter Review Even Problems*** section provides extra detail in the problem solutions.

FIRST THINGS FIRST

OBJECTIVES

- Statistics is a way of thinking that can lead to better decision making
- Statistics requires analytics skills and is an important part of your business education
- Recent developments such as the use of business analytics and "big data" have made knowing statistics even more critical
- The DCOVA framework guides your application of statistics
- The opportunity business analytics represents for business students

OVERVIEW AND KEY CONCEPTS

What is Statistics?

Statistics is a way of thinking that can help you make better decisions based on data that have been collected. It helps transform data into useful information for decision makers.

Why Statistics in the Business World?

- To summarize and visualize business data
- To draw conclusions from the data
- To make reliable forecasts about business activities
- To improve business processes

How to Use Statistics in the Business World (DCOVA)?

The **D**efine **C**ollect **O**rganize **V**isualize **A**nalyze framework helps minimize possible errors of thinking and analysis.

- **D**efine the data that you want to study in order to solve a problem or meet an objective
- **C**ollect the data from appropriate sources
- **O**rganize the data collected by developing tables
- **V**isualize the data collected by developing charts
- **A**nalyze the data collected to reach conclusions and present those results

Key Definitions

- **Data:** The set of individual values associated with a variable.
- **Variable:** A characteristic of an item or individual.
- **Statistics:** The methods that help transform data into useful information for decision makers.

Business Analytics

Business analytics combine "traditional" statistical methods with methods and techniques from management science and information systems to form an interdisciplinary tool that supports fact-based management decision making. It enables a manager to

- Use statistical methods to analyze and explore data to uncover unforeseen relationships.
- Use management science methods to develop models that impact an organization's strategy, planning, and operations.
- Use information systems methods to collect and process data sets of all sizes, including very large data sets that would otherwise be hard to examine efficiently.

Chapter 1

1.2 Business size represents a categorical variable because each size represents a particular category. Because of the different sizes, order is implied, but this variable includes no information about the quantity of differences among the three sizes.

1.4 (a) The number of cellphones is a numerical variable that is discrete because the outcome is a count.
(b) Monthly data usage is a numerical variable that is continuous because any value within a range of values can occur.
(c) Number of text messages exchanged per month is a numerical variable that is discrete because the outcome is a count.
(d) Voice usage per month is a numerical variable that is continuous because any value within a range of values can occur.
(e) Whether a cellphone is used for streaming video is a categorical variable because the answer can be only yes or no.

1.6 (a) Categorical, nominal scale
(b) Numerical, continuous, ratio scale
(c) Categorical, nominal scale
(d) Numerical, discrete, ratio scale
(e) Categorical, nominal scale

1.8 (a) numerical, continuous, ratio scale
(b) numerical, discrete, ratio scale
(c) numerical, continuous, ratio scale
(d) categorical, nominal scale

1.10 The underlying variable, ability of the students, may be continuous, but the measuring device, the test, does not have enough precision to distinguish between the two students.

1.12 (a) Data distributed by an organization or individual.
(b) The American Community Survey is based on a sample.

1.14 The answer depends on the specific story.

1.16 The information presented there is based mainly on a mixture of data distributed by an organization and data collected by ongoing business activities.

1.18 Sample without replacement: Read from left to right in 3-digit sequences and continue unfinished sequences from end of row to beginning of next row.
Row 05: 338 505 855 551 438 855 077 186 579 488 767 833 170
Rows 05–06: 897
Row 06: 340 033 648 847 204 334 639 193 639 411 095 924
Rows 06–07: 707
Row 07: 054 329 776 100 871 007 255 980 646 886 823 920 461
Row 08: 893 829 380 900 796 959 453 410 181 277 660 908 887
Rows 08–09: 237
Row 09: 818 721 426 714 050 785 223 801 670 353 362 449
Rows 09–10: 406
Note: All sequences above 902 and duplicates are discarded.

1.20 A simple random sample would be less practical for personal interviews because of travel costs (unless interviewees are paid to attend a central interviewing location).

1.22 Here all members of the population are equally likely to be selected and the sample selection mechanism is based on chance. But not every sample of size 2 has the same chance of being selected. For example the sample "B and C" is impossible.

1.24 (a)

Row 16: 2323 6737 5131 8888 1718 0654 6832 4647 6510 4877
Row 17: 4579 4269 2615 1308 2455 7830 5550 5852 5514 7182
Row 18: 0989 3205 0514 2256 8514 4642 7567 8896 2977 8822
Row 19: 5438 2745 9891 4991 4523 6847 9276 8646 1628 3554
Row 20: 9475 0899 2337 0892 0048 8033 6945 9826 9403 6858
Row 21: 7029 7341 3553 1403 3340 4205 0823 4144 1048 2949
Row 22: 8515 7479 5432 9792 6575 5760 0408 8112 2507 3742
Row 23: 1110 0023 4012 8607 4697 9664 4894 3928 7072 5815
Row 24: 3687 1507 7530 5925 7143 1738 1688 5625 8533 5041
Row 25: 2391 3483 5763 3081 6090 5169 0546

Note: All sequences above 5000 are discarded. There were no repeating sequences.

(b)

089 189 289 389 489 589 689 789 889 989
1089 1189 1289 1389 1489 1589 1689 1789 1889 1989
2089 2189 2289 2389 2489 2589 2689 2789 2889 2989
3089 3189 3289 3389 3489 3589 3689 3789 3889 3989
4089 4189 4289 4389 4489 4589 4689 4789 4889 4989

(c) With the single exception of invoice #0989, the invoices selected in the simple random sample are not the same as those selected in the systematic sample. It would be highly unlikely that a random process would select the same units as a systematic process.

1.26 (a) For the third value, Apple is spelled incorrectly. The twelfth value should be Blackberry not Blueberry. The fifteenth value, APPLE, may lead to an irregularity. The eighteenth value should be Samsung not Samsun.

(b) This list contains 19 names, where one would expect to find 20 names.

1.28 (a) The times for each of the hotels would be arranged in separate columns.

(b) The hotel names would be in one column and the times would be in a second column.

1.30 Before accepting the results of a survey of college students, you might want to know, for example:
Who funded the survey? Why was it conducted? What was the population from which the sample was selected? What sampling design was used? What mode of response was used: a personal interview, a telephone interview, or a mail survey? Were interviewers trained?
Were survey questions field-tested? What questions were asked? Were they clear, accurate, unbiased, valid? What operational definition of "vast majority" was used? What was the response rate? What was the sample size?

1.32 Coverage error could result if bank executives are systematically excluded from the population thereby not allowing them to be part of any sample that is used to generate the results. This could lead to selection bias. Non-response error that results in non-response bias could result if not all bank executives who were selected for inclusion in the sample are contacted even after multiple attempts to do so. In this case, data that was desired and necessary for inclusion in the sample would then not be present. Sampling error reflects the variability in outcomes when taking different samples. Sampling error is unavoidable. One can obtain an impression of the size of the sampling error by creating interval estimates. Measurement error could arise if the bank executives self-report results or if the methods of reporting are not standardized, i.e. if questions are not asked in the same manner from respondent to respondent, or if those conducting the survey do not do so in a consistent manner.

1.34 Before accepting the results of the survey, you might want to know, for example:
Who funded the survey? Why was it conducted? What was the population from which the sample was selected? What sampling design was used? What mode of response was used: a personal interview, a telephone interview, or a mail survey? Were interviewers trained? Were survey questions field-tested? What questions were asked? Were they clear, accurate, unbiased, valid? What was the response rate? What was the margin of error? What was the sample size? What frame was used?

1.36 A statistic is a summary measure describing a sample whereas a parameter is a summary measure describing an entire population.

1.38 Discrete random variables produce numerical responses that arise from a counting process. Continuous random variables produce numerical responses that arise from a measuring process.

1.40 Both interval scaled and ratio scaled variables are numerical variables in which the difference between measurements is meaningful but an interval scaled variable does not involve a true zero such as standardized exam scores while a ratio scaled variable involves a true zero such as height.

1.42 Missing values are values that were not collected for a variable. Outliers are values that seem excessively different from most of the other values

1.44 Coverage error is error generated due to an improperly or inappropriately framed population which can result in a sample that may not be representative of the population that one wishes to study. Non-response error is error generated due to members of a chosen sample not being contacted even after repeated attempts so that information that should be provided is missing.

1.46 Microsoft Excel:
This product features a spreadsheet-based interface that allows users to organize, calculate, and organize data. Excel also contains many statistical functions to assist in the description of a dataset. Excel can be used to develop worksheets and workbooks to calculate a variety of statistics including introductory and advanced statistics. Excel also includes interactive tools to create graphs, charts, and pivot tables. Excel can be used to summarize data to better understand a population of interest, compare across groups, predict outcomes, and to develop forecasting models. These capabilities represent those that are generally relevant to the current course.

Excel also includes many other statistical capabilities that can be further explored on the Microsoft Office Excel official website.

1.48 The answers are based on an article titled “U.S. Satisfaction Still Running at Improved Level” and written by Lydia Saad (August 15, 2018). The article is located on the following site: https://news.gallup.com/poll/240911/satisfaction-running-improved-level.aspx?g_source=link_NEWSV9&g_medium=NEWSFEED&g_campaign=item_&g_content=U.S.%2520Satisfaction%2520Still%2520Running%2520at%2520Improved%2520Level

(a) The population of interest includes all individuals aged 18 and older who live within the 50 U.S. states and the District of Columbia.

(b) The collected sample includes a random sample of 1,024 individuals aged 18 and older who live within the 50 U.S. states and the District of Columbia.

(c) A parameter of interest is the percentage of the population of individuals aged 18 and older and live within the 50 U.S. states and the District of Columbia who are satisfied with the direction of the U.S.

(d) A statistic used to the estimate the parameter in (c) is the percentage of the 1,024 individuals included in the sample. In this case, the statistic is 36%.

1.50 (a) One variable collected with the American Community Survey is marital status with the following possible responses: now married, widowed, divorced, separated, and never married.

(b) The variable in (a) represents a categorical variable.

(c) Because the variable in (a) is a categorical, this question is not applicable. If one had chosen age in years from the American Community Survey as the variable, the answer to (c) would be discrete.

1.52 (a) The population of interest consisted of 10,000 benefited employees of the University of Utah.

(b) The sample consisted of 3,095 employees of the University of Utah.

(c) Gender, marital status, and employment category represent categorical variables. Age in years, education level in years completed, and household income represent numerical variables.

Chapter 2

2.2 (a) Table frequencies for all student responses

	Student Major Categories			
Gender	A	C	M	Totals
Male	14	9	2	25
Female	6	6	3	15
Totals	20	15	5	40

(b) Table percentages based on overall student responses

	Student Major Categories			
Gender	A	C	M	Totals
Male	35.0%	22.5%	5.0%	62.5%
Female	15.0%	15.0%	7.5%	37.5%
Totals	50.0%	37.5%	12.5%	100.0%

Table based on row percentages

	Student Major Categories			
Gender	A	C	M	Totals
Male	56.0%	36.0%	8.0%	100.0%
Female	40.0%	40.0%	20.0%	100.0%
Totals	50.0%	37.5%	12.5%	100.0%

Table based on column percentages

	Student Major Categories			
Gender	A	C	M	Totals
Male	70.0%	60.0%	40.0%	62.5%
Female	30.0%	40.0%	60.0%	37.5%
Totals	100.0%	100.0%	100.0%	100.0%

2.4 (a)

Category	Total	Percentages
Bank Account or Service	202	9.330%
Consumer Loan	132	6.097%
Credit Card	175	8.083%
Credit Reporting	581	26.836%
Debt Collection	486	22.448%
Mortgage	442	20.416%
Student Loan	75	3.464%
Other	72	3.326%
Grand Total	2165	

(b) There are more complaints for credit reporting, debt collection, and mortgage than the other categories. These categories account for about 70% of all the complaints.

2.4 cont. (c)

Company	Total	Percentage
Bank of America	42	3.64%
Capital One	93	8.07%
Citibank	59	5.12%
Ditech Financial	31	2.69%
Equifax	217	18.82%
Experian	177	15.35%
JPMorgan	128	11.10%
Nationstar Mortgage	39	3.38%
Navient	38	3.30%
Ocwen	41	3.56%
Synchrony	43	3.73%
Trans-Union	168	14.57%
Wells Fargo	77	6.68%
Grand Total	1153	

(d) Equifax, Trans-Union, and Experion, all of which are credit score companies, have the most complaints.

2.6 The largest sources of electricity in the United States are Natural gas followed by Coal. Nuclear is the third most used source of energy. Hydropower and Wind are about the same followed by Solar, Biomass, Petroleum coke and liquids, Geothermal, and Other sources.

2.8 (a) Table of row percentages:

	GENDER		
OVERLOADED	**Male**	**Female**	**Total**
Yes	44.08%	55.92%	100.00%
No	53.54%	46.46%	100.00%
Total	51.64%	48.36%	100.00%

Table of column percentages:

	GENDER		
OVERLOADED	**Male**	**Female**	**Total**
Yes	17.07%	23.13%	20.00%
No	82.93%	76.87%	80.00%
Total	100.00%	100.00%	100.00%

2.8 cont. (a) Table of total percentages:

	GENDER		
OVERLOADED	Male	Female	Total
Yes	8.82%	11.18%	20.00%
No	42.83%	37.17%	80.00%
Total	51.64%	48.36%	100.00%

(b) Approximately the same percentages of males and females as a percentage of the total number of people surveyed feel overloaded with too much information. As percentages of those who do and do not feel overloaded, the genders differ mildly. However, four times as many people do not feel overloaded at work than those that do.

2.10 Approximately 11.7% of the total people surveyed answered window tinting as their preferred luxury upgrade. A higher percentage of women than men prefer window tinting as a luxury upgrade.

2.12 Ordered array: 73 78 78 78 85 88 91

2.14 $\frac{261,000-61,000}{6}=33,333.33$ so choose 40,000 as interval width

(a) \$60,000 – under \$100,000; \$100,000 – under \$140,000; \$140,000 – under \$180,000; \$180,000 – under \$220,000; \$220,000 – under \$260,000; \$260,000 – under \$300,000

(b) \$40,000

(c) $\frac{60,000+100,000}{2}=\$80,000$ similarly, the remaining class midpoints are \$120,000; \$160,000; \$200,000; \$240,000; \$280,000

2.16 (a)

Electricity Costs

Electricity Costs	Frequency	Percentage
\$80 but less than \$100	4	8%
\$100 but less than \$120	7	14%
\$120 but less than \$140	9	18%
\$140 but less than \$160	13	26%
\$160 but less than \$180	9	18%
\$180 but less than \$200	5	10%
\$200 but less than \$220	3	6%

2.16 cont. (b)

Electricity Costs	Frequency	Percentage	Cumulative %
$ 99	4	8.00%	8.00%
$119	7	14.00%	22.00%
$139	9	18.00%	40.00%
$159	13	26.00%	66.00%
$179	9	18.00%	84.00%
$199	5	10.00%	94.00%
$219	3	6.00%	100.00%

(c) The majority of utility charges are clustered between $120 and $180.

2.18 (a), (b)

Credit Score	Frequency	Percent (%)	Cumulative Percent (%)
560 – under 580	4	0.16	0.16
580 – under 600	24	0.93	1.09
600 – under 620	68	2.65	3.74
620 – under 640	290	11.28	15.02
640 – under 660	548	21.32	36.34
660 – under 680	560	21.79	58.13
680 – under 700	507	19.73	77.86
700 – under 720	378	14.71	92.57
720 – under 740	168	6.54	99.11
740 – under 760	22	0.86	99.96
760 – under 780	1	0.04	100.00

(c) The average credit scores are concentrated between 620 and 720.

2.20 (a), (b)

Time in Seconds	Frequency	Percent (%)
5 – under 10	8	16%
10 – under 15	15	30%
15 – under 20	18	36%
20 – under 25	6	12%
25 – under 30	3	6%

2.20 cont. (b)

Time in Seconds	Percentage Less Than
5	0
10	16
15	46
20	82
25	94
30	100

(c) The target is being met since 82% of the calls are being answered in less than 20 seconds

2.22 (a)

Bulb Life			Frequency Mftr A	Percentage Mftr A	Frequency Mftr B	Percentage Mftr B
46,500	but less than	47,500	3	7.5%	0	0.0%
47,500	but less than	48,500	5	12.5%	2	5.0%
48,500	but less than	49,500	20	50.0%	8	20.0%
49,500	but less than	50,500	9	22.5%	16	40.0%
50,500	but less than	51,500	3	7.5%	9	22.5%
51,500	but less than	52,500	0	0.0%	5	12.5%
			40	100.0%	40	100.0%

(b)

% less than	Percentage Less than, Mftr A	Percentage Less than, Mftr B
47,500	7.5%	0.0%
48,500	20.0%	5.0%
49,500	70.0%	25.0%
50,500	92.5%	65.0%
51,500	100.0%	87.5%
52,500	100.0%	100.0%

(c) Manufacturer B produces bulbs with longer lives than Manufacturer A. The cumulative percentage for Manufacturer B shows 65% of its bulbs lasted less than 50,500 hours, contrasted with 70% of Manufacturer A's bulbs, which lasted less than 49,500 hours. None of Manufacturer A's bulbs lasted more than 51,500 hours, but 12.5% of Manufacturer B's bulbs lasted between 51,500 and 52,500 hours. At the same time, 7.5% of Manufacturer A's bulbs lasted less than 47,500 hours, whereas all of Manufacturer B's bulbs lasted at least 47,500 hours

2.24 (a)

How Purchases Were Made
Search and buy online
Search and buy in store
Research online and in store, buy online
Research online and in store, buy in store
0 5 10 15 20 25 30 35 40 45

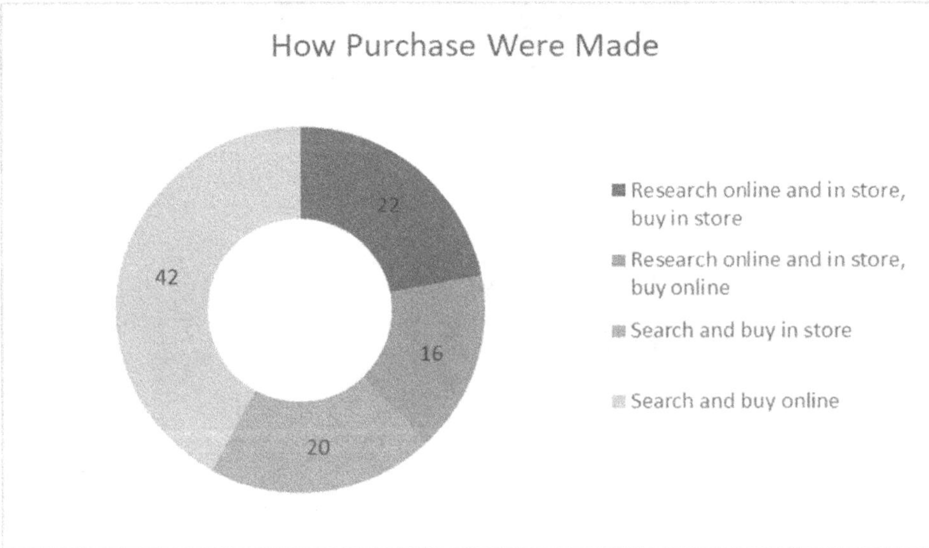
How Purchase Were Made
22
16
20
42
Research online and in store, buy in store
Research online and in store, buy online
Search and buy in store
Search and buy online

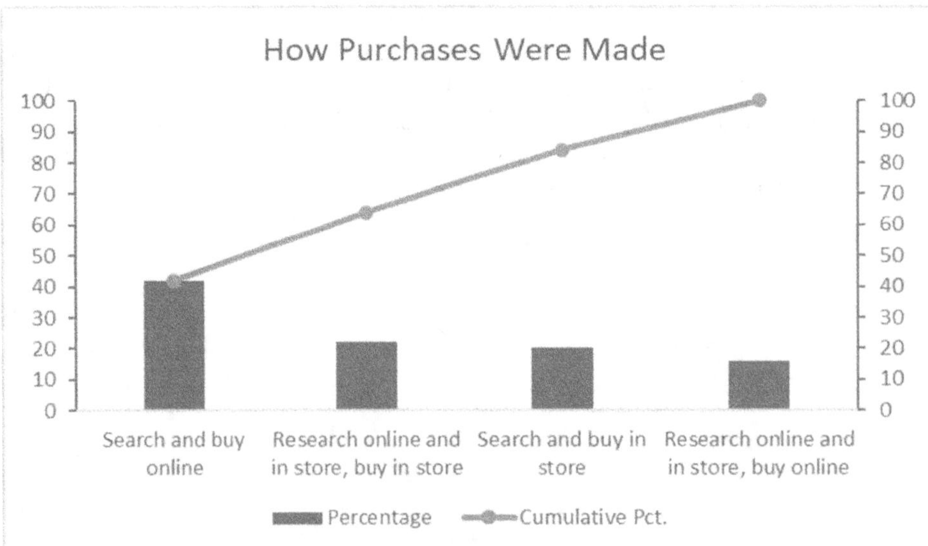
How Purchases Were Made
100 90 80 70 60 50 40 30 20 10 0
Search and buy online
Research online and in store, buy in store
Search and buy in store
Research online and in store, buy online
Percentage
Cumulative Pct.

2.24 cont. (b) The Pareto chart is best for portraying these data because it not only sorts the frequencies in descending order but also provides the cumulative line on the same chart.

(c) You can conclude that searching and buying online was the highest category and the other three were equally likely.

2.26 (a)

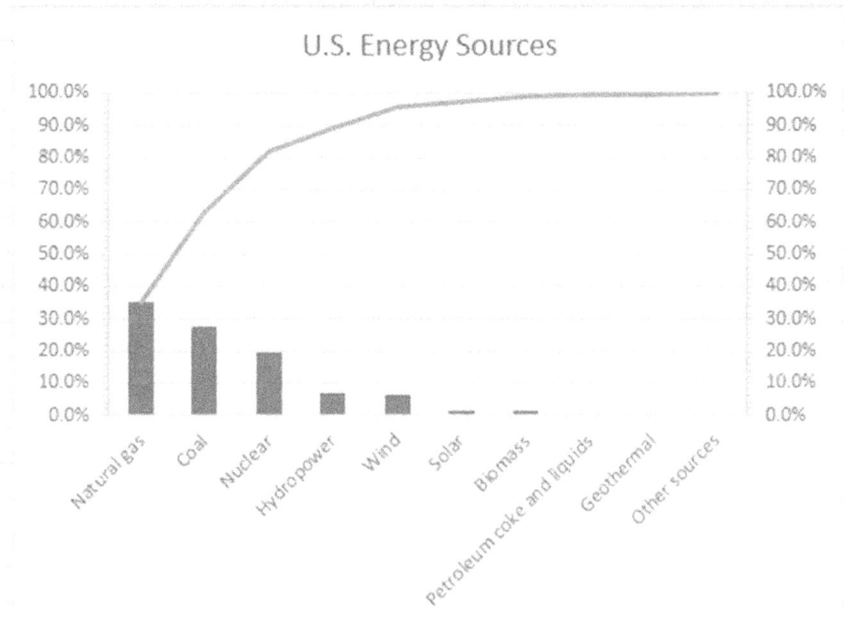

(b) 27.4% + 19.3% + 35.2% = 81.9%

(c)

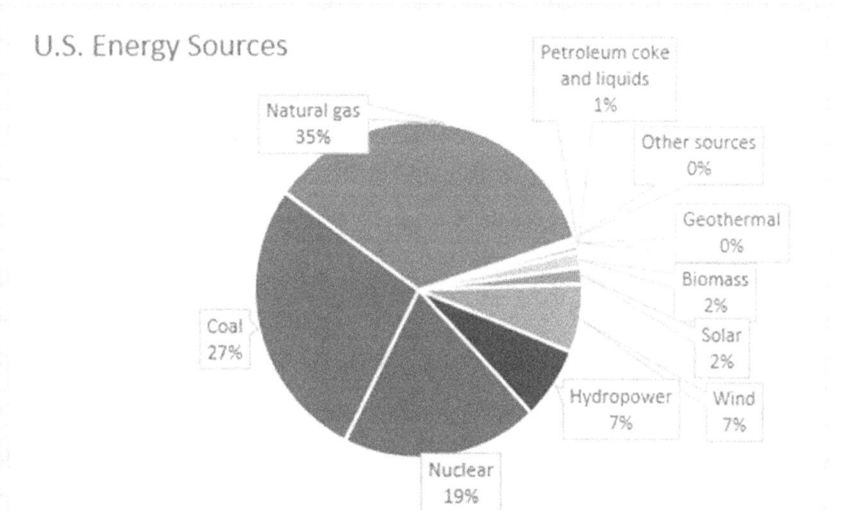

(d) The Pareto diagram is better than the pie chart because it not only sorts the frequencies in descending order, it also provides the cumulative polygon on the same scale.

2.28 (a)

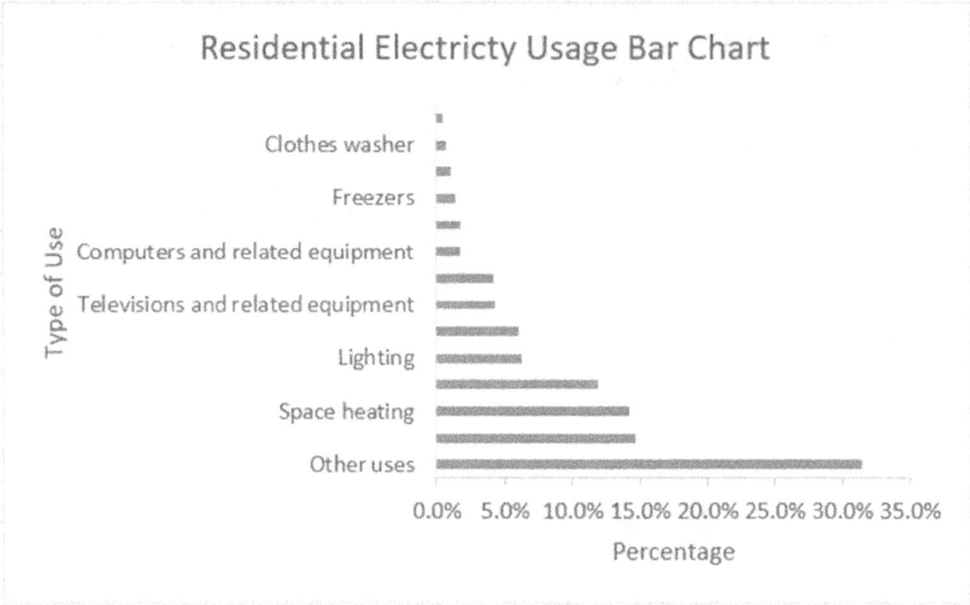
Residential Electricty Usage Bar Chart
Type of Use
Clothes washer
Freezers
Computers and related equipment
Televisions and related equipment
Lighting
Space heating
Other uses
0.0% 5.0% 10.0% 15.0% 20.0% 25.0% 30.0% 35.0%
Percentage

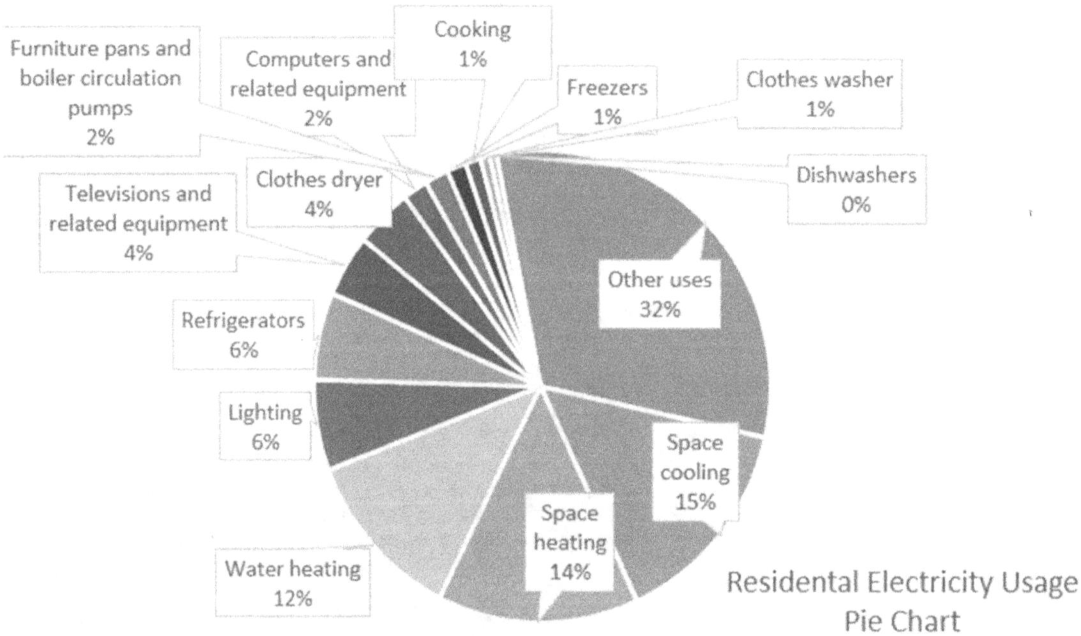
Furniture pans and boiler circulation pumps 2%
Computers and related equipment 2%
Cooking 1%
Freezers 1%
Clothes washer 1%
Dishwashers 0%
Televisions and related equipment 4%
Clothes dryer 4%
Other uses 32%
Refrigerators 6%
Lighting 6%
Space cooling 15%
Space heating 14%
Water heating 12%
Residental Electricity Usage Pie Chart

2.28 cont. (a)

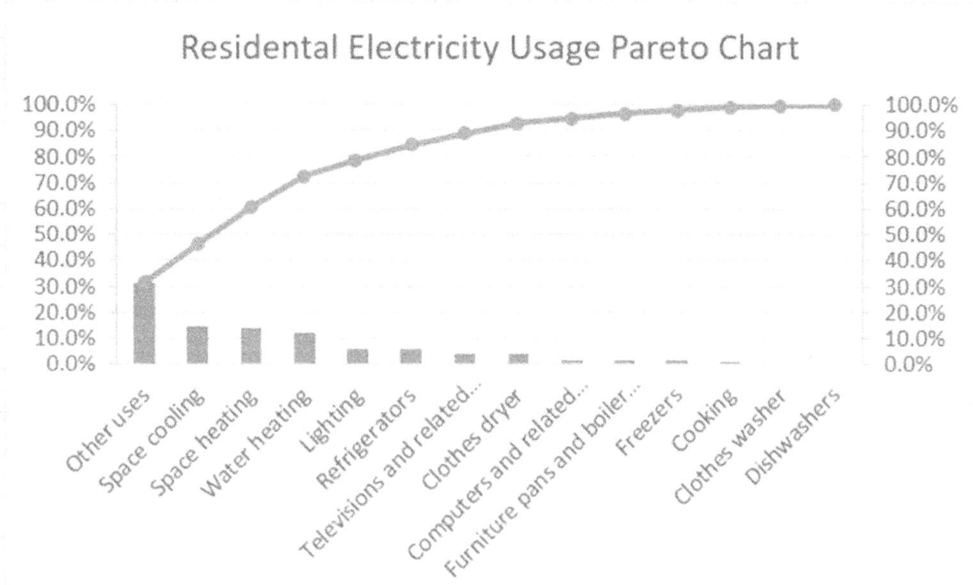

(b) The Pareto diagram is better than the pie chart and bar chart because it not only sorts the frequencies in descending order; it also provides the cumulative polygon on the same scale.

(c) Other, cooling, heating and lighting accounted for 78.5% of the residential electricity consumption in the United States.

2.30 (a)

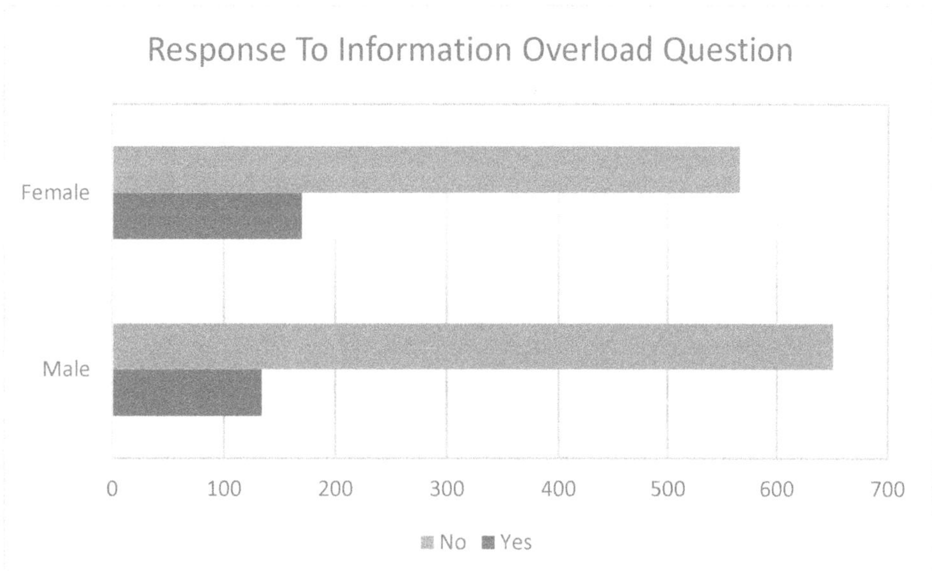

(b) Females are more likely to be overloaded with information.

2.32 (a)

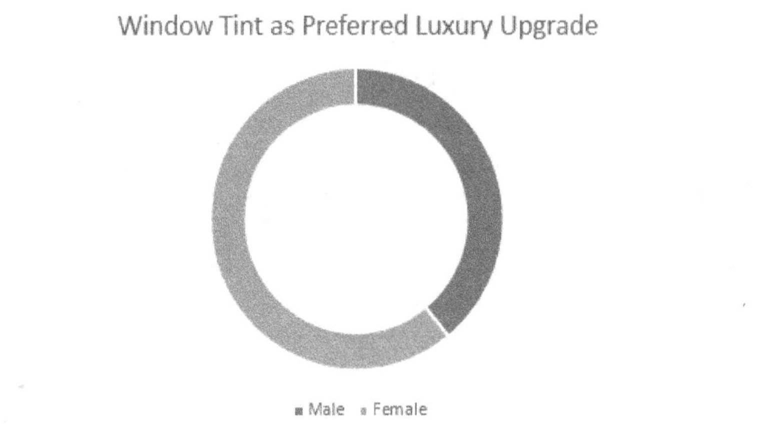

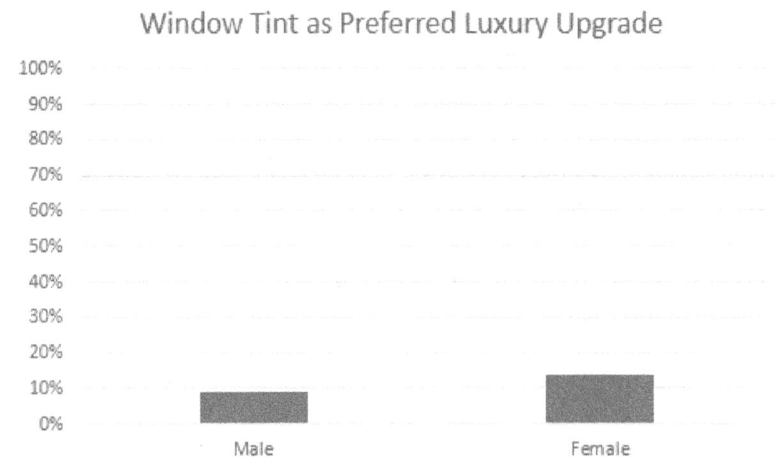

(b) More females then men prefer window tint as a luxury upgrade.

2.34 Ordered array: 50 74 74 76 81 89 92

2.36 (a)

stem	leaf
4	0
5	0056889
6	0133457
7	3388899
8	048
9	
10	25
11	
12	8
13	3
14	3

(b) The results are concentrated between 5 hours and 8 hours.

2.38 (a)

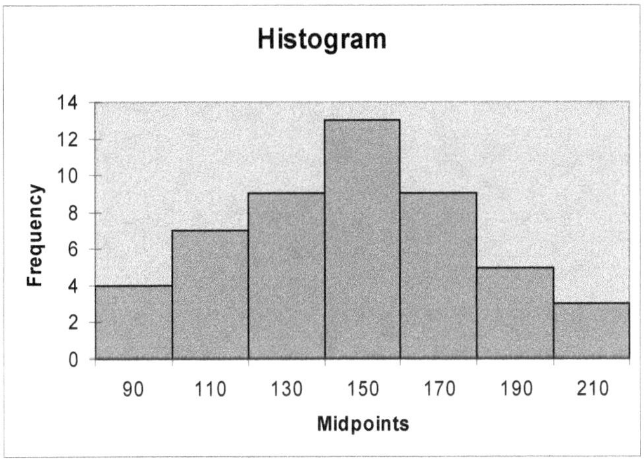

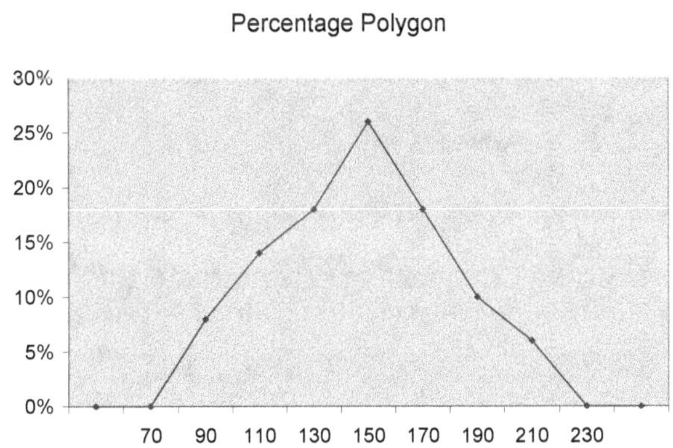

(b)

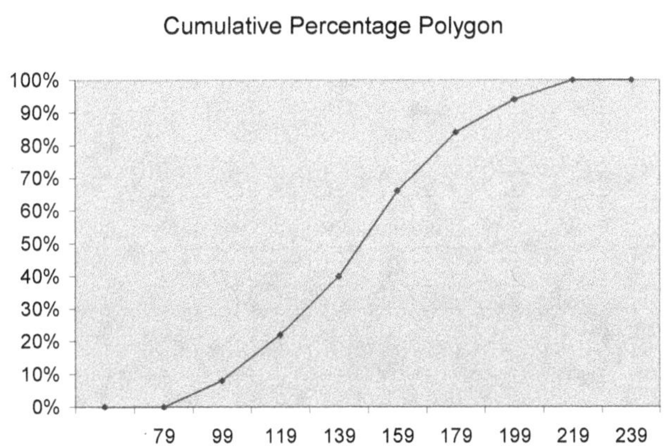

(c) The majority of utility charges are clustered between \$120 and \$180.

2.40 Property taxes on a \$176K home seem concentrated between \$700 and \$2,200 and also between \$3,200 and \$3,700.

2.42 (a)

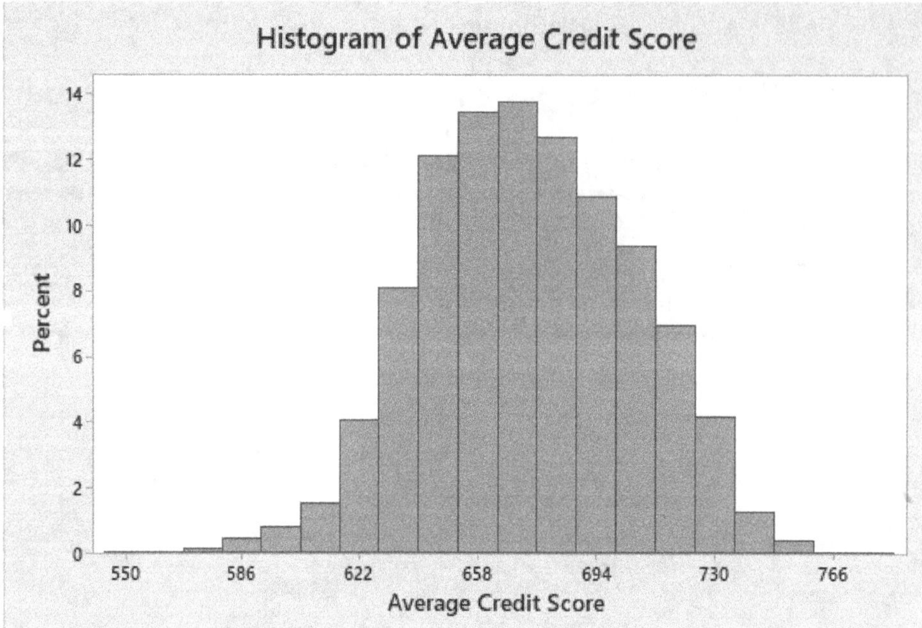

(b)

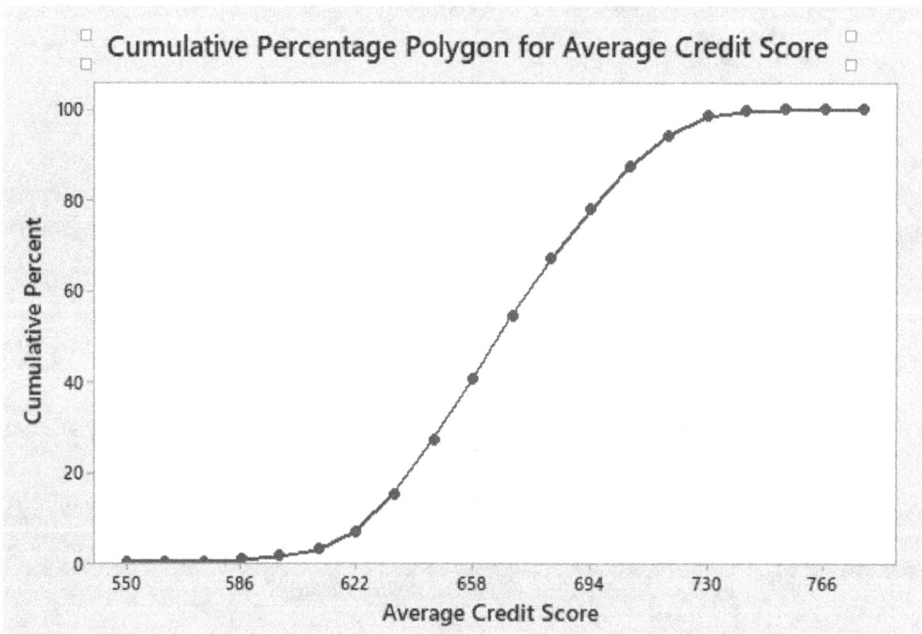

(c) The average credit scores are concentrated between 622 and 730.

2.44 (a)

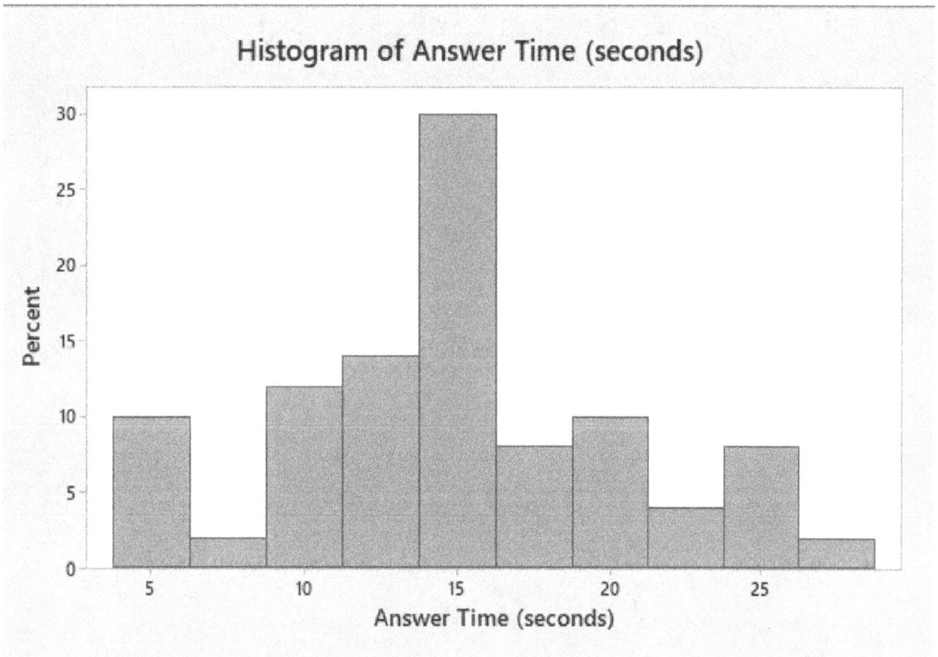
Histogram of Answer Time (seconds)
Percent
0
5
10
15
20
25
30
5
10
15
20
25
Answer Time (seconds)

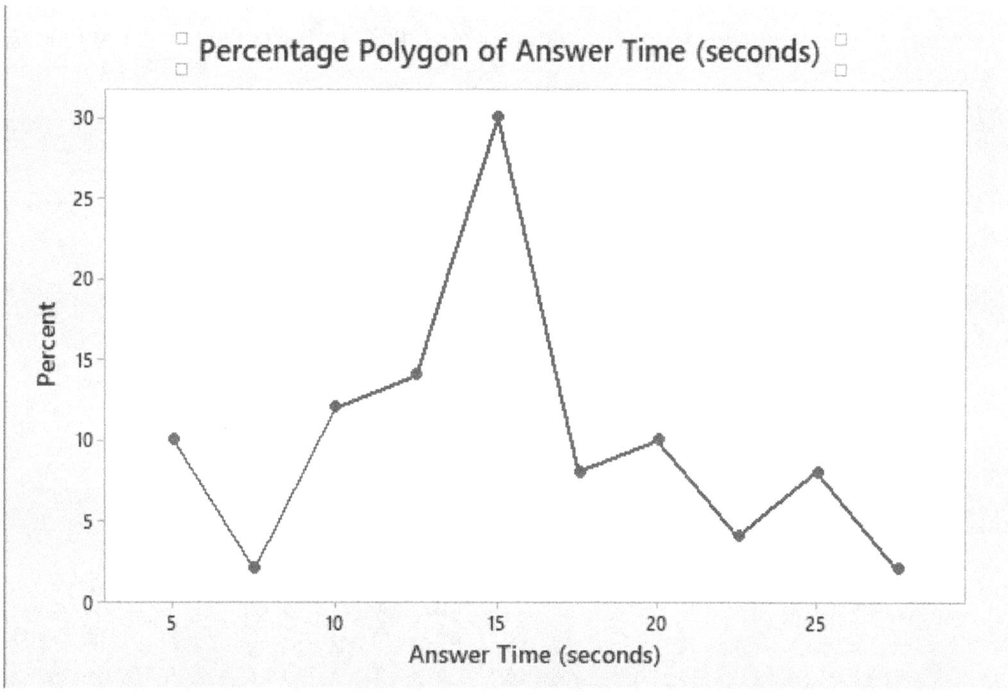
Percentage Polygon of Answer Time (seconds)
Percent
0
5
10
15
20
25
30
5
10
15
20
25
Answer Time (seconds)

2.44 cont. (b)

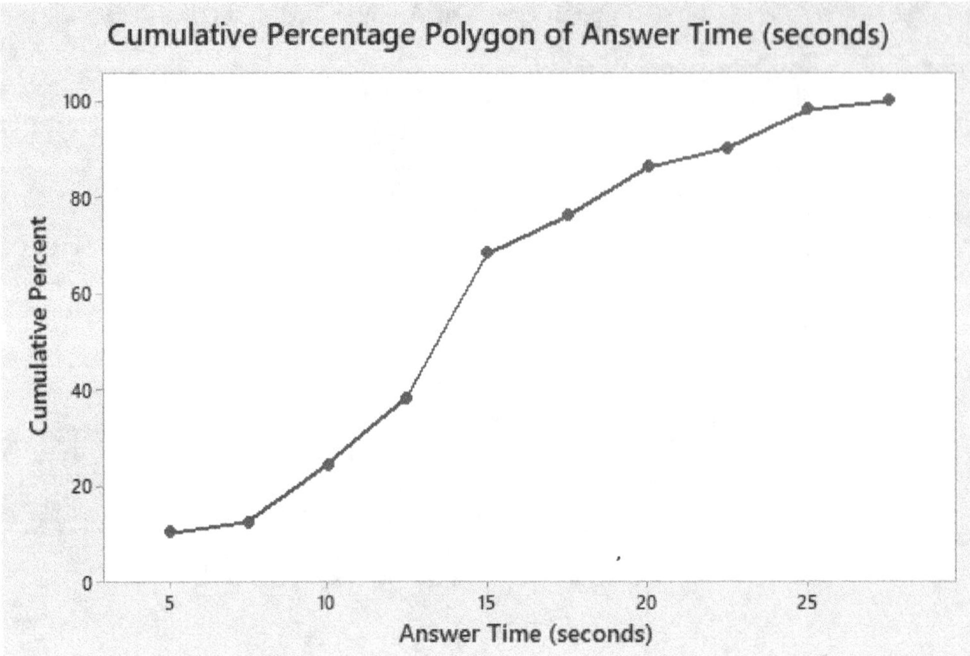

(c) The target is being met since 82% of the calls are being answered in less than 20 seconds.

2.46 (a)

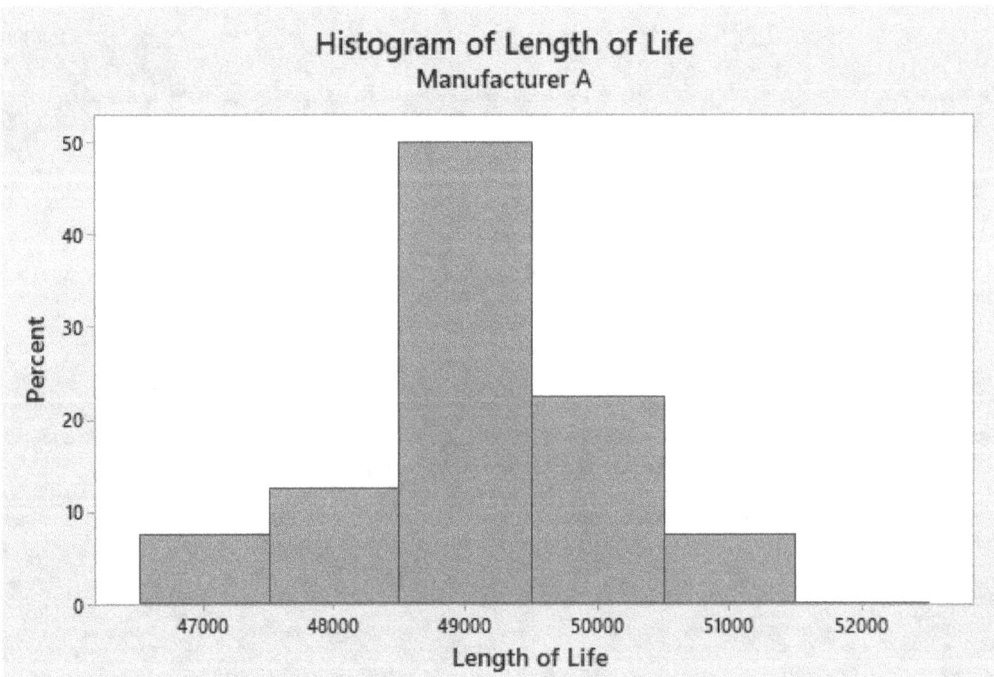

2.46 cont. (a)

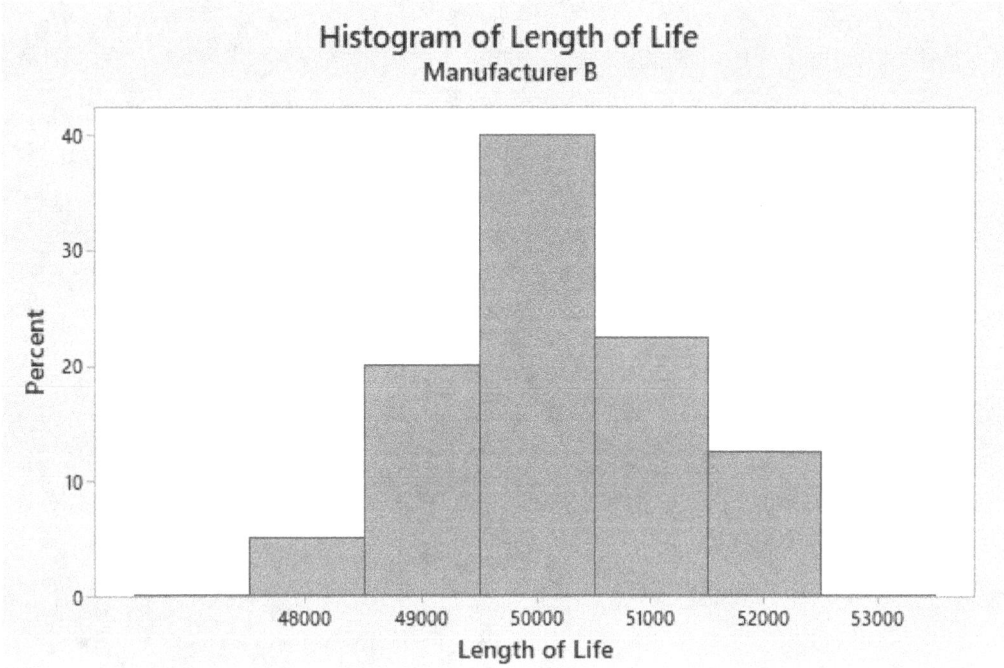
Histogram of Length of Life
Manufacturer B
Percent
0
10
20
30
40
48000
49000
50000
51000
52000
53000
Length of Life

(b)

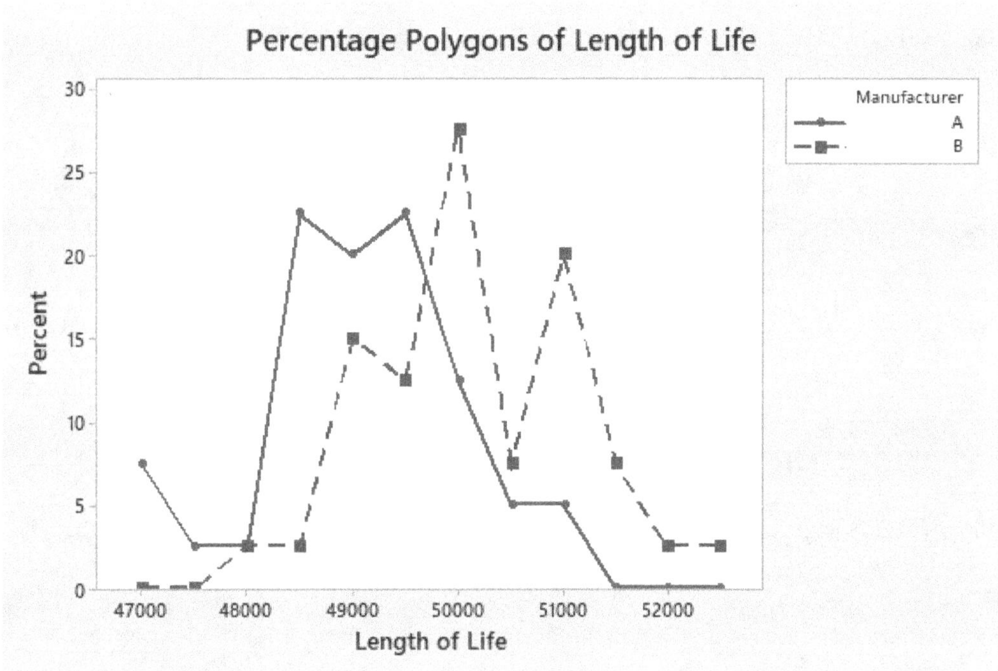
Percentage Polygons of Length of Life
Percent
0
5
10
15
20
25
30
47000
48000
49000
50000
51000
52000
Length of Life
Manufacturer
A
B

2.46 cont. (b)

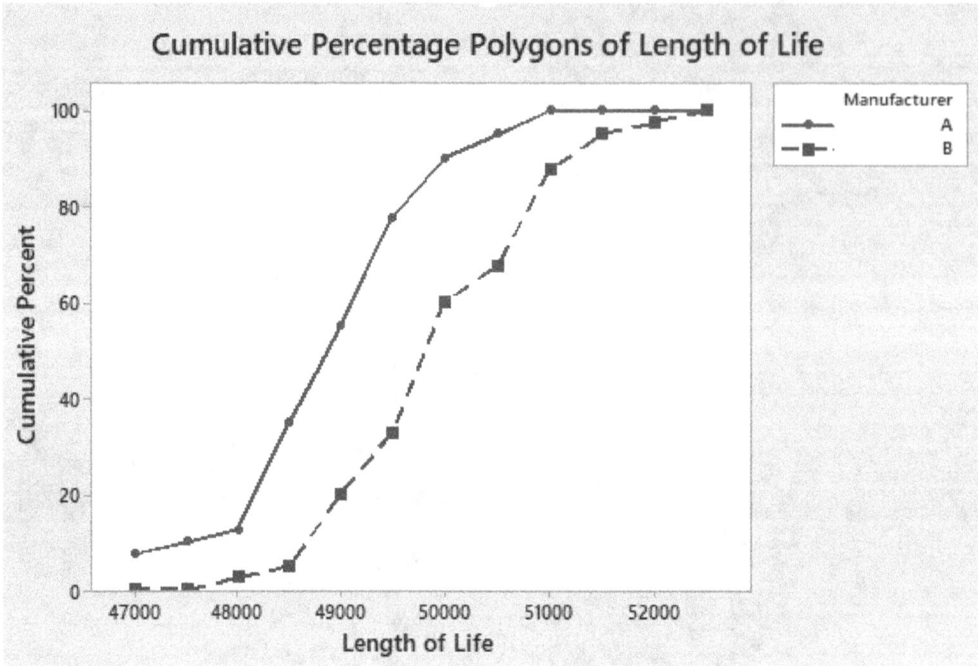

(c) Manufacturer B produces bulbs with longer lives than Manufacturer A

2.48 (a)

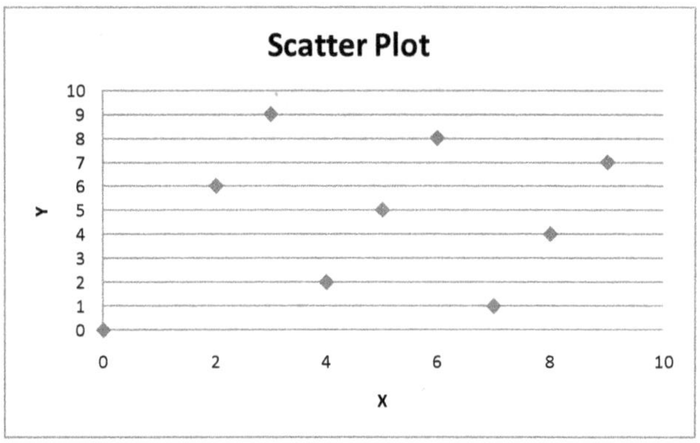

(b) There is no relationship between X and Y.

2.50 (a)

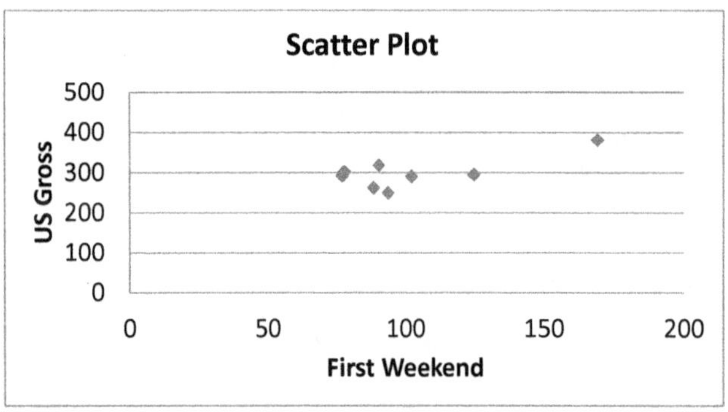

2.50 cont. (b)

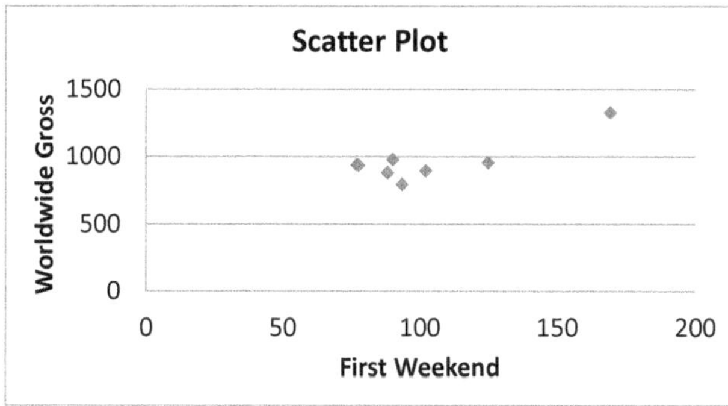

(c) There appears to be a linear relationship between the first weekend gross and either the U.S. gross or the worldwide gross of Harry Potter movies. However, this relationship is greatly affected by the results of the last movie, *Deathly Hallows*, *Part II.*

2.52 (a) There appears to be a positive relationship between the download speed and the upload speed.

(b)

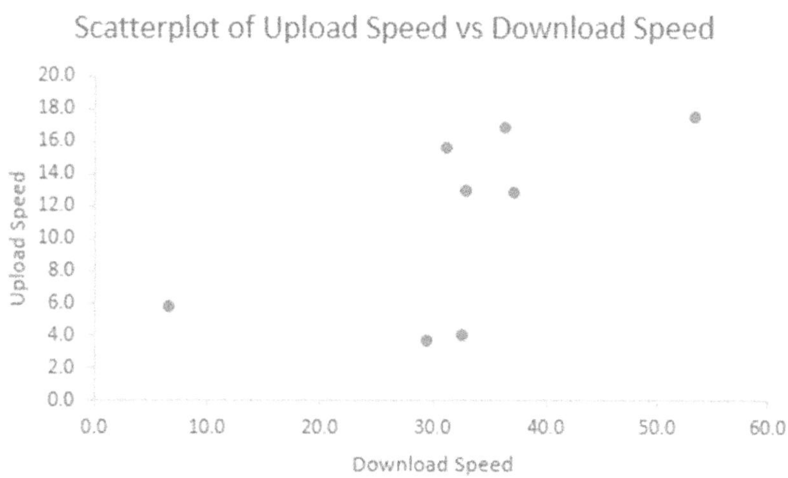

(c) Yes, this is borne out by the data

2.54 (a) Excel output:

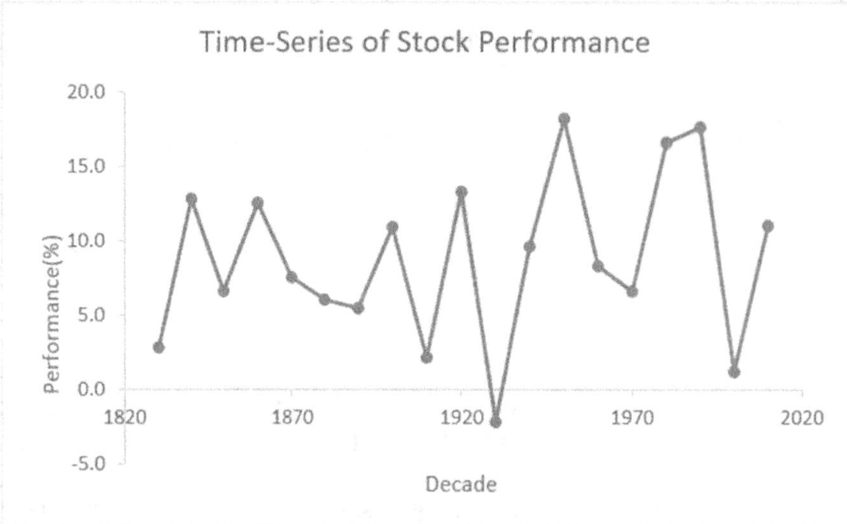

(b) There is a great deal of variation in the returns from decade to decade. Most of the returns are between 5% and 15%. The 1950s, 1980s, and 1990s had exceptionally high returns, and only the 1930s had negative returns.

2.56 (a)

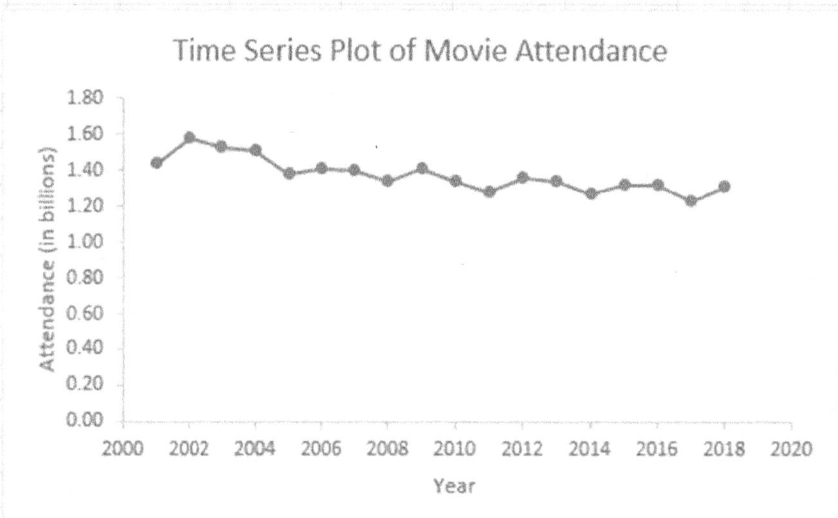

(b) There was a decline in movie attendance from 2002 to 2018. Movie attendance increased from 2001 to 2002 but then by 2018 decreased to a level below 2001.

2.58 (a) Pivot Table in terms of %

Count of Type	Star Rating					
Type	One	Two	Three	Four	Five	Grand Total
Growth	**5.43%**	**17.12%**	**27.35%**	**11.27%**	**2.71%**	**63.88%**
Large	3.76%	7.72%	13.57%	5.43%	1.67%	32.15%
Mid-Cap	1.25%	5.43%	7.52%	3.13%	0.63%	17.96%
Small	0.42%	3.97%	6.26%	2.71%	0.42%	13.78%
Value	**2.92%**	**10.65%**	**13.99%**	**7.31%**	**1.25%**	**36.12%**
Large	2.09%	6.68%	9.19%	3.97%	1.25%	23.18%
Mid-Cap	0.63%	2.09%	2.71%	1.04%	0.00%	6.47%
Small	0.21%	1.88%	2.09%	2.30%	0.00%	6.48%
Grand Total	**8.35%**	**27.77%**	**41.34%**	**18.58%**	**3.97%**	**100.00%**

(b) The growth and value funds have similar patterns in terms of star rating and type. Both growth and value funds have more funds with a rating of three. Very few funds have ratings of five.

(c) Pivot Table in terms of Average Three-Year Return

Count of Type	Star Rating					
Type	One	Two	Three	Four	Five	Grand Total
Growth	**5.41**	**7.04**	**8.94**	**10.14**	**12.83**	**8.51**
Large	6.97	9.43	10.62	11.83	14.25	10.30
Mid-Cap	2.27	5.07	7.93	8.77	11.22	6.93
Small	0.78	5.09	6.52	8.35	9.53	6.39
Value	**4.43**	**5.49**	**7.29**	**8.34**	**10.23**	**6.84**
Large	5.23	6.05	7.58	8.85	10.23	7.29
Mid-Cap	2.79	5.77	7.32	9.26	–	6.69
Small	1.33	3.20	5.93	7.04	–	5.39
Grand Total	**5.07**	**6.45**	**8.38**	**9.43**	**12.01**	**7.91**

(d) There are 65 large cap growth funds with a rating of three. Their average three year return is 10.62.

2.60 (a)

Count of Type	Star Rating					
Type	One	Two	Three	Four	Five	Grand Total
Growth	**5.43%**	**17.12%**	**27.35%**	**11.27%**	**2.71%**	**63.88%**
Large	1.25%	2.09%	4.80%	3.55%	1.46%	13.15%
Mid-Cap	1.67%	7.72%	15.87%	6.05%	0.42%	31.73%
Small	2.51%	7.31%	6.68%	1.67%	0.84%	19.00%
Value	**2.92%**	**10.65%**	**13.99%**	**7.31%**	**1.25%**	**36.12%**
Large	0.84%	4.38%	7.10%	4.38%	0.84%	17.54%
Mid-Cap	1.25%	4.80%	5.85%	2.71%	0.42%	15.03%
Small	0.84%	1.46%	1.04%	0.21%	0.00%	3.55%
Grand Total	**8.35%**	**27.77%**	**41.34%**	**18.58%**	**3.96%**	**100.00%**

(b) Patterns of star rating conditioned on risk:
For the growth funds as a group, most are rated as three-star, followed by two-star, four-star, one-star, and five-star. The pattern of star rating is different among the various risk growth funds.

For the value funds as a group, most are rated as three-star, followed by two-star, four-star, one-star and five-star. Among the high-risk value funds, more are two-star than three-star.

Most of the growth funds are rated as average-risk, followed by high-risk and then low-risk. The pattern is not the same among all the rating categories.

Most of the value funds are rated as low-risk, followed by average-risk and then high-risk. The pattern is the same among the three-star, four-star, and five-star value funds. Among the one-star and two-star funds, there are more average risk funds than low risk funds.

2.60 cont. (c)

Count of Type	Star Rating					
Type	One	Two	Three	Four	Five	Grand Total
Growth	**5.41**	**7.04**	**8.94**	**10.14**	**12.83**	**8.51**
Large	7.53	8.60	9.89	10.29	12.64	9.87
Mid-Cap	6.17	7.99	9.28	10.43	11.96	9.06
Small	3.83	5.59	7.45	8.76	13.59	6.64
Value	**4.43**	**5.49**	**7.29**	**8.34**	**10.23**	**6.84**
Large	5.29	7.00	7.66	8.57	10.74	7.76
Mid-Cap	5.01	4.98	6.97	7.96	9.23	6.41
Small	2.71	2.63	6.53	8.39	–	4.13
Grand Total	**5.07**	**6.45**	**8.38**	**9.43**	**12.01**	**7.91**

The three-year returns for growth funds is higher than for value funds. The return is higher for funds with higher ratings than lower ratings. This pattern holds for the growth funds for each risk level. For the low risk and average risk value funds, the return is lowest for the funds with a two-star rating.

(d) There are 32 growth funds with high risk with a rating of three. These funds have an average three-year return of 7.45.

2.62 The fund with the highest five-year return of 15.72 is a large cap growth fund that has a four-star rating and low risk.

2.64 Funds 479, 471, 347, 443, and 477 have the lowest five-year return.

2.66 The five funds with the lowest five-year return have (1) midcap growth, average risk, one-star rating, (2) midcap growth, high risk, two-star rating, (3) large value, average risk, two-star rating, (4) midcap growth, high risk, one-star rating, and (5) small value, average risk, two-star rating.

2.68 (a)

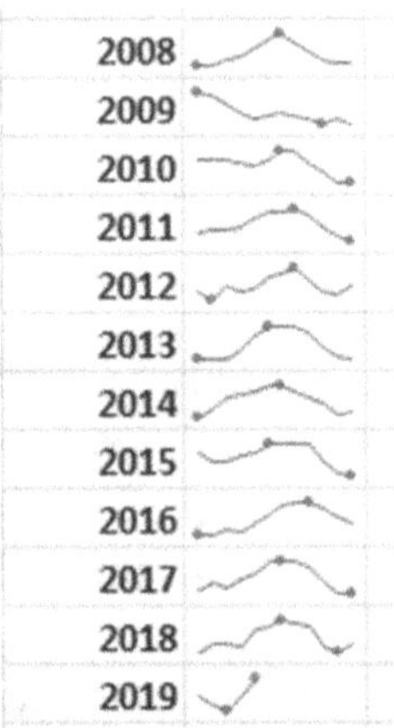

(b) There has been a decline in the price of natural gas over time. However, there is no pattern within the years. For some years, the price is higher in the beginning of the year. For other years, the price is higher in the latter part of the year. Sometimes, there is little variation within the year.

2.70 Student project answers will vary

2.72 (a) There is a title.
(b) The simplest possible visualization is not used.
(c)

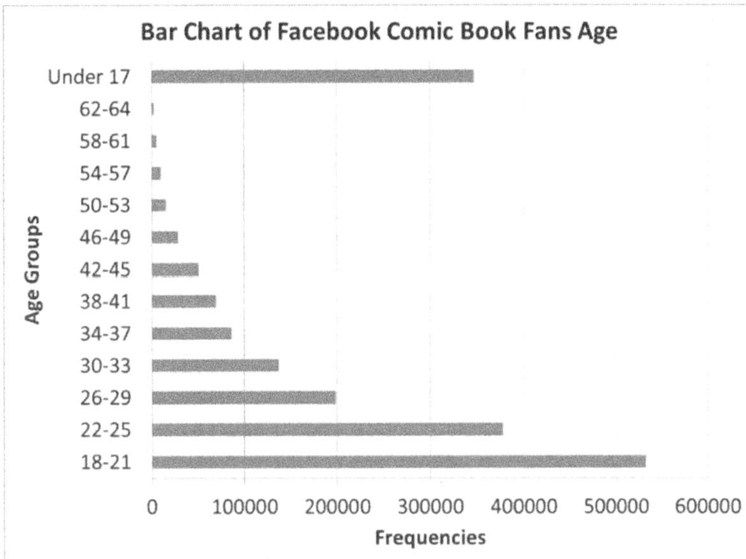

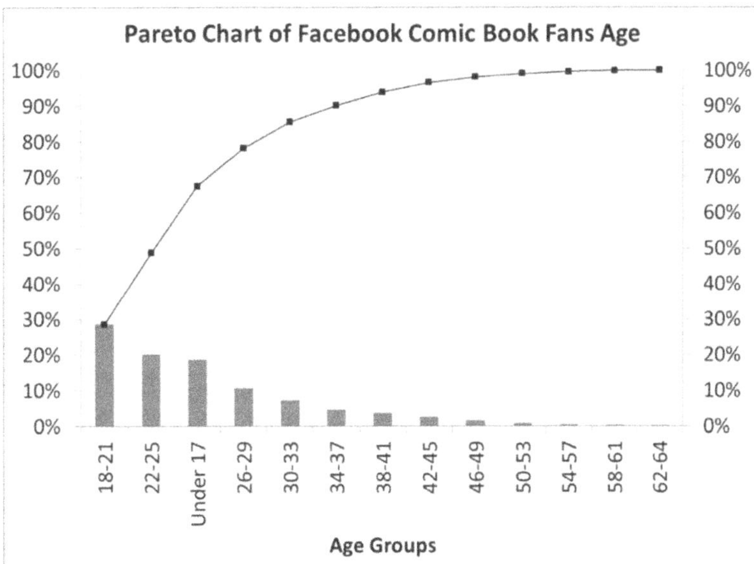

2.74 Answers will vary depending on selection of source.

2.76 (a)

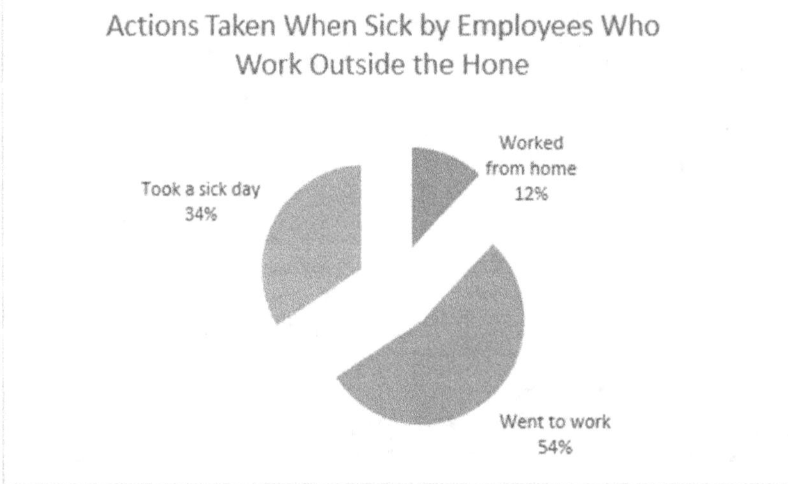

2.76 cont. (b) The bar chart and the pie chart should be preferred over the exploded pie chart, the cone chart and the pyramid chart since the former set is simpler and easier to interpret.

2.78 A summary table allows one to determine the frequency or percentage of occurrences in each category.

2.80 The bar chart for categorical data is plotted with the categories on the vertical axis and the frequencies or percentages on the horizontal axis. In addition, there is a separation between categories. The histogram is plotted with the class grouping on the horizontal axis and the frequencies or percentages on the vertical axis. This allows one to more easily determine the distribution of the data. In addition, there are no gaps between classes in the histogram.

2.82 Because the categories are arranged according to frequency or importance, it allows the user to focus attention on the categories that have the greatest frequency or importance.

2.84 A contingency table contains information on two categorical variables whereas a multidimensional table can display information on more than two categorical variables.

2.86 In a PivotTable in Excel, double-clicking a cell drills down and causes Excel to display the underlying data in a new worksheet to enable you to then observe the data for patterns. In Excel, a slicer is a panel of clickable buttons that appears superimposed over a worksheet to enable you to work with many variables at once in a way that avoids creating an overly complex multidimensional contingency table that would be hard to comprehend and interpret.

2.88 (a)

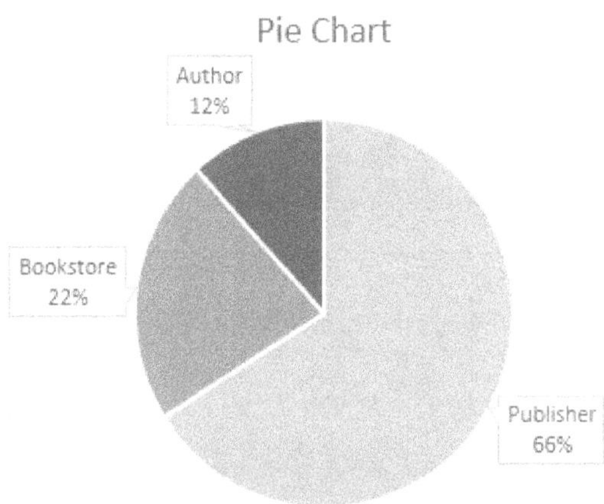

2.88 cont. (a)

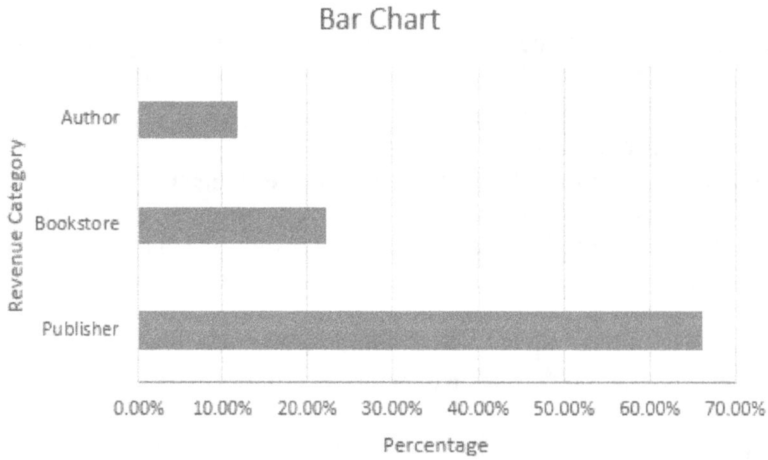
Bar Chart
Author
Bookstore
Publisher
Revenue Category
0.00%
10.00%
20.00%
30.00%
40.00%
50.00%
60.00%
70.00%
Percentage

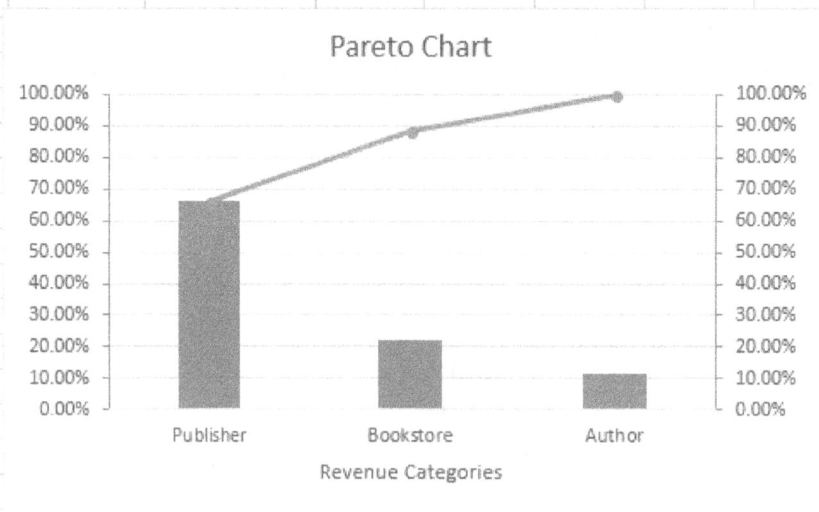
Pareto Chart
100.00%
90.00%
80.00%
70.00%
60.00%
50.00%
40.00%
30.00%
20.00%
10.00%
0.00%
Publisher
Bookstore
Author
Revenue Categories

2.88 cont. (b)

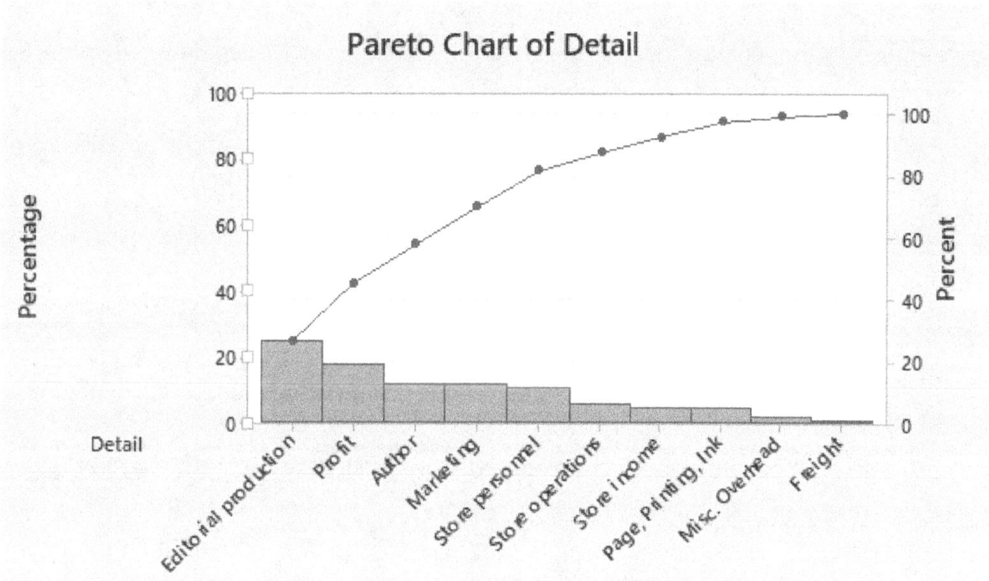

(c) The publisher gets the largest portion (66.06%) of the revenue. 24.93% is editorial production manufacturing costs. The publisher's marketing accounts for the next largest share of the revenue, at 11.6%. Author and bookstore personnel each account for around 11 to 12% of the revenue, whereas the publisher and bookstore profit and income account for more than 26% of the revenue. Yes, the bookstore gets almost twice the revenue of the authors.

2.90 (a)

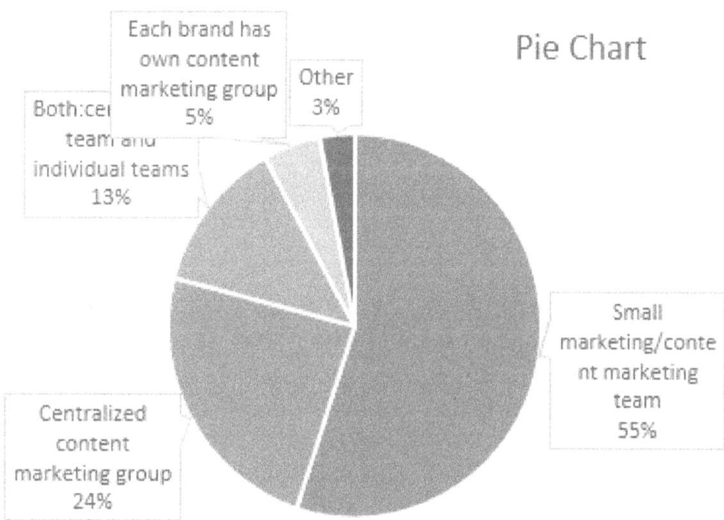

2.90 cont. (a)

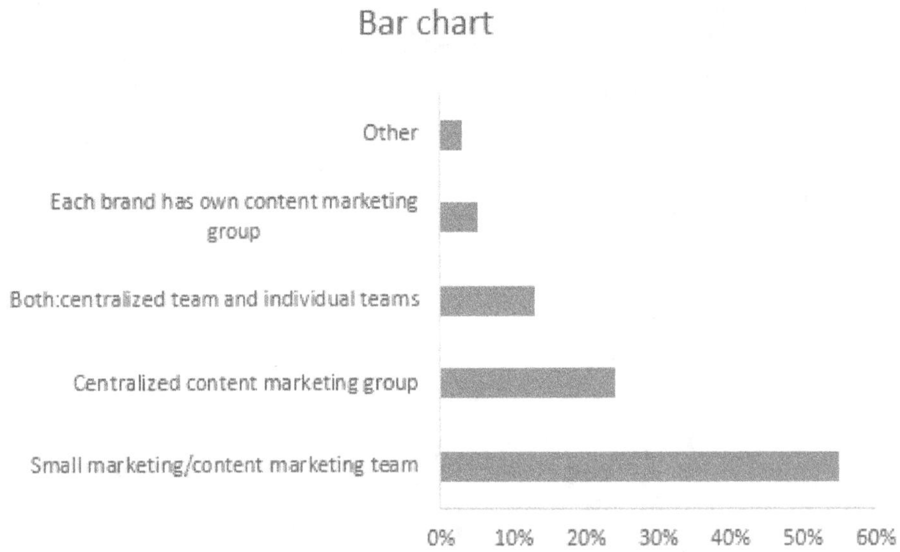

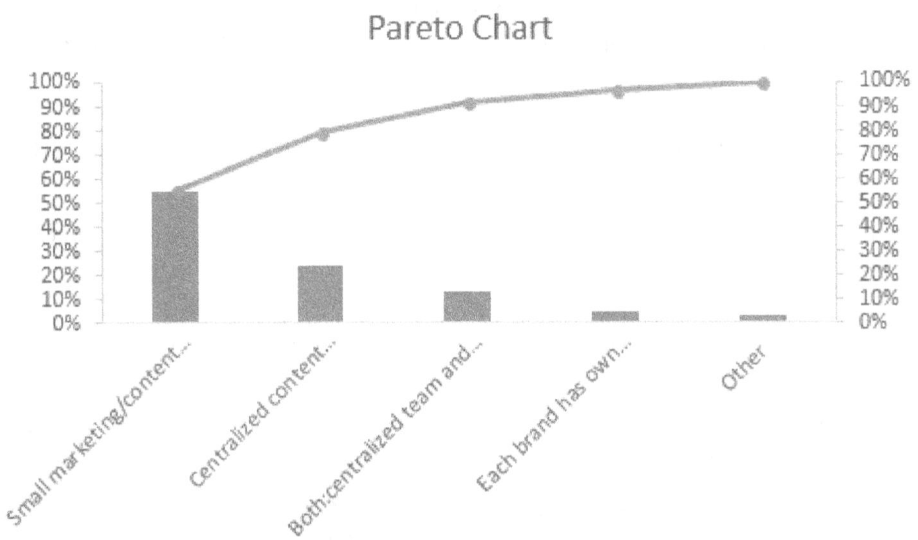

(b) The pie chart or the Pareto chart would be best. The pie chart would allow you to see each category as part of the whole, while the Pareto chart would enable you to see that Small marketing/content marketing team is the dominant category.

2.90 (c)
cont.

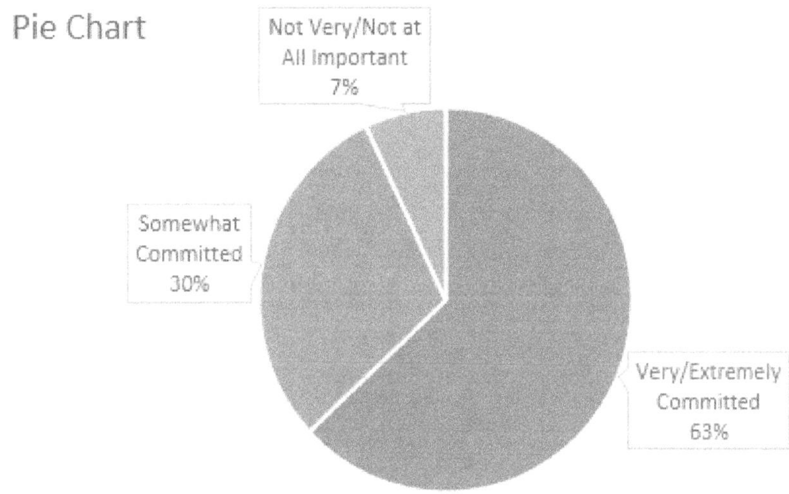
Pie Chart
Not Very/Not at All Important 7%
Somewhat Committed 30%
Very/Extremely Committed 63%

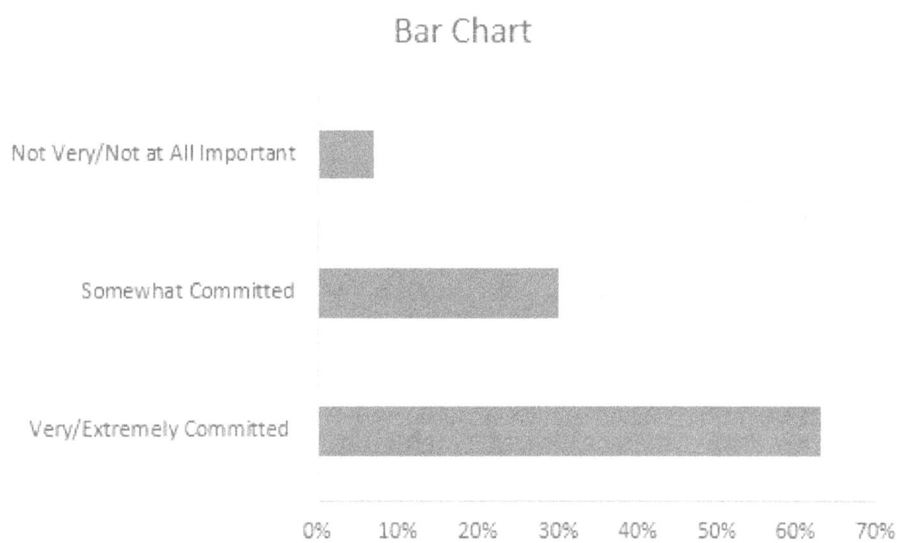
Bar Chart
Not Very/Not at All Important
Somewhat Committed
Very/Extremely Committed
0%
10%
20%
30%
40%
50%
60%
70%

2.90 (c)

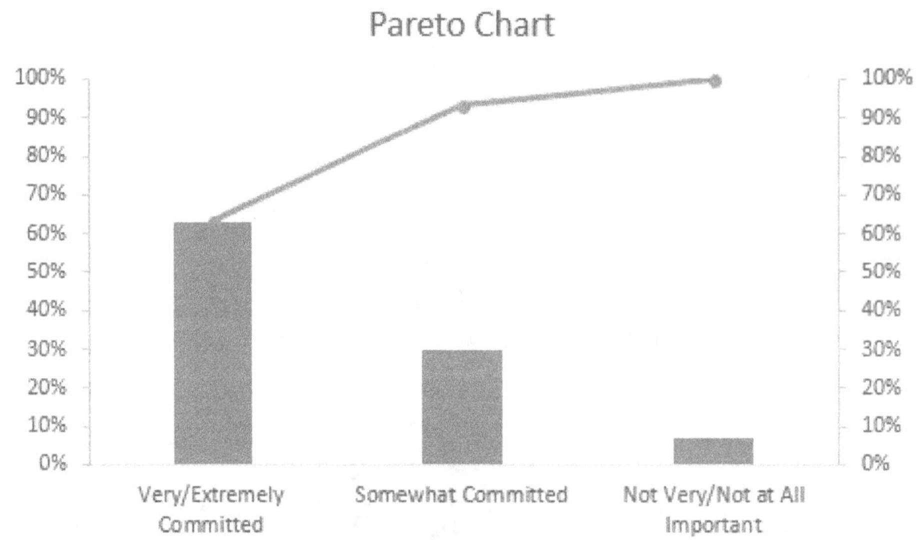

(d) The pie chart or the Pareto chart would be best. The pie chart would allow you to see each category as part of the whole while the Pareto chart would enable you to see that very committed to content marketing is the dominant category.

(e) Most organizations have a small marketing/content marketing team and are very committed to content marketing.

2.92 (a)

Dessert Ordered	Gender Male	Female	Total
Yes	66%	34%	100%
No	48%	52%	100%
Total	52%	48%	100%

Dessert Ordered	Gender Male	Female	Total
Yes	29%	34%	100%
No	71%	52%	100%
Total	100%	48%	100%

Dessert Ordered	Gender Male	Female	Total
Yes	15%	8%	23%
No	37%	40%	77%
Total	52%	48%	100%

Dessert Ordered	Gender Male	Female	Total
Yes	52%	48%	100%
No	25%	75%	100%
Total	31%	69%	100%

Dessert Ordered	Gender Male	Female	Total
Yes	38%	16%	23%
No	62%	84%	77%
Total	100%	100%	100%

2.92 cont. (a)

Dessert Ordered	Gender		
	Male	Female	Total
Yes	11.75%	10.79%	22.54%
No	19.52%	57.94%	77.46%
Total	31.27%	68.73%	100%

(b) If the owner is interested in finding out the percentage of males and females who order dessert or the percentage of those who order a beef entrée and a dessert among all patrons, the table of total percentages is most informative. If the owner is interested in the effect of gender on ordering of dessert or the effect of ordering a beef entrée on the ordering of dessert, the table of column percentages will be most informative. Because dessert is usually ordered after the main entrée, and the owner has no direct control over the gender of patrons, the table of row percentages is not very useful here.

(c) 29% of the men ordered desserts, compared to 17 of the women; men are almost twice as likely to order dessert as women. Almost 38% of the patrons ordering a beef entrée ordered dessert, compared to 16% of patrons ordering all other entrées. Patrons ordering beef are more than 2.3 times as likely to order dessert as patrons ordering any other entrée.

2.94 (a)

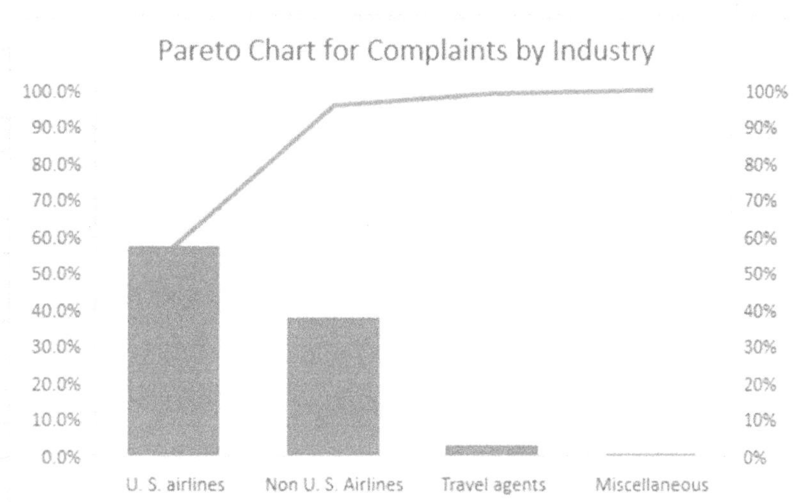

Most complaints were against U.S. airlines.

2.94 cont. (b)

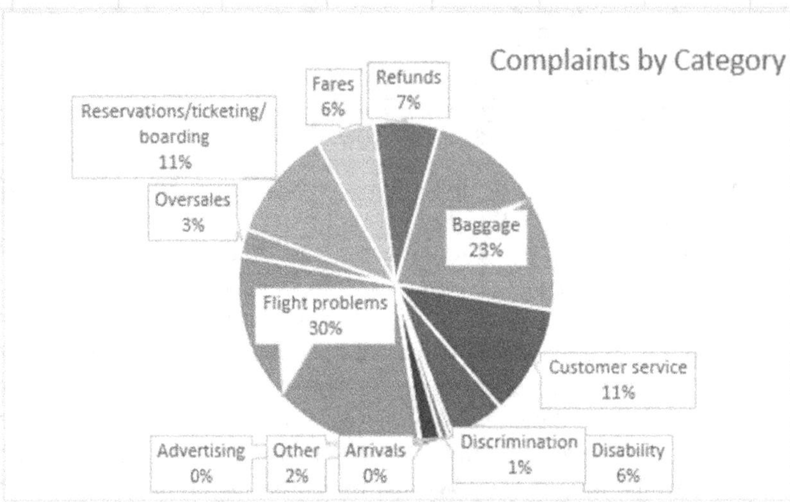

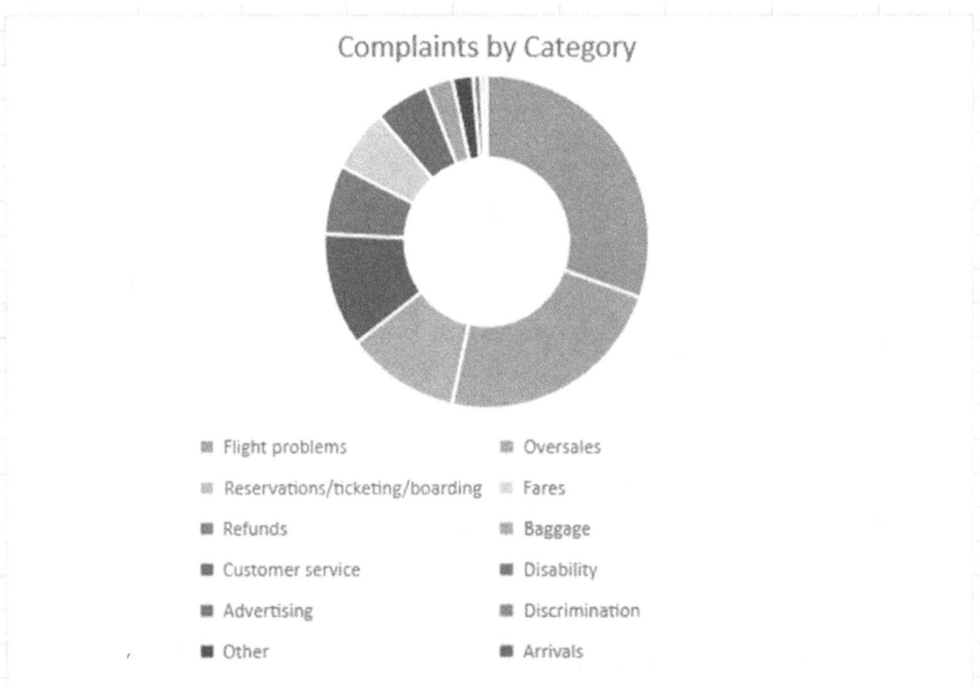

Most of the complaints were due to flight problems.

2.96 (a)

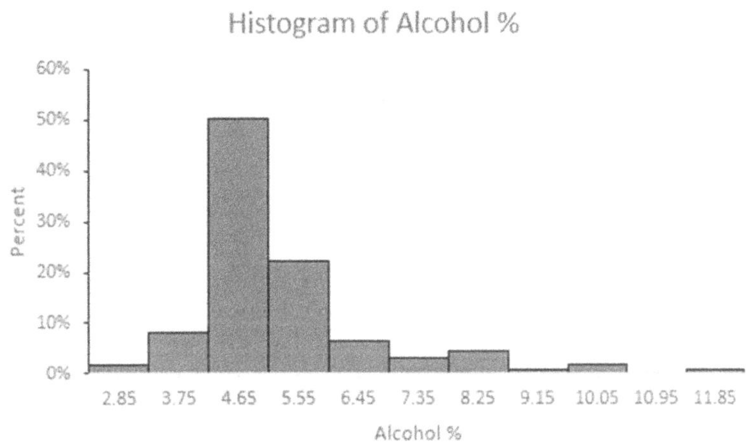
Histogram of Alcohol %
60%
50%
40%
30%
20%
10%
0%
Percent
2.85 3.75 4.65 5.55 6.45 7.35 8.25 9.15 10.05 10.95 11.85
Alcohol %

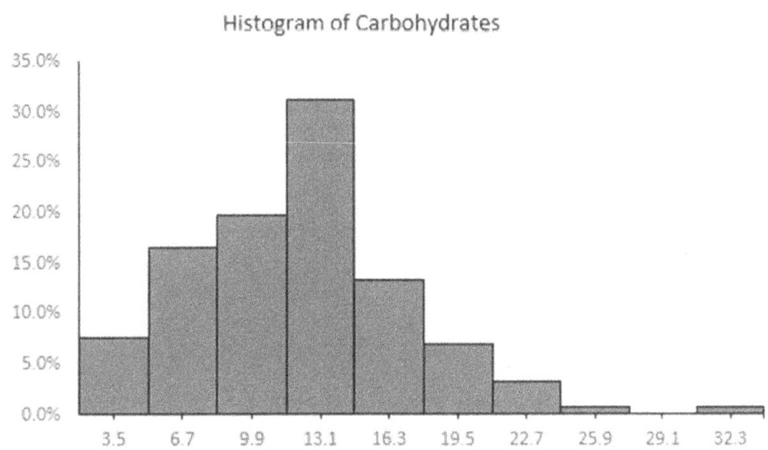
Histogram of Carbohydrates
35.0%
30.0%
25.0%
20.0%
15.0%
10.0%
5.0%
0.0%
3.5 6.7 9.9 13.1 16.3 19.5 22.7 25.9 29.1 32.3

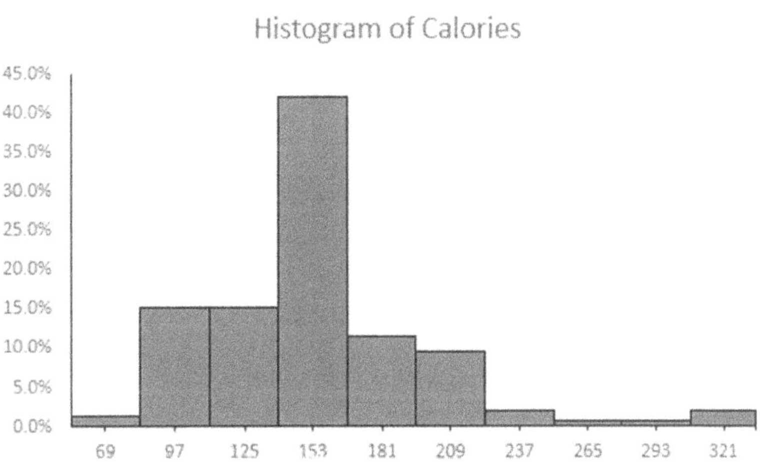
Histogram of Calories
45.0%
40.0%
35.0%
30.0%
25.0%
20.0%
15.0%
10.0%
5.0%
0.0%
69 97 125 153 181 209 237 265 293 321

2.96 (b)
cont.

Scatterplot Alcohol % vs Calories
Alcohol %
14.0
12.0
10.0
8.0
6.0
4.0
2.0
0.0
0
50
100
150
200
250
300
350
Calories

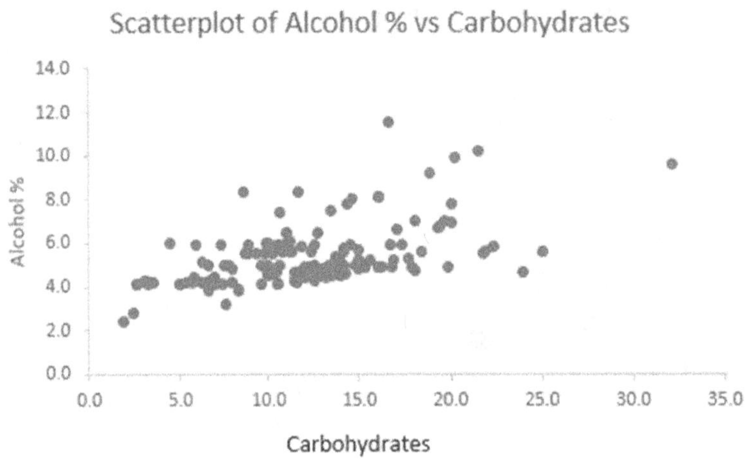
Scatterplot of Alcohol % vs Carbohydrates
Alcohol %
14.0
12.0
10.0
8.0
6.0
4.0
2.0
0.0
0.0
5.0
10.0
15.0
20.0
25.0
30.0
35.0
Carbohydrates

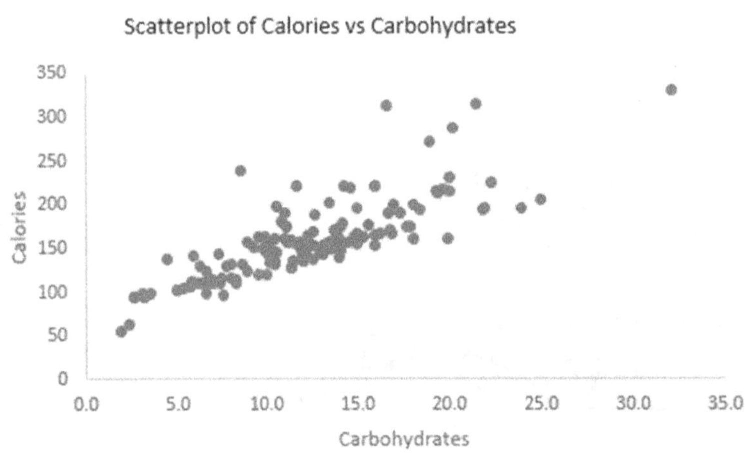
Scatterplot of Calories vs Carbohydrates
Calories
350
300
250
200
150
100
50
0
0.0
5.0
10.0
15.0
20.0
25.0
30.0
35.0
Carbohydrates

2.96 cont. (c) The alcohol percentage is concentrated between 4% and 6%, with more between 4% and 5%. The calories are concentrated between 140 and 160. The carbohydrates are concentrated between 8 and 15. There are outliers in the percentage of alcohol in both tails. There are a few beers with alcohol content as high as around 11.5%. There are a few beers with calorie content as high as around 320 and carbohydrates as high as 32. There is a positive relationship between percentage of alcohol and calories and between calories and carbohydrates, and positive relationship between percentage alcohol and carbohydrates.

2.98 (a) Stem-and -leaf of One Year CD, leaf unit = 0.1

Stems	Leaf
0	01111
0	22233
0	55
0	7
0	
1	1
1	
1	445
1	667
1	889
2	111
2	2233
2	44555
2	777
2	88888899

Stem-and -leaf of five Year CD, leaf unit = 0.1

Stems	Leaf
0	
0	23
0	5
0	66
0	88
1	001
1	33
1	
1	66
1	889
2	01
2	223
2	
2	
2	88888899
3	0000000011111
3	223

(b) The yield of one-year CDs shows that most values are at least 1.0. The yield of five-year CDs shows that most values are at least 1.6.

2.98 cont. (c)

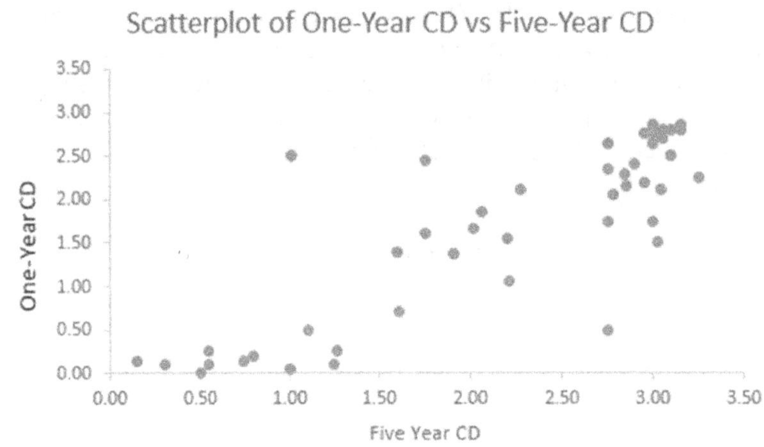

(d) There appears to be a positive relationship between the yield of the one-year CD and the five-year CD.

2.100 (a)

Frequencies (Boston)

Weight (Boston)	*Frequency*	*Percentage*
3015 but less than 3050	2	0.54%
3050 but less than 3085	44	11.96%
3085 but less than 3120	122	33.15%
3120 but less than 3155	131	35.60%
3155 but less than 3190	58	15.76%
3190 but less than 3225	7	1.90%
3225 but less than 3260	3	0.82%
3260 but less than 3295	1	0.27%

(b)

Frequencies (Vermont)

Weight (Vermont)	*Frequency*	*Percentage*
3550 but less than 3600	4	1.21%
3600 but less than 3650	31	9.39%
3650 but less than 3700	115	34.85%
3700 but less than 3750	131	39.70%
3750 but less than 3800	36	10.91%
3800 but less than 3850	12	3.64%
3850 but less than 3900	1	0.30%

2.100 (c)
cont.

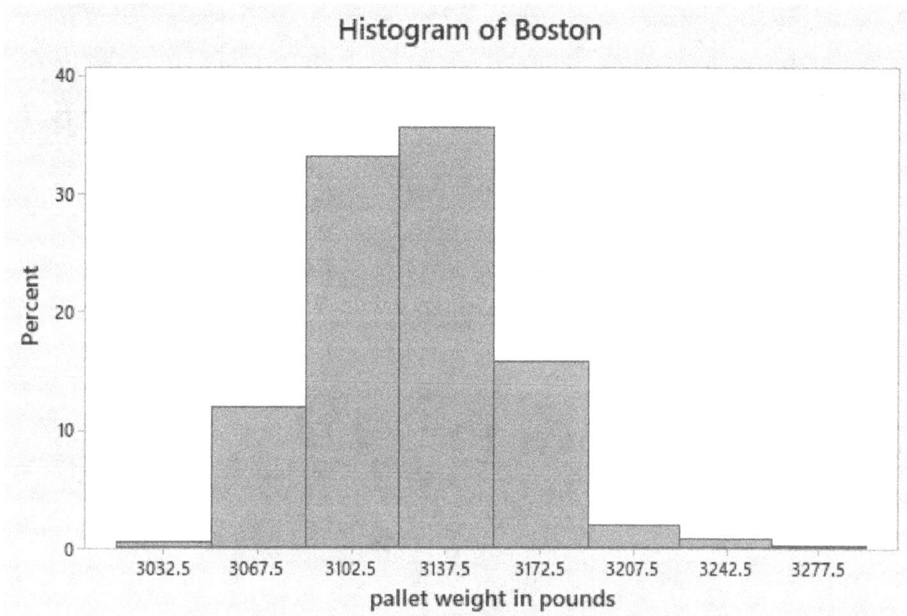

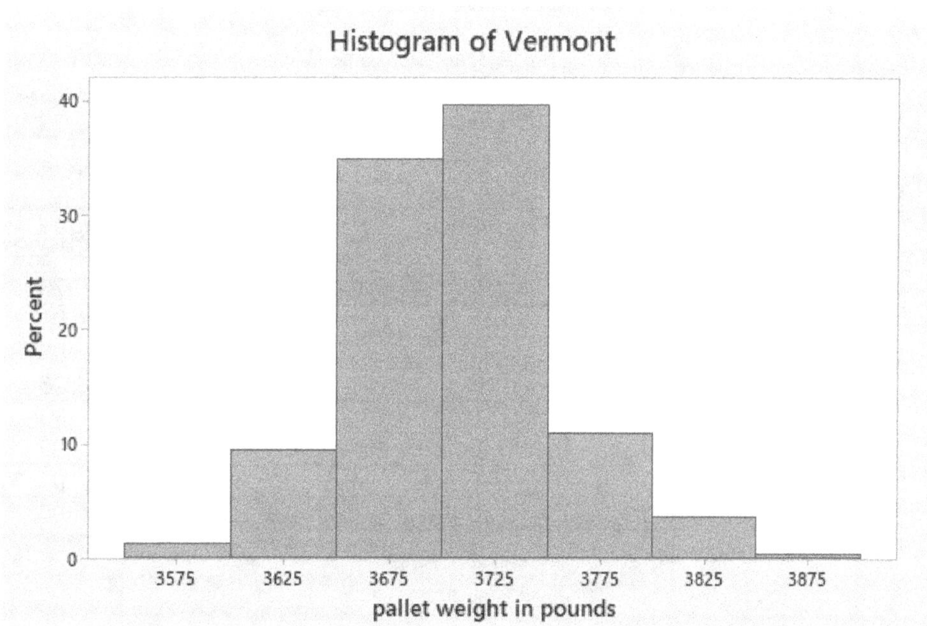

(d) 0.54% of the "Boston" shingles pallets are underweight while 0.27% are overweight. 1.21% of the "Vermont" shingles pallets are underweight while 3.94% are overweight.

2.102 (a)

Calories	*Frequency*	*Percentage*	*Percentage Less Than*
50 up to 100	3	12%	12%
100 up to 150	3	12	24
150 up to 200	9	36	60
200 up to 250	6	24	84
250 up to 300	3	12	96
300 up to 350	0	0	96
350 up to 400	1	4	100

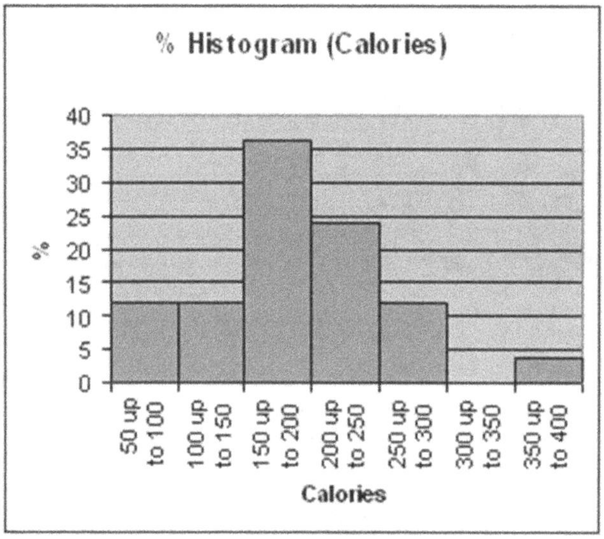

(b)

Cholesterol	*Frequency*	*Percentage*	*Percentage Less Than*
0 up to 50	2	8	8%
50 up to 100	17	68	76
100 up to 150	4	16	92
150 up to 200	1	4	96
200 up to 250	0	0	96
250 up to 300	0	0	96
300 up to 350	0	0	96
350 up to 400	0	0	96
400 up to 450	0	0	96
450 up to 500	1	4	100

2.102 cont. (b)

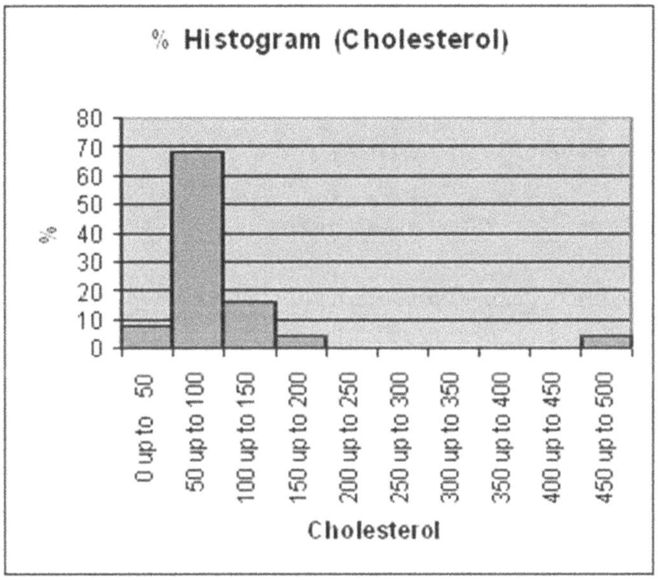

(c) The sampled fresh red meats, poultry, and fish vary from 98 to 397 calories per serving, with the highest concentration between 150 to 200 calories. One protein source, spareribs, with 397 calories, is more than 100 calories above the next highest caloric food. The protein content of the sampled foods varies from 16 to 33 grams, with 68% of the data values falling between 24 and 32 grams. Spareribs and fried liver are both very different from other foods sampled—the former on calories and the latter on cholesterol content.

2.104 (a)

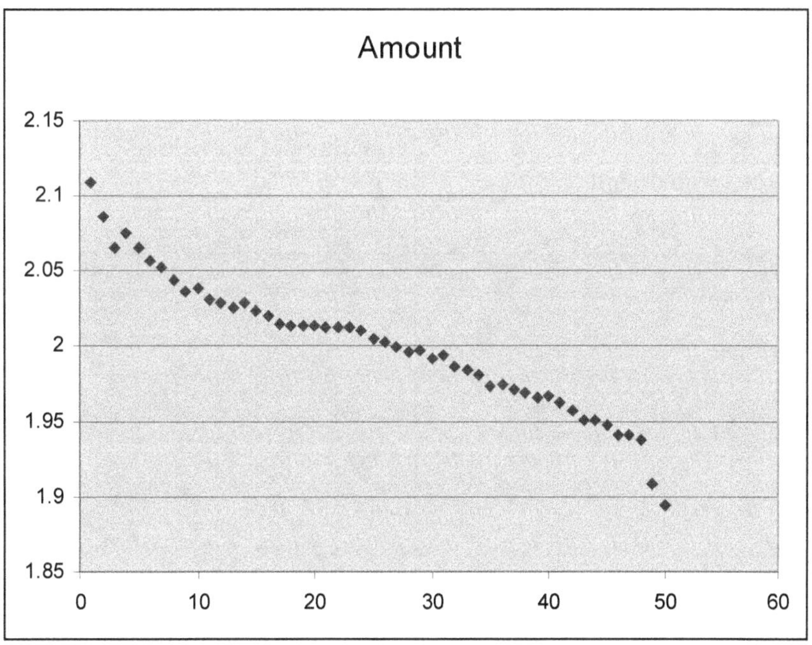

(b) There is a downward trend in the amount filled.

(c) The amount filled in the next bottle will most likely be below 1.894 liter.

2.104 cont. (d) The scatter plot of the amount of soft drink filled against time reveals the trend of the data, whereas a histogram only provides information on the distribution of the data.

2.106 (a)

Variations	Percentage of Download
Original Call to Action Button	9.64%
New Call to Action Button	13.64%

(b)

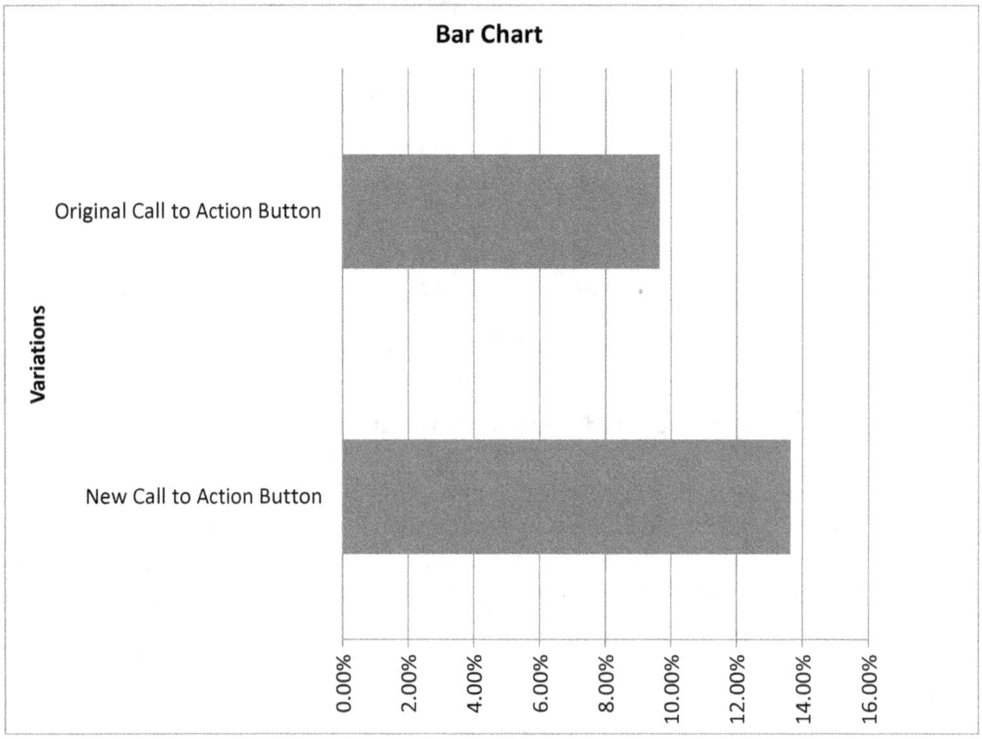

(c) The New Call to Action Button has a higher percentage of downloads at 13.64% when compared to the Original Call to Action Button with a 9.64% of downloads.

(d)

Variations	Percentage of Download
Original web design	8.90%
New web design	9.41%

2.106 cont. (e)

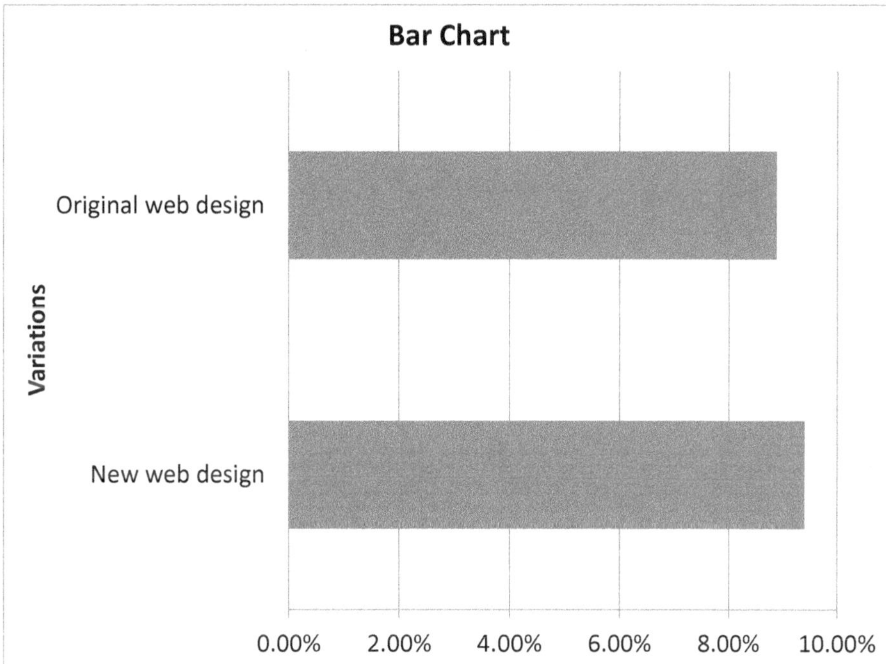

(f) The New web design has only a slightly higher percentage of downloads at 9.41% when compared to the Original web design with an 8.90% of downloads.

(g) The New web design is only slightly more successful than the Original web design while the New Call to Action Button is much more successful than the Original Call to Action Button with about 41% higher percentage of downloads.

(h)

Call to Action Button	Web Design	Percentage of Download
Old	Old	8.30%
New	Old	13.70%
Old	New	9.50%
New	New	17.00%

(i) The combination of the New Call to Action Button and the New web design results in slightly more than twice as high a percentage of downloads than the combination of the Old Call to Action Button and Old web design.

(j) The New web design is only slightly more successful than the Original web design while the New Call to Action Button is much more successful than the Original Call to Action Button with about 41% higher percentage of downloads. However, the combination of the New Call to Action Button and New web design results in more than twice as high a percentage of downloads than the combination of the Old Call to Action Button and Old web design.

2.108 Class project – answers will vary depending on student responses.

Chapter 3

3.2 (a) Excel output:

X	
Mean	7
Median	7
Mode	7
Standard Deviation	3.286335
Sample Variance	10.8
Range	9
Minimum	3
Maximum	12
Sum	42
Count	6
First Quartile	4
Third Quartile	9
Interquartile Range	5
Coefficient of Variation	46.9476%

Mean = 7 Median = 7 Mode = 7

(b) Range = 9 Variance = 10.8
Standard deviation = 3.286
Coefficient of variation = (3.286/7) • 100% = 46.948%

(c) Z scores: 0, –0.913, 0.609, 0, –1.217, 1.522
None of the Z scores is larger than 3.0 or smaller than –3.0. There is no outlier.

(d) Since the mean equals the median, the distribution is symmetrical.

3.4 Excel output:

X	
Mean	2
Median	7
Mode	7
Standard Deviation	7.874007874
Sample Variance	62
Range	17
Minimum	–8
Maximum	9
Sum	10
Count	5
First Quartile	–6.5
Third Quartile	8
Interquartile Range	14.5
Coefficient of Variation	393.7004%

(a) Mean = 2 Median = 7 Mode = 7

(b) Range = 17 Variance = 62
Standard deviation = 7.874 Coefficient of variation = (7.874/2) • 100% = 393.7%

3.4 cont. (c) Z scores: 0.635, –0.889, –1.270, 0.635, 0.889. No outliers.
(d) Since the mean is less than the median, the distribution is left-skewed.

3.6 $\bar{R}_G = \left[(1+0.2)(1-0.3)\right]^{1/2} - 1 = -8.348\%$

3.8 (a)

	Grade *X*	Grade *Y*
Mean	575	575.4
Median	575	575
Standard deviation	6.4	2.1

(b) If quality is measured by central tendency, Grade *X* tires provide slightly better quality because *X*'s mean and median are both equal to the expected value, 575 mm. If, however, quality is measured by consistency, Grade *Y* provides better quality because, even though *Y*'s mean is only slightly larger than the mean for Grade *X*, *Y*'s standard deviation is much smaller. The range in values for Grade *Y* is 5 mm compared to the range in values for Grade *X*, which is 16 mm.

(c) Excel output:

Grade X	
Mean	575
Median	575
Mode	#N/A
Standard Deviation	6.403124
Sample Variance	41
Range	16
Minimum	568
Maximum	584
Sum	2875
Count	5

Grade Y	
Mean	577.4
Median	575
Mode	#N/A
Standard Deviation	6.107373
Sample Variance	37.3
Range	15
Minimum	573
Maximum	588
Sum	2887
Count	5

	Grade *X*	Grade *Y*, Altered
Mean	575	577.4
Median	575	575
Standard deviation	6.4	6.1

When the fifth *Y* tire measures 588 mm rather than 578 mm, *Y*'s mean inner diameter becomes 577.4 mm, which is larger than *X*'s mean inner diameter, and *Y*'s standard deviation increases from 2.1 mm to 6.1 mm. In this case, *X*'s tires are providing better quality in terms of the mean inner diameter, with only slightly more variation among the tires than *Y*'s.

3.10 (a), (b)

Download Speed		Upload Speed	
Mean	32.375	Mean	11.175
Standard Error	4.542999	Standard Error	2.048148118
Median	32.65	Median	12.95
Mode	#N/A	Mode	#N/A
Standard Deviation	12.84954	Standard Deviation	5.793037693
Sample Variance	165.1107	Sample Variance	33.55928571
Kurtosis	3.158892	Kurtosis	-1.951578447
Skewness	-0.72039	Skewness	-0.39562811
Range	46.8	Range	13.8
Minimum	6.5	Minimum	3.7
Maximum	53.3	Maximum	17.5
Sum	259	Sum	89.4
Count	8	Count	8

(c) The mean is about the same as the median for the download speed. The upload speed is indicating a left or negative skewed distribution (the skewness statistic is also negative). The kurtosis statistic is positive for the upload speed, indicating a distribution that is more peaked than a normal (bell-shaped) distribution. The kurtosis statistic is negative for download speed, indicating a distribution that is less peaked than a normal distribution.

(d) The mean download speed is much higher than the mean upload speed. The median download speed indicates that half the carriers have a download speed of at least 32.65 Mbps as compared to a median upload speed of 12.95 Mbps that indicates that half the carriers have an upload speed of at least 12.95 Mbps. There is much more variation in the download speed than the upload speed because the standard deviation is 12.8495 as compared to 5.7930.

3.12 (a), (b)

	Household Hours
Mean	7.5667
Median	7
Minimum	4
Maximum	14.3
Range	10.3
Variance	6.1444
Standard deviation	2.4788
Coefficient of variation	32.76%
Skewness	1.3521
Kurtosis	1.5387
Sample size	30

(c) (d) The mean work hours needed is greater than the median, indicating a right or positive skewed distribution (the skewness statistic is also positive). The kurtosis statistic is positive, indicating a distribution that is more peaked than a normal (bell-shaped) distribution.

3.14 (a), (b)

	A	B	C
1	Mobil Commerce Penetration %		
2			
3		Mobile Commerce Penetration (%)	
4	Mean	45.08333333	
5	Median	45	
6	Mode	46	
7	Minimum	30	
8	Maximum	60	
9	Range	30	
10	Variance	58.5145	
11	Standard Deviation	7.6495	
12	Coeff. of Variation	16.97%	
13	Skewness	-0.0469	
14	Kurtosis	-0.2779	
15	Count	24	
16	Standard Error	1.5614	
17			

	A	B	C
1	Country	Mobile Commerce Penetration (%)	Z-Scores
2	Australia	46	0.119834
3	Austria	44	-0.14162
4	Belgium	38	-0.92599
5	Brazil	43	-0.27235
6	Canada	33	-1.57963
7	Denmark	51	0.773473
8	Finland	49	0.512018
9	France	39	-0.79526
10	Germany	50	0.642745
11	Italy	41	-0.53381
12	Japan	55	1.296385
13	Netherlands	49	0.512018
14	New Zealand	44	-0.14162
15	Norway	57	1.557841
16	Poland	33	-1.57963
17	Russia	30	-1.97181
18	South Korea	47	0.250562
19	Spain	48	0.38129
20	Sweden	60	1.950024
21	Switzerland	43	-0.27235
22	Taiwan	42	-0.40308
23	Turkey	46	0.119834
24	United Kingdom	55	1.296385
25	United States	39	-0.79526

(a), (b) Because there are no Z values below –3.0 or above 3.0, there are no outliers.

(c) The mean is approximately the same the median, so Mobile Commerce Penetration is symmetrical.

(d) The mean Mobile Commerce Penetration is 45.0833% and half the countries have values greater than or equal to 45%. The average scatter around the mean is 7.6495%. The lowest value is 30% (Russia), and the highest value is 60% (Sweden).

3.16 (a),(b)

Time	
Mean	232.78
Standard Error	22.441676
Median	228
Mode	243
Standard Deviation	158.68661
Sample Variance	25181.44
Kurtosis	21.834832
Skewness	3.923888
Range	1076
Minimum	65
Maximum	1141
Sum	11639
Count	50

(c) The mean time is 232.78 seconds, and half the calls last greater than or equal to 228 seconds, so call duration is slightly right-skewed. The average scatter around the mean is 158.6866 seconds. The shortest call lasted 65 seconds, and the longest call lasted 1141 seconds.

3.18 (a) Mean = 7.11 Median = 6.68

(b) Variance = 4.336 Standard Deviation = 2.082 Range = 6.67

Coefficient of variation = 29.27%

Waiting Time	Z Score
9.66	1.222431
5.90	–0.58336
8.02	0.434799
5.79	–0.63619
8.73	0.775786
3.82	–1.58231
8.01	0.429996
8.35	0.593286

Waiting Time	Z Score
10.49	1.62105
6.68	–0.20875
5.64	–0.70823
4.08	–1.45744
6.17	–0.45369
9.91	1.342497
5.47	–0.78987

Since there are no Z values below –3.0 or above 3.0, there are no outliers.

(c) Because the mean is greater than the median, the distribution is right-skewed.

(d) The mean and median are both greater than five minutes. The distribution is right-skewed, meaning that there are some unusually high values. Further, 13 of the 15 bank customers sampled (or 86.7%) had waiting times greater than five minutes. So the customer is likely to experience a waiting time in excess of five minutes. The manager overstated the bank's service record in responding that the customer would "almost certainly" not wait longer than five minutes for service.

3.20 (a) $\overline{R}_G = \left[(1+0.758)(1-0.257)\right]^{1/2} - 1 = 14.29\%$

(b) 1000(1+0.1429) = \$1142.90

(c) The rate of return was much better than that of GE, which declined in price.

3.22 (a)

	A	B	C	D	E	F
1	Year	Platinum	Gold	Silver		
2	2016	8.50	8.50	15.70		
3	2017	-0.44	10.10	2.30		
4	2018	-14.80	-2.10	-9.50		
5	Geometric Mean	-2.7%	5.4%	2.3%		
6	Excel formula	=((1+B2/100)*(1+B3/100)*(1+B4/100))^(1/3)-1				
7	for Platinum					
8						

(b) Gold had the best rate of return followed by silver. Only platinum had a negative rate of return.

(c) The return on the metals was much worse than the rate of the stock indices.

3.24 (a)

Mean of 3YrReturn%	Rating					
Type	One	Two	Three	Four	Five	Grand Total
Growth	**5.41**	**7.04**	**8.94**	**10.14**	**12.83**	**8.51**
Large	6.97	9.43	10.62	11.83	14.25	10.30
Mid-Cap	2.27	5.07	7.93	8.77	11.22	6.93
Small	0.78	5.09	6.52	8.35	9.53	6.39
Value	**4.43**	**5.49**	**7.29**	**8.34**	**10.23**	**6.84**
Large	5.23	6.05	7.58	8.85	10.23	7.29
Mid-Cap	2.79	5.77	7.32	9.26	–	6.69
Small	1.33	3.20	5.93	7.04	–	5.39

(b)

StdDev of 3Yr Return%	Rating					
Type	One	Two	Three	Four	Five	Grand Total
Growth	**3.72**	**2.85**	**2.71**	**2.23**	**2.12**	**3.19**
Large	2.86	1.34	2.23	1.43	0.89	2.56
Mid-Cap	3.49	2.04	2.08	1.03	1.02	2.86
Small	0.84	2.40	2.08	2.11	0.62	2.52
Value	**2.07**	**2.40**	**1.20**	**2.09**	**1.32**	**2.33**
Large	1.81	1.68	0.98	1.63	1.32	1.93
Mid-Cap	1.00	2.90	1.13	0.99	–	2.51
Small	–	2.88	1.36	2.62	–	2.35
Grand Total	**3.24**	**2.78**	**2.44**	**2.34**	**2.24**	**3.02**

(c) The mean three-year return of small-cap funds is much lower than mid-cap and large funds. Five-star funds for all market cap categories show the highest mean three-year returns. The mean three-year returns for all combinations of type and market cap rises as the star rating rises, consistent to the mean three-year returns for all growth and value funds. The standard deviations of the three-year return for large-cap and mid-cap value funds vary greatly among star rating categories.

3.26 (a)

Mean of 3Yr Return%	Rating					
Type	One	Two	Three	Four	Five	Grand Total
Growth	**5.41**	**7.04**	**8.94**	**10.14**	**12.83**	**8.51**
Low	7.53	8.60	9.89	10.29	12.64	9.87
Average	6.17	7.99	9.28	10.43	11.96	9.06
High	3.83	5.59	7.45	8.76	13.59	6.64
Value	**4.43**	**5.49**	**7.29**	**8.34**	**10.23**	**6.84**
Low	5.29	7.00	7.66	8.57	10.74	7.76
Average	5.01	4.98	6.97	7.96	9.23	6.41
High	2.71	2.63	6.53	8.39	–	4.13
Grand Total	**5.07**	**6.45**	**8.38**	**9.43**	**12.01**	**7.91**

(b)

StdDev of 3Yr Return%	Rating					
	One	Two	Three	Four	Five	Grand Total
Growth	3.72	2.85	2.71	2.23	2.12	3.19
Low	3.27	1.57	2.02	2.05	2.04	2.42
Average	4.37	2.43	2.67	2.42	2.51	2.86
High	2.98	2.92	2.73	1.43	2.47	3.39
Value	**2.07**	**2.40**	**1.20**	**2.09**	**1.32**	**2.33**
Low	1.46	1.12	1.00	2.15	0.85	1.72
Average	2.11	2.43	1.25	2.09	1.87	2.27
High	–	2.88	1.36	2.62	–	2.35
Grand Total	**3.24**	**2.78**	**2.44**	**2.34**	**2.24**	**3.02**

(c) The mean three-year return of high-risk funds is much lower than the other risk categories except for five-star funds. In all risk categories, five-star funds have the highest mean three-year return. The mean three-year returns for high-risk growth and value funds for one-, two-, and three-star rating funds are lower than the means for the other risk categories.

The standard deviations of the three-year return for low-risk funds show the most consistency across star rating categories and the standard deviations of the three-year return for low-risk funds are the lowest across categories. They also vary greatly among star rating categories.

3.28 (a) $Q_1 = 4$, $Q_3 = 9$, interquartile range = 5

(b) Five-number summary: 3 4 7 9 12

(c)

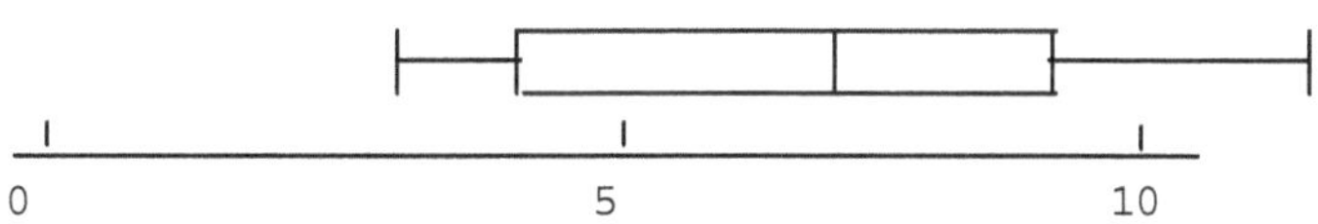

The distances between the median and the extremes are close, 4 and 5, but the differences in the tails are different (1 on the left and 3 on the right), so this distribution is slightly right-skewed.

(d) In 3.2 (d), because the mean and median are equal, the distribution is symmetric. The box part of the graph is symmetric, but the tails show right-skewness.

3.30 (a) $Q_1 = -6.5$, $Q_3 = 8$, interquartile range = 14.5

(b) Five-number summary: – 8 – 6.5 7 8 9

3.30 (c)
cont.

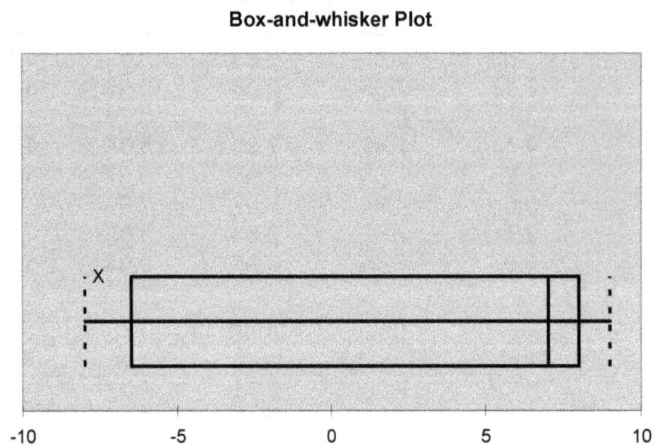

The distribution is left-skewed.

(d) This is consistent with the answer in 3.4 (d).

3.32 (a) $Q_1 = 39$, $Q_3 = 50$, interquartile range = 11

(b)

	Five-Number Summary	
4	Minimum	30
5	First Quartile	39
6	Median	45
7	Third Quartile	50
8	Maximum	60

3.32 (c)
cont.

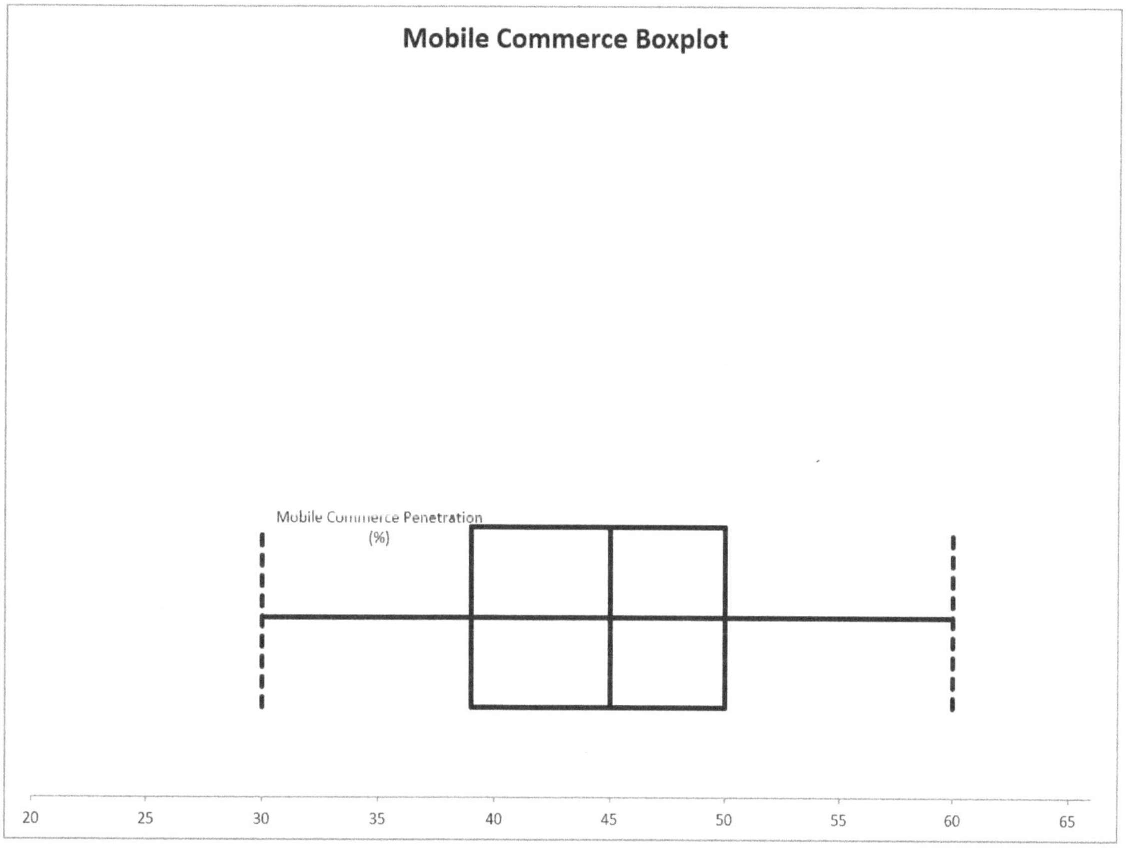

The distribution is symmetric

3.34 (a),(b)

Five-Number Summary		
	Halftime or After	First Half
Minimum	3.63	4.22
First Quartile	4.96	4.81
Median	5.59	5.34
Third Quartile	6.41	6.14
Maximum	7.69	6.51
Interquartile Range	1.45	1.33

3.34 cont. (c)

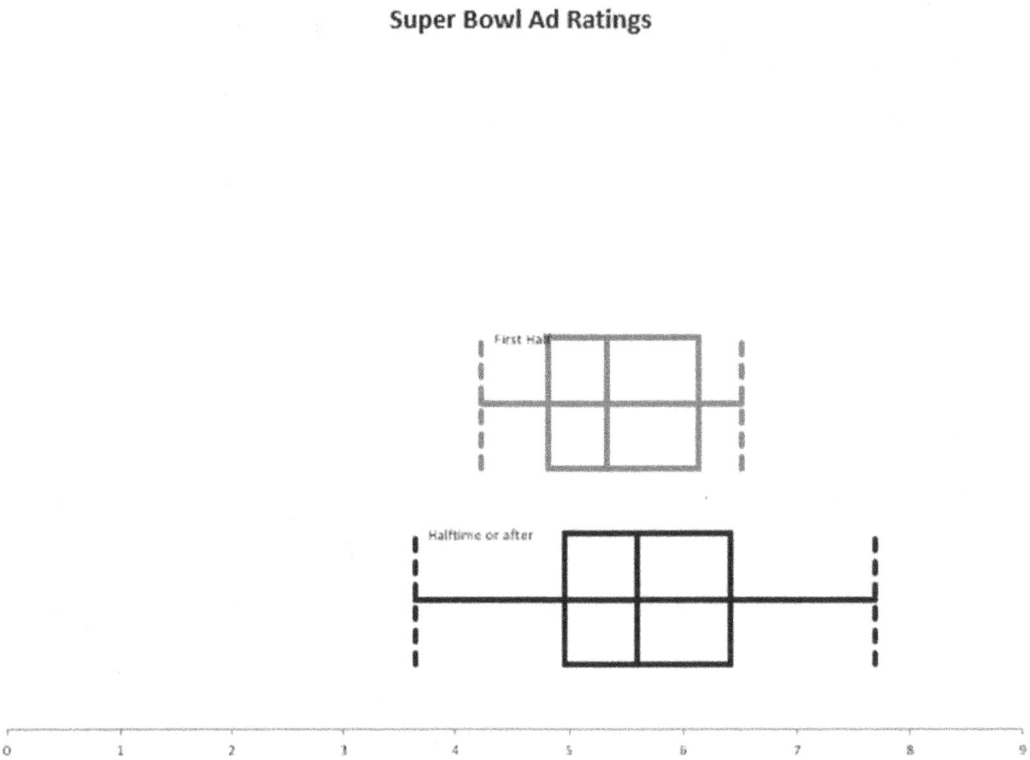

The boxplot plot for halftime or after is approximately symmetrical and the boxplot for the first or second quarter is also approximately symmetric

3.36 (a)

Variable	Minimum	Q1	Median	Q3	Maximum
Bank 1 Waiting Time	0.380	3.200	4.500	5.550	6.460
Bank 2 Waiting Time	3.820	5.640	6.680	8.730	10.490

(b)

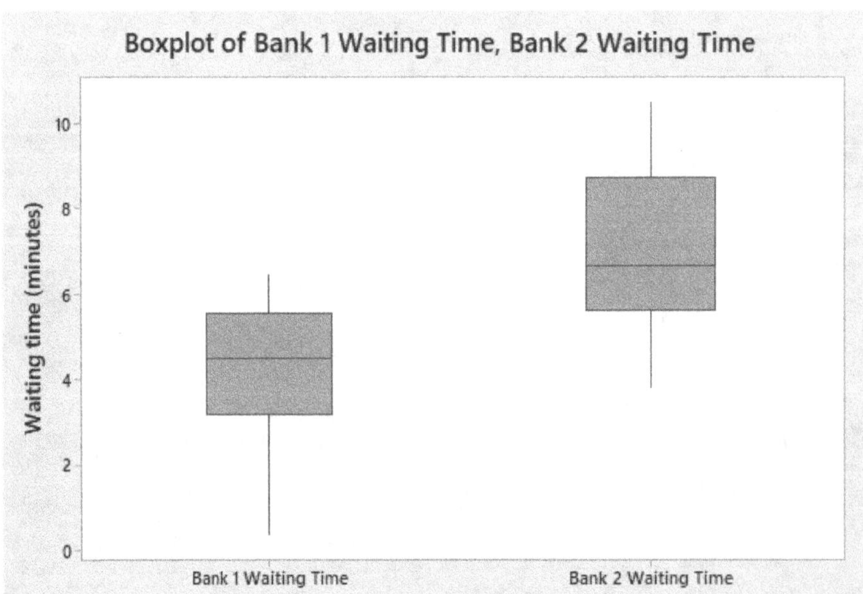

3.36 cont.

(b) The waiting time for bank 1 in the commercial district of a city is skewed to the left. The waiting time for bank 2 in the residential area is skewed right.

(c) The central tendency of the waiting times for the bank branch located in the commercial district (bank 1) of a city is lower than that of the branch located in the residential area (bank 2). There are a few longer than normal waiting times for the branch located in the residential area whereas there are a few exceptionally short waiting times for the branch located in the commercial area.

3.38 (a) Population Mean = 6

(b) $\sigma^2 = 2.8$ $\sigma = 1.67$

3.40 (a) 68%

(b) 95%

(c) at least 0 75% 88.89%

(d) $\mu - 4\sigma$ to $\mu + 4\sigma$ or –2.8 to 19.2

3.42 (a)

	Average Residential Price
Mean	13.48
Standard Deviation	3.4515

(b) Within one standard deviation of the mean is (10.03,16.93), counting the data reveals 40 states or 40/51*100 = 78.43% of the states are within this range.

Within two standad deviations of the mean is (6.57,20.38), counting the data reveals 49 states or 49/51*100 = 96.08% of the states are within this range.

Within three standad deviations of the mean is (3.12,23.83), counting the data reveals 50 states or 50/51*100 = 98.04% of the states are within this range.

(c) This is slightly different from 68%, 95% and 99.7% of the empirical rule.

Excel Output:

Variability in a Distribution

Data	
Mean	13.47706
Standard Deviation	3.451484

Results	Range	
±1 standard deviations	10.03	16.93
±2 standard deviations	6.57	20.38
±3 standard deviations	3.12	23.83

% of Values Found in Intervals Around the Mean

Chebyshev Rule (any distribution)	Empirical Rule (normal distribution)
At least 0%	Approximately 68%
At least 75%	Approximately 95%
At least 88.89%	Approximately 99.7%

3.44 (a) $cov(X,Y) = 65.2909$

(b) $S_X^2 = 21.7636,\ S_Y^2 = 195.8727$

$$r = \frac{\operatorname{cov}(X,Y)}{\sqrt{S_X^2}\sqrt{S_Y^2}} = \frac{65.2909}{\sqrt{21.7636}\sqrt{195.8727}} = +1.0$$

3.44 cont. (c) There is a perfect positive linear relationship between X and Y; all the points lie exactly on a straight line with a positive slope.

3.46 (a) $cov(X,Y) = 133.3333$

(b) $S_X^2 = 2200,\ S_Y^2 = 11.4762$

$$r = \frac{\text{cov}(X,Y)}{S_X S_Y} = 0.8391$$

(c) The correlation coefficient is more valuable for expressing the relationship between calories and sugar because it does not depend on the units used to measure calories and sugar.

(d) There is a strong positive linear relationship between calories and sugar.

3.48 Excel Output:

	A	B	C	D	E	F
1	**Carrier**	**Download Speed**	**Upload Speed**			
2	Verizon	53.3	17.5			
3	T-Mobile	36.3	16.9			
4	AT&T	37.1	12.9			
5	Metro PCS	32.8	13.0			
6	Sprint	32.5	4.0			
7	Boost	29.4	3.7			
8	Straight Talk	31.1	15.6			
9	Cricket	6.5	5.8			
10						
11	Covariance	45.5036	=COVARIANCE.S(B2:B9,C2:C9)			
12	r	0.6113	=CORREL(B2:B9,C2:C9)			
13						
14						

(a) $\text{cov}(X,Y) = 45.5036$

(b) Correlation $= r = 0.6113$

(c) The is a positive linear relationship between download speed and upload speed.

3.50 We should look for ways to describe the typical value, the variation, and the distribution of the data within a range.

3.52 The arithmetic mean is a simple average of all the values, but is subject to the effect of extreme values. The median is the middle ranked value, but varies more from sample to sample than the arithmetic mean, although it is less susceptible to extreme values. The mode is the most common value, but is extremely variable from sample to sample.

3.54 Variation is the amount of dispersion, or "spread," in the data.

3.56 The range is a simple measure, but only measures the difference between the extremes. The interquartile range measures the range of the center fifty percent of the data. The standard deviation measures variation around the mean while the variance measures the squared variation around the mean, and these are the only measures that take into account each observation. The coefficient of variation measures the variation around the mean relative to the mean. The range, standard deviation, variance and coefficient of variation are all sensitive to outliers while the interquartile range is not.

3.58 Chebyshev's theorem applies to any type of distribution while the empirical rule applies only to data sets that are approximately bell-shaped. The empirical rule is more accurate than the Chebyshev rule in approximating the concentration of data around the mean.

3.60 Skewness measures the extent to which the data values are not symmetrical around the mean. Kurtosis measures the extent to which values that are very different from the mean affect the shape of the distribution of a set of data.

3.62 The covariance measures the strength of the linear relationship between two numerical variables while the coefficient of correlation measures the relative strength of the linear relationship. The value of the covariance depends very much on the units used to measure the two numerical variables while the value of the coefficient of correlation is totally free from the units used.

3.64 The geometric mean is used to measure the rate of change of a variable over time. It is calculated by taking the nth root of the product of the n data values, where n is the number of data values. The geometric rate of return measures the mean percentage return of an investment per time period.

3.66 Minitab Output:

Statistics

Variable	Mean	StDev	Variance	CoefVar	Q1	Median	Q3	Range	IQR
Time	45.22	23.15	535.79	51.19	25.00	45.00	63.00	83.00	38.00

(a) Mean = 45.22 Median = 45 first quartile = 25 third quartile = 63

(b) Range = 83 Interquartile range = 38 Variance = 535.79
Standard Deviation = 23.15 Coefficient of variation = 51.19%

3.66 cont. (c)

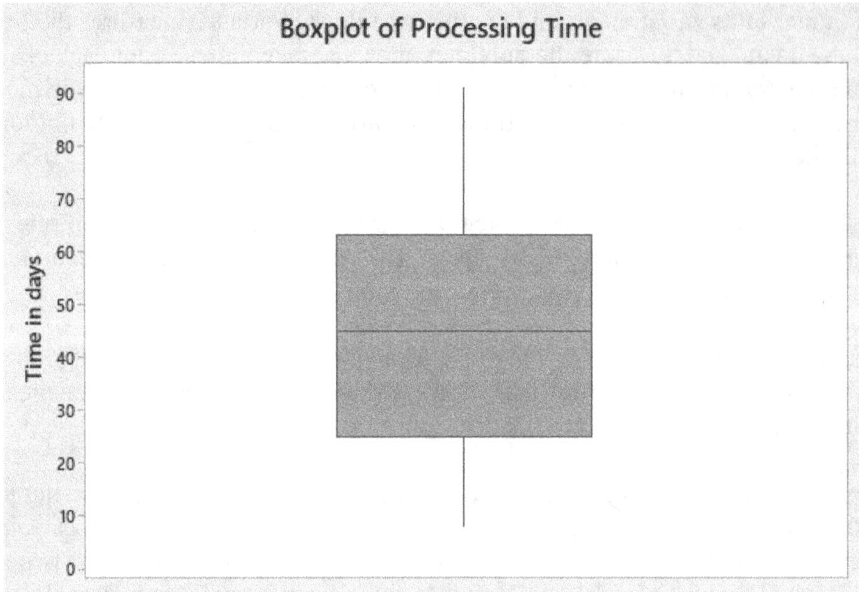

The distribution is approximately symmetric.

(d) The mean approval process takes 45.22 days with 50% of the policies being approved in less than 45 days. 50% of the applications are approved between 25 and 63 days. About 25% of the applicants are approved in no more than 25 days.

3.68 (a) Excel output:

Statistic	r Time (seconds)
Nbr. of observations	50
Minimum	5.000
Maximum	28.000
1st Quartile	12.000
Median	15.000
3rd Quartile	18.000
Mean	14.980
Standard deviation (n-1)	5.557

Box plots:

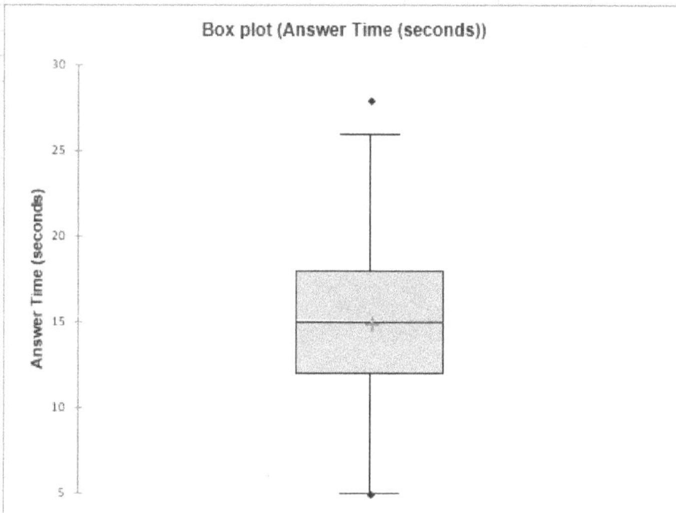

Minitab Output:

Variable	Mean	StDev	Median	Range
Answer Time (seconds)	14.980	5.557	15.000	23.000

(b) Using the formulas in the text with n= 50, Q1 = (50+1)/4 ranked value = 12.75 ranked value so choose 13th ranked value which is 12. Q3 = 3(50+1)/4 ranked value = 38.25 ranked value so choose 38th ranked value which is 18
Therefore 5 number summary is min, Q1, median, Q3, max = 5, 12, 15, 18, 28

* Note Minitab uses a slightly different formula to calculate the quartiles

Variable	Minimum	Q1	Median	Q3	Maximum
Answer Time (seconds)	5.000	11.750	15.000	18.250	28.000

(c) The distribution is symmetric.
(d) The service level is met because 75% of the class are answered in less than 18 seconds.

3.70 (a), (b)

	Bundle Score	*Typical Cost ($)*
Mean	54.775	24.175
Standard Error	4.367344951	2.866224064
Median	62	20
Mode	75	8
Standard Deviation	27.62151475	18.12759265
Sample Variance	762.9480769	328.6096154
Kurtosis	-0.845357193	2.766393511
Skewness	-0.48041728	1.541239625
Range	98	83
Minimum	2	5
Maximum	100	88
Sum	2191	967
Count	40	40
First Quartile	34	9
Third Quartile	75	31
Interquartile Range	41	22
CV	50.43%	74.98%

(c)

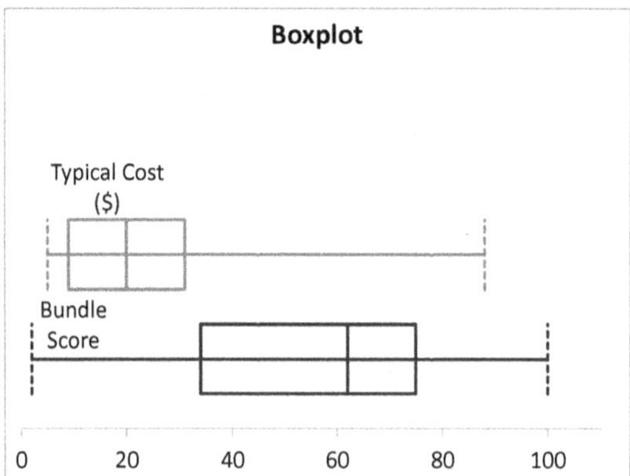

The typical cost is right-skewed, while the bundle score is left-skewed.

(d) $r = \dfrac{\text{cov}(X, Y)}{S_X S_Y} = 0.3465$

(e) The mean typical cost is $24.18, with an average spread around the mean equaling $18.13. The spread between the lowest and highest costs is $83. The middle 50% of the typical cost fall over a range of $22 from $9 to $31, while half of the typical cost is below $20. The mean bundle score is 54.775, with an average spread around the mean equaling 27.6215. The spread between the lowest and highest scores is 98. The middle 50% of the scores fall over a range of 41 from 34 to 75, while half of the scores are below 62. The typical cost is right-skewed, while the bundle score is left-skewed. There is a weak positive linear relationship between typical cost and bundle score.

3.72 (a) Excel output:

Five-number Summary	Boston	Vermont
Minimum	0.04	0.02
First Quartile	0.17	0.13
Median	0.23	0.2
Third Quartile	0.32	0.28
Maximum	0.98	0.83

(b)

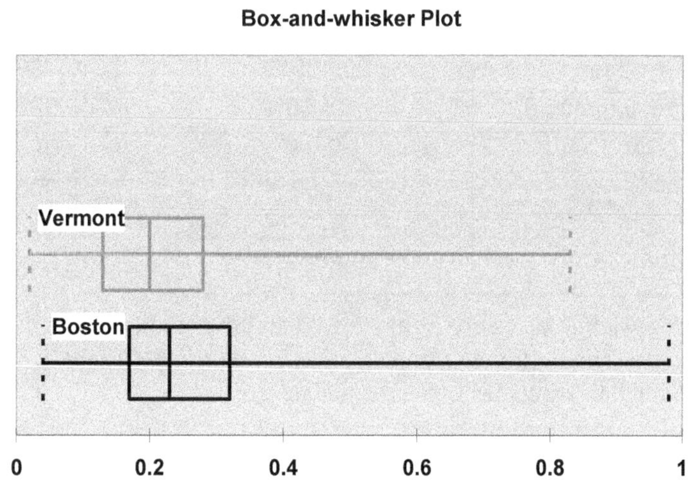

Both distributions are right skewed.

(c) Both sets of shingles did quite well in achieving a granule loss of 0.8 gram or less. The Boston shingles had only two data points greater than 0.8 gram. The next highest to these was 0.6 gram. These two data points can be considered outliers. Only 1.176% of the shingles failed the specification. In the Vermont shingles, only one data point was greater than 0.8 gram. The next highest was 0.58 gram. Thus, only 0.714% of the shingles failed to meet the specification.

3.74 (a), (b), (c)

	Calories	*Protein*	*Cholesterol*
Calories	1		
Protein	0.464411	1	
Cholesterol	0.177665	0.141673	1

(d) There is a rather weak positive linear relationship between calories and protein with a correlation coefficient of 0.46. The positive linear relationship between calories and cholesterol is quite weak at .178.

3.76 (a), (b)

	Annual Taxes on $176 Home	*Median Home Value ($000)*
Mean	1,979.490196	195.6509804
Median	1,763	165.9
Mode	#NA	#NA
Minimum	489	100.2
Maximum	4,029	504.5
Range	3,540	404.3
Variance	11,065.8549	7,418.7265
Standard Deviation	900.5919	86.1320
Coefficient of variance	45.50%	44.02%
Skewness	0.6423	1.6988
Kurtosis	–0.5014	3.3069
Count	51	51
Standard Error	126.1081	12.0609

(c) The boxplot shows that taxes are right skewed and the median value of homes is highly right skewed.(d) The coefficient of correlation is –0.041. (e) There is a large variation in taxes and the median value of homes from state to state.

3.78 (a), (b)

	Abandonment rate in % (7:00AM-3:00PM)
Mean	13.86363636
Standard Error	1.625414306
Median	10
Mode	9
Standard Deviation	7.623868875
Sample Variance	58.12337662
Kurtosis	0.723568739
Skewness	1.180708144
Range	29
Minimum	5
Maximum	34
Sum	305
Count	22
First Quartile	9
Third Quartile	20
Interquartile Range	11
CV	54.99%

3.78 cont. (c)

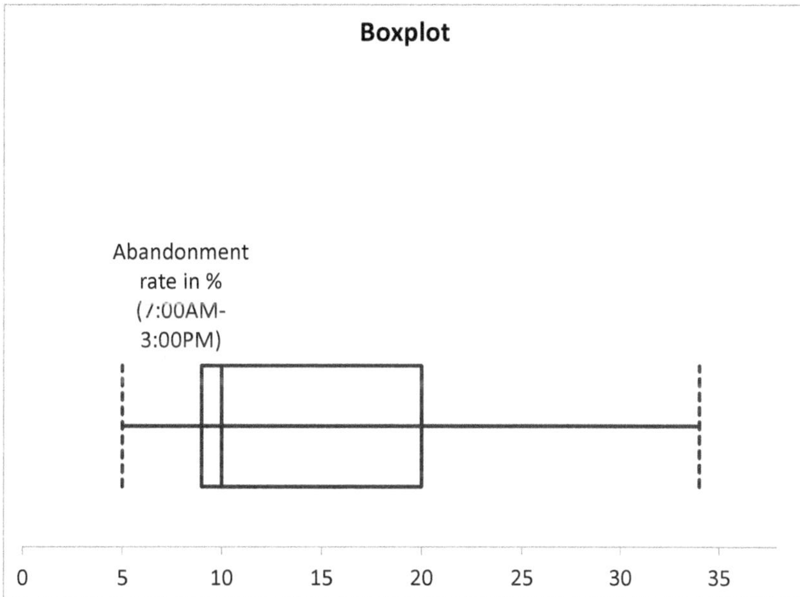

The data are right-skewed.

(d) $r = 0.7575$

(e) The average abandonment rate is 13.86%. Half of the abandonment rates are less than 10%. One-quarter of the abandonment rates are less than 9% while another one-quarter are more than 20%. The overall spread of the abandonment rates is 29%. The middle 50% of the abandonment rates are spread over 11%. The average spread of abandonment rates around the mean is 7.62%. The abandonment rates are right-skewed.

3.80 (a)–(c) Excel output:

Statistic	verage Credit Score
Range	214.510
1st Quartile	649.835
Median	672.015
3rd Quartile	697.195
Mean	673.244
Variance (n-1)	1005.878
Standard deviation (n-1)	31.716
IQR	47.360
Variation coefficient	0.047

3.80 cont. (a)–(c)

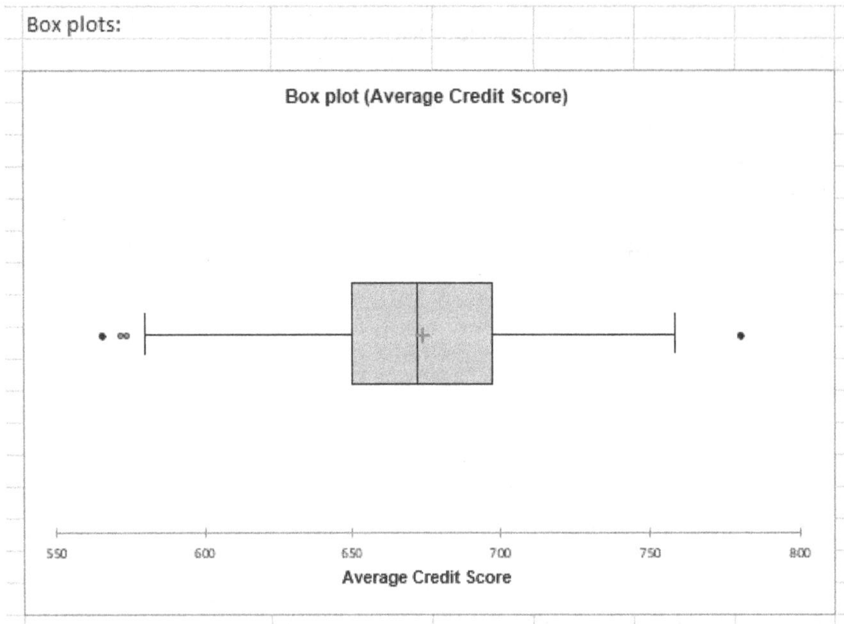

The data are symmetrical.

(d) The mean of the average credit scores is 673.24. Half of the average credit scores are less than 672.02. One-quarter of the average credit scores are less than 649.84 while another one-quarter is more than 697.2. The range of the average credit score is 214.51. The middle 50% of the average credit scores is spread over 47.36. The typical spread of the average credit scores around the mean is 31.716.

3.82 Minitab Output:

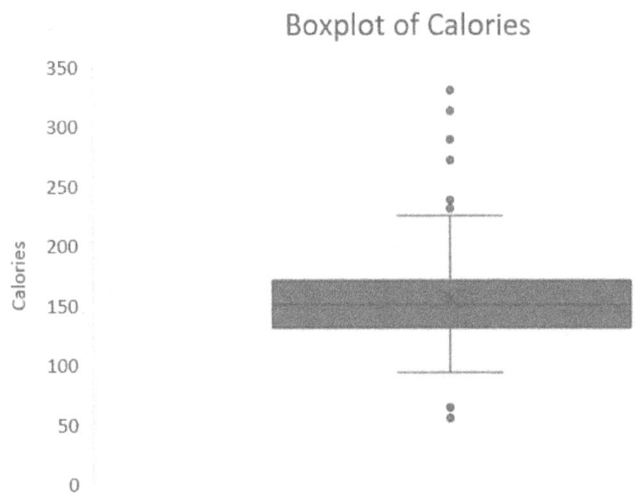

3.82
cont.

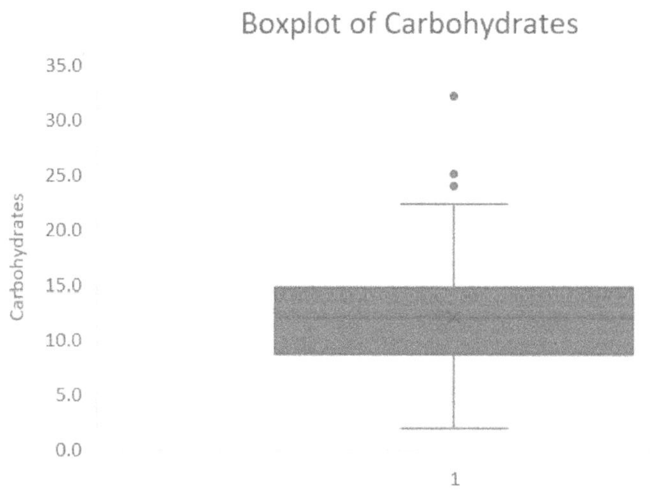
Boxplot of Carbohydrates
35.0
30.0
25.0
20.0
15.0
10.0
5.0
0.0
Carbohydrates
1

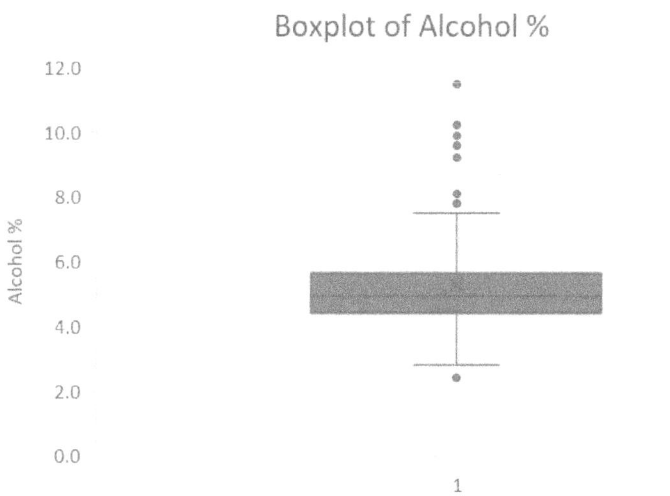
Boxplot of Alcohol %
12.0
10.0
8.0
6.0
4.0
2.0
0.0
Alcohol %
1

3.82
cont.

	A	B
1	Alcohol %	
2		
3	Five-Number Summary	
4	Minimum	2.4
5	First Quartile	4.4
6	Median	4.92
7	Third Quartile	5.65
8	Maximum	11.5
9	IQR	1.25
10	Range	9.1

	A	B
1	Alcohol	
2		
3		Alcohol %
4	Mean	5.270127389
5	Median	4.92
6	Mode	4.2
7	Minimum	2.4
8	Maximum	11.5
9	Range	9.1
10	Variance	1.8337
11	Standard Deviation	1.3541
12	Coeff. of Variation	25.69%
13	Skewness	1.8403
14	Kurtosis	4.5833
15	Count	157
16	Standard Error	0.1081
17		

	A	B
1	Carbohydrates	
2		
3	Five-Number Summary	
4	Minimum	1.9
5	First Quartile	8.65
6	Median	12
7	Third Quartile	14.7
8	Maximum	32.1
9	IQR	6.05
10	Range	30.2
11		

	A	B
1	Carbohydrates	
2		
3		Carbohydrates
4	Mean	12.05235669
5	Median	12
6	Mode	12
7	Minimum	1.9
8	Maximum	32.1
9	Range	30.2
10	Variance	24.8119
11	Standard Deviation	4.9812
12	Coeff. of Variation	41.33%
13	Skewness	0.4908
14	Kurtosis	1.0801
15	Count	157
16	Standard Error	0.3975
17		

	A	B
1	Calories	
2		
3	Five-Number Summary	
4	Minimum	55
5	First Quartile	130.5
6	Median	150
7	Third Quartile	170.5
8	Maximum	330
9	IQR	40
10	Range	275
11		
12		

	A	B
1	Calories	
2		
3		Calories
4	Mean	155.5095541
5	Median	150
6	Mode	110
7	Minimum	55
8	Maximum	330
9	Range	275
10	Variance	1918.6746
11	Standard Deviation	43.8027
12	Coeff. of Variation	28.17%
13	Skewness	1.2148
14	Kurtosis	2.9712
15	Count	157
16	Standard Error	3.4958
17		

3.82 cont. The amount of % alcohol is right skewed with an average at 5.278%. Half of the beers have % alcohol below 4.92%. The middle 50% of the beers have alcohol content spread over a range of 1.25%. The highest alcohol content is at 11.5% while the lowest is at 2.4%. The typical spread of alcohol content around the mean is 1.354%.

The number of calories is symmetric with an average at 155.51. Half of the beers have calories below 150.00. The middle 50% of the beers have calories spread over a range of 40. The highest number of calories is 330 while the lowest is 55. The typical spread of calories around the mean is 43.80.

The number of carbohydrates is symmetric with three high outliers from the boxplot with an average at 12.052, which is almost identical to the median at 12.000. Half of the beers have carbohydrates below 12.000. The middle 50% of the beers have carbohydrates spread over a range of 6.05. The highest number of carbohydrates is 32.10 while the lowest is 1.9. The typical spread of carbohydrates around the mean is 4.98.

Chapter 4

4.2 (a) Simple events include selecting a red ball.
(b) Selecting a white ball
(c) The sample space is the collection of "a red ball being selected" and "a white ball being selected."

4.4 (a) $\frac{60}{100}=\frac{3}{5}=0.6$
(b) $\frac{10}{100}=\frac{1}{10}=0.1$
(c) $\frac{35}{100}=\frac{7}{20}=0.35$
(d) $\frac{60}{100}+\frac{65}{100}-\frac{35}{100}=\frac{90}{100}=\frac{9}{10}=0.9$

4.6 (a) Mutually exclusive, not collectively exhaustive.
(b) Not mutually exclusive, not collectively exhaustive.
(c) Mutually exclusive, not collectively exhaustive.
(d) Mutually exclusive, collectively exhaustive

4.8 (a) Is a millennial.
(b) Is a millennial and has a retirement account.
(c) Does not have a retirement account.
(d) Is a millennial and has a retirement account is a joint event because it consists of two characteristics.

4.10 Answers will vary.
(a) A marketer who plans to increase use of LinkedIn.
(b) A B2B marketer who plans to increase use of LinkedIn.
(c) A marketer who does not plan to increase use of LinkedIn.
(d) A marketer who plans to increase use of LinkedIn and is a B2C marketer is a joint event because it consists of two characteristics, plans to increase use of LinkedIn and is a B2C marketer.

4.12 (a) *P*(fully supports increased use of educational technologies in higher ed)
$=\frac{686}{1,803}=0.3805$
(b) *P*(is a digital learning leader) $=\frac{206}{1,803}=0.1143$
(c) *P*(fully supports increased use of educational technologies *or* is a digital learning leader)
$=\frac{686+206-175}{1,803}=\frac{717}{1,803}=0.3977$
(d) The probability in (c) includes those who fully support increased use of educational technologies in higher education and those who are digital learning leaders.

4.14

Important to Understand Privacy Policy	Older adults	Younger adults	Total
Yes	911	195	1106
No	90	65	155
Total	1001	260	1261

(a) *P*(is important to have a clear understanding of a company's privacy policy before signing up for its service online) $= \frac{1,106}{1,261} = 0.8771$

(b) *P*(is an older adult and indicates it is important to have a clear understanding of a company's privacy policy before signing up for its service online) $= \frac{911}{1,261} = 0.7224$

(c) *P*(is an older adult or indicates it is important to have a clear understanding of a company's privacy policy before signing up for its service online)
$= \frac{1,001 + 1,106 - 911}{1,261} = \frac{1,196}{1,261} = 0.9485$

(d) *P*(is an older adult or a younger adult) $= \frac{1,261}{1,261} = 1.00$

4.16 (a) $P(A \mid B) = \frac{10}{30} = \frac{1}{3} = 0.33$

(b) $P(A \mid B') = \frac{20}{60} = \frac{1}{3} = 0.33$

(c) $P(A' \mid B') = \frac{40}{60} = \frac{2}{3} = 0.67$

(d) Since $P(A \mid B) = P(A) = \frac{1}{3}$, events *A* and *B* are statistically independent.

4.18 $P(A \mid B) = \frac{P(A \text{ and } B)}{P(B)} = \frac{0.4}{0.8} = \frac{1}{2} = 0.5$

4.20 Since *P*(*A and B*) = 0.20 and *P*(*A*) *P*(*B*) = 0.12, events *A* and *B* are not statistically independent.

4.22 (a) *P*(Increased use of LinkedIn | B2B marketer) $= \frac{1,266}{1,947} = 0.6502$

(b) *P*(Increased use of LinkedIn | B2C marketer) $= \frac{1,625}{3,779} = 0.4300$

(c) *P*(Increased use of LinkedIn) = 0.5049 and *P*(Increased use of LinkedIn | B2B marketer) = 0.6502 are not equal. Therefore, increased use of LinkedIn and business focus are not independent.

4.24 (a) *P*(fully supports increased use of educational technologies in higher ed | faculty member) $= \frac{511}{1,597} = 0.3200$

4.24 cont.

(b) P(does not fully supports increased use of educational technologies in higher ed | faculty member) $= \dfrac{1{,}086}{1{,}597} = 0.6800$

(c) P(fully supports increased use of educational technologies in higher ed | digital learning leader) $= \dfrac{175}{206} = 0.8495$

(d) P(does not fully supports increased use of educational technologies in higher ed | digital learning leader) $= \dfrac{31}{206} = 0.1505$

4.26

Needs Warranty-Related Repair	U.S.	Non-U.S.	Total
Yes	0.025	0.015	0.04
No	0.575	0.385	0.96
Total	0.600	0.400	1.00

(a) P(needs warranty repair | manufacturer based in U.S.) $= \dfrac{0.025}{0.6} = 0.0417$

(b) P(needs warranty repair | manufacturer not based in U.S.) $= \dfrac{0.015}{0.4} = 0.0375$

(c) Since P(needs warranty repair | manufacturer based in U.S.) $= \dfrac{0.025}{0.6} = 0.0417$ is not equal to P(needs warranty repair) = 0.04, the two events are not independent.

4.28 (a) $P(\text{both queens}) = \dfrac{4}{52}\cdot\dfrac{3}{51} = \dfrac{12}{2{,}652} = \dfrac{1}{221} = 0.0045$

(b) $P(10 \text{ followed by 5 or 6}) = \dfrac{4}{52}\cdot\dfrac{8}{51} = \dfrac{32}{2{,}652} = \dfrac{8}{663} = 0.012$

(c) $P(\text{both queens}) = \dfrac{4}{52}\cdot\dfrac{4}{52} = \dfrac{16}{2{,}704} = \dfrac{1}{169} = 0.0059$

(d) $P(\text{blackjack}) = \dfrac{16}{52}\cdot\dfrac{4}{51} + \dfrac{4}{52}\cdot\dfrac{16}{51} = \dfrac{128}{2{,}652} = \dfrac{32}{663} = 0.0483$

4.30 With *a priori* probability, the probability of success is based on prior knowledge of the process involved. With empirical probability, outcomes are based on observed data. Subjective probability refers to the chance of occurrence assigned to an event by a particular individual.

4.32 The general addition rule is used by adding the probability of *A* and the probability of *B* and then subtracting the joint probability of *A* and *B*.

4.34 If events *A* and *B* are statistically independent, the conditional probability of event *A* given *B* is equal to the probability of *A*.

4.36 (a)

Prefer Hybrid Advice	Generation: Boomers	Generation: Millennials	Total
Yes	140	320	460
No	360	180	540
Total	500	500	1,000

(b) A simple event is "prefers hybrid investment advice." A joint event is "being a baby boomer and preferring hybrid investment advice."

(c) $P(\text{prefers hybrid advice}) = \frac{460}{1{,}000} = 0.46$

(d) $P(\text{prefers hybrid advice } \textit{and} \text{ is a baby boomer}) = \frac{140}{1{,}000} = 0.14$

(e) They are not independent because baby boomers and millennials have different probabilities of preferring hybrid investment advice.

4.38 (a) $P(\text{creative display}) = \frac{82}{276} = 0.2971$

(b) $P(\text{creative display } \textit{or} \text{ informational resources}) = \frac{82+33}{276} = \frac{115}{276} = 0.4167$

(c) $P(\text{business website } \textit{or} \text{ online sales}) = \frac{129+45-32}{276} = \frac{142}{276} = 0.5145$

(d) $P(\text{business website } \textit{and} \text{ online sales}) = \frac{32}{276} = 0.1159$

(e) $P(\text{online business presence} \mid \text{personal website}) = \frac{4}{147} = 0.0272$

Chapter 5

5.2 PHStat output:

Probabilities & Outcomes:	P	X
	0.1	0
	0.2	1
	0.45	2
	0.15	3
	0.05	4
	0.05	5
Statistics		
E(X)	2	
E(Y)	0	
Variance(X)	1.4	
Standard Deviation(X)	1.183216	
Variance(Y)	0	
Standard Deviation(Y)	0	
Covariance(XY)	0	
Variance(X+Y)	1.4	
Standard Deviation(X+Y)	1.183216	

(a)–(b)

X	$P(X)$	$X*P(X)$	$(X-\mu_X)^2$	$(X-\mu_X)^2*P(X)$
0	0.10	0.00	4	0.40
1	0.20	0.20	1	0.20
2	0.45	0.90	0	0.00
3	0.15	0.45	1	0.15
4	0.05	0.20	4	0.20
5	0.05	0.25	9	0.45
	(a) Mean =	2.00	Variance =	1.40
			(b) Stdev =	1.18321596

(c) $P(X \geq 2) = 0.45 + 0.15 + 0.05 + 0.05 = 0.70$

5.4 (a)

X	$P(X)$
\$ – 1	21/36
\$ + 1	15/36

(b)

X	$P(X)$
\$ – 1	21/36
\$ + 1	15/36

(c)

X	$P(X)$
\$ – 1	30/36
\$ + 4	6/36

(d) \$ – 0.167 for each method of play

5.6 Excel Output:

	A	B	C	D	E	F
1	Arrivals = X	Frequency	Probability = Frequency/n	[X-E(X)]^2		
2	0	13	0.125	4.434	=(A2-B12)^2	
3	1	25	0.240384615	1.223	=(A3-B12)^2	
4	2	32	0.307692308	0.011	=(A4-B12)^2	
5	3	17	0.163461538	0.800	=(A5-B12)^2	
6	4	9	0.086538462	3.588	=(A6-B12)^2	
7	5	6	0.057692308	8.377	=(A7-B12)^2	
8	6	1	0.009615385	15.165	=(A8-B12)^2	
9	7	1	0.009615385	23.953	=(A9-B12)^2	
10		Statistics				
11	n	104	=SUM(B2:B9)			
12	E(x)	2.105769231	=SUMPRODUCT(A2:A9,C2:C9)			
13	Variance (X)	2.152274408	=SUMPRODUCT(C2:C9,D2:D9)			
14	Standard Deviation (X)	1.467063192	=SQRT(B13)			
15	P(X>1)	0.634615385	=SUM(C4:C9)			

(a) $\mu = E(X) = 2.1058$

(b) $\sigma = 1.4671$

(c) $P(X > 1) = P(X = 2) + P(X = 3) + P(X = 4) + P(X = 5) + P(X = 6) + P(X = 7) = 0.6346$

5.8 Excel Output:

	A	B	C	D	E
1	Corporate Bond Fund X	Probability	[X-E(X)]^2		
2	-300	0.01	128307.24	=(A2-B12)^2	
3	-70	0.09	16435.24	=(A3-B12)^2	
4	30	0.15	795.24	=(A4-B12)^2	
5	60	0.35	3.24	=(A5-B12)^2	
6	100	0.3	1747.24	=(A6-B12)^2	
7	120	0.1	3819.24	=(A7-B12)^2	
8					
9					
10					
11		Statistics			
12	E(X)	58.2	=SUMPRODUCT(A2:A7,B2:B7)		
13	Variance(X)	3788.76	=SUMPRODUCT(B2:B7,C2:C7)		
14	Standard Deviation (X)	61.55290407	=SQRT(B13)		
15					
16					

5.8 cont.

	A	B	C	D	E
1	Common Stock Fund X	Probability	[X-E(X)]^2		
2	-999	0.01	1127865.24	=(A2-B12)^2	
3	-300	0.09	131776.2601	=(A3-B12)^2	
4	-100	0.15	26572.2601	=(A4-B12)^2	
5	100	0.35	1368.2601	=(A5-B12)^2	
6	150	0.3	7567.2601	=(A6-B12)^2	
7	350	0.1	82363.2601	=(A7-B12)^2	
8					
9					
10					
11		Statistics			
12	E(X)	63.01	=SUMPRODUCT(A2:A7,B2:B7)		
13	Variance(X)	38109.7499	=SUMPRODUCT(B2:B7,C2:C7)		
14	Standard Deviation (X)	195.2171865	=SQRT(B13)		
15					

(a) E(Bond Fund) = \$58.20; E(Common Stock Fund) = \$63.01

(b) $\sigma_{\text{bond fund}} = \$61.55$; $\sigma_{\text{common stock fund}} = \$195.22$

(c) Based on the expected value criteria, you would choose the common stock fund. However, the common stock fund also has a standard deviation more than three times higher than that for the corporate bond fund. An investor should carefully weigh the increased risk.

(d) If you chose the common stock fund, you would need to assess your reaction to the small possibility that you could lose virtually all of your entire investment.

5.10 (a) $\mu = 4(0.10) = 0.40$ $\sigma = \sqrt{4 \cdot 0.1 \cdot 0.9} = 0.60$

(b) $\mu = 4(0.40) = 1.60$ $\sigma = \sqrt{4 \cdot 0.4 \cdot 0.6} = 0.98$

(c) $\mu = 5(0.80) = 0.40$ $\sigma = \sqrt{5 \cdot 0.8 \cdot 0.2} = 0.894$

(d) $\mu = 3(0.5) = 1.50$ $\sigma = \sqrt{3 \cdot 0.5 \cdot 0.5} = 0.866$

5.12 Excel Output:

	A	B	C
1	**Binomial Probabilities**		
2			
3	**Data**		
4	**Sample size**	**6**	
5	**Probability of an event of interest**	**0.47**	
6			
7	**Parameters**		
8	**Mean**	**2.82**	
9	**Variance**	**1.4946**	
10	**Standard deviation**	**1.22254**	
11			
12	**Binomial Probabilities Table**		
13	***X***	***P(X)***	
14	**0**	**0.0222**	
15	**1**	**0.1179**	
16	**2**	**0.2615**	
17	**3**	**0.3091**	
18	**4**	**0.2056**	
19	**5**	**0.0729**	
20	**6**	**0.0108**	
21			
22	Prob(at least 4) = P(X>=4)	0.2893	=SUM(B18:B20)

(a) $P(X = 4) = 0.2056$
(b) $P(X = 6) = 0.0108$
(c) $P(X \geq 4) = 0.2056 + 0.0729 + 0.0108 = 0.2893$
(d) $\mu = 2.82$, $\sigma = 1.22254$
(e) That each American adult owns an iPhone or does not own an iPhone and that next six adults selected are independent.

5.14 Excel Output:

	A	B	C	D
1	Binomial Probabilities			
2				
3	Data			
4	Sample size	10		
5	Probability of an event of interest	0.03		
6				
7	Parameters			
8	Mean	0.3		
9	Variance	0.291		
10	Standard deviation	0.53944		
11				
12	Binomial Probabilities Table			
13	*X*	*P(X)*		
14	0	0.7374		
15	1	0.2281		
16	2	0.0317		
17	3	0.0026		
18	4	0.0001		
19	5	0.0000		
20	6	0.0000		
21	7	0.0000		
22	8	0.0000		
23	9	0.0000		
24	10	0.0000		
25				
26	Prob(two or fewer) = P(X<=2)	0.9972	=SUM(B14:B16)	
27	Prob(Three or more) = P(X>=3)	0.0028	=SUM(B17:B24)	

(a) $P(X = 0) = 0.7374$
(b) $P(X = 1) = 0.2281$
(c) $P(X \leq 2) = 0.9972$
(d) $P(X \geq 3) = 0.0028$

5.16 Excel Output:

	A	B	C	D
1	Binomial Probabilities			
2				
3	Data			
4	Sample size	3		
5	Probability of an event of interest	0.909		
6				
7	Parameters			
8	Mean	2.727		
9	Variance	0.24816		
10	Standard deviation	0.49815		
11				
12	Binomial Probabilities Table			
13	X	P(X)		
14	0	0.0008		
15	1	0.0226		
16	2	0.2256		
17	3	0.7511		
18				
19	Prob(at least 2) = P(X>=2)	0.9767	=SUM(B16:B17)	

(a) $P(X = 3) = 0.7511$
(b) $P(X = 0) = 0.0008$
(c) $P(X \geq 2) = 0.9767$
(d) $\mu = 2.727$ $\sigma_X = 0.49815$
On the average, over the long run, you theoretically expect 2.727 orders to be filled correctly in a sample of 3 orders with a standard deviation of 0.49815
(e) McDonald's has a slightly higher probability of filling orders correctly and Wendy's has a slightly lower probability

5.18 (a) Partial PHStat output:

Poisson Probabilities					
Data					
Average/Expected number of successes:			2.5		
Poisson Probabilities Table					
X	P(X)	P(<=X)	P(<X)	P(>X)	P(>=X)
2	0.256516	0.543813	0.287297	0.456187	0.712703

Using the equation, if $\lambda = 2.5$, $P(X = 2) = \dfrac{e^{-2.5} \cdot (2.5)^2}{2!} = 0.2565$

5.18 cont. (b) Partial PHStat output:

Poisson Probabilities					
Data					
Average/Expected number of successes:			8		
Poisson Probabilities Table					
	X	P(X)	P(<=X)	P(<X)	P(>X)	P(>=X)
	8	0.139587	0.592547	0.452961	0.407453	0.547039

If $\lambda = 8.0$, $P(X = 8) = 0.1396$

(c) Partial PHStat output:

Poisson Probabilities						
Data						
Average/Expected number of successes:				0.5		
Poisson Probabilities Table						
	X	P(X)	P(<=X)	P(<X)	P(>X)	P(>=X)
	0	0.606531	0.606531	0.000000	0.393469	1.000000
	1	0.303265	0.909796	0.606531	0.090204	0.393469

If $\lambda = 0.5$, $P(X = 1) = 0.3033$

(d) Partial PHStat output:

Poisson Probabilities						
Data						
Average/Expected number of successes:				3.7		
Poisson Probabilities Table						
	X	P(X)	P(<=X)	P(<X)	P(>X)	P(>=X)
	0	0.024724	0.024724	0.000000	0.975276	1.000000

If $\lambda = 3.7$, $P(X = 0) = 0.0247$

5.20 PHStat output for (a) – (d)

Poisson Probabilities Table						
	X	P(X)	P(<=X)	P(<X)	P(>X)	P(>=X)
	0	0.006738	0.006738	0.000000	0.993262	1.000000
	1	0.033690	0.040428	0.006738	0.959572	0.993262
	2	0.084224	0.124652	0.040428	0.875348	0.959572
	3	0.140374	0.265026	0.124652	0.734974	0.875348
	4	0.175467	0.440493	0.265026	0.559507	0.734974
	5	0.175467	0.615961	0.440493	0.384039	0.559507
	6	0.146223	0.762183	0.615961	0.237817	0.384039
	7	0.104445	0.866628	0.762183	0.133372	0.237817
	8	0.065278	0.931906	0.866628	0.068094	0.133372
	9	0.036266	0.968172	0.931906	0.031828	0.068094
	10	0.018133	0.986305	0.968172	0.013695	0.031828
	11	0.008242	0.994547	0.986305	0.005453	0.013695
	12	0.003434	0.997981	0.994547	0.002019	0.005453
	13	0.001321	0.999302	0.997981	0.000698	0.002019
	14	0.000472	0.999774	0.999302	0.000226	0.000698
	15	0.000157	0.999931	0.999774	0.000069	0.000226
	16	0.000049	0.999980	0.999931	0.000020	0.000069
	17	0.000014	0.999995	0.999980	0.000005	0.000020
	18	0.000004	0.999999	0.999995	0.000001	0.000005
	19	0.000001	1.000000	0.999999	0.000000	0.000001
	20	0.000000	1.000000	1.000000	0.000000	0.000000

Given $\lambda = 5.0$,

(a) $P(X = 1) = 0.0337$

(b) $P(X < 1) = 0.0067$

(c) $P(X > 1) = 0.9596$

(d) $P(X \leq 1) = 0.0404$

5.22 (a)–(c) Portion of PHStat output

Data					
Average/Expected number of successes:			6		
Poisson Probabilities Table					
X	P(X)	P(<=X)	P(<X)	P(>X)	P(>=X)
0	0.002479	0.002479	0.000000	0.997521	1.000000
1	0.014873	0.017351	0.002479	0.982649	0.997521
2	0.044618	0.061969	0.017351	0.938031	0.982649
3	0.089235	0.151204	0.061969	0.848796	0.938031
4	0.133853	0.285057	0.151204	0.714943	0.848796
5	(b) 0.160623	0.445680	(a) 0.285057	0.554320	(c) 0.714943
6	0.160623	0.606303	0.445680	0.393697	0.554320
7	0.137677	0.743980	0.606303	0.256020	0.393697
8	0.103258	0.847237	0.743980	0.152763	0.256020
9	0.068838	0.916076	0.847237	0.083924	0.152763
10	0.041303	0.957379	0.916076	0.042621	0.083924
11	0.022529	0.979908	0.957379	0.020092	0.042621
12	0.011264	0.991173	0.979908	0.008827	0.020092
13	0.005199	0.996372	0.991173	0.003628	0.008827
14	0.002228	0.998600	0.996372	0.001400	0.003628
15	0.000891	0.999491	0.998600	0.000509	0.001400
16	0.000334	0.999825	0.999491	0.000175	0.000509
17	0.000118	0.999943	0.999825	0.000057	0.000175

(a) $P(X < 5) = P(X = 0) + P(X = 1) + P(X = 2) + P(X = 3) + P(X = 4)$

$$= \frac{e^{-6}(6)^0}{0!} + + \frac{e^{-6}(6)^2}{2!} + \frac{e^{-6}(6)^3}{3!} + \frac{e^{-6}(6)^4}{4!}$$

$$= 0.002479 + 0.014873 + 0.044618 + 0.089235 + 0.133853 = 0.2851$$

(b) $P(X = 5) = \frac{e^{-6}(6)^5}{5!} = 0.1606$

(c) $P(X \geq 5) = 1 - P(X < 5) = 1 - 0.2851 = 0.7149$

(d) $P(X = 4 \text{ or } X = 5) = P(X = 4) + P(X = 5) = \frac{e^{-6}(6)^4}{4!} + \frac{e^{-6}(6)^5}{5!} = 0.2945$

$$= \frac{e^{-6}(6)^1}{1!}$$

5.24 Excel Output:

	A	B	C	D	E
1	Poisson Probabilities				
2					
3	Data				
4	Mean/Expected number of events of interest:				0.32
5					
6	Poisson Probabilities Table				
7	X	P(X)			
8	0	0.7261			
9	1	0.2324			
10	2	0.0372			
11	3	0.0040			
12	4	0.0003			
13	5	0.0000			
14	6	0.0000			

(a) $P(X = 0) = 0.7261$
(b) $P(X \geq 1) = 1 - P(X = 0) = 1 - 0.7261 = 0.2739$
(c) $P(X \geq 2) = 1 - P(X \leq 1) = 1 - [0.7261 + 0.2324] = 0.0415$

5.26 Excel Output:

	A	B	C	D	E	F	G
1	Poisson Probabilities						
2							
3	Data						
4	Mean/Expected number of events of interest:				3.5		
5							
6	Poisson Probabilities Table						
7	X	P(X)		(c) P(more than 1) = 1- P(X <=1)		0.8641	
8	0	0.0302		(d) P(fewer than 2) = P(X <=1)		0.1359	
9	1	0.1057					
10	2	0.1850					
11	3	0.2158					
12	4	0.1888					
13	5	0.1322					
14	6	0.0771					
15	7	0.0385					
16	8	0.0169					
17	9	0.0066					
18	10	0.0023					
19	11	0.0007					
20	12	0.0002					
21	13	0.0001					

(a) $P(X = 0) = 0.0302$
(b) $P(X = 1) = 0.1057$
(c) $P(X > 1) = 1 - P(X \leq 1) = 1 - [0.0302 + 0.1057] = 0.8641$
(d) $P(X < 2) = P(X \leq 1) = 0.0302 + 0.1057 = 0.1359$

5.28 Excel Output:

	A	B	C	D	E
1	Poisson Probabilities				
2					
3	Data				
4	Mean/Expected number of events of interest:				1.08
5					
6	Poisson Probabilities Table				
7	X	P(X)			
8	0	0.3396			
9	1	0.3668			
10	2	0.1981			
11	3	0.0713			
12	4	0.0193			
13	5	0.0042			
14	6	0.0007			
15	7	0.0001			
16	8	0.0000			

(a) $P(X = 0) = 0.3396$

(b) $P(X \leq 2) = P(X = 0) + P(X = 1) + P(X = 2) = 0.9044$

(c) Because Ford had a higher mean rate of problems per car than Toyota, the probability of a randomly selected Ford having zero problems and the probability of no more than two problems are both lower than for Toyota.

5.30 The expected value is the average of a probability distribution. It is the value that can be expected to occur on the average, in the long run.

5.32 The four properties of a situation that must be present in order to use the Poisson distribution are
(i) you are interested in counting the number of times a particular event occurs in a given area of opportunity (defined by time, length, surface area, and so forth),
(ii) the probability that an event occurs in a given area of opportunity is the same for all of the areas of opportunity,
(iii) the number of events that occur in one area of opportunity is independent of the number of events that occur in other areas of opportunity and
(iv) the probability that two or more events will occur in an area of opportunity approaches zero as the area of opportunity becomes smaller.

5.34 (a) 0.664

(b) 0.664

Excel Output

	A	B
1	Binomial Probabilities	
2		
3	Data	
4	Sample size	5
5	Probability of an event of interest	0.664
6		
7	Parameters	
8	Mean	3.32
9	Variance	1.11552
10	Standard deviation	1.05618
11		
12	Binomial Probabilities Table	
13	X	P(X)
14	0	0.0043
15	1	0.0423
16	2	0.1672
17	3	0.3305
18	4	0.3266
19	5	0.1291

$\pi = 0.664,\ n = 5$

(c) $P(X = 4) = 0.3266$

(d) $P(X = 0) = 0.0043$

(e) Stock prices tend to rise in the years when the economy is expanding and fall in the years of recession or contraction. Hence, the probability that the price will rise in one year is not independent from year to year.

5.36 Excel Output

Binomial Probabilities	
Data	
Sample size	14
Probability of an event of interest	0.5
Parameters	
Mean	7
Variance	3.5
Standard deviation	1.87083
Binomial Probabilities Table	
X	*P(X)*
0	0.0001
1	0.0009
2	0.0056
3	0.0222
4	0.0611
5	0.1222
6	0.1833
7	0.2095
8	0.1833
9	0.1222
10	0.0611
11	0.0222
12	0.0056
13	0.0009
14	0.0001
P(X>=11)	0.0287 =SUM(B25:B28)

(a) $P(X \geq 11) = 0.0287$

5.36 cont. (b) Excel Output

	A	B	C	D
1	Binomial Probabilities			
2				
3	Data			
4	Sample size	14		
5	Probability of an event of interest	0.75		
6				
7	Parameters			
8	Mean	10.5		
9	Variance	2.625		
10	Standard deviation	1.62019		
11				
12	Binomial Probabilities Table			
13	*X*	*P(X)*		
14	0	0.0000		
15	1	0.0000		
16	2	0.0000		
17	3	0.0000		
18	4	0.0003		
19	5	0.0018		
20	6	0.0082		
21	7	0.0280		
22	8	0.0734		
23	9	0.1468		
24	10	0.2202		
25	11	0.2402		
26	12	0.1802		
27	13	0.0832		
28	14	0.0178		
29				
30	P(X>=11)	0.5213	=SUM(B25:B28)	
31				

$P(X \geq 11) = 0.5213$

5.38 Excel Output:

	A	B	C	D
1	Binomial Probabilities			
2				
3	Data			
4	Sample size	10		
5	Probability of an event of interest	0.4		
6				
7	Parameters			
8	Mean	4		
9	Variance	2.4		
10	Standard deviation	1.54919		
11				
12	Binomial Probabilities Table			
13	X	P(X)		
14	0	0.0060		
15	1	0.0403		
16	2	0.1209		
17	3	0.2150		
18	4	0.2508		
19	5	0.2007		
20	6	0.1115		
21	7	0.0425		
22	8	0.0106		
23	9	0.0016		
24	10	0.0001		
25				
26	P(x >5)	0.1662	=SUM(B20:B24)	

(a) $P(X = 0) = 0.0060$

(b) $P(X = 5) = 0.2007$

(c) $P(X > 5) = 0.1662$

(d) $\mu = 4, \ \sigma = 1.54919$

(e) Since the percentage of bills containing an error is lower in this problem, the probability is higher in (a) and (b) of this problem and lower in (c).

5.40 Excel Output:

	A	B	C	D
1	Binomial Probabilities			
2				
3	Data			
4	Sample size	20		
5	Probability of an event of interest	0.46		
6				
7	Parameters			
8	Mean	9.2		
9	Variance	4.968		
10	Standard deviation	2.2289		
11				
12	Binomial Probabilities Table			
13	X	P(X)		
14	0	0.0000		
15	1	0.0001		
16	2	0.0006		
17	3	0.0031		
18	4	0.0113		
19	5	0.0309		
20	6	0.0658		
21	7	0.1122		
22	8	0.1553		
23	9	0.1763		
24	10	0.1652		
25	11	0.1280		
26	12	0.0818		
27	13	0.0429		
28	14	0.0183		
29	15	0.0062		
30	16	0.0017		
31	17	0.0003		
32	18	0.0000		
33	19	0.0000		
34	20	0.0000		
35				
36	P(No more than 5) = P(X<=5)	0.0461	=SUM(B14:B19)	
37	P(5 or more) = P(X>=5)	0.9848	=SUM(B19:B34)	

(a) $E(X) = \mu = 9.2$

(b) $\sigma = 2.2289$

(c) $P(X = 10) = 0.1652$

(d) $P(X \leq 5) = 0.0461$

(e) $P(X \geq 5) = 0.9848$

5.42 Excel Output:

(a)	0.0000	=1-BINOM.DIST(35,44,0.5,1)
(b)	0.0564	=1-BINOM.DIST(35,44,0.7,1)
(c)	0.9720	=1-BINOM.DIST(35,44,0.9,1)

(a) $\pi = 0.5$, $P(X \geq 36) = 0.0000$
(b) $\pi = 0.7$, $P(X \geq 36) = 0.0564$
(c) $\pi = 0.9$, $P(X \geq 36) = 0.9720$
(d) Based on the results in (a)–(c), the probability that the Standard & Poor's 500 index will increase if there is an early gain in the first five trading days of the year is very likely to be close to 0.90 because that yields a probability of 97.20% that at least 36 of the 44 years the Standard & Poor's 500 index will increase the entire year.

5.44 Excel Output

	A	B	C	D	E
1	Poisson Probabilities				
2					
3	Data				
4	Mean/Expected number of events of interest:				7
5					
6	Poisson Probabilities Table				
7	X	P(X)			
8	0	0.0009			
9	1	0.0064			
10	2	0.0223			
11	3	0.0521			
12	4	0.0912			
13	5	0.1277			
14	6	0.1490			
15	7	0.1490			
16	8	0.1304			
17	9	0.1014			
18	10	0.0710			
19	11	0.0452			
20	12	0.0263			
21	13	0.0142			
22	14	0.0071			
23	15	0.0033			
24	16	0.0014			
25	17	0.0006			
26	18	0.0002			
27	19	0.0001			
28	20	0.0000			
29					
30	P(10 or fewer)	0.9015	=SUM(B8:B18)		
31	P(11 or more))	0.0985	=SUM(B19:B28)		

5.44 cont.

(a) The assumptions needed are (i) the probability that a questionable claim is referred by an investigator is constant, (ii) the probability that a questionable claim is referred by an investigator approaches 0 as the interval gets smaller, and (iii) the probability that a questionable claim is referred by an investigator is independent from interval to interval.

(b) $P(X = 5) = 0.1277$

(c) $P(X \leq 10) = 0.9015$

(d) $P(X \geq 11) = 0.0985$

Chapter 6

6.2 PHStat output:

Normal Probabilities			
Common Data			
Mean	0		
Standard Deviation	1		
		Probability for a Range	
Probability for X <=		From X Value	1.57
X Value	–1.57	To X Value	1.84
Z Value	–1.57	Z Value for 1.57	1.57
P(X<=–1.57)	0.0582076	Z Value for 1.84	1.84
		P(X<=1.57)	0.9418
Probability for X >		P(X<=1.84)	0.9671
X Value	1.84	P(1.57<=X<=1.84)	0.0253
Z Value	1.84		
P(X>1.84)	0.0329	Find X and Z Given Cum. Pctage.	
		Cumulative Percentage	84.13%
Probability for X<–1.57 or X >1.84		Z Value	0.999815
P(X<–1.57 or X >1.84)	0.0911	X Value	0.999815

(a) $P(-1.57 < Z < 1.84) = 0.9671 - 0.0582 = 0.9089$

(b) $P(Z < -1.57) + P(Z > 1.84) = 0.0582 + 0.0329 = 0.0911$

(c) If $P(Z > A) = 0.025$, $P(Z < A) = 0.975$. $A = +1.96$.

(d) If $P(-A < Z < A) = 0.6826$, $P(Z < A) = 0.8413$. So 68.26% of the area is captured between $-A = -1.00$ and $A = +1.00$.

6.4 PHStat output:

Normal Probabilities			
Common Data			
Mean	0		
Standard Deviation	1		
		Probability for a Range	
Probability for X <=		From X Value	–1.96
X Value	–0.21	To X Value	–0.21
Z Value	–0.21	Z Value for –1.96	–1.96
P(X<=–0.21)	0.4168338	Z Value for –0.21	–0.21
		P(X<=–1.96)	0.0250
Probability for X >		P(X<=–0.21)	0.4168
X Value	1.08	P(–1.96<=X<=–0.21)	0.3918
Z Value	1.08		
P(X>1.08)	0.1401	Find X and Z Given Cum. Pctage.	
		Cumulative Percentage	84.13%
Probability for X<–0.21 or X >1.08		Z Value	0.999815
P(X<–0.21 or X >1.08)	0.5569	X Value	0.999815

(a) $P(Z > 1.08) = 1 - 0.8599 = 0.1401$

6.4 cont.

(b) $P(Z < -0.21) = 0.4168$

(c) $P(-1.96 < Z < -0.21) = 0.4168 - 0.0250 = 0.3918$

(d) $P(Z > A) = 0.1587$, $P(Z < A) = 0.8413$. $A = +1.00$.

6.6

(a) Partial PHStat output:

Common Data			
Mean	50		
Standard Deviation	4		
		Probability for a Range	
Probability for X <=		From X Value	42
X Value	42	To X Value	43
Z Value	–2	Z Value for 42	–2
P(X<=42)	0.0227501	Z Value for 43	–1.75
		P(X<=42)	0.0228
Probability for X >		P(X<=43)	0.0401
X Value	43	P(42<=X<=43)	0.0173
Z Value	–1.75		
P(X>43)	0.9599	Find X and Z Given Cum. Pctage.	
		Cumulative Percentage	5.00%
Probability for X<42 or X >43		Z Value	–1.644854
P(X<42 or X >43)	0.9827	X Value	43.42059

$P(X > 43) = P(Z > -1.75) = 1 - 0.0401 = 0.9599$

(b) $P(X < 42) = P(Z < -2.00) = 0.0228$

(c) $P(X < A) = 0.05$,

$$Z = -1.645 = \frac{A - 50}{4} \qquad A = 50 - 1.645(4) = 43.42$$

(d) Partial PHStat output:

Find X and Z Given Cum. Pctage.	
Cumulative Percentage	80.00%
Z Value	0.841621
X Value	53.36648

$P(X_{lower} < X < X_{upper}) = 0.60$

$P(Z < -0.84) = 0.20$ and $P(Z < 0.84) = 0.80$

$$Z = -0.84 = \frac{X_{lower} - 50}{4} \qquad Z = +0.84 = \frac{X_{upper} - 50}{4}$$

$X_{lower} = 50 - 0.84(4) = 46.64$ and $X_{upper} = 50 + 0.84(4) = 53.36$

6.8 Partial PHStat output:

Common Data	
Mean	50
Standard Deviation	12

Probability for X <=	
X Value	30
Z Value	–1.666667
P(X<=30)	0.0477904

Probability for X >	
X Value	60
Z Value	0.8333333
P(X>60)	0.2023

Probability for X<30 or X >60	
P(X<30 or X >60)	0.2501

Probability for a Range	
From X Value	34
To X Value	50
Z Value for 34	–1.333333
Z Value for 50	0
P(X<=34)	0.0912
P(X<=50)	0.5000
P(34<=X<=50)	0.4088

Find X and Z Given Cum. Pctage.	
Cumulative Percentage	20.00%
Z Value	–0.841621
X Value	39.90055

(a) $P(34 < X < 50) = P(-1.33 < Z < 0) = 0.4088$

(b) $P(X < 30) + P(X > 60) = P(Z < -1.67) + P(Z > 0.83)$
$= 0.0475 + (1.0 - 0.7967) = 0.2508$

(c) $P(X > \text{A}) = 0.80$ $\quad P(Z < -0.84) \cong 0.20$ $\quad Z = -0.84 = \dfrac{A - 50}{12}$

$A = 50 - 0.84(12) = 39.92$ thousand miles or 39,920 miles

(d) Partial PHStat output:

Common Data	
Mean	50
Standard Deviation	10

Probability for X <=	
X Value	30
Z Value	–2
P(X<=30)	0.0227501

Probability for X >	
X Value	60
Z Value	1
P(X>60)	0.1587

Probability for X<30 or X >60	
P(X<30 or X >60)	0.1814

Probability for a Range	
From X Value	34
To X Value	50
Z Value for 34	–1.6
Z Value for 50	0
P(X<=34)	0.0548
P(X<=50)	0.5000
P(34<=X<=50)	0.4452

Find X and Z Given Cum. Pctage.	
Cumulative Percentage	20.00%
Z Value	–0.841621
X Value	41.58379

The smaller standard deviation makes the *Z*-values larger.

(a) $P(34 < X < 50) = P(-1.60 < Z < 0) = 0.4452$

(b) $P(X < 30) + P(X > 60) = P(Z < -2.00) + P(Z > 1.00)$
$= 0.0228 + (1.0 - 0.8413) = 0.1815$

(c) $A = 50 - 0.84(10) = 41.6$ thousand miles or 41,600 miles

6.10 PHStat output:

Common Data	
Mean	73
Standard Deviation	8

Probability for X <=	
X Value	91
Z Value	2.25
P(X<=91)	0.9877755

Probability for X >	
X Value	81
Z Value	1
P(X>81)	0.1587

Probability for X<91 or X >81	
P(X<91 or X >81)	1.1464

Probability for a Range	
From X Value	65
To X Value	89
Z Value for 65	–1
Z Value for 89	2
P(X<=65)	0.1587
P(X<=89)	0.9772
P(65<=X<=89)	0.8186

Find X and Z Given Cum. Pctage.	
Cumulative Percentage	95.00%
Z Value	1.644854
X Value	86.15883

(a) $P(X < 91) = P(Z < 2.25) = 0.9878$

(b) $P(65 < X < 89) = P(-1.00 < Z < 2.00) = 0.9772 - 0.1587 = 0.8185$

(c) $P(X > A) = 0.05$ $\quad$ $P(Z < 1.645) = 0.9500$

$$Z = 1.645 = \frac{A - 73}{8} \qquad A = 73 + 1.645(8) = 86.16\%$$

(d) Option 1: $P(X > A) = 0.10$ $\quad$ $P(Z < 1.28) \cong 0.9000$

$$Z = \frac{81 - 73}{8} = 1.00$$

Since your score of 81% on this exam represents a Z-score of 1.00, which is below the minimum Z-score of 1.28, you will not earn an "A" grade on the exam under this grading option.

Option 2: $Z = \frac{68 - 62}{3} = 2.00$

Since your score of 68% on this exam represents a Z-score of 2.00, which is well above the minimum Z-score of 1.28, you will earn an "A" grade on the exam under this grading option. You should prefer Option 2.

6.12 (a) $P(X > 50) = P(Z > 1.5625) = 0.0591$

Probability for X >	
X Value	50
Z Value	1.5625
P(X>50)	0.0591

6.12 cont. (b) $P(25 < X < 40) = P(-1.5625 < Z < 0.3125) = 0.5636$

Probability for a Range	
From X Value	25
To X Value	40
Z Value for 25	-1.5625
Z Value for 40	0.3125
P(X<=25)	0.0591
P(X<=40)	0.6227
P(25<=X<=40)	0.5636

(c) $P(X < 10) = P(Z < -3.4375) = 0.0003$

Probability for X <=	
X Value	10
Z Value	-3.4375
P(X<=10)	0.0003

(d) $P(X < A) = 0.99$ $Z = 2.33$ $A = 56.11$

Find X and Z Given a Cum. Pctage.	
Cumulative Percentage	99.00%
Z Value	2.33
X Value	56.11

6.14 With 39 values, the smallest of the standard normal quantile values covers an area under the normal curve of 0.025. The corresponding Z value is -1.96. The middle (20th) value has a cumulative area of 0.50 and a corresponding Z value of 0.0. The largest of the standard normal quantile values covers an area under the normal curve of 0.975, and its corresponding Z value is $+1.96$.

6.16 (a) Excel output:
Before Halftime Ad Ratings

	A	B	C	D	E
1	**Before Halftime Ad Ratings**				
2					
3		**Variable**			
4	**Mean**	5.382903226			
5	**Median**	5.34			
6	**Mode**	5.34			
7	**Minimum**	4.22			
8	**Maximum**	6.51			
9	**Range**	2.29		**6*stand dev**	4.291523
10	**Variance**	0.5116			
11	**Standard Deviation**	0.7153			
12	**Coeff. of Variation**	13.29%			
13	**Skewness**	0.0358			
14	**Kurtosis**	-1.2567			
15	**Count**	31			
16	**Standard Error**	0.1285			
17					
18	Five-Number Summary				
19	Minimum	4.22			
20	First Quartile	4.81			
21	Median	5.34			
22	Third Quartile	6.14			
23	Maximum	6.51			
24	IQR	1.33		**1.33*stand dev**	0.951288
25					

Ad Ratings Before Halftime

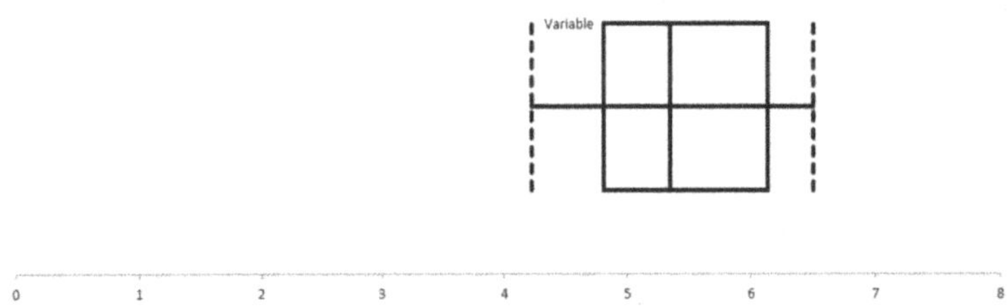

6.16 cont. (a) Halftime and after Ad Ratings

	A	B	C	D	E	F
1	**Descriptive Summary**					
2						
3		**Rating**				
4	**Mean**	5.65				
5	**Median**	5.59				
5	**Mode**	4.96				
7	**Minimum**	3.63				
3	**Maximum**	7.69				
9	**Range**	4.06	**6*stand dev**	6.246562952		
0	**Variance**	1.0839	**mean + 1 SD**	6.6918		63% within 1 SD
1	**Standard Deviation**	1.0411	**mean - 1SD**	4.6096		
2	**Coeff. of Variation**	18.42%	**mean +1.28SD**	6.98		77.78% within 1.28SD
3	**Skewness**	0.1406	**mean - 1.28SD**	4.3181		
4	**Kurtosis**	-0.5910	**mean +2SD**	7.7329	all values within 2SD	
5	**Count**	27	**mean - 2SD**	3.56855309		
6	**Standard Error**	0.2004				
7	**First Quartile**	4.96				
8	**Third Quartile**	6.41				
9	**IQR**	1.45	**1.33*stand dev**	1.384654788		
:0						

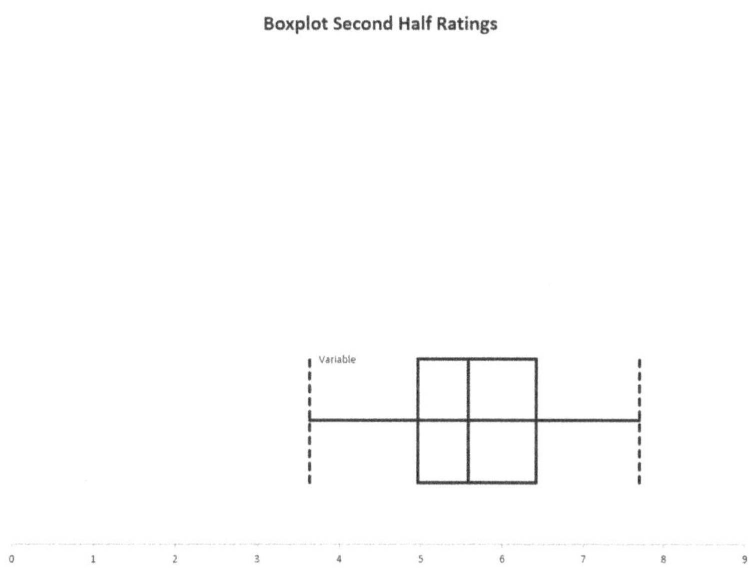

Super Bowl Ad Ratings First and Second Period: (a) Mean = 5.38, median = 5.34, S = 0.7153, range = 2.29, 6S = 4.2918, interquartile range = 1.33, 1.33(0.7153) = 0.9513. The mean is approximately the same as the median. The range is much less than 6S, and the interquartile range is more than 1.33S. The skewness statistic is 0.0358, indicating a symmetric distribution, and the kurtosis statistic is –1.2567, indicating a platykurtic distribution.

6.16 cont. (a) Super Bowl Ad Ratings Halftime and Afterward: (a) Mean = 5.65, median = 5.59, S = 1.0411, range = 4.06, 6S = 6.2466, interquartile range = 1.45, 1.33(1.0411) = 1.3847. The mean is approximately the same as the median. The range is much less than 6S, and the interquartile range is slightly more than 1.33S. The skewness statistic is 0.1406, indicating an approximately symmetric distribution, and the kurtosis statistic is –0.5910, indicating a platykurtic distribution.

(b)

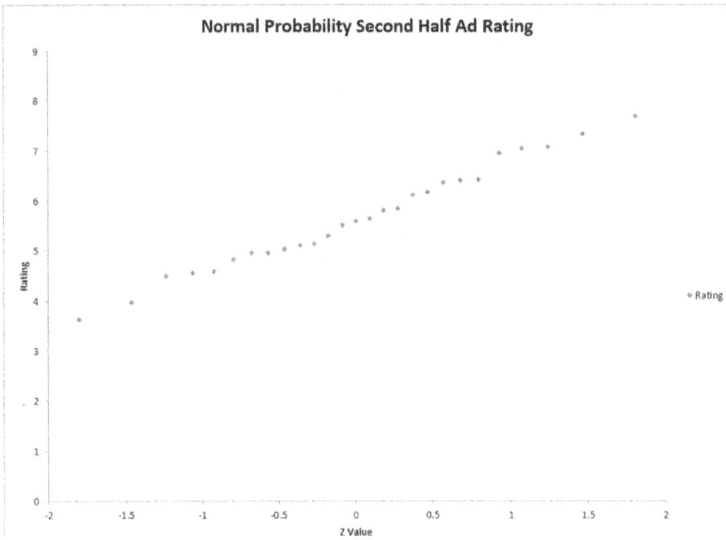

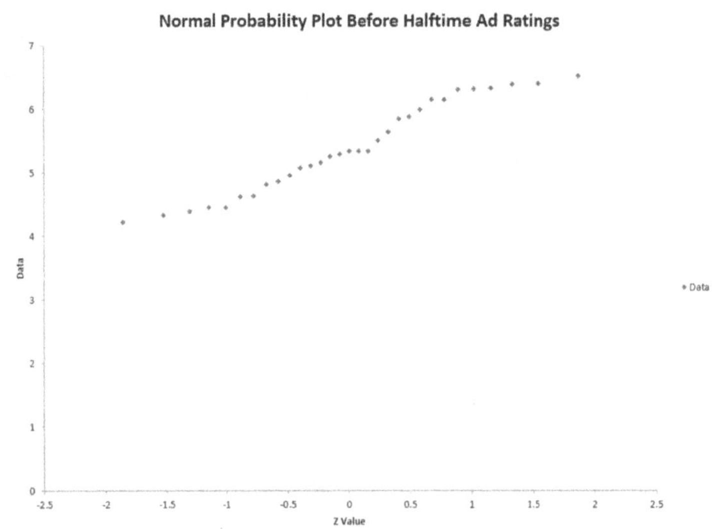

The data for the second half appear to follow a normal distribution.

6.18 (a)(b) Excel Output:

Descriptive statistics (Quantitative data):

Statistic	Taxes on $176K House		
Nbr. of observations	51		
Minimum	489.000		
Maximum	4029.000		
Range	3540.000	6S	5405.362
1st Quartile	1334.000		
Median	1763.000		
3rd Quartile	2614.500		
Mean	1979.941		
IQR	1280.500	1.33S	1198.189
Variance (n-1)	811609.376		
Standard deviation (n-1)	900.894		
Variation coefficient	0.451		
Skewness (Fisher)	0.641		
Skewness (Bowley)	0.330		
Kurtosis (Fisher)	-0.506		

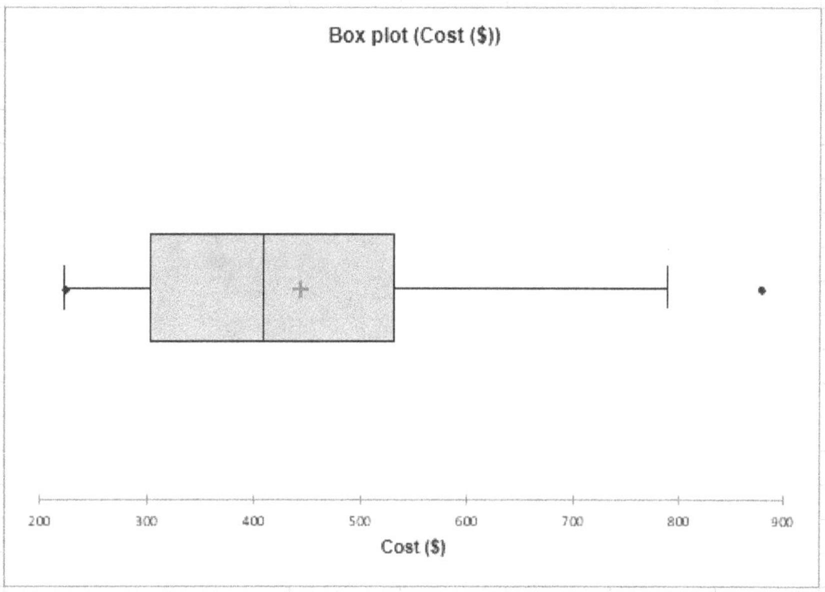

6.18 cont. (a)(b)

Normal Q-Q plots:

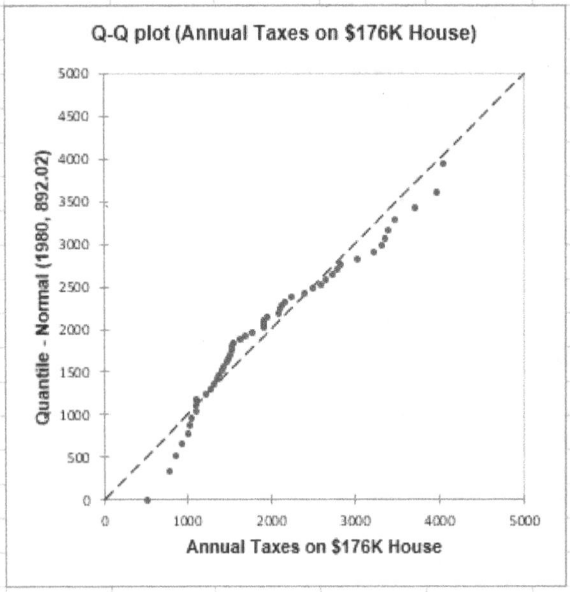

The mean is greater than the median. The range is much less than 6S, and the IQR is more than 1.33S. The box plot is right skewed. The normal probability plot along with the skewness and kurtosis statistics indicate a departure from the normal distribution.

6.20 Excel output:

Error	
Mean	–0.00023
Median	0
Mode	0
Standard Deviation	0.001696
Sample Variance	2.88E-06
Range	0.008
Minimum	–0.003
Maximum	0.005
First Quartile	–0.0015
Third Quartile	0.001
1.33 Std Dev	0.002255
Interquartile Range	0.0025
6 Std Dev	0.010175

(a) Because the interquartile range is close to 1.33S and the range is also close to 6S, the data appear to be approximately normally distributed.

6.20 (b)
cont.

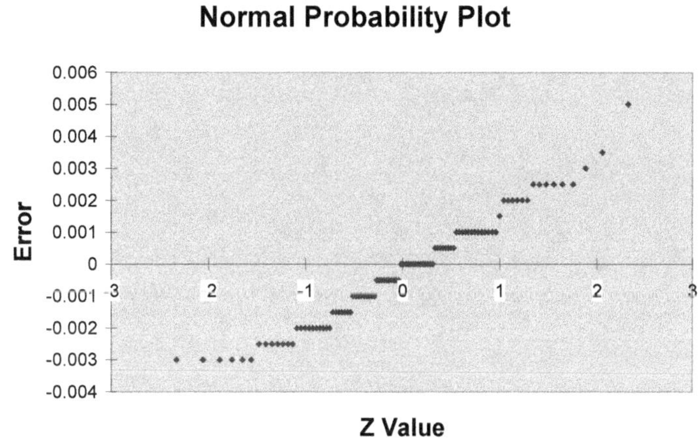

The normal probability plot suggests that the data appear to be approximately normally distributed.

6.22 (a) Five-number summary: 82 127 148.5 168 213 mean = 147.06
range = 131 interquartile range = 41 standard deviation = 31.69

The mean is very close to the median. The five-number summary suggests that the distribution is quite symmetrical around the median. The interquartile range is very close to 1.33 times the standard deviation. The range is about $50 below 6 times the standard deviation. In general, the distribution of the data appears to closely resemble a normal distribution.
Note: The quartiles are obtained using PHStat without any interpolation.

(b)

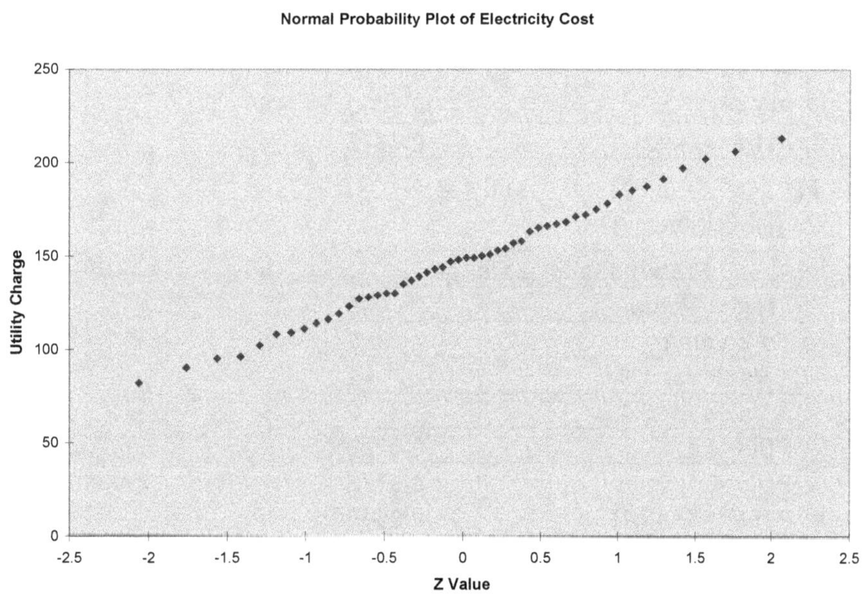

The normal probability plot confirms that the data appear to be approximately normally distributed.

6.24 (a) $P(0 < X < 20) = (20 - 0) / 120 = 0.1667$
(b) $P(10 < X < 30) = (30 - 10)/120 = 0.1667$
(c) $P(35 < X < 120) = (120 - 35)/120 = 0.7083$
(d) $\mu = \dfrac{0+120}{2} = 60 \qquad \sigma = \sqrt{\dfrac{(120-0)^2}{12}} = 34.6410$

6.26 (a) $P(X < 4.5) = (4.5 - 3.5)/(5.5 - 3.5) = 0.5$
(b) $P(X > 4) = (5.5 - 4)/(5.5 - 3.5) = 0.75$
(c) $P(4.0 < X < 4.5) = (4.5 - 4.0)/(5.5 - 3.5) = 0.25$
(d) $\mu = \dfrac{3.5+5.5}{2} = 4.5 \qquad \sigma = \sqrt{\dfrac{(5.5-3.5)^2}{12}} = 0.5774$

6.28 Using Table E.2, first find the cumulative area up to the larger value, and then subtract the cumulative area up to the smaller value.

6.30 The normal distribution is bell-shaped; its measures of central tendency are all equal; its middle 50% is within 1.33 standard deviations of its mean; and 99.7% of its values are contained within three standard deviations of its mean.

6.32 If the distribution is normal, the plot of the Z values on the horizontal axis and the original values on the vertical axis will be a straight line.

6.34 (a) Partial PHStat output:

Probability for a Range	
From X Value	1.9
To X Value	2
Z Value for 1.9	−2
Z Value for 2	0
P(X<=1.9)	0.0228
P(X<=2)	0.5000
P(1.9<=X<=2)	0.4772

$P(1.90 < X < 2.00) = P(-2.00 < Z < 0) = 0.4772$

(b) Partial PHStat output:

Probability for a Range	
From X Value	1.9
To X Value	2.1
Z Value for 1.9	−2
Z Value for 2.1	2
P(X<=1.9)	0.0228
P(X<=2.1)	0.9772
P(1.9<=X<=2.1)	0.9545

$P(1.90 < X < 2.10) = P(-2.00 < Z < 2.00) = 0.9772 - 0.0228 = 0.9544$

(c) Partial PHStat output:

Probability for X<1.9 or X >2.1	
P(X<1.9 or X >2.1)	0.0455

$P(X < 1.90) + P(X > 2.10) = 1 - P(1.90 < X < 2.10) = 0.0456$

6.34 cont. (d) Partial PHStat output:

Find X and Z Given Cum. Pctage.	
Cumulative Percentage	1.00%
Z Value	–2.326348
X Value	1.883683

$P(X > A) = P(Z > -2.33) = 0.99 A = 2.00 - 2.33(0.05) = 1.8835$

(e) Partial PHStat output:

Find X and Z Given Cum. Pctage.	
Cumulative Percentage	99.50%
Z Value	2.575829
X Value	2.128791

$P(A < X < B) = P(-2.58 < Z < 2.58) = 0.99$

$A = 2.00 - 2.58(0.05) = 1.8710$ $B = 2.00 + 2.58(0.05) = 2.1290$

6.36 (a) Partial PHStat output:

Probability for X <=	
X Value	210
Z Value	-2
P(X<=210)	0.0228

$P(X < 210) = P(Z < -2) = 0.0228$

(b)

Probability for a Range	
From X Value	270
To X Value	300
Z Value for 270	1
Z Value for 300	2.5
P(X<=270)	0.8413
P(X<=300)	0.9938
P(270<=X<=300)	0.1524

$P(270 < X < 300) = P(1.0 < Z < 2.5) = 0.1524$

(c)

Find X and Z Given Cum. Pctage.	
Cumulative Percentage	90.00%
Z Value	1.2816
X Value	275.6310

$P(X < A) = P(Z < 1.2816) = 0.90 A = 250 + 20(1.2816) = \$275.63$

(d)

Find X Values Given a Percentage	
Percentage	80.00%
Z Value	-1.28
Lower X Value	224.37
Upper X Value	275.63

6.36 cont. (d) $P(A < X < B) = P(-1.2816 < Z < 1.2816) = 0.80$
$A = 250 - 1.28(500) = \$224.37$
$B = 250 + 1.28(500) = \$275.63$

6.38 (a) Waiting time will more closely resemble an exponential distribution.
(b) Seating time will more closely resemble a normal distribution.
(c)

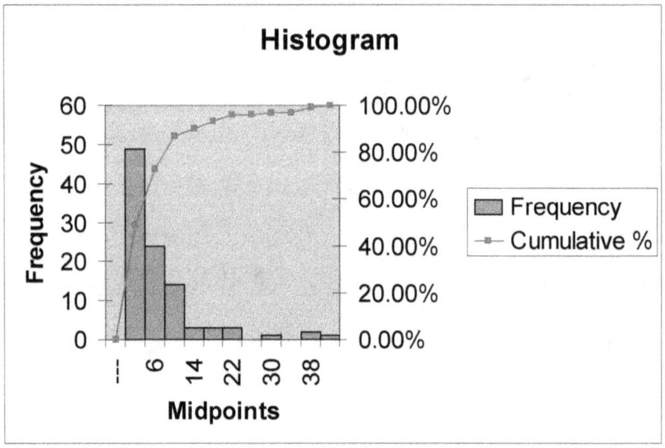

(c)

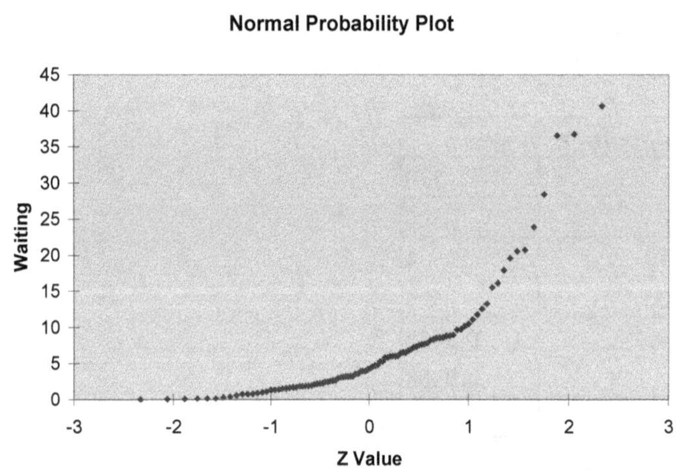

Both the histogram and normal probability plot suggest that waiting time more closely resembles an exponential distribution.

6.38 (d)
cont.

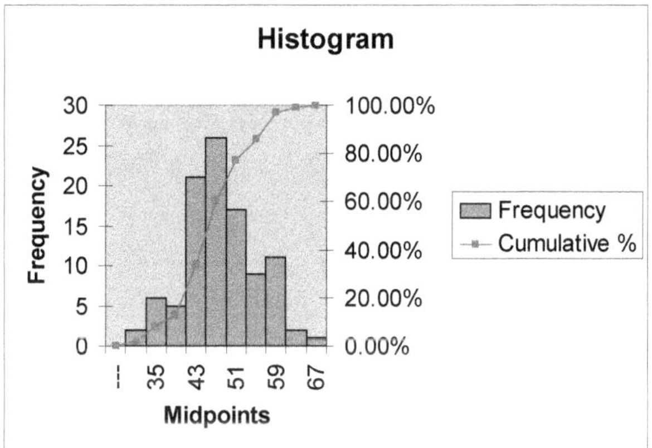

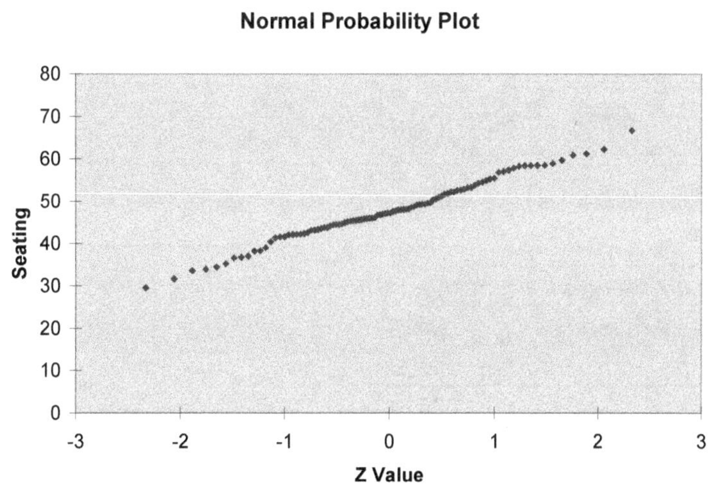

Both the histogram and normal probability plot suggest that seating time more closely resembles a normal distribution.

6.40 (a) Excel Output:

Probability for X <=	
X Value	5900
Z Value	-0.1
P(X<=5900)	0.4602

$P(X < \$5900) = P(Z < -0.1) = 0.4602$

6.40 cont. (b) Excel Output:

Probability for a Range	
From X Value	5700
To X Value	6100
Z Value for 5700	-0.6
Z Value for 6100	0.4
P(X<=5700)	0.2743
P(X<=6100)	0.6554
P(5700<=X<=6100)	0.3812

$P(\$5700 < X < \$6100) = P(-0.6 < Z < 0.4) = 0.3812$

(c) Excel Output:

Probability for X >	
X Value	6500
Z Value	1.4
P(X>6500)	0.0808

$P(X > \$6500) = P(Z > 1.4) = 0.0808$

(d) Excel Output:

Find X and Z Given a Cum. Pctage.	
Cumulative Percentage	1.00%
Z Value	-2.33
X Value	5009.46

$P(A < X) = 0.01$ $Z = -2.33$ $A = \$5009.46$

(e) Excel Output:

Find X Values Given a Percentage	
Percentage	95.00%
Z Value	-1.96
Lower X Value	5156.01
Upper X Value	6723.99

$P(A < X < B) = 0.95$ $Z = -1.9600$ $A = \$5156.01$

$Z = 1.96$ $B = \$6723.99$

6.42 *Class project solutions may vary.*

Chapter 7

7.2 PHStat output:

Common Data	
Mean	50
Standard Deviation	0.5

Probability for X <=	
X Value	47
Z Value	–6
P(X<=47)	9.866E-10

Probability for X >	
X Value	51.5
Z Value	3
P(X>51.5)	0.0013

Probability for X<47 or X >51.5	
P(X<47 or X >51.5)	0.0013

Probability for X >	
X Value	51.1
Z Value	2.2
P(X>51.1)	0.0139

Probability for a Range	
From X Value	47
To X Value	49.5
Z Value for 47	–6
Z Value for 49.5	–1
P(X<=47)	0.0000
P(X<=49.5)	0.1587
P(47<=X<=49.5)	0.1587

Find X and Z Given Cum. Pctage.	
Cumulative Percentage	65.00%
Z Value	0.38532
X Value	50.19266

(a) $P(\overline{X} < 47) = P(Z < -6.00) =$ virtually zero

(b) $P(47 < \overline{X} < 49.5) = P(-6.00 < Z < -1.00) = 0.1587 - 0.00 = 0.1587$

(c) $P(\overline{X} > 51.1) = P(Z > 2.20) = 1.0 - 0.9861 = 0.0139$

(d) $P(\overline{X} > A) = P(Z > 0.39) = 0.35$ $\overline{X} = 50 + 0.39(0.5) = 50.195$

7.4 (a) Sampling Distribution of the Mean for $n = 2$ (without replacement)

Sample Number	Outcomes	Sample Means $\overline{X}_i$
1	1, 3	$\overline{X}_1 = 2$
2	1, 6	$\overline{X}_2 = 3.5$
3	1, 7	$\overline{X}_3 = 4$
4	1, 9	$\overline{X}_4 = 5$
5	1, 10	$\overline{X}_5 = 5.5$
6	3, 6	$\overline{X}_6 = 4.5$
7	3, 7	$\overline{X}_7 = 5$
8	3, 9	$\overline{X}_8 = 6$
9	3, 10	$\overline{X}_9 = 6.5$
10	6, 7	$\overline{X}_{10} = 6.5$
11	6, 9	$\overline{X}_{11} = 7.5$
12	6, 10	$\overline{X}_{12} = 8$
13	7, 9	$\overline{X}_{13} = 8$
14	7, 10	$\overline{X}_{14} = 8.5$
15	9, 10	$\overline{X}_{15} = 9.5$

Mean of All Possible Sample Means: $\mu_{\overline{X}} = \frac{90}{15} = 6$

Mean of All Population Elements: $\mu = \frac{1+3+6+7+9+10}{6} = 6$

Both means are equal to 6. This property is called unbiasedness.

7.4 cont. (b) Sampling Distribution of the Mean for $n = 3$ (without replacement)

Sample Number	Outcomes	Sample Means $\overline{X}_i$
1	1, 3, 6	$\overline{X}_1 = 3\ 1/3$
2	1, 3, 7	$\overline{X}_2 = 3\ 2/3$
3	1, 3, 9	$\overline{X}_3 = 4\ 1/3$
4	1, 3, 10	$\overline{X}_4 = 4\ 2/3$
5	1, 6, 7	$\overline{X}_5 = 4\ 2/3$
6	1, 6, 9	$\overline{X}_6 = 5\ 1/3$
7	1, 6, 10	$\overline{X}_7 = 5\ 2/3$
8	3, 6, 7	$\overline{X}_8 = 5\ 1/3$
9	3, 6, 9	$\overline{X}_9 = 6$
10	3, 6, 10	$\overline{X}_{10} = 6\ 1/3$
11	6, 7, 9	$\overline{X}_{11} = 7\ 1/3$
12	6, 7, 10	$\overline{X}_{12} = 7\ 2/3$
13	6, 9, 10	$\overline{X}_{13} = 8\ 1/3$
14	7, 9, 10	$\overline{X}_{14} = 8\ 2/3$
15	1, 7, 9	$\overline{X}_{15} = 5\ 2/3$
16	1, 7, 10	$\overline{X}_{16} = 6$
17	1, 9, 10	$\overline{X}_{17} = 6\ 2/3$
18	3, 7, 9	$\overline{X}_{18} = 6\ 1/3$
19	3, 7, 10	$\overline{X}_{19} = 6\ 2/3$
20	3, 9, 10	$\overline{X}_{20} = 7\ 1/3$

$\mu_{\overline{X}} = \dfrac{120}{20} = 6$ This is equal to μ, the population mean.

(c) The distribution for $n = 3$ has less variability. The larger sample size has resulted in sample means being closer to μ.

(d) (a) Sampling Distribution of the Mean for $n = 2$ (with replacement)

Sample Number	Outcomes	Sample Means $\overline{X}_i$
1	1, 1	$\overline{X}_1 = 1$
2	1, 3	$\overline{X}_2 = 2$
3	1, 6	$\overline{X}_3 = 3.5$
4	1, 7	$\overline{X}_4 = 4.5$
5	1, 9	$\overline{X}_5 = 5$
6	1, 10	$\overline{X}_6 = 5.5$
7	3,1	$\overline{X}_7 = 2$
8	3, 3	$\overline{X}_8 = 3$
9	3, 6	$\overline{X}_9 = 4.5$

(table continues on next page)

7.4 cont. (d) (a)

Sample Number	Outcomes	Sample Means $\overline{X}_i$
10	3, 7	$\overline{X}_{10} = 5$
11	3, 9	$\overline{X}_{11} = 6$
12	3, 10	$\overline{X}_{12} = 6.5$
13	6, 1	$\overline{X}_{13} = 3.5$
14	6, 3	$\overline{X}_{14} = 4.5$
15	6, 6	$\overline{X}_{15} = 6$
16	6, 7	$\overline{X}_{16} = 6.5$
17	6, 9	$\overline{X}_{17} = 7.5$
18	6, 10	$\overline{X}_{18} = 8$
19	7, 1	$\overline{X}_{19} = 4$
20	7,3	$\overline{X}_{20} = 5$
21	7, 6	$\overline{X}_{21} = 6.5$
22	7, 7	$\overline{X}_{22} = 7$
23	7, 9	$\overline{X}_{23} = 8$
24	7, 10	$\overline{X}_{24} = 8.5$
25	9, 1	$\overline{X}_{25} = 5$
26	9, 3	$\overline{X}_{26} = 6$
27	9, 6	$\overline{X}_{27} = 7.5$
28	9, 7	$\overline{X}_{28} = 8$
29	9, 9	$\overline{X}_{29} = 9$
30	9, 10	$\overline{X}_{30} = 9.5$
31	10, 1	$\overline{X}_{31} = 5.5$
32	10, 3	$\overline{X}_{32} = 6.5$
33	10, 6	$\overline{X}_{33} = 8$
34	10, 7	$\overline{X}_{34} = 8.5$
35	10, 9	$\overline{X}_{35} = 9.5$
36	10, 10	$\overline{X}_{36} = 10$

Mean of All Possible Sample Means:

$$\mu_{\overline{X}} = \frac{216}{36} = 6$$

Mean of All Population Elements:

$$\mu = \frac{1+3+6+7+7+12}{6} = 6$$

Both means are equal to 6. This property is called unbiasedness.

(b) Repeat the same process for the sampling distribution of the mean for $n = 3$ (with replacement). There will be $6^3 = 216$ different samples.
$\mu_{\overline{X}} = 6$ This is equal to μ, the population mean.

(c) The distribution for $n = 3$ has less variability. The larger sample size has resulted in more sample means being close to μ.

7.6 (a) $P(X < 42.035) = P(Z < -0.6) = 0.2743$

Excel Output:

	A	B
4	Mean	42.05
5	Standard Deviation	0.025
6		
7	Probability for X <=	
8	X Value	42.035
9	Z Value	-0.6
10	P(X<=42.035)	0.2743

(b) Because the weight of an energy bar is approximately normally distributed, the sampling distribution of samples of 4 will also be approximately normal with a mean of

$\mu_{\overline{X}} = \mu = 42.05$ and $\sigma_{\overline{X}} = \dfrac{\sigma}{\sqrt{n}} = 0.0125.$

$P(\overline{X} < 42.035) = P(Z < -1.2) = 0.1151$

Excel Output:

	A	B
4	Mean	42.05
5	Standard Deviation	0.0125
6		
7	Probability for X <=	
8	X Value	42.035
9	Z Value	-1.2
10	P(X<=42.035)	0.1151

(c) Because the weight of an energy bar is approximately normally distributed, the sampling distribution of samples of 25 will also be approximately normal with a mean of

$\mu_{\overline{X}} = \mu = 42.05$ and $\sigma_{\overline{X}} = \dfrac{\sigma}{\sqrt{n}} = 0.005.$

$P(\overline{X} < 42.035) = P(Z < -3) = 0.0013$

Excel Output:

	A	B
4	Mean	42.05
5	Standard Deviation	0.005
6		
7	Probability for X <=	
8	X Value	42.035
9	Z Value	-3
10	P(X<=42.035)	0.0013
11		

(d) (a) refers to an individual energy bar while (c) refers to the mean of a sample of 25 energy bars. There is a 27.43% chance that an individual energy bar will have a weight below 42.05 grams but only a chance of 0.135% that a mean of 25 energy bars will have a weight below 42.05 grams.

(e) Increasing the sample size from four to 25 reduced the probability the mean will have a weight below 42.05 grams from 11.51% to 0.135%.

7.8 (a) When $n = 4$, the shape of the sampling distribution of $\overline{X}$ should closely resemble the shape of the distribution of the population from which the sample is selected. Because the mean is larger than the median, the distribution of the sales price of new houses is skewed to the right, and so is the sampling distribution of $\overline{X}$ although it will be less skewed than the population.

(b) If you select samples of $n = 100$, the shape of the sampling distribution of the sample mean will be very close to a normal distribution with a mean of \$382,700 and a standard deviation of $\sigma_{\overline{X}} = \frac{\sigma}{\sqrt{n}}$ = \$9,000.

(c) $P(\overline{X} < 370{,}000) = P(Z < -1.411) = .0791$

Excel Output:

Normal Probabilities	
Common Data	
Mean	382700
Standard Deviation	9000
Probability for X <=	
X Value	370000
Z Value	-1.411111
P(X<=370000)	0.0791

(d) $P(350{,}000 < \overline{X} < 365{,}000) = P(-3.63 < Z < -1.97) = 0.0245$

Excel Output:

	Probability for a Range	
20		
21	From X Value	350000
22	To X Value	365000
23	Z Value for 350000	-3.633333
24	Z Value for 365000	-1.966667
25	P(X<=350000)	0.0001
26	P(X<=365000)	0.0246
27	P(350000<=X<=365000)	0.0245

7.10 (a) $\mu_{\overline{X}} = \mu = 15$ and $\sigma_{\overline{X}} = \frac{\sigma}{\sqrt{n}} = 1$

$P(\overline{X} > 14) = P(Z > -1) = 0.8413$

Excel Output:

	Probability for X >	
12		
13	X Value	14
14	Z Value	-1
15	P(X>14)	0.8413

7.10 cont. (b) $P(\overline{X} < A) = P(Z < 1.04) = 0.85$ $\overline{X} = 15 + 1.04\,(1) = 16.04$

Excel Output:

29	Find X and Z Given a Cum. Pctage.	
30	Cumulative Percentage	85.00%
31	Z Value	1.04
32	X Value	16.04

(c) To be able to use the standardized normal distribution as an approximation for the area under the curve, you must assume that the population is approximately symmetrical.

(d) $P(\overline{X} < A) = P(Z < 1.04) = 0.85$ $\overline{X} = 15 + 1.04\,(0.5) = 15.52$

Excel Output:

29	Find X and Z Given a Cum. Pctage.	
30	Cumulative Percentage	85.00%
31	Z Value	1.04
32	X Value	15.52

7.12 (a) $p = \frac{20}{50} = 0.40$

(b) $\sigma_p = \sqrt{\frac{(0.45)(0.55)}{50}} = 0.0704$

7.14 (a) $\mu_p = \pi = 0.501,\ \sigma_p = \sqrt{\frac{\pi(1-\pi)}{n}} = \sqrt{\frac{0.501(1-0.501)}{100}} = 0.05$

Partial PHstat output:

Probability for X >	
X Value	0.55
Z Value	0.98
P(X>0.55)	0.1635

$P(p > 0.55) = P\,(Z > 0.98) = 1 - 0.8365 = 0.1635$

(b) $\mu_p = \pi = 0.60,\ \sigma_p = \sqrt{\frac{\pi(1-\pi)}{n}} = \sqrt{\frac{0.6(1-0.6)}{100}} = 0.04899$

Partial PHstat output:

Probability for X >	
X Value	0.55
Z Value	–1.020621
P(X>0.55)	0.8463

$P(p > 0.55) = P\,(Z > -1.021) = 1 - 0.1539 = 0.8461$

7.14 cont. (c) $\mu_p = \pi = 0.49$, $\sigma_p = \sqrt{\frac{\pi(1-\pi)}{n}} = \sqrt{\frac{0.49(1-0.49)}{100}} = 0.05$

Partial PHstat output:

Probability for X >	
X Value	0.55
Z Value	1.2002401
P(X>0.55)	0.1150

$P(p > 0.55) = P(Z > 1.20) = 1 - 0.8849 = 0.1151$

(d) Increasing the sample size by a factor of 4 decreases the standard error by a factor of 2.

(a) Partial PHstat output:

Probability for X >	
X Value	0.55
Z Value	1.9600039
P(X>0.55)	0.0250

$P(p > 0.55) = P(Z > 1.96) = 1 - 0.9750 = 0.0250$

(b) Partial PHstat output:

Probability for X >	
X Value	0.55
Z Value	–2.041241
P(X>0.55)	0.9794

$P(p > 0.55) = P(Z > -2.04) = 1 - 0.0207 = 0.9793$

(c) Partial PHstat output:

Probability for X >	
X Value	0.55
Z Value	2.4004801
P(X>0.55)	0.0082

$P(p > 0.55) = P(Z > 2.40) = 1 - 0.9918 = 0.0082$

If the sample size is increased to 400, the probably in (a), (b) and (c) is smaller, larger, and smaller, respectively because the standard error of the sampling distribution of the sample proportion becomes smaller and, hence, the sampling distribution is more concentrated around the true population proportion.

7.16 $\mu_p = \pi = 0.65$, $\sigma_p = \sqrt{\frac{\pi(1-\pi)}{n}} = \sqrt{\frac{0.65(1-0.65)}{100}} = 0.0477$

(a) $P(p < 0.7) = P(Z < 1.0483) = 0.8527$

7.16 cont. (a) Excel Output:

	Probability for X <=	
8	X Value	0.7
9	Z Value	1.0482848
10	P(X<=0.7)	0.8527

(b) $P(0.6 < p < 0.7) = P(-1.05 < Z < 1.05) = 0.7055$

Excel Output:

20	Probability for a Range	
21	From X Value	0.6
22	To X Value	0.7
23	Z Value for 0.6	-1.048285
24	Z Value for 0.7	1.0482848
25	P(X<=0.6)	0.1473
26	P(X<=0.7)	0.8527
27	P(0.6<=X<=0.7)	0.7055

(c) $P(p > 0.7) = P(Z > 1.048) = 0.1473$

Excel Output:

2	Probability for X >	
3	X Value	0.7
4	Z Value	1.0482848
5	P(X>0.7)	0.1473

(d) $\mu_p = \pi = 0.65,\ \sigma_p = \sqrt{\dfrac{\pi(1-\pi)}{n}} = \sqrt{\dfrac{0.65(1-0.65)}{400}} = 0.0238$

$P(p < 0.7) = P(Z < 2.0966) = 0.982$

$P(0.6 < p < 0.7) = P(-2.0966 < Z < 2.0966) = 0.9640$

$P(p > 0.7) = P(Z > 2.0966) = 0.0180$

Excel Output:

1	Normal Probabilities	
2		
3	Common Data	
4	Mean	0.65
5	Standard Deviation	0.0238485
6		
7	Probability for X <=	
8	X Value	0.7
9	Z Value	2.0965697
10	P(X<=0.7)	0.9820
11		
12	Probability for X >	
13	X Value	0.7
14	Z Value	2.0965697
15	P(X>0.7)	0.0180

7.16 cont. (d)

20	Probability for a Range	
21	From X Value	0.6
22	To X Value	0.7
23	Z Value for 0.6	-2.09657
24	Z Value for 0.7	2.0965697
25	P(X<=0.6)	0.0180
26	P(X<=0.7)	0.9820
27	P(0.6<=X<=0.7)	0.9640

7.18 (a) $\mu_p = \pi = 0.392,\ \sigma_p = \sqrt{\frac{\pi(1-\pi)}{n}} = \sqrt{\frac{0.392(1-0.392)}{200}} = 0.0345207$

$P(0.30 < p < 0.38) = P(-2.665 < Z < -0.3476) = 0.3602$

Excel Output:

Probability for a Range	
From X Value	0.3
To X Value	0.38
Z Value for 0.3	-2.665066
Z Value for 0.38	-0.347617
P(X<=0.3)	0.0038
P(X<=0.38)	0.3641
P(0.3<=X<=0.38)	0.3602

(b) The probability is 90% that the sample percentage will be contained between 0.3352 and 0.4488.

Excel Output:

Find X Values Given a Percentage	
Percentage	90.00%
Z Value	-1.64
Lower X Value	0.3352
Upper X Value	0.4488

(c) The probability is 95% that the sample percentage will be contained between 0.3243 and 0.4597.

Excel Output:

34	Find X Values Given a Percentage	
35	Percentage	95.00%
36	Z Value	-1.96
37	Lower X Value	0.3243
38	Upper X Value	0.4597

7.20 $\mu_p = \pi = 0.80,\ \sigma_p = \sqrt{\frac{\pi(1-\pi)}{n}} = \sqrt{\frac{0.80(1-0.80)}{200}} = 0.02828$

(a) $P(0.70 < p < 0.78) = P(-3.5355 < Z < -0.7071) = 0.2395$

Probability for a Range	
From X Value	0.7
To X Value	0.78
Z Value for 0.7	-3.535534
Z Value for 0.78	-0.707107
P(X<=0.7)	0.0002
P(X<=0.78)	0.2398
P(0.7<=X<=0.78)	0.2395

(b) The probability is 90% that the sample percentage will be contained between 0.7535 and 0.8465

34	Find X Values Given a Percentage	
35	Percentage	90.00%
36	Z Value	-1.64
37	Lower X Value	0.7535
38	Upper X Value	0.8465

(c) The probability is 95% that the sample percentage will be contained between 0.7446 and 0.8554

Find X Values Given a Percentage	
Percentage	95.00%
Z Value	-1.96
Lower X Value	0.7446
Upper X Value	0.8554

7.22 The standard error of the sample means becomes smaller as larger sample sizes are taken. This is due to the fact that an extreme observation will have a smaller effect on the mean in a larger sample than in a small sample. Thus, the sample means will tend to be closer to the population mean as the sample size increases.

7.24 The population distribution is the distribution of a particular variable of interest, while the sampling distribution represents the distribution of a statistic.

7.26 $\mu_{\overline{X}} = 0.753$ $\sigma_{\overline{X}} = \frac{\sigma}{\sqrt{n}} = \frac{0.004}{5} = 0.0008$

PHStat output:

Common Data	
Mean	0.753
Standard Deviation	0.0008

Probability for X <=	
X Value	0.74
Z Value	–16.25
P(X<=0.74)	1.117E-59

Probability for X >	
X Value	0.76
Z Value	8.75
P(X>0.76)	0.0000

Probability for X<0.74 or X >0.76	
P(X<0.74 or X >0.76)	0.0000

Probability for a Range	
From X Value	0.74
To X Value	0.75
Z Value for 0.74	–16.25
Z Value for 0.75	–3.75
P(X<=0.74)	0.0000
P(X<=0.75)	0.0001
P(0.74<=X<=0.75)	0.00009

Probability for a Range	
From X Value	0.75
To X Value	0.753
Z Value for 0.75	–3.75
Z Value for 0.753	0
P(X<=0.75)	0.0001
P(X<=0.753)	0.5000
P(0.75<=X<=0.753)	0.4999

Find X and Z Given Cum. Pctage.	
Cumulative Percentage	7.00%
Z Value	–1.475791
X Value	0.751819

(a) $P(0.75 < \overline{X} < 0.753) = P(-3.75 < Z < 0) = 0.5 - 0.00009 = 0.4999$

(b) $P(0.74 < \overline{X} < 0.75) = P(-16.25 < Z < -3.75) = 0.00009$

(c) $P(\overline{X} > 0.76) = P(Z > 8.75) =$ virtually zero

(d) $P(\overline{X} < 0.74) = P(Z < -16.25) =$ virtually zero

(e) $P(\overline{X} < A) = P(Z < -1.48) = 0.07$ $X = 0.753 - 1.48(0.0008) = 0.7518$

7.28 $\mu_{\overline{X}} = 4.7$ $\sigma_{\overline{X}} = \frac{\sigma_X}{\sqrt{n}} = \frac{0.40}{5} = 0.08$

PHstat output:

Common Data	
Mean	4.7
Standard Deviation	0.08
Probability for X >	
X Value	4.6
Z Value	–1.25
P(X>4.6)	0.8944

Find X and Z Given Cum. Pctage.	
Cumulative Percentage	23.00%
Z Value	–0.738847
X Value	4.640892

Find X and Z Given Cum. Pctage.	
Cumulative Percentage	15.00%
Z Value	–1.036433
X Value	4.6170853

Find X and Z Given Cum. Pctage.	
Cumulative Percentage	85.00%
Z Value	1.036433
X Value	4.782915

(a) $P(4.60 < \overline{X}) = P(-1.25 < Z) = 1 - 0.1056 = 0.8944$

(b) $P(A < \overline{X} < B) = P(-1.04 < Z < 1.04) = 0.70$

$A = 4.70 - 1.04(0.08) = 4.6168$ ounces $X = 4.70 + 1.04(0.08) = 4.7832$ ounces

(c) $P(\overline{X} > A) = P(Z > -0.74) = 0.77$ $A = 4.70 - 0.74(0.08) = 4.6408$

7.30 $\mu_{\overline{X}} = 21.19$ $\sigma_{\overline{X}} = \frac{\sigma}{\sqrt{n}} = \frac{20}{4} = 5$

Excel Output:

1	Normal Probabilities	
2		
3	Common Data	
4	Mean	21.19
5	Standard Deviation	5
6		
7	Probability for X <=	
8	X Value	0
9	Z Value	-4.238
10	P(X<=0)	0.0000
11		
12	Probability for X >	
13	X Value	10
14	Z Value	-2.238
15	P(X>10)	0.9874

20	Probability for a Range	
21	From X Value	0
22	To X Value	10
23	Z Value for 0	-4.238
24	Z Value for 10	-2.238
25	P(X<=0)	0.0000
26	P(X<=10)	0.0126
27	P(0<=X<=10)	0.0126

(a) $P(\overline{X} < 0) = P(Z < -4.238) = 0.0000$

(b) $P(0 < \overline{X} < 10) = P(-4.238 < Z < -2.238) = 0.0126$

(c) $P(\overline{X} > 10) = P(Z > -2.238) = 0.9874$

7.32 Class Project answers will vary. The mean of the uniform distribution is $\frac{a+b}{2}$, since the random numbers in the table range from 0 to 9 the mean is 4.5. When $n = 2$, the frequency distribution of the sample means for the class should be centered around 4.5 and have a shape similar to column B with $n = 2$ in Figure 7.4 page 232 of text. As the sample size increases the frequency distribution of the sample means should have the shape similar to a normal distribution centered around 4.5.

7.34 Class Project answers will vary. Population mean is 1.310 and population standard deviation is 1.13

X	P(X=x)	x*P(X=x)	(x-mean)^2*P(X=x)
0.00	0.25	0.000	0.429025
1.00	0.40	0.400	0.03844
2.00	0.20	0.400	0.09522
3.00	0.10	0.300	0.28561
4.00	0.04	0.160	0.289444
5.00	0.01	0.050	0.136161
mean	1.310		
standard deviation	1.12867179		

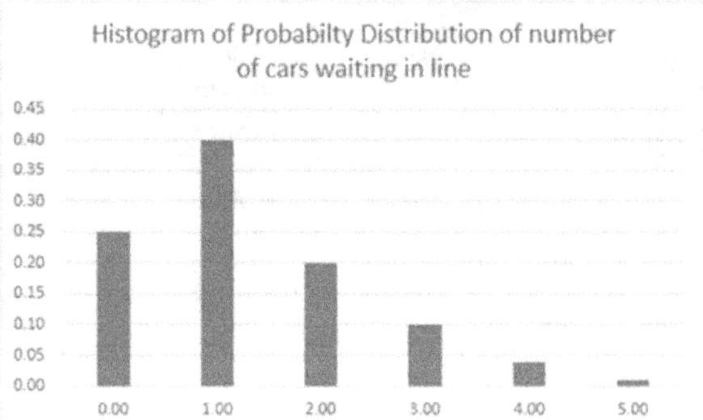

Depending on class results, one should expect similar results to example 7.5 on page 233 of text. The frequency distributions of the sample means for each sample size should progress from a skewed population toward a bell-shaped distribution as the sample size increases.

Chapter 8

8.2 $\bar{X} \pm Z \cdot \frac{\sigma}{\sqrt{n}} = 125 \pm 2.58 \cdot \frac{24}{\sqrt{36}}$ $114.68 \le \mu \le 135.32$

8.4 Yes, it is true since 5% of intervals will not include the population mean.

8.6 (a) You would compute the mean first because you need the mean to compute the standard deviation. If you had a sample, you would compute the sample mean. If you had the population mean, you would compute the population standard deviation.

(b) If you have a sample, you are computing the sample standard deviation not the population standard deviation needed in Equation 8.1. If you have a population, and have computed the population mean and population standard deviation, you don't need a confidence interval estimate of the population mean since you already have computed it.

8.8 Equation (8.1) assumes that you know the population standard deviation. Because you are selecting a sample of 100 from the population, you are computing a sample standard deviation, not the population standard deviation.

8.10 (a) $\bar{X} \pm Z \cdot \frac{\sigma}{\sqrt{n}} = 49{,}875 \pm 1.96 \cdot \frac{1500}{\sqrt{64}}$ $49{,}507.51 \le \mu \le 50{,}242.49$

Excel Output:

	A	B
1	**Confidence Estimate for the Mean**	
2		
3	**Data**	
4	**Population Standard Deviation**	**1500**
5	**Sample Mean**	**49875**
6	**Sample Size**	**64**
7	**Confidence Level**	**95%**
8		
9	Intermediate Calculations	
10	Standard Error of the Mean	187.5
11	Z Value	-1.9600
12	Interval Half Width	367.4932
13		
14	**Confidence Interval**	
15	**Interval Lower Limit**	**49507.5068**
16	**Interval Upper Limit**	**50242.4932**

(b) Yes, because the confidence interval includes 50,000 hours the manufacturer can support a claim that the bulbs have a mean of 50,000 hours.

(c) No. Because σ is known and $n = 64$, from the Central Limit Theorem, you know that the sampling distribution of $\bar{X}$ is approximately normal.

(d) $\bar{X} \pm Z \cdot \frac{\sigma}{\sqrt{n}} = 49{,}875 \pm 1.96 \cdot \frac{500}{\sqrt{64}}$ $49{,}752.50 \le \mu \le 49{,}997.50$

The confidence interval is narrower, based on the population standard deviation of 500 hours and the confidence interval no longer includes 50,000 so the manufacturer could not state that the LED bulbs have a mean life of 50,000 hours.

8.10 cont. (d) Excel Output:

	A	B
1	**Confidence Estimate for the Mean**	
2		
3	**Data**	
4	**Population Standard Deviation**	500
5	**Sample Mean**	49875
6	**Sample Size**	64
7	**Confidence Level**	95%
8		
9	Intermediate Calculations	
10	Standard Error of the Mean	62.5
11	Z Value	-1.9600
12	Interval Half Width	122.4977
13		
14	**Confidence Interval**	
15	**Interval Lower Limit**	49752.5023
16	**Interval Upper Limit**	49997.4977
17		

8.12 (a) $df = 9,\ \alpha = 0.05,\ t_{\alpha/2} = 2.2622$

(b) $df = 9,\ \alpha = 0.01,\ t_{\alpha/2} = 3.2498$

(c) $df = 31,\ \alpha = 0.05,\ t_{\alpha/2} = 2.0395$

(d) $df = 64,\ \alpha = 0.05,\ t_{\alpha/2} = 1.9977$

(e) $df = 15,\ \alpha = 0.1,\ t_{\alpha/2} = 1.7531$

8.14 Original data: $5.8571 \pm 2.4469 \cdot \frac{6.4660}{\sqrt{7}}$ $\quad -0.1229 \le \mu \le 11.8371$

Altered data: $4.00 \pm 2.4469 \cdot \frac{2.1602}{\sqrt{7}}$ $\quad 2.0022 \le \mu \le 5.9978$

The presence of an outlier in the original data increases the value of the sample mean and greatly inflates the sample standard deviation.

8.16 (a) $\bar{X} \pm t \cdot \frac{S}{\sqrt{n}} = 87 \pm 1.9781 \cdot \frac{9}{\sqrt{133}}$ $85.46 \le \mu \le 88.54$

3	Data	
4	Sample Standard Deviation	9
5	Sample Mean	87
6	Sample Size	133
7	Confidence Level	95%
8		
9	Intermediate Calculations	
10	Standard Error of the Mean	0.7804
11	Degrees of Freedom	132
12	t Value	1.9781
13	Interval Half Width	1.5437
14		
15	Confidence Interval	
16	Interval Lower Limit	85.46
17	Interval Upper Limit	88.54

(b) You can be 95% confident that the population mean one-time gift donations is somewhere between \$85.46 and \$88.54.

8.18 (a) $6.32 \le \mu \le 7.87$

Minitab Output:

One-Sample T: Cost (\$)

Descriptive Statistics

N	Mean	StDev	SE Mean	95% CI for μ
15	7.093	1.406	0.363	(6.315, 7.872)

μ: mean of Cost (\$)

(b) You can be 95% confident that the population mean amount spent for lunch at a fast-food restaurant is between \$6.31 and \$7.87.

(c) That the population distribution is normally distributed.

(d) The assumption of normality is not seriously violated and with a sample of 15, the validity of the confidence interval is not seriously impacted.

8.20 (a) For First and Second Quarter ads: $5.12 \le \mu \le 5.65$

For Halftime and Second half ads: $5.24 \le \mu \le 6.06$

8.20 cont. (a) Excel Output:

	A	B	C
1	Estimate for the Mean Ad Ratings First and Second Quarter		
2			
3	Data		
4	Sample Standard Deviation	0.715253771	
5	Sample Mean	5.38	
6	Sample Size	31	
7	Confidence Level	95%	
8			
9	Intermediate Calculations		
10	Standard Error of the Mean	0.1285	
11	Degrees of Freedom	30	
12	*t* Value	2.0423	
13	Interval Half Width	0.2624	
14			
15	Confidence Interval		
16	Interval Lower Limit	5.12	
17	Interval Upper Limit	5.65	

	A	B	C
1	Estimate for the Mean Ad Ratings halftime and Second half		
2			
3	Data		
4	Sample Standard Deviation	1.041093825	
5	Sample Mean	5.65	
6	Sample Size	27	
7	Confidence Level	95%	
8			
9	Intermediate Calculations		
10	Standard Error of the Mean	0.2004	
11	Degrees of Freedom	26	
12	*t* Value	2.0555	
13	Interval Half Width	0.4118	
14			
15	Confidence Interval		
16	Interval Lower Limit	5.24	
17	Interval Upper Limit	6.06	

(b) You are 95% confident that the mean rating for first and second quarter ads is between 5.12 and 5.65. You are 95% confident that the mean rating for halftime and second half ads is between 5.24 and 6.06.

(c) The confidence intervals for the two groups of ads are similar.

(d) You need to assume that the distributions of the rating for the two groups of ads are normally distributed.

(e) The distribution of each group of ads appears approximately normally distributed.

8.22 (a) $\bar{X} \pm t \cdot \frac{S}{\sqrt{n}} = 43.04 \pm 2.0096 \cdot \frac{41.9261}{\sqrt{50}}$ $\quad 31.12 \le \mu \le 54.96$

(b) The population distribution needs to be normally distribution.

(c)

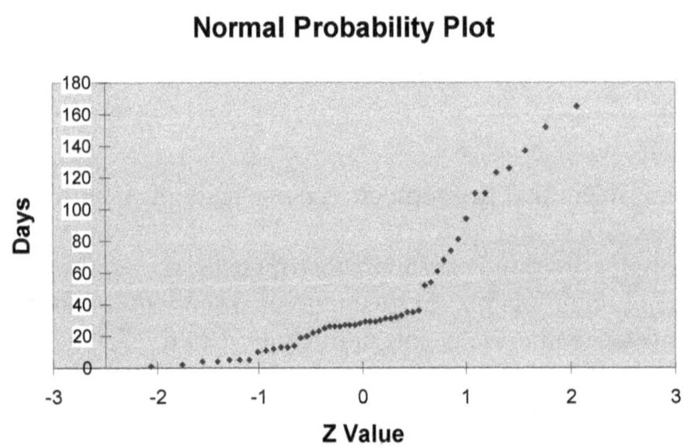

8.22 cont. (c)

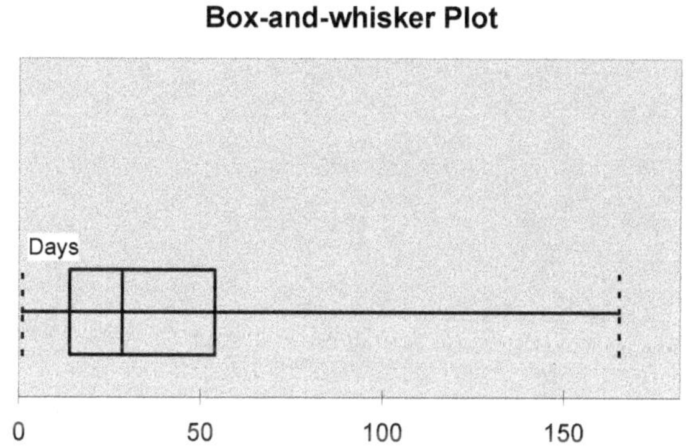

Both the normal probability plot and the boxplot suggest that the distribution is skewed to the right.

(d) Even though the population distribution is not normally distributed, with a sample of 50, the t distribution can still be used due to the Central Limit Theorem.

8.24 Excel Output:

	A	B	C
1	**Estimate for the Mean Mobile Commerce Penetration %**		
2			
3	**Data**		
4	**Sample Standard Deviation**	**7.649476633**	
5	**Sample Mean**	**45.08**	
6	**Sample Size**	**24**	
7	**Confidence Level**	**95%**	
8			
9	Intermediate Calculations		
10	Standard Error of the Mean	1.5614	
11	Degrees of Freedom	23	
12	*t* Value	2.0687	
13	Interval Half Width	3.2301	
14			
15	**Confidence Interval**		
16	**Interval Lower Limit**	**41.85**	
17	**Interval Upper Limit**	**48.31**	

8.24
cont.

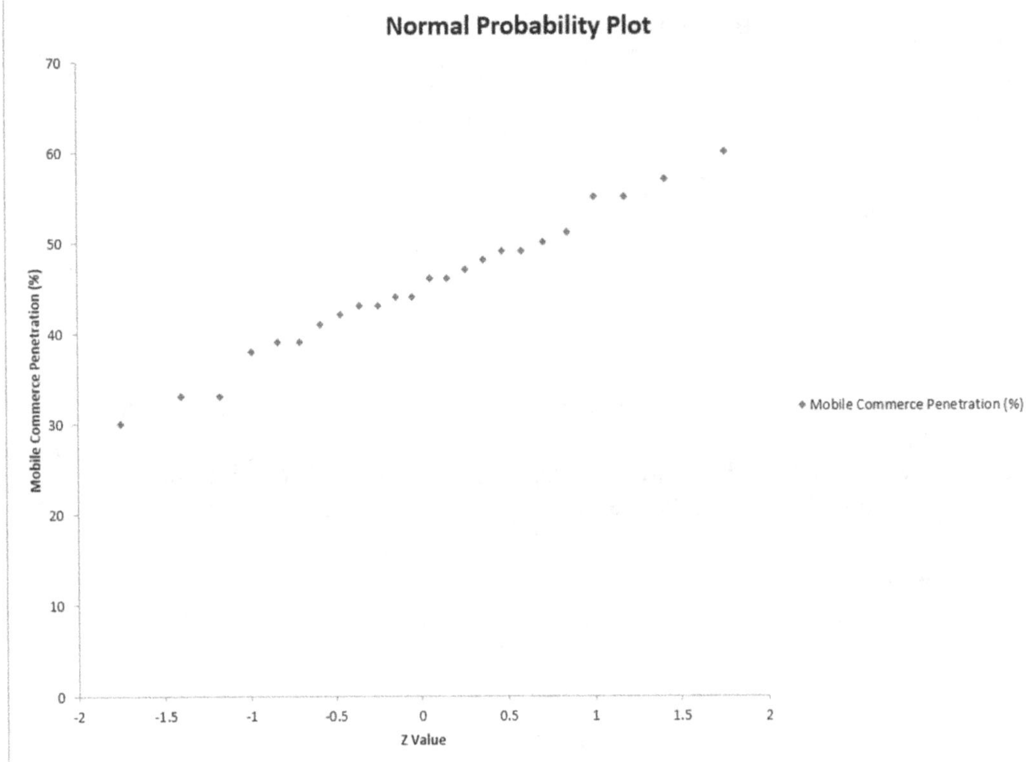

(a) $41.85 \le \mu \le 48.31$
(b) The populations distribution is normally distributed.
(c) The normal probability plot appears to be approximately normally distributed

8.26 $p = \frac{X}{n} = \frac{50}{200} = 0.25 \qquad p \pm Z \cdot \sqrt{\frac{p(1-p)}{n}} = 0.25 \pm 1.96\sqrt{\frac{0.25(0.75)}{200}}$

$0.19 \le \pi \le 0.31$

8.28 (a)

	A	B
1	**Purchase Additional Telephone Line**	
2		
3	**Sample Size**	**500**
4	**Number of Successes**	**135**
5	**Confidence Level**	**99%**
6	Sample Proportion	0.27
7	Z Value	-2.57583451
8	Standard Error of the Proportion	0.019854471
9	Interval Half Width	0.05114183
10	**Interval Lower Limit**	**0.21885817**
11	**Interval Upper Limit**	**0.32114183**

$p = \frac{X}{n} = \frac{135}{500} = 0.27 \qquad p \pm Z \cdot \sqrt{\frac{p(1-p)}{n}} = 0.27 \pm 2.5758\sqrt{\frac{0.27(1-0.27)}{500}}$

$0.22 \le \pi \le 0.32$

8.28 cont. (b) The manager in charge of promotional programs concerning residential customers can infer that the proportion of households that would purchase a new cellphone if it were made available at a substantially reduced installation cost is between 0.22 and 0.32 with a 99% level of confidence.

8.30 (a) Excel Output:

	Data	
4	**Sample Size**	**1000**
5	**Number of Successes**	**260**
6	**Confidence Level**	**95%**
7		
8	Intermediate Calculations	
9	Sample Proportion	0.26
10	Z Value	-1.9600
11	Standard Error of the Proportion	0.013871
12	Interval Half Width	0.0272
13		
14	**Confidence Interval**	
15	**Interval Lower Limit**	**0.2328**
16	**Interval Upper Limit**	**0.2872**
17		

$$p = 0.26 \quad p \pm Z\sqrt{\frac{p(1-p)}{n}} = 0.26 \pm 1.96\sqrt{\frac{0.26(1-0.26)}{1000}}$$

$$0.2328 \le \pi \le 0.2872$$

(b) No, you cannot because the interval estimate includes 0.25 (25%).

(c) Excel Output:

	Data	
4	**Sample Size**	**10000**
5	**Number of Successes**	**2600**
6	**Confidence Level**	**95%**
7		
8	Intermediate Calculations	
9	Sample Proportion	0.26
10	Z Value	-1.9600
11	Standard Error of the Proportion	0.004386
12	Interval Half Width	0.0086
13		
14	**Confidence Interval**	
15	**Interval Lower Limit**	**0.2514**
16	**Interval Upper Limit**	**0.2686**
17		

$$p = 0.26 \quad p \pm Z\sqrt{\frac{p(1-p)}{n}} = 0.26 \pm 1.96\sqrt{\frac{0.26(1-0.26)}{10{,}000}}$$

$$0.2514 \le \pi \le 0.2686$$

8.30 cont. (c) Yes, you can claim more than a quarter of all consumers value personalized experience most when shopping in retail store because the interval is above 0.25 (25%)

(d) The larger the sample size, the narrower the confidence interval, holding everything else constant.

8.32 (a) Excel Output:

Data	
Sample Size	**4787**
Number of Successes	**4178**
Confidence Level	**95%**
Intermediate Calculations	
Sample Proportion	0.87278
Z Value	-1.9600
Standard Error of the Proportion	0.004816
Interval Half Width	0.0094
Confidence Interval	
Interval Lower Limit	**0.8633**
Interval Upper Limit	**0.8822**

$p = 0.87 \quad p \pm Z\sqrt{\frac{p(1-p)}{n}} = 0.87 \pm 1.96\sqrt{\frac{0.87(1-0.87)}{4787}}$

$0.8633 \le \pi \le 0.8822$

(b) Excel Output:

Data	
Sample Size	**4178**
Number of Successes	**789**
Confidence Level	**95%**
Intermediate Calculations	
Sample Proportion	0.188846
Z Value	-1.9600
Standard Error of the Proportion	0.006055
Interval Half Width	0.0119
Confidence Interval	
Interval Lower Limit	**0.1770**
Interval Upper Limit	**0.2007**

$p = 0.19 \quad p \pm Z\sqrt{\frac{p(1-p)}{n}} = 0.19 \pm 1.96\sqrt{\frac{0.19(1-0.19)}{4178}}$

$0.1770 \le \pi \le 0.2007$

8.32 cont. (c) Because almost 90% of adults have purchased something online, but only about 20% are weekly online shoppers, the director of e-commerce sales may want to focus on those adults who are weekly online shoppers.

8.34 $n = \frac{Z^2\sigma^2}{e^2} = \frac{1.96^2 \cdot 15^2}{5^2} = 34.57$ Use $n = 35$

8.36 $n = \frac{Z^2\pi(1-\pi)}{e^2} = \frac{2.58^2(0.5)(0.5)}{(0.04)^2} = 1{,}040.06$ Use $n = 1{,}041$

8.38 (a) $n = \frac{Z^2\sigma^2}{e^2} = \frac{1.96^2 \cdot 400^2}{50^2} = 245.86$ Use $n = 246$

(b) $n = \frac{Z^2\sigma^2}{e^2} = \frac{1.96^2 \cdot 400^2}{25^2} = 983.41$ Use $n = 984$

8.40 Excel Output:

3	Data	
4	Population Standard Deviation	1500
5	Sampling Error	400
6	Confidence Level	95%
7		
8	Intemediate Calculations	
9	Z Value	-1.9600
10	Calculated Sample Size	54.0205
11		
12	Result	
13	Sample Size Needed	55
14		

$n = \frac{Z^2\sigma^2}{e^2} = \frac{1.96^2 \cdot 1500^2}{400^2} = 54.0225$ Use $n = 55$

8.42 (a) $n = \frac{Z^2\sigma^2}{e^2} = \frac{2.5758^2 \cdot 20^2}{5^2} = 106.1583$ Use $n = 107$

(b) $n = \frac{Z^2\sigma^2}{e^2} = \frac{1.96^2 \cdot 20^2}{5^2} = 61.4633$ Use $n = 62$

8.44 Note: All the answers are computed using PHStat. Answers computed otherwise may be slightly different due to rounding.

(a) $n = \frac{Z^2\sigma^2}{e^2} = \frac{1.96^2 \cdot 2^2}{0.25^2} = 245.85$ Use $n = 246$

(b) $n = \frac{Z^2\sigma^2}{e^2} = \frac{1.96^2 \cdot 2.5^2}{0.25^2} = 384.15$ Use $n = 385$

(c) $n = \frac{Z^2\sigma^2}{e^2} = \frac{1.96^2 \cdot 3.0^2}{0.25^2} = 553.17$ Use $n = 554$

8.44 cont. (d) When there is more variability in the population, a larger sample is needed to accurately estimate the mean.

8.46 (a) Excel Output:

Data	
Sample Size	115
Number of Successes	81
Confidence Level	95%
Intermediate Calculations	
Sample Proportion	0.704348
Z Value	-1.9600
Standard Error of the Proportion	0.042553
Interval Half Width	0.0834
Confidence Interval	
Interval Lower Limit	0.6209
Interval Upper Limit	0.7878

$$p = 0.70 \quad p \pm Z\sqrt{\frac{p(1-p)}{n}} = 0.70 \pm 1.96\sqrt{\frac{0.70(1-0.70)}{115}}$$

$0.6209 \le \pi \le 0.7878$

(b) Excel Output

Data	
Sample Size	115
Number of Successes	68
Confidence Level	95%
Intermediate Calculations	
Sample Proportion	0.591304
Z Value	-1.9600
Standard Error of the Proportion	0.045841
Interval Half Width	0.0898
Confidence Interval	
Interval Lower Limit	0.5015
Interval Upper Limit	0.6812

$$p = 0.59 \quad p \pm Z\sqrt{\frac{p(1-p)}{n}} = 0.59 \pm 1.96\sqrt{\frac{0.59(1-0.59)}{115}}$$

$0.5015 \le \pi \le 0.6812$

8.46 cont. (c) Excel Output:

Data	
Sample Size	**115**
Number of Successes	**16**
Confidence Level	**95%**

Intermediate Calculations	
Sample Proportion	0.13913
Z Value	-1.9600
Standard Error of the Proportion	0.032272
Interval Half Width	0.0633

Confidence Interval	
Interval Lower Limit	**0.0759**
Interval Upper Limit	**0.2024**

$$p = 0.14 \quad p \pm Z\sqrt{\frac{p(1-p)}{n}} = 0.14 \pm 1.96\sqrt{\frac{0.14(1-0.14)}{115}}$$

$0.0759 \le \pi \le 0.2024$

(d) (a) Excel Output:

Data	
Estimate of True Proportion	**0.7**
Sampling Error	**0.02**
Confidence Level	**95%**

Intermediate Calculations	
Z Value	-1.9600
Calculated Sample Size	2016.7659

Result	
Sample Size Needed	**2017**

$$n = \frac{Z^2\pi(1-\pi)}{e^2} = \frac{1.96^2 \cdot (0.7)(1-0.7)}{0.02^2} = 2016.84 \qquad \text{Use } n = 2017$$

8.46 cont. (d) (b) Excel Output:

3	Data	
4	**Estimate of True Proportion**	**0.59**
5	**Sampling Error**	**0.02**
6	**Confidence Level**	**95%**
7		
8	Intermediate Calculations	
9	Z Value	-1.9600
10	Calculated Sample Size	2323.1222
11		
12	**Result**	
13	**Sample Size Needed**	**2324**

$$n = \frac{Z^2\pi(1-\pi)}{e^2} = \frac{1.96^2 \cdot (0.59)(1-0.59)}{0.02^2} = 2323.208 \text{ Use } n = 2324$$

(c) Excel Output:

3	Data	
4	**Estimate of True Proportion**	**0.14**
5	**Sampling Error**	**0.02**
6	**Confidence Level**	**95%**
7		
8	Intermediate Calculations	
9	Z Value	-1.9600
10	Calculated Sample Size	1156.2791
11		
12	**Result**	
13	**Sample Size Needed**	**1157**

$$n = \frac{Z^2\pi(1-\pi)}{e^2} = \frac{1.96^2 \cdot (0.14)(1-0.14)}{0.02^2} = 1156.322 \text{ Use } n = 1157$$

8.48 (a) If you conducted a follow-up study, you would use $\pi = 0.38$ in the sample size formula because it is based on past information on the proportion.

8.48 cont. (b) Excel Output:

	Data	
3	**Data**	
4	**Estimate of True Proportion**	**0.38**
5	**Sampling Error**	**0.03**
6	**Confidence Level**	**95%**
7		
8	Intermediate Calculations	
9	Z Value	-1.9600
10	Calculated Sample Size	1005.6086
11		
12	**Result**	
13	**Sample Size Needed**	**1006**

$$n = \frac{Z^2\pi(1-\pi)}{e^2} = \frac{1.96^2 \cdot (0.38)(1-0.38)}{0.03^2} = 1005.646 \qquad \text{Use } n = 1006$$

8.50 The only way to have 100% confidence is to obtain the parameter of interest, rather than a sample statistic. From another perspective, the range of the normal and t distribution is infinite, so a Z or t value that contains 100% of the area cannot be obtained.

8.52 If the confidence level is increased, a greater area under the normal or t distribution needs to be included. This leads to an increased value of Z or t, and thus a wider interval.

8.54 (a) PC/laptop Excel Output:

	Data	
3	**Data**	
4	**Sample Size**	**1000**
5	**Number of Successes**	**840**
6	**Confidence Level**	**95%**
7		
8	Intermediate Calculations	
9	Sample Proportion	0.84
10	Z Value	-1.9600
11	Standard Error of the Proportion	0.011593
12	Interval Half Width	0.0227
13		
14	**Confidence Interval**	
15	**Interval Lower Limit**	**0.8173**
16	**Interval Upper Limit**	**0.8627**

$$p = 0.84 \quad p \pm Z\sqrt{\frac{p(1-p)}{n}} = 0.84 \pm 1.96\sqrt{\frac{0.84(1-0.84)}{1000}}$$

$$0.8173 \le \pi \le 0.8627$$

8.54 cont. (a) Smartphone Excel Output:

Data	
Sample Size	**1000**
Number of Successes	**910**
Confidence Level	**95%**
Intermediate Calculations	
Sample Proportion	0.91
Z Value	-1.9600
Standard Error of the Proportion	0.00905
Interval Half Width	0.0177
Confidence Interval	
Interval Lower Limit	**0.8923**
Interval Upper Limit	**0.9277**

$p = 0.91 \quad p \pm Z\sqrt{\frac{p(1-p)}{n}} = 0.91 \pm 1.96\sqrt{\frac{0.91(1-0.91)}{1000}}$

$0.8923 \leq \pi \leq 0.9277$

Tablet Excel Output:

Data	
Sample Size	**1000**
Number of Successes	**500**
Confidence Level	**95%**
Intermediate Calculations	
Sample Proportion	0.5
Z Value	-1.9600
Standard Error of the Proportion	0.015811
Interval Half Width	0.0310
Confidence Interval	
Interval Lower Limit	**0.4690**
Interval Upper Limit	**0.5310**

$p = 0.5 \quad p \pm Z\sqrt{\frac{p(1-p)}{n}} = 0.5 \pm 1.96\sqrt{\frac{0.5(1-0.5)}{1000}}$

$0.469 \leq \pi \leq 0.5310$

8.54 cont. (a) Smart Watch Excel Output:

Data	
Sample Size	1000
Number of Successes	100
Confidence Level	95%
Intermediate Calculations	
Sample Proportion	0.1
Z Value	-1.9600
Standard Error of the Proportion	0.009487
Interval Half Width	0.0186
Confidence Interval	
Interval Lower Limit	0.0814
Interval Upper Limit	0.1186

$p = 0.1 \quad p \pm Z\sqrt{\frac{p(1-p)}{n}} = 0.1 \pm \sqrt{\frac{0.1(1-0.1)}{100}}$

$0.0814 \le \pi \le 0.1186$

(b) Most adults have a PC/laptop and a smartphone. Some adults have a tablet computer and very few have a smart watch.

8.56 Note: All the answers are computed using PHStat. Answers computed otherwise may be slightly different due to rounding.

(a) PHStat output:

Confidence Interval Estimate for the Mean

Data	
Sample Standard Deviation	3.5
Sample Mean	51
Sample Size	40
Confidence Level	95%
Intermediate Calculations	
Standard Error of the Mean	0.553398591
Degrees of Freedom	39
t Value	2.0227
Interval Half Width	1.1194
Confidence Interval	
Interval Lower Limit	49.88
Interval Upper Limit	52.12

$49.88 \le \mu \le 52.12$

8.56 cont. (b) PHStat output:

Confidence Interval Estimate for the Proportio

Data	
Sample Size	40
Number of Successes	32
Confidence Level	95%

Intermediate Calculations	
Sample Proportion	0.8000
Z Value	-1.9600
Standard Error of the Proportion	0.0632
Interval Half Width	0.1240

Confidence Interval	
Interval Lower Limit	0.6760
Interval Upper Limit	0.9240

$0.6760 \le \pi \le 0.9240$

(c) $n = \dfrac{Z^2 \cdot \sigma^2}{e^2} = \dfrac{1.96^2 \cdot 5^2}{2^2} = 24.01$ Use $n = 25$

(d) $n = \dfrac{Z^2 \cdot \pi \cdot (1-\pi)}{e^2} = \dfrac{1.96^2 \cdot (0.5) \cdot (0.5)}{(0.06)^2} = 266.7680$ Use $n = 267$

(e) If a single sample were to be selected for both purposes, the larger of the two sample sizes ($n = 267$) should be used.

8.58 (a) PHStat output:

Confidence Interval Estimate for the Mean

Data	
Sample Standard Deviation	7.3
Sample Mean	6.2
Sample Size	25
Confidence Level	95%

Intermediate Calculations	
Standard Error of the Mean	1.46
Degrees of Freedom	24
t Value	2.0639
Interval Half Width	3.0133

Confidence Interval	
Interval Lower Limit	3.19
Interval Upper Limit	9.21

$3.19 \le \mu \le 9.21$

8.58 cont. (b) PHStat output:

Confidence Interval Estimate for the Proportio

Data	
Sample Size	25
Number of Successes	13
Confidence Level	95%

Intermediate Calculations	
Sample Proportion	0.52
Z Value	-1.9600
Standard Error of the Proportion	0.0999
Interval Half Width	0.1958

Confidence Interval	
Interval Lower Limit	0.3242
Interval Upper Limit	0.7158

$0.3241 \le \pi \le 0.7158$

(c) $n = \frac{Z^2 \cdot \sigma^2}{e^2} = \frac{1.96^2 \cdot 8^2}{1.5^2} = 109.2682$ Use $n = 110$

(d) $n = \frac{Z^2 \cdot \pi \cdot (1-\pi)}{e^2} = \frac{1.645^2 \cdot (0.5) \cdot (0.5)}{(0.075)^2} = 120.268$ Use $n = 121$

(e) If a single sample were to be selected for both purposes, the larger of the two sample sizes ($n = 121$) should be used.

8.60 (a) $p \pm Z \cdot \sqrt{\frac{p(1-p)}{n}} = 0.31 \pm 1.645 \cdot \sqrt{\frac{0.31(0.69)}{200}}$ $0.2562 \le \pi \le 0.3638$

(b) $\bar{X} \pm t \cdot \frac{S}{\sqrt{n}} = 3.5 \pm 1.9720 \cdot \frac{2}{\sqrt{200}}$ $3.22 \le \mu \le 3.78$

(c) $\bar{X} \pm t \cdot \frac{S}{\sqrt{n}} = 18000 \pm 1.9720 \cdot \frac{3000}{\sqrt{200}}$ $\$17,581.68 \le \mu \le \$18,418.32$

8.62 (a) $\bar{X} \pm t \cdot \frac{S}{\sqrt{n}} = \$38.54 \pm 2.0010 \cdot \frac{\$7.26}{\sqrt{60}}$ $\$36.66 \le \mu \le \$40.42$

(b) $p \pm Z \cdot \sqrt{\frac{p(1-p)}{n}} = 0.30 \pm 1.645 \cdot \sqrt{\frac{0.30(0.70)}{60}}$ $0.2027 \le \pi \le 0.3973$

(c) $n = \frac{Z^2\sigma^2}{e^2} = \frac{1.96^2 \cdot 8^2}{1.5^2} = 109.27$ Use $n = 110$

(d) $n = \frac{Z^2 \cdot \pi \cdot (1-\pi)}{e^2} = \frac{1.645^2 \cdot (0.5) \cdot (0.5)}{(0.04)^2} = 422.82$ Use $n = 423$

(e) If a single sample were to be selected for both purposes, the larger of the two sample sizes ($n = 423$) should be used.

8.64 (a)

Confidence Interval Estimate for the Proportio

Data	
Sample Size	90
Number of Successes	51
Confidence Level	95%

Intermediate Calculations	
Sample Proportion	0.566666667
Z Value	-1.9600
Standard Error of the Proportion	0.0522
Interval Half Width	0.1024

Confidence Interval	
Interval Lower Limit	**0.4643**
Interval Upper Limit	**0.6690**

$$p \pm Z \cdot \sqrt{\frac{p(1-p)}{n}} = 0.5667 \pm 1.96 \cdot \sqrt{\frac{0.5667(1-0.5667)}{90}}$$

$0.4643 \le \pi \le 0.6690$

(b)

Confidence Interval Estimate for the Mean

Data	
Sample Standard Deviation	1103.6491
Sample Mean	563.38
Sample Size	51
Confidence Level	95%

Intermediate Calculations	
Standard Error of the Mean	154.5417855
Degrees of Freedom	50
t Value	2.0086
Interval Half Width	310.4063

Confidence Interval	
Interval Lower Limit	**252.97**
Interval Upper Limit	**873.79**

$$\bar{X} \pm t \cdot \frac{S}{\sqrt{n}} = 563.38 \pm 2.0086 \left(\frac{1103.6491}{\sqrt{51}} \right)$$

$\$252.97 \le \mu \le \$873.79$

8.66 (a) MiniTab Output

One-Sample T: Answer Time (seconds)

Descriptive Statistics

N	Mean	StDev	SE Mean	95% CI for μ
50	14.980	5.557	0.786	(13.401, 16.559)

μ: mean of Answer Time (seconds)

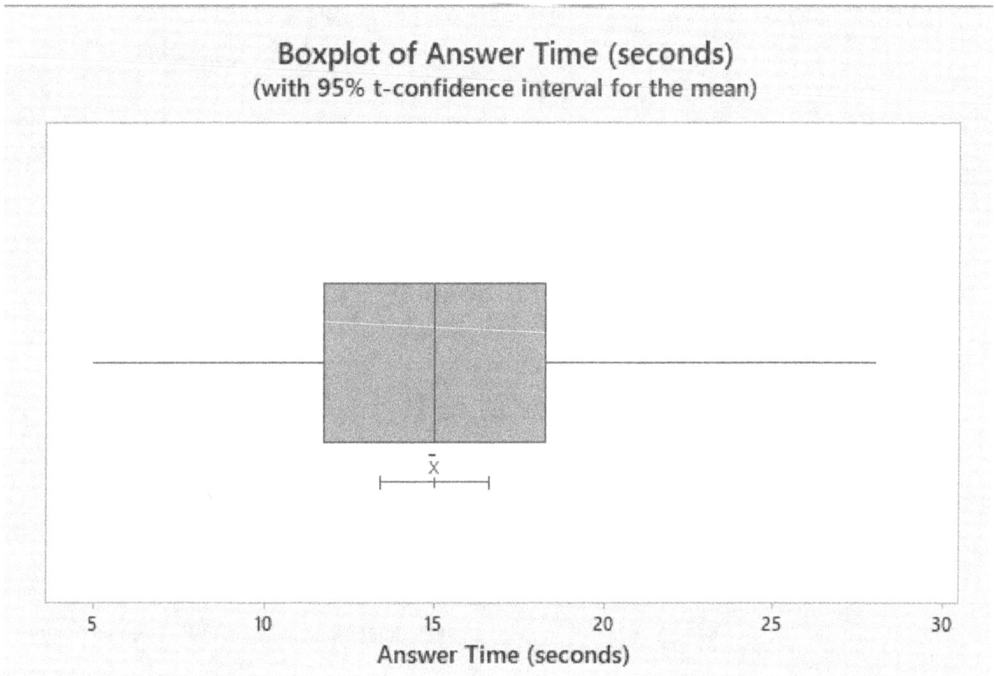

$13.4001 \le \mu \le 16.559$

(b) With 95% confidence, the population mean answer time is somewhere between 13.40 and 16.56 seconds.

(c) The assumption is valid as the answer time is approximately normally distributed.

8.68 (a) $\bar{X} \pm t \cdot \frac{S}{\sqrt{n}} = 0.2641 \pm 1.9741 \cdot \frac{0.1424}{\sqrt{170}}$ $\quad 0.2425 \le \mu \le 0.2856$

(b) $\bar{X} \pm t \cdot \frac{S}{\sqrt{n}} = 0.218 \pm 1.9772 \cdot \frac{0.1227}{\sqrt{140}}$ $\quad 0.1975 \le \mu \le 0.2385$

8.68 cont. (c)

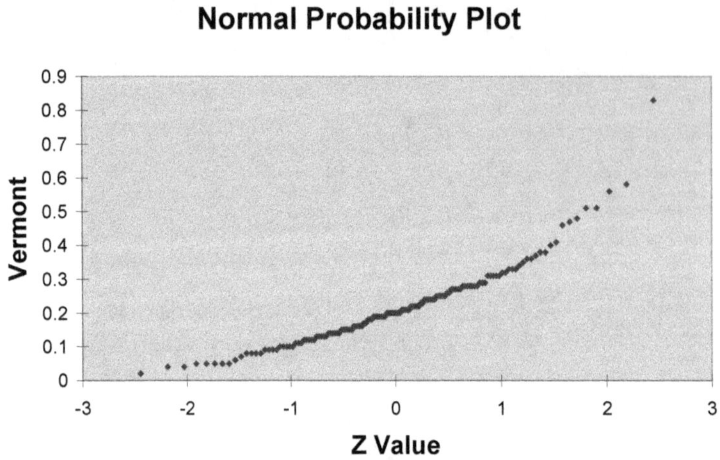

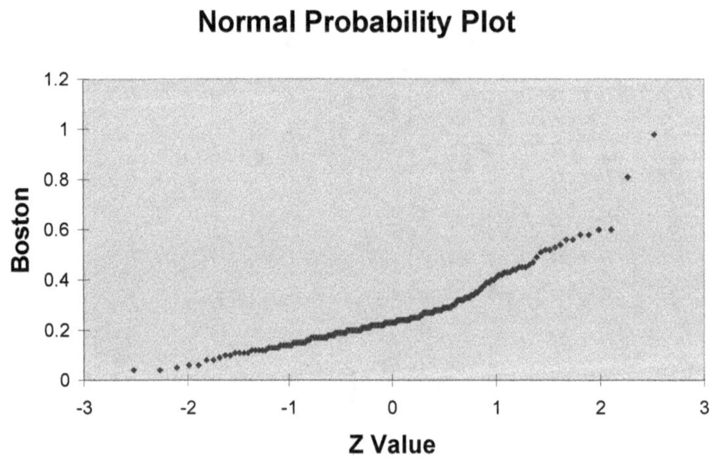

The amount of granule loss for both brands are skewed to the right but the sample sizes are large enough so the violation of the normality assumption is not critical.

(d) Because the two confidence intervals do not overlap, you can conclude that the mean granule loss of Boston shingles is higher than that of Vermont shingles

Chapter 9

9.2 Decision rule: Reject H_0 if $Z_{STAT} < -1.96$ or $Z_{STAT} > +1.96$.
Decision: Since $Z_{STAT} = +2.21$ is greater than the upper critical value of + 1.96, reject H_0.

9.4 Decision rule: Reject H_0 if $Z_{STAT} < -2.58$ or $Z_{STAT} > +2.58$.

9.6 p-value = 2(1 – 0.9772) = 0.0456

9.8 p-value = 0.1676

9.10 Under the French judicial system, unlike the United States, the null hypothesis assumes the defendant is guilty, the alternative hypothesis assumes the defendant is innocent. A Type I error would be not convicting a guilty person and a Type II error would be convicting an innocent person.

9.12 H_0: $\mu = 20$ minutes. 20 minutes is adequate travel time between classes.
H_1: $\mu \neq 20$ minutes. 20 minutes is not adequate travel time between classes.

9.14 (a) Minitab Output:

One-Sample Z

Descriptive Statistics

N	Mean	SE Mean	95% CI for μ
64	49875	188	(49508, 50242)

μ: mean of Sample
Known standard deviation = 1500

Test

Null hypothesis	H₀: μ = 50000
Alternative hypothesis	H₁: μ ≠ 50000

Z-Value	P-Value
-0.67	0.505

H_0: $\mu = 50{,}000$. The mean life of a large shipment of LEDs is equal to 50,000 hours.
H_1: $\mu \neq 50{,}000$. The mean life of a large shipment of LEDs differs from 50,000 hours.
Decision rule: Reject H_0 if $|Z_{STAT}| > 1.96$

Test statistic: $$Z_{STAT} = \frac{\overline{X} - \mu}{\frac{\sigma}{\sqrt{n}}} = -0.67$$

Decision: Since $-1.96 < Z_{STAT} = -0.67 < 1.96$, do not reject H_0. There is not enough evidence to conclude that the mean life of a large shipment of LEDs differs from 50,000 hours.

(b) p-value = 0.505. If the population mean life of a large shipment of LEDs is indeed equal to 50,000 hours, there is a 50.5% chance of observing a test statistic at least as contradictory to the null hypothesis as the sample result.

9.14 cont.

(c) $\overline{X} \pm Z_{\alpha/2}\frac{\sigma}{\sqrt{n}} = 49875 \pm 1.96\frac{1500}{\sqrt{64}}$ $\quad 49508 \le \mu \le 50242$

(d) Because the interval includes the hypothesized value of 50000 hours, you do not reject the null hypothesis. There is insufficient evidence that the mean life of a large shipment of LEDs differs from 50,000 hours. The same decision was reached using the two-tailed hypothesis test.

9.16 (a) PHStat output:

Data	
Null Hypothesis μ =	**1**
Level of Significance	**0.01**
Population Standard Deviation	**0.02**
Sample Size	**50**
Sample Mean	**0.995**
Intermediate Calculations	
Standard Error of the Mean	0.002828427
Z Test Statistic	**–1.767766953**
Two-Tail Test	
Lower Critical Value	**–2.575829304**
Upper Critical Value	**2.575829304**
***p*-Value**	**0.077099872**
Do not reject the null hypothesis	

H_0: $\mu = 1$. The mean amount of water is 1 gallon.

H_1: $\mu \ne 1$. The mean amount of water differs from 1 gallon.

Decision rule: Reject H_0 if $|Z_{STAT}| > 2.5758$

Test statistic: $Z_{STAT} = \frac{\overline{X} - \mu}{\frac{\sigma}{\sqrt{n}}} = \frac{0.995 - 1}{\frac{0.02}{\sqrt{50}}} = -1.7678$

Decision: Since $|Z_{STAT}| < 2.5758$, do not reject H_0. There is not enough evidence to conclude that the mean amount of water contained in 1-gallon bottles purchased from a nationally known water bottling company is different from 1 gallon.

(b) p-value $= 0.0771$. If the population mean amount of water contained in 1-gallon bottles purchased from a nationally known water bottling company is actually 1 gallon, the probability of obtaining a test statistic that is more than 1.7678 standard error units away from 0 is 0.0771.

9.16 cont. (c) PHStat output:

Data	
Population Standard Deviation	**0.02**
Sample Mean	**0.995**
Sample Size	**50**
Confidence Level	**99%**
Intermediate Calculations	
Standard Error of the Mean	0.002828427
Z Value	–2.5758293
Interval Half Width	0.007285545
Confidence Interval	
Interval Lower Limit	**0.987714455**
Interval Upper Limit	**1.002285545**

(c) $\bar{X} \pm Z_{a/2}\frac{\sigma}{\sqrt{n}} = 0.995 \pm 2.5758\frac{0.02}{\sqrt{50}}$ $\quad 0.9877 \leq \mu \leq 1.0023$

You are 99% confident that population mean amount of water contained in 1-gallon bottles purchased from a nationally known water bottling company is somewhere between 0.9877 and 1.0023 gallons.

(d) Since the 99% confidence interval does contain the hypothesized value of 1, you will not reject H_0. The conclusions are the same.

9.18 $t_{STAT} = \frac{\bar{X}-\mu}{\frac{S}{\sqrt{n}}} = \frac{56-50}{\frac{12}{\sqrt{16}}} = 2.00$

9.20 For a two-tailed test with a 0.05 level of confidence, the critical values are ± 2.1315.

9.22 No, you should not use the *t* test to test the null hypothesis that $\mu = 60$ on a population that is left-skewed because the sample size (n = 16) is less than 30. The *t* test assumes that, if the underlying population is not normally distributed, the sample size is sufficiently large to enable the test to be valid. If sample sizes are small (n < 30), the *t* test should not be used because the sampling distribution does not meet the requirements of the Central Limit Theorem.

9.24 PHStat output:

t Test for Hypothesis of the Mean		
Data		
Null Hypothesis	**μ =**	**3.7**
Level of Significance		**0.05**
Sample Size		**64**
Sample Mean		**3.57**
Sample Standard Deviation		**0.8**
Intermediate Calculations		
Standard Error of the Mean		0.1
Degrees of Freedom		63
***t* Test Statistic**		**–1.3**
Two-Tail Test		
Lower Critical Value		**–1.9983405**
Upper Critical Value		**1.9983405**
***p*-Value**		**0.1983372**
Do not reject the null hypothesis		

(a) $H_0: \mu = 3.7 \quad H_1: \mu \neq 3.7$

Decision rule: Reject H_0 if $|t_{STAT}| > 1.9983 \quad d.f. = 63$

Test statistic: $t_{STAT} = \dfrac{\overline{X} - \mu}{\dfrac{S}{\sqrt{n}}} = \dfrac{3.57 - 3.7}{\dfrac{0.8}{\sqrt{64}}} = -1.3$

Decision: Since $|t_{STAT}| < 1.9983$, do not reject H_0. There is not enough evidence to conclude that the population mean waiting time is different from 3.7 minutes at the 0.05 level of significance.

(b) The sample size of 64 is large enough to apply the Central Limit Theorem, hence, you do not need to be concerned about the shape of the population distribution when conducting the *t*-test in (a). In general, the *t* test is appropriate for this sample size except for the case where the population is extremely skewed or bimodal.

9.26 PHStat output:

t Test for Hypothesis of the Mean

Data	
Null Hypothesis μ=	1475
Level of Significance	0.05
Sample Size	100
Sample Mean	1500
Sample Standard Deviation	200

Intermediate Calculations	
Standard Error of the Mean	20.0000
Degrees of Freedom	99
t Test Statistic	1.2500

Two-Tail Test	
Lower Critical Value	-1.9842
Upper Critical Value	1.9842
p-Value	0.2142
Do not reject the null hypothesis	

(a) $H_0 : \mu = \$1,475$ $H_1 : \mu \neq \$1,475$

Decision rule: Reject H_0 if *p*-value < 0.05

Test statistic: $t_{STAT} = \dfrac{\overline{X} - \mu}{\dfrac{S}{\sqrt{n}}} = 1.2500$

p-value = 0.2142

Decision: Since the *p*-value of 0.2142 > 0.05, do not reject H_0. There is not enough evidence to conclude that the population mean amount spent on Amazon.com by Amazon Prime member shoppers is different from \$1,475.

(b) The *p*-value is 0.2142. If the population mean is indeed \$1,475, the probability of obtaining a test statistic that is more than 1.25 standard error units away from 0 in either direction is 0.2142.

9.28 PHStat output:

t Test for Hypothesis of the Mean

Data	
Null Hypothesis μ=	6.5
Level of Significance	0.05
Sample Size	15
Sample Mean	7.09
Sample Standard Deviation	1.406031226

Intermediate Calculations	
Standard Error of the Mean	0.3630
Degrees of Freedom	14
t Test Statistic	1.6344

Two-Tail Test	
Lower Critical Value	-2.1448
Upper Critical Value	2.1448
p-Value	0.1245
Do not reject the null hypothesis	

(a) $H_0: \mu = \$6.50 \quad H_1: \mu \neq \$6.50$

Decision rule: Reject H_0 if $|t_{STAT}| > 2.1448$ or p-value < 0.05

Test statistic: $t_{STAT} = \dfrac{\overline{X} - \mu}{\dfrac{S}{\sqrt{n}}} = 1.6344$

Decision: Since $|t_{STAT}| < 2.1448$, do not reject H_0. There is not enough evidence to conclude that the mean amount spent for lunch is different from \$6.50.

(b) The p-value is 0.1245. If the population mean is indeed \$6.50, the probability of obtaining a test statistic that is more than 1.6344 standard error units away from 0 in either direction is 0.4069.

(c) That the distribution of the amount spent on lunch is normally distributed.

(d) With a sample size of 15, it is difficult to evaluate the assumption of normality. However, the distribution may be fairly symmetric because the mean and the median are close in value. Also, the boxplot appears only slightly skewed so the normality assumption does not appear to be seriously violated.

9.30 (a) $H_0: \mu = 2 \qquad H_1: \mu \neq 2 \qquad d.f. = 49$

Decision rule: Reject H_0 if $|t_{STAT}| > 2.0096$

Test statistic: $t_{STAT} = \dfrac{\overline{X} - \mu}{\dfrac{S}{\sqrt{n}}} = \dfrac{2.0007 - 2}{\dfrac{0.0446}{\sqrt{50}}} = 0.1143$

Decision: Since $|t_{STAT}| < 2.0096$, do not reject H_0. There is not enough evidence to conclude that the mean amount of soft drink filled is different from 2.0 liters.

9.30 cont. (b) p-value = 0.9095. If the population mean amount of soft drink filled is indeed 2.0 liters, the probability of observing a sample of 50 soft drinks that will result in a sample mean amount of fill more different from 2.0 liters is 0.9095.

(c)

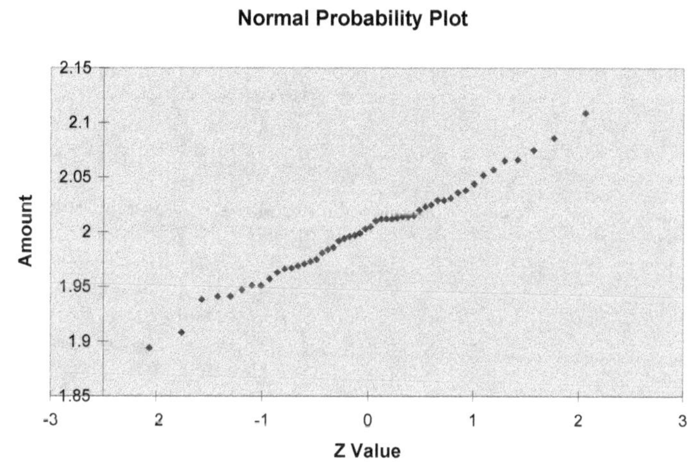

(d) The normal probability plot suggests that the data are rather normally distributed. Hence, the results in (a) are valid in terms of the normality assumption.

(e)

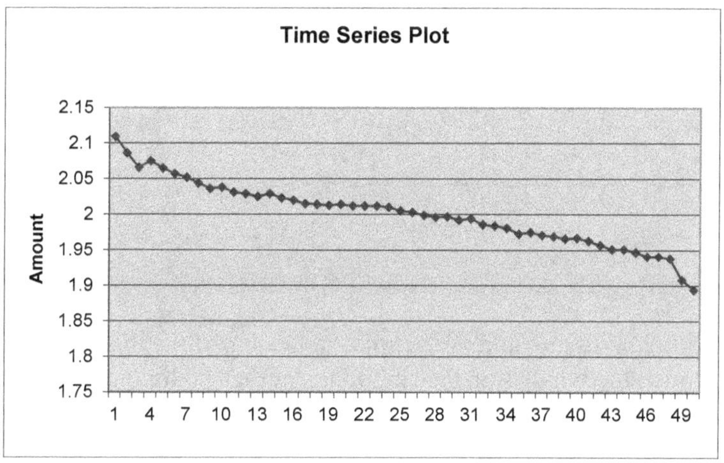

The time series plot of the data reveals that there is a downward trend in the amount of soft drink filled. This violates the assumption that data are drawn independently from a normal population distribution because the amount of fill in consecutive bottles appears to be closely related. As a result, the t test in (a) becomes invalid.

9.32 (a) $H_0: \mu = 8.46 \qquad H_1: \mu \neq 8.46$

Decision rule: Reject H_0 if $|t_{STAT}| > 2.0106 \quad d.f. = 48$

Test statistic: $t_{STAT} = \dfrac{\overline{X} - \mu}{\dfrac{S}{\sqrt{n}}} = \dfrac{8.4209 - 8.46}{\dfrac{0.0461}{\sqrt{49}}} = -5.9355$

Decision: Since $|t_{STAT}| > 2.0106$, reject H_0. There is enough evidence to conclude that mean widths of the troughs is different from 8.46 inches.

(b) The population distribution needs to be normal.

9.32 cont. (c)

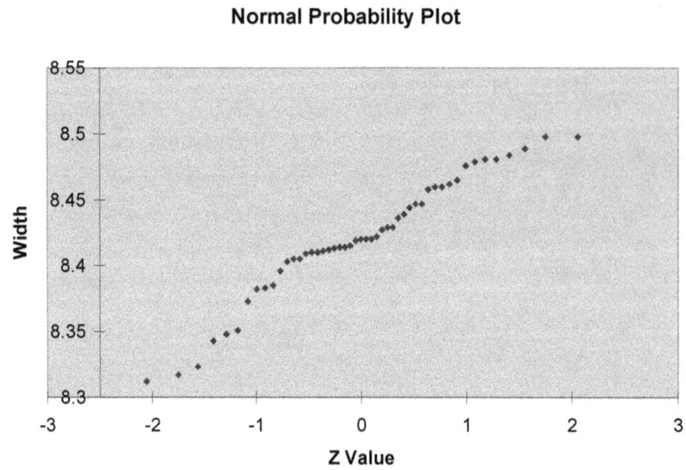

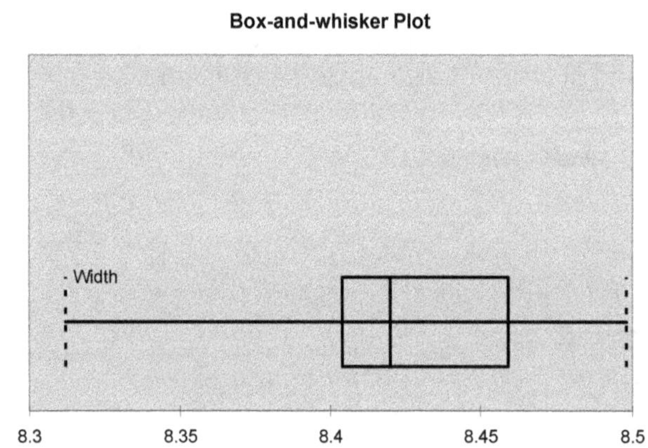

(d) The normal probability plot and the boxplot indicate that the distribution is skewed to the left. Even though the population distribution is not normally distributed, the result obtained in (a) should still be valid due to the Central Limit Theorem as a result of the relatively large sample size of 49.

9.34 (a) $H_0: \mu = 5.5 \qquad H_1: \mu \neq 5.5$

Decision rule: Reject H_0 if $|t_{STAT}| > 2.680 \quad d.f. = 49$

Test statistic: $t_{STAT} = \dfrac{\overline{X} - \mu}{\dfrac{S}{\sqrt{n}}} = \dfrac{5.5014 - 5.5}{\dfrac{0.1058}{\sqrt{50}}} = 0.0935$

Decision: Since $|t_{STAT}| < 2.680$, do not reject H_0. There is not enough evidence to conclude that the mean amount of tea per bag is different from 5.5 grams.

(b) $\overline{X} \pm t \cdot \dfrac{S}{\sqrt{n}} = 5.5014 \pm 2.6800 \cdot \dfrac{0.1058}{\sqrt{50}} \qquad 5.46 < \mu < 5.54$

With 99% confidence, you can conclude that the population mean amount of tea per bag is somewhere between 5.46 and 5.54 grams.

(c) The conclusions are the same.

9.36 p-value = 1 – 0.9772 = 0.0228

9.38 p-value = 0.0838

9.40 p-value = $P(Z < 1.38) = 0.9162$

9.42 $t = 2.7638$

9.44 $t = -2.5280$

9.46 (a)

One-Sample T

Descriptive Statistics

N	Mean	StDev	SE Mean	95% Lower Bound for μ
64	8210.0	625.0	78.1	8079.6

μ: mean of Sample

Test

Null hypothesis H₀: μ = 8000
Alternative hypothesis H₁: μ > 8000

T-Value	P-Value
2.69	0.005

$H_0: \mu \le 8000$ $H_1: \mu > 8000$

Decision rule: Reject H_0 if p-value < 0.05 $d.f. = 63$

Test statistic: $t_{STAT} = \dfrac{\overline{X} - \mu}{\dfrac{S}{\sqrt{n}}} = 2.69$

p-value = 0.005

Decision: $t_{STAT} = 2.69 > 1.6694$, reject H_0. There is evidence to conclude that the population mean bus miles is more than 8000 bus miles.

(b) The p-value is 0.005 < 0.05. The probability of getting a t_{STAT} statistic greater than 2.69 given that the null hypothesis is true, is 0.005.

9.48 (a) Minitab Output:

One-Sample T

Descriptive Statistics

N	Mean	StDev	SE Mean	99% Upper Bound for μ
860	24.050	16.500	0.563	25.361

μ: mean of Sample

Test

Null hypothesis H₀: μ = 30
Alternative hypothesis H₁: μ < 30

T-Value	P-Value
-10.58	0.000

(a) $H_0: \mu \geq 30 \qquad H_1: \mu < 30$

Decision rule: Reject H_0 if p-value < 0.01 $\quad d.f. = 859$

Test statistic: $t_{STAT} = \dfrac{\overline{X} - \mu}{\dfrac{S}{\sqrt{n}}} = -10.58$

p-value = 0.000

Decision: $t_{STAT} = -10.58 < -2.3307$, reject H_0. p-value = 0.000 < 0.01, reject H_0. There is evidence to conclude that the population mean wait time is less than 30 minutes.

(b) The probability of getting a sample mean of 24.05 minutes or less if the population mean is 30 minutes is 0.000.

9.50 (a) Minitab Output:

One-Sample T

Descriptive Statistics

N	Mean	StDev	SE Mean	99% Lower Bound for μ
133	87.000	9.000	0.780	85.162

μ: mean of Sample

Test

Null hypothesis H₀: μ = 85.5
Alternative hypothesis H₁: μ > 85.5

T-Value	P-Value
1.92	0.028

9.50 cont. (a) $H_0: \mu \le 85.5 \qquad H_1: \mu > 85.5$

Decision rule: Reject H_0 if p-value $< 0.01 \quad d.f. = 132$

Test statistic: $t_{STAT} = \dfrac{\bar{X} - \mu}{\dfrac{S}{\sqrt{n}}} = 1.92$

p-value = 0.028

Decision: $t_{STAT} = 1.92 < 2.35493$, do not reject H_0. p-value = 0.028 > 0.01, do not reject H_0. There is insufficient evidence to conclude that the population mean one-time gift donation is greater than $85.50.

(b) The probability of getting a sample mean of $87 or more if the population mean is $85.5 is 0.028.

9.52 $p = \dfrac{X}{n} = \dfrac{88}{400} = 0.22$

9.54 H_0: $\pi = 0.20$

H_1: $\pi \neq 0.20$

Decision rule: If $Z < -1.96$ or $Z > 1.96$, reject H_0.

Test statistic: $Z_{STAT} = \dfrac{p - \pi}{\sqrt{\dfrac{\pi(1-\pi)}{n}}} = \dfrac{0.22 - 0.20}{\sqrt{\dfrac{0.20(0.8)}{400}}} = 1.00$

Decision: Since $Z = 1.00$ is between the critical bounds of ± 1.96, do not reject H_0.

9.56 (a) Excel Output:

	A	B
1	**Z Test of Hypothesis for the Proportion**	
2		
3	**Data**	
4	**Null Hypothesis** π=	**0.6952**
5	**Level of Significance**	**0.05**
6	**Number of Items of Interest**	**60**
7	**Sample Size**	**100**
8		
9	Intermediate Calculations	
10	Sample Proportion	0.6000
11	Standard Error	0.0460
12	**Z Test Statistic**	**-2.0681**
13		
14	**Lower-Tail Test**	
15	**Lower Critical Value**	**-1.6449**
16	***p*-Value**	**0.0193**
17	**Reject the null hypothesis**	
18		

H_0: $\pi \ge 0.6952$

H_1: $\pi < 0.6952$

9.56 cont. (a) Decision rule: p-value < 0.05, reject H_0.

Test statistic: $Z_{STAT} = \dfrac{p-\pi}{\sqrt{\dfrac{\pi(1-\pi)}{n}}} = -2.0681$ p-value $= 0.0193$

Decision: Since p-value $= 0.0193 < 0.05$, Reject H_0. There is evidence to show that less than 69.52% of students at your university use the Chrome web browser.

(b) Excel Output:

	A	B
1	**Z Test of Hypothesis for the Proportion**	
2		
3	**Data**	
4	**Null Hypothesis** π=	**0.6952**
5	**Level of Significance**	**0.05**
6	**Number of Items of Interest**	**360**
7	**Sample Size**	**600**
8		
9	Intermediate Calculations	
10	Sample Proportion	0.6000
11	Standard Error	0.0188
12	**Z Test Statistic**	**-5.0658**
13		
14	**Lower-Tail Test**	
15	**Lower Critical Value**	**-1.6449**
16	***p*-Value**	**0.0000**
17	**Reject the null hypothesis**	

H_0: $\pi \geq 0.6952$
H_1: $\pi < 0.5643$
Decision rule: p-value < 0.05, reject H_0.

Test statistic: $Z_{STAT} = \dfrac{p-\pi}{\sqrt{\dfrac{\pi(1-\pi)}{n}}} = -5.0658$ p-value $= 0.000$

Decision: Since p-value $= 0.000 < 0.05$, Reject H_0. There is evidence to show that less than 69.52% of students at your university use the Chrome web browser.

(c) The sample size had an effect on being able to reject the null hypothesis.

(d) You would be very unlikely to reject the null hypothesis with a sample of 20.

9.58 Minitab Output:

Test and CI for One Proportion

Method

p: event proportion
Normal approximation method is used for this analysis.

Descriptive Statistics

N	Event	Sample p	95% CI for p
703	464	0.660028	(0.625012, 0.695045)

Test

Null hypothesis H₀: p = 0.6
Alternative hypothesis H₁: p ≠ 0.6

Z-Value	P-Value
3.25	0.001

H_0: $\pi = 0.60$
H_1: $\pi \neq 0.60$
Decision rule: p-value < 0.05, reject H_0.

Test statistic: $Z_{STAT} = \dfrac{p-\pi}{\sqrt{\dfrac{\pi(1-\pi)}{n}}} = 3.25$ $\quad$ p-value = 0.001

Decision: Since p-value = 0.001 < 0.05, reject H_0. There is evidence that the proportion of all talent acquisition professionals who report competition is the biggest obstacle to attracting the best talent at their company is different from 0.60.

9.60 (a) H_0: $\pi \geq 0.294$. H_1: $\pi < 0.294$.

9.60 cont. (b) Minitab Output:

Test and CI for One Proportion

Method

p: event proportion
Normal approximation method is used for this analysis.

Descriptive Statistics

N	Event	Sample p	95% Upper Bound for p
100	27	0.270000	0.343025

Test

Null hypothesis H₀: p = 0.294
Alternative hypothesis H₁: p < 0.294

Z-Value	P-Value
-0.53	0.299

H_0: $\pi \geq 0.294$
H_1: $\pi < 0.294$
Decision rule: p-value < 0.05, reject H_0 or $Z_{STAT} < -1.645$, reject H_0

Test statistic: $Z_{STAT} = \dfrac{p-\pi}{\sqrt{\dfrac{\pi(1-\pi)}{n}}} = -0.53$ p-value = 0.299

Decision: Because $Z_{STAT} = -0.53 > -1.645$ or p-value = 0.299 > 0.05, Do not reject H_0. There is not enough evidence that the proportion is less than 0.294.

9.62 A Type I error represents rejecting a true null hypothesis, while a Type II error represents not rejecting a false null hypothesis.

9.64 In a one-tailed test for a mean or proportion, the entire rejection region is contained in one tail of the distribution. In a two-tailed test, the rejection region is split into two equal parts, one in the lower tail of the distribution, and the other in the upper tail.

9.66 Assuming a two-tailed test is used, if the hypothesized value for the parameter does not fall into the confidence interval, then the null hypothesis can be rejected.

9.68 The following are the 6-step p-value approach to hypothesis testing: (1) State the null hypothesis, H_0, and the alternative hypothesis, H_1. (2) Choose the level of significance, α, and the sample size, n. (3) Determine the appropriate test statistic and the sampling distribution. (4) Collect the sample data, compute the value of the test statistic. (5) compute the p-value. (6) Make the statistical decision and state the managerial conclusion. If the p-value is greater than or equal to α, you do not reject the null hypothesis, H_0. If the p-value is less than α, you reject the null hypothesis.

9.70 (a) A Type I error occurs when a firm is predicted to be a bankrupt firm when it will not.

(b) A Type II error occurs when a firm is predicted to be a non-bankrupt firm when it will go bankrupt.

(c) The executives are trying to avoid a Type I error by adopting a very stringent decision criterion. Only firms that show significant evidence of being in financial stress will be predicted to go bankrupt within the next two years at the chosen level of the possibility of making a Type I error.

(d) If the revised model results in more moderate or large Z scores, the probability of committing a Type I error will increase. Many more of the firms will be predicted to go bankrupt than will go bankrupt. On the other hand, the revised model that results in more moderate or large Z scores will lower the probability of committing a Type II error because few firms will be predicted to go bankrupt than will actually go bankrupt.

9.72 (a) PHStat output:

t Test for Hypothesis of the Mean

Data	
Null Hypothesis μ=	6.5
Level of Significance	0.05
Sample Size	60
Sample Mean	7.25
Sample Standard Deviation	1.75

Intermediate Calculations	
Standard Error of the Mean	0.2259
Degrees of Freedom	59
t Test Statistic	3.3197

Two-Tail Test	
Lower Critical Value	-2.0010
Upper Critical Value	2.0010
p-Value	0.0015
Reject the null hypothesis	

H_0: $\mu = \$6.50$

H_1: $\mu \neq \$6.50$

Decision rule: $d.f. = 59$. If p-value < 0.05, reject H_0.

Test statistic: $t_{STAT} = \dfrac{\overline{X} - \mu}{\dfrac{S}{\sqrt{n}}} = = 3.3197$ p-value $= 0.0015$

Decision: Since p-value < 0.05, reject H_0. There is enough evidence to conclude that the mean amount spent differs from \$6.50

(b) p-value $= 0.0015$.

Note: The p-value was found using Excel.

9.72 cont. (c) PHStat output:

Z Test of Hypothesis for the Proportion

Data	
Null Hypothesis $\pi =$	0.5
Level of Significance	0.05
Number of Items of Interest	31
Sample Size	60

Intermediate Calculations	
Sample Proportion	0.516666667
Standard Error	0.0645
Z Test Statistic	0.2582

Upper-Tail Test	
Upper Critical Value	1.6449
p-Value	0.3981
Do not reject the null hypothesis	

(c) H_0: $\pi \leq 0.50$.
H_1: $\pi > 0.50$.
Decision rule: If p-value < 0.05, reject H_0.

Test statistic: $Z_{STAT} = \frac{p-\pi}{\sqrt{\frac{\pi(1-\pi)}{n}}} = = 0.2582$ p-value = 0.3981

Decision: Since p-value > 0.05, do not reject H_0. There is not sufficient evidence to conclude that more than 50% of customers say they "definitely will" recommend the specialty coffee shop to family and friends.

(d) PHStat output:

t Test for Hypothesis of the Mean

Data	
Null Hypothesis $\mu=$	6.5
Level of Significance	0.05
Sample Size	60
Sample Mean	6.25
Sample Standard Deviation	1.75

Intermediate Calculations	
Standard Error of the Mean	0.2259
Degrees of Freedom	59
t Test Statistic	-1.1066

Two-Tail Test	
Lower Critical Value	-2.0010
Upper Critical Value	2.0010
p-Value	0.2730
Do not reject the null hypothesis	

9.72 cont. (d) H_0: $\mu = \$6.50$

H_1: $\mu \neq \$6.50$

Decision rule: $d.f. = 59$. If p-value < 0.05, reject H_0.

Test statistic: $t = \dfrac{\bar{X} - \mu}{\dfrac{S}{\sqrt{n}}} = \dfrac{6.25 - 6.5}{\dfrac{1.75}{\sqrt{60}}} = -1.1066$ p-value = 0.2730

Decision: Since the p-value > 0.05, do not reject H_0. There is not enough evidence to conclude that the mean amount spent differs from \$6.50.

(e) PHStat output:

Z Test of Hypothesis for the Proportion

Data	
Null Hypothesis π =	0.5
Level of Significance	0.05
Number of Items of Interest	39
Sample Size	60

Intermediate Calculations	
Sample Proportion	0.65
Standard Error	0.0645
Z Test Statistic	**2.3238**

Upper-Tail Test	
Upper Critical Value	1.6449
***p*-Value**	0.0101
Reject the null hypothesis	

H_0: $\pi \leq 0.50$.

H_1: $\pi > 0.50$.

Decision rule: If p-value < 0.05, reject H_0.

Test statistic: $Z_{STAT} = \dfrac{p - \pi}{\sqrt{\dfrac{\pi(1-\pi)}{n}}} = = 2.3238$ p-value = 0.0101

Decision: Since p-value < 0.05, reject H_0. There is sufficient evidence to conclude that more than 50% of customers say they "definitely will" recommend the specialty coffee shop to family and friends.

9.74 (a) H_0: $\mu \geq 5$ minutes. The mean waiting time at a bank branch in a commercial district of the city is at least 5 minutes during the 12:00 p.m. to 1 p.m. peak lunch period.

H_1: $\mu < 5$ minutes. The mean waiting time at a bank branch in a commercial district of the city is less than 5 minutes during the 12:00 p.m. to 1 p.m. peak lunch period.

Decision rule: $d.f. = 14$. If $t_{STAT} < -1.7613$, reject H_0.

$$\text{Test statistic: } t_{STAT} = \frac{\bar{X} - \mu}{\dfrac{S}{\sqrt{n}}} = \frac{4.28\overline{6} - 5.0}{\dfrac{1.637985}{\sqrt{15}}} = -1.6867$$

Decision: Since $t_{STAT} = -1.6867$ is greater than the critical bound of -1.7613, do not reject H_0. There is not enough evidence to conclude that the mean waiting time at a bank branch in a commercial district of the city is less than 5 minutes during the 12:00 p.m. to 1 p.m. peak lunch period.

9.74 cont. (b) To perform the t-test on the population mean, you must assume that the observed sequence in which the data were collected is random and that the data are approximately normally distributed.

(c) Normal probability plot:

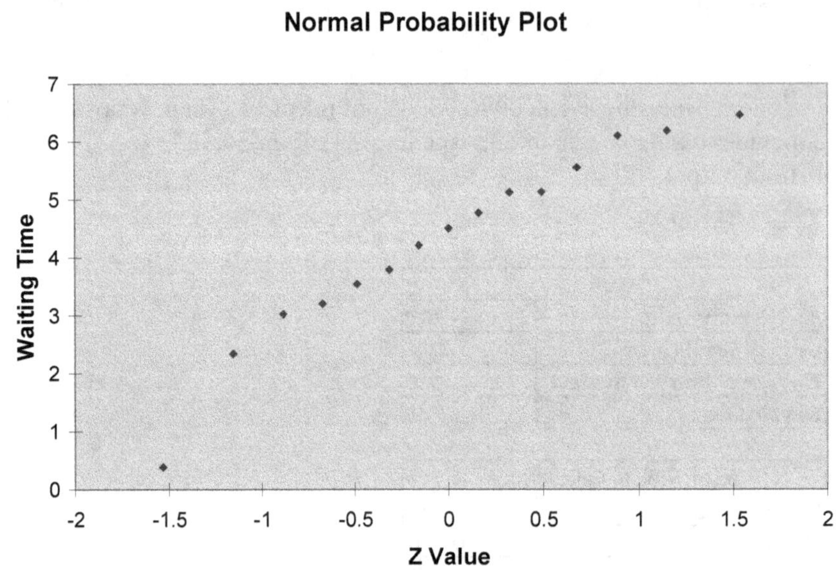

(d) With the exception of one extreme point, the data are approximately normally distributed.

(e) Based on the results of (a), the manager does not have enough evidence to make that statement.

9.76 (a) $H_0: \mu \geq 0.35 \qquad H_1: \mu < 0.35$

Decision rule: Reject H_0 if $t_{STAT} < -1.690 \quad d.f. = 35$

Test statistic: $t_{STAT} = \dfrac{\overline{X} - \mu}{\dfrac{S}{\sqrt{n}}} = \dfrac{0.3167 - 0.35}{\dfrac{0.1357}{\sqrt{36}}} = -1.4735$

Decision: Since $t_{STAT} > -1.690$, do not reject H_0.

There is not enough evidence to conclude that the mean moisture content for Boston shingles is less than 0.35 pounds per 100 square feet.

(b) p-value = 0.0748. If the population mean moisture content is in fact no less than 0.35 pounds per 100 square feet, the probability of observing a sample of 36 shingles that will result in a sample mean moisture content of 0.3167 pounds per 100 square feet or less is 0.0748.

(c) $H_0: \mu \geq 0.35 \qquad H_1: \mu < 0.35$

Decision rule: Reject H_0 if $t_{STAT} < -1.6973 \quad d.f. = 30$

Test statistic: $t_{STAT} = \dfrac{\overline{X} - \mu}{\dfrac{S}{\sqrt{n}}} = \dfrac{0.2735 - 0.35}{\dfrac{0.1373}{\sqrt{31}}} = -3.1003$

Decision: Since $t_{STAT} < -1.6973$, reject H_0. There is enough evidence to conclude that the mean moisture content for Vermont shingles is less than 0.35 pounds per 100 square feet.

9.76 cont.

(d) p-value = 0.0021. If the population mean moisture content is in fact no less than 0.35 pounds per 100 square feet, the probability of observing a sample of 31 shingles that will result in a sample mean moisture content of 0.2735 pounds per 100 square feet or less is 0.0021.

(e) In order for the t test to be valid, the data are assumed to be independently drawn from a population that is normally distributed. Since the sample sizes are 36 and 31, respectively, which are considered quite large, the t distribution will provide a good approximation to the sampling distribution of the mean as long as the population distribution is not very skewed.

(f)

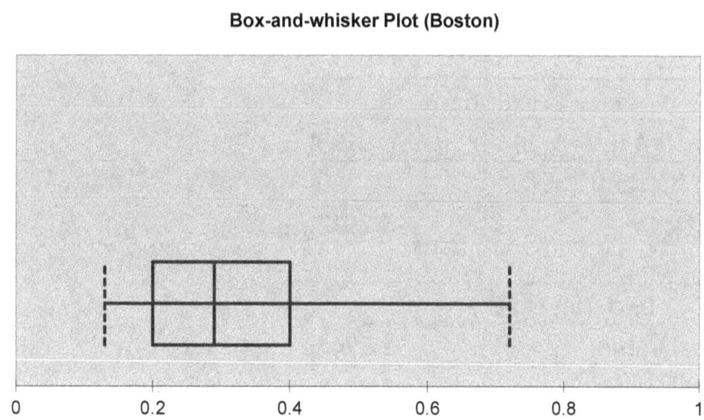

(f)

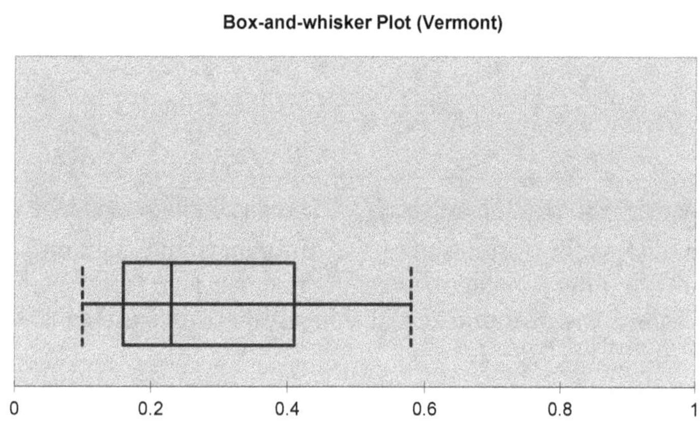

Both boxplots suggest that the data are skewed slightly to the right, more so for the Boston shingles. However, the very large sample sizes mean that the results of the t test are relatively insensitive to the departure from normality.

9.78 (a) $H_0: \mu = 0.3$ $H_1: \mu \neq 0.3$

t Test for Hypothesis of the Mean

Data	
Null Hypothesis μ=	0.3
Level of Significance	0.05
Sample Size	170
Sample Mean	0.26
Sample Standard Deviation	0.142382504

Intermediate Calculations	
Standard Error of the Mean	0.0109
Degrees of Freedom	169
t Test Statistic	-3.2912

Two-Tail Test	
Lower Critical Value	-1.9741
Upper Critical Value	1.9741
p-Value	0.0012
Reject the null hypothesis	

Decision rule: Reject H_0 if $|t_{STAT}| > 1.9741$ $d.f. = 169$

Test statistic: $t_{STAT} = \dfrac{\bar{X} - \mu}{\dfrac{S}{\sqrt{n}}} = -3.2912,$ p-value = 0.0012

Decision: Since $t_{STAT} < -1.9741$, reject H_0. There is enough evidence to conclude that the mean granule loss for Boston shingles is different from 0.3 grams.

(b) p-value is 0.0012. If the population mean granule loss is in fact 0.3 grams, the probability of observing a sample of 170 shingles that will yield a test statistic more extreme than –3.2912 is 0.0012.

9.78 cont. (c) $H_0: \mu = 0.3 \qquad H_1: \mu \neq 0.3$

t Test for Hypothesis of the Mean

Data	
Null Hypothesis μ=	**0.3**
Level of Significance	**0.05**
Sample Size	**140**
Sample Mean	**0.22**
Sample Standard Deviation	**0.122698672**

Intermediate Calculations	
Standard Error of the Mean	0.0104
Degrees of Freedom	139
***t* Test Statistic**	**-7.9075**

Two-Tail Test	
Lower Critical Value	**-1.9772**
Upper Critical Value	**1.9772**
***p*-Value**	**0.0000**
Reject the null hypothesis	

Decision rule: Reject H_0 if $|t_{STAT}| > 1.9772 \quad d.f. = 139$

Test statistic: $t_{STAT} = \dfrac{\overline{X} - \mu}{\dfrac{S}{\sqrt{n}}} = -7.9075$

Decision: Since $t_{STAT} < -1.977$, reject H_0. There is enough evidence to conclude that the mean granule loss for Vermont shingles is different from 0.3 grams.

(d) *p*-value is virtually zero. The probability of observing a sample of 140 shingles that will yield a test statistic more extreme than –1.977 is virtually zero if the population mean granule loss is in fact 0.3 grams.

(e) In order for the *t* test to be valid, the data are assumed to be independently drawn from a population that is normally distributed. Both normal probability plots indicate that the data are slightly right-skewed. Since the sample sizes are 170 and 140, respectively, which are considered large enough, the *t* distribution will provide a good approximation to the sampling distribution of the mean even if the population is not normally distributed.

Chapter 10

10.2 (a)

$$S_p^2 = \frac{(n_1-1)\cdot S_1^2+(n_2-1)\cdot S_2^2}{(n_1-1)+(n_2-1)} = \frac{(7)\cdot 4^2+(14)\cdot 5^2}{7+14} = 22$$

$$t_{STAT} = \frac{(\bar{X}_1-\bar{X}_2)-(\mu_1-\mu_2)}{\sqrt{S_p^2\left(\frac{1}{n_1}+\frac{1}{n_2}\right)}} = \frac{(42-34)-0}{\sqrt{22\left(\frac{1}{8}+\frac{1}{15}\right)}} = 3.8959$$

(b) $d.f. = (n_1 - 1) + (n_2 - 1) = 7 + 14 = 21$

(c) Decision rule: $d.f. = 21$. If $t_{STAT} > 2.5177$, reject H_0.

(d) Decision: Since $t = 3.8959$ is greater than the critical bound of 2.5177, reject H_0. There is enough evidence to conclude that the first population mean is larger than the second population mean.

10.4 $$(\bar{X}_1-\bar{X}_2)\pm t\sqrt{S_p^2\left(\frac{1}{n_1}+\frac{1}{n_2}\right)} = (42-34)\pm 2.0796\sqrt{22\left(\frac{1}{8}+\frac{1}{15}\right)} \quad 3.7296 \le \mu_1-\mu_2 \le 12.2704$$

10.6

Pooled-Variance t Test for Differences in Two Means
(assumes equal population variances)

Data	
Hypothesized Difference	0
Level of Significance	0.01
Population 1 Sample	
Sample Size	5
Sample Mean	42
Sample Standard Deviation	4.0000
Population 2 Sample	
Sample Size	4
Sample Mean	34
Sample Standard Deviation	5.0000

Intermediate Calculations	
Population 1 Sample Degrees of Freedom	4
Population 2 Sample Degrees of Freedom	3
Total Degrees of Freedom	7
Pooled Variance	19.8571
Standard Error	2.9893
Difference in Sample Means	8
t Test Statistic	2.6762

10.6
cont.

Two-Tail Test	
Lower Critical Value	-3.4995
Upper Critical Value	3.4995
p-Value	0.0317
Do not reject the null hypothesis	

Decision: Since $t_{STAT} = 2.6762$ is smaller than the upper critical bounds of 2.9979, do not reject H_0. There is not enough evidence of a difference in the means of the two populations.

10.8 (a) Because $t_{STAT} = 2.8990 > 1.6620$ or p-value $= 0.0024 < 0.05$, reject H_0. There is evidence that the mean amount of Walker Crisps eaten by children who watched a commercial featuring a long-standing sports celebrity endorser is higher than for those who watched a commercial for an alternative food snack.

(b) $3.4616 \le \mu_1 - \mu_2 \le 18.5384$

(c) The results cannot be compared because (a) is a one-tail test and (b) is a confidence interval that is comparable only to the results of a two-tail test.

(d) You would choose the commercial featuring a long-standing celebrity endorser.

10.10 (a)

Two-Sample T-Test and CI: Number of Partners, Region

Method

μ_1: mean of Number of Partners when Region = Gulf Coast
μ_2: mean of Number of Partners when Region = Southeast
Difference: $\mu_1 - \mu_2$

Equal variances are assumed for this analysis.

Descriptive Statistics: Number of Partners

Region	N	Mean	StDev	SE Mean
Gulf Coast	22	40.8	62.3	13
Southeast	22	45.0	51.9	11

Estimation for Difference

Difference	Pooled StDev	95% CI for Difference
-4.2	57.3	(-39.1, 30.6)

Test

Null hypothesis $H_0: \mu_1 - \mu_2 = 0$
Alternative hypothesis $H_1: \mu_1 - \mu_2 \ne 0$

T-Value	DF	P-Value
-0.24	42	0.808

10.10 cont. (a) The results from a pooled-variance t test revealed that there is no evidence at the 0.05 level of significance that there is a difference between the Southeast region accounting firms and the Gulf Coast accounting firms with respect to the mean number of partners. Because $t_{STAT} = -0.24$ or p-value = 0.808, do not reject H_0.

(b) The p-value was 0.808, well above the 0.05 level. This means that the probability of obtaining an equal or larger value than the observed test statistic, when H_0 is true, is 80.8%.

(c) The pooled-variance t test assumes that the variance associated with the two populations of accounting firms are equal and that the number of partners data are approximately normally distributed for the two populations.

10.12 (a) $H_0 : \mu_1 = \mu_2$ Mean waiting times of Bank 1 and Bank 2 are the same.
$H_1 : \mu_1 \neq \mu_2$ Mean waiting times of Bank 1 and Bank 2 are different.

Two-Sample T-Test and CI: Bank1, Bank2

Method

μ_1: mean of Bank1
μ_2: mean of Bank2
Difference: $\mu_1 - \mu_2$

Equal variances are assumed for this analysis.

Descriptive Statistics

Sample	N	Mean	StDev	SE Mean
Bank1	15	4.29	1.64	0.42
Bank2	15	7.11	2.08	0.54

Estimation for Difference

Difference	Pooled StDev	95% CI for Difference
-2.828	1.873	(-4.229, -1.427)

Test

Null hypothesis $H_0: \mu_1 - \mu_2 = 0$
Alternative hypothesis $H_1: \mu_1 - \mu_2 \neq 0$

T-Value	DF	P-Value
-4.13	28	0.000

Since the p-value of 0.000 is less than the 5% level of significance, reject the null hypothesis. There is enough evidence to conclude that the mean waiting time is different in the two banks.

(b) p-value = 0.000. The probability of obtaining a sample that will yield a t test statistic more extreme than 4.13 is 0.000 if, in fact, the mean waiting times of Bank 1 and Bank 2 are the same.

(c) We need to assume that the two populations are normally distributed.

10.12 (d) $\left(\bar{X}_1-\bar{X}_2\right)+t\sqrt{S_p^2\left(\frac{1}{n_1}+\frac{1}{n_2}\right)}=(4.2867-7.1147)+2.0484\sqrt{3.5093\left(\frac{1}{15}+\frac{1}{15}\right)}$

cont. $-4.2292 \le \mu_1-\mu_2 \le -1.4268$

You are 95% confident that the difference in mean waiting time between Bank 1 and Bank 2 is between −4.2292 and −1.4268 minutes.

10.14 (a) Because $t_{STAT} = 2.7349 > 2.0484$, reject H_0. There is evidence of a difference in the meantime to start a business between developed and emerging countries.

(b) p-value = 0.0107. The probability that two samples have a mean difference of 14.62 or more is 0.0107 if there is no difference in the meantime to start a business between developed and emerging countries.

(c) You need to assume that the population distribution of the time to start a business of both developed and emerging countries is normally distributed.

(d) $3.6700 \le \mu_1-\mu_2 \le 25.5700$

10.16 (a) Because $t_{STAT} = -2.1554 < -2.0017$ or p-value $= 0.03535 < 0.05$, reject H_0. There is evidence of a difference in the mean time per day accessing the Internet via a mobile device between males and females.

(b) You must assume that each of the two independent populations is normally distributed.

10.18 The degrees of freedom is 20 – 1, or 19.

10.20 (a)

Paired T-Test and CI: A, B

Descriptive Statistics

Sample	N	Mean	StDev	SE Mean
A	9	24.000	2.646	0.882
B	9	25.556	1.878	0.626

Estimation for Paired Difference

Mean	StDev	SE Mean	95% CI for μ_difference
-1.556	1.424	0.475	(-2.650, -0.461)

μ_difference: mean of (A - B)

Test

Null hypothesis H₀: μ_difference = 0
Alternative hypothesis H₁: μ_difference ≠ 0

T-Value	P-Value
-3.28	0.011

10.20 (a) $t_{STAT} = \frac{(-1.5566)}{\left(\frac{1.424}{\sqrt{9}}\right)} = -3.2772$. Because $t_{STAT} = -3.2772 < -2.306$ or

cont. p-value $= 0.0112 < 0.05$, reject H_0. There is enough evidence of a difference in the mean summated ratings between the two brands.

(b) You must assume that the distribution of the differences between the two ratings is approximately normal.

(c) p-value $= 0.0112$. The probability of obtaining a mean difference in ratings that results in a test statistic that deviates from 0 by 3.2772 or more in either direction is 0.0112 if there is no difference in the mean summated ratings between the two brands.

(d) $-2.6501 \le \mu_D \le -0.4610$. You are 95% confident that the mean difference in summated ratings between brand A and brand B is somewhere between –2.6501 and –0.4610.

10.22 (a)

Paired T-Test and CI: AT&T Download Speed, Verizon Download Speed

Descriptive Statistics

Sample	N	Mean	StDev	SE Mean
AT&T Download Speed	39	7.140	1.429	0.229
Verizon Download Speed	39	9.111	2.694	0.431

Estimation for Paired Difference

Mean	StDev	SE Mean	95% CI for μ_difference
-1.971	2.976	0.476	(-2.936, -1.007)

μ_difference: mean of (AT&T Download Speed - Verizon Download Speed)

Test

Null hypothesis	H₀: μ_difference = 0
Alternative hypothesis	H₁: μ_difference ≠ 0

T-Value	P-Value
-4.14	0.000

(a) Because $t_{STAT} = -4.14$ or p-value $= 0.000$, reject H_0. There is evidence to conclude that the mean download speed at AT&T is different than at Verizon Wireless.

(b) You must assume that the distribution of the differences between the ratings is approximately normal.

10.22 (c)
cont.

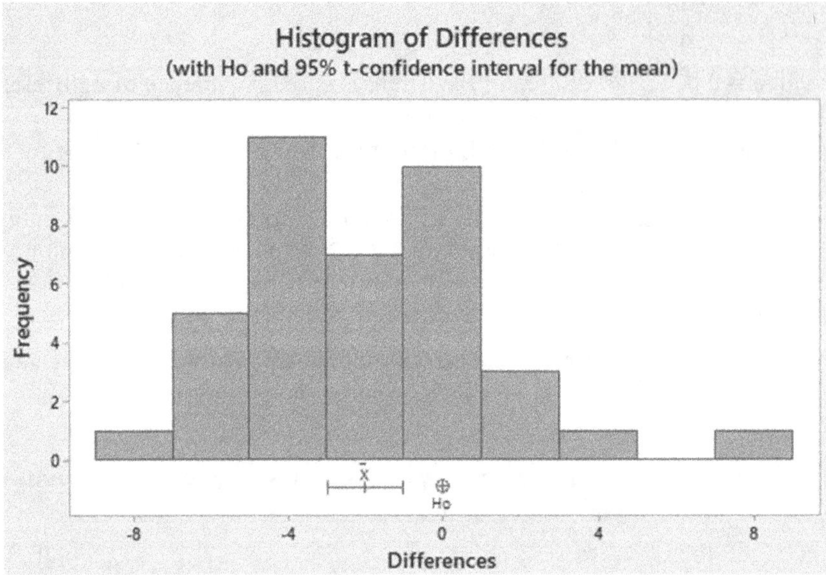

Although a histogram of differences reveals slight skewness to the right, there does not appear to be a substantial violation of the normality assumption.

(d) The confidence interval is from –2.936 to –1.007.

Estimation for Paired Difference

Mean	StDev	SE Mean	95% CI for μ_difference
-1.971	2.976	0.476	(-2.936, -1.007)

μ_difference: mean of (AT&T Download Speed - Verizon Download Speed)

10.24 (a) Define the difference in bone marrow microvessel density as the density before the transplant minus the density after the transplant and assume that the difference in density is normally distributed.

$H_0 : \mu_D \le 0$ vs. $H_1 : \mu_D > 0$

t-Test: Paired Two Sample for Means

	Before	***After***
Mean	312.1429	226
Variance	15513.14	4971
Observations	7	7
Pearson Correlation	0.295069	
Hypothesized Mean Difference	0	
df	6	
t Stat	1.842455	
P(T<=t) one-tail	0.057493	
t Critical one-tail	1.943181	
P(T<=t) two-tail	0.114986	
t Critical two-tail	2.446914	

10.24 (a) Test statistic: $t_{STAT} = \dfrac{\bar{D} - \mu_D}{\dfrac{S_D}{\sqrt{n}}} = 1.8425$

cont. Decision: Since $t_{STAT} = 1.8425$ is less than the critical value of 1.943, do not reject H_0. There is not enough evidence to conclude that the mean bone marrow microvessel density is higher before the stem cell transplant than after the stem cell transplant.

(b) p-value = 0.0575. The probability of obtaining a mean difference in density that gives rise to a t test statistic that deviates from 0 by 1.8425 or more is 0.0575 if the mean density is not higher before the stem cell transplant than after the stem cell transplant.

(c) $\bar{D} \pm t\dfrac{S_D}{\sqrt{n}} = 86.1429 \pm 2.4469\dfrac{123.7005}{\sqrt{7}}$ $\quad -28.26 \le \mu_D \le 200.55$

You are 95% confident that the mean difference in bone marrow microvessel density before and after the stem cell transplant is somewhere between –28.26 and 200.55.

(d) You must assume that the distribution of differences between the mean density of before and after stem cell transplant is approximately normal.

10.26 (a)

Paired T-Test and CI: Two Days, Seven Days

Descriptive Statistics

Sample	N	Mean	StDev	SE Mean
Two Days	40	2.9910	0.4961	0.0784
Seven Days	40	3.5441	0.5036	0.0796

Estimation for Paired Difference

Mean	StDev	SE Mean	95% Upper Bound for μ_difference
-0.5531	0.3733	0.0590	-0.4537

μ_difference: mean of (Two Days - Seven Days)

Test

Null hypothesis H_0: μ_difference = 0
Alternative hypothesis H_1: μ_difference < 0

T-Value	P-Value
-9.37	0.000

H_0: $\mu_{\bar{D}} \ge 0$

H_1: $\mu_{\bar{D}} < 0$

Decision rule: $d.f. = 39$. If $t_{STAT} < -2.4258$, reject H_0.

Test statistic: $t_{STAT} = \dfrac{\bar{D} - \mu_D}{\dfrac{S_D}{\sqrt{n}}} = -9.372$

Decision: Since $t_{STAT} = -9.372$ is less than the critical bound of –2.4258, reject H_0. There is enough evidence to conclude that the mean strength is lower at two days than at seven days.

10.26 cont. (b) You must assume that the distribution of the differences between the mean strength of the concrete is approximately normal.

(c) p-value is virtually 0. The probability of obtaining a mean difference that gives rise to a test statistic that is –9.372 or less when the null hypothesis is true is virtually 0.

10.28 (a) $p_1 = \frac{X_1}{n_1} = \frac{45}{100} = 0.45,\ p_2 = \frac{X_2}{n_2} = \frac{25}{50} = 0.50,\ \text{and}\ \bar{p} = \frac{X_1 + X_2}{n_1 + n_2} = \frac{45+25}{100+50} = 0.467$

H_0: $\pi_1 = \pi_2$ H_1: $\pi_1 \neq \pi_2$

Decision rule: If $Z < -2.58$ or $Z > 2.58$, reject H_0.

$$Z_{STAT} = \frac{(p_1 - p_2) - (\pi_1 - \pi_2)}{\sqrt{\bar{p}(1-\bar{p})\left(\frac{1}{n_1} + \frac{1}{n_2}\right)}} = \frac{(0.45\text{-}0.50) - 0}{\sqrt{0.467(1\text{-}0.467)\left(\frac{1}{100} + \frac{1}{50}\right)}} = -0.58$$

Decision: Since $Z_{STAT} = -0.58$ is between the critical bound of ±2.58, do not reject H_0. There is insufficient evidence to conclude that the population proportion differs for group 1 and group 2

(b) $$(p_1 - p_2) \pm Z\sqrt{\left(\frac{p_1(1-p_1)}{n_1} + \frac{p_2(1-p_2)}{n_2}\right)} = -0.05 \pm 2.5758\sqrt{\left(\frac{.45(.55)}{100} + \frac{.5(.5)}{50}\right)}$$

$-0.2727 \leq \pi_1 - \pi_2 \leq 0.1727$

10.30 (a) H_0: $\pi_1 \leq \pi_2$ H_1: $\pi_1 > \pi_2$

Population 1 = following VOD D+4 viewing, 2 = general TV viewing

(b)

Z Test for Differences in Two Proportions

Data	
Hypothesized Difference	0
Level of Significance	0.01
Group 1	
Number of Items of Interest	147
Sample Size	250
Group 2	
Number of Items of Interest	35
Sample Size	201
Intermediate Calculations	
Group 1 Proportion	0.5880
Group 2 Proportion	0.1741
Difference in Two Proportions	0.4139
Average Proportion	0.4035
Z Test Statistic	8.9045
Two-Tail Test	
Lower Critical Value	-2.5758
Upper Critical Value	2.5758
p-Value	0.0000
Reject the null hypothesis	

10.30 cont. (b) Decision rule: If $Z_{STAT} > 1.6449$, reject H_0.

Test statistic:

$$Z_{STAT} = \frac{(p_1 - p_2) - (\pi_1 - \pi_2)}{\bar{p}(1-\bar{p})\left(\frac{1}{n_1}+\frac{1}{n_2}\right)} = 8.9045 \quad p\text{-value is essentially 0.}$$

Decision: Since p-value < 0.05, reject H_0. There is sufficient evidence to conclude that the population proportion of those who viewed the brand on VOD D4 were more likely to visit the brand website.

(c) Yes, the result in (b) make it appropriate to claim that ad impact is stronger following VOD D4+ than following general TV viewing.

10.32 (a)

Test and CI for Two Proportions

Method

p_1: proportion where Sample 1 = Event
p_2: proportion where Sample 2 = Event
Difference: $p_1 - p_2$

Descriptive Statistics

Sample	N	Event	Sample p
Sample 1	423	326	0.770686
Sample 2	192	167	0.869792

Estimation for Difference

Difference	95% CI for Difference
-0.0991061	(-0.161323, -0.036890)

CI based on normal approximation

Test

Null hypothesis $H_0: p_1 - p_2 = 0$
Alternative hypothesis $H_1: p_1 - p_2 \neq 0$

Method	Z-Value	P-Value
Normal approximation	-2.86	0.004
Fisher's exact		0.004

The pooled estimate of the proportion (0.801626) is used for the tests.

At the 0.01 level of significance level, there is evidence of a significant difference between organizations with 500 to 2,499 employees and organizations with 10,000+ employees with respect to the proportion that have employee recognition programs. Because $Z_{STAT} = -2.86$ or p-value = 0.004, reject H_0.

(b) p-value = 0.004. The probability of obtaining a test statistic that gives rise to a test statistic below –2.86 or above +2.86 if there is no difference in the proportion based on the size of the organization is 0.4%.

(c) One can be 99% confident that the difference in the proportion based on the size of the organization is between 1.73% and 18.09%.

10.34 (a) H_0: $\pi_1 = \pi_2$ H_1: $\pi_1 \neq \pi_2$ Where Population: 1 = cobrowsing, 2 = Non-cobrowsing

Z Test for Differences in Two Proportions	
Data	
Hypothesized Difference	0
Level of Significance	0.05
Group 1	
Number of Items of Interest	81
Sample Size	129
Group 2	
Number of Items of Interest	65
Sample Size	176
Intermediate Calculations	
Group 1 Proportion	0.6279
Group 2 Proportion	0.3693
Difference in Two Proportions	0.2586
Average Proportion	0.4787
Z Test Statistic	4.4662
Two-Tail Test	
Lower Critical Value	-1.9600
Upper Critical Value	1.9600
p-Value	0.0000
Reject the null hypothesis	

Decision rule: If *p*-value < 0.05, reject H_0.
Decision: Since *p*-value = 0.0000 < 0.05, reject H_0. There is sufficient evidence of a difference between cobrowsing organizations and non-cobrowsing organizations in the proportion that use skills-based routing to match the caller with the right agent.

(b) *p*-value is 0.0000. The probability of obtaining a difference in proportions that gives rise to a test statistic that deviates from 0 by 4.4662 or more in either direction is 0.0000 if there is not a difference between cobrowsing organizations and non-cobrowsing organizations in the proportion that use skills-based routing to match the caller with the right agent.

10.36 (a) 2.20
(b) 2.57
(c) 3.50

10.38 (a) Population B: $S^2 = 25$
(b) 1.5625

10.40 $df_{\text{numerator}} = 24,\ df_{\text{denominator}} = 24,$

10.42 Because $F_{STAT} = 1.2109 < 2.27,$ do not reject H_0.

10.44 (a) Because $F_{STAT} = 1.2995 < 3.18,$ do not reject H_0.
(b) Because $F_{STAT} = 1.2995 < 2.62,$ do not reject H_0.

10.46 (a)

F Test for Differences in Two Variances	
Data	
Level of Significance	0.05
Larger-Variance Sample	
Sample Size	22
Sample Variance	3876.156
Smaller-Variance Sample	
Sample Size	22
Sample Variance	2690.331
Intermediate Calculations	
F Test Statistic	1.4408
Population 1 Sample Degrees of Freedom	21
Population 2 Sample Degrees of Freedom	21
Two-Tail Test	
Upper Critical Value	2.4086
p-Value	0.4096
Do not reject the null hypothesis	

Test and CI for Two Variances: Number of Partners vs Region

Method

σ_1: standard deviation of Number of Partners when Region = Gulf Coast
σ_2: standard deviation of Number of Partners when Region = Southeast
Ratio: σ_1/σ_2
F method was used. This method is accurate for normal data only.

Descriptive Statistics

Region	N	StDev	Variance	95% CI for σ^2
Gulf Coast	22	62.259	3876.156	(2294.302, 7915.986)
Southeast	22	51.868	2690.331	(1592.411, 5494.264)

Ratio of Variances

Estimated Ratio	95% CI for Ratio using F
1.44077	(0.598, 3.470)

Test

Null hypothesis $H_0: \sigma_1^2 / \sigma_2^2 = 1$
Alternative hypothesis $H_1: \sigma_1^2 / \sigma_2^2 \neq 1$
Significance level $\alpha = 0.05$

Method	Test Statistic	DF1	DF2	P-Value
F	1.44	21	21	0.410

10.46 cont.

(a) At the 0.05 level, there is no evidence that there is a difference between the variances of the Southeast and Gulf Coast regions. One would fail to reject the null hypothesis. The F_{STAT} of 1.44 is below the upper critical value. Because F_{STAT} = 1.44 or p-value = 0.410, do not reject H_0.

(b) The p-value is 0.410, which means that the probability of obtaining an equal or larger value than the observed test statistic, when H_0 is true, is 41%.

(c) To justify the use of the F test, it was assumed that the rating data from both populations were normally distributed.

(d) Because the results from (a) and (b) revealed that there was no significant difference between the variances of the Southeast and Gulf Coast regions, one would use the pooled-variance t test.

10.48

F Test for Differences in Two Variances	
Data	
Level of Significance	0.05
Larger-Variance Sample	
Sample Size	27
Sample Variance	1.083876
Smaller-Variance Sample	
Sample Size	31
Sample Variance	0.511588
Intermediate Calculations	
F Test Statistic	2.1187
Population 1 Sample Degrees of Freedom	26
Population 2 Sample Degrees of Freedom	30
Two-Tail Test	
Upper Critical Value	2.1124
p-Value	0.0491
Reject the null hypothesis	

10.48 cont.

Test and CI for Two Variances: Rating vs First Half

Method

σ_1: standard deviation of Rating when First Half = No
σ_2: standard deviation of Rating when First Half = Yes
Ratio: σ_1/σ_2
F method was used. This method is accurate for normal data only.

Descriptive Statistics

First Half	N	StDev	Variance	95% CI for σ^2
No	27	1.041	1.084	(0.672, 2.036)
Yes	31	0.715	0.512	(0.327, 0.914)

Ratio of Variances

Estimated Ratio	95% CI for Ratio using F
2.11865	(1.003, 4.569)

Test

Null hypothesis $H_0: \sigma_1^2 / \sigma_2^2 = 1$
Alternative hypothesis $H_1: \sigma_1^2 / \sigma_2^2 \neq 1$
Significance level $\alpha = 0.05$

Method	Test Statistic	DF1	DF2	P-Value
F	2.12	26	30	0.049

At the 0.05 level, there is sufficient evidence that there is a difference between the variances in the rating scores between ads in first half and ads in the second half. The F_{STAT} of 2.12 is above the upper critical value. Because $F_{STAT} = 2.12$ or p-value = 0.049, reject H_0.

The p-value is 0.049, which means that the probability of obtaining an equal or larger value than the observed test statistic, when H_0 is true, is a 4.9%. The p-value is just below 0.05 indicating that F_{STAT} is statistically significant at the 0.05 level.

To justify the use of the F test, it was assumed that the rating data from both groups were normally distributed.

10.48 cont.

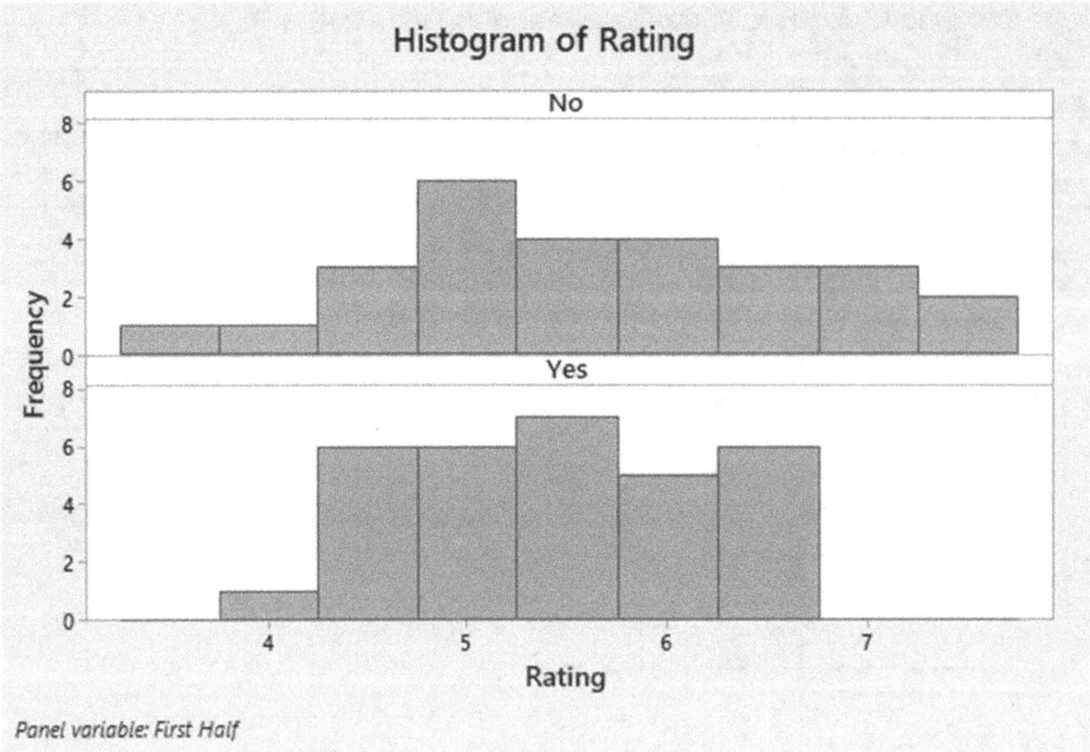

Descriptive Statistics: Rating

Statistics

Variable	First Half	N	N*	Mean	SE Mean	StDev	Minimum	Q1	Median	Q3	Maximum
Rating	No	27	0	5.651	0.200	1.041	3.630	4.960	5.590	6.410	7.690
	Yes	31	0	5.383	0.128	0.715	4.220	4.810	5.340	6.140	6.510

Variable	First Half	Skewness
Rating	No	0.14
	Yes	0.04

Ratings for ads that were not shown in the first half of the game were slightly skewed to the right while ratings for ads shown in the first half were generally uniform.

Because the results from (a) revealed that there was a significant difference between the two types of ads, one would use separate-variance *t* test.

10.50 (a) Because $F_{STAT} = 69.50001 > 1.9811$ or *p*-value = $0.0000 < 0.05$, reject H_0. There is evidence of a difference in the variance of the delay times between the two drivers.

(b) You assume that the delay times are normally distributed.

(c) From the boxplots and the normal probability plots, the delay times appear to be approximately normally distributed.

(d) Because there is a difference in the variance of the delay times between the two drivers, you should use the separate-variance *t* test to determine whether there is evidence of a difference in the mean delay time between the two drivers.

10.52 The pooled-variance t test should be used when the populations are approximately normally distributed and the variances of the two populations are assumed equal.

10.54 With independent populations, the outcomes in one population do not depend on the outcomes in the second population. With two related populations, either repeated measurements are obtained on the same set of items or individuals, or items or individuals are paired or matched according to some characteristic.

10.56 The hypothesis test for the difference between two means provides a single test statistic upon which a decision is made to reject or fail to reject the hypothesis. The confidence interval estimate provides the low end and high end of the mean differences assuming a given confidence level such as 95%. The confidence interval estimate can also be used to decide whether to accept or reject the null hypothesis. If the hypothesized value of 0 for the difference in two population means is not in the confidence interval, then, assuming a two-tailed test is used, the null hypothesis of no difference in the two population means can be rejected.

10.58 (a)

Test and CI for Two Variances

Method

σ_1: standard deviation of Sample 1
σ_2: standard deviation of Sample 2
Ratio: σ_1/σ_2
F method was used. This method is accurate for normal data only.

Descriptive Statistics

Sample	N	StDev	Variance	95% CI for σ
Sample 1	96	33.354	1112.489	(29.211, 38.877)
Sample 2	29	19.344	374.190	(15.351, 26.162)

Ratio of Standard Deviations

Estimated Ratio	95% CI for Ratio using F
1.72426	(1.242, 2.276)

Test

Null hypothesis $H_0: \sigma_1 / \sigma_2 = 1$
Alternative hypothesis $H_1: \sigma_1 / \sigma_2 \neq 1$
Significance level $\alpha = 0.05$

Method	Test Statistic	DF1	DF2	P-Value
F	2.97	95	28	0.002

At the 0.05 level, there is evidence that there is a statistically significant difference in variances for the two types of jobs. Because $F_{STAT} = 2.97$ or p-value = 0.002, reject H_0.

(b) Based on the results from (a), one would reject the null hypothesis and choose the separate-variance t test.

10.58 (c)
cont.

Two-Sample T-Test and CI

Method

μ_1: mean of Sample 1
μ_2: mean of Sample 2
Difference: $\mu_1 - \mu_2$

Equal variances are not assumed for this analysis.

Descriptive Statistics

Sample	N	Mean	StDev	SE Mean
Sample 1	96	101.8	33.4	3.4
Sample 2	29	72.3	19.3	3.6

Estimation for Difference

Difference	95% CI for Difference
29.44	(19.59, 39.29)

Test

Null hypothesis H_0: $\mu_1 - \mu_2 = 0$
Alternative hypothesis H_1: $\mu_1 - \mu_2 \neq 0$

T-Value	DF	P-Value
5.95	81	0.000

At the 0.05 level, there is evidence that the mean salary for Black belt jobs are significantly higher than the mean salary for Green belt jobs. The t_{STAT} of 5.95 is above the critical value. The *p*-value is 0.000. Because $t_{STAT} = 5.95$ or *p*-value = 0.000, reject H_0.

10.60 (a)

Test and CI for Two Variances

Method

σ_1: standard deviation of Sample 1
σ_2: standard deviation of Sample 2
Ratio: σ_1/σ_2
F method was used. This method is accurate for normal data only.

Descriptive Statistics

Sample	N	StDev	Variance	95% CI for σ^2
Sample 1	100	70.000	4900.000	(3777.391, 6612.498)
Sample 2	100	60.000	3600.000	(2775.226, 4858.162)

Ratio of Variances

Estimated Ratio	95% CI for Ratio using F
1.36111	(0.916, 2.023)

Test

Null hypothesis	H_0: $\sigma_1^2 / \sigma_2^2 = 1$
Alternative hypothesis	H_1: $\sigma_1^2 / \sigma_2^2 \neq 1$
Significance level	$\alpha = 0.05$

Method	Test Statistic	DF1	DF2	P-Value
F	1.36	99	99	0.127

Using a 0.01 level of significance, there is insufficient evidence that there is a difference in the variances in time spent online between males and females. Because $F_{STAT} = 1.36$ or p-value = 0.127, do not reject H_0.

10.60 cont. (b) It is most appropriate to use the pooled-variance t test to test for differences in mean online time between males and females.

Two-Sample T-Test and CI

Method

μ_1: mean of Sample 1
μ_2: mean of Sample 2
Difference: $\mu_1 - \mu_2$

Equal variances are assumed for this analysis.

Descriptive Statistics

Sample	N	Mean	StDev	SE Mean
Sample 1	100	1254.0	60.0	6.0
Sample 2	100	1344.0	70.0	7.0

Estimation for Difference

Difference	Pooled StDev	95% CI for Difference
-90.00	65.19	(-108.18, -71.82)

Test

Null hypothesis $H_0: \mu_1 - \mu_2 = 0$
Alternative hypothesis $H_1: \mu_1 - \mu_2 \neq 0$

T-Value	DF	P-Value
-9.76	198	0.000

At the 0.01 significance level, the t_{STAT} of –9.76 is well below the lower critical value. Because $t_{STAT} = -9.76$ or p-value = 0.000, one would reject the null hypothesis that there is no difference between the mean online time between males and females. The results indicate that men spent significantly more time online compared to women.

10.60 (c)
cont.

Test and CI for Two Variances

Method

σ_1: standard deviation of Sample 1
σ_2: standard deviation of Sample 2
Ratio: σ_1/σ_2
F method was used. This method is accurate for normal data only.

Descriptive Statistics

Sample	N	StDev	Variance	95% CI for σ^2
Sample 1	100	20.000	400.000	(308.358, 539.796)
Sample 2	100	15.000	225.000	(173.452, 303.635)

Ratio of Variances

Estimated Ratio	95% CI for Ratio using F
1.77778	(1.196, 2.642)

Test

Null hypothesis H_0: $\sigma_1^2 / \sigma_2^2 = 1$
Alternative hypothesis H_1: $\sigma_1^2 / \sigma_2^2 \neq 1$
Significance level $\alpha = 0.05$

Method	Test Statistic	DF1	DF2	P-Value
F	1.78	99	99	0.005

Using a 0.01 level of significance, there is evidence that there is a difference in the variances in time spent playing online games between males and females. Because $F_{STAT} = 1.78$ or p-value = 0.005, reject H_0.

10.60 cont. (d)

Two-Sample T-Test and CI

Method

μ_1: mean of Sample 1
μ_2: mean of Sample 2
Difference: $\mu_1 - \mu_2$

Equal variances are not assumed for this analysis.

Descriptive Statistics

Sample	N	Mean	StDev	SE Mean
Sample 1	100	360.0	20.0	2.0
Sample 2	100	294.0	15.0	1.5

Estimation for Difference

Difference	95% CI for Difference
66.00	(61.07, 70.93)

Test

Null hypothesis H_0: $\mu_1 - \mu_2 = 0$
Alternative hypothesis H_1: $\mu_1 - \mu_2 \neq 0$

T-Value	DF	P-Value
26.40	183	0.000

A separate-variance t test revealed that at the 0.01 significance level, there is evidence that men and women differ significantly in amount of time spent playing online games. Men spent significantly more time playing online games than women. Because $F_{STAT} = 26.40$ or p-value = 0.000, reject H_0.

10.62 (a) H_0: $\mu \leq 10$ minutes. Introductory computer students required no more than a mean of 10 minutes to write and run a program in Python.
H_1: $\mu > 10$ minutes. Introductory computer students required more than a mean of 10 minutes to write and run a program in Python.
Decision rule: $d.f. = 8$. If $t_{STAT} > 1.8595$, reject H_0.

Test statistic: $$t_{STAT} = \frac{\bar{X} - \mu}{\frac{S}{\sqrt{n}}} = \frac{12 - 10}{\frac{1.8028}{\sqrt{9}}} = 3.3282$$

10.62 cont.

(a) Decision: Since $t_{STAT} = 3.3282$ is greater than the critical bound of 1.8595, reject H_0. There is enough evidence to conclude that the introductory computer students required more than a mean of 10 minutes to write and run a program in Python.

(b) H_0: $\mu \le 10$ minutes. Introductory computer students required no more than a mean of 10 minutes to write and run a program in Python.

H_1: $\mu > 10$ minutes. Introductory computer students required more than a mean of 10 minutes to write and run a program in Python.

Decision rule: $d.f. = 8$. If $t_{STAT} > 1.8595$, reject H_0.

Test statistic: $t_{STAT} = \dfrac{\overline{X} - \mu}{\dfrac{S}{\sqrt{n}}} = \dfrac{16 - 10}{\dfrac{13.2004}{\sqrt{9}}} = 1.3636$

Decision: Since $t_{STAT} = 1.3636$ is less than the critical bound of 1.8595, do not reject H_0. There is not enough evidence to conclude that the introductory computer students required more than a mean of 10 minutes to write and run a program in Python.

(c) Although the mean time necessary to complete the assignment increased from 12 to 16 minutes as a result of the increase in one data value, the standard deviation went from 1.8 to 13.2, which in turn brought the t-value down because of the increased denominator.

(d) H_0: $\sigma_{IC}^2 = \sigma_{CS}^2$ $\quad$ H_1: $\sigma_{IC}^2 \ne \sigma_{CS}^2$

Decision rule: If $F_{STAT} > 3.8549$, reject H_0.

Test statistic: $F_{STAT} = \dfrac{S_{CS}^2}{S_{IC}^2} = \dfrac{2.0^2}{1.8028^2} = 1.2307$

Decision: Since $F_{STAT} = 1.2307$ is lower than the critical bound 3.8549, do not reject H_0. There is not enough evidence to conclude that the population variances are different for the Introduction to Computers students and computer majors. Hence, the pooled-variance t test is a valid test to see whether computer majors can write a Python program (on average) in less time than introductory students, assuming that the distributions of the time needed to write a Python program for both the Introduction to Computers students and the computer majors are approximately normal.

H_0: $\mu_{IC} \le \mu_{CS}$ The mean amount of time needed by Introduction to Computers students is not greater than the mean amount of time needed by computer majors.

H_1: $\mu_{IC} > \mu_{CS}$ The mean amount of time needed by Introduction to Computers students is greater than the mean amount of time needed by computer majors.

10.62 (d)
cont.

Pooled-Variance *t* Test for the Difference Between Two Means	
(assumes equal population variances)	
Data	
Hypothesized Difference	**0**
Level of Significance	**0.05**
Population 1 Sample	
Sample Size	**9**
Sample Mean	**12**
Sample Standard Deviation	**1.802776**
Population 2 Sample	
Sample Size	**11**
Sample Mean	**8.5**
Sample Standard Deviation	**2**
Intermediate Calculations	
Population 1 Sample Degrees of Freedom	8
Population 2 Sample Degrees of Freedom	10
Total Degrees of Freedom	18
Pooled-Variance	3.666667
Difference in Sample Means	3.5
***t* Test Statistic**	**4.066633**
Upper-Tail Test	
Upper Critical Value	**1.734064**
***p*-Value**	**0.000362**
Reject the null hypothesis	

Decision rule: $d.f. = 18$. If $t_{STAT} > 1.7341$, reject H_0.
Test statistic:

$$S_p^2 = \frac{(n_{IC}-1)\cdot S_{IC}^2 + (n_{CS}-1)\cdot S_{CS}^2}{(n_{IC}-1)+(n_{CS}-1)} = \frac{9\cdot 1.8028^2 + 11\cdot 2.0^2}{8+10} = 3.6667$$

$$t_{STAT} = \frac{(\bar{X}_{IC}-\bar{X}_{CS})-(\mu_{IC}-\mu_{CS})}{\sqrt{S_p^2\left(\frac{1}{n_{IC}}+\frac{1}{n_{CS}}\right)}} = \frac{12.0-8.5}{\sqrt{3.6667\left(\frac{1}{9}+\frac{1}{11}\right)}} = 4.0666$$

Decision: Since $t_{STAT} = 4.0666$ is greater than 1.7341, reject H_0. There is enough evidence to support a conclusion that the mean time is higher for Introduction to Computers students than for computer majors.

(e) p-value = 0.0052. If the true population mean amount of time needed for Introduction to Computer students to write a Python program is indeed no more than 10 minutes, the probability for observing a sample mean greater than the 12 minutes in the current sample is 0.0052, which means it will be a quite unlikely event. Hence, at a 95% level of confidence, you can conclude that the population mean amount of time needed for Introduction to Computer students to write a Python program is more than 10 minutes.

10.62 cont. (e) As illustrated in part (d) in which there is not enough evidence to conclude that the population variances are different for the Introduction to Computers students and computer majors, the pooled-variance *t* test performed is a valid test to determine whether computer majors can write a Python program in less time than in introductory students, assuming that the distributions of the time needed to write a Python program for both the Introduction to Computers students and the computer majors are approximately normal.

10.64 Because an *F* test for the ratio of two variances revealed no significant differences between the variances of the two manufacturers, a pooled-variance *t* test is appropriate for these data.

Test and CI for Two Variances: man2, man1

Method

σ_1: standard deviation of man2
σ_2: standard deviation of man1
Ratio: σ_1/σ_2
F method was used. This method is accurate for normal data only.

Descriptive Statistics

Variable	N	StDev	Variance	95% CI for σ
man2	40	969.014	938987.436	(793.778, 1244.248)
man1	40	943.052	889346.410	(772.511, 1210.912)

Ratio of Standard Deviations

Estimated Ratio	95% CI for Ratio using F
1.02753	(0.747, 1.413)

Test

Null hypothesis $H_0: \sigma_1 / \sigma_2 = 1$
Alternative hypothesis $H_1: \sigma_1 / \sigma_2 \neq 1$
Significance level $\alpha = 0.05$

Method	Test Statistic	DF1	DF2	P-Value
F	1.06	39	39	0.866

10.64
cont.

Two-Sample T-Test and CI: Length of Life, Manufacturer

Method

μ_1: mean of Length of Life when Manufacturer = 1
μ_2: mean of Length of Life when Manufacturer = 2
Difference: $\mu_1 - \mu_2$

Equal variances are assumed for this analysis.

Descriptive Statistics: Length of Life

Manufacturer	N	Mean	StDev	SE Mean
1	40	49097	943	149
2	40	50184	969	153

Estimation for Difference

Difference	Pooled StDev	95% CI for Difference
-1087	956	(-1513, -661)

Test

Null hypothesis H_0: $\mu_1 - \mu_2 = 0$
Alternative hypothesis H_1: $\mu_1 - \mu_2 \neq 0$

T-Value	DF	P-Value
-5.08	78	0.000

The mean length of life was significantly longer for Manufacturer 2 compared to Manufacturer 1. Because $t_{STAT} = -5.08$ or p-value = 0.000, one would reject the null hypothesis that the mean length of bulb life is the same for the two manufacturers.

10.66 H_0: $\pi_1 = \pi_2$ H_1: $\pi_1 \neq \pi_2$ where Populations: 1 = Males, 2 = Females
Decision rule: If p-value < 0.05, reject H_0.

Gender:

Z Test for Differences in Two Proportions

Data	
Hypothesized Difference	0
Level of Significance	0.05
Group 1	
Number of Items of Interest	50
Sample Size	300
Group 2	
Number of Items of Interest	96
Sample Size	330

Intermediate Calculations	
Group 1 Proportion	0.166666667
Group 2 Proportion	0.290909091
Difference in Two Proportions	-0.12424242
Average Proportion	0.2317
Z Test Statistic	-3.6911

Two-Tail Test	
Lower Critical Value	-1.9600
Upper Critical Value	1.9600
p-Value	0.0002
Reject the null hypothesis	

Decision: Since the p-value is smaller than 0.05, reject H_0. There is enough evidence of a difference between males and females in the proportion who order dessert.

10.66 cont. **Beef Entrée:**

Z Test for Differences in Two Proportions	
Data	
Hypothesized Difference	0
Level of Significance	0.05
Group 1	
Number of Items of Interest	74
Sample Size	197
Group 2	
Number of Items of Interest	68
Sample Size	433
Intermediate Calculations	
Group 1 Proportion	0.375634518
Group 2 Proportion	0.15704388
Difference in Two Proportions	0.218590638
Average Proportion	0.2254
Z Test Statistic	6.0873
Two-Tail Test	
Lower Critical Value	-1.9600
Upper Critical Value	1.9600
p-Value	0.0000
Reject the null hypothesis	

Decision: Since the p-value = 0.0000 is smaller than 0.05, reject H_0. There is enough evidence of a difference in the proportion who order dessert based on whether a beef entrée has been ordered.

10.68 The normal probability plots suggest that the two populations are not normally distributed. An F test is inappropriate for testing the difference in the two variances. The sample variances for Boston and Vermont shingles are 0.0203 and 0.015, respectively. Because $t_{STAT} = 3.015 > 1.967$ or p-value = $0.0028 < \alpha = 0.05$, reject H_0. There is sufficient evidence to conclude that there is a difference in the mean granule loss of Boston and Vermont shingles.

10.70 An analysis of the data in 10.67 revealed that a pallet of Vermont shingles weighed significantly more than a pallet of Boston shingles. Assuming that a heavier weight shingle is associated with higher quality, the Vermont shingle might be perceived as a higher quality shingle compared to the Boston shingle. The below figure shows the results from a separate-variance *t* test.

Descriptive Statistics

Sample	N	Mean	StDev	SE Mean
Boston	368	3124.2	34.7	1.8
Vermont	330	3704.0	46.7	2.6

Estimation for Difference

Difference	95% CI for Difference
-579.83	(-586.01, -573.65)

Test

Null hypothesis $H_0: \mu_1 - \mu_2 = 0$
Alternative hypothesis $H_1: \mu_1 - \mu_2 \neq 0$

T-Value	DF	P-Value
-184.32	602	0.000

An analysis of the data in 10.68 revealed that the Vermont shingles were associated with less granule loss compared to the Boston shingles following accelerated-life testing. Shingles with less weight loss are assumed to have a longer life expectancy. Both shingles would be expected to outperform the length of the warranty period because their weight losses were well below the 0.8 gram threshold. However, the Vermont shingles would be expected to have a longer life expectancy given that they loss less weight relative to the Boston shingles. The below figure shows the results from a pooled-variance *t* test.

Descriptive Statistics

Sample	N	Mean	StDev	SE Mean
Boston	170	0.264	0.142	0.011
Vermont	140	0.218	0.123	0.010

Estimation for Difference

Difference	Pooled StDev	95% CI for Difference
0.0461	0.1339	(0.0160, 0.0761)

Test

Null hypothesis $H_0: \mu_1 - \mu_2 = 0$
Alternative hypothesis $H_1: \mu_1 - \mu_2 \neq 0$

T-Value	DF	P-Value
3.01	308	0.003

Taken together, the results from 10.67 and 10.68 suggest that the Vermont shingle may be a higher quality shingle based on pallet weight and life expectancy as determined by granule loss associated with accelerated-life testing. These conclusions suggest that the manufacturer may be able to charge more for the Vermont shingle compared to the Boston shingle.

CHAPTER 11

11.2 (a) $SSW = SST - SSA = 210 - 60 = 150$

(b) $MSA = \dfrac{SSA}{c-1} = \dfrac{60}{5-1} = 15$

(c) $MSW = \dfrac{SSW}{n-c} = \dfrac{150}{35-5} = 5$

(d) $F_{STAT} = \dfrac{MSA}{MSW} = \dfrac{15}{5} = 3$

11.4 (a) $df\,A = c - 1 = 3 - 1 = 2$

(b) $df\,W = n - c = 21 - 3 = 18$

(c) $df\,T = n - 1 = 21 - 1 = 20$

11.6 (a) Decision rule: If $F_{STAT} > 2.95$, reject H_0.

(b) Since $F_{STAT} = 4$ is greater than the critical bound of 2.95, reject H_0.

(c) There are $c = 4$ degrees of freedom in the numerator and $n - c = 32 - 4 = 28$ degrees of freedom in the denominator. The table does not have 28 degrees of freedom in the denominator so use the next larger critical value, $Q_\alpha = 3.90$.

(d) To perform the Tukey-Kramer procedure, the critical range is

$$Q_\alpha\sqrt{\frac{MSW}{2}\left(\frac{1}{n_j}+\frac{1}{n_{j'}}\right)} = 3.90\sqrt{\frac{20}{2}\left(\frac{1}{8}+\frac{1}{8}\right)} = 6.166.$$

11.8

One-way ANOVA: Cost to import (US$) versus Region

Method

Null hypothesis	All means are equal
Alternative hypothesis	Not all means are equal
Significance level	α = 0.05

Equal variances were assumed for the analysis.

Factor Information

Factor	Levels	Values
Region	4	East Asia & Pacific, Eastern Europe & Central Asia, Latin American & Carribbean, Middle East & North Africa

Analysis of Variance

Source	DF	Adj SS	Adj MS	F-Value	P-Value
Region	3	1151016	383672	4.66	0.007
Error	36	2961835	82273		
Total	39	4112852			

Model Summary

S	R-sq	R-sq(adj)	R-sq(pred)
286.833	27.99%	21.98%	11.09%

Means

Region	N	Mean	StDev	95% Upper Bound
East Asia & Pacific	10	380.1	176.7	533.2
Eastern Europe & Central Asia	10	334	334	487
Latin American & Carribbean	10	755	383	908
Middle East & North Africa	10	594.4	199.3	747.5

Pooled StDev = 286.833

11.8 cont. (a) At the 0.05 level of significance, there is evidence there are differences in import costs among the four regions. Because $F_{STAT} = 4.66$ OR p-value = 0.007, reject H_0. The ANOVA F_{STAT} indicates that there is a difference among the four regions. However, it does not indicate which groups differ from one another.

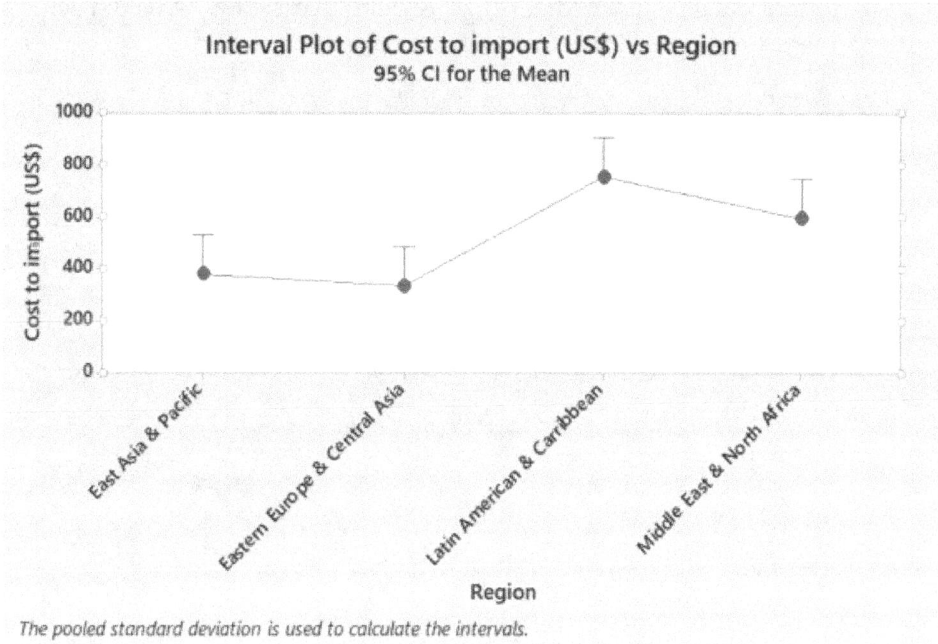

Tukey Pairwise Comparisons

Grouping Information Using the Tukey Method and 95% Confidence

Region	N	Mean	Grouping	
Latin American & Carribbean	10	755	A	
Middle East & North Africa	10	594.4	A	B
East Asia & Pacific	10	380.1		B
Eastern Europe & Central Asia	10	334		B

Means that do not share a letter are significantly different.

11.8 cont. (b) Pairwise comparisons with the Tukey test revealed that the Latin American & Caribbean region had higher import costs compared to the East Asia & Pacific and Eastern Europe & Central Asia regions. The Latin American & Caribbean region and the Middle East & North Africa did not differ significantly in import costs. There were no other pairwise differences among the Middle East & North Africa, East Asia & Pacific and Eastern Europe & Central Asia regions.

Test for Equal Variances: Cost to import (US$) versus Region

Method

Null hypothesis	All variances are equal
Alternative hypothesis	At least one variance is different
Significance level	$\alpha = 0.05$

95% Bonferroni Confidence Intervals for Standard Deviations

Region	N	StDev	CI
East Asia & Pacific	10	176.739	(60.618, 686.85)
Eastern Europe & Central Asia	10	333.606	(99.291, 1494.05)
Latin American & Carribbean	10	383.221	(187.382, 1044.66)
Middle East & North Africa	10	199.262	(90.062, 587.64)

Individual confidence level = 98.75%

Tests

Method	Test Statistic	P-Value
Multiple comparisons	—	0.284
Levene	1.56	0.216

(c) Because the Levene test $F_{STAT} = 1.56$ or p-value = 0.216, there is no evidence that the variances are different among the four regions.

(d) East Asia & Pacific, Eastern Europe & Central Asia, and Middle East & North Africa would all be appropriate for foreign market entry. While Eastern Europe & Central Asia had the lowest import costs, these three regions did not differ significantly from each other due to high standard deviations associated within each region. The Latin American & Caribbean would be less appropriate to consider because it had the highest import costs that were significantly different compared to the East Asia & Pacific and Eastern Europe & Central Asia regions.

11.10 (a) H_0: $\mu_A = \mu_B = \mu_C = \mu_D = \mu_E$ H_1: At least one mean is different.

One-way ANOVA: Rating versus Ad

Method

Null hypothesis	All means are equal
Alternative hypothesis	Not all means are equal
Significance level	α = 0.05

Equal variances were assumed for the analysis.

Factor Information

Factor	Levels	Values
Ad	5	A, B, C, D, E

Analysis of Variance

Source	DF	Adj SS	Adj MS	F-Value	P-Value
Ad	4	377.9	94.467	12.56	0.000
Error	25	188.0	7.520		
Total	29	565.9			

Model Summary

S	R-sq	R-sq(adj)	R-sq(pred)
2.74226	66.78%	61.46%	52.16%

Means

Ad	N	Mean	StDev	95% CI
A	6	18.000	1.789	(15.694, 20.306)
B	6	17.667	1.966	(15.361, 19.972)
C	6	11.33	3.44	(9.03, 13.64)
D	6	9.00	3.03	(6.69, 11.31)
E	6	15.33	3.08	(13.03, 17.64)

Pooled StDev = 2.74226

Since the p-value is essentially zero, reject H_0. There is evidence of a difference in the mean rating of the five advertisements.

11.10 (b)
cont.

Tukey Pairwise Comparisons

Grouping Information Using the Tukey Method and 95% Confidence

Ad	N	Mean	Grouping		
A	6	18.000	A		
B	6	17.667	A		
E	6	15.33	A	B	
C	6	11.33		B	C
D	6	9.00			C

Means that do not share a letter are significantly different.

Tukey Simultaneous Tests for Differences of Means

Difference of Levels	Difference of Means	SE of Difference	95% CI	T-Value	Adjusted P-Value
B - A	-0.33	1.58	(-4.98, 4.31)	-0.21	1.000
C - A	-6.67	1.58	(-11.31, -2.02)	-4.21	0.002
D - A	-9.00	1.58	(-13.65, -4.35)	-5.68	0.000
E - A	-2.67	1.58	(-7.31, 1.98)	-1.68	0.461
C - B	-6.33	1.58	(-10.98, -1.69)	-4.00	0.004
D - B	-8.67	1.58	(-13.31, -4.02)	-5.47	0.000
E - B	-2.33	1.58	(-6.98, 2.31)	-1.47	0.588
D - C	-2.33	1.58	(-6.98, 2.31)	-1.47	0.588
E - C	4.00	1.58	(-0.65, 8.65)	2.53	0.117
E - D	6.33	1.58	(1.69, 10.98)	4.00	0.004

Individual confidence level = 99.29%

There is a difference in the mean rating between advertisement A and C, between A and D, between B and C, between B and D and between D and E.

(c) H_0: $\sigma_A^2 = \sigma_B^2 = \sigma_C^2 = \sigma_D^2 = \sigma_E^2$ H_1: At least one variance is different.

ANOVA output for Levene's test for homogeneity of variance:

ANOVA

Source of Variation	*SS*	*df*	*MS*	*F*	*P-value*	*F crit*
Between Groups	14.13333	4	3.533333	1.927273	0.137107	2.758711
Within Groups	45.83333	25	1.833333			
Total	59.96667	29				

Since the p-value = 0.137 > 0.05, do not reject H_0. There is not enough evidence to conclude there is a difference in the variation in rating among the five advertisements.

(d) There is no significant difference between advertisements A and B, and they have the highest mean rating among the five and should be used. There is no significant difference between advertisements C and D, and they are among the lowest in mean rating and should be avoided.

11.12 (a)

Source	Degrees of Freedom	Sum of Squares	Mean Squares	F
Among Groups	2	15,671,226,037.72	7,835,613,018.86	1.702052
Within Groups	50	230,181,430,044.96	4,603,628,600.90	
Total	52	245,852,656,082.68	4,727,935,693.90	

(b) Because $F_{STAT} = 1.7021 < 3.23$, do not reject H_0. There is insufficient evidence that there are significant differences in mean brand value among the financial institution, technology, and telecom sectors.

(c) Because the results in (b) indicated that there were no differences in mean brand value among the three sectors, it would not be appropriate to use the Tukey-Kramer procedure.

11.14

One-way ANOVA: Asia, Europe, North America, South America

Method

Null hypothesis	All means are equal
Alternative hypothesis	Not all means are equal
Significance level	α = 0.05

Equal variances were assumed for the analysis.

Factor Information

Factor	Levels	Values
Factor	4	Asia, Europe, North America, South America

Analysis of Variance

Source	DF	Adj SS	Adj MS	F-Value	P-Value
Factor	3	1172	390.83	6.23	0.002
Error	36	2259	62.76		
Total	39	3432			

Model Summary

S	R-sq	R-sq(adj)	R-sq(pred)
7.92202	34.17%	28.68%	18.72%

Means

Factor	N	Mean	StDev	95% Upper Bound
Asia	10	49.20	5.98	53.43
Europe	10	40.60	3.86	44.83
North America	10	37.90	11.08	42.13
South America	10	34.60	8.81	38.83

Pooled StDev = 7.92202

11.14 cont. (a) At the 0.05 level of significance, there is evidence there are differences in congestion levels among the four continents. Because $F_{STAT} = 6.23$ or p-value = 0.002, reject H_0. The ANOVA F_{STAT} indicates that there are differences in congestion levels among the four continents. However, it does not indicate which groups differ from one another.

Tukey Pairwise Comparisons

Grouping Information Using the Tukey Method and 95% Confidence

Factor	N	Mean	Grouping	
Asia	10	49.20	A	
Europe	10	40.60	A	B
North America	10	37.90		B
South America	10	34.60		B

Means that do not share a letter are significantly different.

(b) Because the results from (a) revealed a significant difference in congestion levels among the four continents, the Tukey-Kramer procedure is appropriate. This test revealed that Asia had significantly higher congestion levels than North America and South America. There is no significant difference in congestion level between Asia and Europe. There are no significant differences in pairwise comparisons among Europe, North America, and South America.

(c) The ANOVA F test assumes randomness and independence of samples, normally distributed data in all groups, and equal variances among groups.

Test for Equal Variances: Asia, Europe, North America, South America

Method

Null hypothesis	All variances are equal
Alternative hypothesis	At least one variance is different
Significance level	α = 0.05

95% Bonferroni Confidence Intervals for Standard Deviations

Sample	N	StDev	CI
Asia	10	5.9777	(2.34648, 20.2984)
Europe	10	3.8644	(1.10956, 17.9395)
North America	10	11.0800	(2.90555, 56.3195)
South America	10	8.8091	(5.47314, 18.8987)

Individual confidence level = 98.75%

Tests

Method	Test Statistic	P-Value
Multiple comparisons	—	0.131
Levene	1.52	0.226

(d) Because the Levene test $F_{STAT} = 1.52$ or p-value = 0.226, there is no evidence that the variances are different among the four regions.

11.16

Source	df	SS	MS	F
Factor A	2	120	(b) 120 ÷ 2 = 60	60 ÷ 10 = 6
Factor B	2	110	(b) 110 ÷ 2 = 55	55 ÷ 10 = 5.5
Interaction, AB	4	(a) 540 – 120 – 110 – 270 = 40	(c) 40 ÷ 4 = 10	10 ÷ 10 = 1
Error, E	27	270	(d)270 ÷ 27 = 10	
Total, T	35	540		

(a) 40
(b) 60 and 55
(c) 10
(d) 10

11.18 $F_{(2, 27)} = 3.35$ $F_{(4, 27)} = 2.73$

(a) Decision: Since $F_{STAT} = 6.00$ is greater than the critical bound of 3.35, reject H_0. There is evidence of a difference among factor A means.

(b) Decision: Since $F_{STAT} = 5.50$ is greater than the critical bound of 3.35, reject H_0. There is evidence of a difference among factor B means.

(c) Decision: Since $F_{STAT} = 1.00$ is less than the critical bound of 2.73, do not reject H_0. There is insufficient evidence to conclude there is an interaction effect.

11.20

Source	df	SS	MS	F
Factor A	2	2×80 = 160	80	80 ÷ 5 = 16
Factor B	8 ÷ 2 = 4	220	220 ÷ 4 = 55	11
Interaction, AB	8	8×10 = 80	10	10 ÷ 5 = 2
Error, E	30	30×5 = 150	55 ÷ 11 = 5	
Total, T	44	160 + 220 + 80 + 150 = 610		

11.22 Two-way ANOVA output:

General Linear Model: result versus Die Temperature, Diameter

Method

Factor coding (-1, 0, +1)

Factor Information

Factor	Type	Levels	Values
Die Temperature	Fixed	2	145, 155
Diameter	Fixed	2	3, 4

Analysis of Variance

Source	DF	Adj SS	Adj MS	F-Value	P-Value
Die Temperature	1	214.3	214.3	1.85	0.189
Diameter	1	1095.3	1095.3	9.45	0.006
Die Temperature*Diameter	1	394.2	394.2	3.40	0.080
Error	20	2316.8	115.8		
Total	23	4020.6			

(a) H_0: There is no interaction between die temperature and die diameter.
H_1: There is an interaction between die temperature and die diameter.
Decision: Since $F_{STAT} = 3.4032 < 4.3512$, do not reject H_0. There is insufficient evidence to conclude that there is any interaction between die temperature and die diameter.

11.22 cont. (b) H_0: $\mu_{145..} = \mu_{155..}$ H_1: $\mu_{145} \neq \mu_{155}$

Decision: Since $F_{STAT} = 1.85 < 4.3512$, do not reject H_0. There is insufficient evidence to conclude that there is an effect due to die temperature.

(c) H_0: $\mu_{3mm.} = \mu_{4mm.}$ H_1: $\mu_{3mm} \neq \mu_{4mm}$

Decision: Since $F_{STAT} = 9.45 > 4.3512$, reject H_0. There is sufficient evidence to conclude that there is an effect due to die diameter.

(d)

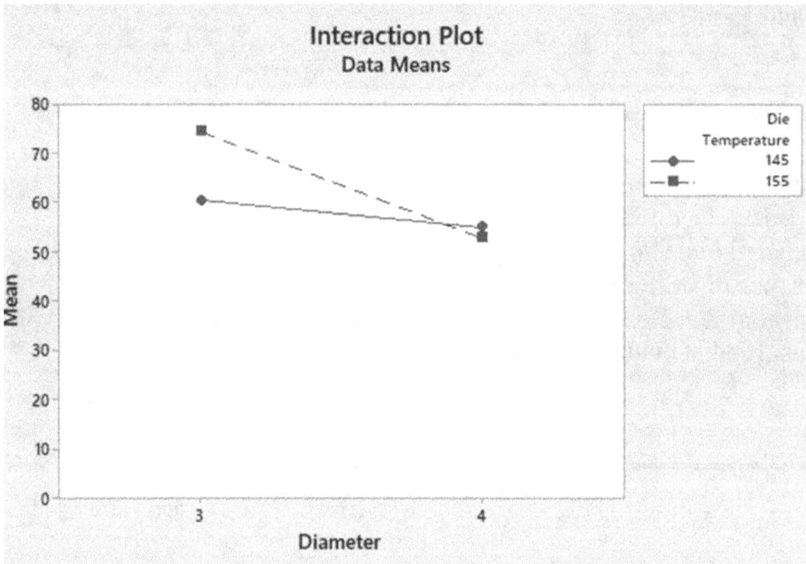

(e) At 5% level of significance, die diameter has an effect on the density while the die temperature does not have any impact on the density. There is no significant interaction between die diameter and die temperature.

11.24 (a)

General Linear Model: Warpage versus Filling Time, Temp

Method

Factor coding (-1, 0, +1)

Factor Information

Factor	Type	Levels	Values
Filling Time	Fixed	3	1, 2, 3
Temp	Fixed	3	60.0, 72.5, 85.0

Analysis of Variance

Source	DF	Adj SS	Adj MS	F-Value	P-Value
Filling Time	2	0.9031	0.45153	9.02	0.002
Temp	2	0.4234	0.21172	4.23	0.031
Filling Time*Temp	4	0.4544	0.11361	2.27	0.102
Error	18	0.9008	0.05005		
Total	26	2.6818			

11.24 cont.

(a) H_0: There is no interaction between filling time and mold temperature. H_1: There is an interaction between filling time and mold temperature.

Because $F_{STAT} = \frac{0.1136}{0.05} = 2.27 < 2.9277$ or the p-value $= 0.102 > 0.05$, do not reject H_0.
There is insufficient evidence of interaction between filling time and mold temperature.

(b) $F_{STAT} = 9.02 > 3.5546$, reject H_0. There is evidence of a difference in the warpage due to the filling time.

(c) $F_{STAT} = 4.23 > 3.5546$, reject H_0. There is evidence of a difference in the warpage due to the mold temperature.

(d)

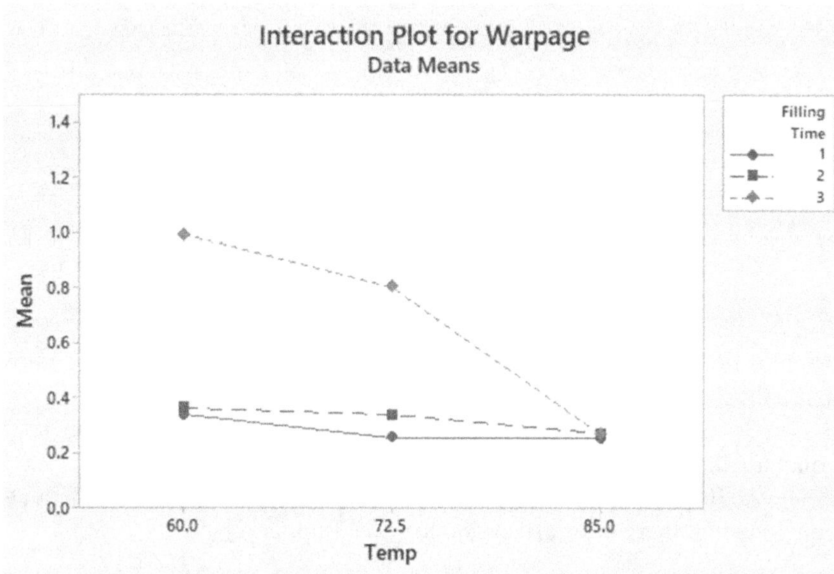

(e) The Tukey procedure revealed that the 3 sec filling time group was significantly higher than the 2 sec and 1 sec groups, which were not significant from each other. The Tukey procedure also revealed that the 60°C group was different than the 85°C group.

(f) Both filling time and temperature had main effects on warpage. Although the interaction plot appeared to show an interaction between filling time and temperature, it was not significant at the 0.05 significance level. The warpage for a three-second filling time seems to be much higher at 60°C and 72.5°C but not at 85°C. Caution should be used in interpreting this non-significant interaction due to relatively small sample sizes.

11.26 (a)

General Linear Model: Result versus Zone 1 Lower, Zone 3 upper

Method

Factor coding (-1, 0, +1)

Factor Information

Factor	Type	Levels	Values
Zone 1 Lower	Fixed	2	630, 650
Zone 3 upper	Fixed	2	695, 715

Analysis of Variance

Source	DF	Adj SS	Adj MS	F-Value	P-Value
Zone 1 Lower	1	689.1	689.1	0.38	0.548
Zone 3 upper	1	189.1	189.1	0.10	0.752
Zone 1 Lower*Zone 3 upper	1	1501.6	1501.6	0.83	0.380
Error	12	21643.7	1803.6		
Total	15	24023.4			

(a) $F_{STAT} = 0.83$, p-value $= 0.38 > 0.05$, do not reject H_0.
There is not enough evidence to conclude that there is an interaction between zone lower and zone 3 upper.

(b) $F_{STAT} = 0.38$, p-value is $0.548 > 0.05$, do not reject H_0. There is insufficient evidence to conclude that there is an effect due to zone 1 lower.

(c) $F_{STAT} = 0.10$, p-value $= 0.752 > 0.05$, do not reject H_0. There is inadequate evidence to conclude that there is an effect due to zone 3 upper.

(d)

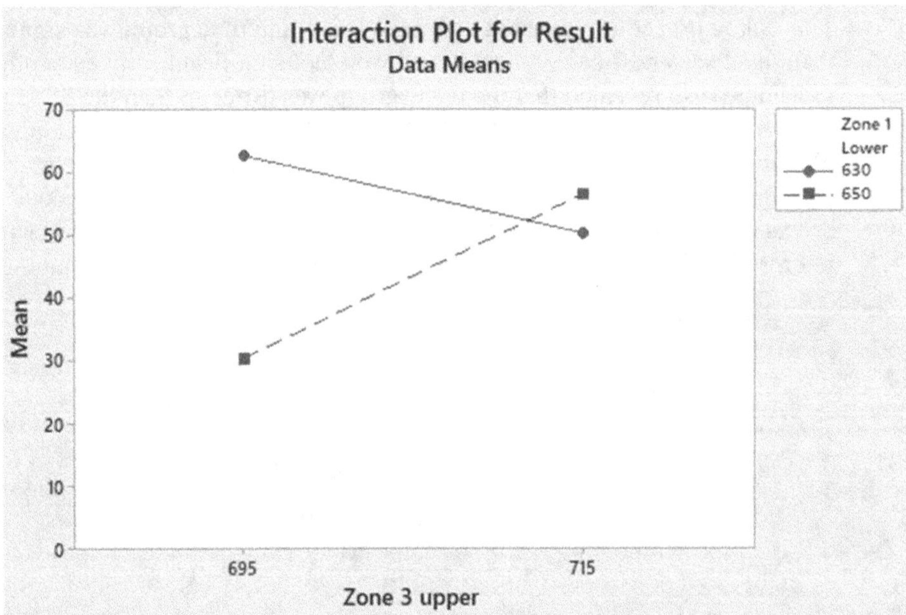

A large difference at a zone 3 upper of 695°C but only a small difference at zone 3 upper of 715°C.

11.26 cont. (e) Because this difference appeared on the cell means plot but the interaction was not statistically significant because of the large *MSE*. Caution should be used in interpreting these findings due to small sample sizes. Further testing should be done with larger sample sizes.

11.28 The completely randomized design evaluates one factor of interest, in which sample observations are randomly and independently drawn. The randomized block design also evaluates one factor of interest, but sample observations are divided into blocks according to common characteristics to reduce within group variation. The two-factor factorial design evaluates two factors of interest and the interaction between these two factors.

11.30 If the populations are approximately normally distributed and the variances of the groups are approximately equal, you select the one-way ANOVA *F* test to examine possible differences among the means of *c* independent populations.

11.32 The one-way ANOVA *F* test for a completely randomized design is used to test for the existence of treatment effect of the treatment variable on the mean level of the dependent variable, while the Levene test is used to test whether the amounts of variation of the dependent variable are the same across the different categories of the treatment variable.

11.34 Interaction measures the difference in the effect of one variable for the different levels of the second factor. If there is no interaction, any difference between levels of one factor will be the same at each level of the second factor.

11.36 (a)

General Linear Model: Strength versus Loom, Supplier

Method

Factor coding (-1, 0, +1)

Factor Information

Factor	Type	Levels	Values
Loom	Fixed	2	jetta, turk
Supplier	Fixed	4	1, 2, 3, 4

Analysis of Variance

Source	DF	Adj SS	Adj MS	F-Value	P-Value
Loom	1	6.972	6.9722	0.81	0.375
Supplier	3	134.349	44.7829	5.20	0.005
Loom*Supplier	3	0.287	0.0956	0.01	0.998
Error	32	275.592	8.6123		
Total	39	417.200			

H_0: There is no interaction
H_1: There is an interaction
Decision: Since $F_{STAT} = 0.01 < 2.9011$, do not reject H_0. There is not enough evidence to conclude that there is an interaction between supplier and loom.

11.36 cont.

(b) H_0: $\mu_{jetta..} = \mu_{turk..}$ H_1: At least one mean differs.

Decision: Since $F_{STAT} = 0.81 < 4.1491$, do not reject H_0. There is insufficient evidence to conclude that there is an effect due to loom.

(c) H_0: $\mu_{.1.} = \mu_{.2.} = \mu_{.3.} = \mu_{.4.}$ H_1: At least one mean differs.

Decision: Since $F_{STAT} = 5.20 > 2.9011$, reject H_0. There is adequate evidence to conclude that there is an effect due to suppliers.

(d)

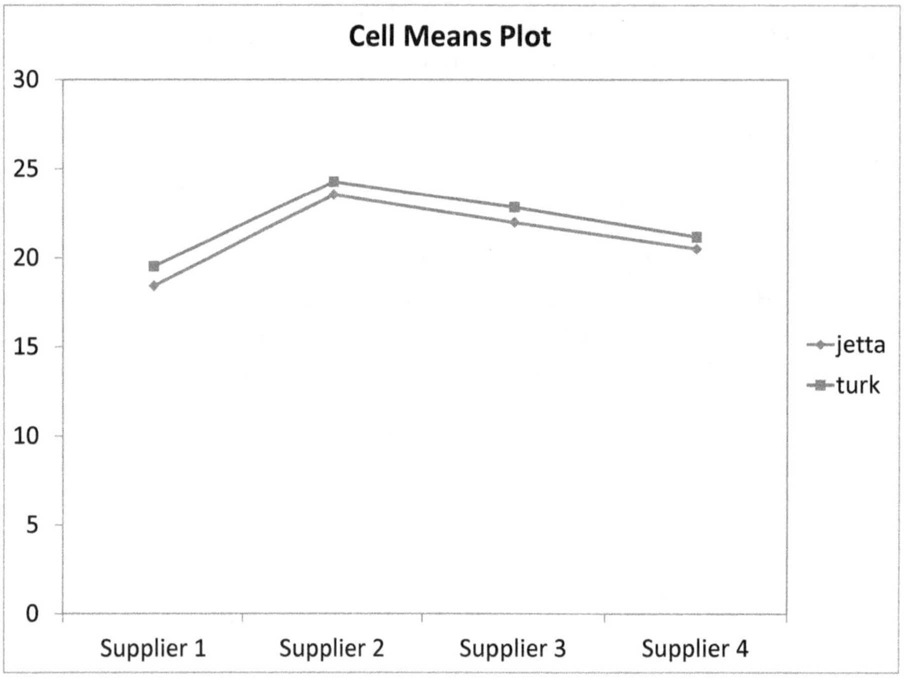

(e) Output of the Tukey Procedure:

For different suppliers, $Q_{\alpha} = 3.84$ with numerator d.f. = 4 and denominator d.f. = 32.

Tukey-Kramer Multiple Comparisons

Group	Sample Mean	Sample Size	Comparison	Absolute Difference	Std. Error of Difference	Critical Range	Results
1: Supplier 1	18.97	10	**Group 1 to Group 2**	4.93	0.92802209	3.5636	**Means are different**
2: Supplier 2	23.9	10	**Group 1 to Group 3**	3.44	0.92802209	3.5636	**Means are not different**
3: Supplier 3	22.41	10	**Group 1 to Group 4**	1.86	0.92802209	3.5636	**Means are not different**
4: Supplier 4	20.83	10	**Group 2 to Group 3**	1.49	0.92802209	3.5636	**Means are not different**
			Group 2 to Group 4	3.07	0.92802209	3.5636	**Means are not different**
			Group 3 to Group 4	1.58	0.92802209	3.5636	**Means are not different**

Other Data	
Level of significance	0.05
Numerator d.f.	4
Denominator d.f.	32
MSE	8.61225
Q Statistic	3.84

There is a difference in mean strength between supplier 1 and supplier 2 only.

11.36 (f) cont.

One-way ANOVA: Supplier 1, Supplier 2, Supplier 3, Supplier 4

Method

Null hypothesis	All means are equal
Alternative hypothesis	Not all means are equal
Significance level	α = 0.05

Equal variances were assumed for the analysis.

Factor Information

Factor	Levels	Values
Factor	4	Supplier 1, Supplier 2, Supplier 3, Supplier 4

Analysis of Variance

Source	DF	Adj SS	Adj MS	F-Value	P-Value
Factor	3	134.3	44.783	5.70	0.003
Error	36	282.9	7.857		
Total	39	417.2			

H_0: $\mu_1 = \mu_2 = \mu_3 = \mu_4$ H_1: At least one mean differs.

Decision: Since $F_{STAT} = 5.70 > 2.8663$, reject H_0. There is adequate evidence to conclude that there is an effect due to suppliers.

Output of Tukey-Kramer Procedure:

Tukey-Kramer Multiple Comparisons

Group	Sample Mean	Sample Size
1: Supplier 1	18.97	10
2: Supplier 2	23.9	10
3: Supplier 3	22.41	10
4: Supplier 4	20.83	10

Comparison	Absolute Difference	Std. Error of Difference	Critical Range	Results
Group 1 to Group 2	4.93	0.88639564	3.3594	Means are different
Group 1 to Group 3	3.44	0.88639564	3.3594	Means are different
Group 1 to Group 4	1.86	0.88639564	3.3594	Means are not different
Group 2 to Group 3	1.49	0.88639564	3.3594	Means are not different
Group 2 to Group 4	3.07	0.88639564	3.3594	Means are not different
Group 3 to Group 4	1.58	0.88639564	3.3594	Means are not different

Other Data	
Level of significance	0.05
Numerator d.f.	4
Denominator d.f.	36
MSW	7.856972
Q Statistic	3.79

The result is consistent with that in (b) and (e) except the Turkey-Kramer Procedure in the one-way ANOVA concludes that not only there is a difference in mean strength between supplier 1 and supplier 2, but there is also a difference in mean strength between supplier 1 and suppler 3.

11.38 (a) To test the homogeneity of variance, you perform a Levene's Test.

H_0: $\sigma_1^2 = \sigma_2^2 = \sigma_3^2$ H_1: Not all σ_j^2 are the same

Excel output:

ANOVA

Source of Variation	SS	df	MS	F	P-value	F crit
Between Groups	0.07	2	0.035	0.07468	0.928383	3.682317
Within Groups	7.03	15	0.468667			
Total	7.1	17				

Since the p-value = 0.928 > 0.05, do not reject H_0. There is not enough evidence of a significant difference in the variances of the breaking strengths for the three air-jet pressures.

(b) H_0: $\mu_1 = \mu_2 = \mu_3$ H_1: At least one of the means differs.

Decision rule: If $F_{STAT} > 3.68$, reject H_0.

One-way ANOVA: 30 psi, 40 psi, 50 psi

Method

Null hypothesis	All means are equal
Alternative hypothesis	Not all means are equal
Significance level	α = 0.05

Equal variances were assumed for the analysis.

Factor Information

Factor	Levels	Values
Factor	3	30 psi, 40 psi, 50 psi

Analysis of Variance

Source	DF	Adj SS	Adj MS	F-Value	P-Value
Factor	2	8.074	4.0372	4.09	0.038
Error	15	14.815	0.9877		
Total	17	22.889			

Decision: Since $F_{STAT} = 4.09$ is greater than the critical bound of 3.68, reject H_0. There is enough evidence to conclude that the mean breaking strengths differ for the three air-jet pressures.

11.38 (c)
cont.

Tukey Pairwise Comparisons

Grouping Information Using the Tukey Method and 95% Confidence

Factor	N	Mean	Grouping	
30 psi	6	24.833	A	
40 psi	6	23.533	A	B
50 psi	6	23.317		B

Means that do not share a letter are significantly different.

Tukey Simultaneous Tests for Differences of Means

Difference of Levels	Difference of Means	SE of Difference	95% CI	T-Value	Adjusted P-Value
40 psi - 30 psi	-1.300	0.574	(-2.789, 0.189)	-2.27	0.092
50 psi - 30 psi	-1.517	0.574	(-3.006, -0.028)	-2.64	0.046
50 psi - 40 psi	-0.217	0.574	(-1.706, 1.272)	-0.38	0.925

Individual confidence level = 97.97%

Breaking strength scores under 30 psi are significantly higher than those under 50 psi. No other pairwise comparisons were significant at the 0.05 significance level.

(d) Other things being equal, use 30 psi.

11.40

ANOVA

Source of Variation	*SS*	*Df*	*MS*	*F*	*P-value*	*F crit*
Sample	112.5603	1	112.5603	30.4434	3.07E-06	4.113165
Columns	46.01025	1	46.01025	12.4441	0.001165	4.113165
Interaction	0.70225	1	0.70225	0.1899	0.665575	4.113165
Within	133.105	36	3.697361			
Total	292.3778	39				

(a) H_0: There is no interaction between type of breakfast and desired time.
H_1: There is an interaction between type of breakfast and desired time.
Decision rule: If $F_{STAT} > 4.1132$, reject H_0.
Test statistic: $F_{STAT} = 0.1899$.
Decision: Since $F_{STAT} = 0.1899$ is less than the critical bound of 4.1132, do not reject H_0. There is insufficient evidence to conclude that there is any interaction between type of breakfast and desired time.

(b) H_0: $\mu_1 = \mu_2$ H_1: $\mu_1 \neq \mu_2$ Population 1 = Continental, 2 = American
Decision rule: If $F_{STAT} > 4.1132$, reject H_0.
Test statistic: $F_{STAT} = 30.4434$.
Decision: Since $F_{STAT} = 30.4434$ is greater than the critical bound of 4.1132, reject H_0. There is sufficient evidence to conclude that there is an effect that is due to type of breakfast.

11.40 cont. (c) H_0: $\mu_1 = \mu_2$ H_1: $\mu_1 \neq \mu_2$ Population 1 = Early, 2 = Late
Decision rule: If $F_{STAT} > 4.1132$, reject H_0.
Test statistic: $F_{STAT} = 12.4441$.
Decision: Since $F_{STAT} = 12.4441$ is greater than the critical bound of 4.1132, reject H_0. There is sufficient evidence to conclude that there is an effect that is due to desired time

(d)

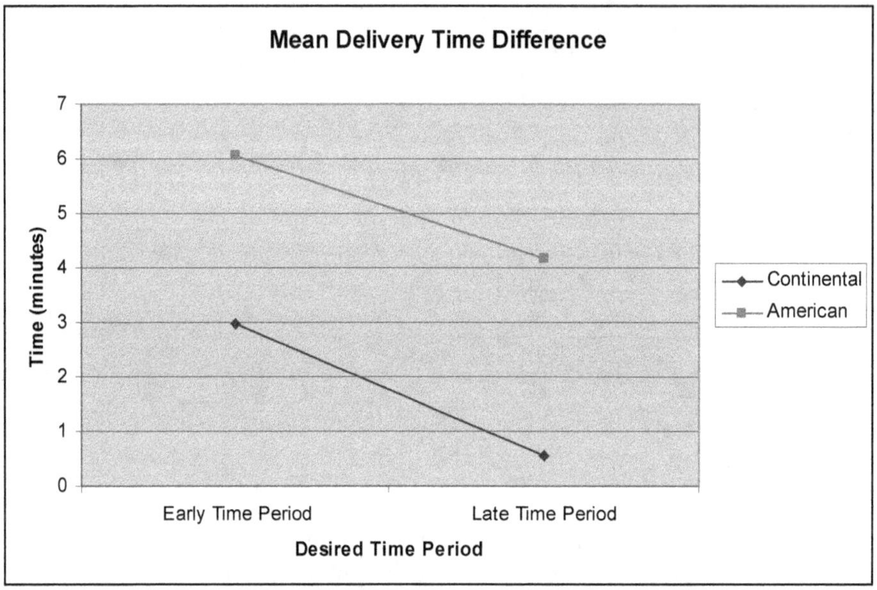

(e) At the 5% level of significance, both the type of breakfast ordered and the desired time have an effect on delivery time difference. There is no interaction between the type of breakfast ordered and the desired time.

11.42 H_0: There is no interaction between the size of the pieces and the can fill height.
H_1: There is an interaction between the size of the pieces and the can fill height.
Decision rule: If p-value < 0.05, reject H_0.

General Linear Model: Result versus Piece size, Fill Height

Method

Factor coding (-1, 0, +1)

Factor Information

Factor	Type	Levels	Values
Piece size	Fixed	2	C, F
Fill Height	Fixed	2	Current, Low

Analysis of Variance

Source	DF	Adj SS	Adj MS	F-Value	P-Value
Piece size	1	100.666	100.666	842.22	0.000
Fill Height	1	25.946	25.946	217.08	0.000
Piece size*Fill Height	1	0.026	0.026	0.22	0.643
Error	76	9.084	0.120		
Total	79	135.722			

Test statistic: $F_{STAT} = 0.2169$

11.42 cont. Decision: Since p-value is 0.6428, do not reject H_0. There is not sufficient evidence to conclude there is an interaction between the size of the pieces and the can fill height.

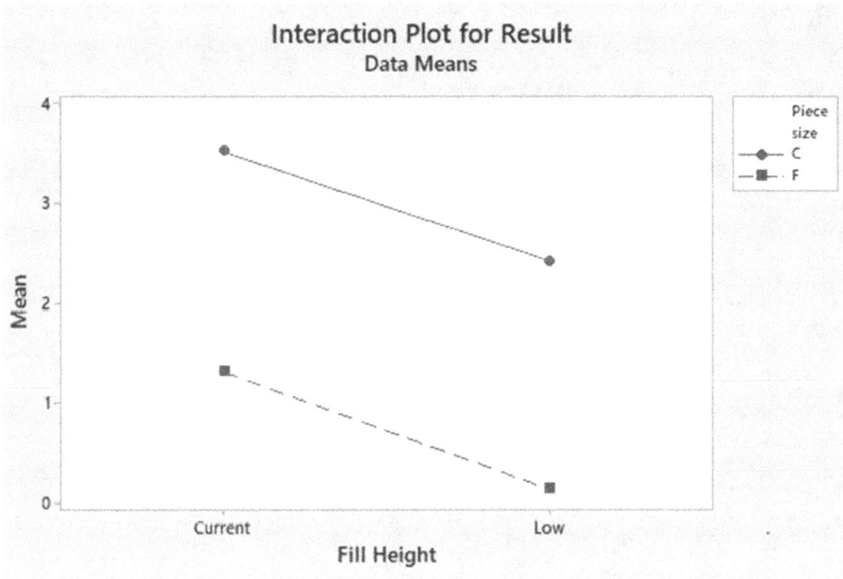

Both piece size and fill height had significant main effects. The F_{STAT} was much higher for piece size, which suggest that this factor may be of more importance relative to fill height. Filling cans with fine cut size led to more accuracy in relation to the weight of the can compared to the label weight. Filling cans with fine cut size and lower fill height led to the most accuracy in relation to the weight of the can compared to the label weight. Based on these results, one would recommend that the pet food company use the fine cut size and the lower fill height.

One-way ANOVA: Low, Current

Method

Null hypothesis	All means are equal
Alternative hypothesis	Not all means are equal
Significance level	α = 0.05

Equal variances were assumed for the analysis.

Factor Information

Factor	Levels	Values
Factor	2	Low, Current

Analysis of Variance

Source	DF	Adj SS	Adj MS	F-Value	P-Value
Factor	1	25.95	25.946	18.44	0.000
Error	78	109.78	1.407		
Total	79	135.72			

A One-Way Anova on fill height produced a $F_{STAT} = 18.44$. Because $F_{STAT} = 18.44$ or p-value = 0.000, reject H_0.

11.42
cont.

One-way ANOVA: F, C

Method

Null hypothesis	All means are equal
Alternative hypothesis	Not all means are equal
Significance level	α = 0.05

Equal variances were assumed for the analysis.

Factor Information

Factor	Levels	Values
Factor	2	F, C

Analysis of Variance

Source	DF	Adj SS	Adj MS	F-Value	P-Value
Factor	1	100.67	100.666	223.98	0.000
Error	78	35.06	0.449		
Total	79	135.72			

A One-Way Anova on cut size produced a $F_{STAT} = 223.98$. Because $F_{STAT} = 223.98$ or p-value = 0.000, reject H_0.

CHAPTER 12

12.2 (a) For $df = 1$ and $\alpha = 0.05$, $\chi^2 = 3.841$.

(b) For $df = 1$ and $\alpha = 0.025$, $\chi^2 = 5.024$.

(c) For $df = 1$ and $\alpha = 0.01$, $\chi^2 = 6.635$.

12.4 (a)

Observed Freq	*Expected Freq*	Observed Freq	*Expected Freq*	Total Obs, Row 1
20	25	30	25	50
chi-sq contrib=	1.00	chi-sq contrib=	1.00	
Observed Freq	*Expected Freq*	Observed Freq	*Expected Freq*	Total Obs, Row 2
30	25	20	25	50
chi-sq contrib=	1.00	chi-sq contrib=	1.00	
Total Obs, Col 1		Total Obs, Col 2		GRAND TOTAL
50		50		100

(b) Decision rule: If $\chi^2 > 3.841$, reject H_0.

Test statistic: $\chi^2_{STAT} = \sum_{\text{All Cells}} \frac{(f_0 - f_e)^2}{f_e} = 1.00 + 1.00 + 1.00 + 1.00 = 4$

Decision: Since $\chi^2_{STAT} = \sum_{\text{All Cells}} \frac{(f_0 - f_e)^2}{f_e} = 4$ is greater than the critical value of 3.841, it is significant at the 5% level of significance.

12.6 (a)

Chi-Square Test

Observed Frequencies			
	Made me want to		
Viewing Audience	Yes	No	Total
General TV	35	166	201
VOD D4+	147	103	250
Total	182	269	451

Expected Frequencies			
	itMade Me Want to Buy		
Viewing Audience	Yes	No	Total
General TV	81.11308	119.886918	201
VOD D4+	100.8869	149.113082	250
Total	182	269	451

Data	
Level of Significance	0.05
Number of Rows	2
Number of Columns	2
Degrees of Freedom	1

Results	
Critical Value	3.841459
Chi-Square Test Statistic	79.28996
p-Value	5.36E-19
Reject the null hypothesis	

H_0: $\pi_1 = \pi_2$ H_1: $\pi_1 \neq \pi_2$

(b) Decision rule: $df = 1$. If $\chi^2_{STAT} > 3.8415$ or p-value < 0.05, reject H_0.

Test statistic: $\chi^2_{STAT} = 79.2900$

Decision: Since χ^2 STAT = 79.2900 is larger than the upper critical bound of 3.8415, reject H_0. There is enough evidence of difference in ad impact between general TV viewing and VOD D4+ viewing.

(c) You should not compare the results in (a) to those of Problem 10.30 part (b) because Problem 10.30 was a one-tail test.

12.8 (a) H_0: $\pi_1 = \pi_2$. H_1: $\pi_1 \neq \pi_2$.

Because $\chi^2_{STAT} = (326 - 339.0878)^2/339.0878 + (97 - 83.9122)^2/83.9122 + (167 - 153.9122)^2/153.9122 + (25 - 38.0878)^2/38.0878 = 8.1566 > 6.635$, reject H_0. There is evidence of a difference in the proportion of organizations with 500 to 2,499 employees and organizations with 2,500+ employees with respect to the proportion that have employee recognition programs.

(b) p-value = 0.0043. The probability of obtaining a difference in proportions that gives rise to a test statistic above 8.1566 is 0.0043 if there is no difference in the proportion in the two groups.

12.8 cont. (c) The results of (a) and (b) are exactly the same as those of Problem 10.32. The χ^2 in (a) and the Z in Problem 10.32 (a) satisfy the relationship that $\chi^2 = 8.1566 = Z^2 = (-2.856)^2$, and the *p*-value in (b) is exactly the same as the *p*-value computed in Problem 10.32 (b).

12.10 (a)

Observed Frequencies			
	co-browsing		
use skills-based routing	Yes	No	Total
Yes	81	65	146
No	48	111	159
Total	129	176	305

(b) Because $\chi^2_{STAT} = 19.9467 > 3.841$, reject H_0. There is evidence that there is a significant difference between the proportion of cobrowsing organizations and noncobrowsing organizations that use skills-based routing to match the caller with the *right* agent.

(c) *p*-value is virtually zero. The probability of obtaining a test statistic of 19.9467 or larger when the null hypothesis is true is 0.0000.

(d) The results are identical because $(4.4662)^2 = 19.9467$.

12.12 (a) The expected frequencies in the first row are 20, 30, and 40. The expected frequencies in the second row are 30, 45, and 60.

(b) $\chi^2_{STAT} = 12.500$. The critical value with 2 degrees of freedom and $\alpha = 0.05$ is 5.991. The result is deemed significant.

12.14 (a)

Tabulated Statistics: Worksheet rows, Worksheet columns

Rows: Worksheet rows Columns: Worksheet columns

	18-29	30-49	50-64	65+	All
1	116	94	54	30	294
	73.50	73.50	73.50	73.50	
2	84	106	146	170	506
	126.50	126.50	126.50	126.50	
All	200	200	200	200	800

Cell Contents
Count
Expected count

Chi-Square Test

	Chi-Square	DF	P-Value
Pearson	96.776	3	0.000
Likelihood Ratio	101.136	3	0.000

Because the calculated test statistic 96.776 is greater than the critical value of 7.8147, you reject H_0 and conclude that there is evidence of a difference among the age groups in the proportion smartphone owners who have reached the maximum amount of data they are allowed to use as part of their plan, at least on occasion.

12.14 cont. (b) p-value = 0.0000. The probability of obtaining a data set that gives rise to a test statistic of 96.776 or more is 0.0000 if there is no difference in the proportion who have reached the maximum amount of data they are allowed to use as part of their plan, at least on occasion.

(c)

Marascuilo Procedure

Level of Significance	0.05
Square Root of Critical Value	2.795483483

Group Sample Proportions	
1: C1	0.58
2: C2	0.47
3: C3	0.27
4: C4	0.15

MARASCUILO TABLE			
Proportions	Absolute Differences	Critical Range	
| Group 1 - Group 2 |	0.11	0.138750071	Not significant
| Group 1 - Group 3 |	0.31	0.131224056	Significant
| Group 1 - Group 4 |	0.43	0.120416891	Significant
| Group 2 - Group 3 |	0.2	0.132040365	Significant
| Group 2 - Group 4 |	0.32	0.121305946	Significant
| Group 3 - Group 4 |	0.12	0.112620173	Significant

There is a significant difference between 18- to 29-year-olds and 50- to 64-years-olds and those 65 and older. There is a significant difference between 30- to 49-year-olds and 50- to 64-years-olds and those 65 and older. There is a significant difference between those who are between 50 and 64 years old and those 65 or older.

12.16 (a) H_0: $\pi_1 = \pi_2 = \pi_3$. H_1: At least one proportion differs.

Observed Frequencies				
	Group			
Compensation value	BE	HR	Employees	Total
Yes	28	76	66	170
No	172	124	134	430
Total	200	200	200	600

Expected Frequencies				
	Global Region			
Compensation Value	BE	HR	Employees	Total
Yes	56.6667	56.6667	56.6667	170
No	143.3333	143.3333	143.3333	430
Total	200	200	200	600

Data	
Level of Significance	0.05
Number of Rows	2
Number of Columns	3
Degrees of Freedom	2

Results	
Critical Value	5.9915
Chi-Square Test Statistic	31.5841
p-Value	0.0000
Reject the null hypothesis	

Because 31.5841 > 5.9915, reject H_0.
There is a significant difference among business groups with respect to the proportion that say compensation (pay and rewards) makes for a unique and compelling EVP.

(b) p-value = 0.0000. The probability of a test statistic greater than 31.5841 is 0.0000.

(c)

Level of Significance	0.05
Square Root of Critical Value	2.4477

Sample Proportions	
Group 1	0.14
Group 2	0.38
Group 3	0.33

Marascuilo Table

Proportions	Absolute Differences	Critical Range	
| Group 1 – Group 2 |	0.124	0.1033	Significant
| Group 1 – Group 3 |	0.19	0.1011	Significant
| Group 2 – Group 3 |	0.05	0.1170	Not significant

Business executives are different from HR leaders and from employees.

12.18 (a)

Tabulated Statistics: Worksheet rows, Worksheet columns

Rows: Worksheet rows Columns: Worksheet columns

	Smartphone	Computer	Tablet	All
1	320	194	141	655
	276.4	216.1	162.5	
2	124	153	120	397
	167.6	130.9	98.5	
All	444	347	261	1052

Cell Contents
Count
Expected count

Chi-Square Test

	Chi-Square	DF	P-Value
Pearson	31.689	2	0.000
Likelihood Ratio	32.201	2	0.000

Because $\chi^2_{STAT} = 31.6888 > 5.9915$, reject H_0. There is evidence of a difference in the percentage who use their device to check social media while watching TV between the groups.

(b) p-value = 0.0000.

(c)

Marascuilo Procedure for Guest Satisfaction Analysis

Level of Significance	0.05
Square Root of Critical Value	2.4477

Group Sample Proportions	
c1	0.7207
c2	0.5591
c3	0.5402

MARASCUILO TABLE			
Proportions	**Absolute Differences**	**Critical Range**	
| Group 1 - Group 2 |	**0.1616**	**0.0835**	**Significant**
| Group 1 - Group 3 |	**0.1805**	**0.0917**	**Significant**
| Group 2 - Group 3 |	**0.0188**	**0.0998**	**Not significant**

(c) Cellphone versus computer 0.1616 > 0.0835. Significant. Smartphone versus tablet: 0.1805 > 0.0917. Significant. Computer versus tablet: 0.0188 < 0.0998. Not significant. The smartphone group is different from the computer and tablet groups.

12.20 $df = (r - 1)(c - 1) = (3 - 1)(4 - 1) = 6$

12.22 H_0: There is no relationship between type of dessert and type of entrée.
H_1: There is a relationship between type of dessert and type of entrée.

$$\text{Test statistic: } \chi^2_{STAT} = \sum_{All\ cells} \frac{(f_0 - f_e)^2}{f_e}\ 92.1028$$

Decision: Since the calculated test statistic 92.1028 is larger than the critical value of 16.9190, you reject H_0 and conclude that there is enough evidence of a relationship between type of dessert and type of entrée.

12.24

Tabulated Statistics: Times Per Week, Worksheet columns

Rows: Times Per Week Columns: Worksheet columns

	18-24	35-44	45-54	55-64	65+	All
Less than 1 hour	35	25	33	10	5	108
	13.41	15.15	20.50	8.26	23.81	14.81
	38.67	24.44	23.85	17.93	3.11	
1 to less than 3	95	55	32	34	7	223
	36.40	33.33	19.88	28.10	33.33	30.59
	79.84	50.47	49.25	37.01	6.42	
3 to less than 6	60	44	42	33	5	184
	22.99	26.67	26.09	27.27	23.81	25.24
	65.88	41.65	40.64	30.54	5.30	
6 to less than 8	37	19	34	24	3	117
	14.18	11.52	21.12	19.83	14.29	16.05
	41.89	26.48	25.84	19.42	3.37	
9 hours or more	34	22	20	20	1	97
	13.03	13.33	12.42	16.53	4.76	13.31
	34.73	21.95	21.42	16.10	2.79	
All	261	165	161	121	21	729
	100.00	100.00	100.00	100.00	100.00	100.00

Cell Contents
Count
% of Column
Expected count

Chi-Square Test

	Chi-Square	DF	P-Value
Pearson	27.651	16	0.035
Likelihood Ratio	28.739	16	0.026

3 cell(s) with expected counts less than 5.

Decision: Because $\chi^2_{STAT} = 27.651$ or p-value = 0.035, reject H_0. There is evidence to conclude that there is a relationship between age and willingness to devote time to healthy activities.

12.26 Because $\chi^2_{STAT} = 81.6061 > 47.3999$ reject H_0. There is evidence of a relationship between identified main opportunity and geographic region.

12.28 (a) The lower critical value is 31.
(b) The lower critical value is 29.
(c) The lower critical value is 27.
(d) The lower critical value is 25.

12.30 The lower and upper critical values are 40 and 79, respectively.

12.32 (a) The ranks for Sample 1 are 1, 2, 4, 5, and 10, respectively.
The ranks for Sample 2 are 3, 6.5, 6.5, 8, 9, and 11, respectively.
(b) $T_1 = 1 + 2 + 4 + 5 + 10 = 22$
(c) $T_2 = 3 + 6.5 + 6.5 + 8 + 9 + 11 = 44$
(d) $T_1 + T_2 = \dfrac{n(n+1)}{2} = \dfrac{11(12)}{2} = 66 \qquad T_1 + T_2 = 22 + 44 = 66$

12.34 Decision: Since $T_1 = 22$ is greater than the lower critical bound of 20, do not reject H_0.

12.36 (a) The data are ordinal.
(b) The two-sample t test is inappropriate because the data are ordinal, the sample size is small and the distribution of the ordinal data is not normally distributed.
(c) $H_0: M_1 = M_2$ where Populations: 1 = California, 2 = Washington
$H_1: M_1 \neq M_2$

Data	
Level of Significance	0.05
Population 1 Sample	
Sample Size	8
Sum of Ranks	47

(c)

Population 2 Sample	
Sample Size	8
Sum of Ranks	89
Intermediate Calculations	
Total Sample Size n	16
T1 Test Statistic	47
T1 Mean	68
Standard Error of *T1*	9.521905
Z Test Statistic	–2.20544
Two-Tailed Test	
Lower Critical Value	**–1.95996**
Upper Critical Value	**1.959964**
***p*-value**	**0.027423**
Reject the null hypothesis	

$$\mu_{T1} = \frac{n_1(n+1)}{2} = \frac{8(16+1)}{2} = 68$$

$$\sigma_{T_1} = \sqrt{\frac{n_1 n_2 (n+1)}{12}} = \sqrt{\frac{8(8)(16+1)}{12}} = 9.5219$$

12.36 (c) $$Z_{STAT} = \frac{T_1 - \mu_{T_1}}{\sigma_{T_1}} = -2.2054$$

cont. Decision: Since $Z_{STAT} = -2.2054$ is lower than the lower critical bounds of -1.96, reject H_0. There is enough evidence of a significant difference in the median rating of California Cabernets and Washington Cabernets.

12.38 (a) H_0: $M_1 = M_2$, where Populations: 1 = Wing A, 2 = Wing B.
H_1: $M_1 \neq M_2$.
Population 1 sample: Sample size 20, sum of ranks 561
Population 2 sample: Sample size 20, sum of ranks 259

$$\mu_{T_1} = \frac{n_1(n+1)}{2} = \frac{20(40+1)}{2} = 410$$

$$\sigma_{T_1} = \sqrt{\frac{n_1 n_2 (n+1)}{12}} = \sqrt{\frac{20(20)(40+1)}{12}} = 36.9685$$

$$Z_{STAT} = \frac{T_1 - \mu_{T_1}}{S_{T_1}} = \frac{561 - 410}{36.9685} = 4.0846$$

Decision: Because $Z_{STAT} = 4.0846 > 1.96$ (or p-value $= 0.0000 < 0.05$), reject H_0. There is sufficient evidence of a difference in the median delivery time in the two wings of the hotel.

(b) The results of (a) are consistent with the results of Problem 10.65.

12.40 (a)

Wilcoxon Rank Sum Test	
Data	
Level of Significance	0.05
Population 1 Sample	
Sample Size	14
Sum of Ranks	224
Population 2 Sample	
Sample Size	19
Sum of Ranks	337
Intermediate Calculations	
Total Sample Size	33
T_1 Test Statistic	224
T_1 Mean	238
Standard Error of T_1	27.4530
Z Test Statistic	-0.5100
Two-Tail Test	
Lower Critical Value	-1.9600
Upper Critical Value	1.9600
p-Value	0.6101
Do not reject the null hypothesis	

Because $Z_{STAT} = -0.5100 > 1.96$, do not reject H_0. There is insufficient evidence to conclude that there is a difference in the median brand value between the two sectors.

12.40 cont. (b) You must assume approximately equal variability in the two populations.

(c) Using the pooled-variance t test and the separate-variance t test, the decision was to not reject the null hypothesis. From all three tests, the decision was the same, to not reject the null hypothesis and to conclude that there is no difference in median brand value for the two sectors.

12.42 (a)

Wilcoxon Rank Sum Test	
Data	
Level of Significance	0.05
Population 1 Sample	
Sample Size	27
Sum of Ranks	859
Population 2 Sample	
Sample Size	31
Sum of Ranks	852
Intermediate Calculations	
Total Sample Size	58
T_1 Test Statistic	859
T_1 Mean	796.5
Standard Error of T_1	64.1502
Z Test Statistic	0.9743
Two-Tail Test	
Lower Critical Value	-1.9600
Upper Critical Value	1.9600
p-Value	0.3299
Do not reject the null hypothesis	

Because $-1.96 < Z_{STAT} = 0.9743 < 1.96$, do not reject H_0. There is not enough evidence to conclude that there is a difference in the median rating of 60-second and 30-second ads.

(b) You must assume approximately equal variability in the two populations.

(c) Using the pooled-variance t test, you do not reject the null hypothesis ($t = -2.0032 < t_{STAT} = 1.15 < 2.0032$; p-value $= 0.4301 > 0.05$) and conclude that there is insufficient evidence of a difference in the mean rating of ads before and after halftime in Problem 10.11 (a).

12.44 (a) Decision rule: If $H > \chi^2_\alpha = 15.086$, reject H_0.

(b) Decision: Since $H_{calc} = 13.77$ is less than the critical bound of 15.086, do not reject H_0.

12.46 Kruskal-Wallis rank test:

Data	
Level of Significance	0.05
Group 1	
Sum of Ranks	640
Sample Size	15
Group 2	
Sum of Ranks	291
Sample Size	15
Group 3	
Sum of Ranks	468
Sample Size	15
Group 4	
Sum of Ranks	431
Sample Size	15
Intermediate Calculations	
Sum of Squared Ranks/Sample Size	59937.73
Sum of Sample Sizes	60
Number of groups	4
H Test Statistic	13.51716
Test Result	
Critical Value	**7.814728**
***p*-Value**	**0.003642**
Reject the null hypothesis	

(a) H_0: $M_{main} = M_{Sat1} = M_{Sat2} = M_{Sat3}$ H_1: At least one of the medians differs.
Since the *p*-value = 0.0036 is lower than 0.05, reject H_0. There is sufficient evidence of a difference in the median waiting time in the four locations.

(b) The results are consistent with those of Problem 11.9.

12.48 Kruskal-Wallis rank test:

Data	
Level of Significance	0.05
Intermediate Calculations	
Sum of Squared Ranks/Sample Size	8705.333
Sum of Sample Sizes	30
Number of Groups	5
Test Result	
H Test Statistic	19.32688
Critical Value	9.487729
p-Value	0.000678
Reject the null hypothesis	

(a) H_0: $M_A = M_B = M_C = M_D = M_E$ H_1: At least one of the medians differs.
Since the *p*-value = 0.0007 < 0.05, reject H_0. There is sufficient evidence of a difference in the median rating of the five advertisements.

(b) In (a), you conclude that there is evidence of a difference in the median rating of the five advertisements, while in problem 11.10 (a), you conclude that there is evidence of a difference in the mean rating of the five advertisements.

(c) Since the combined scores are not true continuous variables, the nonparametric Kruskal-Wallis rank test is more appropriate because it does not require the scores to be normally distributed.

12.50

Kruskal-Wallis Test: Cost to import (US$) versus Region

Descriptive Statistics

Region	N	Median	Mean Rank	Z-Value
East Asia & Pacific	10	352.0	15.3	-1.62
Eastern Europe & Central Asia	10	228.0	12.6	-2.47
Latin American & Carribbean	10	635.5	28.3	2.44
Middle East & North Africa	10	645.0	25.8	1.66
Overall	40		20.5	

Test

Null hypothesis H₀: All medians are equal

Alternative hypothesis H₁: At least one median is different

DF	H-Value	P-Value
3	13.05	0.005

(a) Because $H = 13.0522 > 7.815$ or the p-value is 0.0045, reject H_0. There is sufficient evidence of a difference in the median cost associated with importing a standardized cargo of goods by sea transport across the global regions.

(b) The results are similar. The ANOVA F_{STAT} also indicates that there is a difference in import costs among the four regions.

12.52 The Chi-square test can be used for c populations as long as all expected frequencies are at least one.

12.54 The Wilcoxon rank sum test should be used when you are unable to assume that each of two independent populations are normally distributed.

12.56

Chi-Square Test for Association: gender, Worksheet columns

Rows: gender Columns: Worksheet columns

	pizza hut	other	All
f	4	13	17
	4.857	12.143	
m	6	12	18
	5.143	12.857	
All	10	25	35

Cell Contents
Count
Expected count

Chi-Square Test

	Chi-Square	DF	P-Value
Pearson	0.412	1	0.521
Likelihood Ratio	0.414	1	0.520

1 cell(s) with expected counts less than 5.

(a) H_0: There is no relationship between a student's gender and his/her pizzeria selection.
H_1: There is a relationship between a student's gender and his/her pizzeria selection.
Decision rule: $d.f. = 1$. If $\chi^2_{STAT} > 3.841$, reject H_0. Test statistic: $\chi^2_{STAT} = 0.412$
Decision: Since the $\chi^2_{STAT} = 0.412$ is smaller than the critical bound of 3.841, do not reject H_0. There is not enough evidence to conclude that there is a relationship between a student's gender and his/her pizzeria selection.

12.56 cont. (a)

Chi-Square Test for Association: gender, Worksheet columns

Rows: gender Columns: Worksheet columns

	pizza hut	other	All
f	4	13	17
	6.314	10.686	
m	9	9	18
	6.686	11.314	
All	13	22	35

Cell Contents
Count
Expected count

Chi-Square Test

	Chi-Square	DF	P-Value
Pearson	2.624	1	0.105
Likelihood Ratio	2.676	1	0.102

(b) Test statistic: $\chi^2_{STAT} = 2.624$

Decision: Since the $\chi^2_{STAT} = 2.624$ is less than the critical bound of 3.841, do not reject H_0. There is not enough evidence to conclude that there is a relationship between a student's gender and his/her pizzeria selection.

Chi-Square Test for Association: Pizzeria, Worksheet columns

Rows: Pizzeria Columns: Worksheet columns

	\$8.49	\$11.49	\$14.49	All
Pizza Hut	10	5	2	17
	6.467	5.174	5.359	
Other	25	23	27	75
	28.533	22.826	23.641	
All	35	28	29	92

Cell Contents
Count
Expected count

Chi-Square Test

	Chi-Square	DF	P-Value
Pearson	4.956	2	0.084
Likelihood Ratio	5.346	2	0.069

(c) H_0: There is no relationship between price and pizzeria selection.
H_1: There is a relationship between price and pizzeria selection.

12.56 (c) Decision rule: $d.f. = 2$. If $\chi^2_{STAT} > 5.991$, reject H_0. Test statistic: $\chi^2_{STAT} = 4.956$

cont. Decision: Since the $\chi^2_{STAT} = 4.956$ is smaller than the critical bound of 5.991, do not reject H_0. There is not enough evidence to conclude that there is a relationship between price and pizzeria selection.

(d) p-value = 0.0839. The probability of obtaining a sample that gives a test statistic equal to or greater than 4.956 is 0.0839 if the null hypothesis of no relationship between price and pizzeria selection is true.

12.58

Chi-Square Test for Association: Embarked, Worksheet columns

Rows: Embarked Columns: Worksheet columns

	Finance	Healthcare	Manufacturing	Transport	Wholesale/Retail	All
Yes	70	51	149	26	50	346
	64.09	46.44	145.83	26.01	63.63	
No	68	49	165	30	87	399
	73.91	53.56	168.17	29.99	73.37	
All	138	100	314	56	137	745

Cell Contents
Count
Expected count

Chi-Square Test

	Chi-Square	DF	P-Value
Pearson	7.430	4	0.115
Likelihood Ratio	7.515	4	0.111

12.58 cont. (a) Because $\chi^2_{STAT} = 7.4298 < 9.4877$; p-value $= 0.1148 > 0.05$ do not reject H_0. There is not enough evidence to conclude that there is evidence of a difference in the proportion of organizations that have embarked on digital transformation on the basis of industry sector.

Chi-Square Test for Association: Progress, Worksheet columns

Rows: Progress Columns: Worksheet columns

	Finance	Healthcare	Manufacturing	Transport	Wholesale/Retail	All
Planning	7	15	15	5	10	52
	10.52	7.66	22.39	3.91	7.51	
Testing	31	12	24	5	11	83
	16.79	12.23	35.74	6.24	11.99	
Implementing	12	12	54	9	15	102
	20.64	15.03	43.92	7.66	14.74	
Outcomes delivered	20	12	56	7	14	109
	22.05	16.07	46.94	8.19	15.75	
All	70	51	149	26	50	346

Cell Contents
Count
Expected count

Chi-Square Test

	Chi-Square	DF	P-Value
Pearson	38.090	12	0.000
Likelihood Ratio	35.567	12	0.000

(b) Because $\chi^2_{STAT} = 38.09 > 21.0261$; p-value $= 0.0001 < 0.05$ reject H_0. There is evidence of a relationship between digital transformation progress and industry sector.

CHAPTER 13

13.2 (a) yes
(b) no
(c) no
(d) yes

13.4 (a)

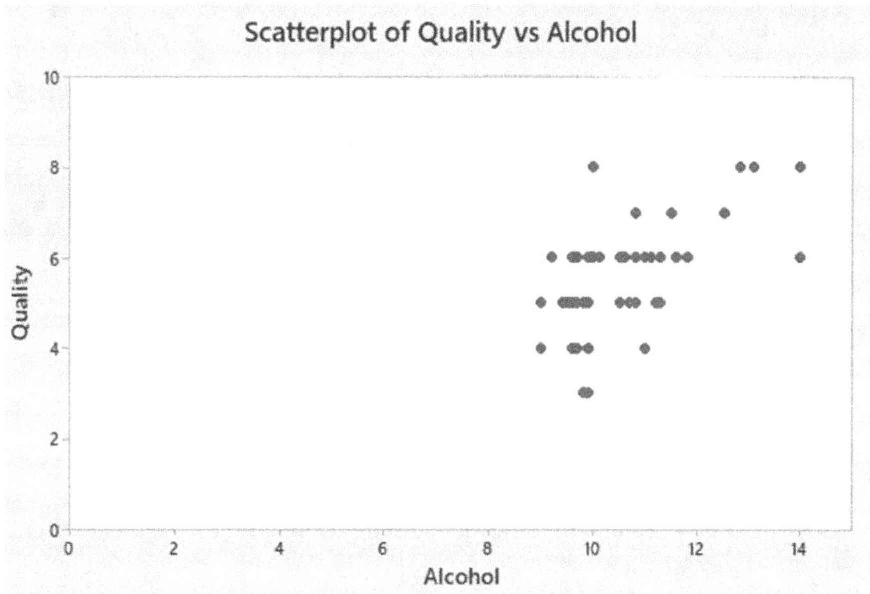

The scatter plot shows a positive linear relationship.

(b) For each % increase in alcohol content, there is an expected increase in quality of an estimated 0.5624.

(c) $\hat{Y} = -0.3529 + 0.5624X = -0.3529 + 0.5624(10) = 5.2715$

(d) There appears to be a positive linear relationship between quality and % alcohol content. For each % increase in alcohol content, there is an expected increase in quality of an estimated 0.5624.

13.6 (a)

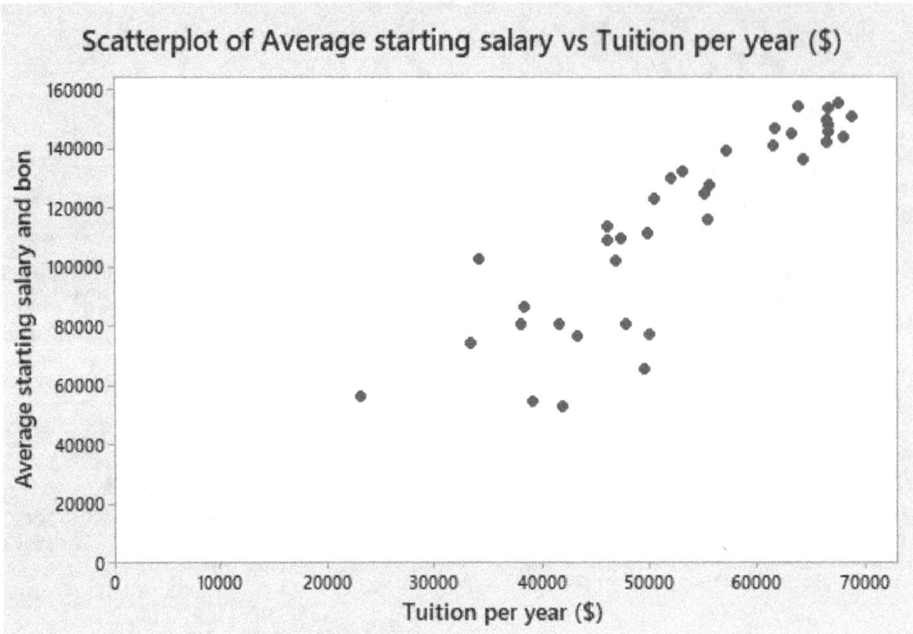

(b) $b_0 = -13{,}130.6592$, $b_1 = 2.4218$.

(c) For each increase of $1,000 in tuition, the mean starting salary is predicted to increase by $2,421.80.

(d) $109,047.01

(e) Starting salary seems higher for those schools that have a higher tuition.

13.8 (a)

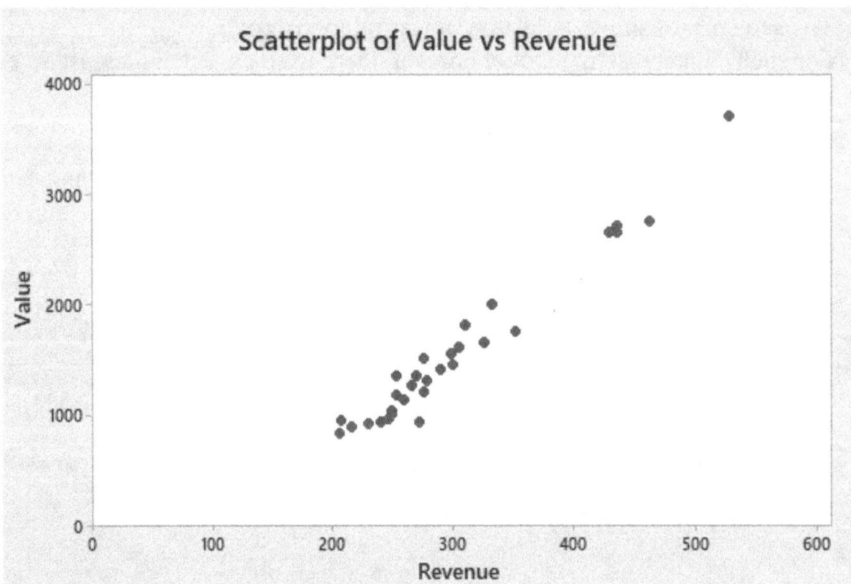

(b) $b_0 = -1{,}039.5317$, $b_1 = 8.5816$.

(c) For each additional million dollar increase in revenue, the mean value is predicted to increase by an estimated $8.5816 million. Literal interpretation of b_0 is not meaningful because an operating franchise cannot have zero revenue.

(d) $1,105.864 million.

(e) That the value of the franchise can be expected to increase as revenue increases.

13.10 (a)

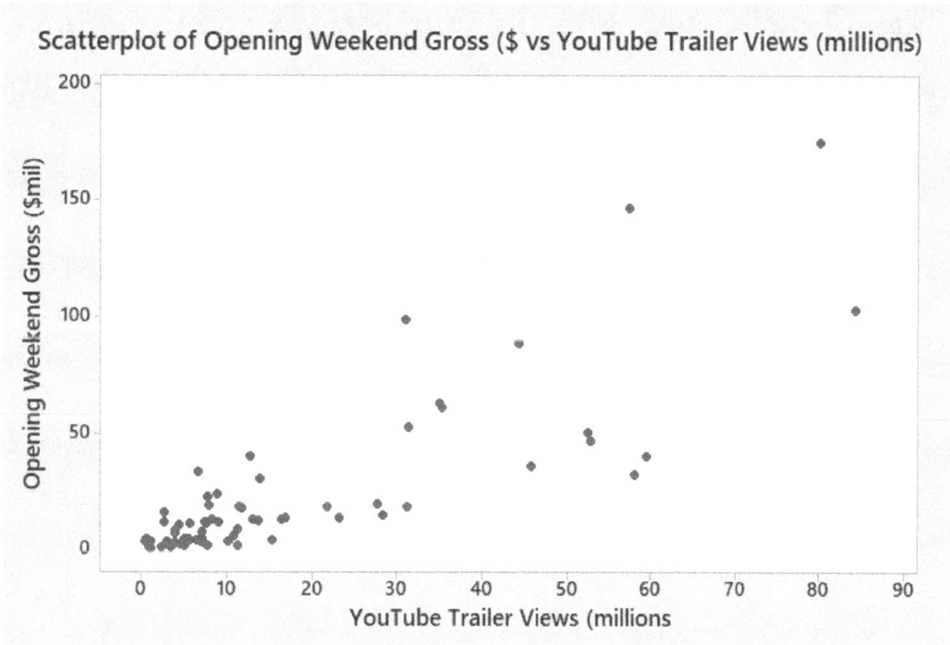

(b) $b_0 = -0.7744$, $b_1 = 1.4030$.

(c) For each increase of one million YouTube trailer views, the predicted weekend box office gross is estimated to increase by \$1.4030 million.

(d) \$27.2847 million.

(e) You can conclude that the mean predicted increase in weekend box office gross is \$1.4030 million for each one million increase in YouTube trailer views.

13.12 $SST = 40$ and $r^2 = 0.90$. So, 90% of the variation in the dependent variable can be explained by the variation in the independent variable.

13.14 $r^2 = 0.75$. So, 75% of the variation in the dependent variable can be explained by the variation in the independent variable.

13.16 (a) $r^2 = \frac{SSR}{SST} = 0.3417$. So, 34.17% of the variation in wine quality can be explained by the variation in alcohol content.

(b) $S_{YX} = \sqrt{\frac{42.1323}{48}} = 0.9369$

(c) Based on (a) and (b), the model should be moderately useful for predicting wine quality.

13.18

Regression Analysis: Average starting salary and bon ... on per year ($)

Analysis of Variance

Source	DF	Adj SS	Adj MS	F-Value	P-Value
Regression	1	29201020760	29201020760	114.86	0.000
Tuition per year ($)	1	29201020760	29201020760	114.86	0.000
Error	35	8897814652	254223276		
Lack-of-Fit	34	8879343610	261157165	14.14	0.208
Pure Error	1	18471042	18471042		
Total	36	38098835411			

Model Summary

S	R-sq	R-sq(adj)	R-sq(pred)
15944.4	76.65%	75.98%	74.05%

Coefficients

Term	Coef	SE Coef	T-Value	P-Value	VIF
Constant	-13131	12161	-1.08	0.288	
Tuition per year ($)	2.422	0.226	10.72	0.000	1.00

Regression Equation

Average starting salary and bon = -13131 + 2.422 Tuition per year ($)

(a) $r^2 = 0.7665$. 76.65% of the variation in starting salary can be explained by the variation in tuition.

(b) $S_{YX} = 15{,}944.3807$.

(c) Based on (a) and (b), the model should be very useful for predicting the starting salary.

13.20

Regression Analysis: Value versus Revenue

Analysis of Variance

Source	DF	Adj SS	Adj MS	F-Value	P-Value
Regression	1	13752399	13752399	693.52	0.000
Revenue	1	13752399	13752399	693.52	0.000
Error	28	555238	19830		
Lack-of-Fit	25	493675	19747	0.96	0.608
Pure Error	3	61563	20521		
Total	29	14307637			

Model Summary

S	R-sq	R-sq(adj)	R-sq(pred)
140.819	96.12%	95.98%	95.31%

Coefficients

Term	Coef	SE Coef	T-Value	P-Value	VIF
Constant	-1040	101	-10.26	0.000	
Revenue	8.582	0.326	26.33	0.000	1.00

Regression Equation

Value = -1040 + 8.582 Revenue

(a) $r^2 = 0.9612$, 96.12% of the variation in the value of a baseball franchise can be explained by the variation in its annual revenue.

(b) $S_{YX} = 140.8188$

(c) Based on (a) and (b), the model should be very useful for predicting the value of a baseball franchise.

13.22

Regression Analysis: Opening Weekend Gross ($mil) ... Views (millions

Analysis of Variance

Source	DF	Adj SS	Adj MS	F-Value	P-Value
Regression	1	48605	48605.0	128.55	0.000
YouTube Trailer Views (millions	1	48605	48605.0	128.55	0.000
Error	64	24198	378.1		
Total	65	72803			

Model Summary

S	R-sq	R-sq(adj)	R-sq(pred)
19.4447	66.76%	66.24%	60.90%

Coefficients

Term	Coef	SE Coef	T-Value	P-Value	VIF
Constant	-0.77	3.21	-0.24	0.810	
YouTube Trailer Views (millions	1.403	0.124	11.34	0.000	1.00

Regression Equation

Opening Weekend Gross ($mil) = -0.77 + 1.403 YouTube Trailer Views (millions

(a) $r^2 = 0.6676$, 66.76% of the variation in weekend box office gross can be explained by the variation in YouTube trailer views.

(b) $S_{YX} = 19.4447$.

(c) Based on (a) and (b), the model should be useful for predicting weekend box office gross.

(d) Other variables that might explain the variation in weekend box office gross could be the amount spent on advertising, the timing of the release of the movie, and the type of movie.

13.24 A residual analysis of the data indicates a pattern, with sizable clusters of consecutive residuals that are either all positive or all negative. This pattern indicates a violation of the assumption of linearity. A curvilinear model should be investigated.

13.26

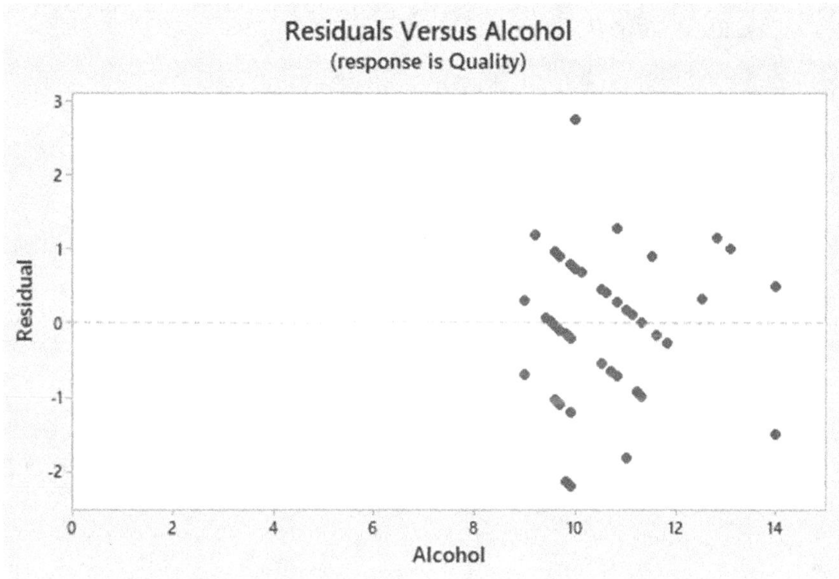

Based on the residual plot, there does not appear to be a pattern in the residual plot. There is no apparent violation of the linearity and equal variance assumptions.

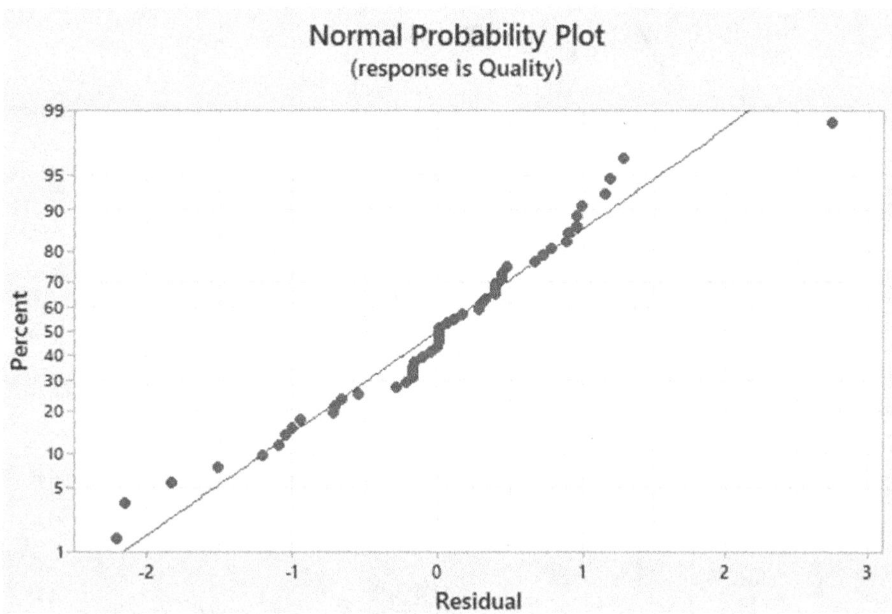

The normal probability plot suggests possible departure from the normality assumption.

13.28

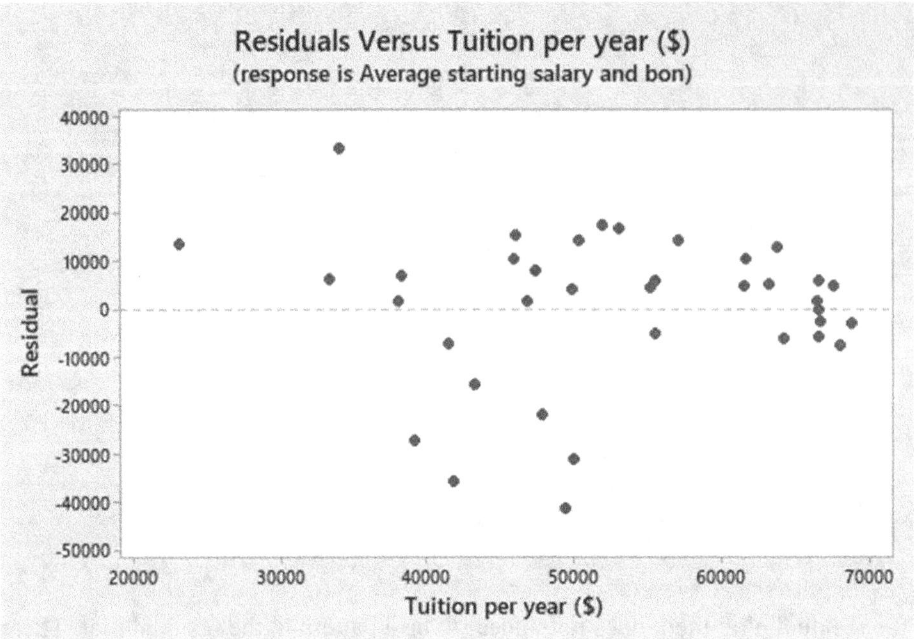

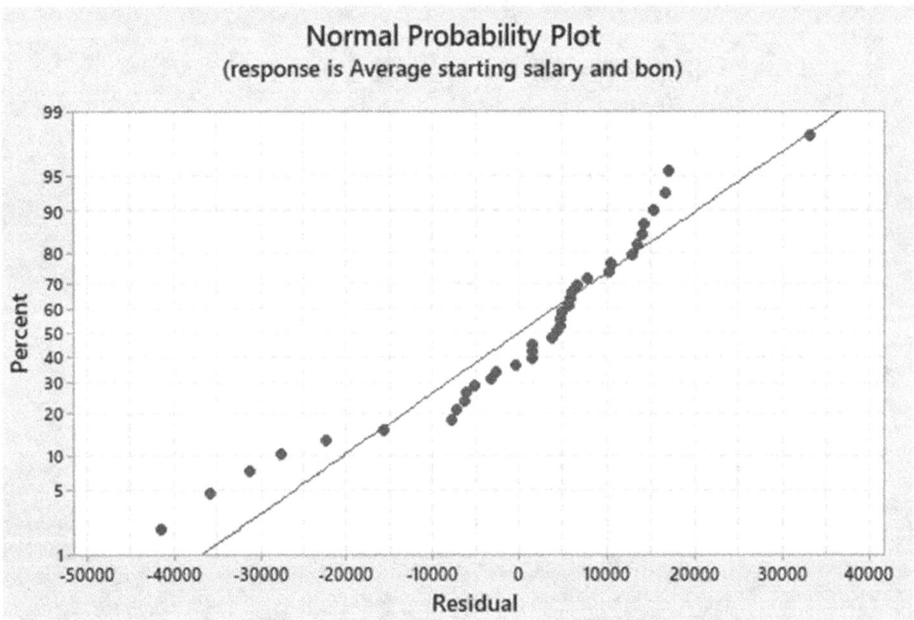

Based on the residual plot, the assumption of equal variance may be violated. The normal probability plot suggests possible departure from the normality assumption.

13.30

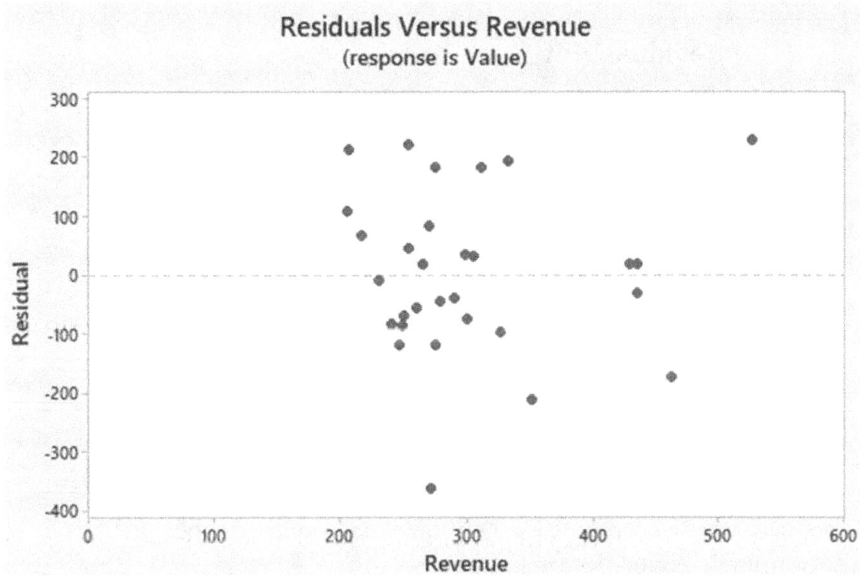

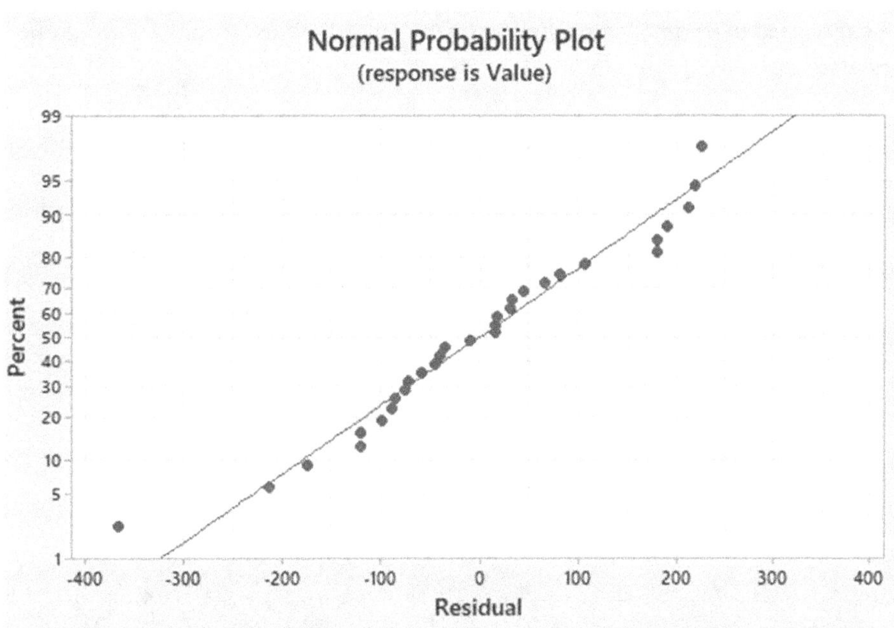

Based on the residual plot, there is no evidence of a pattern. There is no evidence of a violation of the linearity and equal variance assumptions. The normal probability plot reveals no evidence of substantial departure from the normality assumption.

13.32 (a)

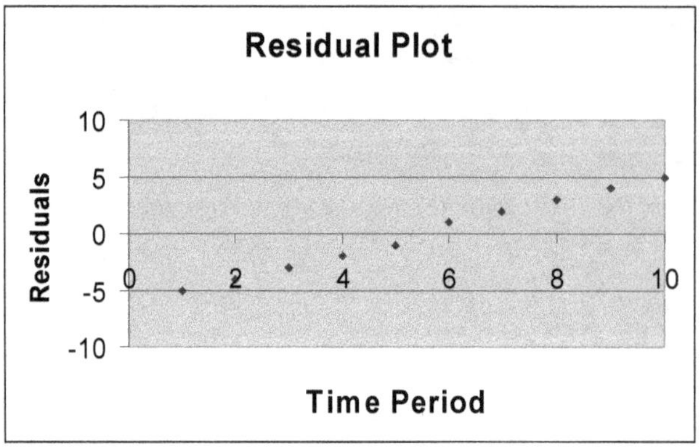

An increasing linear relationship exists.

(b) There appears to be strong positive autocorrelation among the residuals.

13.34 (a) No, it is not necessary to compute the Durbin-Watson statistic since the data have been collected for a single period for a set of bags.

(b) If a single bag-sealing equipment was studied over a period of time and the amount of plate gap varied over time, computation of the Durbin-Watson statistic would be necessary.

13.36 (a) $b_1 = \frac{SSXY}{SSX} = \frac{201399.05}{12495626} = 0.0161$

$b_0 = \overline{Y} - b_1\overline{X} = 71.2621 - 0.0161(4393) = 0.458$

(b) $\hat{Y} = 0.458 + 0.0161X = 0.458 + 0.0161(4500) =$ 72.908 or \$72,908

(c)

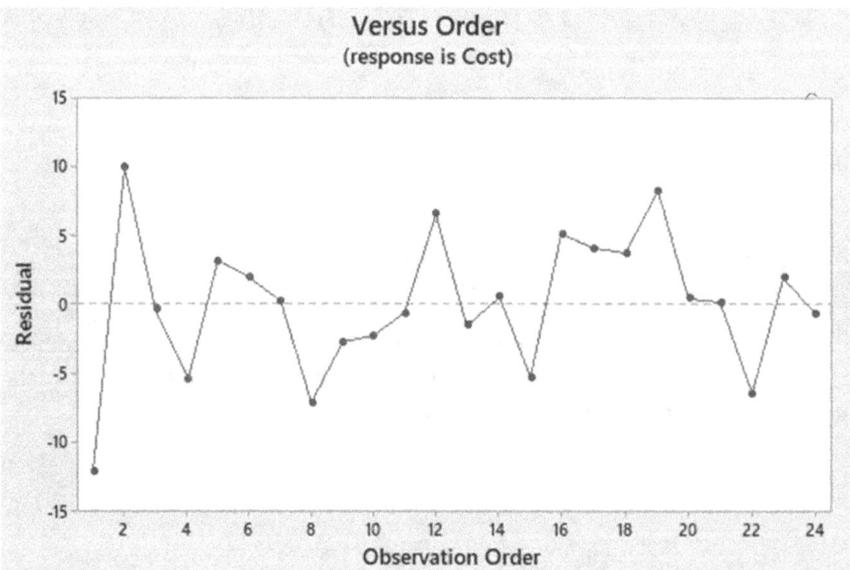

13.36 (d) $D = \frac{\sum_{i=2}^{n}(e_i - e_{i-1})^2}{\sum_{i=1}^{n} e_i^2} = \frac{1243.2244}{599.0683} = 2.08 > 1.45.$

cont. There is no evidence of positive autocorrelation among the residuals.

(e) Based on a residual analysis, the model appears to be adequate.

(f) It appears that the number of orders affects the monthly distribution costs.

13.38 (a) $b_0 = -2.535$, $b_1 = 0.060728$

(b) $\hat{Y} = -2.535 + 0.060728X = -2.535 + 0.060728(83) = 2.5054$

(c)

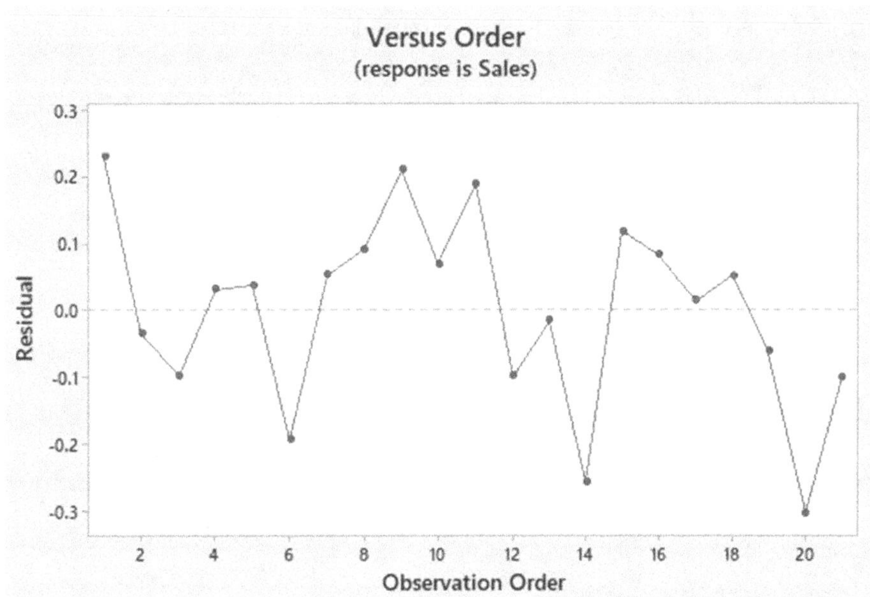

(d) $D = 1.64 > 1.42$. There is no evidence of positive autocorrelation among the residuals.

(e) The plot of the residuals versus time period shows some clustering of positive and negative residuals for intervals in the domain, suggesting a nonlinear model might be better. Otherwise, the model appears to be adequate.

(f) There appears to be a positive relationship between sales and atmospheric temperature.

13.40 (a) $H_0 : \beta_1 = 0 \qquad H_1 : \beta_1 \neq 0$

Test statistic: $t_{STAT} = (b_1 - 0)/s_{b_1} = 4.5/1.5 = 3.00$

(b) With $n = 18$, df $= 18 - 2 = 16$, $t_{0.05/2} = \pm 2.1199$.

(c) Reject H_0. There is evidence that the fitted linear regression model is useful.

(d) $b_1 - t_{0.05/2}s_{b_1} \leq \beta_1 \leq b_1 + t_{0.05/2}s_{b_1}$

$4.5 - 2.1199(1.5) \leq \beta_1 \leq 4.5 + 2.1199(1.5)$

$1.32 \leq \beta_1 \leq 7.68$

13.42 (a) $H_0 : \beta_1 = 0$ $H_1 : \beta_1 \neq 0$

	Coefficients	Standard Error	t Stat	P-value	Lower 95%	Upper 95%
Intercept	-0.3529	1.2000	-0.2941	0.7700	-2.7656	2.0599
alcohol	0.5624	0.1127	4.9913	0.0000	0.3359	0.7890

$t_{STAT} = \frac{b_1 - \beta_1}{S_{b_1}}$ = 4.9913 with a p-value = 0.0000 < 0.05. Reject H_0. There is enough evidence to conclude that the fitted linear regression model is useful.

(b) $b_1 \pm t_{\alpha/2} S_{b_1}$ $0.3359 \leq \beta_1 \leq 0.7890$

13.44

Regression Analysis: Average starting salary and bon ... on per year ($)

Analysis of Variance

Source	DF	Adj SS	Adj MS	F-Value	P-Value
Regression	1	29201020760	29201020760	114.86	0.000
Tuition per year ($)	1	29201020760	29201020760	114.86	0.000
Error	35	8897814652	254223276		
Lack-of-Fit	34	8879343610	261157165	14.14	0.208
Pure Error	1	18471042	18471042		
Total	36	38098835411			

Model Summary

S	R-sq	R-sq(adj)	R-sq(pred)
15944.4	76.65%	75.98%	74.05%

Coefficients

Term	Coef	SE Coef	T-Value	P-Value	VIF
Constant	-13131	12161	-1.08	0.288	
Tuition per year ($)	2.422	0.226	10.72	0.000	1.00

(a) t_{STAT} = 10.7174 > 2.0301; p-value = 0.0000 < 0.05 reject H_0. There is evidence of a linear relationship between tuition and starting salary.

(b) $1.963 \leq \beta_1 \leq 2.8805$

13.46

Regression Analysis: Value versus Revenue

Analysis of Variance

Source	DF	Adj SS	Adj MS	F-Value	P-Value
Regression	1	13752399	13752399	693.52	0.000
Revenue	1	13752399	13752399	693.52	0.000
Error	28	555238	19830		
Lack-of-Fit	25	493675	19747	0.96	0.608
Pure Error	3	61563	20521		
Total	29	14307637			

Model Summary

S	R-sq	R-sq(adj)	R-sq(pred)
140.819	96.12%	95.98%	95.31%

Coefficients

Term	Coef	SE Coef	T-Value	P-Value	VIF
Constant	-1040	101	-10.26	0.000	
Revenue	8.582	0.326	26.33	0.000	1.00

(a) $t_{STAT} = 26.3347 > 2.0484$ or because the p-value is 0.0000, reject H_0 at the 5% level of significance. There is evidence of a linear relationship between annual revenue and franchise value.

(b) $7.9141 \le \beta_1 \le 9.2491$

13.48

Regression Analysis: Opening Weekend Gross ($mil) ... Views (millions

Analysis of Variance

Source	DF	Adj SS	Adj MS	F-Value	P-Value
Regression	1	48605	48605.0	128.55	0.000
YouTube Trailer Views (millions	1	48605	48605.0	128.55	0.000
Error	64	24198	378.1		
Total	65	72803			

Model Summary

S	R-sq	R-sq(adj)	R-sq(pred)
19.4447	66.76%	66.24%	60.90%

Coefficients

Term	Coef	SE Coef	T-Value	P-Value	VIF
Constant	-0.77	3.21	-0.24	0.810	
YouTube Trailer Views (millions	1.403	0.124	11.34	0.000	1.00

(a) $t_{STAT} = 11.3381 > 1.9977$ or because the p-value $= 0.0000 < 0.05$; reject H_0. There is evidence of a linear relationship between YouTube trailer views and weekend box office gross.

(b) $1.1558 \le \beta_1 \le 1.6501$

13.50 (a) (% daily change in SPUU) = b_0 + 2.0 (% daily change in S&P 500 index).
(b) If the S&P 500 gains 10% in a year, SPUU is expected to gain an estimated 20%.
(c) If the S&P 500 loses 20% in a year, SPUU is expected to lose an estimated 40%.
(d) Risk takers will be attracted to leveraged funds, and risk-averse investors will stay away.

13.52 (a) **First weekend gross and the U. S. gross**
$r = 0.7284$. There appears to be a strong positive linear relationship.
First weekend gross and the worldwide gross
$r = 0.8233$. There appears to be a strong positive linear relationship.
U. S. gross, and worldwide gross
$r = 0.9642$ There appears to be a very strong positive linear relationship.
(b) **First weekend gross and the U. S. gross**
Since $t_{stat} = 2.6042 > 2.4469$ and p-value $= 0.0404 < 0.05$, reject H_0. At the 0.05 level of significance, there is evidence of a linear relationship between first weekend sales and U.S. gross.
First weekend gross and the worldwide gross
Since $t_{stat} = 3.5532 > 2.4469$ and p-value $= 0.0120 < 0.05$, reject H_0. At the 0.05 level of significance, there is evidence of a linear relationship between first weekend sales and worldwide gross.
U. S. gross, and worldwide gross
Since $t_{stat} = 8.9061 > 2.4469$ and p-value $= 0.0001 < 0.05$, reject H_0. At the 0.05 level of significance, there is evidence of a linear relationship between U.S. gross and worldwide gross.

13.54

Correlation: GDP per capita, Social Media Usage (%)

Correlations

Pearson correlation	0.567
P-value	0.002

(a) $r = 0.567$ with p-value of 0.002 indicates that there is a moderate linear relationship between social media networking and the GDP per capita.
(b) $t_{STAT} = 3.45$, p-value $= 0.002 < 0.05$. Reject H_0. At the 0.05 level of significance, there is sufficient evidence of a linear relationship between social media networking and the GDP per capita.
(c) There appears to be a significant linear relationship.

13.56 (a) When $X = 4$, $\hat{Y} = 5 + 3X = 5 + 3(4) = 17$

$$h = \frac{1}{n} + \frac{(X_i - \bar{X})^2}{\sum_{i=1}^{n}(X_i - \bar{X})^2} = \frac{1}{20} + \frac{(4-2)^2}{20} = 0.25$$

95% confidence interval: $\hat{Y} \pm t_{0.05/2} S_{YX}\sqrt{h} = 17 \pm 2.1009 \cdot 1 \cdot \sqrt{0.25}$
$15.95 \le \mu_{Y|X=4} \le 18.05$

(b) 95% prediction interval: $\hat{Y} \pm t_{0.05/2} S_{YX}\sqrt{1+h} = 17 \pm 2.1009 \cdot 1 \cdot \sqrt{1.25}$
$14.651 \le Y_{X=4} \le 19.349$

13.56 cont. (c) The intervals in this problem are wider than the intervals in Exercise 13.55 because the value of X is farther from $\bar{X}$.

13.58 (a) $4.9741 \le \mu_{Y|X=10} \le 5.568984094$

(b) $3.3645 \le Y_{X=10} \le 7.178609919$

(c) Part (b) provides a prediction interval for the individual response given a specific value of the independent variable, and part (a) provides an interval estimate for the mean value, given a specific value of the independent variable. Because there is much more variation in predicting an individual value than in estimating a mean value, a prediction interval is wider than a confidence interval estimate.

13.60 (a) $\$103{,}638.95 \le \mu_{Y|X=50,450} \le \$114{,}455.06$

(b) $\$76{,}229.52 \le Y_{X=50,450} \le \$141{,}864.49$

(c) You can estimate a mean more precisely than you can predict a single observation.

13.62 (a) $1{,}043.1911 \le \mu_{Y|X=250} \le 1{,}168.5370$

(b) $810.6799 \le Y_{X=250} \le 1{,}401.0480$

(c) Because there is much more variation in predicting an individual value than in estimating a mean, the prediction interval is wider than the confidence interval.

13.64 The slope of the line, b_1, represents the estimated expected change in Y per unit change in X. It represents the estimated mean amount that Y changes (either positively or negatively) for a particular unit change in X. The Y intercept b_0 represents the estimated mean value of Y when X equals 0.

13.66 The unexplained variation or error sum of squares (SSE) will be equal to zero only when the regression line fits the data perfectly and the coefficient of determination equals 1.

13.68 Unless a residual analysis is undertaken, you will not know whether the model fit is appropriate for the data. In addition, residual analysis can be used to check whether the assumptions of regression have been seriously violated.

13.70 The normality of error assumption can be evaluated by obtaining a histogram, boxplot, and/or normal probability plot of the residuals. The homoscedasticity assumption can be evaluated by plotting the residuals on the vertical axis and the X variable on the horizontal axis. The independence of errors assumption can be evaluated by plotting the residuals on the vertical axis and the time order variable on the horizontal axis. This assumption can also be evaluated by computing the Durbin-Watson statistic.

13.72 The confidence interval for the mean response estimates the mean response for a given X value. The prediction interval estimates the value for a single item or individual.

13.74 (a) $b_0 = 24.84$, $b_1 = 0.14$

(b) 24.84 is the portion of estimated mean delivery time that is not affected by the number of cases delivered. For each additional case, the estimated mean delivery time increases by 0.14 minutes.

(c) $\hat{Y} = 24.84 + 0.14 \quad X = 24.84 + 0.14(150) = 45.84$

(d) No, 500 cases is outside the relevant range of the data used to fit the regression equation.

13.74 cont. (e) $r^2 = 0.972$. So, 97.2% of the variation in delivery time can be explained by the variation in the number of cases.

(f) Based on a visual inspection of the graphs of the distribution of residuals and the residuals versus the number of cases, there is no pattern. The model appears to be adequate.

(g) $t = 24.88 > t_{0.05/2} = 2.1009$ with 18 degrees of freedom for $\alpha = 0.05$. Reject H_0. There is evidence that the fitted linear regression model is useful.

(h) $44.88 \le \mu_{Y|X=150} \le 46.80$

$41.56 \le Y_{X=150} \le 50.12$

13.76 (a) $b_0 = 326.5935$, $b_1 = 0.0835$.

(b) For each additional square foot of living space in the house, the mean asking price is predicted to increase by \$83.50. The estimated asking price of a house with 0 living space is 326.5935 thousand dollars. However, this interpretation is not meaningful because the living space of the house cannot be 0.

(c) $\hat{Y} = 493.6769$ thousand dollars.

(d) $r^2 = 0.3979$. So 39.79% of the variation in asking price is explained by the variation in living space.

(e) Neither the residual plot nor the normal probability plot reveals any potential violation of the linearity, equal variance, and normality assumptions.

(f) $t_{STAT} = 6.2436 > 2.0010$, p-value is 0.0000. Because p-value < 0.05, reject H_0. There is evidence of a linear relationship between asking price and living space.

(g) $0.0568 \le \beta_1 \le 0.1103$

(h) The living space in the house is somewhat useful in predicting the asking price, but because only 39.79% of the variation in asking price is explained by variation in living space, other variables should be considered.

13.78 (a) $b_0 = 21.2034$, $b_1 = -0.1517$.

(b) For each additional point on the efficiency ratio, the predicted mean tangible common equity (ROATCE) is estimated to decrease by 0.1517. For an efficiency of 0, the predicted mean tangible common equity (ROATCE) is 21.2034.

(c) 12.0989.

(d) $r^2 = 0.1882$.

(e) There is no obvious pattern in the residuals, so the assumptions of regression are met. The model appears to be adequate.

(f) $t_{STAT} = -4.7662 < -1.9845$; reject H_0. There is evidence of a linear relationship between efficiency ratio and tangible common equity (ROATCE).

(g) $11.4060 \le \mu_{Y|X=60} \le 12.7918$, $5.1534 \le Y_{X=60} \le 19.0444$

(h) $-0.2149 \le \beta_1 \le -0.0886$ (i) There is a small relationship between efficiency ratio and tangible common equity (ROATCE).

13.80 (a)

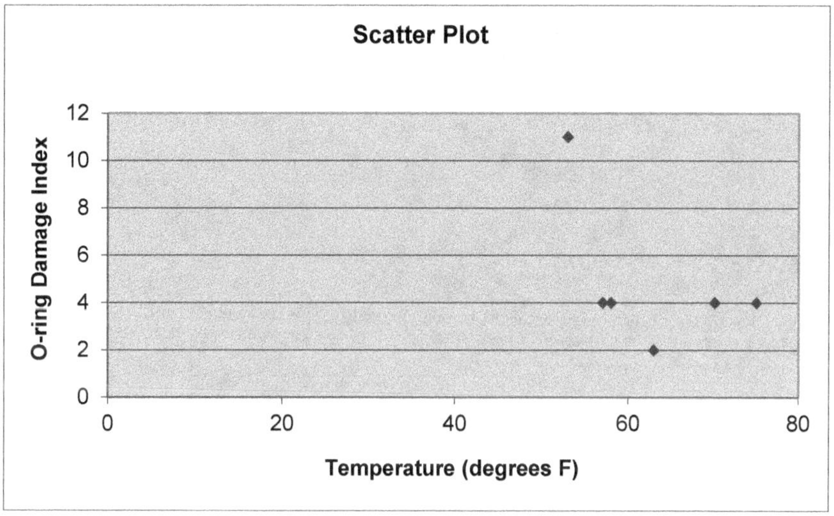

There is not any clear relationship between atmospheric temperature and O-ring damage from the scatter plot.

(b)

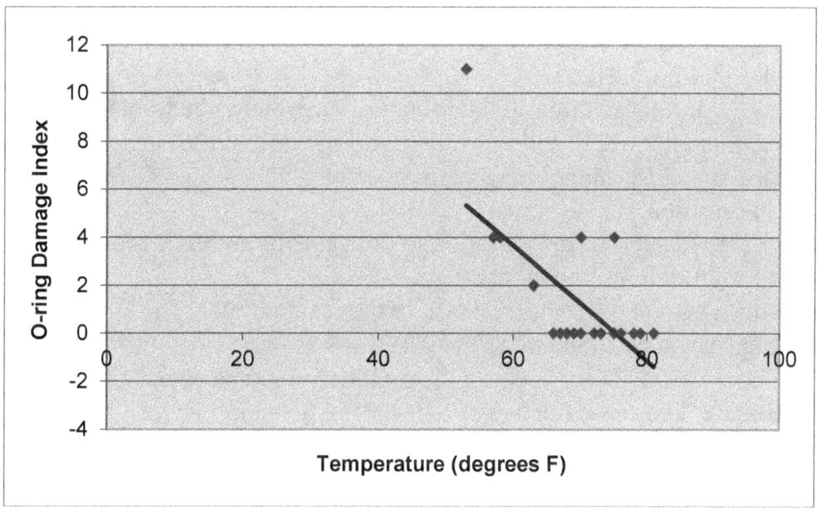

(c) In (b), there are 16 observations with an O-ring damage index of 0 for a variety of temperatures. If one concentrates on these observations with no O-ring damage, there is obviously no relationship between O-ring damage index and temperature. If all observations are used, the observations with no O-ring damage will bias the estimated relationship. If the intention is to investigate the relationship between the degrees of O-ring damage and atmospheric temperature, it makes sense to focus only on the flights in which there was O-ring damage.

(d) Prediction should not be made for an atmospheric temperature of 31 ^{0}F because it is outside the range of the temperature variable in the data. Such prediction will involve extrapolation, which assumes that any relationship between two variables will continue to hold outside the domain of the temperature variable.

(e) $\hat{Y} = 18.036 - 0.240X$

(g) A nonlinear model is more appropriate for these data.

13.80 (h)
cont.

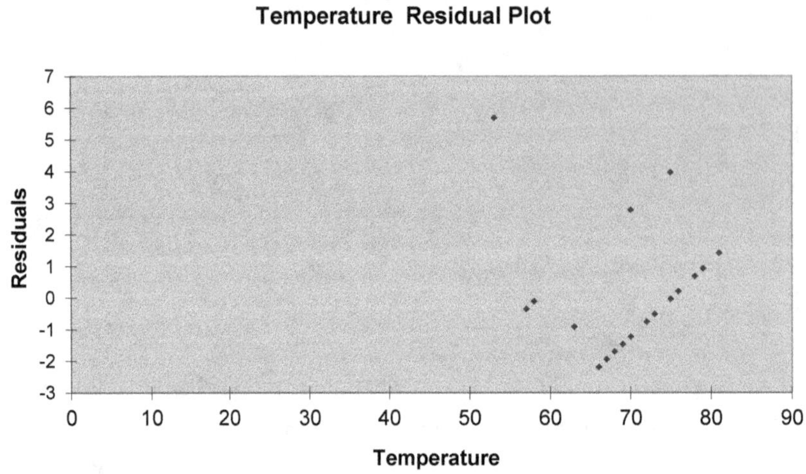

The string of negative residuals and positive residuals that lie on a straight line with a positive slope in the lower-right corner of the plot is a strong indication that a nonlinear model should be used if all 23 observations are to be used in the fit.

13.82 (a) $b_0 = -1.348$, $b_1 = 0.01211$.

(b) For each additional million-dollar increase in revenue, the franchise value will increase by an estimated 0.01211 billion. Literal interpretation of b_0 is not meaningful because an operating franchise cannot have zero revenue.

(c) \$469.117 million.

(d) $r^2 = 0.8288$. 82.88% of the variation in the value of an NBA franchise can be explained by the variation in its annual revenue.

(e) There does not appear to be a pattern in the residual plot. The assumptions of regression do not appear to be seriously violated.

(f) $t_{STAT} = 11.64 > 2.0484$ or because the p-value is 0.0000, reject H_0 at the 5% level of significance. There is evidence of a linear relationship between annual revenue and franchise value.

(g) $0.1913 \le \mu_{Y|X=150} \le 0.74697$ billons

(h) $-0.2569 \le Y_{X=150} \le 1.1951$ billons

(i) The strength of the relationship between revenue and value is approximately the same for NBA franchises and for European soccer teams but lower than for Major League Baseball teams.

13.84 (a) $b_0 = -2{,}629.222$, $b_1 = 82.472$.

(b) For each additional centimeter in circumference, the weight is estimated to increase by 82.472 grams.

(c) 2,319.08 grams.

(d) Yes, because circumference is a very strong predictor of weight.

(e) $r^2 = 0.937$.

(f) There appears to be a nonlinear relationship between circumference and weight.

(g) p-value is virtually $0 < 0.05$; reject H_0.

(h) $72.7875 \le \beta_1 \le 92.156$.

CHAPTER 14

14.2 (a) Holding constant the effect of X_2, for each increase of one unit in X_1, the response variable Y is estimated to decrease an average of 2 units. Holding constant the effect of X_1, for each increase of one unit in X_2, the response variable Y is estimated to increase an average of 7 units.

(b) The Y-intercept 50 is the estimate of the mean value of Y if X_1 and X_2 are both 0.

14.4 (a) $\hat{Y} = 1.3960 - 0.0117X_1 + 0.0286X_2$

(b) For a given capital adequacy, for each increase of 1% in efficiency ratio, ROAA decreases by 0.0117%. For a given efficiency ratio, for each increase of 1% in capital adequacy, ROAA increases by 0.0286%

(c) $\hat{Y} = 1.1214$

(d) $1.0798 \le \mu_{Y|X} \le 1.1629$

(e) $0.5679 \le Y_X \le 1.6749$

(f) The interval in (e) is narrower because it is estimating the mean value, not an individual value.

(g) The model uses both the efficiency ratio and capital adequacy to predict ROAA. This may produce a better model than if only one of these independent variables is included.

14.6 (a) $\hat{Y} = 301.78 + 3.4771X_1 + 41.041X_2$

(b) For a given amount of voluntary turnover, for each increase of \$1 billion in worldwide revenue, the mean number of full-time jobs added is predicted to increase by 3.4771. For a given \$1 billion in worldwide revenue, for each increase of 1% in voluntary turnover, the mean number of full-time jobs added is predicted to increase by 41.041.

(c) The Y intercept has no meaning in this problem.

(d) Holding the other independent variable constant, voluntary turnover has a higher slope than worldwide revenue.

14.8 (a) $\hat{Y} = 532.2883 + 407.1346X_1 - 2.8257X_2$ where $X_1 = \text{Land}$, $X_2 = \text{Age}$

(b) For a given age, each increase by one acre in land area is estimated to result in a mean increase in fair market value of \$407.1346 thousands. For a given acreage, each increase of one year in age is estimated to result in the mean decrease in fair market value of \$2.8257 thousands.

(c) The interpretation of b_0 has no practical meaning here because it would have meant the estimated mean fair market value of a new house that has no land area.

(d) $\hat{Y} = 532.2883 + 407.1346(.25) - 2.8257(55) = \$478.6577$ thousands.

(e) $446.8367 \le \mu_{Y|X} \le 510.4788$

(f) $307.2577 \le Y_X \le 650.0577$

14.10 (a) $MSR = SSR / k = 30 / 2 = 15$
$MSE = SSE / (n - k - 1) = 120 / 10 = 12$

(b) $F_{STAT} = MSR / MSE = 15 / 12 = 1.25$

(c) $F_{STAT} = 1.25 < F_{U(2,13-2-1)} = 4.103$. Do not reject H_0. There is not sufficient evidence of a significant linear relationship.

14.10 (d) $r^2 = \frac{SSR}{SST} = \frac{30}{150} = 0.2$

cont. (e) $r^2_{adj} = 1 - \left[\left(1 - r^2_{Y.12}\right) \frac{n-1}{n-k-1} \right] = 0.04$

14.12 p-value for revenue is 0.0395 < 0.05 and the p-value for efficiency is less than 0.0001 < 0.05. Reject H_0 for each of the independent variables. There is evidence of a significant linear relationship with each of the independent variables.

14.14

Regression Analysis: ROAA (%) versus Efficiency Ratio ... Capital Ratio

Analysis of Variance

Source	DF	Adj SS	Adj MS	F-Value	P-Value
Regression	2	5.927	2.96353	37.84	0.000
Efficiency Ratio (%)	1	2.235	2.23477	28.53	0.000
Total Risk-Based Capital Ratio	1	2.200	2.19954	28.08	0.000
Error	196	15.352	0.07833		
Total	198	21.279			

Model Summary

S	R-sq	R-sq(adj)	R-sq(pred)
0.279869	27.85%	27.12%	23.99%

(a) $F_{STAT} = 37.8384 > 3.00$; reject H_0.

(b) p-value = 0.0000. The probability of obtaining an F_{STAT} value > 37.8384 if the null hypothesis is true is 0.0000.

(c) $r^2 = 0.2785$. 27.85% of the variation in ROAA can be explained by variation in efficiency ratio and variation in risk-based capital.

(d) $r^2_{adj} = 0.2712$

14.16 (a) $F_{STAT} = 1.95 < 3.15$; Do not reject H_0. There is insufficient evidence of a significant linear relationship.

(b) p-value = 0.1512. The probability of obtaining an F_{STAT} value > 1.95 if the null hypothesis is true is 0.1512.

(c) $r^2 = 0.0610$. 6.10% of the variation in full-time jobs added can be explained by variation in worldwide revenue and variation in full-time voluntary turnover.

(d) $r^2_{adj} = 0.0297$

14.18

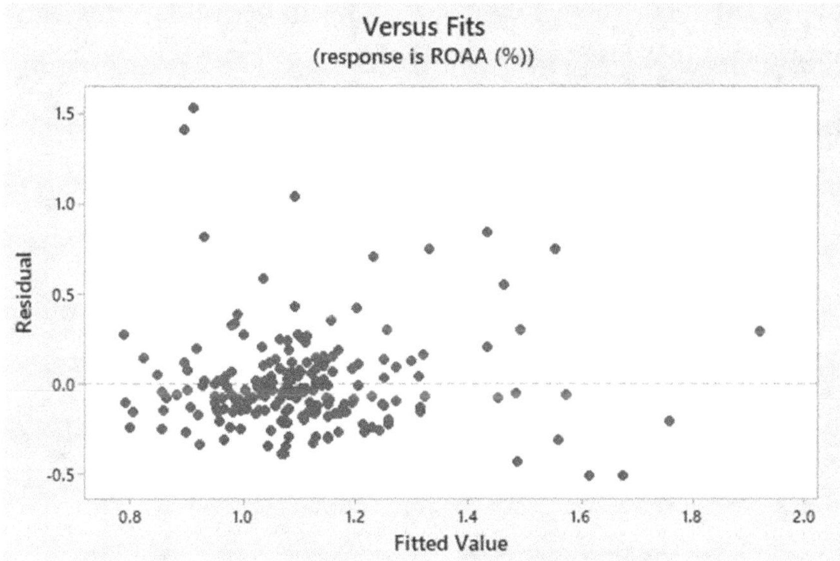
Versus Fits
(response is ROAA (%))
Residual
1.5
1.0
0.5
0.0
-0.5
0.8
1.0
1.2
1.4
1.6
1.8
2.0
Fitted Value

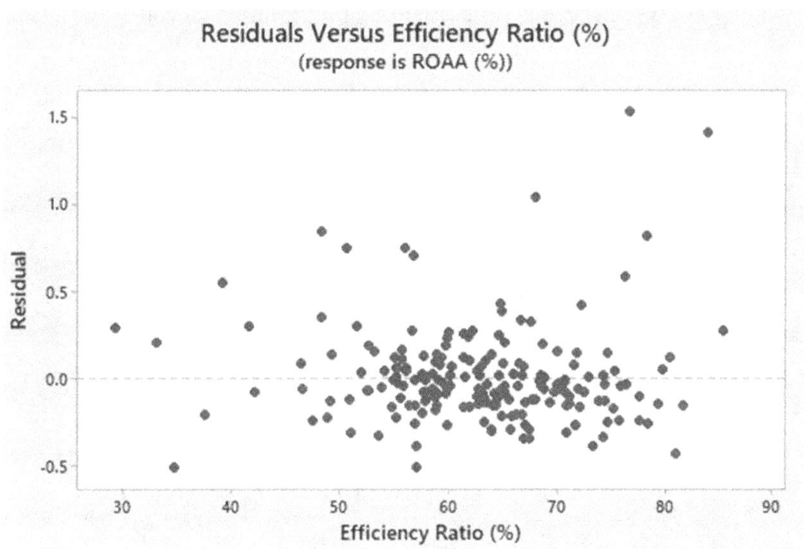
Residuals Versus Efficiency Ratio (%)
(response is ROAA (%))
Residual
1.5
1.0
0.5
0.0
-0.5
30
40
50
60
70
80
90
Efficiency Ratio (%)

14.18
cont.

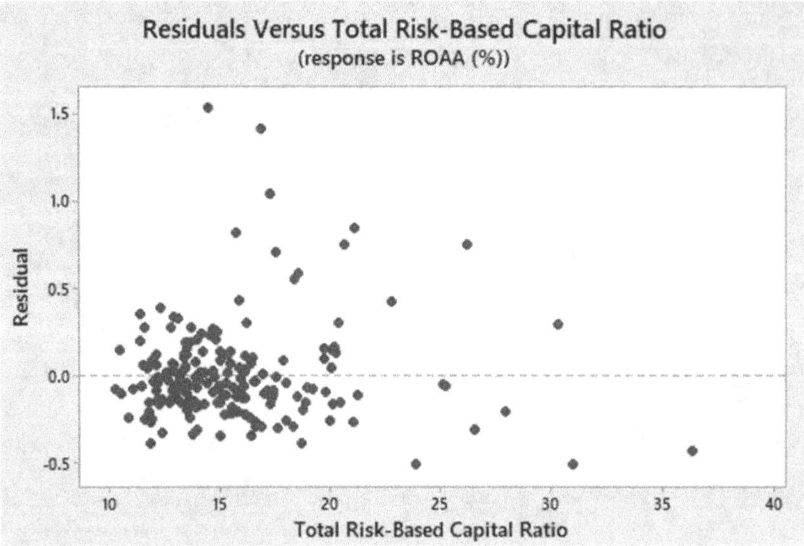

(a)–(d) Based on a residual analysis, there is no evidence of a violation of the assumptions of regression.

14.20

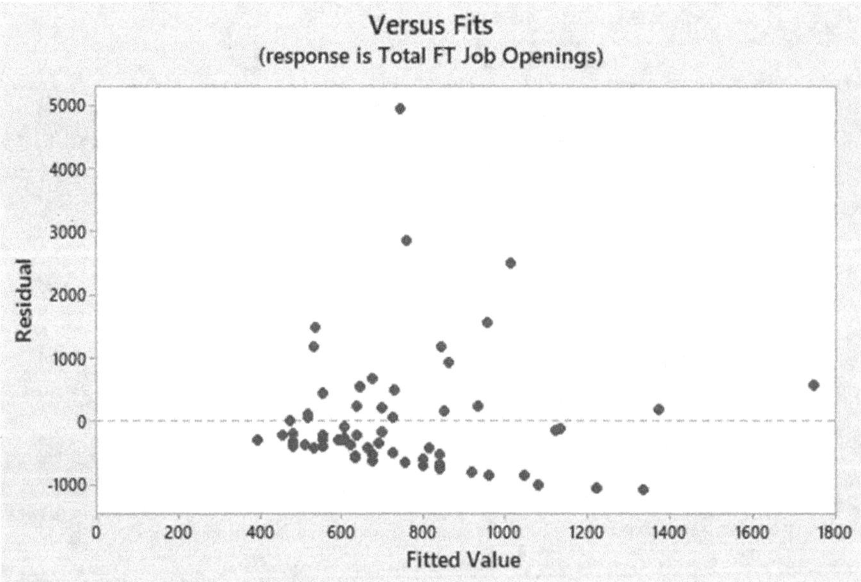

14.20
cont.

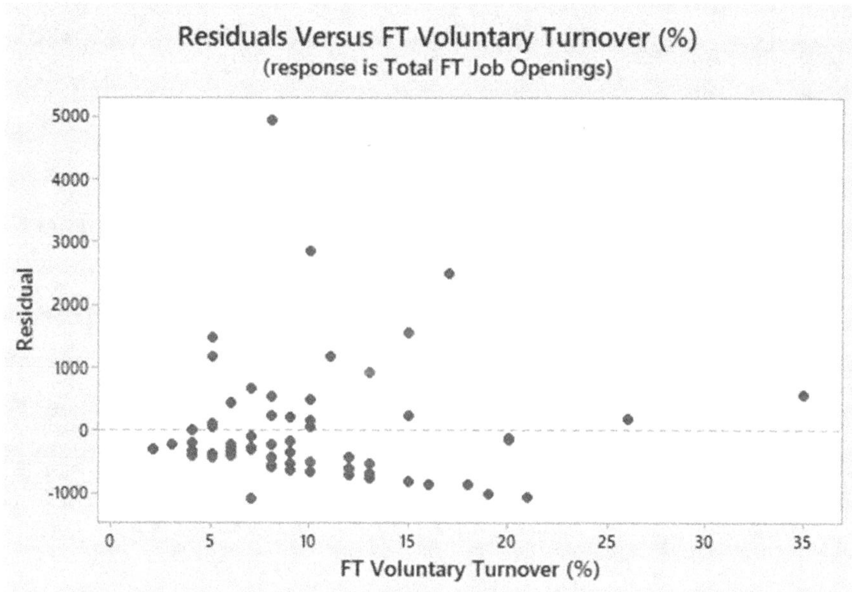

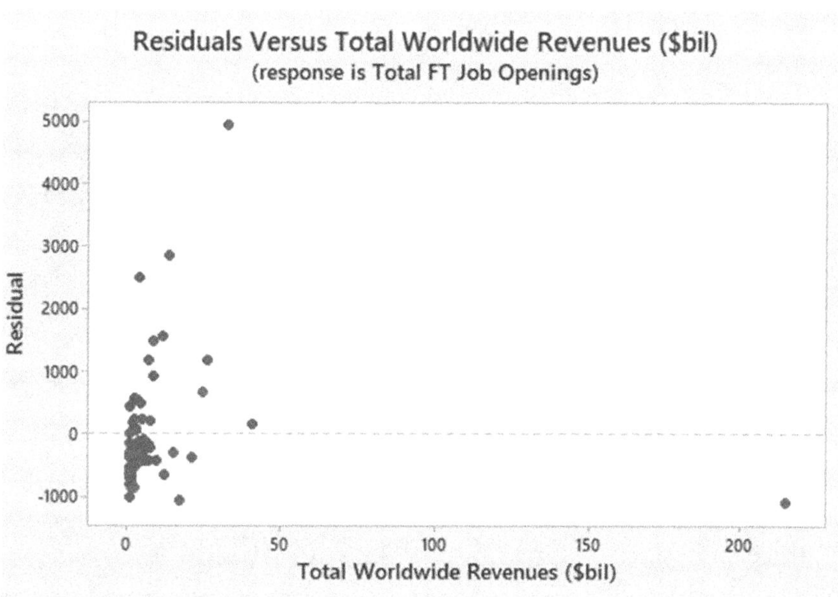

(a) Because the residual plots revealed patterns, there is evidence of a potential violation of the assumptions
(b) Because the data are not collected over time, the Durbin-Watson test is not appropriate.
(c) They may not be valid

14.22 (a)

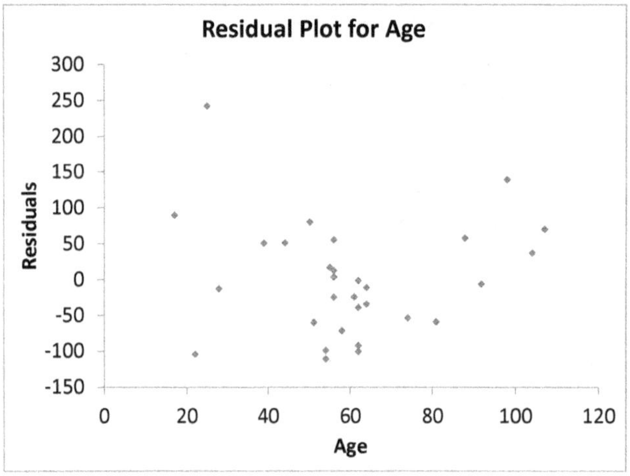

The residual analysis reveals no patterns.

(b) Since the data set is cross-sectional, the Durbin-Watson test is not appropriate.

(c) There are no apparent violations of the assumptions.

14.24 (a) The slope of X_2 in terms of the t statistic is 3.75 which is larger than the slope of X_1 in terms of the t statistic which is 3.33.

(b) 95% confidence interval on β_1 : $b_1 \pm t_{n-k-1} s_{b_1}$, $4 \pm 2.1098(1.2)$

$1.46824 \le \beta_1 \le 6.53176$

(c) For X_1: $t_{STAT} = \frac{b_1}{s_{b_1}} = \frac{4}{1.2} = 3.33 > t_{17} = 2.1098$ with 17 degrees of freedom for $\alpha = 0.05$.

Reject H_0. There is evidence that the variable X_1 contributes to a model already containing X_2.

For X_2: $t_{STAT} = \frac{b_2}{s_{b_2}} = \frac{3}{0.8} = 3.75 > t_{17} = 2.1098$ with 17 degrees of freedom for $\alpha = 0.05$.

Reject H_0. There is evidence that the variable X_2 contributes to a model already containing X_1. Both variables X_1 and X_2 should be included in the model.

14.26 (a) 95% confidence interval on β_1: $b_1 \pm tS_{b_1}$, $-0.0117 \pm 1.98(0.0022)$,

$-0.0161 \le \beta_1 \le -0.0074$

(b) For X_1 : $t_{STAT} = \frac{b_1}{S_{b_1}} = \frac{-0.0177}{0.0022} = -5.3415 < -1.98$. Reject H_0. There is evidence that X_1 contributes to a model already containing X_2.

For X_2 : $t_{STAT} = \frac{b_2}{S_{b_2}} = \frac{0.0286}{0.0054} = 5.2992 > 1.98$. Reject H_0.

There is evidence that X_2 contributes to a model already containing X_1. Both X_1 (efficiency ratio) and X_2 (total risk-based capital) should be included in the model.

14.28 (a) $-5.8682 \le \beta_1 \le 12.8225$

(b) For X_1 : t_{STAT} =0.7443 < 2.0003. Do not reject H_0. There is insufficient evidence that X_1 contributes to a model already containing X_2.
For X_2 : t_{STAT} = 1.8835 < 2.0003. Do not reject H_0. There is insufficient evidence that X_2 contributes to a model already containing X_1. Neither variable contributes to a model that includes the other variable. You should consider using only a simple linear regression model.

14.30 (a)

	Coefficients	Standard Error	t Stat	P-value	Lower 95%	Upper 95%
Intercept	532.2883	48.6661	10.9376	0.0000	432.4338	632.1428
Property Size (acre:	407.1346	64.8028	6.2827	0.0000	274.1702	540.0990
Age	-2.8257	0.6813	-4.1475	0.0003	-4.2236	-1.4278

$274.1702 \le \beta_1 \le 540.0990$

(b) For X_1: $t_{STAT} = \frac{b_1}{s_{b_1}} = 6.2827$ and p-value = 0.0000. Since p-value < 0.05, reject H_0.

There is evidence that the variable X_1 contributes to a model already containing X_2.

For X_2: $t_{STAT} = \frac{b_2}{s_{b_2}} = -4.1475$ and p-value = 0.0003. Since p-value < 0.05, reject H_0.

There is evidence that the variable X_2 contributes to a model already containing X_1. Both variables X_1 and X_2 should be included in the model.

14.32 (a) For X_1: $SSR(X_1|X_2) = SSR(X_1 \text{ and } X_2) - SSR(X_2) = 30 - 15 = 15$

$F_{STAT} = \frac{SSR(X_1|X_2)}{MSE} = \frac{15}{120/10} = 1.25 < F_{U(1,10)} = 4.965$ with 1 and 10 degrees of freedom and $\alpha = 0.05$. Do not reject H_0. There is not sufficient evidence that the variable X_1 contributes to a model already containing X_2.

For X_2: $SSR(X_2|X_1) = SSR(X_1 \text{ and } X_2) - SSR(X_1) = 30 - 20 = 10$

$F_{STAT} = \frac{SSR(X_2|X_1)}{MSE} = \frac{10}{120/10} = 0.833 < F_{U(1,10)} = 4.965$ with 1 and 10 degrees of freedom and $\alpha = 0.05$. Do not reject H_0. There is not sufficient evidence that the variable X_2 contributes to a model already containing X_1.

14.32 cont. (a) Neither independent variable X_1 nor X_2 makes a significant contribution to the model in the presence of the other variable. Also the overall regression equation involving both independent variables is not significant:

$$F_{STAT} = \frac{MSR}{MSE} = \frac{30/2}{120/10} = 1.25 < F_{U(2,10)} = 4.103$$

Neither variable should be included in the model and other variables should be investigated.

(b) $$r^2_{Y1.2} = \frac{SSR(X_1|X_2)}{SST - SSR(X_1 \text{ and } X_2) + SSR(X_1|X_2)} = \frac{15}{150-30+15} = 0.1111.$$

Holding constant the effect of variable X_2, 11.11% of the variation in Y can be explained by the variation in variable X_1.

$$r^2_{Y2.1} = \frac{SSR(X_2|X_1)}{SST - SSR(X_1 \text{ and } X_2) + SSR(X_2|X_1)} = \frac{10}{150-30+10} = 0.0769.$$

Holding constant the effect of variable X_1, 7.69% of the variation in Y can be explained by the variation in variable X_2.

14.34 (a) For X_1: $SSR(X_1|X_2) = SSR(X_1 \text{ and } X_2) - SSR(X_2) = 5.9271 - 3.6923 = 2.2348$

$$F_{STAT} = \frac{SSR(X_1|X_2)}{MSE} = \frac{2.2348}{15.3521/196} = 28.5227 > 3.897$$

Reject H_0. There is evidence that X1 contributes to a model already containing X2.

For X_2: $SSR(X_2|X_1) = SSR(X_1 \text{ and } X_2) - SSR(X_1) = 5.9271 - 3.7275 = 2.1996,$

$$F_{STAT} = \frac{SSR(X_2|X_1)}{MSE} = \frac{2.1996}{15.3521/196} = 28.0823 \; 7 \; 3.897.$$

Reject H_0. There is evidence that X_2 contributes to a model already containing X_1. Because both X_1 and X_2 make a significant contribution to the model in the presence of the other variable, both variables should be included in the model.

(b) $$r^2_{Y1.2} = \frac{SSR(X_1|X_2)}{SST - SSR(X_1 \text{ and } X_2) + SSR(X_1|X_2)} = \frac{2.2348}{21.2791\text{-}5.9271\text{+}2.2348} = 0.1271.$$

Holding constant the effect of the total risk based capital, 12.71% of the variation in ROAA can be explained by the variation in efficiency ratio.

$$r^2_{Y2.1} = \frac{SSR(X_2|X_1)}{SST - SSR(X_1 \text{ and } X_2) + SSR(X_2|X_1)} = \frac{2.1996}{21.2791\text{-}5.9271\text{+}2.1996} = 0.1253.$$

Holding constant the effect of efficiency ratio 12.53% of the variation in ROAA can be explained by the variation in the total risk-based capital.

14.36 (a) For X_1: $F_{STAT} = 0.554 < 4.00$; Don't reject H_0. There is insufficient evidence that X_1 contributes to a model containing X_2. For X_2: $F_{STAT} = 3.5476 < 4.00$. Do not reject H_0. There is insufficient evidence that X_2 contributes to a model already containing X_1. Because only X_1 makes a significant contribution to the model in the presence of the other variable, only X_1 should be included in the model.

14.36 cont. (b) $r^2_{Y1.2} = 0.0091$. Holding constant the effect of full-time voluntary turnover, 0.91% of the variation in full-time jobs added be explained by the variation in total worldwide revenue. $r^2_{Y2.1} = 0.0558$. Holding constant the effect of total worldwide revenue, 5.58% of the variation in full-time jobs created can be explained by the variation in full-time voluntary turnover.

14.38 (a) Holding constant the effect of X_2, the estimated mean value of the dependent variable will increase by 4 units for each increase of one unit of X_1.

(b) Holding constant the effects of X_1, the presence of the condition represented by $X_2 = 1$ is estimated to increase the mean value of the dependent variable by 2 units.

(c) $t = 3.27 > t_{17} = 2.1098$. Reject H_0. The presence of X_2 makes a significant contribution to the model.

14.40 (a) $\hat{Y} = 243.7371 + 9.2189X_1 + 12.6967X_2$, where X_1 = number of rooms and X_2 = neighborhood (east = 0).

(b) Holding constant the effect of neighborhood, for each additional room, the selling price is estimated to increase by a mean of 9.2189 thousands of dollars, or \$9218.9. For a given number of rooms, a west neighborhood is estimated to increase mean selling price over an east neighborhood by 12.6967 thousands of dollars, or \$12,696.7.

(c) $\hat{Y} = 243.7371 + 9.2189(9) + 12.6967(0) = 326.70758$ or \$326,707.58

$\$309{,}560.04 \le Y_{X=X_i} \le \$343{,}855.11 \qquad \$321{,}471.44 \le \mu_{Y|X=X_i} \le \$331{,}943.71$

(d)

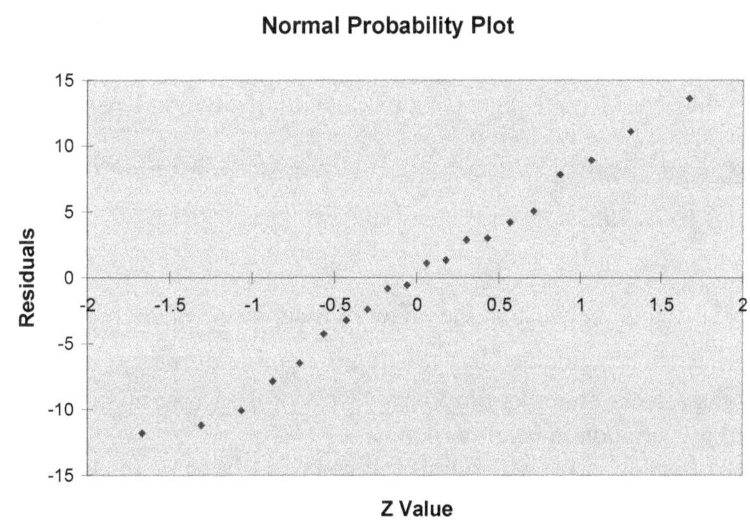

14.40 (d)
cont.

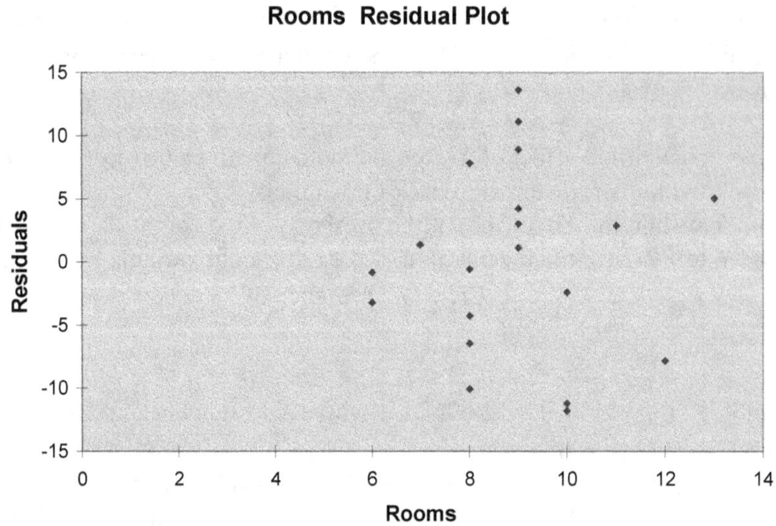

Based on a residual analysis, the model appears adequate.

(e) $F_{STAT} = 55.39$, p-value is virtually 0. Since p-value < 0.05, reject H_0. There is evidence of a significant relationship between selling price and the two independent variables (rooms and neighborhood).

(f) For X_1: $t_{STAT} = 8.9537$, p-value is virtually 0. Reject H_0. Number of rooms makes a significant contribution and should be included in the model.
For X_2: $t_{STAT} = 3.5913$, p-value $= 0.0023 < 0.05$. Reject H_0. Neighborhood makes a significant contribution and should be included in the model.
Based on these results, the regression model with the two independent variables should be used.

(g) $7.0466 \le \beta_1 \le 11.3913$

(h) $5.2378 \le \beta_2 \le 20.1557$

(i) $r^2_{adj} = 0.851$

(j) $r^2_{Y1.2} = 0.825$. Holding constant the effect of neighborhood, 82.5% of the variation in selling price can be explained by variation in number of rooms. $r^2_{Y2.1} = 0.431$. Holding constant the effect of number of rooms, 43.1% of the variation in selling price can be explained by variation in neighborhood.

(k) The slope of selling price with number of rooms is the same regardless of whether the house is located in an east or west neighborhood.

(l) $\hat{Y} = 253.95 + 8.032X_1 - 5.90X_2 + 2.089X_1X_2$.
For $X_1 X_2$: the p-value is 0.330. Do not reject H_0. There is no evidence that the interaction term makes a contribution to the model.

(m) The two-variable model in (f) should be used.

(n) The real estate association can conclude that the number of rooms and the neighborhood both significantly affect the selling price, but the number of rooms has a greater effect.

14.42 (a) $\hat{Y} = 8.0100 + 0.0052X_1 - 2.1052X_2$, where X_1 = depth (in feet) and X_2 = type of drilling (wet = 0, dry = 1).

14.42 cont.

(b) Holding constant the effect of type of drilling, for each foot increase in depth of the hole, the additional drilling time is estimated to increase by a mean of 0.0052 minute . For a given depth, a dry drilling is estimated to reduce mean additional drilling time over wet drilling by 2.1052 minutes.

(c) Dry drilling: $\hat{Y} = 8.0101 + 0.0052(100) - 2.1052 = 6.4276$ minutes.

$6.2096 \le \mu_{Y|X=X_i} \le 6.6457$, $4.9230 \le Y_{X=X_i} \le 7.9322$

(d)

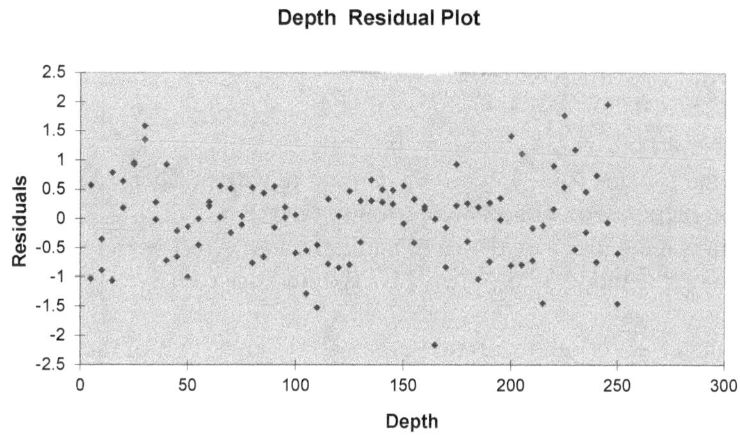

Based on a residual analysis, the model appears adequate.

(e) $F_{STAT} = 111.109$ with 2 and 97 degrees of freedom, $F_{2,97} = 3.09$ using Excel. p-value is virtually 0. Reject H_0 at 5% level of significance. There is evidence of a relationship between additional drilling time and the two dependent variables.

(f) For X_1: $t_{STAT} = 5.0289 > t_{97} = 1.9847$. Reject H_0. Depth of the hole makes a significant contribution and should be included in the model.

For X_2: $t_{STAT} = -14.0331 < t_{97} = -1.9847$. Reject H_0. Type of drilling makes a significant contribution and should be included in the model.

Based on these results, the regression model with the two independent variables should be used.

(g) $0.0032 \le \beta_1 \le 0.0073$

(h) $-2.4029 \le \beta_2 \le -1.8075$

(i) $r^2_{adj} = 0.6899$

(j) $r^2_{Y1.2} = 0.2068$. Holding constant the effect of type of drilling, 20.68% of the variation in additional drilling time can be explained by variation in depth of the hole. $r^2_{Y2.1} = 0.6700$. Holding constant the effect of the depth of the hole, 67% of the variation in additional drilling time can be explained by variation in type of drilling.

(k) The slope of additional drilling time with depth of the hole is the same regardless of whether it is a dry drilling hole or a wet drilling hole.

(l) $\hat{Y} = 7.9120 + 0.0060X_1 - 1.9091X_2 - 0.0015X_1X_2$.

For X_1X_2: the p-value is $0.4624 > 0.05$. Do not reject H_0. There is not evidence that the interaction term makes a contribution to the model.

(m) The two-variable model in (a) should be used.

(n) Both variables affect the drilling time. Dry drilling holes should be used to reduce the drilling time.

14.44 (a) $\hat{Y} = 1.1079 - 0.0070X_1 + 0.0448X_2 - 0.0003X_1X_2$, where X_1 = efficiency ratio, X_2 = total risk-based capital, p-value $=0.4593 > 0.05$. Do not reject H_0. There is not enough evidence that the interaction term makes a contribution to the model.

(b) Because there is insufficient evidence of any interaction effect between efficiency ratio and total risk-based capital, the model in Problem 14.4 should be used.

14.46 (a) The p-value of the interaction term = $0.1650 < 0.05$, so the term is not significant and should be not included in the model.

(b) Use the model developed Problem 14.6.

14.48 (a) $\hat{Y} = 250.4237 + 0.0127X_1 - 1.4785X_2 + 0.004X_3$.
where X_1 = staff present, X_2 = remote hours, $X_3 = X_1 X_2$
For X_1X_2: the p-value is $0.2353 > 0.05$. Do not reject H_0. There is not enough evidence that the interaction term makes a contribution to the model.

(b) Since there is not enough evidence of an interaction effect between total staff present and remote hours, the model in problem 14.7 should be used.

14.50 Holding constant the effect of other variables, the natural logarithm of the estimated odds ratio for the dependent categorical response will increase by a mean of 2.2 for each unit increase in the independent variable to which the coefficient corresponds.

14.52 $$\text{Estimated Probability of Success} = \frac{\text{Estimated Odds Ratio}}{(1+\text{Estimated Odds Ratio})} = \frac{0.75}{(1+0.75)} = 0.4286$$

14.54 (a) ln(estimated odds ratio) $= -6.94 + 0.13947X_1 + 2.774X_2$
$= -6.94 + 0.13947(36) + 2.774(0) = -1.91908$
Estimated odds ratio $= e^{-1.91908} = 0.1467$
Estimated Probability of the Event of Interest =
$$\frac{\text{Estimated Odds Ratio}}{(1+\text{Estimated Odds Ratio})} = \frac{0.1467}{(1+0.1467)} = 0.1280$$

(b) From the text discussion of the example, 70.16% of the individuals who charge \$36,000 per annum and possess additional cards can be expected to purchase the premium card. Only 12.80% of the individuals who charge \$36,000 per annum and do not possess additional cards can be expected to purchase the premium card. For a given amount of money charged per annum, the likelihood of purchasing a premium card is substantially higher among individuals who already possess additional cards than for those who do not possess additional cards.

(c) ln(estimated odds ratio) $= -6.94 + 0.13947X_1 + 2.774X_2$
$= -6.94 + 0.13947(18) + 2.774(0) = -4.42954$
Estimated odds ratio $= e^{-4.42954} = 0.0119$
Estimated Probability of the Event of Interest =
$$\frac{\text{Estimated Odds Ratio}}{(1+\text{Estimated Odds Ratio})} = \frac{0.0119}{(1+0.0119)} = 0.01178$$

(d) Among individuals who do not purchase additional cards, the likelihood of purchasing a premium card diminishes dramatically with a substantial decrease in the amount charged per annum.

14.56 (a)

Binary Logistic Regression

Predictor	Coefficients	SE Coef	Z	p-Value
Intercept	-47.4821	12.0173	-3.9512	0.0001
fixed acidity	1.310179398	0.4139	3.1656	0.0015
chlorides	90.57937563	22.643	4.0003	0.0001
pH	9.779258829	2.9743	3.288	0.0010
Deviance	54.45564087			

(b) Holding constant the effects of chlorides and pH, for each increase of one unit of fixed acidity, ln(odds) increases by an estimate of 1.3102. Holding constant the effects of fixed acidity and pH, for each increase of one unit in chlorides, ln(odds) increases by an estimate of 90.5794. Holding constant the effects of fixed acidity and chlorides, for each increase of one unit in pH, ln(odds) increases by an estimate of 9.7793.

(c) $\ln(\text{estimated odds ratio}) = -47.4821 + 1.3102X_1 + 90.5794X_2 + 9.7793X_3 = -0.4603$

Estimated odds ratio $= e^{-0.4603} = 0.6311$

Estimated Probability of the Event of Interest =

$$\frac{\text{Estimated Odds Ratio}}{(1 + \text{Estimated Odds Ratio})} = \frac{0.6311}{(1 + 0.6311)} = 0.3869$$

(d) The deviance statistic is 54.4556, which has a *p*-value of 0.9998. Do not reject H_0. The model is a good fitting model.

(e) For fixed acidity: $Z_{STAT} = 3.1656$ with a *p*-value = 0.0015. Reject H_0. There is sufficient evidence that fixed acidity makes a significant contribution to the model.
For chlorides: $Z_{STAT} = 4.0003$ with a *p*-value = 0.0001. Reject H_0. There is sufficient evidence that the amount of chlorides makes a significant contribution to the model.
For pH: $Z_{STAT} = 3.2880$ with a *p*-value = 0.0010. Reject H_0. There is sufficient evidence that pH makes a significant contribution to the model.

(f) Based on the *p*-values corresponding to the *Z*-values for the variable coefficients in the logistic regression equation and corresponding to the deviance statistics, the model that includes fixed acidity, chlorides and pH should be used to predict whether the wine is red.

14.58 (a)

Predictor	Coefficients	SE Coef	Z	p-Value
Intercept	-0.6048	0.4194	-1.4421	0.1493
claims/year	0.093769442	0.5029	0.1865	0.8521
new business (1=yes, 0=no):1	1.810770296	0.8134	2.2261	0.0260
Deviance	119.4353239		p-value	0.0457

(b) Holding constant the effects of whether the policy is new, for each increase of the number of claims submitted per year by the policy holder, ln(odds) increases by an estimate of 0.0938. Holding constant the number of claims submitted per year by the policy holder, ln(odds) is estimated to be 1.8108 higher when the policy is new as compared to when the policy is not new.

14.58 (c) $\ln(\text{estimated odds ratio}) = -0.6048 + 0.0938(1) + 1.8108(1) = 1.2998$

cont. Estimated odds ratio $= e^{1.2998} = 3.6684$

$$\text{Estimated Probability of the Event of Interest} = \frac{\text{Estimated Odds Ratio}}{(1 + \text{Estimated Odds Ratio})} = 0.7858$$

(d) The deviance statistic is 119.4353 with a χ^2 distribution of 95 d.f. and p-value = 0.0457 < 0.05. Reject H_0. The model is not a good fitting model.

(e) For claims/year: $Z_{STAT} = 0.1865$, p-value = 0.8521> 0.05. Do not eject H_0. There is not sufficient evidence that the number of claims submitted per year by the policy holder makes a significant contribution to the logistic model.
For new business: $Z_{STAT} = 2.2261$, p-value = 0.0260 < 0.05. Reject H_0. There is sufficient evidence that whether the policy is new makes a significant contribution to the logistic model.

(f) PHStat output:

Predictor	Coefficients	SE Coef	Z	p-Value
Intercept	-1.0125	0.3888	-2.6042	0.0092
claims/year	0.992742206	0.3367	2.9481	0.0032
Deviance	125.0102452		p-value	0.0250

(g) PHStat output:

Predictor	Coefficients	SE Coef	Z	p-Value
Intercept	-0.5423	0.2515	-2.1563	0.0311
new business	1.928618927	0.5211	3.7008	0.0002
Deviance	119.4701921		p-value	0.0526

(h) The deviance statistic for (f) is 125.0102 with a χ^2 distribution of 96 d.f. and p-value = 0.0250 < 0.05. Reject H_0. The model is not a good fitting model.
The deviance statistic for (g) is 119.4702 with a χ^2 distribution of 96 d.f. and p-value = 0.0526 > 0.05. Do not reject H_0. The model is a good fitting model.
The model in (g) should be used to predict a fraudulent claim.

14.60 (a) ln(estimated odds) = 1.252 – 0.0323 Age + 2.2165 subscribes to the wellness newsletters.

(b) Holding constant the effect of subscribes to the wellness newsletters, for each increase of one year in age, ln(estimated odds) decreases by an estimate of 0.0323. Holding constant the effect of age, for a customer who subscribes to the wellness newsletters, ln(estimated odds) increases by an estimate of 2.2165.

(c) 0.912

(d) Deviance = 102.8762, p-value = 0.3264. Do not reject H_0 so model is adequate.

(e) For Age: $Z = -1.8053 > -1.96$, Do not reject H_0. For subscribes to the wellness newsletters: $Z = 4.3286 > 1.96$, Reject H_0.

(f) Only subscribes to wellness newsletters is useful in predicting whether a customer will purchase organic food.

14.62 In the case of the simple linear regression model, the slope b_1 represents the change in the estimated mean of Y per unit change in X and does not take into account any other variables. In the multiple linear regression model, the slope b_1 represents the change in the estimated mean of Y per unit change in X_1, taking into account the effect of all the other independent variables.

14.64 The coefficient of partial determination measures the proportion of variation in Y explained by a particular X variable holding constant the effect of the other independent variables in the model. The coefficient of multiple determination measures the proportion of variation in Y explained by all the X variables included in the model.

14.66 You test whether the interaction of the dummy variable and each of the independent variables in the model make a significant contribution to the regression model.

14.68 It is assumed that the slope of the dependent variable Y with an independent variable X is the same for each of the two levels of the dummy variable.

14.70 In least squares regression the dependent variable is numerical. The use of categorical variables in least squares regression would violate the normality assumption and would not be appropriate with this method. Logistic regression allows one to predict a categorical dependent variable utilizing the odds ratio. The least squares regression uses a numerical dependent variable while logistic regression uses a categorical dependent variable.

14.72 (a) $\hat{Y} = -3.9152 + 0.0319X_1 + 4.2228X_2$, where X_1 = number cubic feet moved and X_2 = number of pieces of large furniture.

(b) Holding constant the number of pieces of large furniture, for each additional cubic foot moved, the mean labor hours are estimated to increase by 0.0319. Holding constant the amount of cubic feet moved, for each additional piece of large furniture, the mean labor hours are estimated to increase by 4.2228.

(c) $\hat{Y} = 20.4926$

(d) Based on a residual analysis, the errors appear to be normally distributed. The equal-variance assumption might be violated because the variances appear to be larger around the center region of both independent variables. There might also be violation of the linearity assumption. A model with quadratic terms for both independent variables might be fitted.

(e) $F_{STAT} = 228.80$, p-value is virtually $0 < 0.05$, reject H_0. There is evidence of a significant relationship between labor hours and the two independent variables (the amount of cubic feet moved and the number of pieces of large furniture).

(f) The p-value is virtually 0. The probability of obtaining a test statistic of 228.80 or greater is virtually 0 if there is no significant relationship between labor hours and the two independent variables (the amount of cubic feet moved and the number of pieces of large furniture).

(g) $r^2 = 0.9327$. 93.27% of the variation in labor hours can be explained by variation in the number of cubic feet moved and the number of pieces of large furniture.

(h) $r^2_{adj} = 0.9287$

(i) For X_1: $t_{STAT} = 6.9339$, the p-value is virtually 0. Reject H_0. The number of cubic feet moved makes a significant contribution and should be included in the model.
For X_2: $t_{STAT} = 4.6192$, the p-value is virtually 0. Reject H_0. The number of pieces of large furniture makes a significant contribution and should be included in the model. Based on these results, the regression model with the two independent variables should be used.

14.72 cont. (j) For X_1: $t_{STAT} = 6.9339$, the p-value is virtually 0. The probability of obtaining a sample that will yield a test statistic greater than 6.9339 is virtually 0 if the number of cubic feet moved does not make a significant contribution, holding the effect of the number of pieces of large furniture constant. For X_2: $t_{STAT} = 4.6192$, the p-value is virtually 0. The probability of obtaining a sample that will yield a test statistic greater than 4.6192 is virtually 0 if the number of pieces of large furniture does not make a significant contribution, holding the effect of the amount of cubic feet moved constant.

(k) $0.0226 \le \beta_1 \le .0413$

(l) $r^2_{Y1.2} = 0.5930$. Holding constant the effect of the number of pieces of large furniture, 59.3% of the variation in labor hours can be explained by variation in the amount of cubic feet moved. $r^2_{Y2.1} = 0.3927$. Holding constant the effect of the number of cubic feet moved, 39.27% of the variation in labor hours can be explained by variation in the number of pieces of large furniture.

(m) Both the number of cubic feet moved and the number of large pieces of furniture are useful in predicting the labor hours, but the cubic feet moved is more important.

14.74 (a) $\hat{Y} = 360.2158 + 0.0775X_1 - 0.4122X_2$, where X_1 = house size and X_2 = age.

(b) Holding constant the age, for each additional square foot in the size of the house, the mean asking price is estimated to increase by 77.50 thousand dollars. Holding constant the living space of the house, for each additional year in age, the asking price is estimated to decrease by 0.4122 thousand dollars.

(c) $\hat{Y} = 492.5316$ thousand dollars.

(d) Based on a residual analysis, the model appears to be adequate.

(e) $F_{STAT} = 19.4909$, the p-value $= 0.0000 < 0.05$, reject H_0. There is evidence of a significant relationship between asking price and the two independent variables (size of the house and age).

(f) The p-value is 0.0000. The probability of obtaining a test statistic of 19.4909 or greater is virtually 0 if there is no significant relationship between asking price and the two independent variables (living space of the house and age).

(g) $r^2 = 0.4019$. 40.19% of the variation in asking price can be explained by variation in the size of the house and age.

(h) $r^2_{adj} = 0.3813$.

(i) For X_1: $t_{STAT} = 4.6904$, the p-value is 0.0000. Reject H_0. The living space of the house makes a significant contribution and should be included in the model.
For X_2: $t_{STAT} = -0.6304$, p-value $= 0.5309 > 0.05$. Do not reject H_0. Age does not make a significant contribution and should not be included in the model. Based on these results, the regression model with only the size of the house should be used.

(j) For X_1: $t_{STAT} = 4.6904$. The probability of obtaining a sample that will yield a test statistic farther away than 4.6904 is 0.0000 if the living space does not make a significant contribution, holding age constant. For X_2: $t_{STAT} = -0.6304$. The probability of obtaining a sample that will yield a test statistic farther away than 0.6304 is 0.5309 if the age does not make a significant contribution holding the effect of the living space constant.

(k) $0.0444 \le \beta_1 \le 0.1106$ You are 95% confident that the asking price will increase by an amount somewhere between \$44.40 thousand and \$110.60 thousand for each additional thousand square foot increase in living space, holding constant the age of the house. In Problem 13.76, you are 95% confident that the assessed value will increase by an amount somewhere between \$56.8 thousand and \$110.30 thousand for each additional 1,000 square foot increase in living space, regardless of the age of the house.

14.74 cont.
(l) $r^2_{Y1.2} = 0.2750$. Holding constant the effect of the age of the house, 27.50% of the variation in asking price can be explained by variation in the living space of the house. $r^2_{Y2.1} = 0.0068$. Holding constant the effect of the size of the house, 0.68% of the variation in asking price can be explained by variation in the age of the house.
(m) Only the living space of the house should be used to predict asking price.

14.76
(a) $\hat{Y} = -90.2166 + 9.2169X_1 + 2.5069X_2$, where X_1 = asking price and X_2 = age.
(b) Holding age constant, for each additional $1,000 in asking price, the taxes are estimated to increase by a mean of $9.2169 thousand. Holding asking price constant, for each additional year, the taxes are estimated to increase by $2.5069
(c) $\hat{Y} = \$3{,}721.90$
(d) Based on a residual analysis, the errors appear to be normally distributed. The equal-variance assumption appears to be valid. However, there is one very large residual that is from the house that is 107 years old. Removing this point, still leaves a residual for the house that has an asking price of $550,000 and is 52 years old. However, because this model is an almost perfect fit, you may want to use this model. In this model, age is no longer significant.
(e) $F_{STAT} = 1{,}677.8619$, p-value = 0.0000 < 0.05, reject H_0. There is evidence of a significant relationship between taxes and the two independent variables (asking price and age).
(f) p-value = 0.0000. The probability of obtaining an F_{STAT} test statistic of 1,677.8619 or greater is virtually 0 if there is no significant relationship between taxes and the two independent variables (asking price and age).
(g) $r^2 = 0.9830$, 98.30% of the variation in taxes can be explained by variation in asking price and age.
(h) $r^2_{adj} = 0.9824$
(i) For X_1: $t_{STAT} = 53.7184$, p-value = 0.0000 < 0.05. Reject H_0. The asking price makes a significant contribution and should be included in the model. For X_2: $t_{STAT} = 2.7873$, p-value = 0.0072 < 0.05. Reject H_0. The age of a house makes a significant contribution and should be included in the model. Based on these results, the regression model with asking price and age should be used.
(j) For X_1: p-value = 0.0000. The probability of obtaining a sample that will yield a test statistic greater than 53.7184 is 0.0000 if the asking price does not make a significant contribution, holding age constant. For X_2: p-value = 0.0072. The probability of obtaining a sample that will yield a test statistic greater than 2.7873 is 0.0072 if the age of a house does not make a significant contribution, holding the effect of the asking price constant.
(k) $8.8735 \le \beta_1 \le 9.5604$. You are 95% confident that the mean taxes will increase by an amount somewhere between $8.87 and $9.56 for each additional $1,000 increase in the asking price, holding constant the age. In Problem 13.77, you are 95% confident that the mean taxes will increase by an amount somewhere between $5.968 and $11.03 for each additional $1,000 increase in asking price, regardless of the age.
(l) $r^2_{Y1.2} = 0.9803$. Holding constant the effect of age, 98.03% of the variation in taxes can be explained by variation in the asking price. $r^2_{Y2.1} = 0.1181$. Holding constant the effect of the asking price, 11.81% of the variation in taxes can be explained by variation in the age.
(m) Based on your answers to (b) through (k), the age of a house has an effect on its taxes. However, given the results when the 107-year-old house is not included, the assessor can state that for houses that are not that old, that age does not have an effect on taxes.

14.78 (a) $\hat{Y} = 160.6120 - 18.7181X_1 - 2.8903X_2$, where X_1 = ERA and X_2 = league (American = 0 National = 1).

(b) Holding constant the effect of the league, for each additional earned run, the number of wins is estimated to decrease by 18.7181. For a given ERA, a team in the National League is estimated to have 2.8903 fewer wins than a team in the American League.

(c) 76.3803 wins.

(d) Based on a residual analysis, there is no pattern in the errors. There is no apparent violation of other assumptions.

(e) $F_{STAT} = 24.306 > 3.35$, p-value $= 0.0000 < 0.05$, reject H_0. There is evidence of a significant relationship between wins and the two independent variables (ERA and league).

(f) For X_1: $t_{STAT} = -6.9184 < -2.0518$, the p-value $= 0.0000$. Reject H_0. ERA makes a significant contribution and should be included in the model.
For X_2: $t_{STAT} = -1.1966 > -2.0518$, p-value $= 0.2419 > 0.05$. Do not reject H_0. The league does not make a significant contribution and should not be included in the model. Based on these results, the regression model with only the ERA as the independent variable should be used.

(g) $-24.2687 \le \beta_1 \le -13.1676$

(h) $-7.8464 \le \beta_2 \le 2.0639$

(i) $r^2_{adj} = 0.6165$ 61.65% of the variation in wins can be explained by the variation in ERA and league after adjusting for number of independent variables and sample size.

(j) $r^2_{Y1.2} = 0.6394$ Holding constant the effect of league, 63.94% of the variation in number of wins can be explained by the variation in ERA. $r^2_{Y2.1} = 0.0504$ Holding constant the effect of ERA, 5.04% of the variation in number of wins can be explained by the variation in league.

(k) The slope of the number of wins with ERA is the same, regardless of whether the team belongs to the American League or the National League.

(l) For X_1X_2: $t_{STAT} = 1.175 < 2.0555$ the p-value is $0.2506 > 0.05$. Do not reject H_0. There is no evidence that the interaction term makes a contribution to the model.

(m) The model with one independent variable (ERA) should be used.

14.80 The multiple regression model is
Predicted base salary = 48,091.7853 + 8,249.2156 (gender) + 1,061.4521 (age).
Holding constant the age of the person, the mean base salary is predicted to be \$8,249.22 higher for males than for females. Holding constant the gender of the person, for each addition year of age, the mean base salary is predicted to be \$1,061.45 higher. The regression model with the two independent variables has $F = 118.0925$ and a p-value $= 0.0000$. So, you can conclude that at least one of the independent variable makes a significant contribution to the model to predict base pay. Each independent variable makes a significant contribution to the regression model given that the other variable is included. ($t_{STAT} = 3.9937$, p-value $= 0.0001$ for gender and $t_{STAT} = 14.8592$, p-value $= 0.0000$ for age). Both independent variables should be included in the model. 37.01% of the variation in base salary can be explained by gender and age. There is no pattern in the residuals and no other violations of the assumptions, so the model appears to be appropriate. Including an interaction term of gender and age does not significantly improve the model (t_{STAT} -0.2371, p-value $= 0.8127 > 0.05$). You can conclude that females are paid less than males holding constant the age of the person. Perhaps other variables such as department, seniority, and score on a performance evaluation can be included in the model to see if the model is improved.

14.82 $b_0 = 18.2892$ (die temperature), $b_1 = 0.5976$, (die diameter), $b_2 = -13.5108$. The r^2 of the multiple regression model is 0.3257 so 32.57% of the variation in unit density can be explained by the variation of die temperature and die diameter. The F test statistic for the combined significance of die temperature and die diameter is 5.0718 with a p-value of 0.0160. Hence, at a 5% level of significance, there is enough evidence to conclude that die temperature and die diameter affect unit density. The p-value of the t test for the significance of die temperature is 0.2117, which is greater than 5%. Hence, there is insufficient evidence to conclude that die temperature affects unit density holding constant the effect of die diameter. The p-value of the t test for the significance of die diameter is 0.0083, which is less than 5%. There is enough evidence to conclude that die diameter affects unit density at the 5% level of significance holding constant the effect of die temperature. After removing die temperature from the model, $b_0 = 107.9267$ (die diameter), $b_1 = -13.5108$. The r^2 of the multiple regression is 0.2724. So 27.24% of the variation in unit density can be explained by the variation of die diameter. The p-value of the t test for the significance of die diameter is 0.0087, which is less than 5%. There is enough evidence to conclude that die diameter affects unit density at the 5% level of significance. There is some lack of equality in the residuals and some departure from normality.

CHAPTER 15

15.2 (a)

GPA	Predicted HOCS	GPA	Predicted HOCS
2	2.8600	3	3.9900
2.1	3.0342	3.1	4.0282
2.2	3.1948	3.2	4.0528
2.3	3.3418	3.3	4.0638
2.4	3.4752	3.4	4.0612
2.5	3.5950	3.5	4.0450
2.6	3.7012	3.6	4.0152
2.7	3.7938	3.7	3.9718
2.8	3.8728	3.8	3.9148
2.9	3.9382	3.9	3.8442
		4	3.7600

(b)

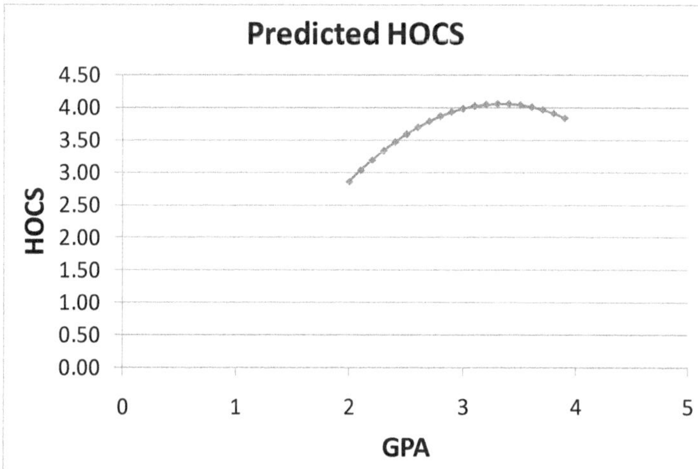

(c) The curvilinear relationship suggests that HOCS increases at a decreasing rate. It reaches its maximum value of 4.0638 at GPA = 3.3 and declines after that as GPA continues to increase.

(d) An r^2 of 0.07 and an adjusted r^2 of 0.06 tell you that GPA has very low explanatory power in explaining the variation in HOCS. You can tell that the individual HOCS scores will have scattered quite widely around the curvilinear relationship plotted in (b) and discussed in (c).

15.4 (a)

Regression Analysis: Calories versus Alcohol %, Carbohydrates

Analysis of Variance

Source	DF	Adj SS	Adj MS	F-Value	P-Value
Regression	2	289506	144753	2273.00	0.000
Alcohol %	1	94227	94227	1479.61	0.000
Carbohydrates	1	41744	41744	655.49	0.000
Error	154	9807	64		
Lack-of-Fit	136	9679	71	10.00	0.000
Pure Error	18	128	7		
Total	156	299313			

Model Summary

S	R-sq	R-sq(adj)	R-sq(pred)
7.98021	96.72%	96.68%	96.56%

Coefficients

Term	Coef	SE Coef	T-Value	P-Value	VIF
Constant	-5.55	2.58	-2.15	0.033	
Alcohol %	21.616	0.562	38.47	0.000	1.42
Carbohydrates	3.911	0.153	25.60	0.000	1.42

Regression Equation

Calories = -5.55 + 21.616 Alcohol % + 3.911 Carbohydrates

15.4 (b)

Regression Equation

Calories = 10.39 + 14.91 Alcohol % + 4.604 Carbohydrates + 0.505 Alcohol%Sq - 0.0229 CarbSq

Coefficients

Term	Coef	SE Coef	T-Value	P-Value	VIF
Constant	10.39	8.25	1.26	0.209	
Alcohol %	14.91	2.94	5.07	0.000	39.83
Carbohydrates	4.604	0.471	9.77	0.000	13.84
Alcohol%Sq	0.505	0.217	2.33	0.021	37.83
CarbSq	-0.0229	0.0164	-1.39	0.166	12.97

Model Summary

S	R-sq	R-sq(adj)	R-sq(pred)
7.88380	96.84%	96.76%	96.58%

Analysis of Variance

Source	DF	Adj SS	Adj MS	F-Value	P-Value
Regression	4	289866	72466.4	1165.91	0.000
Alcohol %	1	1596	1595.8	25.67	0.000
Carbohydrates	1	5929	5928.8	95.39	0.000
Alcohol%Sq	1	337	337.3	5.43	0.021
CarbSq	1	121	120.6	1.94	0.166
Error	152	9447	62.2		
Lack-of-Fit	134	9319	69.5	9.77	0.000
Pure Error	18	128	7.1		
Total	156	299313			

(c) For the model in (b) that includes the quadratic terms, $F_{STAT} = 1{,}165.91$ or p-value = 0.000. Reject H_0. For the quadratic alcohol % term, $t_{STAT} = 2.33$ or p-value = 0.021. Reject H_0. There is sufficient evidence that the quadratic term for alcohol % is significant at the 5% level of significance. For the quadratic carbohydrate term, $t_{STAT} = -1.39$ or p-value = 0.166. Do not reject H_0. There is insufficient evidence that the quadratic term for carbohydrates is significant at the 5% significance level. The model in (b) may represent the better model because it does include a significant quadratic term for alcohol percentage.

(d) The number of calories in a beer depends quadratically on the alcohol percentage but linearly on the number of carbohydrates. The alcohol percentage and number of carbohydrates explain about 96.84% of the variation in the number of calories in a beer.

15.6 (a)

(b)

Regression Analysis: Price ($) versus Age, Age Sq

Analysis of Variance

Source	DF	Adj SS	Adj MS	F-Value	P-Value
Regression	2	494180565	247090283	243.51	0.000
Age	1	95363310	95363310	93.98	0.000
Age Sq	1	23998229	23998229	23.65	0.000
Error	36	36529880	1014719		
Lack-of-Fit	10	13336078	1333608	1.49	0.197
Pure Error	26	23193802	892069		
Total	38	530710445			

Model Summary

S	R-sq	R-sq(adj)	R-sq(pred)
1007.33	93.12%	92.73%	91.28%

Coefficients

Term	Coef	SE Coef	T-Value	P-Value	VIF
Constant	18030	569	31.67	0.000	
Age	-1813	187	-9.69	0.000	18.82
Age Sq	63.2	13.0	4.86	0.000	18.82

Regression Equation

Price ($) = 18030 - 1813 Age + 63.2 Age Sq

$$\hat{Y} = 18030 - 1813X + 63.2X^2$$

15.6 cont. (c)

Prediction

Fit	SE Fit	95% CI	95% PI
10545.6	224.382	(10090.5, 11000.6)	(8452.55, 12638.6)

$\hat{Y} = 18030 - 1813(5) + 63.2(5)^2 = \$10,545.6$

(d)

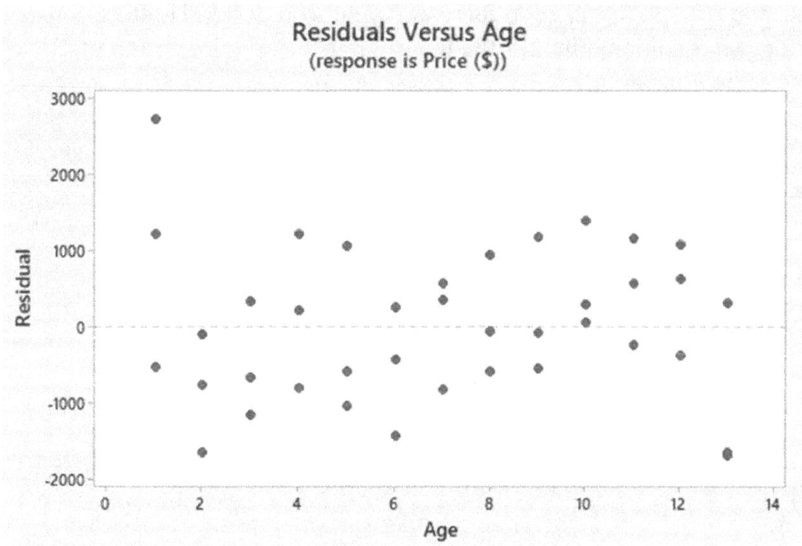

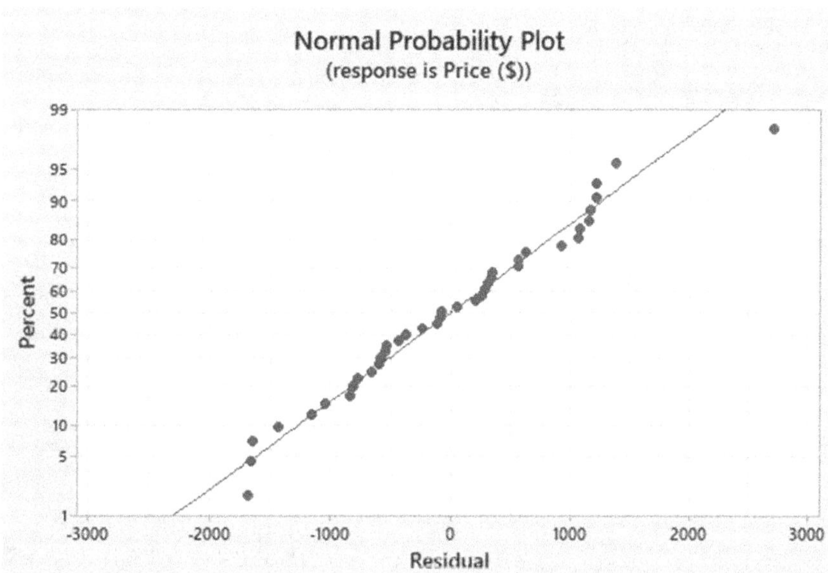

There are no patterns in the residual plots. There does not appear to be any violation of assumptions.

(e) Because $F_{STAT} = 243.51$ or p-value = 0.000, reject H_0.

(f) p-value = 0.000. The probability of $F_{STAT} = 243.51$ or higher is 0.000, given the null hypothesis is true.

15.6 cont.

(g) Because $t_{STAT} = 4.86$ or p-value = 0.000, reject H_0.

(h) The probability of $t_{STAT} < -4.86$ or > 4.86 is 0.000, given the null hypothesis is true.

(i) $r^2 = 0.9312$. 93.12% of the variation in price can be explained by the quadratic relationship between age and price. (j) adjusted $r^2 = 0.9273$.

(k) There is a strong quadratic relationship between age and price.

15.8 (a)

$$\log \hat{Y} = \log(3.07) + 0.9\log(8.5) + 1.41\log(5.2) = 2.33318$$

$$\hat{Y} = 10^{2.33318} = 215.37$$

(b) Holding constant the effects of X_2, for each additional unit of the logarithm of X_1, the logarithm of Y is estimated to increase by a mean of 0.9. Holding constant the effects of X_1, for each additional unit of the logarithm of X_2, the logarithm of Y is estimated to increase by a mean of 1.41.

15.10 (a)

Regression Analysis: sqrt(Calories) versus Alcohol %, Carbohydrates

Analysis of Variance

Source	DF	Seq SS	Contribution	Adj SS	Adj MS	F-Value	P-Value
Regression	2	428.685	95.75%	428.685	214.342	1732.83	0.000
Alcohol %	1	353.400	78.93%	122.581	122.581	991.00	0.000
Carbohydrates	1	75.284	16.81%	75.284	75.284	608.63	0.000
Error	154	19.049	4.25%	19.049	0.124		
Lack-of-Fit	136	18.841	4.21%	18.841	0.139	11.96	0.000
Pure Error	18	0.208	0.05%	0.208	0.012		
Total	156	447.734	100.00%				

Model Summary

S	R-sq	R-sq(adj)	PRESS	R-sq(pred)
0.351703	95.75%	95.69%	20.2200	95.48%

Coefficients

Term	Coef	SE Coef	95% CI	T-Value	P-Value	VIF
Constant	6.245	0.114	(6.020, 6.469)	54.98	0.000	
Alcohol %	0.7796	0.0248	(0.7307, 0.8286)	31.48	0.000	1.42
Carbohydrates	0.16610	0.00673	(0.15280, 0.17940)	24.67	0.000	1.42

Regression Equation

sqrt(Calories) = 6.245 + 0.7796 Alcohol % + 0.16610 Carbohydrates

15.10 cont. (a)

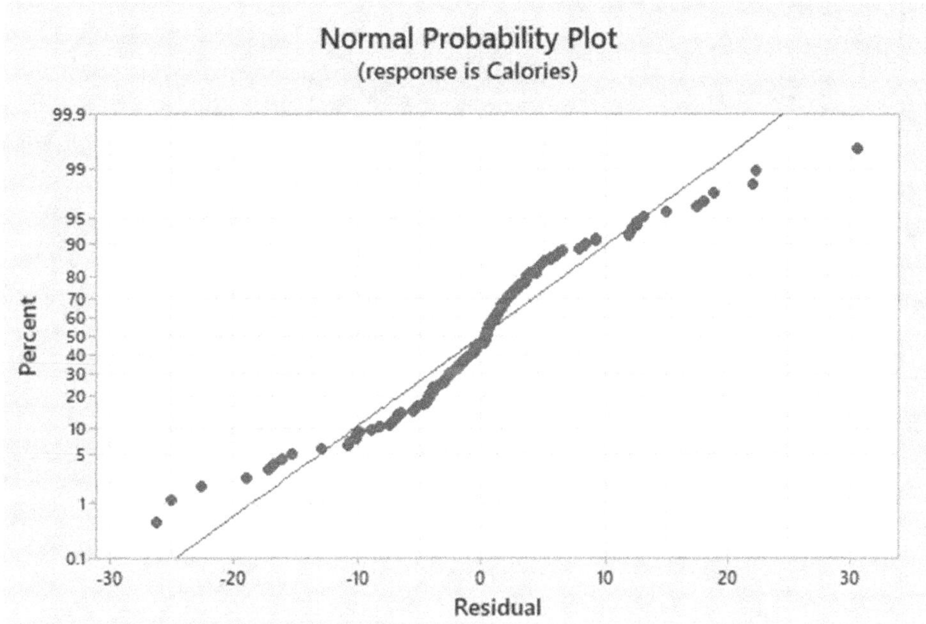

A normal probability plot of the linear model revealed evidence of departure from normality. A square root transformation of the dependent variable (calories) was performed to address the assumption violation.

(b) At the 0.05 level of significance, there is evidence of significant overall relationship between the square root of calories and the percentage of alcohol and the number of carbohydrates. Because $F_{STAT} = 1732.83$ or p-value = 0.000, reject H_0.

(c) $r^2 = 0.9575$. This indicates that 95.75% of the variation in the square root of calories can be explained by the variation in the percentage of alcohol and the variation in the number of carbohydrates.

(d) Adjusted $r^2 = 0.9569$.

(e) The model in 15.10 is better because it is less skewed than the linear model.

15.12 (a) Predicted ln(Price) = 9.7771 – 0.10218 Age.

(b) \$10,574.92

(c)

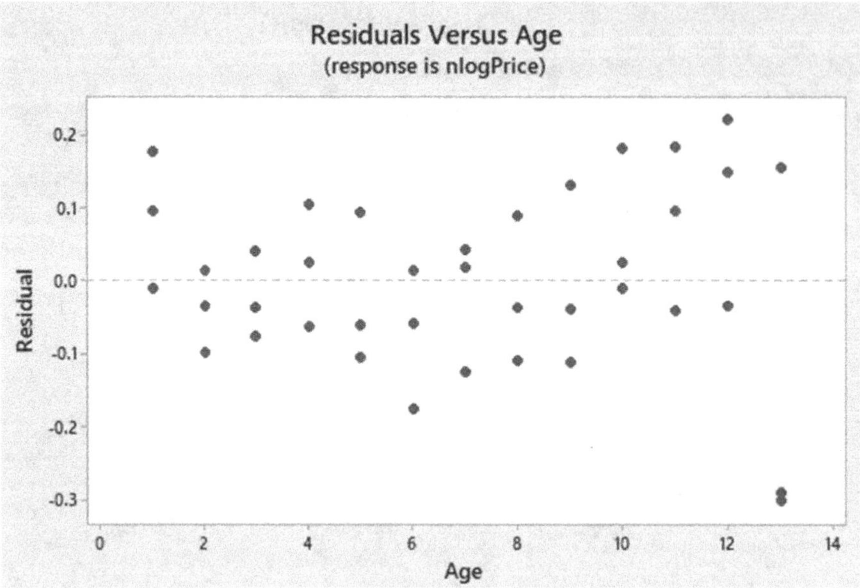

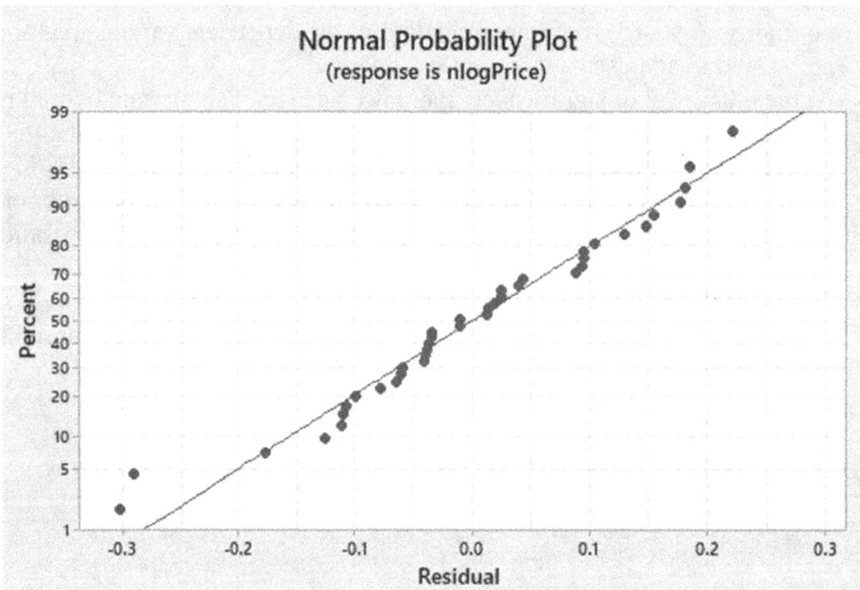

There is no evidence of violations of assumptions. The model is adequate.

(d) t_{STAT} = 19.48 or p-value = 0.000, reject H_0.

(e) 0.9112. 91.12% of the variation in the natural log of price can be explained by the age of the auto.

(f) 0.9088.

(g) Choose the model from Problem 15.6. That model has a higher adjusted r^2 of 92.73%.

15.14 $VIF = \dfrac{1}{1-0.2} = 1.25$

15.16

Coefficients

Term	Coef	SE Coef	T-Value	P-Value	VIF
Constant	1.396	0.179	7.79	0.000	
Efficiency Ratio (%)	-0.01173	0.00220	-5.34	0.000	1.07
Total Risk-Based Capital Ratio	0.02861	0.00540	5.30	0.000	1.07

$R_1^2 = 0.0634$, $VIF_1 = \dfrac{1}{1-0.0634} = 1.0677$

$R_2^2 = 0.0634$, $VIF_2 = \dfrac{1}{1-0.0634} = 1.0677$

There is no reason to suspect the existence of collinearity.

15.18

Coefficients

Term	Coef	SE Coef	T-Value	P-Value	VIF
Constant	302	260	1.16	0.250	
Total Worldwide Revenues ($bil)	3.48	4.67	0.74	0.460	1.01
FT Voluntary Turnover (%)	41.0	21.8	1.88	0.064	1.01

Coefficients

Term	Coef	SE Coef	T-Value	P-Value	VIF
Constant	302	260	1.16	0.250	
Total Worldwide Revenues ($bil)	3.48	4.67	0.74	0.460	1.01
FT Voluntary Turnover (%)	41.0	21.8	1.88	0.064	1.01

$R_1^2 = 0.008464$, $VIF_1 = \dfrac{1}{1-0.008464} = 1.009$

$R_2^2 = 0.008464$, $VIF_2 = \dfrac{1}{1-0.008464} = 1.009$

There is no reason to suspect the existence of collinearity.

15.20 $VIF = \dfrac{1}{1-0.0104} = 1.0105$. There is no reason to suspect the existence of collinearity.

15.22 (a) $C_p = \dfrac{(1-R_k^2)(n-T)}{1-R_T^2} - [n-2(k+1)] = \dfrac{(1-0.274)(40-7)}{1-0.653} - [40-2(2+1)]$

$= 35.04$

(b) C_p overwhelmingly exceeds $k + 1 = 3$, the number of parameters (including the Y-intercept), so this model does not meet the criterion for further consideration as the best model.

15.24

Coefficients

Term	Coef	SE Coef	T-Value	P-Value	VIF
Constant	298.1	76.1	3.92	0.000	
Lot Size	55.5	65.2	0.85	0.399	1.40
Living Space	0.0592	0.0188	3.15	0.003	2.12
Bedrooms	7.1	13.8	0.51	0.610	2.09
Bathrooms	2.5	17.7	0.14	0.888	2.35
Age	-0.268	0.683	-0.39	0.696	1.78
Fireplace	53.5	20.0	2.67	0.010	1.09

A regression analysis revealed that the following six variables had *VIF* values of less than 5.

Best Subsets Regression: Asking Price versus Lot Size, ... Age, Fireplace

Response is Asking Price

Vars	R-Sq	R-Sq (adj)	R-Sq (pred)	Mallows Cp	S	Lot Size	Living Space	Bedrooms	Bathrooms	Age	Fireplace
1	39.8	38.8	36.0	6.2	70.540		X				
1	18.1	16.7	13.2	29.0	82.258	X					
2	46.8	45.0	41.5	0.9	66.869		X				X
2	41.6	39.5	36.1	6.4	70.088	X	X				
3	47.8	45.1	41.0	1.8	66.802	X	X				X
3	47.5	44.7	39.2	2.1	67.007		X	X			X
4	48.4	44.7	38.2	3.2	67.050	X	X	X			X
4	48.2	44.5	38.4	3.4	67.150	X	X		X		X
5	48.6	43.9	34.6	5.0	67.522	X	X	X		X	X
5	48.4	43.8	35.6	5.2	67.606	X	X	X	X		X
6	48.6	42.9	32.0	7.0	68.131	X	X	X	X	X	X

A Best Subsets analysis reveals that the two variable model including living space and whether a house had a fireplace had the lowest C_p value (0.9). The *F*-test of the overall model reveals that the model is significant at the 0.05 significance level. Individual *t*-tests on the independent variables are significant at the 0.05 level, which suggests the two independent variables should be included. Although other models had slightly higher r^2 values, the minimal change does not appear to justify the added complexity. The two variable model (living space and fireplace) with an r^2 of .468 indicates that 46.8% of the variation in starting salary can be explained by the variation in program per-year tuition, acceptance rate, and percent of graduates with job offers.

15.24
cont.

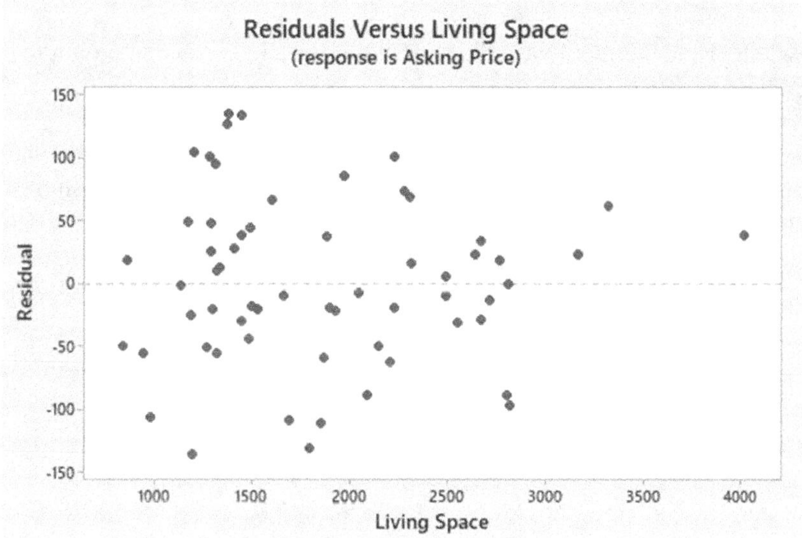
Residuals Versus Living Space
(response is Asking Price)
Residual
Living Space
150
100
50
0
-50
-100
-150
1000
1500
2000
2500
3000
3500
4000

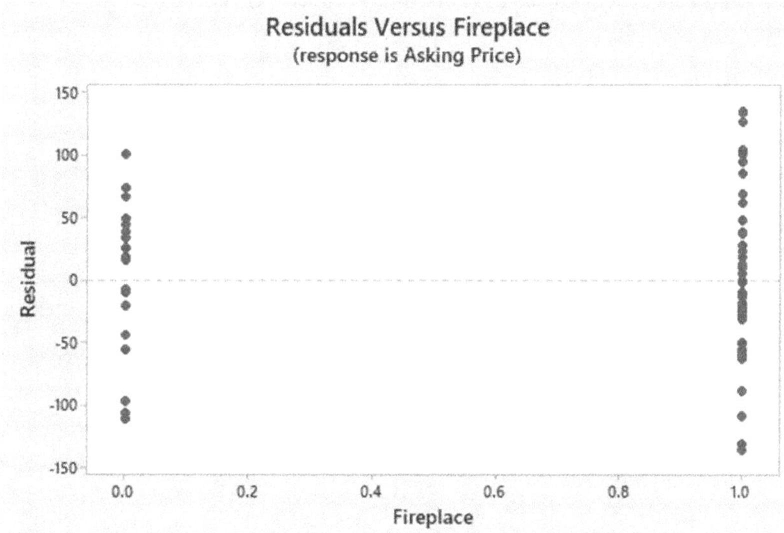
Residuals Versus Fireplace
(response is Asking Price)
Residual
Fireplace
150
100
50
0
-50
-100
-150
0.0
0.2
0.4
0.6
0.8
1.0

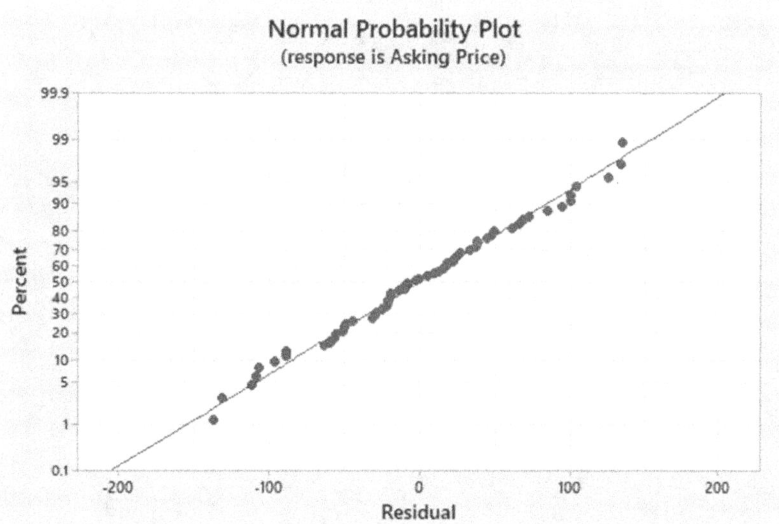
Normal Probability Plot
(response is Asking Price)
Percent
Residual
99.9
99
95
90
80
70
60
50
40
30
20
10
5
1
0.1
-200
-100
0
100
200

15.24 cont. The residual plots reveal no clear pattern, indicating no evidence for violation of the equal variance or linearity assumptions. The normal probability plot shows no sufficient deviation from normality.

15.26 In order to evaluate whether independent variables are intercorrelated, you can compute the Variance Inflationary Factor (*VIF*).

15.28 One way to choose among models that meet these criteria is to determine whether the models contain a subset of variables that are common, and then test whether the contribution of the additional variables is significant.

15.30

Coefficients

Term	Coef	SE Coef	95% CI	T-Value	P-Value	VIF
Constant	-44.6	40.3	(-134.4, 45.2)	-1.11	0.295	
Temperature	0.085	0.121	(-0.184, 0.353)	0.70	0.497	1.03
Pressure	0.800	0.603	(-0.543, 2.143)	1.33	0.214	1.03
Low	-12.48	5.17	(-23.99, -0.96)	-2.41	0.036	1.06

A regression analysis with all three variables reveals that all had VIF values well below five with the largest VIF = 1.06.

Best Subsets Regression: Registration Error versus ... re, Pressure, Low

Response is Registration Error

Vars	R-Sq	R-Sq (adj)	R-Sq (pred)	Mallows Cp	S	Temperature	Pressure	Low
1	39.7	34.7	17.9	2.2	9.4690			X
1	15.4	8.4	0.0	7.1	11.213		X	
1	6.4	0.0	0.0	9.0	11.800	X		
2	48.2	38.7	11.7	2.5	9.1710		X	X
2	41.9	31.3	0.0	3.8	9.7091	X		X
2	21.8	7.6	0.0	7.8	11.263	X	X	
3	50.6	35.8	0.0	4.0	9.3886	X	X	X

15.30 cont. A best subsets regression reveals that the model with pressure and cost had the lowest C_p value and the highest adjusted r^2.

Regression Analysis: Registration Error versus Pressure, Low

Analysis of Variance

Source	DF	Seq SS	Contribution	Adj SS	Adj MS	F-Value	P-Value
Regression	2	859.4	48.16%	859.4	429.68	5.11	0.027
Pressure	1	275.6	15.45%	150.8	150.78	1.79	0.208
Low	1	583.7	32.71%	583.7	583.74	6.94	0.023
Error	11	925.2	51.84%	925.2	84.11		
Lack-of-Fit	3	107.9	6.05%	107.9	35.97	0.35	0.789
Pure Error	8	817.3	45.80%	817.3	102.16		
Total	13	1784.5	100.00%				

Model Summary

S	R-sq	R-sq(adj)	PRESS	R-sq(pred)
9.17097	48.16%	38.73%	1574.96	11.74%

Coefficients

Term	Coef	SE Coef	95% CI	T-Value	P-Value	VIF
Constant	-18.5	15.5	(-52.7, 15.7)	-1.19	0.259	
Pressure	0.788	0.588	(-0.507, 2.083)	1.34	0.208	1.03
Low	-13.10	4.97	(-24.05, -2.16)	-2.63	0.023	1.03

Regression Equation

Registration Error = -18.5 + 0.788 Pressure - 13.10 Low

A regression analysis on the two variable model with pressure and cost reveals that the pressure variable was not significant at the 0.05 significance level.

15.30
cont.

Regression Analysis: Registration Error versus Low

Analysis of Variance

Source	DF	Seq SS	Contribution	Adj SS	Adj MS	F-Value	P-Value
Regression	1	708.6	39.71%	708.6	708.58	7.90	0.016
Low	1	708.6	39.71%	708.6	708.58	7.90	0.016
Error	12	1076.0	60.29%	1076.0	89.66		
Total	13	1784.5	100.00%				

Model Summary

S	R-sq	R-sq(adj)	PRESS	R-sq(pred)
9.46903	39.71%	34.68%	1464.49	17.93%

Coefficients

Term	Coef	SE Coef	95% CI	T-Value	P-Value	VIF
Constant	1.77	3.58	(-6.03, 9.57)	0.49	0.630	
Low	-14.23	5.06	(-25.26, -3.20)	-2.81	0.016	1.00

Regression Equation

Registration Error = 1.77 - 14.23 Low

A regression analysis with cost as the only variable reveals a significant F_{STAT} for the overall model. The cost variable is significant at the 0.05 significance level. Because $t_{STAT} = -2.81$ or p-value = 0.016, reject H_0. The r^2 of 0.3971 indicates that 39.71% of variation in registration errors can be explained by the cost of the material.

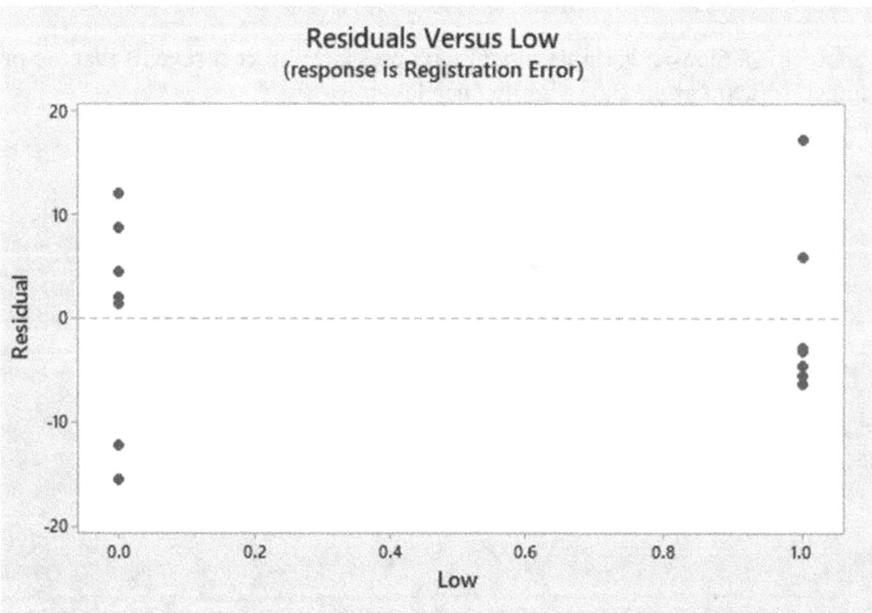

15.30
cont.

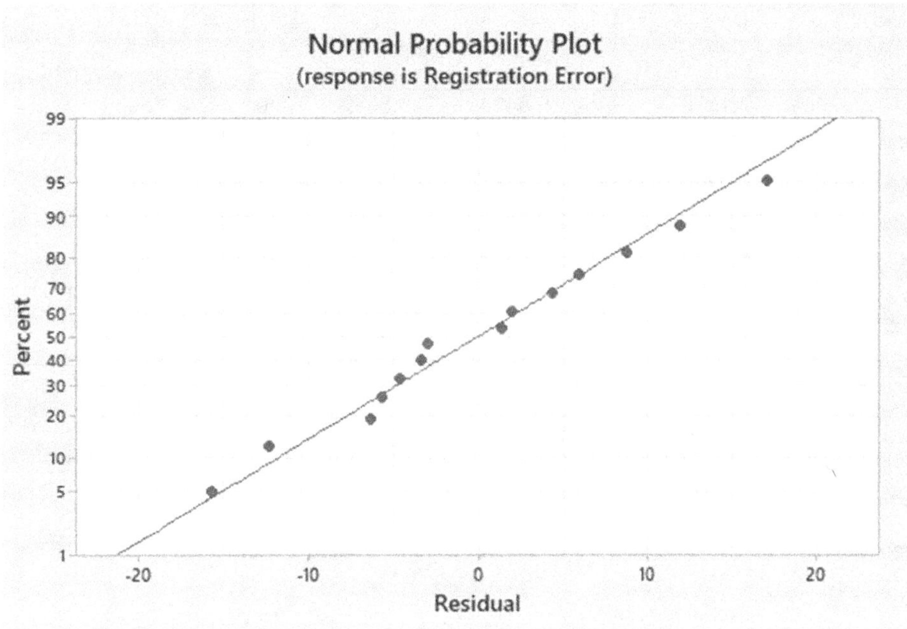

Residual analyses reveal no clear patters, which indicate there appear to be no violations of assumptions.
The best linear model, which contains only the cost as the predictor variable, is:
$\hat{Y} = 1.77 - 14.23X$ where X = cost (low = 1).

15.32 Let Y = fair market value, X_1 = land area, X_2 = interior size, X_3 = age, X_4 = number of rooms, X_5 = number of bathrooms, X_6 = garage size.

Glencove:
Based on a full regression model involving all of the variables:
All *VIF*s are less than 5. So there is no reason to suspect collinearity between any pair of variables.

15.32 cont. The best-subset approach yielded the following models to be considered:

Model	Cp	k+1	R Square	Adj. R Square	Std. Error	Consider This Model?
X1X2X3	**2.1558**	**4**	0.8424	0.8242	60.5007	Yes
X1X2X3X4	**4.1117**	**5**	0.8427	0.8175	61.6425	Yes
X1X2X3X5	**3.2400**	**5**	0.8484	0.8241	60.5180	Yes
X1X2X3X6	**3.8887**	**5**	0.8442	0.8192	61.3567	Yes
X1X2X3X4X5	**5.1832**	**6**	0.8488	0.8173	61.6903	Yes
X1X2X3X4X6	**5.7825**	**6**	0.8449	0.8125	62.4827	Yes
X1X2X3X5X6	**5.1038**	**6**	0.8493	0.8179	61.5846	Yes
X1X2X3X4X5X6	**7.0000**	**7**	0.8500	0.8108	62.7677	Yes

The stepwise regression approach reveals the following best model:

	Coefficients	*Standard Error*	*t Stat*	*P-value*
Intercept	260.6791	66.3288	3.9301	0.0006
Property Size (acres)	362.8318	48.6233	7.4621	0.0000
House Size (square feet)	0.1109	0.0228	4.8682	0.0000
Age	-1.7543	0.5483	-3.1996	0.0036

The p-value of the individual slope coefficients indicate that all the remaining independent variables are significant individually. Combining the results of both approaches, the most appropriate multiple regression model for predicting fair market value in Glencove is:
$\hat{Y} = 260.6791 + 362.8318X_1 + 0.1109X_2 - 1.7543X_3$

15.34 (a) Let Y = fair market value, X_1 = land area, X_2 = interior size, X_3 = age, X_4 = number of rooms, X_5 = number of bathrooms, X_6 = garage size.

Freeport:
Based on a full regression model involving all of the variables:
All *VIF*s are less than 5. So there is no reason to suspect collinearity between any pair of variables.

15.34 cont. (a) The best-subset approach yielded the following models to be considered:

Model	Cp	k+1	R Square	Adj. R Square	Std. Error	Consider This Model?
X1X2	**2.5499**	3	0.8638	0.8538	27.2314	Yes
X1X2X3	**3.8212**	4	0.8676	0.8523	27.3666	Yes
X1X2X5	**2.5555**	4	0.8741	0.8595	26.6875	Yes
X1X2X6	**2.0625**	4	0.8766	0.8624	26.4182	Yes
X1X2X3X5	**4.4527**	5	0.8746	0.8545	27.1590	Yes
X1X2X3X6	**3.9052**	5	0.8774	0.8578	26.8532	Yes
X1X2X4X5	**4.2508**	5	0.8756	0.8557	27.0466	Yes
X1X2X4X6	**3.9937**	5	0.8770	0.8573	26.9029	Yes
X1X2X5X6	**3.5681**	5	0.8791	0.8598	26.6632	Yes
X1X2X3X4X6	**5.6740**	6	0.8786	0.8533	27.2741	Yes
X1X2X3X5X6	**5.3826**	6	0.8801	0.8551	27.1057	Yes
X1X2X4X5X6	**5.4360**	6	0.8798	0.8548	27.1366	Yes
X1X2X3X4X5X6	**7.0000**	7	0.8820	0.8513	27.4612	Yes

The two variable model of property size and house size had the lowest C_p value and the highest adjusted r^2 value. However, the p-value of the t-test for individual coefficient shows that X_1 is not significant at the 5% level of significance.

	Coefficients	*Standard Error*	*t Stat*	*P-value*
Intercept	145.1217	15.1661	9.5688	0.0000
Property size (acres	149.9337	86.1028	1.7413	0.0930
House Size (square	0.0913	0.0120	7.5956	0.0000

Regression Analysis: Fair Market Value($000) versus ... ize (square feet)

Analysis of Variance

Source	DF	Adj SS	Adj MS	F-Value	P-Value
Regression	1	124777	124777	156.88	0.000
House Size (square feet)	1	124777	124777	156.88	0.000
Error	28	22270	795		
Total	29	147047			

Model Summary

S	R-sq	R-sq(adj)	R-sq(pred)
28.2023	84.85%	84.31%	82.40%

Coefficients

Term	Coef	SE Coef	T-Value	P-Value	VIF
Constant	142.7	15.6	9.12	0.000	
House Size (square feet)	0.10664	0.00851	12.53	0.000	1.00

Regression Equation

Fair Market Value($000) = 142.7 + 0.10664 House Size (square feet)

15.34 cont. (a) The best model is:

$\hat{Y} = 142.7398 + 0.1066X_2$

(b) The adjusted r^2 for the best model in 15.32(a), 15.33(a), and 15.34(a) are, respectively, 0.8242, 0.9047 and 0.8431. The model in 15.33(a) has the highest explanatory power after adjusting for the number of independent variables and sample size.

15.36 Let Y = fair market value, X_1 = land area, X_2 = interior size, X_3 = age, X_4 = number of rooms, X_5 = number of bathrooms, X_6 = garage size, X_7 = 1 if GlenCove and 0 otherwise, X_8 = 1 if Roslyn and 0 otherwise.

(a) Based on a full regression model involving all of the variables:
The *VIF* of X_2, X_3 and X_7 are greater than 5.
Dropping X_2 with the largest *VIF*, X_3 still has a *VIF* greater than 5.
After dropping X_2 and X_3, all remaining *VIF*s are less than 5. So there is no reason to suspect collinearity between any pair of variables.

Now let Y = fair market value, X_1 = land area, X_2 = number of rooms, X_3 = number of bathrooms, X_4 = garage size, X_5 = 1 if GlenCove and 0 otherwise, X_6 = 1 if Roslyn and 0 otherwise.

The best-subset approach yielded the following models to be considered:

Model	Cp	k+1	R Square	Adj. R Square	Std. Error	Consider This Model?
X1X3X4X6	4.3211	5	0.6958	0.6815	145.4771	Yes
X1X2X3X4X6	5.3213	6	0.6994	0.6815	145.4702	Yes
X1X2X3X4X5X6	7.0000	7	0.7005	0.6789	146.0615	Yes

The *p*-value of X_2, X_4 and X_5 are all greater than 0.05 in the regression model with X_1, X_2, X_3, X_4, X_5, and X_6.

	Coefficients	*Standard Error*	*t Stat*	*P-value*
Intercept	-19.7877	76.9121	-0.2573	0.7976
Property Size (acre:	551.1974	103.5799	5.3215	0.0000
Rooms	11.3359	10.7931	1.0503	0.2966
Baths	101.7208	26.0074	3.9112	0.0002
Garage	48.1114	29.1443	1.6508	0.1026
Glen Cove	23.1968	40.9252	0.5668	0.5724
Roslyn	226.0072	42.2948	5.3436	0.0000

The stepwise regression approach reveals the following best model:

	Coefficients	*Standard Error*	*t Stat*	*P-value*
Intercept	30.1063	44.6655	0.6740	0.5021
Baths	130.7788	21.7928	6.0010	0.0000
Property Size (acres)	611.6910	98.5954	6.2040	0.0000
Roslyn	214.2567	35.5299	6.0303	0.0000

Combining the results of both approaches, the most appropriate multiple regression model for predicting fair market value is

$\hat{Y} = 30.1063 + 611.6910X_1 + 130.7788X_3 + 214.2567X_6$

15.36 cont. (b) The estimated mean fair market value in Roslyn is \$214.2567 thousands above Freeport for two otherwise identical properties. There is no significant difference in mean fair market value between two otherwise identical properties in Glen Cove and Freeport.

15.38 In the multiple regression model with catalyst, pH, pressure, temperature and voltage as independent variables, none of the variables have a *VIF* value of 5 or larger.

The best-subset approach yielded only the following model to be considered:

Model	Cp	k+1	R Square	Adj. R Square	Std. Error
X1X2X3X4X5	6	6	0.875922	0.861822068	1.293575

where X_1 = catalyst, X_2 = pH, X_3 = pressure, X_4 = temp, and X_5 = voltage.

Looking at the p-values of the t statistics for each slope coefficient of the model that includes X_1 through X_5 reveals that pH level is not significant at 5% level of significance.

	Coefficients	*Standard Error*	*t Stat*	*P-value*
Intercept	4.454255233	8.222983547	0.541683588	0.590769119
Catalyst	0.162669323	0.036277562	4.484020293	5.18724E-05
pH	0.086375011	0.080013101	1.079510851	0.286242198
Pressure	–0.043059299	0.013464369	–3.198018263	0.002564899
Temp	–0.402556214	0.069704281	–5.775200729	7.21416E-07
Voltage	0.422370024	0.028413318	14.86521277	9.13658E-19

The multiple regression model with pH level deleted shows that all coefficients are significant individually at 5% level of significance.

	Coefficients	*Standard Error*	*t Stat*	*P-value*
Intercept	3.683340948	8.206951065	0.44880747	0.655724457
Catalyst	0.154754083	0.035594069	4.347749199	7.77444E-05
Pressure	–0.041971526	0.013451255	–3.120268445	0.003150939
Temp	–0.4035674	0.069825915	–5.779622062	6.62469E-07
Voltage	0.428756573	0.027841579	15.3998654	1.47975E-19

The best linear model is determined to be:

$\hat{Y} = 3.6833 + 0.1548X_1 - 0.04197X_3 - 0.4036X_4 + 0.4288X_5$.

The overall model has $F = 77.0793$ (4 and 45 degrees of freedom) with a p-value that is virtually 0. $r^2 = 0.8726$, $r^2_{adj} = 0.8613$.

The normal probability plot does not suggest possible violation of the normality assumption. A residual analysis reveals a potential non-linear relationship in temperature.

15.38
cont.

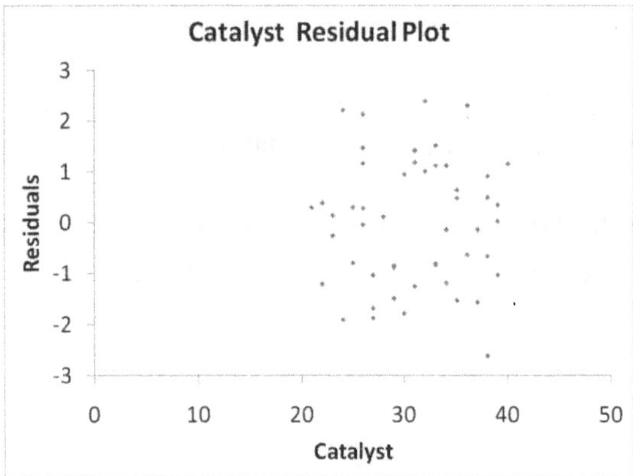
Catalyst Residual Plot
Residuals
3
2
1
0
-1
-2
-3
0
10
20
30
40
50
Catalyst

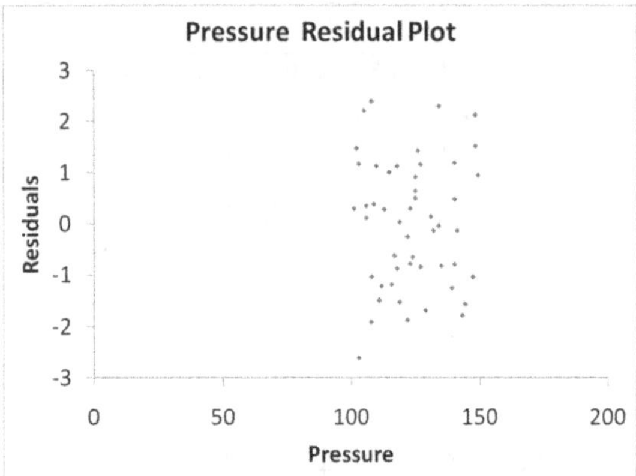
Pressure Residual Plot
Residuals
3
2
1
0
-1
-2
-3
0
50
100
150
200
Pressure

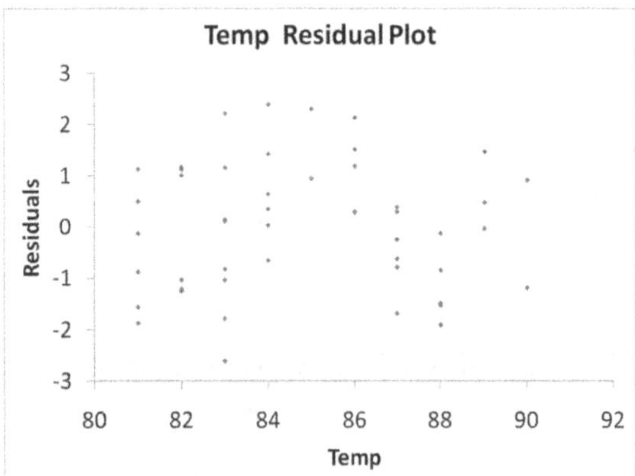
Temp Residual Plot
Residuals
3
2
1
0
-1
-2
-3
80
82
84
86
88
90
92
Temp

15.38
cont.

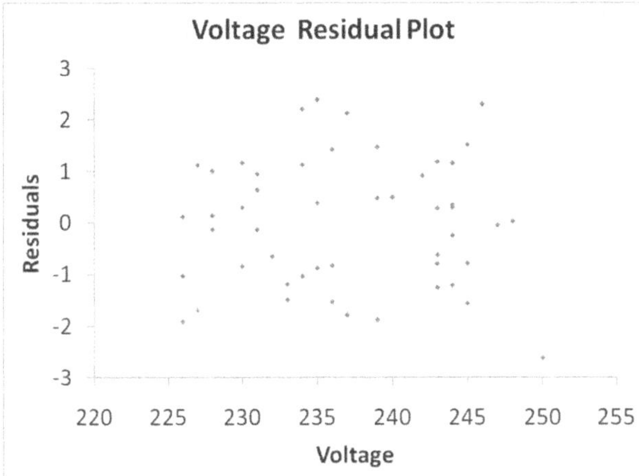

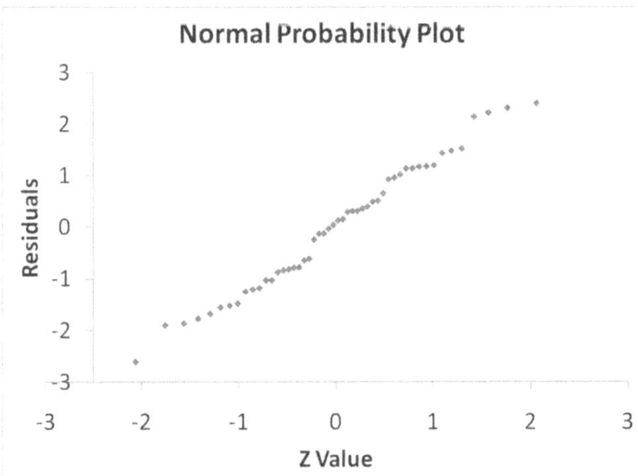

The p-value of the squared term for temperature in the following quadratic transformation of temperature does not support the need for a quadratic transformation at the 5% level of significance.

	Coefficients	*Standard Error*	*t Stat*	*P-value*
Intercept	–322.0541757	209.7341228	–1.535535426	0.131812685
Catalyst	0.16474942	0.035632189	4.623612047	3.30582E-05
Pressure	–0.044452151	0.01334035	–3.332157868	0.001753581
Temp	7.27648367	4.9417966	1.472436901	0.148020497
Temp Squared	–0.04508917	0.029010216	–1.554251433	0.127288634
Voltage	0.424662847	0.027539942	15.41988889	2.34994E-19

15.38 cont. The *p*-value of the interaction term between pressure and temperature below indicates that there is not enough evidence of an interaction at the 5% level of significance.

	Coefficients	*Standard Error*	*t Stat*	*P-value*
Intercept	103.5523674	55.92763384	1.851542078	0.070809822
Catalyst	0.144935857	0.035157935	4.122422311	0.000163315
Pressure	–0.859424944	0.453254189	–1.896121349	0.064522645
Temp	–1.586885548	0.659370559	–2.406667277	0.020363651
Pressure x Temp	0.009640768	0.005343284	1.804277709	0.078035623
Voltage	0.431941042	0.027226309	15.86484039	8.10114E-20

The best model is still the one that includes catalyst, pressure, temperature and voltage which manages to explain 87.26% of the variation in thickness.

15.40

Coefficients

Term	Coef	SE Coef	95% CI	T-Value	P-Value	VIF
Constant	6679	11434	(-17252, 30610)	0.58	0.566	
Unemployment Rate (%)	1181	1214	(-1360, 3722)	0.97	0.343	1.21
Median Home Value ($000)	38.20	5.42	(26.86, 49.54)	7.05	0.000	1.27
Violent Crime per 100,000 resid	-10.42	6.25	(-23.51, 2.67)	-1.67	0.112	1.21
Average Commuter Time (mins)	1012	269	(449, 1575)	3.76	0.001	1.27
Livability Score	117	143	(-183, 417)	0.82	0.423	1.14

15.40 cont. A regression analysis revealed that all five variables had VIF values below 5.

Vars	R-Sq	R-Sq (adj)	R-Sq (pred)	Mallows Cp	S	Unemployment Rate (%)	Median Home Value ($000)	Violent Crime	Average Commuter Time (mins)	Livability Score
1	72.7	71.5	68.4	15.4	4914.8		X			
1	38.2	35.5	30.2	61.3	7397.4				X	
1	6.9	2.9	0.0	102.9	9075.0					X
2	82.8	81.2	73.1	3.9	3992.5		X		X	
2	73.5	71.1	67.2	16.3	4954.1	X	X			
2	73.3	70.9	65.7	16.6	4971.1		X			X
3	84.7	82.5	74.1	3.3	3848.3		X	X	X	
3	83.4	81.1	64.0	5.1	4008.5		X		X	X
3	82.8	80.4	70.0	5.9	4078.5	X	X		X	
4	85.2	82.3	71.7	4.7	3877.2	X	X	X	X	
4	85.0	82.0	65.1	4.9	3904.2		X	X	X	X
4	83.6	80.4	59.9	6.8	4079.3	X	X		X	X
5	85.7	82.0	61.9	6.0	3909.5	X	X	X	X	X

15.40 cont. A best subsets regression analysis reveals that the three variable model with median home value, violent crime, and commuter time has the lowest C_p value and the highest adjusted r^2.

Regression Analysis: Average Annual Salary ($) versus ... r Time (mins)

Analysis of Variance

Source	DF	Seq SS	Contribution	Adj SS	Adj MS	F-Value
Regression	3	1724178553	84.72%	1724178553	574726184	38.81
Median Home Value ($000)	1	1479596447	72.70%	792872643	792872643	53.54
Violent Crime	1	5931696	0.29%	39692207	39692207	2.68
Average Commuter Time (mins)	1	238650410	11.73%	238650410	238650410	16.12
Error	21	310993031	15.28%	310993031	14809192	
Total	24	2035171584	100.00%			

Source	P-Value
Regression	0.000
Median Home Value ($000)	0.000
Violent Crime	0.116
Average Commuter Time (mins)	0.001
Error	
Total	

Model Summary

S	R-sq	R-sq(adj)	PRESS	R-sq(pred)
3848.27	84.72%	82.54%	526877839	74.11%

Coefficients

Term	Coef	SE Coef	95% CI	T-Value	P-Value	VIF
Constant	16830	6289	(3752, 29909)	2.68	0.014	
Median Home Value ($000)	38.26	5.23	(27.38, 49.13)	7.32	0.000	1.22
Violent Crime	-9.53	5.82	(-21.65, 2.58)	-1.64	0.116	1.08
Average Commuter Time (mins)	1053	262	(508, 1599)	4.01	0.001	1.25

Regression Equation

Average Annual Salary ($) = 16830 + 38.26 Median Home Value ($000) - 9.53 Violent Crime + 1053 Average Commuter Time (mins)

15.40 cont. A regression analysis with the three variable model of median home value, violent crime, and commuter time reveals a significant F_{STAT} for the overall model. Because the violent crime variable was not significant at the 0.05 level, it was removed.

Regression Analysis: Average Annual Salary ($) versus ... r Time (mins)

Analysis of Variance

Source	DF	Seq SS	Contribution	Adj SS	Adj MS	F-Value
Regression	2	1684486347	82.77%	1684486347	842243173	52.84
Median Home Value ($000)	1	1479596447	72.70%	907896797	907896797	56.96
Average Commuter Time (mins)	1	204889899	10.07%	204889899	204889899	12.85
Error	22	350685237	17.23%	350685237	15940238	
Total	24	2035171584	100.00%			

Source	P-Value
Regression	0.000
Median Home Value ($000)	0.000
Average Commuter Time (mins)	0.002
Error	
Total	

Model Summary

S	R-sq	R-sq(adj)	PRESS	R-sq(pred)
3992.52	82.77%	81.20%	547073640	73.12%

Coefficients

Term	Coef	SE Coef	95% CI	T-Value	P-Value	VIF
Constant	15708	6486	(2257, 29158)	2.42	0.024	
Median Home Value ($000)	40.04	5.31	(29.04, 51.04)	7.55	0.000	1.17
Average Commuter Time (mins)	943	263	(398, 1489)	3.59	0.002	1.17

Regression Equation

Average Annual Salary ($) = 15708 + 40.04 Median Home Value ($000)
+ 943 Average Commuter Time (mins)

A regression analysis with the two variable model of median home value and commuter time reveals a significant F_{STAT} for the overall model. All variables were significant at the 0.05 level. This model represents the best model to predict average annual salary.

15.40 cont. Residual analyses reveal no potential violations in assumptions.

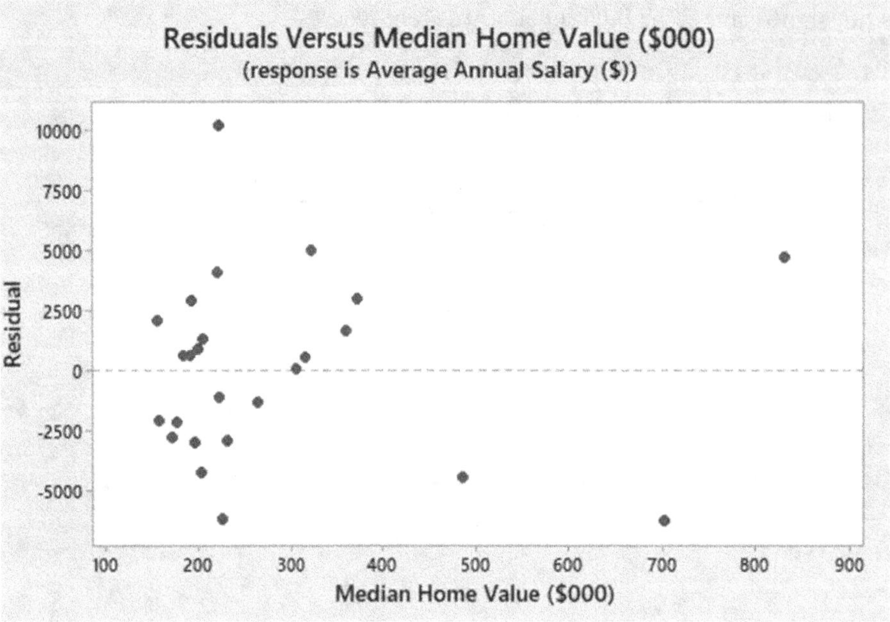

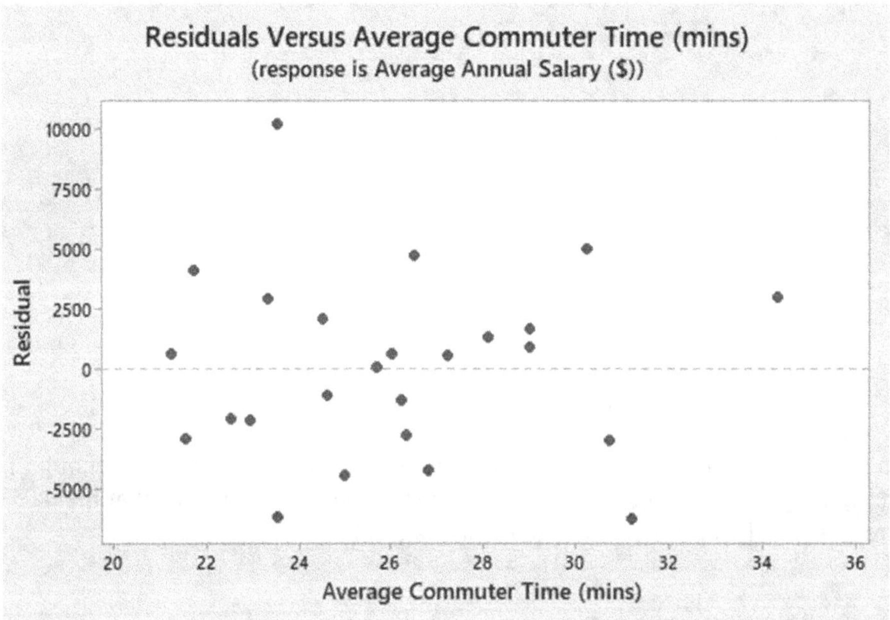

15.40
cont.

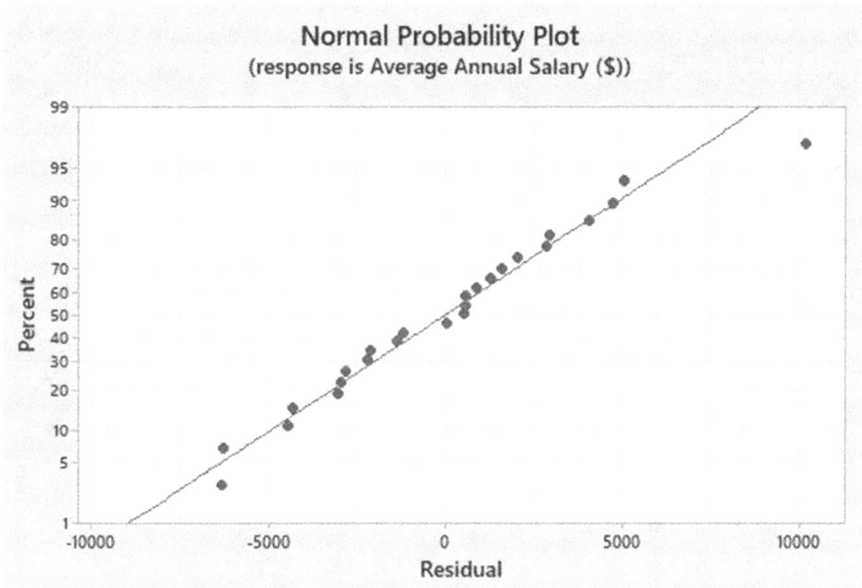

15.42 All analyses and associated summaries are provided with problems 15.32–15.36.

Chapter 16

16.2 (a) Since you need data from four prior years to obtain the centered 9-year moving average for any given year and since the first recorded value is for 1984, the first centered moving average value you can calculate is for 1988.

(b) You would lose four years for the period 1984–1987 since you do not have enough past values to compute a centered moving average. You will also lose the final four years of recorded time series since you do not have enough later values to compute a centered moving average. Therefore, you will lose a total of eight years in computing a series of 9-year moving averages.

16.4 (a)

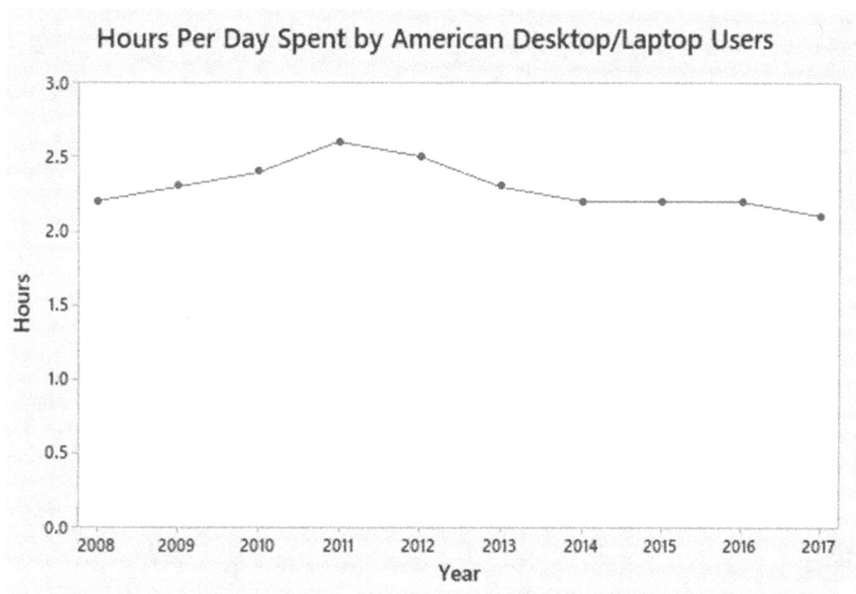

(b)

↓	C1	C2	C3
	Year	Hours	AVER1
1	2008	2.2	*
2	2009	2.3	2.30000
3	2010	2.4	2.43333
4	2011	2.6	2.50000
5	2012	2.5	2.46667
6	2013	2.3	2.33333
7	2014	2.2	2.23333
8	2015	2.2	2.20000
9	2016	2.2	2.16667
10	2017	2.1	*

16.4 cont. (b)

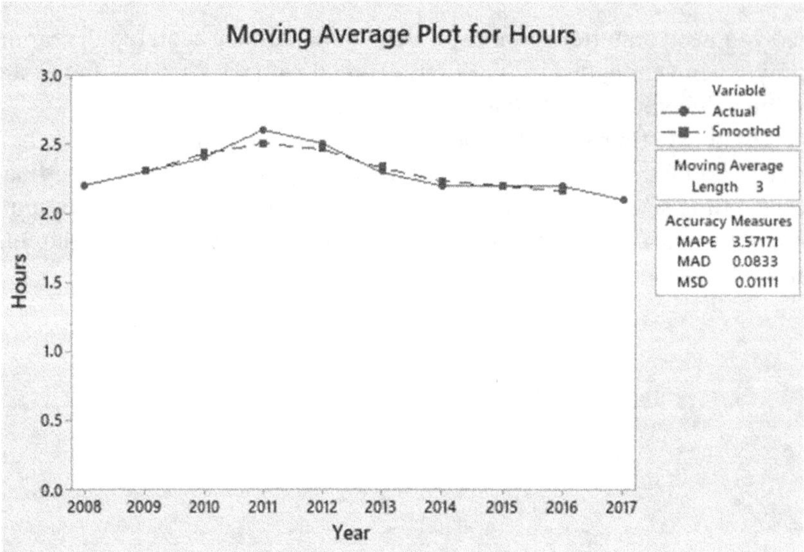

(c)

DATA

↓	C1	C2	C3
	Year	Hours	ES(W=0.50)
1	2008	2.2	2.20000
2	2009	2.3	2.25000
3	2010	2.4	2.32500
4	2011	2.6	2.46250
5	2012	2.5	2.48125
6	2013	2.3	2.39063
7	2014	2.2	2.29531
8	2015	2.2	2.24766
9	2016	2.2	2.22383
10	2017	2.1	2.16191

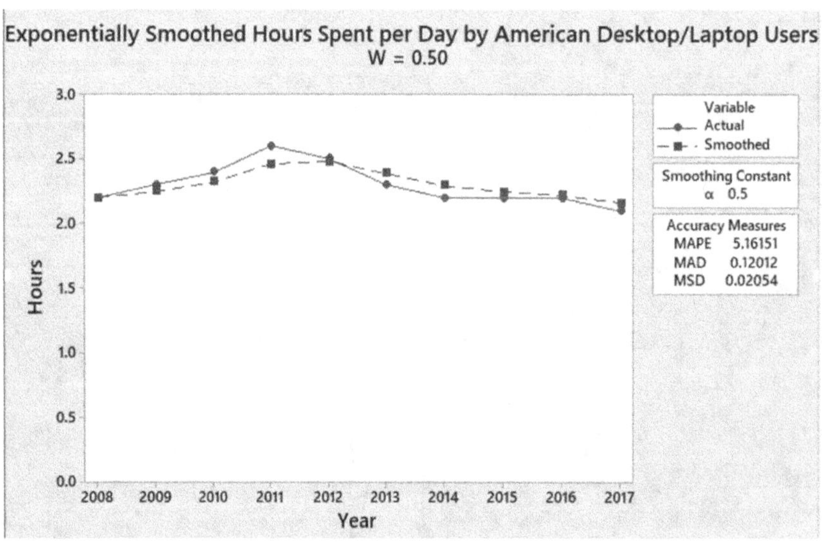

16.4 cont.

(d) $\hat{Y}_{2018} = E_{2017} = 2.1619$

(e)

DATA ***

↓	C1	C2	C4
	Year	Hours	ES (W=0.25)
1	2008	2.2	2.20000
2	2009	2.3	2.22500
3	2010	2.4	2.26875
4	2011	2.6	2.35156
5	2012	2.5	2.38867
6	2013	2.3	2.36650
7	2014	2.2	2.32488
8	2015	2.2	2.29366
9	2016	2.2	2.27024
10	2017	2.1	2.22768

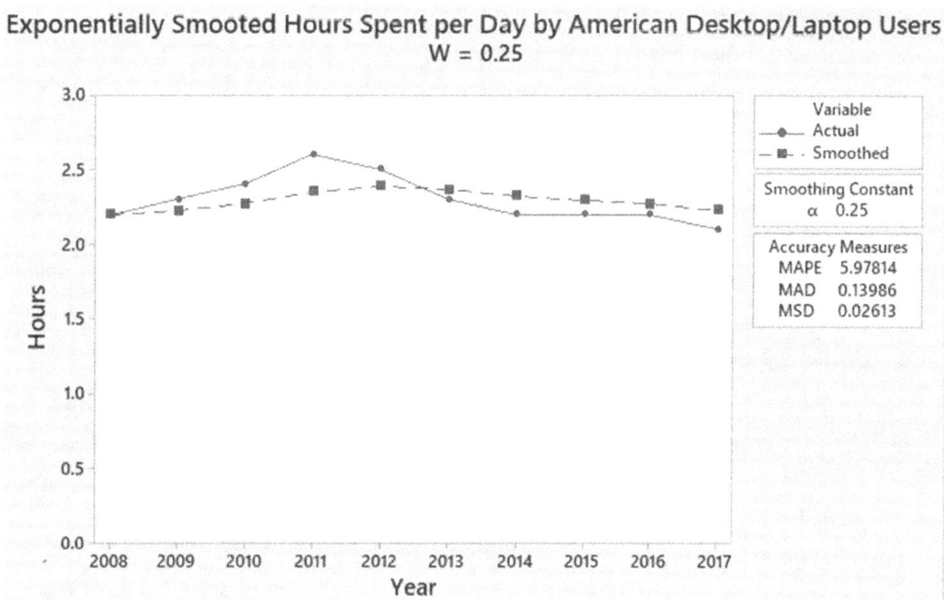

$\hat{Y}_{2018} = E_{2017} = 2.22768$

(f) The exponential smoothing with W = 0.5 assigns more weight to the more recent values and is better for short-term forecasting, while the exponential smoothing with W = 0.25, which assigns more weight to more distant values, is better suited for identifying long-term tendencies.

(g) There is no perceptible trend in the number of hours spent per day by American desktop/laptop users from 2008-1017. American desktop/laptop users have consistently spent between 2 and 2.5 hours per day on their computers.

16.6 (a)

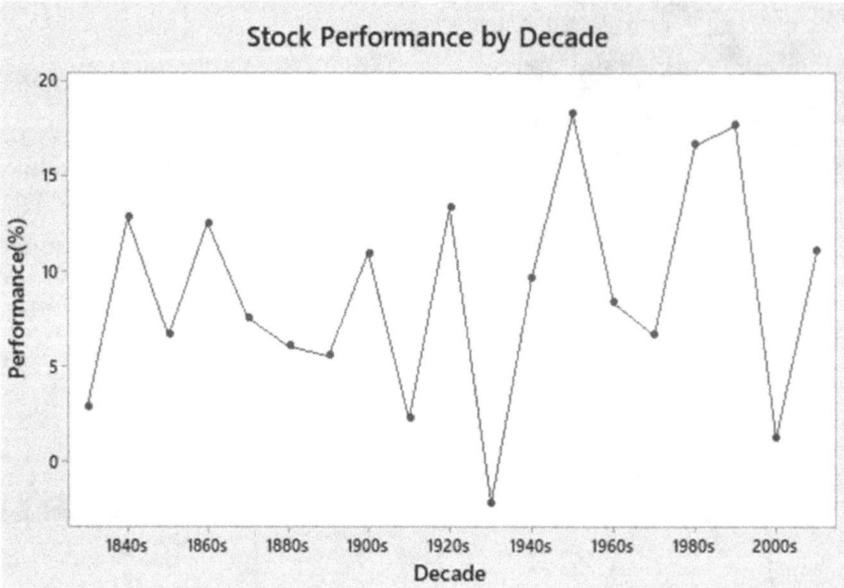

(b)

C1-T	C2	C3
Decade	Performance(%)	MA 3-YR
1830s	2.8	*
1840s	12.8	7.4000
1850s	6.6	10.6333
1860s	12.5	8.8667
1870s	7.5	8.6667
1880s	6.0	6.3333
1890s	5.5	7.4667
1900s	10.9	6.2000
1910s	2.2	8.8000
1920s	13.3	4.4333
1930s	-2.2	6.9000
1940s	9.6	8.5333
1950s	18.2	12.0333
1960s	8.3	11.0333
1970s	6.6	10.5000
1980s	16.6	13.6000
1990s	17.6	11.8000
2000s	1.2	9.9333
2010s	11.0	*

16.6 cont. (b)

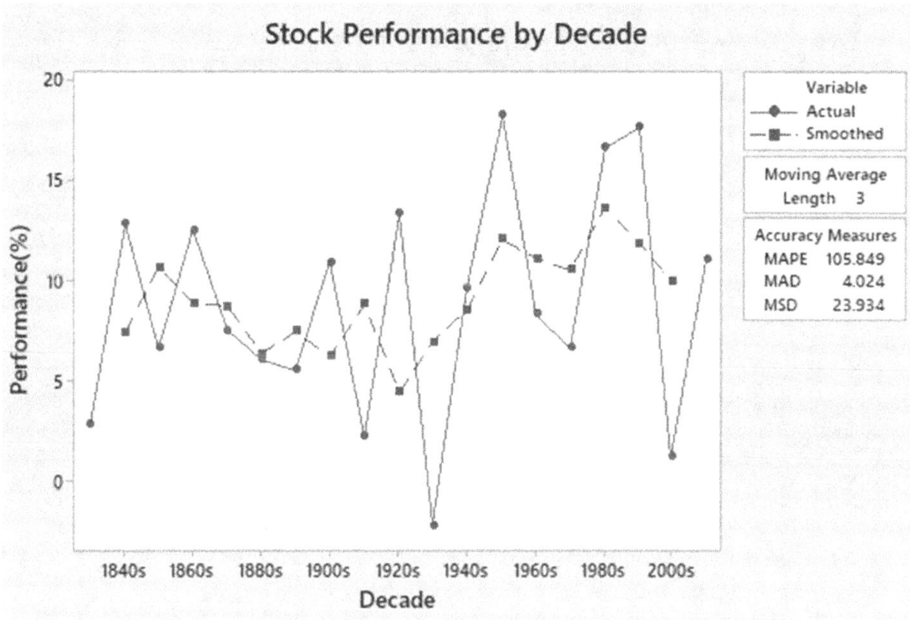

(c)

C1-T	C2	C4
Decade	Performance(%)	ES (W=0.50)
1830s	2.8	2.8000
1840s	12.8	7.8000
1850s	6.6	7.2000
1860s	12.5	9.8500
1870s	7.5	8.6750
1880s	6.0	7.3375
1890s	5.5	6.4188
1900s	10.9	8.6594
1910s	2.2	5.4297
1920s	13.3	9.3648
1930s	-2.2	3.5824
1940s	9.6	6.5912
1950s	18.2	12.3956
1960s	8.3	10.3478
1970s	6.6	8.4739
1980s	16.6	12.5370
1990s	17.6	15.0685
2000s	1.2	8.1342
2010s	11.0	9.5671

16.6 cont. (c)

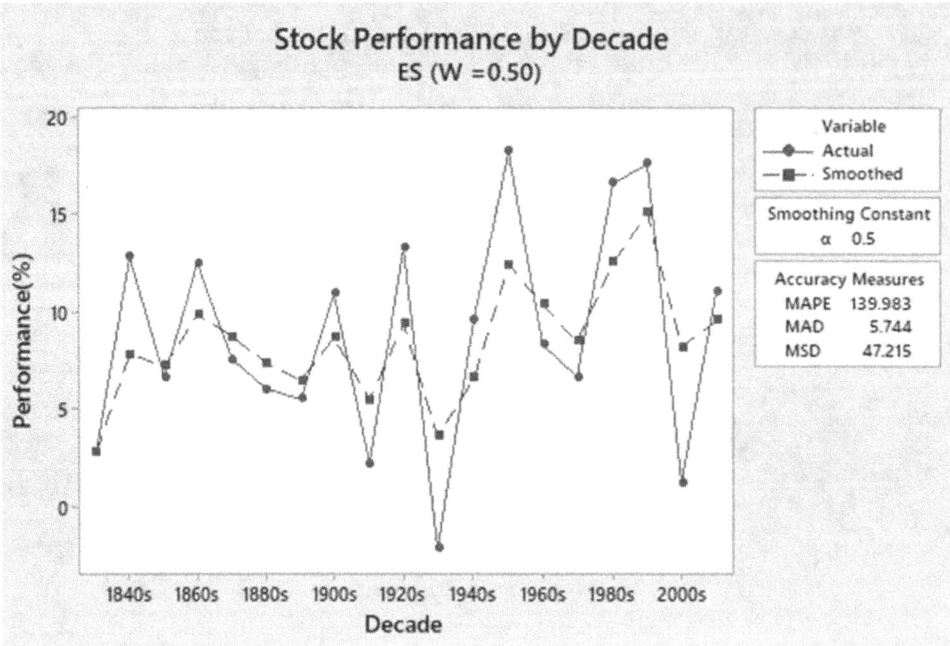

(d) $\hat{Y}_{2020s} = E_{2010s} = 9.5671$

(e)

C1-T	C2	C5
Decade	Performance(%)	ES (W=0.25)
1830s	2.8	2.8000
1840s	12.8	5.3000
1850s	6.6	5.6250
1860s	12.5	7.3438
1870s	7.5	7.3828
1880s	6.0	7.0371
1890s	5.5	6.6528
1900s	10.9	7.7146
1910s	2.2	6.3360
1920s	13.3	8.0770
1930s	-2.2	5.5077
1940s	9.6	6.5308
1950s	18.2	9.4481
1960s	8.3	9.1611
1970s	6.6	8.5208
1980s	16.6	10.5406
1990s	17.6	12.3055
2000s	1.2	9.5291
2010s	11.0	9.8968

16.6 cont. (e)

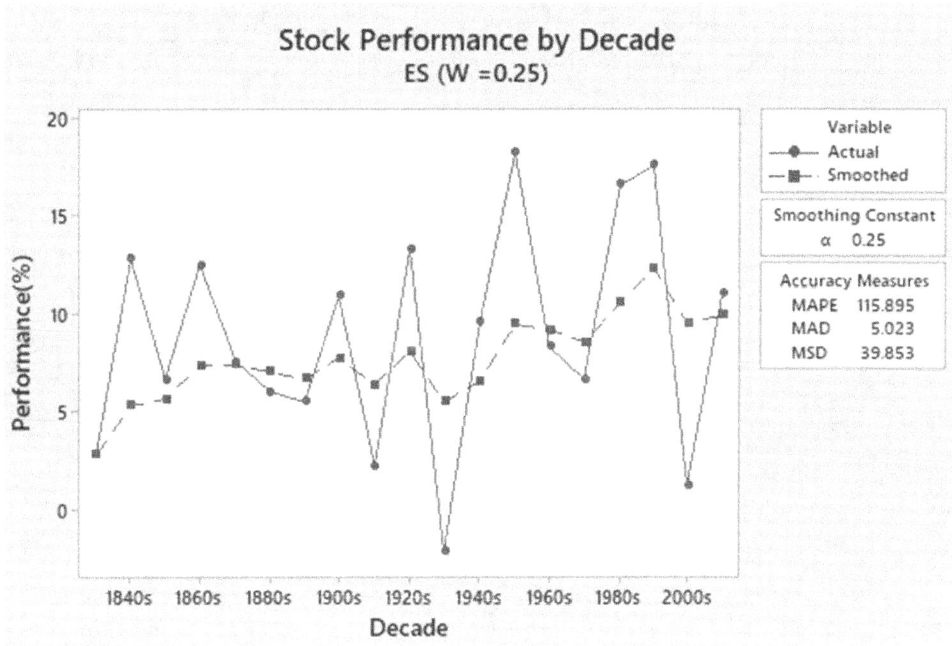

$\hat{Y}_{2020s} = E_{2010s} = 9.8968$

(f) The exponentially smoothed forecast for 2020s is lower with a W of 0.50 compared to a W of 0.25. The exponential smoothing with $W = 0.5$ assigns more weight to the more recent values and is better for short-term forecasting, while the exponential smoothing with $W = 0.25$, which assigns more weight to more distant values, is better suited for identifying long-term tendencies.

(g) Exponential smoothing with a W of 0.25 reveals a general upward trend in the performance of stocks over the last several decades.

16.8 (a)

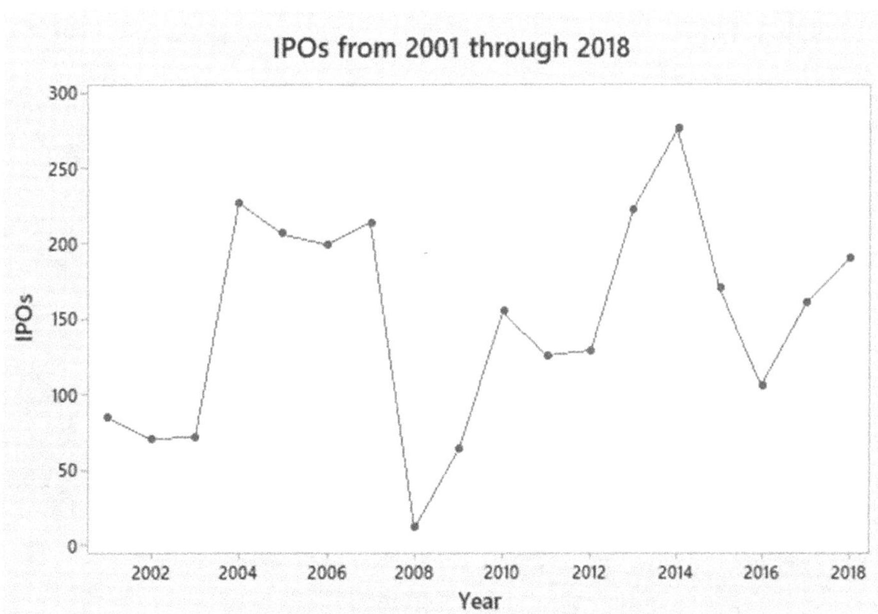

16.8 cont. (b)

Year	IPOs	MA 3-YR
2001	84	*
2002	70	75.000
2003	71	122.333
2004	226	167.667
2005	206	210.333
2006	199	206.000
2007	213	141.000
2008	11	95.667
2009	63	76.000
2010	154	114.000
2011	125	135.667
2012	128	158.333
2013	222	208.333
2014	275	222.333
2015	170	183.333
2016	105	145.000
2017	160	151.667
2018	190	*

(b)

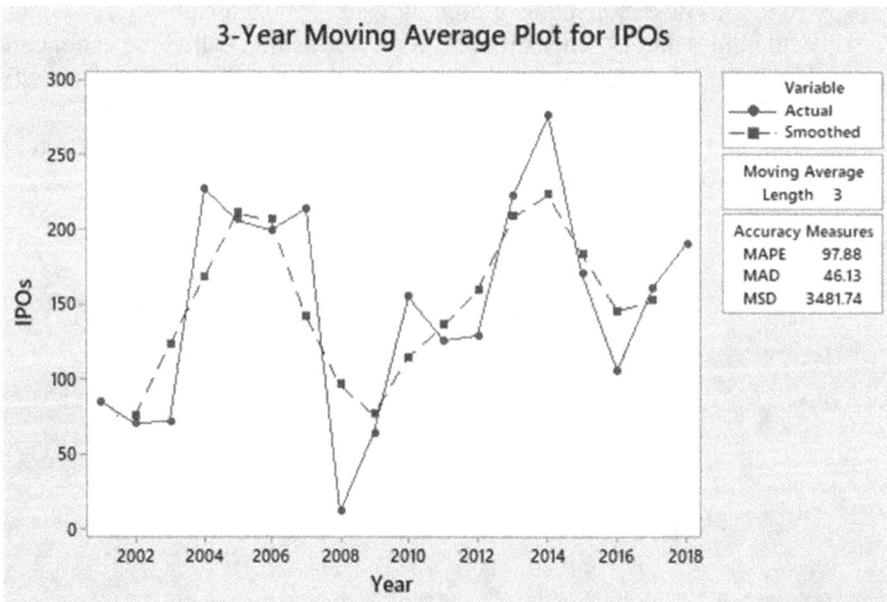

16.8 cont. (c)

Year	IPOs	ES (W=0.50)
2001	84	84.000
2002	70	77.000
2003	71	74.000
2004	226	150.000
2005	206	178.000
2006	199	188.500
2007	213	200.750
2008	11	105.875
2009	63	84.438
2010	154	119.219
2011	125	122.109
2012	128	125.055
2013	222	173.527
2014	275	224.264
2015	170	197.132
2016	105	151.066
2017	160	155.533
2018	190	172.766

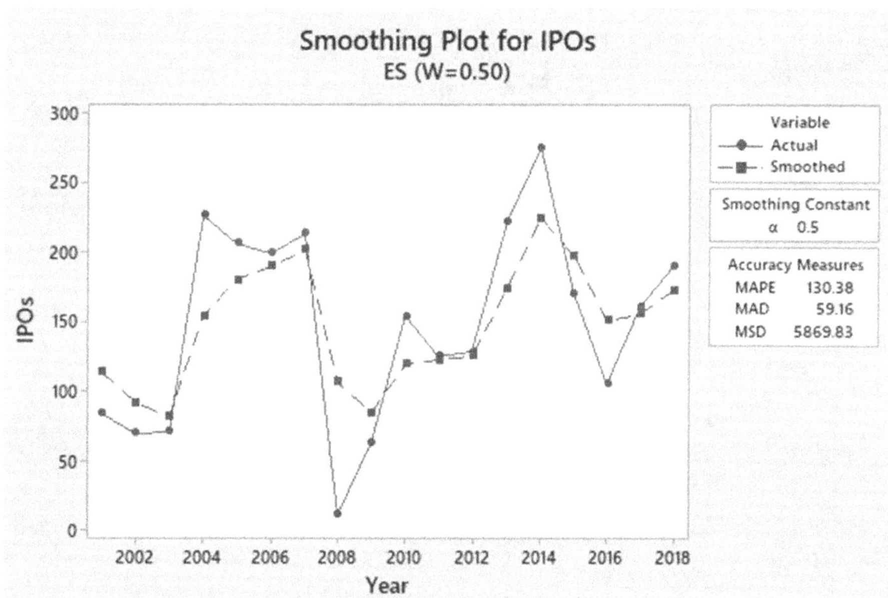

(d) $\hat{Y}_{2019} = E_{2018} = 172.766$ IPOs

16.8 cont. (e)

Year	IPOs	ES (W=0.25)
2001	84	84.000
2002	70	80.500
2003	71	78.125
2004	226	115.094
2005	206	137.820
2006	199	153.115
2007	213	168.086
2008	11	128.815
2009	63	112.361
2010	154	122.771
2011	125	123.328
2012	128	124.496
2013	222	148.872
2014	275	180.404
2015	170	177.803
2016	105	159.602
2017	160	159.702
2018	190	167.276

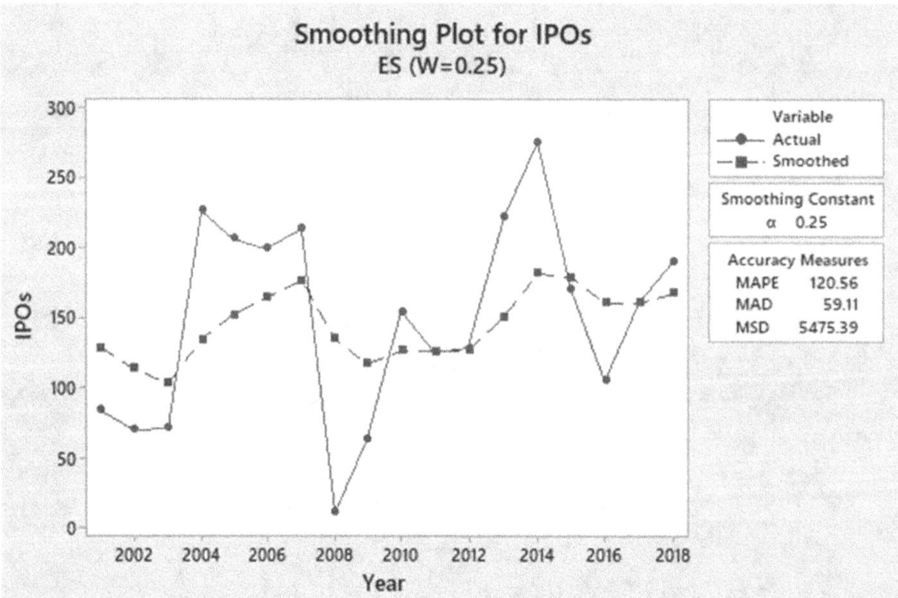

$\hat{Y}_{2019} = E_{2018} = 167.276$ IPOs

(f) The exponentially smoothed 2019 forecast for IPOs is lower with a W of 0.25 compared to a W of 0.50. The exponential smoothing with $W = 0.5$ assigns more weight to the more recent values and is better for short-term forecasting, while the exponential smoothing with $W = 0.25$, which assigns more weight to more distant values, is better suited for identifying long-term tendencies. There appears to be a cyclical component every several years with up and down cycles of the number of IPOs.

16.10 (a) The Y-intercept $b_0 = 4.0$ is the fitted trend value reflecting the real total revenues (in millions of dollars) during the origin or base year 1998.

(b) The slope $b_1 = 1.5$ indicates that the real total revenues are increasing at an estimated rate of 1.5 million per year.

(c) Year is 2002, $X = 2002 - 1998 = 4$

$\hat{Y}_{2002} = 4.0 + 1.5(4) = 10.0$ million dollars

(d) Year is 2019, $X = 2019 - 1998 = 21$,

$\hat{Y}_{2019} = 4.0 + 1.5(21) = 35.5$ million dollars

(e) Year is 2022, $X = 2022 - 1998 = 24$

$\hat{Y}_{2022} = 4.0 + 1.5(24) = 40$ million dollars

16.12 (a)

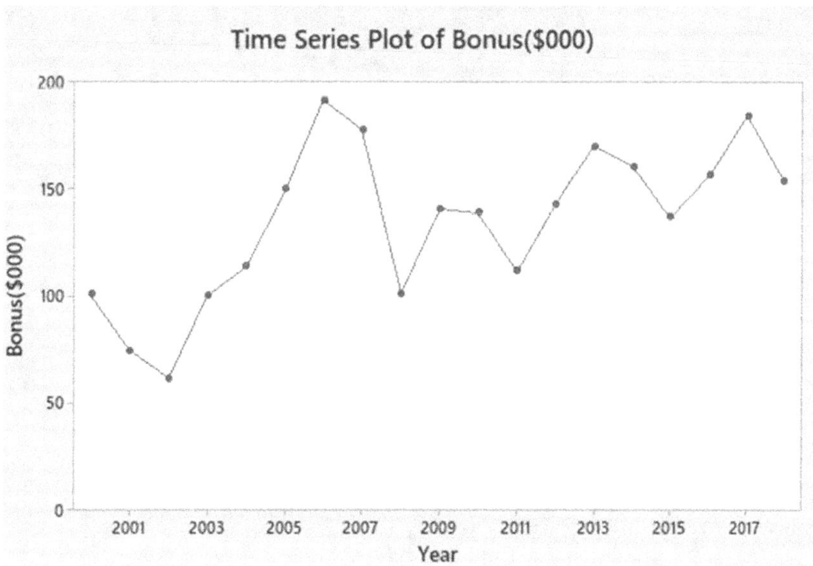

16.12 cont. (b)

Regression Analysis: Bonus($000) versus Coded Year

Analysis of Variance

Source	DF	Adj SS	Adj MS	F-Value	P-Value
Regression	1	9506	9505.6	10.95	0.004
Coded Year	1	9506	9505.6	10.95	0.004
Error	17	14760	868.2		
Total	18	24265			

Model Summary

S	R-sq	R-sq(adj)	R-sq(pred)
29.4654	39.17%	35.60%	26.37%

Coefficients

Term	Coef	SE Coef	T-Value	P-Value	VIF
Constant	98.2	13.0	7.55	0.000	
Coded Year	4.08	1.23	3.31	0.004	1.00

Regression Equation

Bonus($000) = 98.2 + 4.08 Coded Year

$\hat{Y} = 98.2 + 4.08X$ where X = years relative to 2000

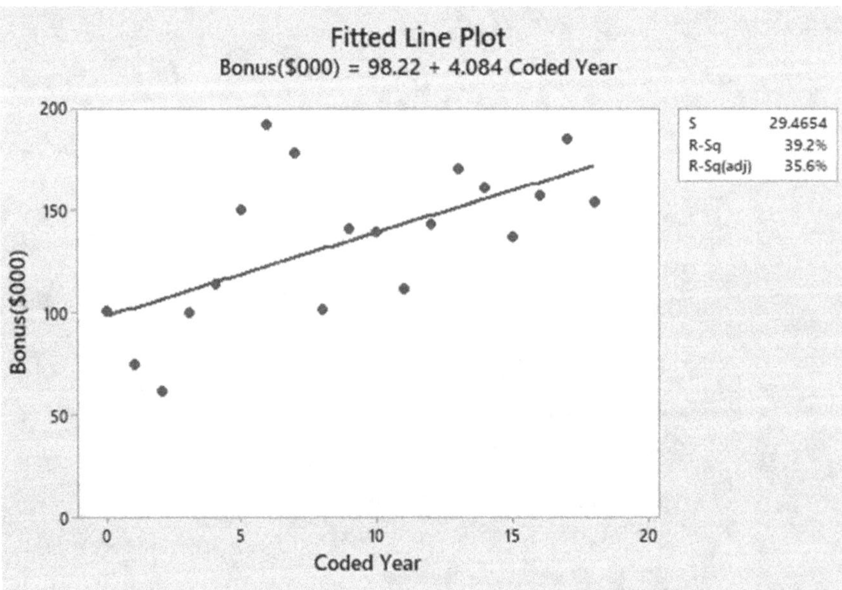

16.12 (c)
cont.

Regression Analysis: Bonus($000) versus Coded Year, Coded Year Sq

Analysis of Variance

Source	DF	Adj SS	Adj MS	F-Value	P-Value
Regression	2	10836	5418.0	6.46	0.009
Coded Year	1	3686	3685.5	4.39	0.052
Coded Year Sq	1	1330	1330.4	1.59	0.226
Error	16	13429	839.3		
Total	18	24265			

Model Summary

S	R-sq	R-sq(adj)	R-sq(pred)
28.9711	44.66%	37.74%	25.25%

Coefficients

Term	Coef	SE Coef	T-Value	P-Value	VIF
Constant	82.2	18.0	4.57	0.000	
Coded Year	9.72	4.64	2.10	0.052	14.61
Coded Year Sq	-0.313	0.249	-1.26	0.226	14.61

Regression Equation

Bonus($000) = 82.2 + 9.72 Coded Year - 0.313 Coded Year Sq

$\hat{Y} = 82.2 + 9.72X - 0.313X^2$ where X = years relative to 2000

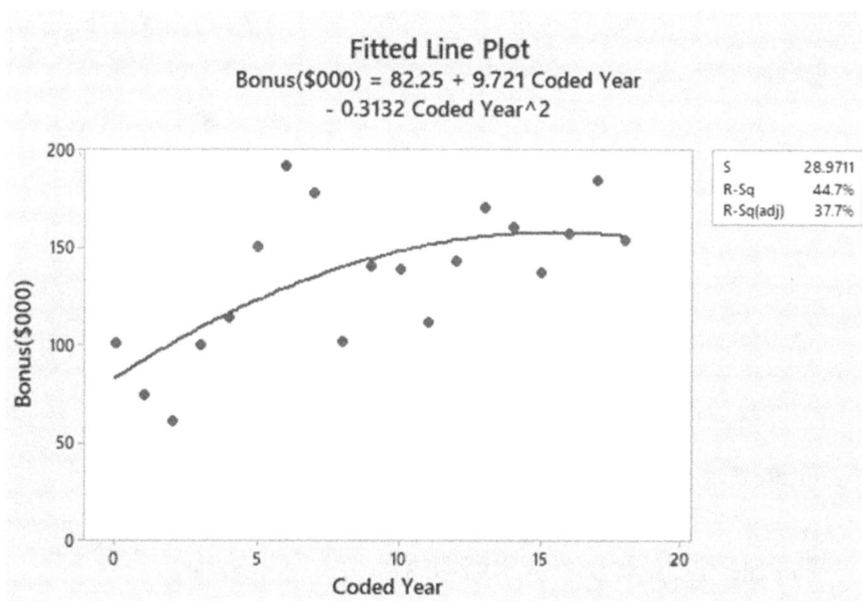

16.12 cont. (d)

Regression Analysis: log Bonus versus Coded Year

Analysis of Variance

Source	DF	Adj SS	Adj MS	F-Value	P-Value
Regression	1	0.1372	0.13716	12.41	0.003
Coded Year	1	0.1372	0.13716	12.41	0.003
Error	17	0.1879	0.01105		
Total	18	0.3251			

Model Summary

S	R-sq	R-sq(adj)	R-sq(pred)
0.105130	42.20%	38.80%	28.52%

Coefficients

Term	Coef	SE Coef	T-Value	P-Value	VIF
Constant	1.9727	0.0464	42.52	0.000	
Coded Year	0.01551	0.00440	3.52	0.003	1.00

Regression Equation

log Bonus = 1.9727 + 0.01551 Coded Year

$\log_{10} \hat{Y} = 1.9727 + 0.01551(X)$ where X = years relative to 2000

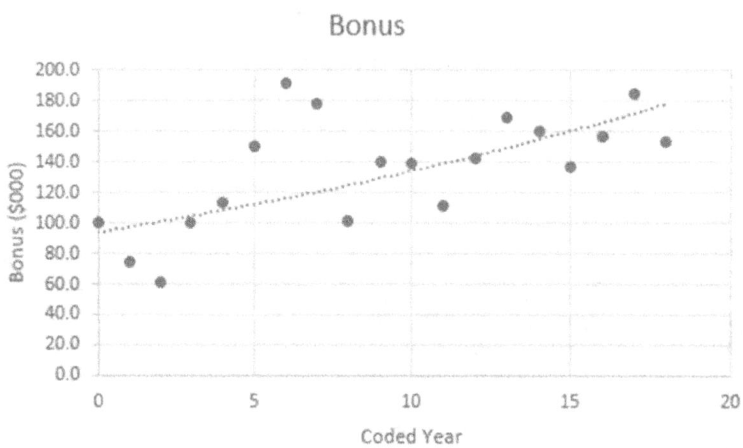

(e) Linear: $\hat{Y}_{2019} = 98.2 + 4.08(19) = 175.72$

$\hat{Y}_{2020} = 98.2 + 4.08(20) = 179.80$

Quadratic: $\hat{Y}_{2019} = 82.2 + 9.72(19) - 0.313(19)^2 = 153.8870$

$\hat{Y}_{2020} = 82.2 + 9.72(20) - 0.313(20)^2 = 151.40$

Exponential: $\log_{10} \hat{Y}_{2019} = 1.9727 + 0.01551(19) = 2.26739$

$\hat{Y}_{2019} = 10^{2.26739} = 185.093$

$\log_{10} \hat{Y}_{2020} = 1.9727 + 0.01551(20) = 2.2829$

16.12 cont. (e) $\hat{Y}_{2020} = 10^{2.2829} = 191.8227$

(f)

Year	Bonuses	First Difference	Second Difference	Percentage Difference
2000	100.5	#N/A	#N/A	#N/A
2001	74.1	-26.4	#N/A	-26.27%
2002	60.9	-13.2	13.2	-17.81%
2003	99.9	39.0	52.2	64.04%
2004	113.5	13.6	-25.4	13.61%
2005	149.8	36.3	22.7	31.98%
2006	191.4	41.6	5.3	27.77%
2007	177.8	-13.6	-55.2	-7.11%
2008	100.9	-76.9	-63.3	-43.25%
2009	140.6	39.7	116.6	39.35%
2010	139.0	-1.6	-41.3	-1.14%
2011	111.4	-27.6	-26.0	-19.86%
2012	142.9	31.5	59.1	28.28%
2013	169.8	26.9	-4.6	18.82%
2014	160.3	-9.5	-36.4	-5.59%
2015	136.8	-23.5	-14.0	-14.66%
2016	156.8	20.0	43.5	14.62%
2017	184.4	27.6	7.6	17.60%
2018	153.7	-30.7	-58.3	-16.65%

A review of 1st, 2nd, and percentage differences reveals no particular model is more appropriate than the other. Based on the principle of parsimony, one might choose the linear model.

16.14 (a)

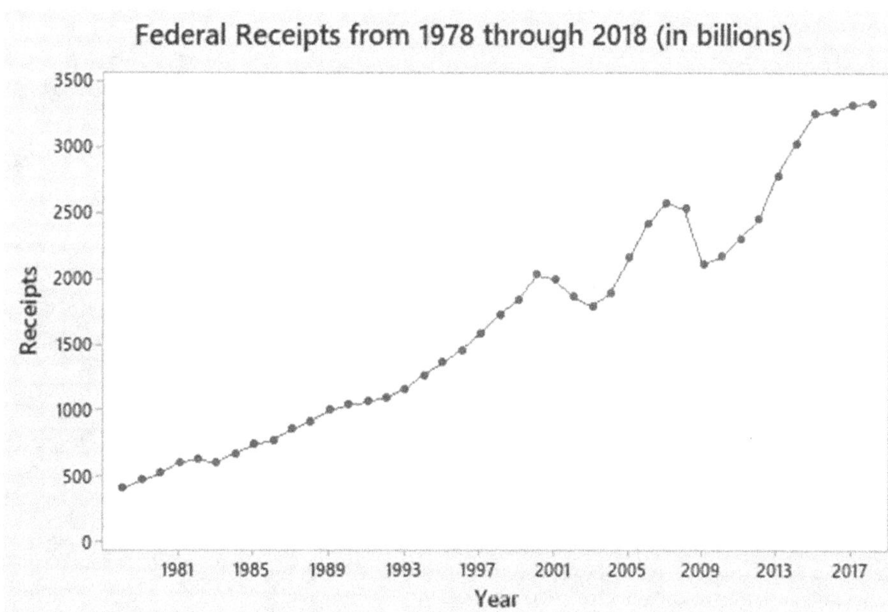

16.14 cont. (b)

Regression Analysis: Receipts versus Coded Year

Analysis of Variance

Source	DF	Adj SS	Adj MS	F-Value	P-Value
Regression	1	30280638	30280638	916.97	0.000
Coded Year	1	30280638	30280638	916.97	0.000
Error	39	1287872	33022		
Total	40	31568511			

Model Summary

S	R-sq	R-sq(adj)	R-sq(pred)
181.721	95.92%	95.82%	95.42%

Coefficients

Term	Coef	SE Coef	T-Value	P-Value	VIF
Constant	225.8	55.7	4.05	0.000	
Coded Year	72.63	2.40	30.28	0.000	1.00

Regression Equation

Receipts = 225.8 + 72.63 Coded Year

$\hat{Y} = 225.8 + 72.63(X)$ where X = years relative to 1978

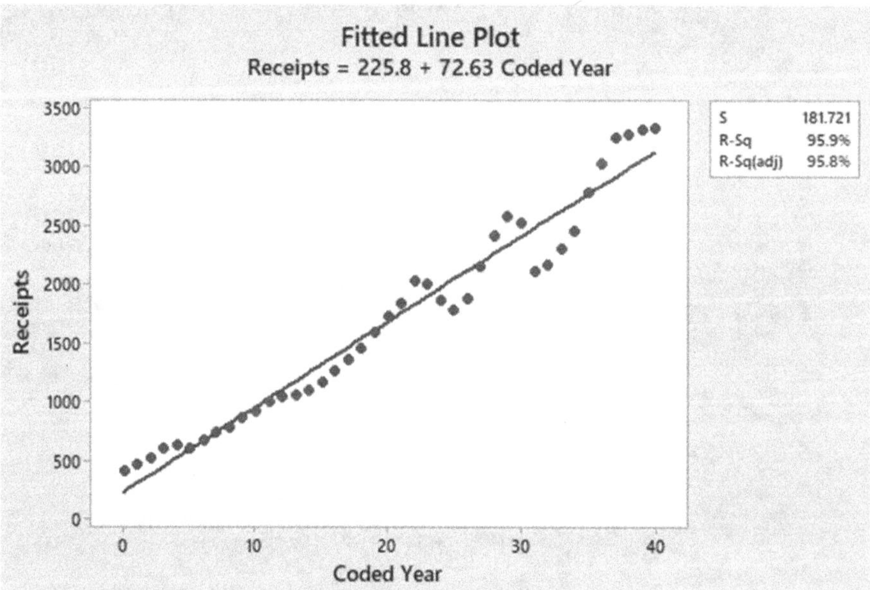

(c) $\hat{Y}_{2019} = 225.8 + 72.63(41) = 3{,}203.63$ billion

$\hat{Y}_{2020} = 225.8 + 72.63(42) = 3{,}276.26$ billion

(d) There is an upward trend in federal receipts from 1978 through 2018, which appears to be linear.

16.16 (a)

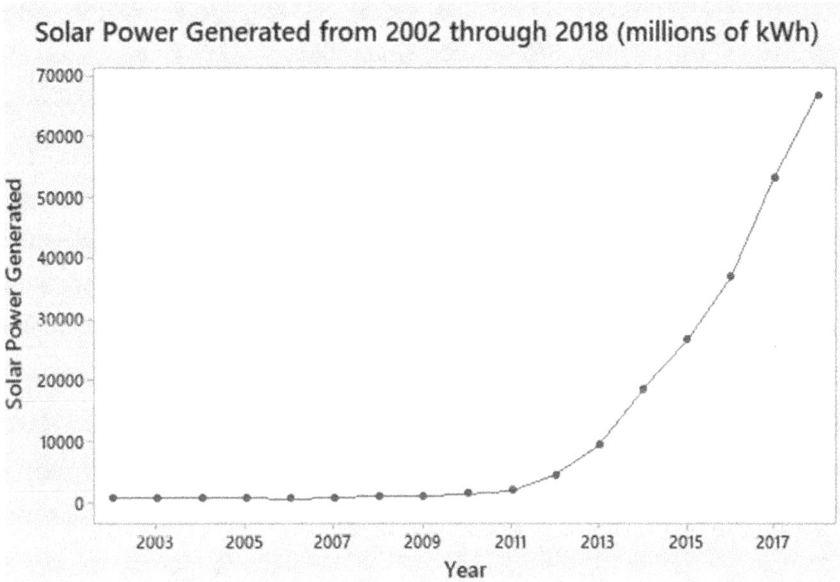

(b) Linear:

Regression Analysis: Solar Power Generated versus Coded Year

Analysis of Variance

Source	DF	Adj SS	Adj MS	F-Value	P-Value
Regression	1	4447549704	4447549704	28.12	0.000
Coded Year	1	4447549704	4447549704	28.12	0.000
Error	15	2372666419	158177761		
Total	16	6820216122			

Model Summary

S	R-sq	R-sq(adj)	R-sq(pred)
12576.9	65.21%	62.89%	51.28%

Coefficients

Term	Coef	SE Coef	T-Value	P-Value	VIF
Constant	-13307	5841	-2.28	0.038	
Coded Year	3302	623	5.30	0.000	1.00

Regression Equation

Solar Power Generated = -13307 + 3302 Coded Year

$\hat{Y} = -13,307 + 3,302(X)$, where X = years relative to 2002

16.16 cont. (b)

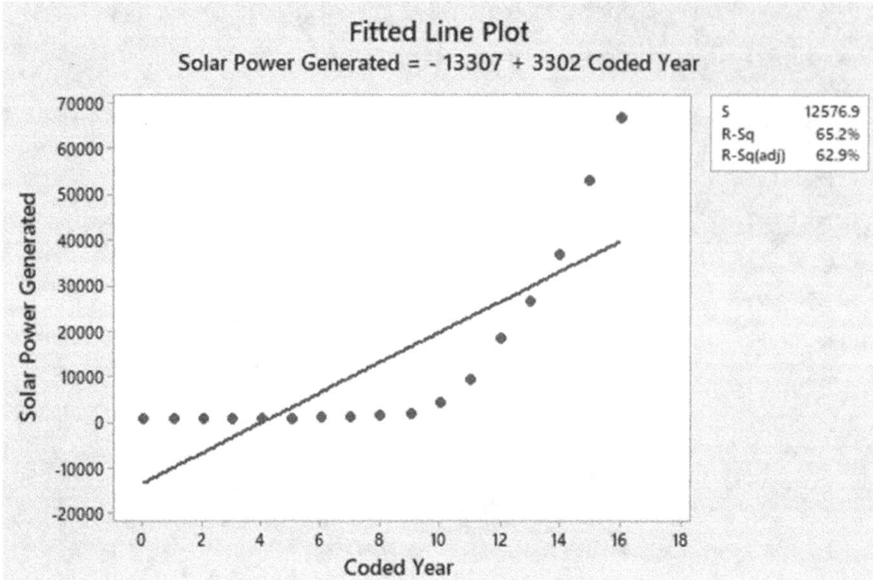

(c) Quadratic:

Regression Analysis: Solar Power Generated versus ... r, Coded Year Sq

Analysis of Variance

Source	DF	Adj SS	Adj MS	F-Value	P-Value
Regression	2	6516476292	3258238146	150.18	0.000
Coded Year	1	694663208	694663208	32.02	0.000
Coded Year Sq	1	2068926589	2068926589	95.36	0.000
Error	14	303739830	21695702		
Total	16	6820216122			

Model Summary

S	R-sq	R-sq(adj)	R-sq(pred)
4657.86	95.55%	94.91%	91.93%

Coefficients

Term	Coef	SE Coef	T-Value	P-Value	VIF
Constant	7358	3026	2.43	0.029	
Coded Year	-4964	877	-5.66	0.000	14.47
Coded Year Sq	516.6	52.9	9.77	0.000	14.47

Regression Equation

Solar Power Generated = 7358 - 4964 Coded Year + 516.6 Coded Year Sq

$\hat{Y} = 7,358 - 4,964X + 516.6X^2$, where X = years relative to 2002

16.16 cont. (c)

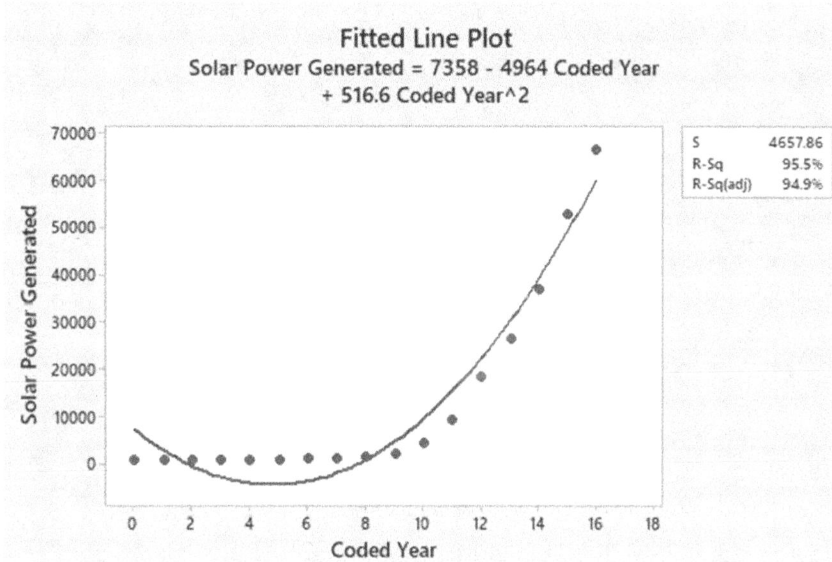

(d) Exponential:

Regression Analysis: Solar Power Log 10 versus Coded Year

Analysis of Variance

Source	DF	Adj SS	Adj MS	F-Value	P-Value
Regression	1	9.218	9.21783	124.71	0.000
Coded Year	1	9.218	9.21783	124.71	0.000
Error	15	1.109	0.07391		
Total	16	10.327			

Model Summary

S	R-sq	R-sq(adj)	R-sq(pred)
0.271872	89.26%	88.55%	85.92%

Coefficients

Term	Coef	SE Coef	T-Value	P-Value	VIF
Constant	2.274	0.126	18.01	0.000	
Coded Year	0.1503	0.0135	11.17	0.000	1.00

Regression Equation

Solar Power Log 10 = 2.274 + 0.1503 Coded Year

$\log_{10} \hat{Y} = 2.274 + 0.1503(X)$, where X = years relative to 2002

16.16 (d)
cont.

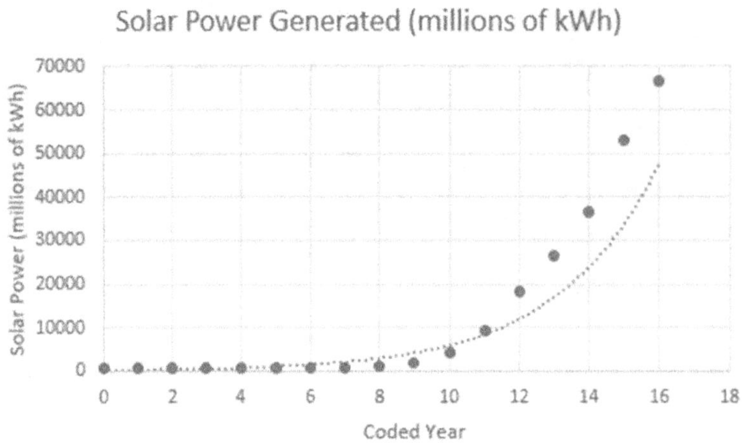

Linear:

$\hat{Y}_{2019} = -13,307 + 3,302(17) = 42,827$ million kWh

$\hat{Y}_{2020} = -13,307 + 3,302(18) = 46,129$ million kWh

Quadratic:

$\hat{Y} = 7,358 - 4,964(17) + 516.6(17)^2 = 72,267.4$ million kWh

$\hat{Y} = 7,358 - 4,964(18) + 516.6(18)^2 = 85,384.4$ million kWh

Exponential:

$\log_{10} \hat{Y}_{2019} = 2.274 + 0.1503(17) = 4.8291$

$\hat{Y}_{2019} = 10^{4.8291} = 67,468.34$ million kWh

$\log_{10} \hat{Y}_{2020} = 2.274 + 0.1503(18) = 4.9794$

$\hat{Y}_{2020} = 10^{4.9794} = 95,367.41$ million kWh

16.18 (a)

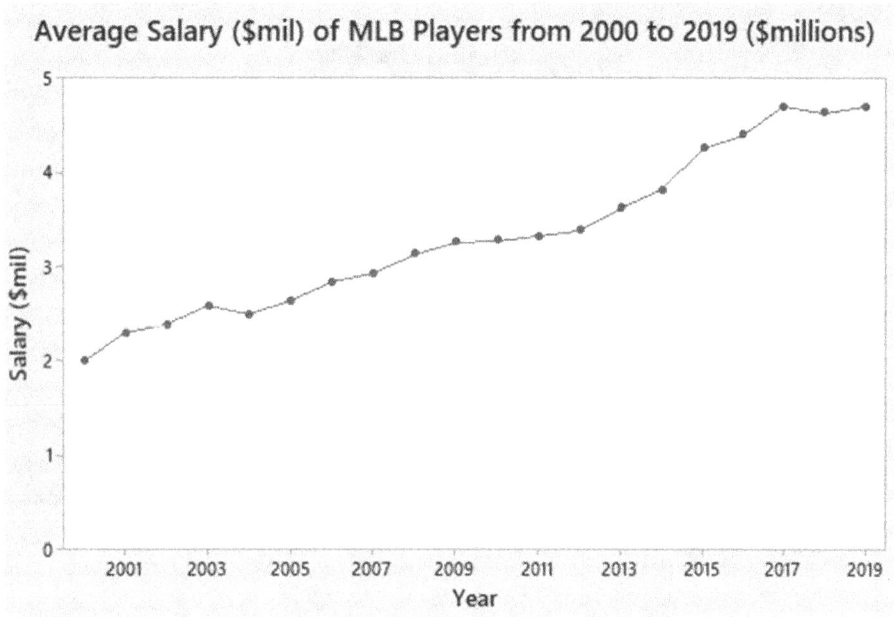

(b) Linear:

Regression Analysis: Salary ($mil) versus Coded Year

Analysis of Variance

Source	DF	Adj SS	Adj MS	F-Value	P-Value
Regression	1	13.3042	13.3042	529.35	0.000
Coded Year	1	13.3042	13.3042	529.35	0.000
Error	18	0.4524	0.0251		
Total	19	13.7566			

Model Summary

S	R-sq	R-sq(adj)	R-sq(pred)
0.158534	96.71%	96.53%	95.96%

Coefficients

Term	Coef	SE Coef	T-Value	P-Value	VIF
Constant	1.9853	0.0683	29.06	0.000	
Coded Year	0.14144	0.00615	23.01	0.000	1.00

Regression Equation

Salary ($mil) = 1.9853 + 0.14144 Coded Year

$\hat{Y} = 1.9853 + 0.14144(X)$, where X = years relative to 2000

16.18 cont. (b)

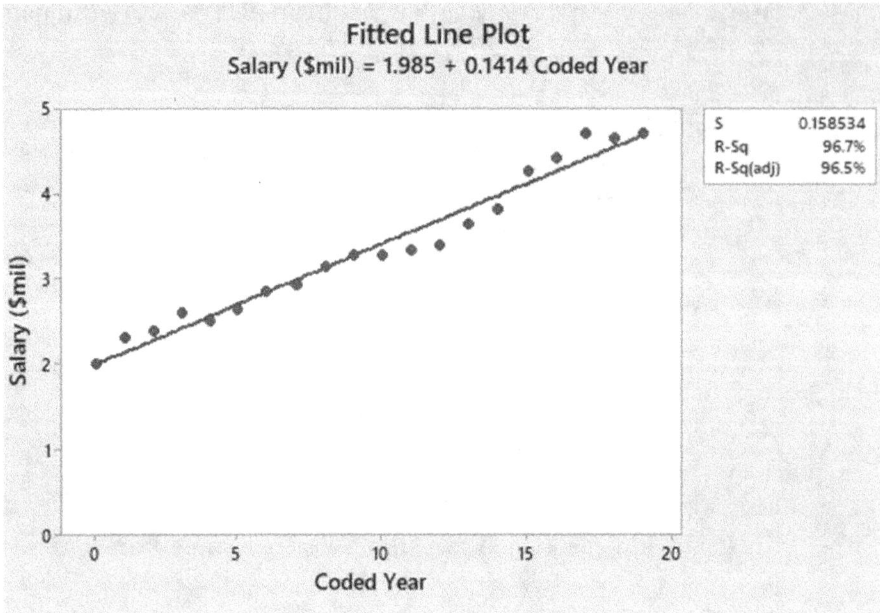

(c) Quadratic:

Regression Analysis: Salary ($mil) versus Coded Year, Coded Year Sq

Analysis of Variance

Source	DF	Adj SS	Adj MS	F-Value	P-Value
Regression	2	13.4579	6.72893	382.93	0.000
Coded Year	1	0.3292	0.32920	18.73	0.000
Coded Year Sq	1	0.1537	0.15367	8.74	0.009
Error	17	0.2987	0.01757		
Total	19	13.7566			

Model Summary

S	R-sq	R-sq(adj)	R-sq(pred)
0.132560	97.83%	97.57%	96.77%

Coefficients

Term	Coef	SE Coef	T-Value	P-Value	VIF
Constant	2.1539	0.0807	26.68	0.000	
Coded Year	0.0852	0.0197	4.33	0.000	14.67
Coded Year Sq	0.00296	0.00100	2.96	0.009	14.67

Regression Equation

Salary ($mil) = 2.1539 + 0.0852 Coded Year + 0.00296 Coded Year Sq

$\hat{Y} = 2.1539 + 0.0852X + 0.00296X^2$, where X = years relative to 2000

16.18 cont. (c)

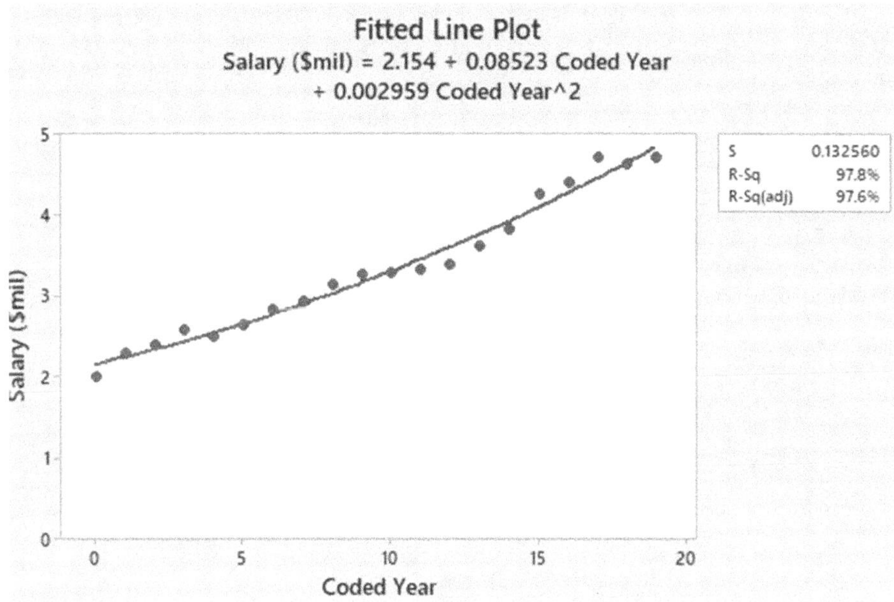

(d) Exponential:

Regression Analysis: Salary log 10 versus Coded Year

Analysis of Variance

Source	DF	Adj SS	Adj MS	F-Value	P-Value
Regression	1	0.232769	0.232769	845.09	0.000
Coded Year	1	0.232769	0.232769	845.09	0.000
Error	18	0.004958	0.000275		
Total	19	0.237726			

Model Summary

S	R-sq	R-sq(adj)	R-sq(pred)
0.0165963	97.91%	97.80%	97.32%

Coefficients

Term	Coef	SE Coef	T-Value	P-Value	VIF
Constant	0.33101	0.00715	46.28	0.000	
Coded Year	0.018709	0.000644	29.07	0.000	1.00

Regression Equation

Salary log 10 = 0.33101 + 0.018709 Coded Year

$\log_{10}\hat{Y} = 0.33101 + 0.018709(X)$, where X = years relative to 2000

16.18 cont. (d)

(e)

Year	Salary ($mil)	First Difference	Second Difference	Percentage Difference
2000	1.99	#N/A	#N/A	#N/A
2001	2.29	0.3	#N/A	15.08%
2002	2.38	0.1	-0.2	3.93%
2003	2.58	0.2	0.1	8.40%
2004	2.49	-0.1	-0.3	-3.49%
2005	2.63	0.1	0.2	5.62%
2006	2.83	0.2	0.1	7.60%
2007	2.92	0.1	-0.1	3.18%
2008	3.13	0.2	0.1	7.19%
2009	3.26	0.1	-0.1	4.15%
2010	3.27	0.0	-0.1	0.31%
2011	3.32	0.0	0.0	1.53%
2012	3.38	0.1	0.0	1.81%
2013	3.62	0.2	0.2	7.10%
2014	3.81	0.2	-0.1	5.25%
2015	4.25	0.4	0.3	11.55%
2016	4.40	0.2	-0.3	3.53%
2017	4.70	0.3	0.1	6.82%
2018	4.63	-0.1	-0.4	-1.49%
2019	4.70	0.1	0.1	1.51%

The first and second differences are relatively consistent across the series. This is not the case for percentage differences. Based on the principle of parsimony, one might choose the linear model.

Linear forecast: $\hat{Y}_{2020} = 1.9853 + 0.14144(20) = 4.8141$ million

16.20 (a)

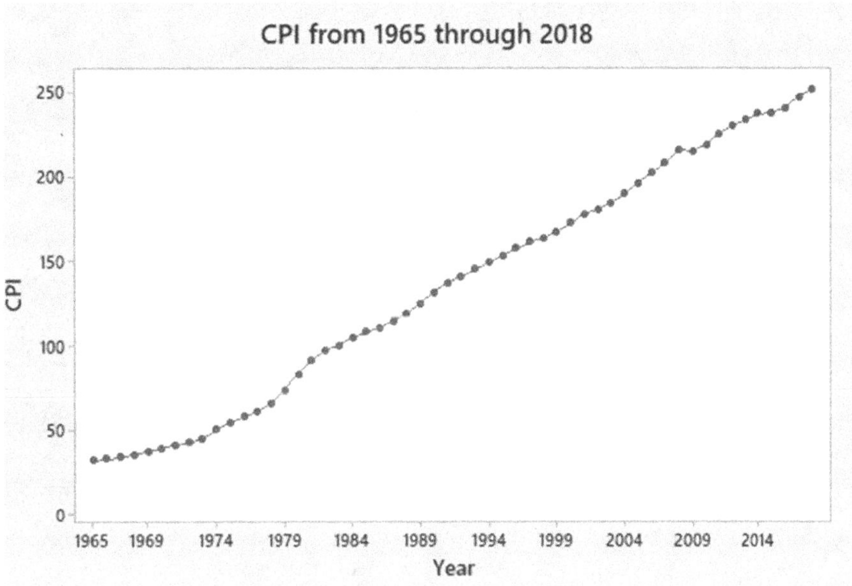

(b) There has been an upward trend in the CPI-U in the United States from 1965 through 2018.

(c) Linear:

Regression Analysis: CPI versus Coded Year

Analysis of Variance

Source	DF	Adj SS	Adj MS	F-Value	P-Value
Regression	1	261479	261479	11402.09	0.000
Coded Year	1	261479	261479	11402.09	0.000
Error	52	1192	23		
Total	53	262671			

Model Summary

S	R-sq	R-sq(adj)	R-sq(pred)
4.78879	99.55%	99.54%	99.50%

Coefficients

Term	Coef	SE Coef	T-Value	P-Value	VIF
Constant	16.71	1.29	13.00	0.000	
Coded Year	4.4647	0.0418	106.78	0.000	1.00

Regression Equation

CPI = 16.71 + 4.4647 Coded Year

$\hat{Y} = 16.71 + 4.4647(X)$, where X = years relative to 1965

16.20 cont. (c)

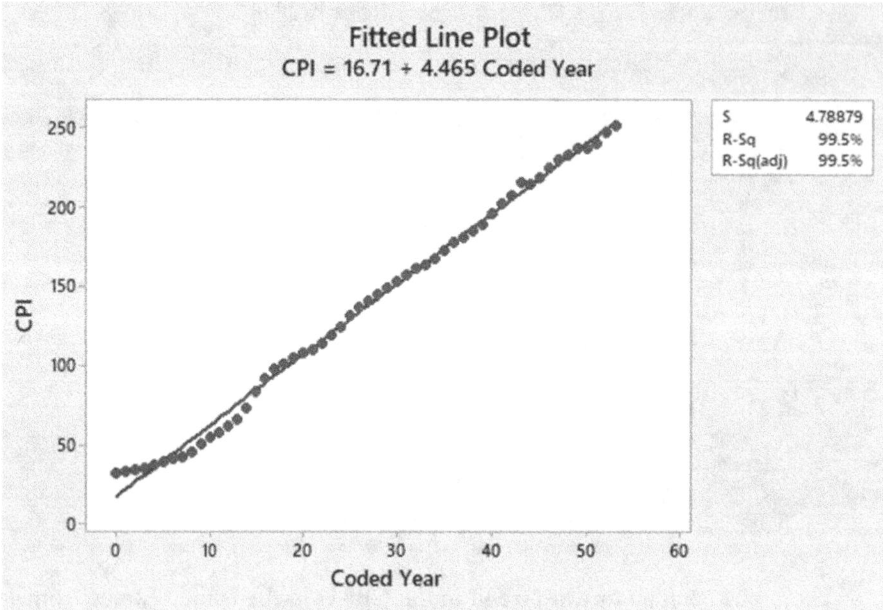

(d) Quadratic:

Regression Analysis: CPI versus Coded Year, Coded Year Sq

Analysis of Variance

Source	DF	Adj SS	Adj MS	F-Value	P-Value
Regression	2	261504	130752	5714.90	0.000
Coded Year	1	15653	15653	684.17	0.000
Coded Year Sq	1	26	26	1.12	0.295
Error	51	1167	23		
Total	53	262671			

Model Summary

S	R-sq	R-sq(adj)	R-sq(pred)
4.78322	99.56%	99.54%	99.48%

Coefficients

Term	Coef	SE Coef	T-Value	P-Value	VIF
Constant	18.17	1.88	9.65	0.000	
Coded Year	4.296	0.164	26.16	0.000	15.47
Coded Year Sq	0.00317	0.00300	1.06	0.295	15.47

Regression Equation

CPI = 18.17 + 4.296 Coded Year + 0.00317 Coded Year Sq

$\hat{Y} = 18.17 + 4.296X + 0.00317X^2$, where X = years relative to 1965

16.20 cont. (d)

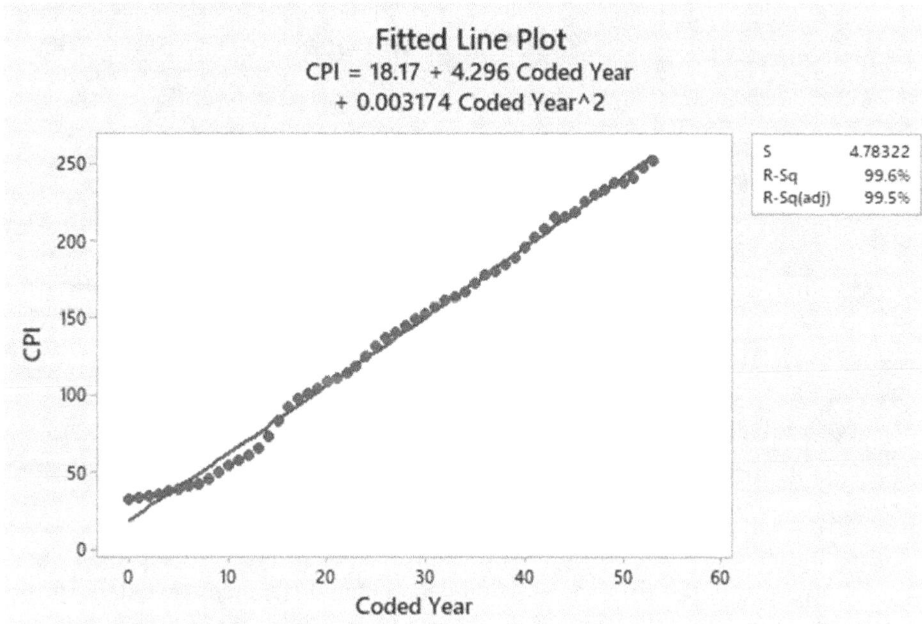

(e) Exponential:

Regression Analysis: CPI log 10 versus Coded Year

Analysis of Variance

Source	DF	Adj SS	Adj MS	F-Value	P-Value
Regression	1	4.0304	4.03041	775.31	0.000
Coded Year	1	4.0304	4.03041	775.31	0.000
Error	52	0.2703	0.00520		
Total	53	4.3007			

Model Summary

S	R-sq	R-sq(adj)	R-sq(pred)
0.0721000	93.71%	93.59%	93.15%

Coefficients

Term	Coef	SE Coef	T-Value	P-Value	VIF
Constant	1.5883	0.0194	82.07	0.000	
Coded Year	0.017529	0.000630	27.84	0.000	1.00

Regression Equation

CPI log 10 = 1.5883 + 0.017529 Coded Year

$\log_{10} \hat{Y} = 1.5883 + 0.017529(X)$, where X = years relative to 1965

16.20 cont. (e)

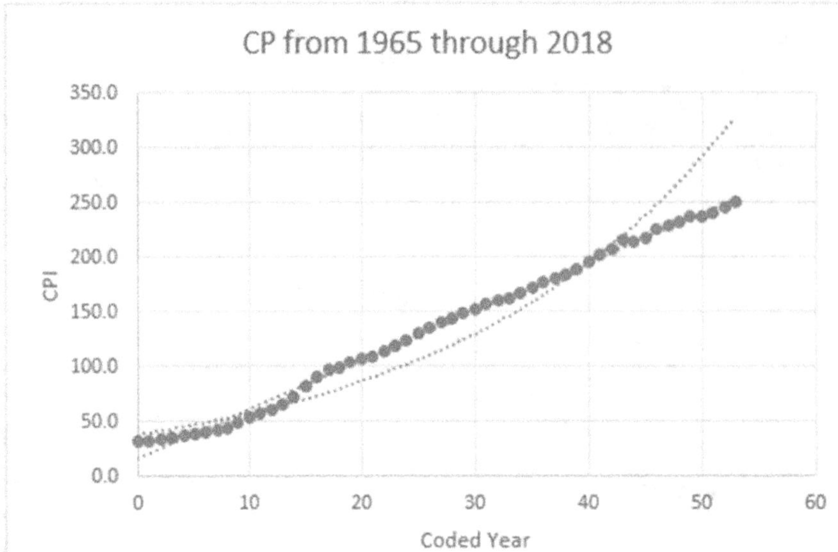

(f) A review of the first, second, and percentage differences revealed similar levels of variation across the time series. Based on the principle of parsimony, one might choose the linear model.

(g) Linear forecast:

$\hat{Y}_{2019} = 16.71 + 4.4647(54) = 257.8038$

$\hat{Y}_{2020} = 16.71 + 4.4647(55) = 262.2685$

16.22 (a) For Time Series I, the graph of Y versus X appears to be more linear than the graph of log Y versus X, so a linear model appears to be more appropriate. For Time Series II, the graph of log Y versus X appears to be more linear than the graph of Y versus X, so an exponential model appears to be more appropriate.

(b) Time Series I: $\hat{Y} = 100.0731 + 14.9776(X)$, where X = years relative to 2007

Time Series II: $\hat{Y} = 10^{1.9982+0.0609(X)}$, where X = years relative to 2007

(c) X = 12 for year 2019 in all models. Forecasts for the year 2019

Time Series I: $\hat{Y} = 100.0731 + 14.9776(12) = 279.8045$

Time Series II $\hat{Y} = 10^{1.9982+0.0609(12)} = 535.6886$

16.24 $t_{STAT} = \frac{a_3}{S_{a_3}} = \frac{0.24}{0.10} = 2.4$ is greater than the critical bound of 2.2281. Reject H_0.

There is sufficient evidence that the third-order regression parameter is significantly different from zero. A third-order autoregressive model is appropriate.

16.26 (a) $t_{STAT} = \frac{a_3}{S_{a_3}} = \frac{0.24}{0.15} = 1.6$ is less than the critical bound of 2.2281. Do not reject H_0. . There is not sufficient evidence that the third-order regression parameter is significantly different than zero. A third-order autoregressive model is not appropriate.

(b) Fit a second-order autoregressive model and test to see if it is appropriate.

16.28 (a)

Regression Analysis: Bonus($000) versus lag1, lag2, lag3

Method

Rows unused 3

Analysis of Variance

Source	DF	Adj SS	Adj MS	F-Value	P-Value
Regression	3	3461.9	1154.0	1.60	0.240
lag1	1	3269.4	3269.4	4.55	0.054
lag2	1	959.3	959.3	1.33	0.271
lag3	1	467.8	467.8	0.65	0.436
Error	12	8628.3	719.0		
Total	15	12090.2			

Model Summary

S	R-sq	R-sq(adj)	R-sq(pred)
26.8147	28.63%	10.79%	0.00%

Coefficients

Term	Coef	SE Coef	T-Value	P-Value	VIF
Constant	91.1	34.2	2.66	0.021	
lag1	0.531	0.249	2.13	0.054	1.61
lag2	-0.336	0.291	-1.16	0.271	2.38
lag3	0.193	0.239	0.81	0.436	1.63

Regression Equation

Bonus($000) = 91.1 + 0.531 lag1 - 0.336 lag2 + 0.193 lag3

For the third order term, $t_{STAT} = 0.81$ with a p-value of 0.436. The third term can be dropped because it is not significant at the 0.05 significance level.

16.28 (b)
cont.

Regression Analysis: Bonus($000) versus lag1, lag2

Method

Rows unused 2

Analysis of Variance

Source	DF	Adj SS	Adj MS	F-Value	P-Value
Regression	2	7041.4	3520.7	4.18	0.038
lag1	1	6232.8	6232.8	7.40	0.017
lag2	1	653.1	653.1	0.78	0.393
Error	14	11794.9	842.5		
Total	16	18836.3			

Model Summary

S	R-sq	R-sq(adj)	R-sq(pred)
29.0257	37.38%	28.44%	0.00%

Coefficients

Term	Coef	SE Coef	T-Value	P-Value	VIF
Constant	79.8	30.0	2.66	0.019	
lag1	0.661	0.243	2.72	0.017	1.59
lag2	-0.221	0.251	-0.88	0.393	1.59

Regression Equation

Bonus($000) = 79.8 + 0.661 lag1 - 0.221 lag2

Fits and Diagnostics for Unusual Observations

Obs	Bonus($000)	Fit	Resid	Std Resid	
9	100.9	154.9	-54.0	-2.12	R

For the second order term, $t_{STAT} = -0.88$ with a p-value of 0.393. The second order term can be dropped because it is not significant at the 0.05 significance level.

16.28 cont. (c)

Regression Analysis: Bonus($000) versus lag1

Method

Rows unused 1

Analysis of Variance

Source	DF	Adj SS	Adj MS	F-Value	P-Value
Regression	1	8520	8519.6	9.41	0.007
lag1	1	8520	8519.6	9.41	0.007
Error	16	14491	905.7		
Total	17	23011			

Model Summary

S	R-sq	R-sq(adj)	R-sq(pred)
30.0948	37.02%	33.09%	19.94%

Coefficients

Term	Coef	SE Coef	T-Value	P-Value	VIF
Constant	56.9	27.0	2.11	0.051	
lag1	0.597	0.195	3.07	0.007	1.00

Regression Equation

Bonus($000) = 56.9 + 0.597 lag1

For the first order term, $t_{STAT} = 3.07$ with a *p*-value of 0.007. The first order term should be retained because it is significant at the 0.05 significance level.

(d) $\hat{Y}_{2019} = 56.9 + 0.597(153.7) = 148.6589$

16.30 (a)

Regression Analysis: Salary ($mil) versus lag1, lag2, lag3

Method

Rows unused 3

Analysis of Variance

Source	DF	Adj SS	Adj MS	F-Value	P-Value
Regression	3	9.07633	3.02544	153.58	0.000
lag1	1	0.27113	0.27113	13.76	0.003
lag2	1	0.01087	0.01087	0.55	0.471
lag3	1	0.01921	0.01921	0.98	0.341
Error	13	0.25609	0.01970		
Total	16	9.33242			

Model Summary

S	R-sq	R-sq(adj)	R-sq(pred)
0.140355	97.26%	96.62%	95.56%

Coefficients

Term	Coef	SE Coef	T-Value	P-Value	VIF
Constant	0.134	0.164	0.82	0.429	
lag1	1.020	0.275	3.71	0.003	34.30
lag2	0.275	0.371	0.74	0.471	57.79
lag3	-0.310	0.314	-0.99	0.341	36.81

Regression Equation

Salary ($mil) = 0.134 + 1.020 lag1 + 0.275 lag2 - 0.310 lag3

For the third order term, $t_{STAT} = -0.99$ with a p-value of 0.341. The third term can be dropped because it is not significant at the 0.05 significance level.

16.30 (b)
cont.

Regression Analysis: Salary ($mil) versus lag1, lag2

Method

Rows unused 2

Analysis of Variance

Source	DF	Adj SS	Adj MS	F-Value	P-Value
Regression	2	10.2940	5.14698	279.70	0.000
lag1	1	0.2725	0.27249	14.81	0.002
lag2	1	0.0009	0.00093	0.05	0.825
Error	15	0.2760	0.01840		
Total	17	10.5700			

Model Summary

S	R-sq	R-sq(adj)	R-sq(pred)
0.135652	97.39%	97.04%	96.26%

Coefficients

Term	Coef	SE Coef	T-Value	P-Value	VIF
Constant	0.102	0.146	0.70	0.495	
lag1	0.955	0.248	3.85	0.002	33.77
lag2	0.057	0.252	0.23	0.825	33.77

Regression Equation

Salary ($mil) = 0.102 + 0.955 lag1 + 0.057 lag2

For the second order term, $t_{STAT} = 0.23$ with a p-value of 0.825. The second term can be dropped because it is not significant at the 0.05 significance level.

16.30 (c)
cont.

Regression Analysis: Salary ($mil) versus lag1

Method

Rows unused 1

Analysis of Variance

Source	DF	Adj SS	Adj MS	F-Value	P-Value
Regression	1	11.5661	11.5661	648.48	0.000
lag1	1	11.5661	11.5661	648.48	0.000
Error	17	0.3032	0.0178		
Total	18	11.8693			

Model Summary

S	R-sq	R-sq(adj)	R-sq(pred)
0.133550	97.45%	97.30%	96.69%

Coefficients

Term	Coef	SE Coef	T-Value	P-Value	VIF
Constant	0.172	0.130	1.32	0.204	
lag1	0.9910	0.0389	25.47	0.000	1.00

Regression Equation

Salary ($mil) = 0.172 + 0.9910 lag1

For the first order term, $t_{STAT} = 25.47$ with a p-value of 0.000. The first order term should be retained because it is significant at the 0.05 significance level.

(d) $\hat{Y}_{2020} = 0.172 + 0.9910(4.7) = 4.8297$ million

16.32 (a) $S_{YX} = \sqrt{\frac{\sum_{i=1}^{n}(Y_i - \hat{Y}_i)^2}{n-p-1}} = \sqrt{\frac{45}{12-1-1}} = 2.121$. The standard error of the estimate is 2.121.

(b) $MAD = \frac{\sum_{i=1}^{n}\left|Y_i - \hat{Y}_i\right|}{n} = \frac{18}{12} = 1.5$. The mean absolute deviation is 1.5.

16.34 (a) Linear

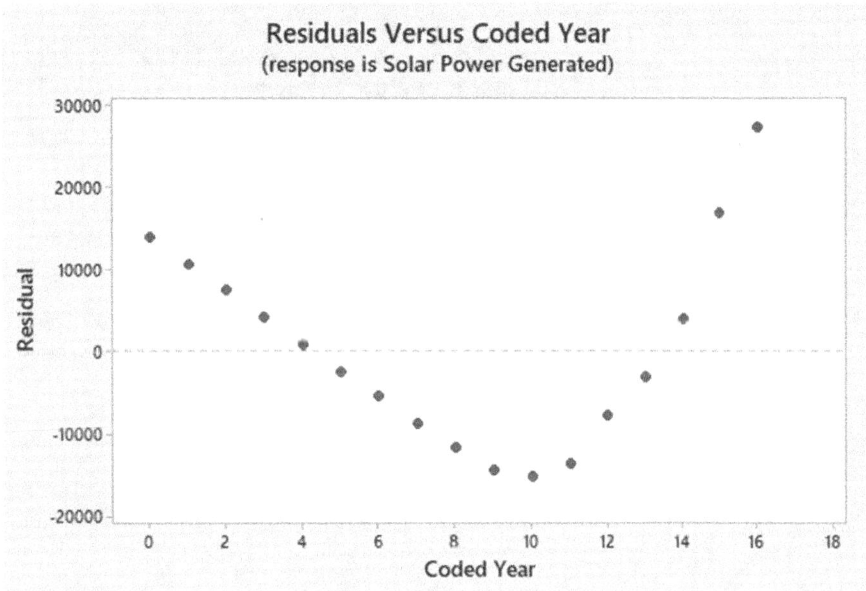

Quadratic

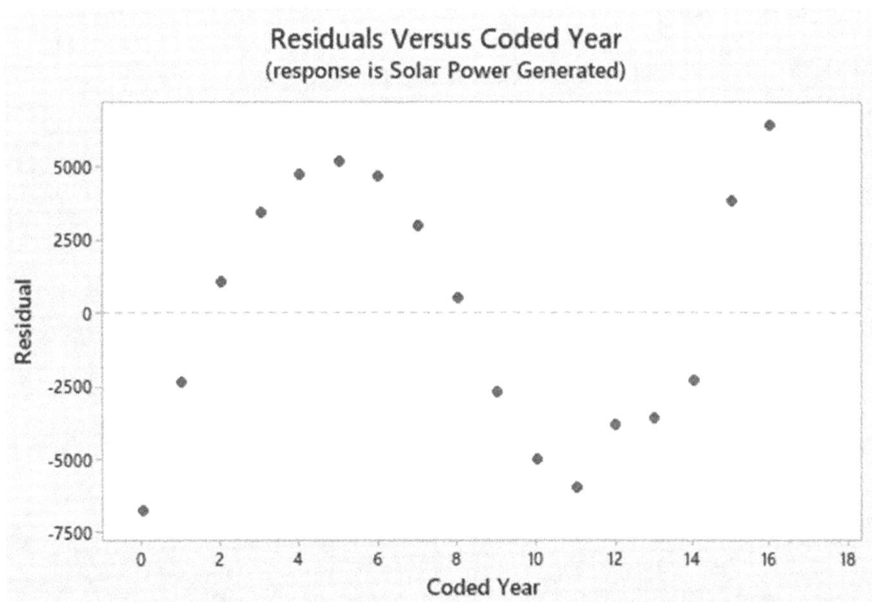

16.34 cont. (a) Exponential

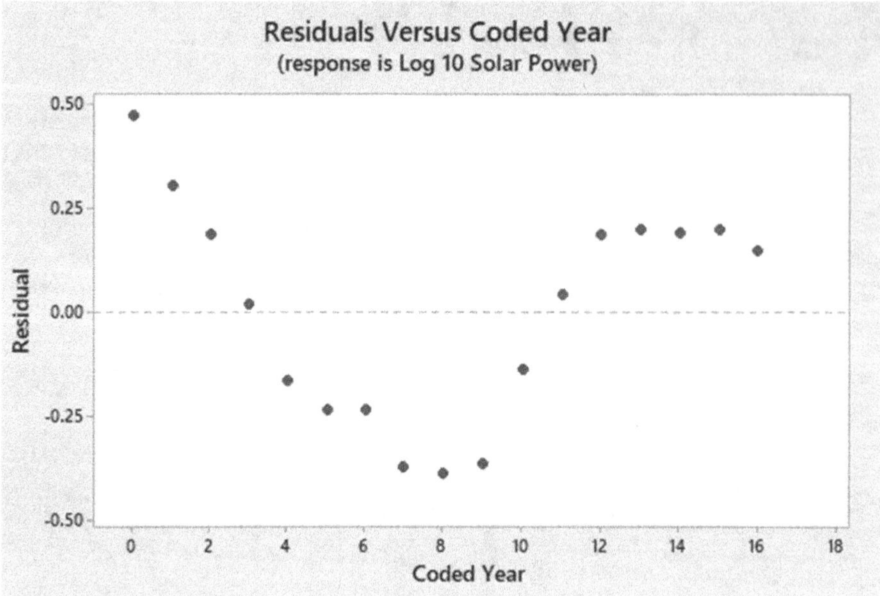

First-order Autoregressive

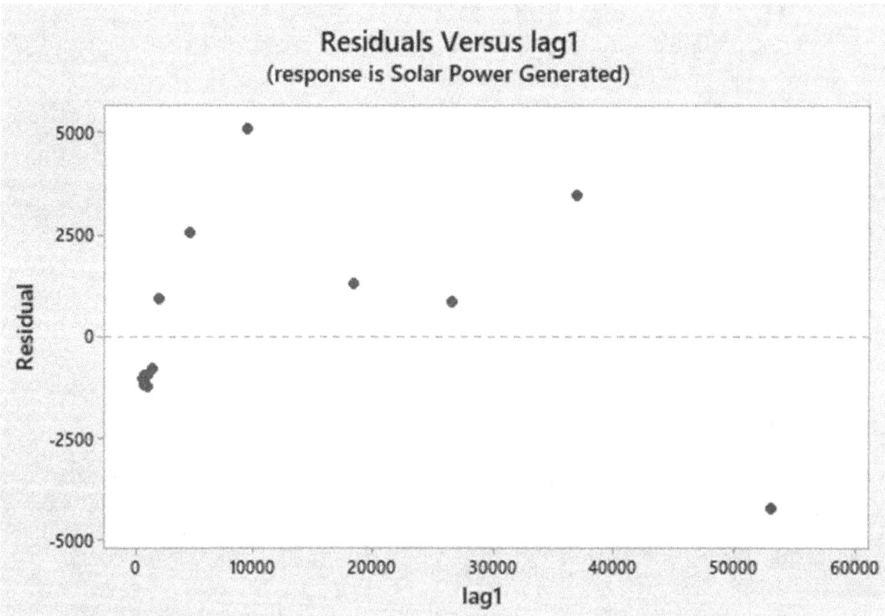

(b–c)

Solar Power		
	S_{yx}	*MAD*
Linear	12576.9	9870.772
Quadratic	4657.86	3861.937
Exponential	8317.774	4526.413
AR - First Order	2342.68	1766.126

16.34 cont. (d) The residual plots for linear, quadratic, and exponential reveal cyclical patterns across coded year. The first-order autoregressive model has no clear pattern but does have one outlier. The first-order autoregressive model has the smallest S_{xy} and *MAD* values. On the basis of (a) through (c) and the principle of parsimony, the first-order autoregressive model would be the best model for forecasting.

16.36 (a) Linear

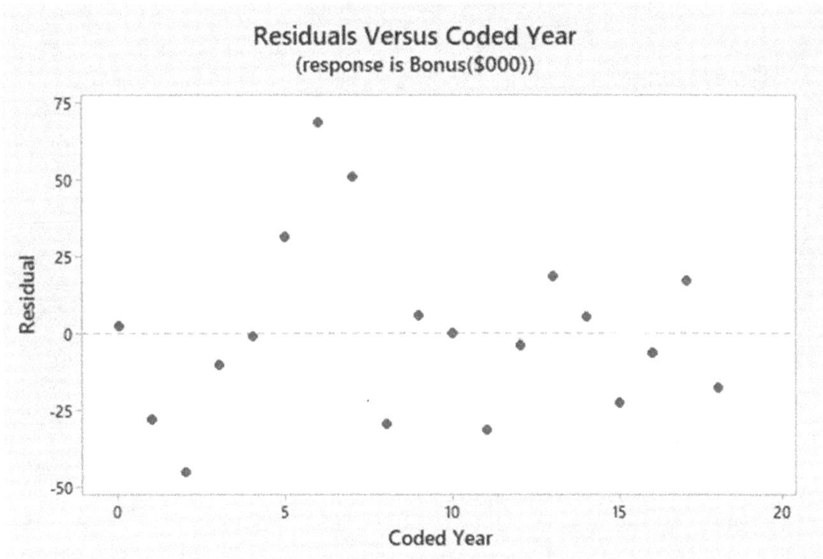

Quadratic

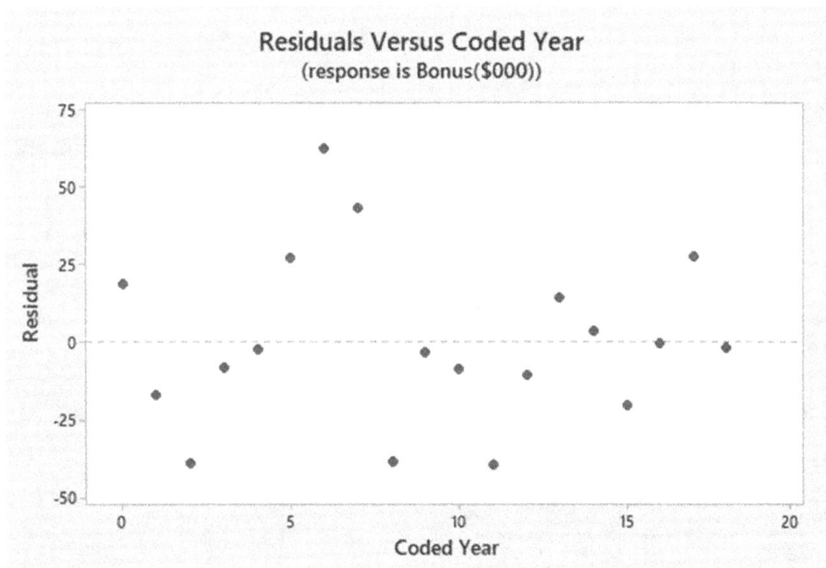

16.36 (a) Exponential
cont.

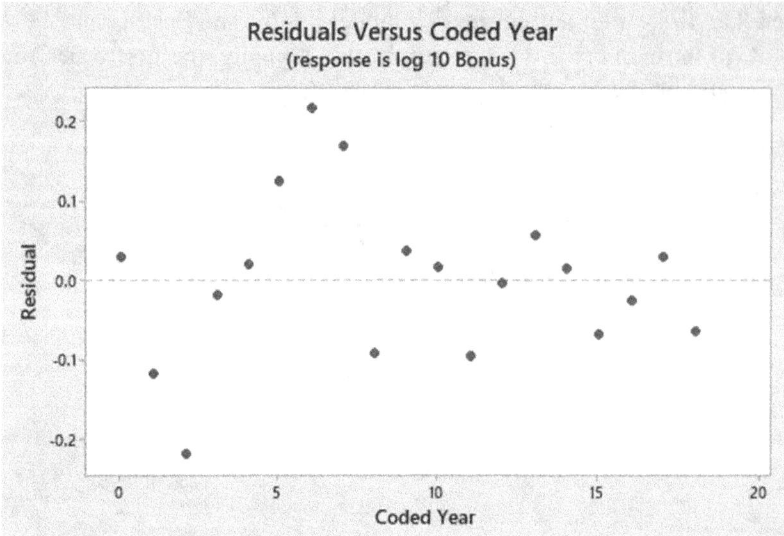

First-Order Autoregressive

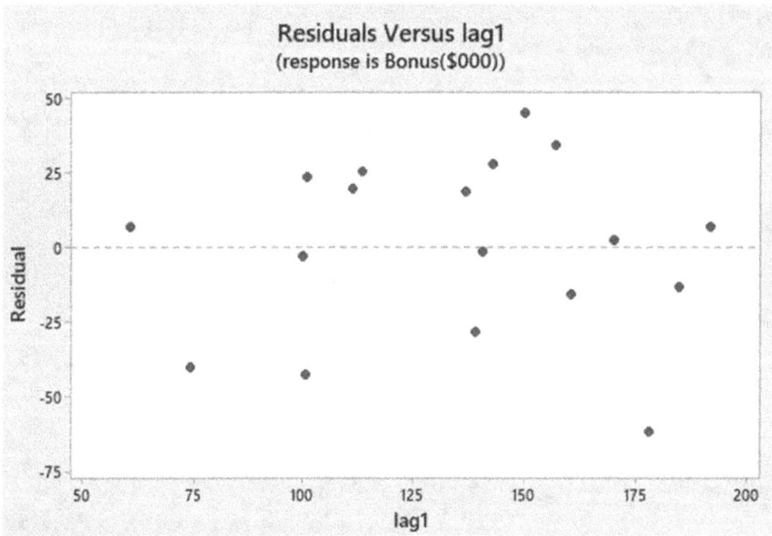

(b–c)

Bonuses		
	S_{yx}	*MAD*
Linear	29.465	20.936
Quadratic	28.971	20.509
Exponential	30.581	21.803
AR - First Order	30.095	23.097

(d) The residual plots for the linear, quadratic, exponential reveal a slight cyclical pattern for the first part of the time series followed by no clear pattern for the remainder of the series. The first-order autoregressive revealed no clear pattern throughout the time series. Each of the models had similar S_{xy} and *MAD* values. On the basis of the residual plots and the principle of parsimony, the first-order autoregressive model might be the best choice for forecasting.

16.38 (a) Linear

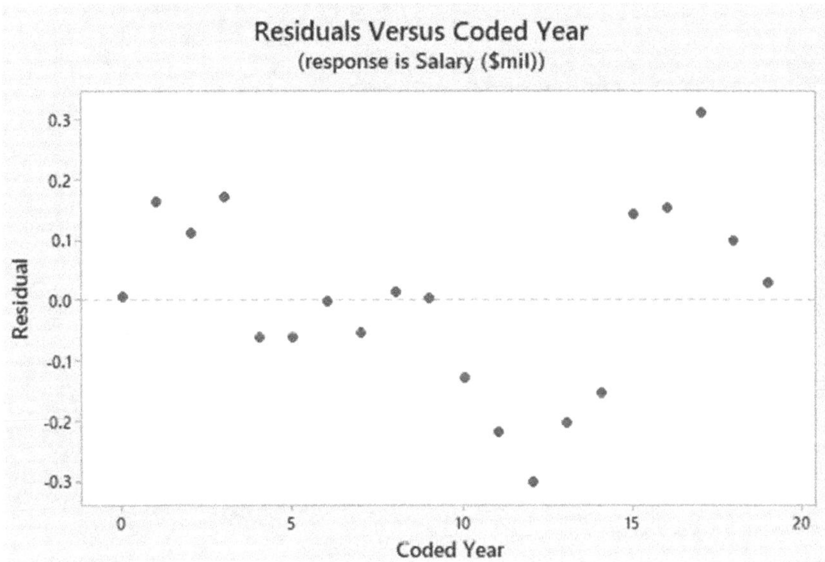

Quadratic

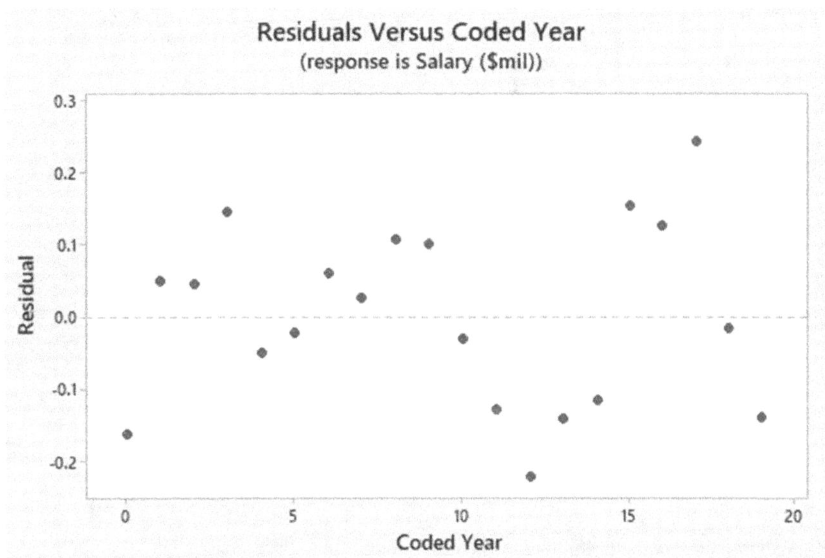

16.38 cont. (a) Exponential

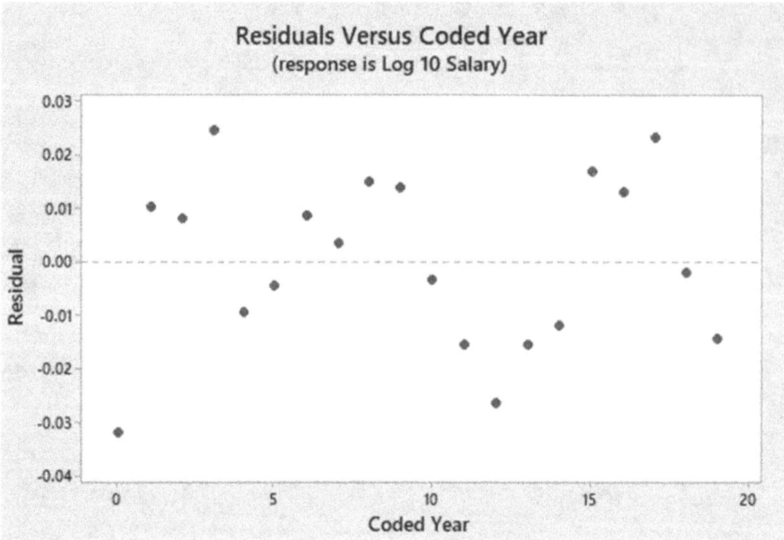

First-Order Autoregressive

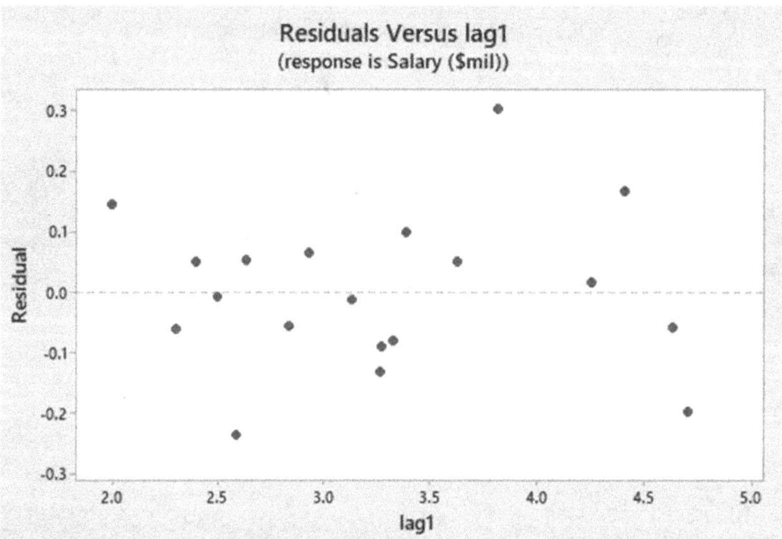

(b–c)

Salary		
	S_{yx}	*MAD*
Linear	0.159	0.12
Quadratic	0.133	0.104
Exponential	0.128	0.104
AR - First Order	0.134	0.1

(d) The residual plots for linear, quadratic, and exponential reveal cyclical patterns across coded year. The first-order autoregressive model has no clear pattern. The S_{xy} and *MAD* values are similar across each of the models. On the basis of (a) through (c) and the principle of parsimony, the first-order autoregressive model might be the best model for forecasting.

16.40 (a) $\log \hat{B}_0 = 2, \hat{B}_0 = 100$

This is the unadjusted forecast.

(b) $\log \hat{B}_1 = 0.01, \hat{B}_1 = 1.0233$

The estimated monthly compound growth rate is 2.33%.

(c) $\log \hat{B}_2 = 0.10, \hat{B}_2 = 1.2589$

The January values in the time series are estimated to have a mean of 25.89% higher than the December values.

16.42 (a) $\log \hat{B}_0 = 3, \hat{B}_0 = 1{,}000$

This is the unadjusted forecast.

(b) $\log \hat{B}_1 = 0.10, \hat{B}_1 = 1.2589$

The estimated quarterly compound growth rate is $(\hat{B}_1 - 1)100\% = 25.89\%$

(c) $\log \hat{B}_3 = 0.20, \hat{B}_3 = 1.5849$

$\hat{B}_3 = 1.5849$ is the seasonal multiplier relative to the fourth quarter. This multiplier indicates that second quarter values are 58.49% greater than the fourth quarter values.

16.44 (a) The revenues for Target appear to be subject to seasonal variation given that revenues are consistently higher in the fourth quarter, which includes several substantial holidays.

(b)

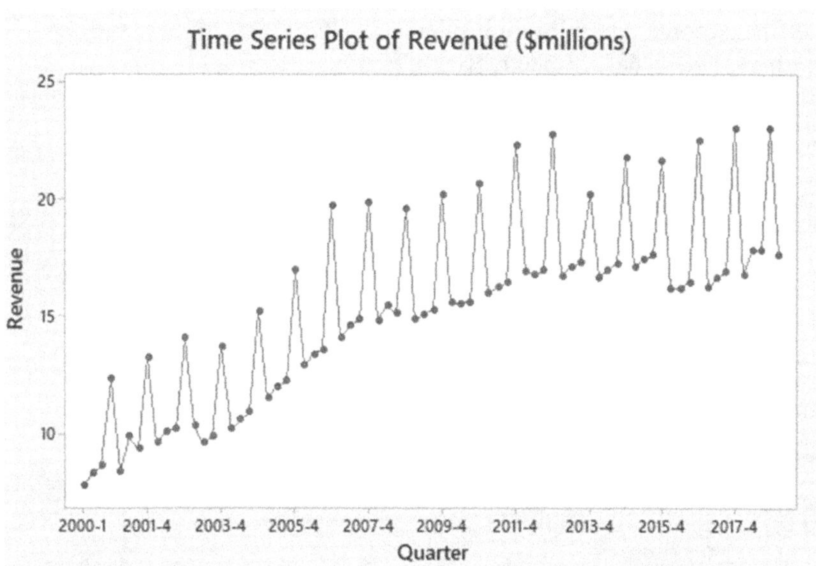

The plot confirms the answer for (a) by clearly revealing a seasonal component to revenues.

16.44 cont. (c)

Coefficients

Term	Coef	SE Coef	T-Value	P-Value	VIF
Constant	1.1091	0.0130	85.63	0.000	
Coded Q	0.004177	0.000218	19.13	0.000	1.00
Q1	-0.1346	0.0136	-9.88	0.000	1.52
Q2	-0.1233	0.0138	-8.93	0.000	1.51
Q3	-0.1233	0.0138	-8.93	0.000	1.51

Regression Equation

LogRevenue = 1.1091 + 0.004177 Coded Q - 0.1346 Q1 - 0.1233 Q2 - 0.1233 Q3

(d) $\log_{10}\hat{\beta}_1 = 0.0042; \hat{\beta}_1 = 10^{0.0042} = 1.0097$

The estimated quarterly compound growth rate is $(\hat{B}_1 - 1)100\% = 0.97\%$

(e)

Quarter	$b_i = \log\hat{\beta}_i$	$\hat{\beta}_i = 10^{b_i}$	$(\hat{\beta}_i - 1)100\%$
First	-0.1346	0.7335	-26.65%
Second	-0.1233	0.7528	-24.72%
Third	-0.1233	0.7528	-24.72%

The first, second, and third multipliers are -26.65%, -24.72%, and -24.72% relative to fourth quarter values, respectively.

(f) 2019 Revenues ($millions)

Quarter	$\hat{Y}$
Second	20.2936
Third	20.4932
Fourth	27.4827

2020 Revenues ($millions)

Quarter	$\hat{Y}$
First	20.3512
Second	21.0892
Third	21.0931
Fourth	28.5601

16.46 (a)

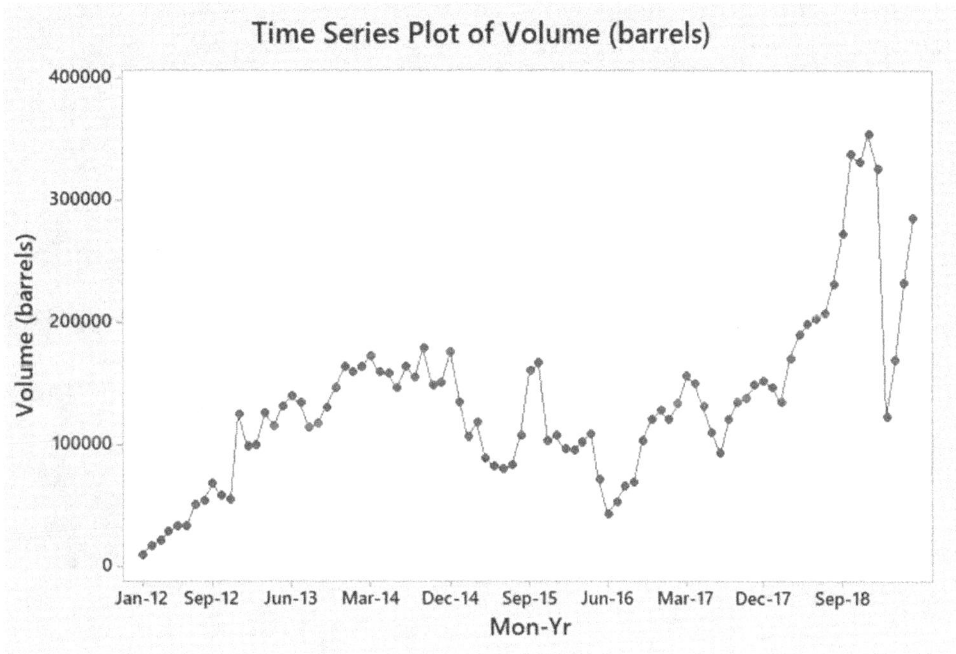

(b)

Coefficients

Term	Coef	SE Coef	T-Value	P-Value	VIF
Constant	4.9069	0.0944	52.00	0.000	
Coded Month	0.006291	0.000918	6.85	0.000	1.00
Month_Jan	-0.167	0.115	-1.45	0.151	1.95
Month_Feb	-0.203	0.115	-1.77	0.081	1.95
Month_Mar	-0.134	0.115	-1.17	0.246	1.95
Month_Apr	-0.125	0.115	-1.09	0.279	1.95
Month_May	-0.137	0.115	-1.19	0.238	1.95
Month_Jun	-0.204	0.119	-1.72	0.089	1.85
Month_Jul	-0.175	0.119	-1.48	0.144	1.85
Month_Aug	-0.139	0.119	-1.17	0.245	1.84
Month_Sep	-0.075	0.119	-0.63	0.529	1.84
Month_Oct	-0.054	0.119	-0.45	0.652	1.84
Month_Nov	-0.073	0.119	-0.62	0.540	1.84

Regression Equation

Log Volume = 4.9069 + 0.006291 Coded Month - 0.167 Month_Jan - 0.203 Month_Feb - 0.134 Month_Mar - 0.125 Month_Apr - 0.137 Month_May - 0.204 Month_Jun - 0.175 Month_Jul - 0.139 Month_Aug - 0.075 Month_Sep - 0.054 Month_Oct - 0.073 Month_Nov

(c) May 2019 Forecast: $\log \hat{Y}_{95} = 5.5045, \hat{Y}_{95} = 319{,}521.4$ barrels

16.46 cont. (d) Forecast for last four months of 2019:

Month	Coded Month	$\hat{Y}$
September	92	257,335.7
October	93	274,283.7
November	94	266,164.4
December	95	319.521.4

(e) $\log_{10}\hat{\beta}_1 = 0.006291; \hat{\beta}_1 = 10^{0.006291} = 1.0146$

The estimated monthly compound growth rate is $(\hat{\beta}_1 - 1)100\% = 1.46\%$ after adjusting for the seasonal component.

(f) The July values are estimated to have a mean of 33.17% below the December values.

16.48 (a)

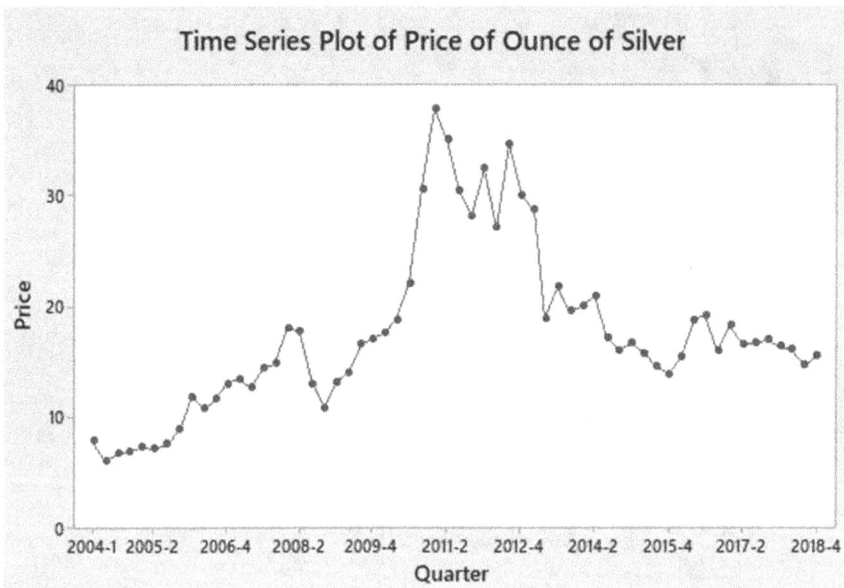

(b)

Coefficients

Term	Coef	SE Coef	T-Value	P-Value	VIF
Constant	1.0212	0.0575	17.75	0.000	
Coded Quarter	0.00574	0.00124	4.63	0.000	1.00
Q1	0.0375	0.0607	0.62	0.539	1.51
Q2	0.0043	0.0606	0.07	0.944	1.50
Q3	0.0074	0.0606	0.12	0.903	1.50

Regression Equation

Log Price = 1.0212 + 0.00574 Coded Quarter + 0.0375 Q1 + 0.0043 Q2 + 0.0074 Q3

(c) $\log_{10}\hat{\beta}_1 = 0.00574; \hat{\beta}_1 = 10^{0.00574} = 1.0133$

The estimated quarterly compound growth rate is $(\hat{\beta}_1 - 1)100\% = 1.33\%$

16.48 cont. (d) $\log_{10} \hat{\beta}_2 = 0.0375; \hat{\beta}_2 = 10^{0.0375} = 1.0902$

The 1st quarter values are estimated to have a mean of 9.02% above the 4th quarter values. A review of the p-values associated with the t test on the slope of the coefficients reveals that the slope coefficients for Quarter 1, Quarter 2, and Quarter 3 are not significant at the 0.05 significance level.

(e) The fitted value is 22.91 (US$)

(f) 2019 Forecasts:

Quarter	Coded Quarter	$\hat{Y}$
First	60	25.3070
Second	61	23.7531
Third	62	24.2443
Fourth	63	24.1513

(g) The forecasts are not likely to be accurate given that that the quarterly exponential trend model did not fit the data particularly well. The adjusted r^2 =0.2308. In addition, the time series contained an irregular component from 2010 through 2013.

16.50 A time series is a set of numerical data obtained at regular periods over time.

16.52 Moving averages take into account the results of a limited number of periods of time. Exponential smoothing takes into account all the time periods but gives increased weight to more recent time periods.

16.54 The linear trend model in this chapter has the time period as the X variable.

16.56 The different methods for choosing an appropriate forecasting model are residual analysis, the standard error of the estimate, the mean absolute deviation, and parsimony.

16.58 Forecasting for monthly or quarterly data uses an exponential trend model with dummy variables to represent either months or quarters.

16.60 (a) Population:

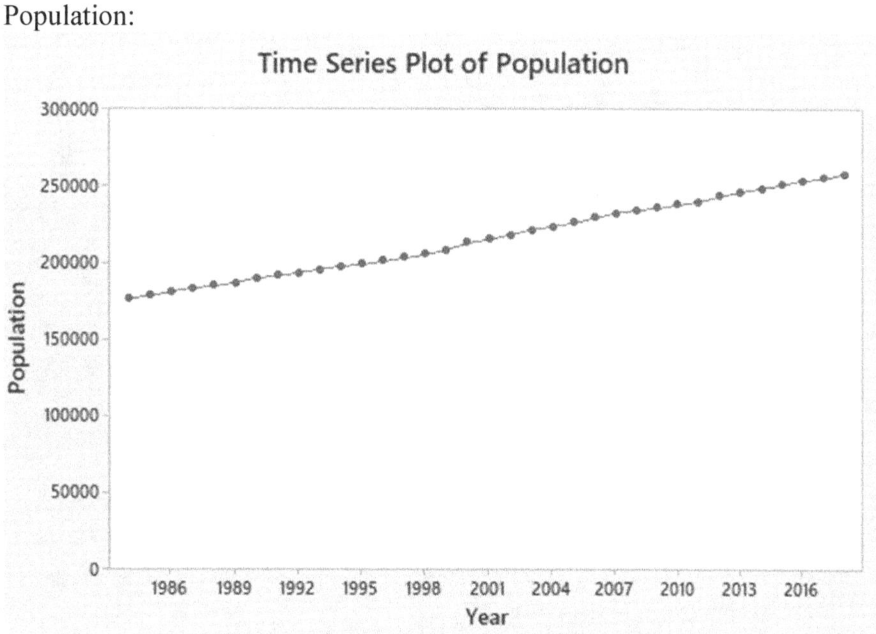

16.60 (b)
cont.

Regression Analysis: Population versus Coded Year

Analysis of Variance

Source	DF	Adj SS	Adj MS	F-Value	P-Value
Regression	1	21635022177	21635022177	10461.18	0.000
Coded Year	1	21635022177	21635022177	10461.18	0.000
Error	33	68248128	2068125		
Total	34	21703270305			

Model Summary

S	R-sq	R-sq(adj)	R-sq(pred)
1438.10	99.69%	99.68%	99.65%

Coefficients

Term	Coef	SE Coef	T-Value	P-Value	VIF
Constant	173763	476	365.10	0.000	
Coded Year	2461.8	24.1	102.28	0.000	1.00

Regression Equation

Population = 173763 + 2461.8 Coded Year

$\hat{Y} = 173,763 + 2,461.8(X)$ where X = years relative to 1984

(c) $\hat{Y}_{2019} = 173,763 + 2,461.8(35) = 259,926$ (thousands)

$\hat{Y}_{2020} = 173,763 + 2,461.8(36) = 262,387.8$ (thousands)

(d) (a) Workforce

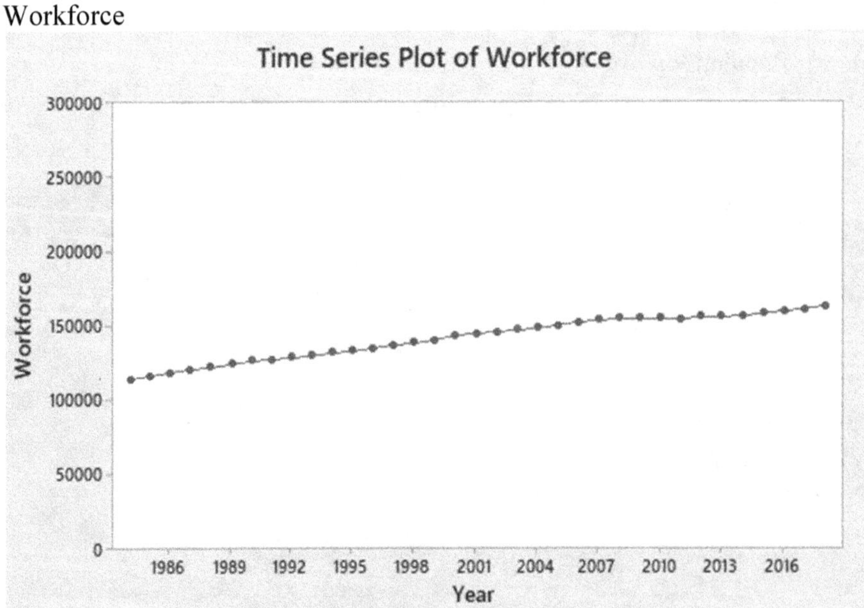

16.60 cont. (d) (b)

Regression Analysis: Workforce versus Coded Year

Analysis of Variance

Source	DF	Adj SS	Adj MS	F-Value	P-Value
Regression	1	7019320655	7019320655	1312.93	0.000
Coded Year	1	7019320655	7019320655	1312.93	0.000
Error	33	176427811	5346297		
Total	34	7195748466			

Model Summary

S	R-sq	R-sq(adj)	R-sq(pred)
2312.21	97.55%	97.47%	97.21%

Coefficients

Term	Coef	SE Coef	T-Value	P-Value	VIF
Constant	117084	765	153.01	0.000	
Coded Year	1402.2	38.7	36.23	0.000	1.00

Regression Equation

Workforce = 117084 + 1402.2 Coded Year

$\hat{Y} = 117,084 + 1,402.2(X)$ where X = years relative to 1984

(c) $\hat{Y}_{2019} = 117,084 + 1402.2(35) = 166,161$ (thousands)

$\hat{Y}_{2020} = 117,084 + 1402.2(35) = 167,563.2$ (thousands)

16.62 (a)

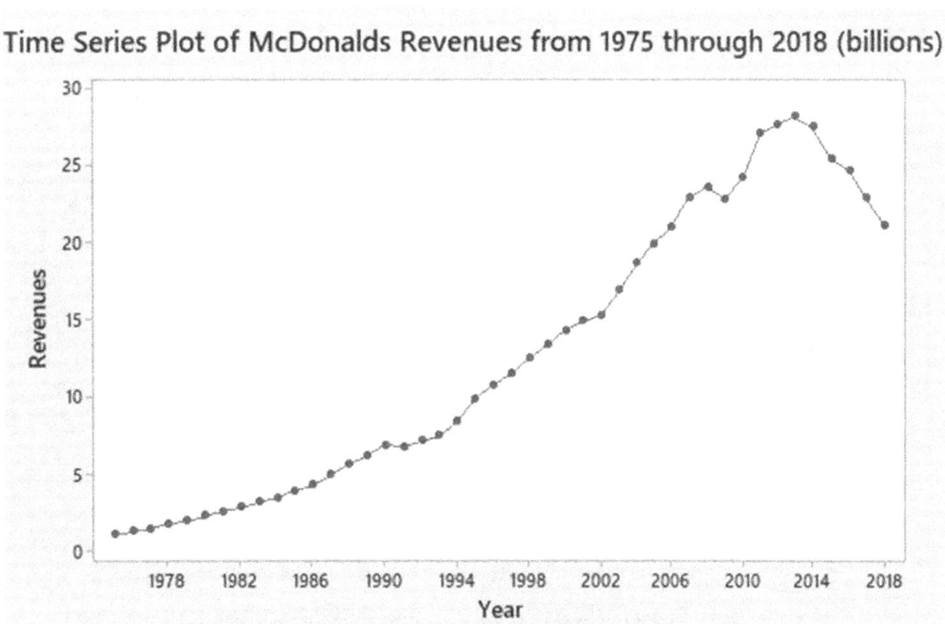

16.62 cont. (b) Linear:

Regression Analysis: Revenues versus Coded Year

Analysis of Variance

Source	DF	Adj SS	Adj MS	F-Value	P-Value
Regression	1	3352.7	3352.65	619.03	0.000
Coded Year	1	3352.7	3352.65	619.03	0.000
Error	42	227.5	5.42		
Total	43	3580.1			

Model Summary

S	R-sq	R-sq(adj)	R-sq(pred)
2.32723	93.65%	93.49%	92.82%

Coefficients

Term	Coef	SE Coef	T-Value	P-Value	VIF
Constant	-2.120	0.690	-3.07	0.004	
Coded Year	0.6874	0.0276	24.88	0.000	1.00

Regression Equation

Revenues = -2.120 + 0.6874 Coded Year

$\hat{Y} = -2.120 + 0.6874(X)$, where X = years relative to 1975

(c) Quadratic:

Regression Analysis: Revenues versus Coded Year, Coded Year Sq

Analysis of Variance

Source	DF	Adj SS	Adj MS	F-Value	P-Value
Regression	2	3370.63	1685.32	329.84	0.000
Coded Year	1	113.98	113.98	22.31	0.000
Coded Year Sq	1	17.98	17.98	3.52	0.068
Error	41	209.49	5.11		
Total	43	3580.13			

Model Summary

S	R-sq	R-sq(adj)	R-sq(pred)
2.26043	94.15%	93.86%	92.48%

Coefficients

Term	Coef	SE Coef	T-Value	P-Value	VIF
Constant	-0.785	0.978	-0.80	0.427	
Coded Year	0.497	0.105	4.72	0.000	15.36
Coded Year Sq	0.00444	0.00236	1.88	0.068	15.36

Regression Equation

Revenues = -0.785 + 0.497 Coded Year + 0.00444 Coded Year Sq

$\hat{Y} = -0.785 + 0.497X + 0.00444X^2$, where X = years relative to 1975

16.62 cont. (d) Exponential:

Regression Analysis: Log Revenues versus Coded Year

Analysis of Variance

Source	DF	Adj SS	Adj MS	F-Value	P-Value
Regression	1	7.4983	7.49834	607.96	0.000
Coded Year	1	7.4983	7.49834	607.96	0.000
Error	42	0.5180	0.01233		
Total	43	8.0164			

Model Summary

S	R-sq	R-sq(adj)	R-sq(pred)
0.111057	93.54%	93.38%	92.59%

Coefficients

Term	Coef	SE Coef	T-Value	P-Value	VIF
Constant	0.2393	0.0329	7.27	0.000	
Coded Year	0.03251	0.00132	24.66	0.000	1.00

Regression Equation

Log Revenues = 0.2393 + 0.03251 Coded Year

$\log_{10}\hat{Y} = 0.2393 + 0.03251(X)$ where X = years relative to 1975

16.62 (e)
cont.

Autoregressive:
For the third order term, $t_{STAT} = 0.08$ with a p-value of 0.935. The third order term can be dropped because it is not significant at the 0.05 significance level.

Regression Analysis: Revenues versus lag1, lag2

Method

Rows unused 2

Analysis of Variance

Source	DF	Adj SS	Adj MS	F-Value	P-Value
Regression	2	3278.23	1639.11	2914.83	0.000
lag1	1	85.42	85.42	151.90	0.000
lag2	1	14.02	14.02	24.93	0.000
Error	39	21.93	0.56		
Total	41	3300.16			

Model Summary

S	R-sq	R-sq(adj)	R-sq(pred)
0.749890	99.34%	99.30%	99.16%

Coefficients

Term	Coef	SE Coef	T-Value	P-Value	VIF
Constant	0.344	0.212	1.62	0.113	
lag1	1.648	0.134	12.32	0.000	107.30
lag2	-0.665	0.133	-4.99	0.000	107.30

Regression Equation

Revenues = 0.344 + 1.648 lag1 - 0.665 lag2

For the second order term, $t_{STAT} = -4.99$ with a p-value of 0.000. The second order term cannot be dropped because it is significant at the 0.05 significance level. The second-order model is appropriate.

$$\hat{Y}_i = 0.344 + 1.648(Y_{i-1}) - 0.665(Y_{i-2})$$

16.62 cont. (f) Linear:

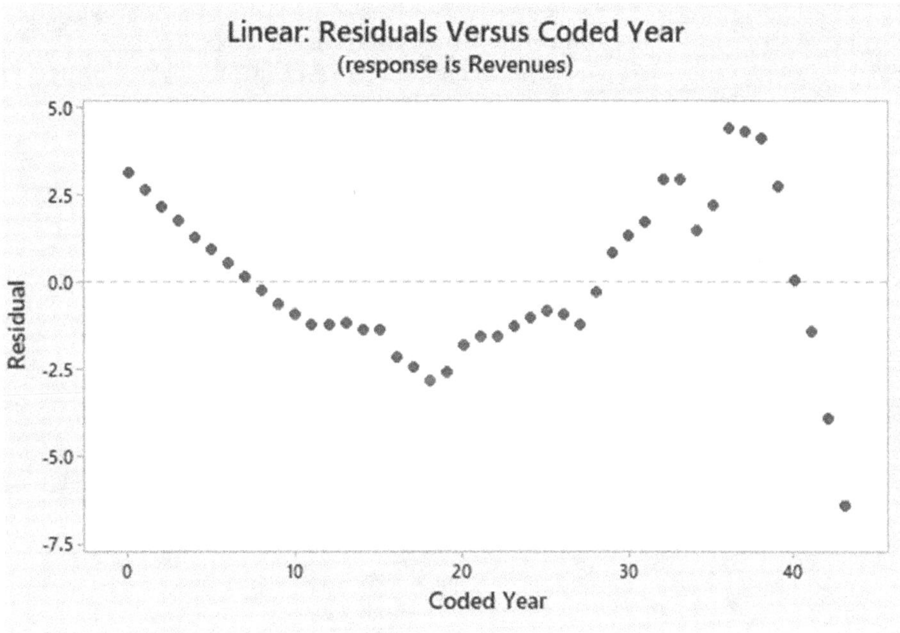

Quadratic:

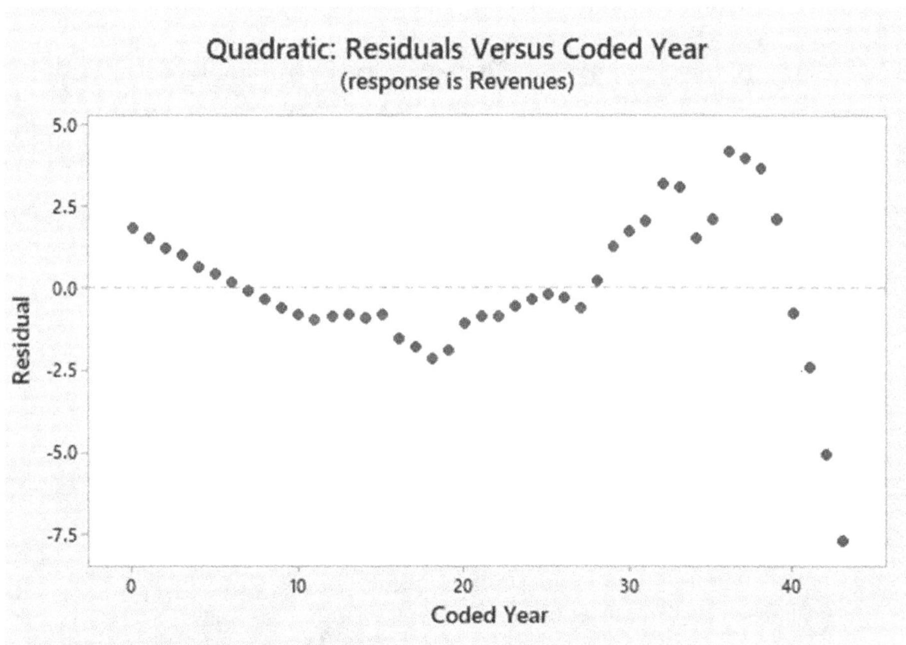

16.62 cont. (f) Exponential:

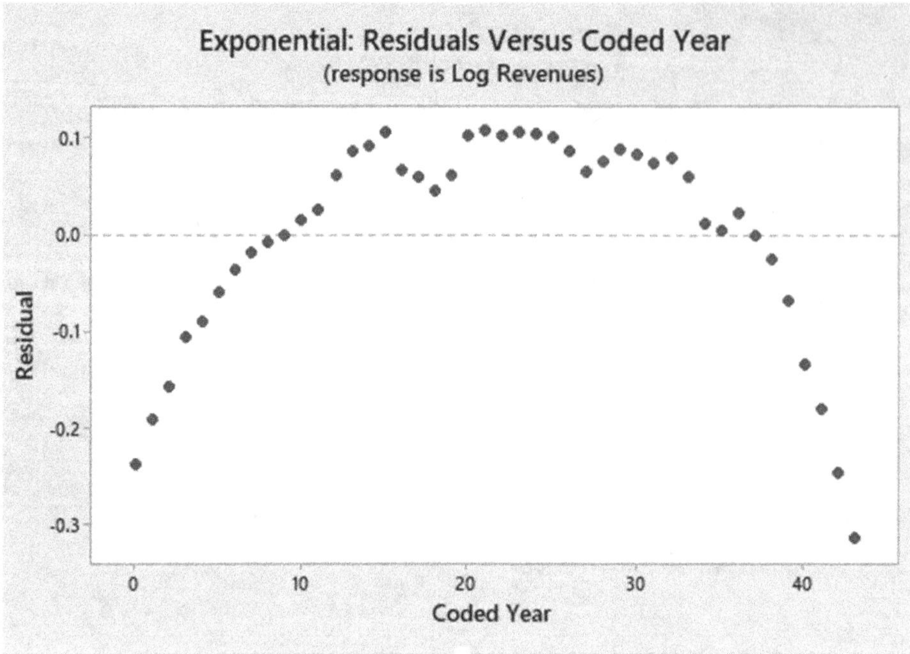

Second-Order Autoregressive:

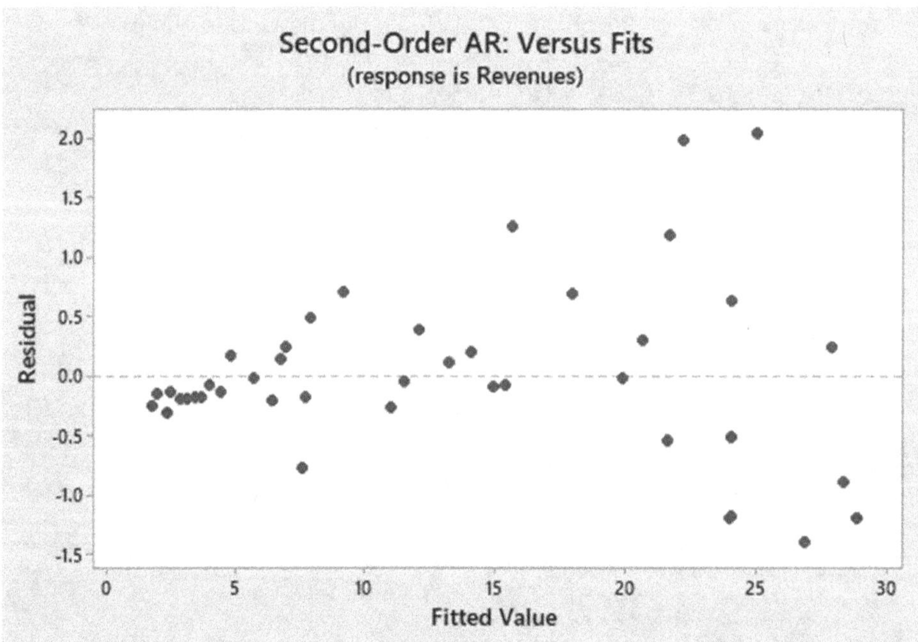

16.62 cont. (g)

Bonuses		
	S_{yx}	*MAD*
Linear	2.3272	1.8713
Quadratic	2.2604	1.6022
Exponential	5.3568	2.7731
AR - Second Order	0.7499	0.5072

(h) The residuals plots reveal clear cyclical patterns for the linear, quadratic, and exponential models. The residual plot for second-order autoregressive model revealed no cyclical pattern. However, the residual plot did reveal a potential equal variance assumption violation discussed in an earlier chapter. The second-order autoregressive model also had the smallest values for the standard error of the estimate and *MAD*. Based on the results from (f), (g), and the principle of parsimony, the second-order autoregressive model would be best suited for forecasting.

(i) $\hat{Y}_{2019} = 0.344 + 1.648(21) - 0.665(22.8) = 19.79$ billion

16.64 A time series analysis of the Canadian dollar reveals a moderate component with up and down cycles of varying durations. Although the currency rate varies in cycles, the 1980 exchange rate is fairly similar to the 2019 exchange rate. A review of residual plots reveals that the linear, quadratic, and exponential models may be problematic due to cyclical variation in the residuals. In contrast, a first-order autoregressive model revealed a random pattern of residuals. In addition, the first-order autoregressive model had the smallest standard error of the estimate and *MAD* values. The first-order autoregressive was the most appropriate model to use for forecasting. Using this model, the forecasted exchange rate is 1.3504 (units per $ U.S.) and 1.3388 (units per $ U.S.) for 2020 and 2021, respectively.

A time series analysis of the Japanese yen exchange rate revealed a steep drop in the rate beginning in 1986. The rate dropped from 238.47 (units per $ U.S.) in 1985 to 128.17 (units per $ U.S.) in 1988. The exchange rate had a cyclical component from that point forward with an overall declining trend. A review of the residual plots, standard error of the estimate and *MAD* values, revealed that the first-order autoregressive model was the most appropriate for forecasting. Using this model, the forecasted exchange rate is 109.278 (units per $ U.S.) and 109.000 (units per $ U.S.) for 2020 and 2021, respectively.

A time series analysis of the English pound reveals a moderate component with up and down cycles of varying durations. Although the currency rate varies in cycles, the 1980 exchange rate has increased from 0.4302 (units per $ U.S.) in 1980 to 0.7847 (units per $ U.S.) in 2019. A review of the residual plots and the standard error of the estimate and *MAD* values revealed that the first-order autoregressive model was the most appropriate for forecasting. Using this model, the forecasted exchange rate is 0.7427 (units per $ U.S.) and 0.7140 (units per $ U.S.) for 2020 and 2021, respectively.

An unexpected irregular component in the future could not be anticipated by the autoregressive models used for each of the currencies.

16.64
cont.

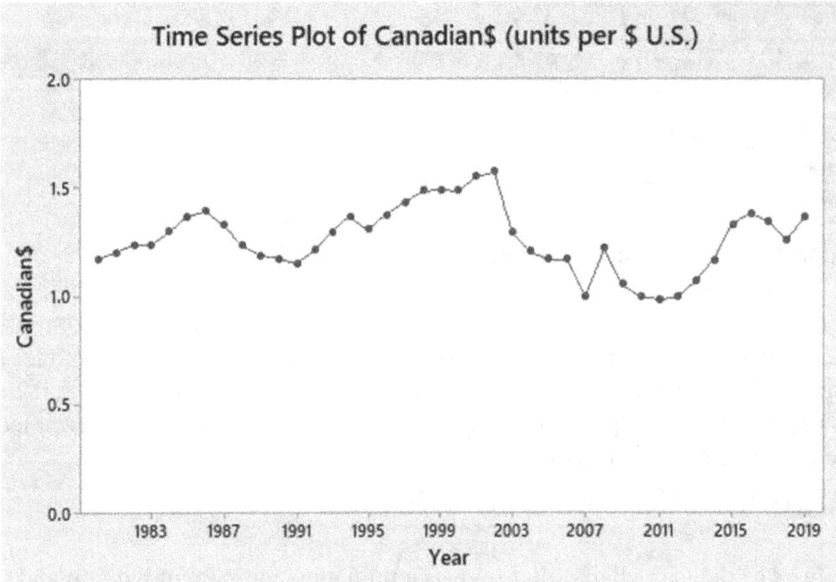

Canadian: Linear

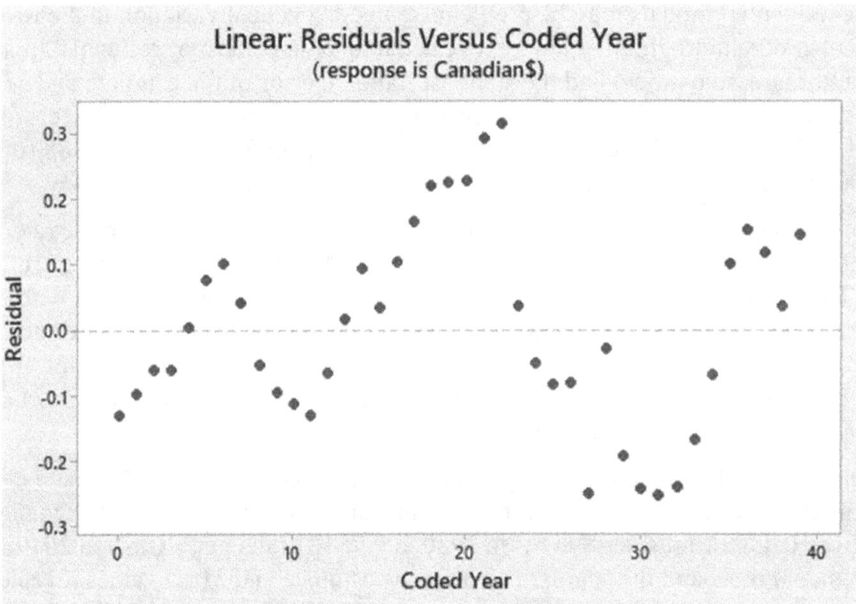

16.64
cont.

Regression Analysis: Canadian$ versus Coded Year

Analysis of Variance

Source	DF	Adj SS	Adj MS	F-Value	P-Value
Regression	1	0.02300	0.02300	0.99	0.327
Coded Year	1	0.02300	0.02300	0.99	0.327
Error	38	0.88559	0.02331		
Total	39	0.90860			

Model Summary

S	R-sq	R-sq(adj)	R-sq(pred)
0.152660	2.53%	0.00%	0.00%

Coefficients

Term	Coef	SE Coef	T-Value	P-Value	VIF
Constant	1.3010	0.0474	27.46	0.000	
Coded Year	-0.00208	0.00209	-0.99	0.327	1.00

Regression Equation

Canadian$ = 1.3010 - 0.00208 Coded Year

Quadratic

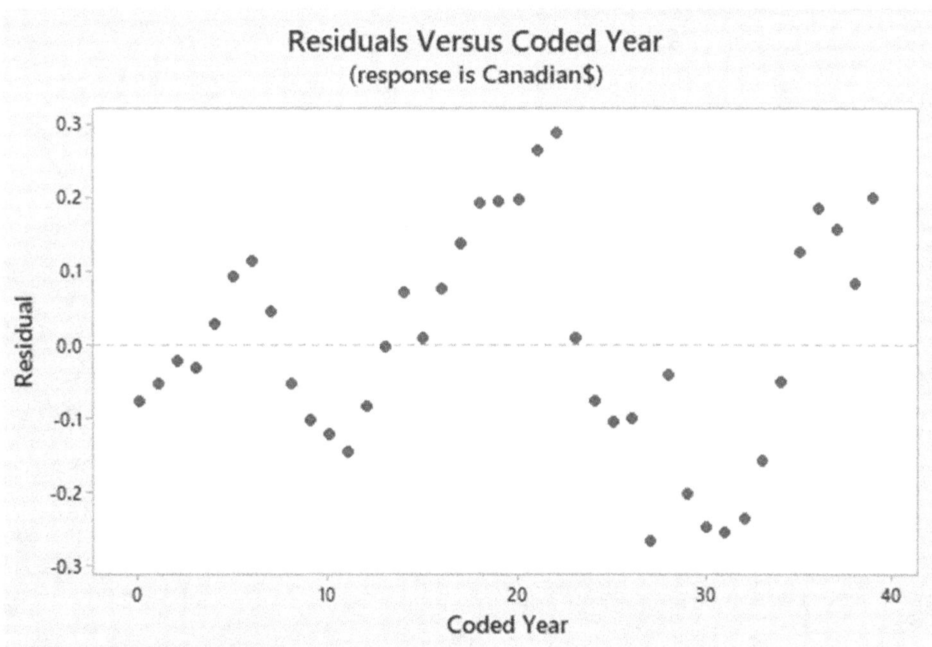

16.64
cont.

Regression Analysis: Canadian$ versus Coded Year, Coded Year Sq

Analysis of Variance

Source	DF	Adj SS	Adj MS	F-Value	P-Value
Regression	2	0.05118	0.02559	1.10	0.342
Coded Year	1	0.01525	0.01525	0.66	0.422
Coded Year Sq	1	0.02818	0.02818	1.22	0.277
Error	37	0.85742	0.02317		
Total	39	0.90860			

Model Summary

S	R-sq	R-sq(adj)	R-sq(pred)
0.152228	5.63%	0.53%	0.00%

Coefficients

Term	Coef	SE Coef	T-Value	P-Value	VIF
Constant	1.2459	0.0687	18.12	0.000	
Coded Year	0.00662	0.00815	0.81	0.422	15.30
Coded Year Sq	-0.000223	0.000202	-1.10	0.277	15.30

Regression Equation

Canadian$ = 1.2459 + 0.00662 Coded Year - 0.000223 Coded Year Sq

Exponential

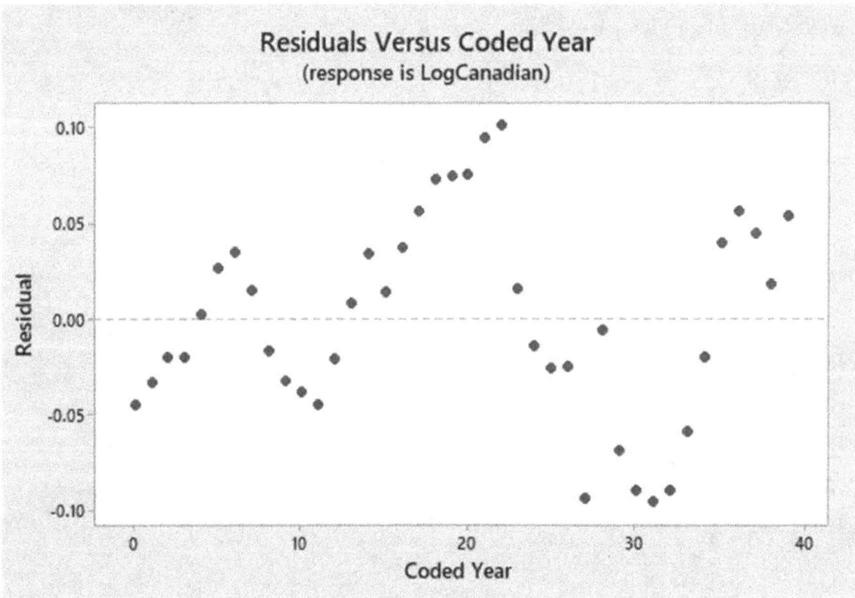

16.64
cont.

Regression Analysis: LogCanadian versus Coded Year

Analysis of Variance

Source	DF	Adj SS	Adj MS	F-Value	P-Value
Regression	1	0.003711	0.003711	1.31	0.259
Coded Year	1	0.003711	0.003711	1.31	0.259
Error	38	0.107412	0.002827		
Total	39	0.111124			

Model Summary

S	R-sq	R-sq(adj)	R-sq(pred)
0.0531662	3.34%	0.80%	0.00%

Coefficients

Term	Coef	SE Coef	T-Value	P-Value	VIF
Constant	0.1136	0.0165	6.89	0.000	
Coded Year	-0.000834	0.000728	-1.15	0.259	1.00

Regression Equation

LogCanadian = 0.1136 - 0.000834 Coded Year

Autoregressive First-Order

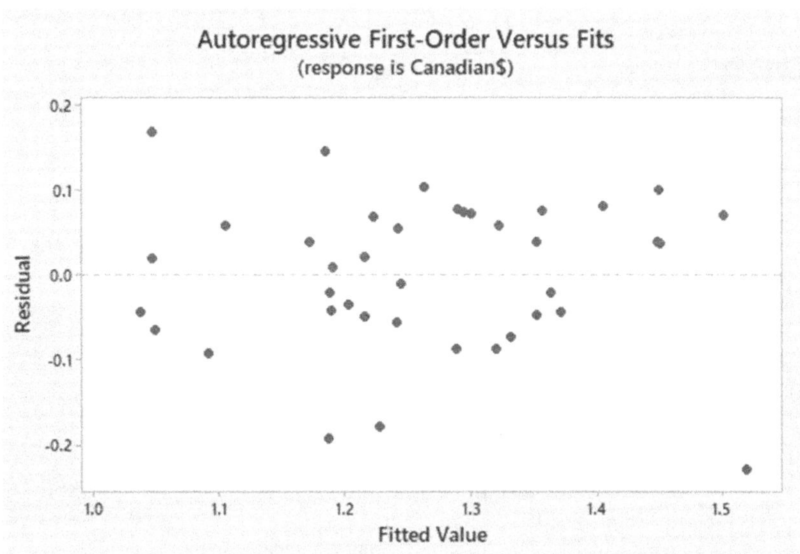

16.64
cont.

Regression Analysis: Canadian$ versus CanLag1

Method

Rows unused 1

Analysis of Variance

Source	DF	Adj SS	Adj MS	F-Value	P-Value
Regression	1	0.6037	0.603656	75.35	0.000
CanLag1	1	0.6037	0.603656	75.35	0.000
Error	37	0.2964	0.008011		
Total	38	0.9001			

Model Summary

S	R-sq	R-sq(adj)	R-sq(pred)
0.0895059	67.07%	66.18%	62.12%

Coefficients

Term	Coef	SE Coef	T-Value	P-Value	VIF
Constant	0.231	0.120	1.93	0.061	
CanLag1	0.8201	0.0945	8.68	0.000	1.00

Regression Equation

Canadian$ = 0.231 + 0.8201 CanLag1

Canadian		
	S_{yx}	*MAD*
Linear	0.1527	0.1245
Quadratic	0.1522	0.1224
Exponential	0.153	0.1247
AR-First Order	0.0895	0.07132

16.64 cont. Yen

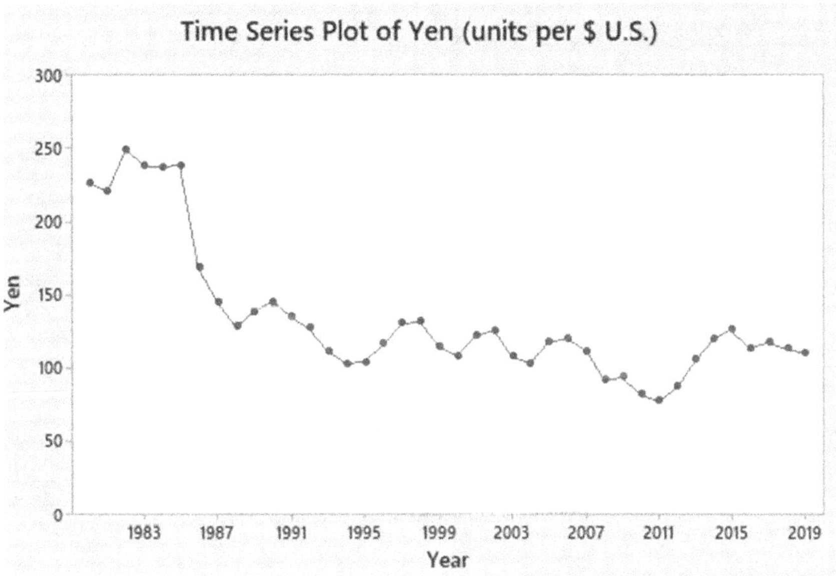

Linear

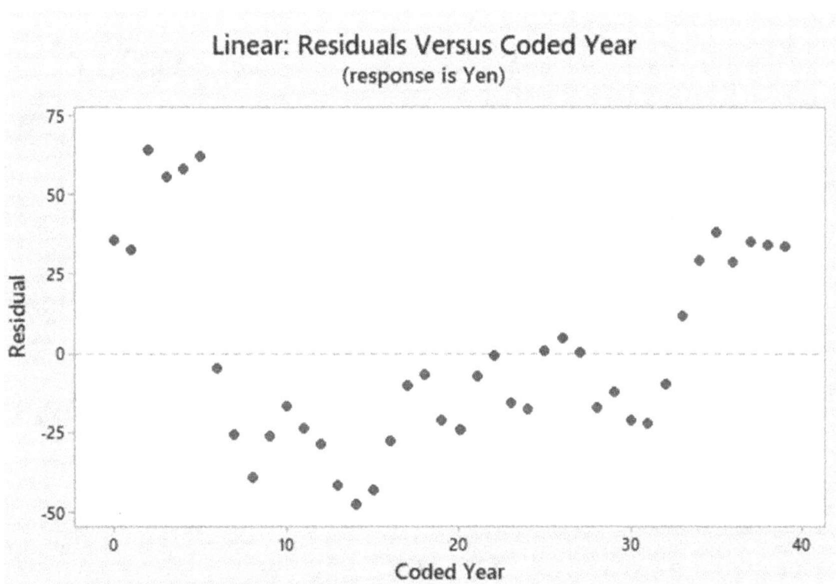

16.64
cont.

Regression Analysis: Yen versus Coded Year

Analysis of Variance

Source	DF	Adj SS	Adj MS	F-Value	P-Value
Regression	1	46637	46637	46.54	0.000
Coded Year	1	46637	46637	46.54	0.000
Error	38	38083	1002		
Total	39	84720			

Model Summary

S	R-sq	R-sq(adj)	R-sq(pred)
31.6572	55.05%	53.87%	48.91%

Coefficients

Term	Coef	SE Coef	T-Value	P-Value	VIF
Constant	191.37	9.83	19.48	0.000	
Coded Year	-2.958	0.434	-6.82	0.000	1.00

Regression Equation

Yen = 191.37 - 2.958 Coded Year

Quadratic

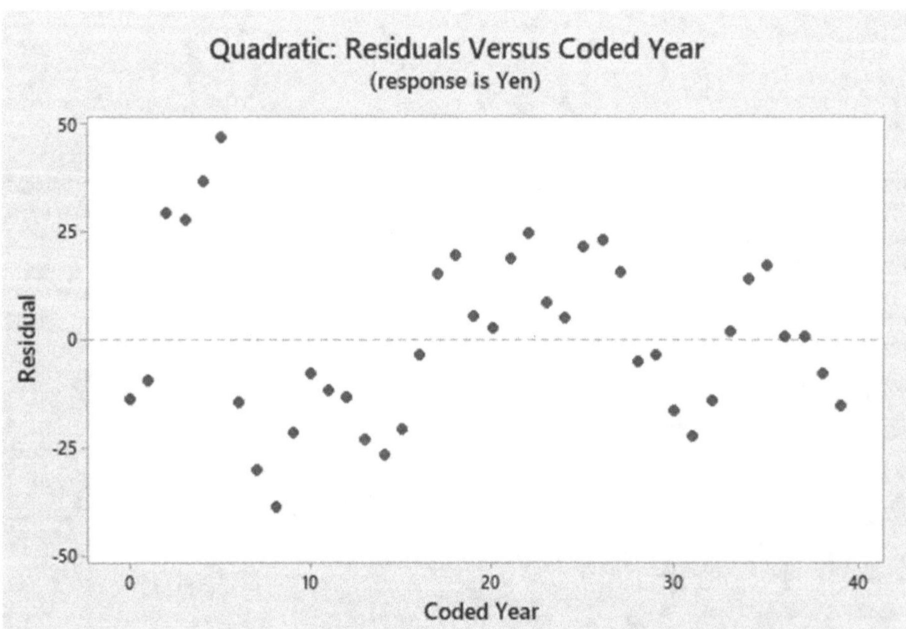

16.64
cont.

Regression Analysis: Yen versus Coded Year, Coded Year Sq

Analysis of Variance

Source	DF	Adj SS	Adj MS	F-Value	P-Value
Regression	2	69339	34669.6	83.40	0.000
Coded Year	1	40354	40353.8	97.08	0.000
Coded Year Sq	1	22702	22702.2	54.61	0.000
Error	37	15381	415.7		
Total	39	84720			

Model Summary

S	R-sq	R-sq(adj)	R-sq(pred)
20.3885	81.85%	80.86%	78.83%

Coefficients

Term	Coef	SE Coef	T-Value	P-Value	VIF
Constant	240.79	9.21	26.15	0.000	
Coded Year	-10.76	1.09	-9.85	0.000	15.30
Coded Year Sq	0.2001	0.0271	7.39	0.000	15.30

Regression Equation

Yen = 240.79 - 10.76 Coded Year + 0.2001 Coded Year Sq

Exponential

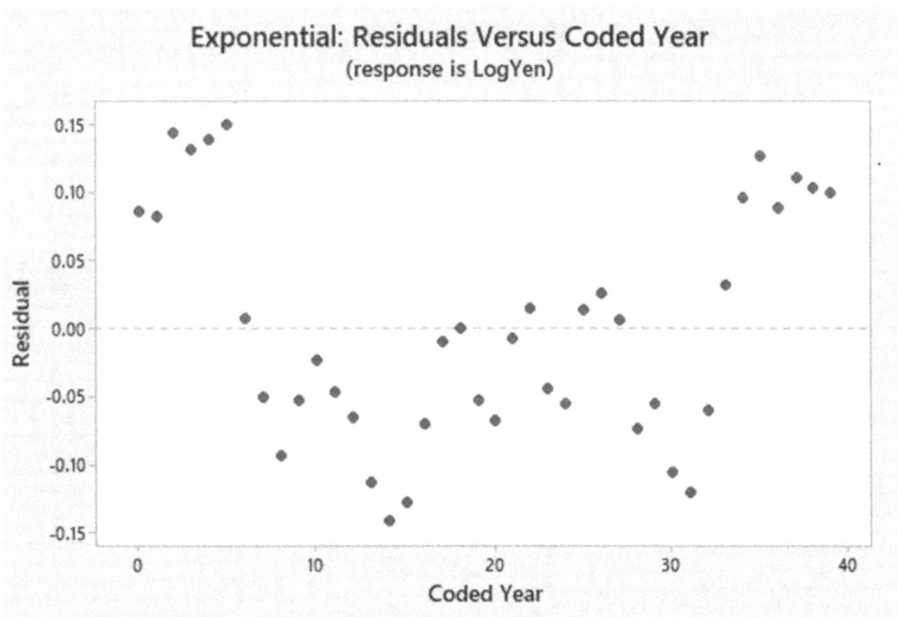

16.64
cont.

Regression Analysis: LogYen versus Coded Year

Analysis of Variance

Source	DF	Adj SS	Adj MS	F-Value	P-Value
Regression	1	0.3822	0.382229	50.24	0.000
Coded Year	1	0.3822	0.382229	50.24	0.000
Error	38	0.2891	0.007608		
Total	39	0.6713			

Model Summary

S	R-sq	R-sq(adj)	R-sq(pred)
0.0872215	56.94%	55.80%	51.23%

Coefficients

Term	Coef	SE Coef	T-Value	P-Value	VIF
Constant	2.2701	0.0271	83.85	0.000	
Coded Year	-0.00847	0.00119	-7.09	0.000	1.00

Regression Equation

LogYen = 2.2701 - 0.00847 Coded Year

Autoregressive First-Order

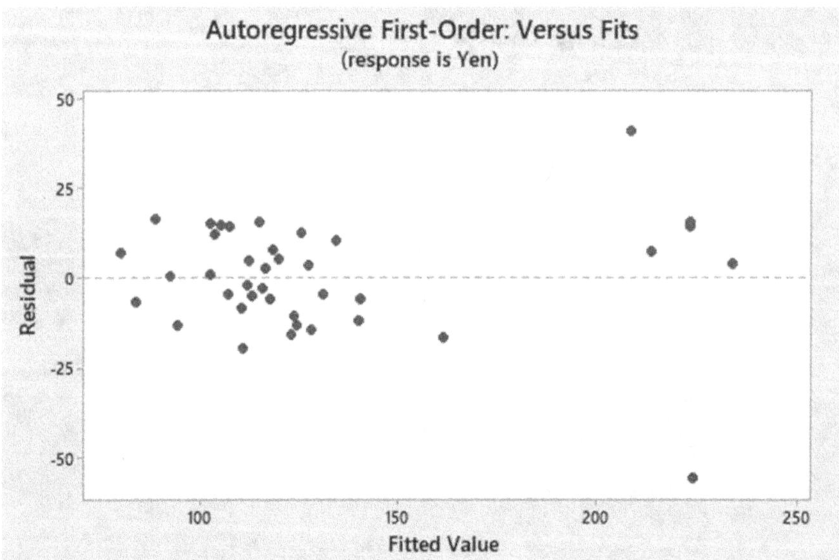

16.64 cont.

Regression Analysis: Yen versus YenLag1

Method

Rows unused 1

Analysis of Variance

Source	DF	Adj SS	Adj MS	F-Value	P-Value
Regression	1	66819	66818.8	273.42	0.000
YenLag1	1	66819	66818.8	273.42	0.000
Error	37	9042	244.4		
Total	38	75861			

Model Summary

S	R-sq	R-sq(adj)	R-sq(pred)
15.6326	88.08%	87.76%	85.23%

Coefficients

Term	Coef	SE Coef	T-Value	P-Value	VIF
Constant	11.61	7.66	1.52	0.138	
YenLag1	0.8912	0.0539	16.54	0.000	1.00

Regression Equation

Yen = 11.61 + 0.8912 YenLag1

Yen		
	S_{YX}	*MAD*
Linear	31.6572	25.9902
Quadratic	20.3885	16.3877
Exponential	29.9896	22.8784
AR - First Order	15.6326	11.3583

16.64 cont. English Pound

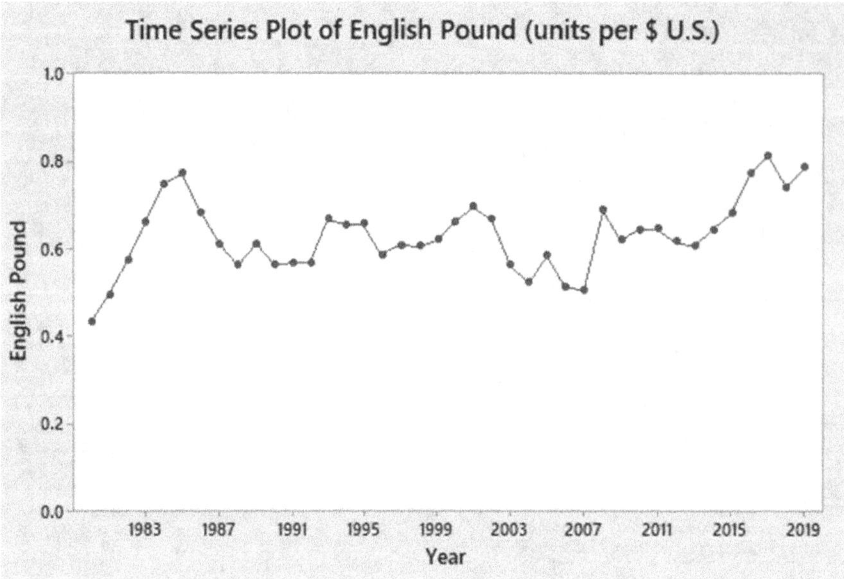

Linear

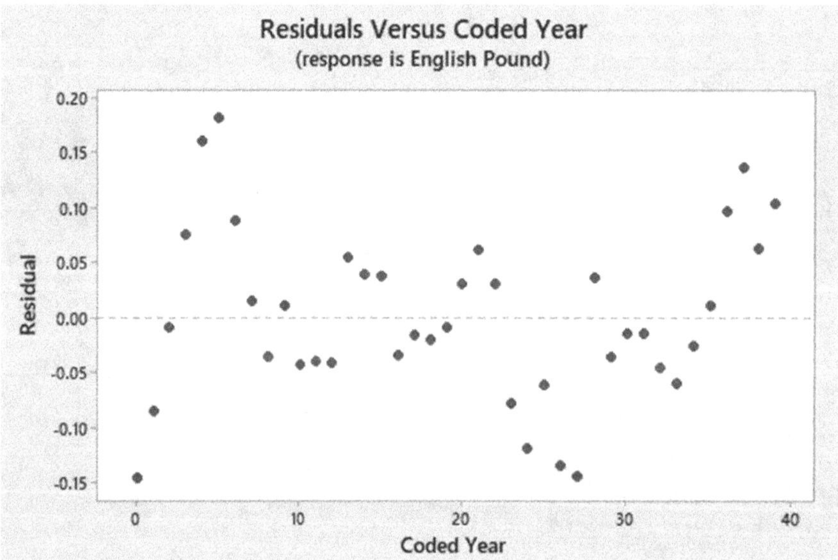

16.64
cont.

Regression Analysis: English Pound versus Coded Year

Analysis of Variance

Source	DF	Adj SS	Adj MS	F-Value	P-Value
Regression	1	0.03801	0.038013	6.09	0.018
Coded Year	1	0.03801	0.038013	6.09	0.018
Error	38	0.23708	0.006239		
Total	39	0.27510			

Model Summary

S	R-sq	R-sq(adj)	R-sq(pred)
0.0789874	13.82%	11.55%	2.13%

Coefficients

Term	Coef	SE Coef	T-Value	P-Value	VIF
Constant	0.5767	0.0245	23.52	0.000	
Coded Year	0.00267	0.00108	2.47	0.018	1.00

Regression Equation

English Pound = 0.5767 + 0.00267 Coded Year

Quadratic

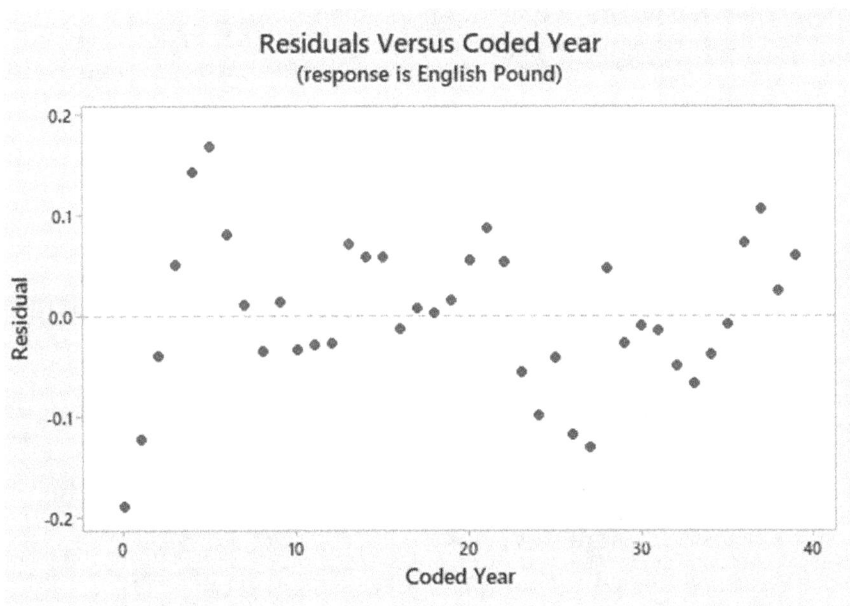

16.64
cont.

Regression Analysis: English Pound versus Coded Year, Coded Year Sq

Analysis of Variance

Source	DF	Adj SS	Adj MS	F-Value	P-Value
Regression	2	0.056616	0.028308	4.79	0.014
Coded Year	1	0.006725	0.006725	1.14	0.293
Coded Year Sq	1	0.018603	0.018603	3.15	0.084
Error	37	0.218479	0.005905		
Total	39	0.275096			

Model Summary

S	R-sq	R-sq(adj)	R-sq(pred)
0.0768430	20.58%	16.29%	0.29%

Coefficients

Term	Coef	SE Coef	T-Value	P-Value	VIF
Constant	0.6215	0.0347	17.91	0.000	
Coded Year	-0.00439	0.00412	-1.07	0.293	15.30
Coded Year Sq	0.000181	0.000102	1.77	0.084	15.30

Regression Equation

English Pound = 0.6215 - 0.00439 Coded Year + 0.000181 Coded Year Sq

Exponential

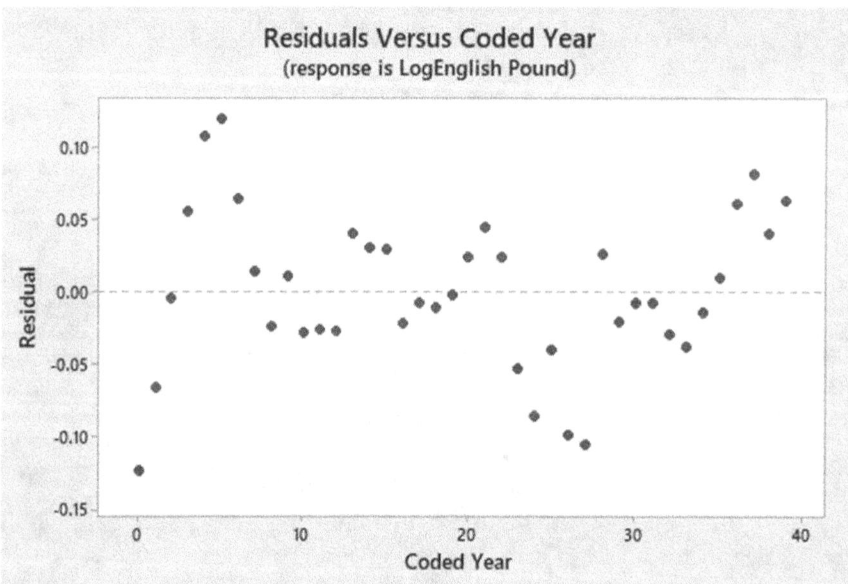

16.64
cont.

Regression Analysis: LogEnglish Pound versus Coded Year

Analysis of Variance

Source	DF	Adj SS	Adj MS	F-Value	P-Value
Regression	1	0.01880	0.018797	6.14	0.018
Coded Year	1	0.01880	0.018797	6.14	0.018
Error	38	0.11626	0.003060		
Total	39	0.13506			

Model Summary

S	R-sq	R-sq(adj)	R-sq(pred)
0.0553133	13.92%	11.65%	2.20%

Coefficients

Term	Coef	SE Coef	T-Value	P-Value	VIF
Constant	-0.2419	0.0172	-14.09	0.000	
Coded Year	0.001878	0.000758	2.48	0.018	1.00

Regression Equation

LogEnglish Pound = -0.2419 + 0.001878 Coded Year

Autoregressive First-order

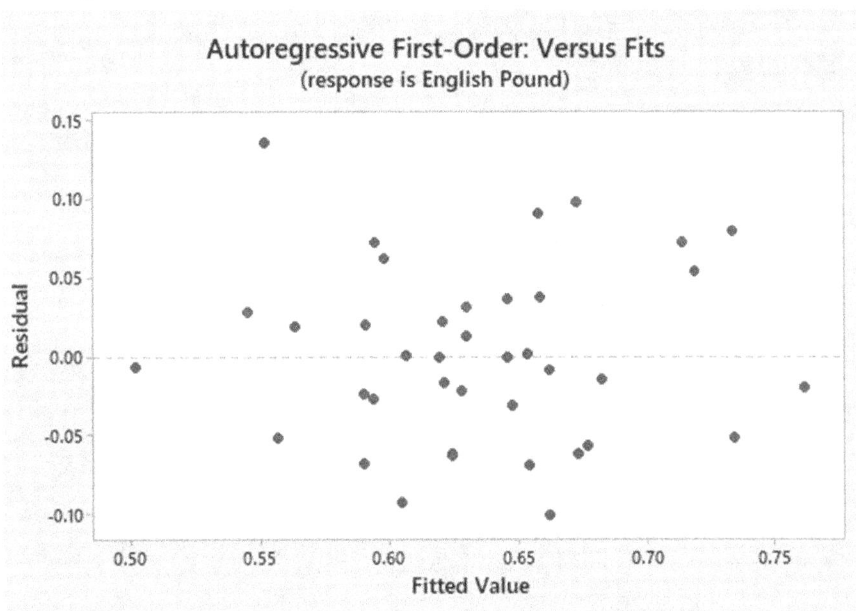

16.64
cont.

Regression Analysis: English Pound versus EngLag1

Method

Rows unused 1

Analysis of Variance

Source	DF	Adj SS	Adj MS	F-Value	P-Value
Regression	1	0.1165	0.116495	36.49	0.000
EngLag1	1	0.1165	0.116495	36.49	0.000
Error	37	0.1181	0.003193		
Total	38	0.2346			

Model Summary

S	R-sq	R-sq(adj)	R-sq(pred)
0.0565043	49.65%	48.29%	43.74%

Coefficients

Term	Coef	SE Coef	T-Value	P-Value	VIF
Constant	0.2075	0.0712	2.92	0.006	
EngLag1	0.682	0.113	6.04	0.000	1.00

Regression Equation

English Pound = 0.2075 + 0.682 EngLag1

English Pound		
	S_{YX}	*MAD*
Linear	0.079	0.0613
Quadratic	0.0768	0.0585
Exponential	0.0789	0.0607
AR - First-Order	0.0565	0.0443

Chapter 17

17.2 Limited information technology and data management systems prevented the widespread adoption of business analytics in the past.

17.4 Artificial intelligence is a type of computer science that utilizes software solutions to simulate human expertice, reasoning, or knowledge. Machine learning is one of the artificial intelligence tools used to automate model building.

17.6 Decision rules compare decision criteria to facilitate prediction.

17.8 Data dimesionality represents the number of variables associated with visualizing a data item. Color, size, and motion represent additional dimensions that can be used to describe a data item.

17.10 Clustering involves the grouping of items into sets based on the similarity of items. A calculated distance is used to determine the similarity of items. Association analyses assesses that similarity of the values that comprise one item.

17.12 The two primary approaches to prescriptive analytics are optimization and simulation. Optimization involves the setting of constraints to assist in the development of a decision modeel that represents the optimal way of managing a business process. Simulation involves the repeating of a predictive analytics model by varying the assumptions or the data associated with the model. Decision criteria are used to select a particular version of the model, which may or may not be optimal. Simulation can be used when a business process is not well understood.

CHAPTER 19 (ONLINE)

19.2 (a) Proportion of nonconformances largest on Day 4, smallest on Day 3.

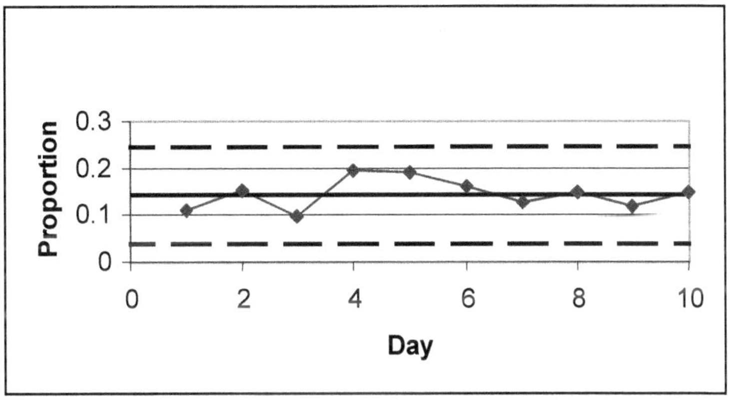

(b) $\bar{n} = 1036/10 = 103.6,\ \bar{p} = 148/1036 = 0.142857,$

$$LCL = \bar{p} - 3\sqrt{\frac{\bar{p}(1-\bar{p})}{\bar{n}}} = 0.142857 - 3\sqrt{\frac{0.142857(1-0.142857)}{103.6}} = 0.039719$$

$$UCL = \bar{p} + 3\sqrt{\frac{\bar{p}(1-\bar{p})}{\bar{n}}} = 0.142857 + 3\sqrt{\frac{0.142857(1-0.142857)}{103.6}} = 0.245995$$

(c) Proportions are within control limits, so there do not appear to be any special causes of variation.

19.4 (a) $n = 500,\ \bar{p} = 761/16000 = 0.0476$

$$LCL = \bar{p} - 3\sqrt{\frac{\bar{p}(1-\bar{p})}{n}} = 0.0476 - 3\sqrt{\frac{0.0476(1-0.0476)}{500}} = 0.0190 > 0$$

$$UCL = \bar{p} + 3\sqrt{\frac{\bar{p}(1-\bar{p})}{n}} = 0.0476 + 3\sqrt{\frac{0.0476(1-0.0476)}{500}} = 0.0761$$

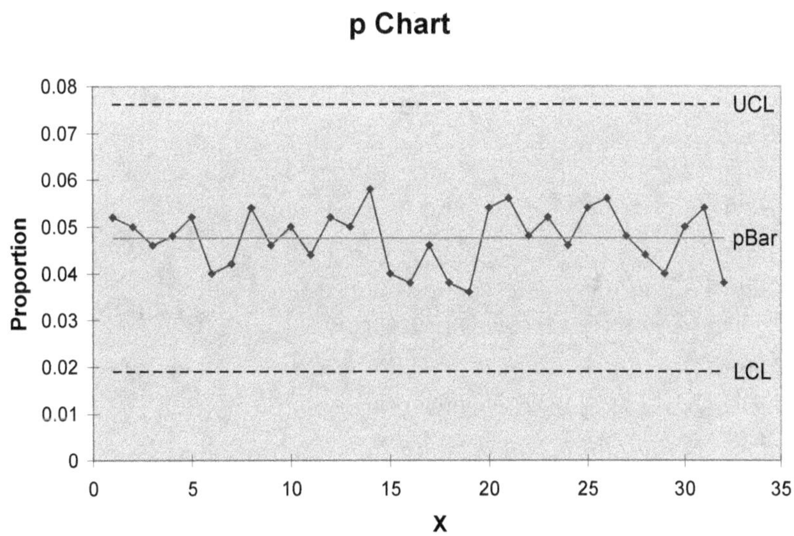

(b) Since the individual points are distributed around $\bar{p}$ without any pattern and all the points are within the control limits, the process is in a state of statistical control.

19.6 (a) $\bar{n} = 113345/22 = 5152.0455$, $\bar{p} = 1460/113345 = 0.01288$,

$$LCL = \bar{p} - 3\sqrt{\frac{\bar{p}(1-\bar{p})}{\bar{n}}} = 0.01288 - 3\sqrt{\frac{0.01288(1-0.01288)}{5152.0455}} = 0.00817$$

$$UCL = \bar{p} + 3\sqrt{\frac{\bar{p}(1-\bar{p})}{\bar{n}}} = 0.01288 + 3\sqrt{\frac{0.01288(1-0.01288)}{5152.0455}} = 0.01759$$

PHStat output:

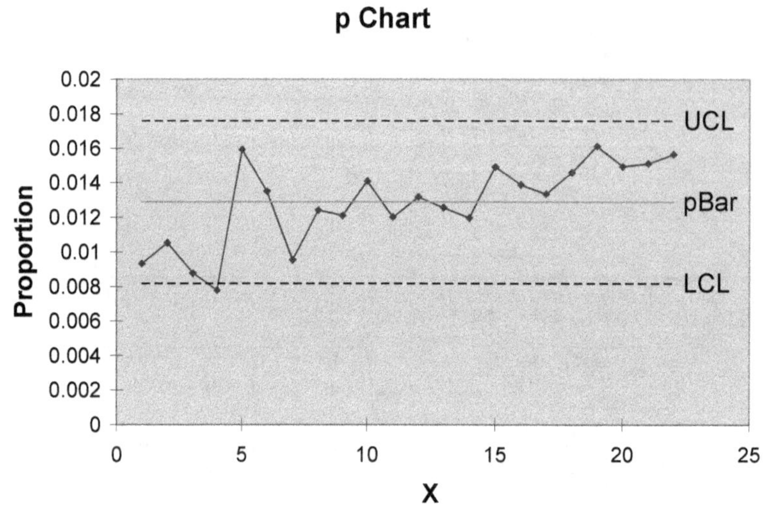

The proportion of unacceptable cans is below the LCL on Day 4. There is evidence of a pattern over time, since the last eight points are all above the mean and most of the earlier points are below the mean. Thus, the special causes that might be contributing to this pattern should be investigated before any change in the system of operation is contemplated.

(b) Once special causes have been eliminated and the process is stable, Deming's fourteen points should be implemented to improve the system. They might also look at day 4 to see if they could identify and exploit the special cause that led to such a low proportion of defects on that day.

19.8 (a)

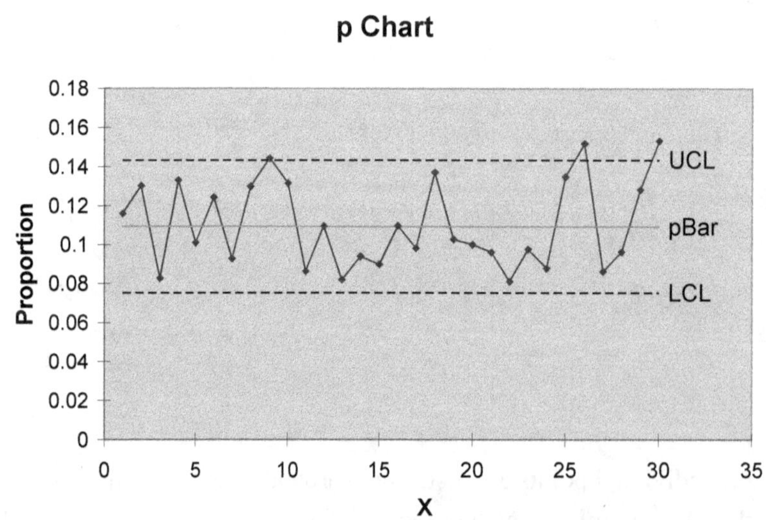

$\bar{p} = 0.1091$, $LCL = 0.0751$, $UCL = 0.1431$. Points 9, 26, and 30 are above the UCL.

19.8 cont. (b) First, the reasons for the special cause variation would need to be determined and local corrective action taken. Once special causes have been eliminated and the process is stable, Deming's fourteen points should be implemented to improve the system.

19.12 (a) $\bar{c} = 115/10 = 11.5$, $LCL = \bar{c} - 3\sqrt{\bar{c}} = 11.5 - 3\sqrt{11.5} = 1.32651$

$UCL = \bar{c} + 3\sqrt{\bar{c}} = 11.5 + 3\sqrt{11.5} = 21.67349$

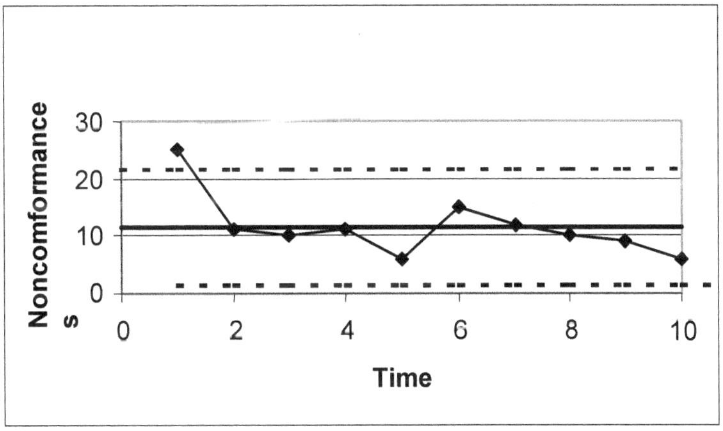

(b) Yes, the number of nonconformances per unit for Time Period 1 is above the upper control limit.

19.14 (a) The twelve errors committed by Gina appear to be much higher than all others, and Gina would need to explain her performance.

(b)

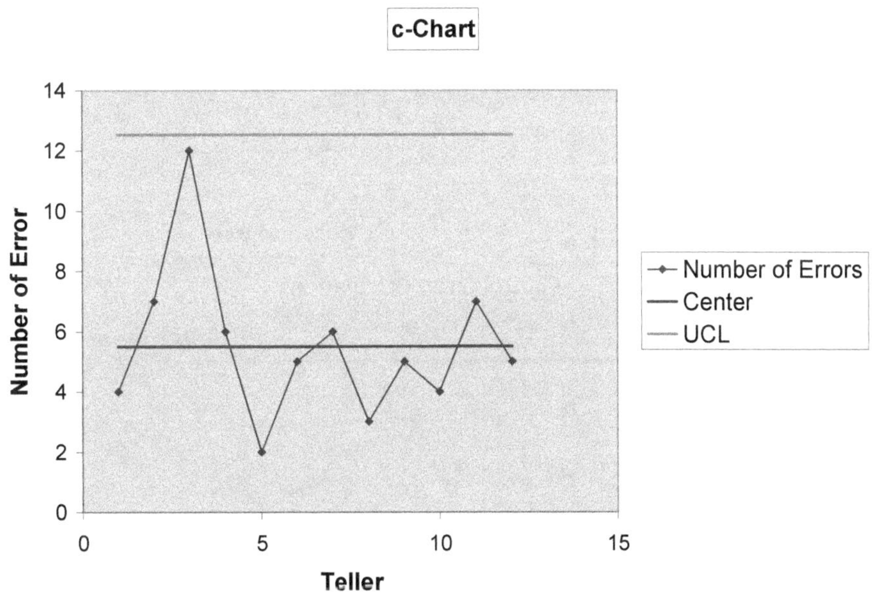

$\bar{c} = 5.5$, $UCL = 12.56$, LCL does not exist. The number of errors is in a state of statistical control since none of the tellers are outside the UCL.

(c) Since Gina is within the control limits, she is operating within the system, and should not be singled out for further scrutiny.

(d) The process needs to be studied and potentially changed using principles of Six Sigma® management and/or Deming's 14 points for management.

19.16 (a) $\bar{c} = 3.057$

(b)

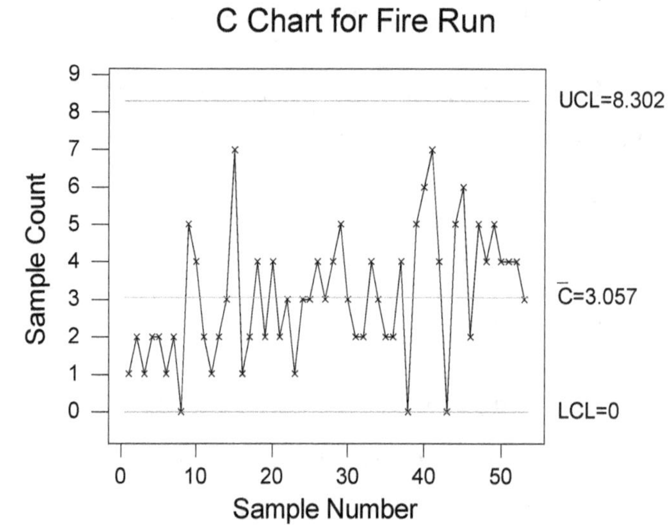

(c) There is evidence of a pattern over time, since the first eight points are all below the mean. Thus, the special causes that might be contributing to this pattern should be investigated before any change in the system of operation is contemplated.

(d) Even though weeks 15 and 41 experienced seven fire runs each, they are both below the upper control limit. They can, therefore, be explained by chance causes.

(e) After having identified the special causes that might have contributed to the first eight points that are below the average, the fire department can use the *c*-chart to monitor the process in future weeks in real-time and identify any potential special causes of variation that might have arisen and could be attributed to increased arson, severe drought, or holiday-related activities.

19.18 (a) $d_2 = 2.059$ (d) $D_4 = 2.282$

(b) $d_3 = 0.88$ (e) $A_2 = 0.729$

(c) $D_3 = 0$

19.20 (a) $\overline{R} = 0.247$, R chart: $UCL = 0.636$; LCL does not exist

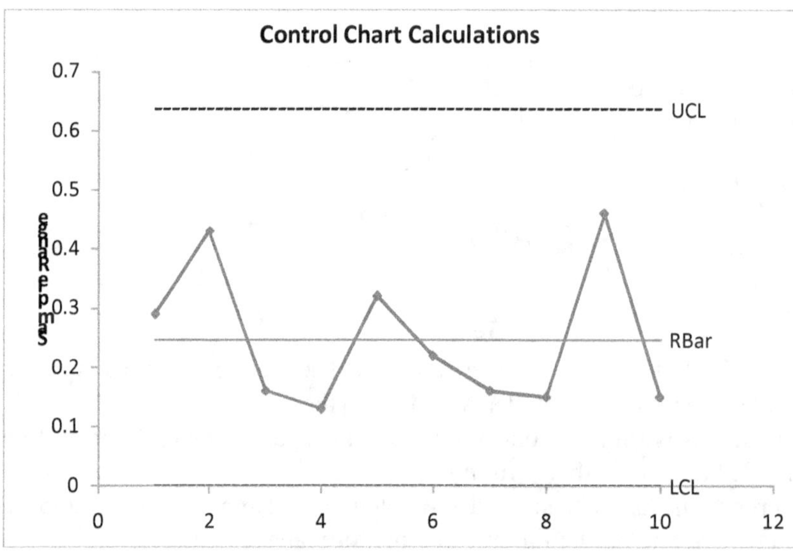

19.20 cont. (b) According to the *R*-charts, the process appears to be in control with all points lying inside the control limits without any pattern and no evidence of special cause variation.

(c) $\overline{\overline{X}} = 47.998$, $\overline{X}$ chart: $UCL = 48.2507$; $LCL = 47.7453$

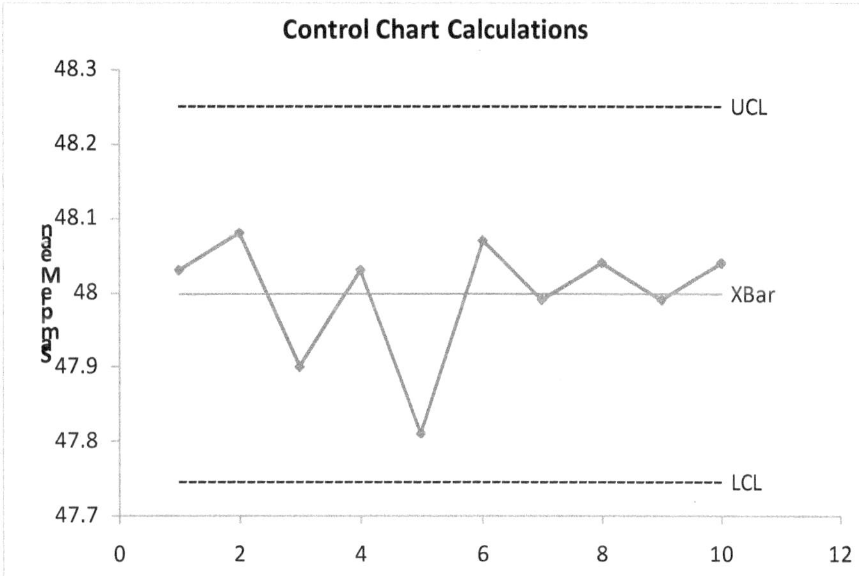

(d) According to the $\overline{X}$-chart, the process appears to be in control with all points lying inside the control limits without any pattern and no evidence of special cause variation.

19.22 (a) $\overline{R} = \frac{\sum_{i=1}^{k} R_i}{k} = 3.275$, $\overline{\overline{X}} = \frac{\sum_{i=1}^{k} \overline{X}_i}{k} = 5.9413$.

R chart:

$$UCL = D_4\overline{R} = 2.282(3.275) = 7.4736$$

LCL does not exist.

$\overline{X}$ chart:

$$UCL = \overline{\overline{X}} + A_2\overline{R} = 5.9413 + 0.729(3.275) = 8.3287$$

$$LCL = \overline{\overline{X}} - A_2\overline{R} = 5.9413 - 0.729(3.275) = 3.5538$$

19.22 cont. (a) **PHStat R Chart output:**

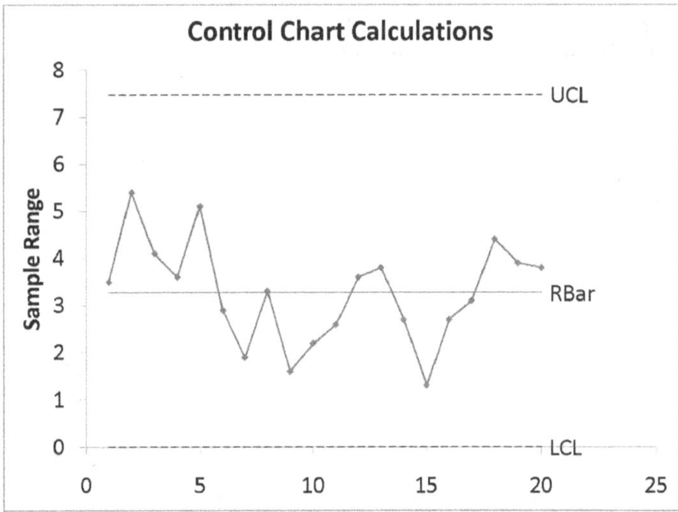

PHStat $\bar{X}$ Chart output:

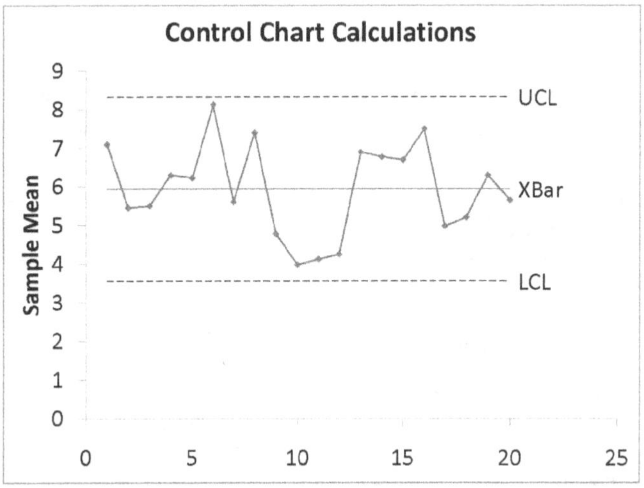

(b) The process appears to be in control since there are no points outside the control limits and there is no evidence of a pattern in the range chart, and there are no points outside the control limits and there is no evidence of a pattern in the $\bar{X}$ chart.

19.24 (a) $\overline{R} = 0.8794$, R chart: $UCL = 2.0068$; LCL does not exist

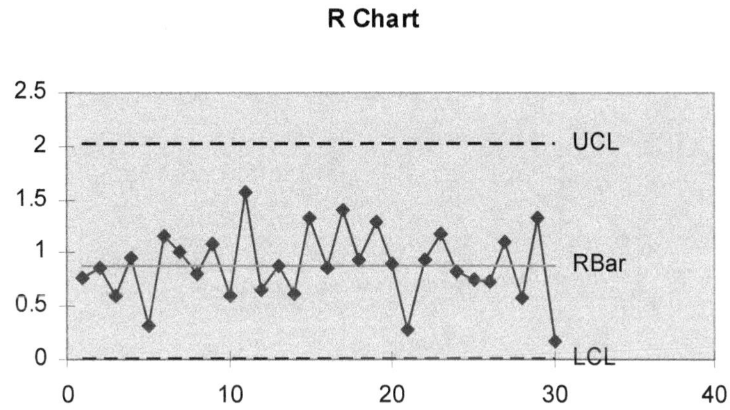

$\overline{\overline{X}} = 20.1065$, $\overline{X}$ chart: $UCL = 20.7476$; $LCL = 18.4654$

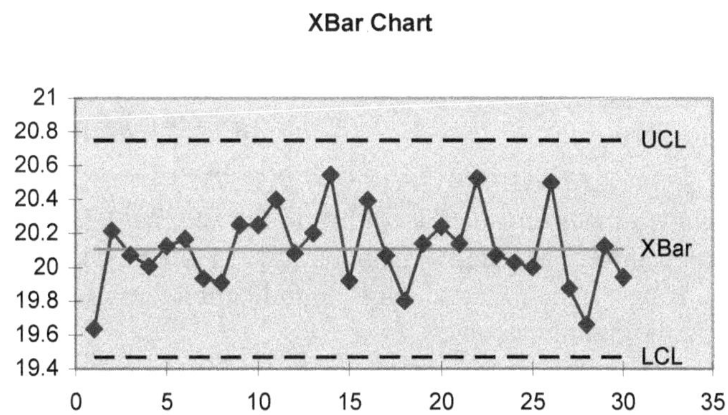

(c) The process appears to be in control since there are no points outside the lower and upper control limits of either the R-chart and Xbar-chart, and there is no pattern in the results over time.

19.26 (a)

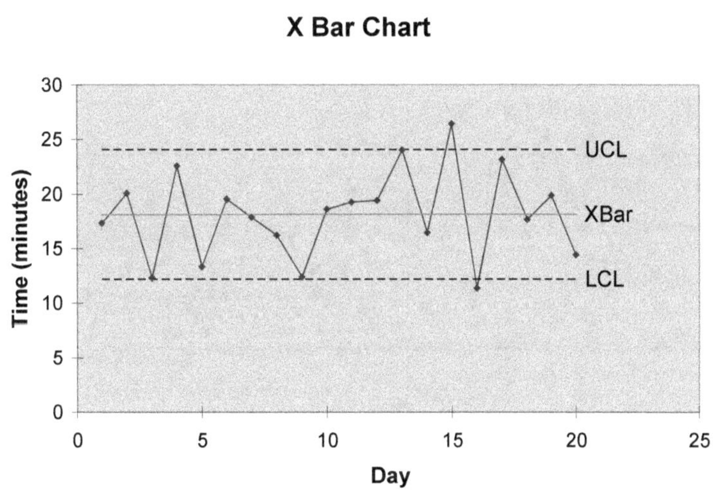

19.26 (a)
cont.

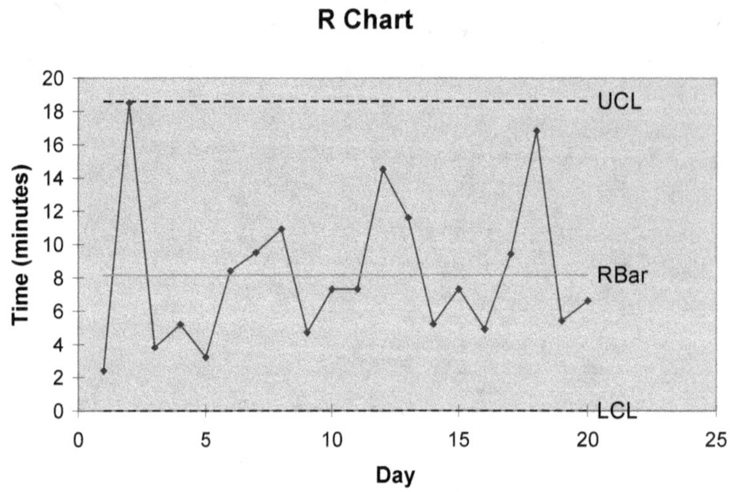

$\overline{R} = 8.145$, $\overline{\overline{X}} = 18.12$.

R chart: $LCL = D_3\,\overline{R} = 0\,(8.145) = 0$. LCL does not exist.

$UCL = D_4\,\overline{R} = (2.282)\,(8.145) = 18.58689$.

For $\overline{X}$ chart: $LCL = \overline{\overline{X}} - A_2\,\overline{R} = 18.12 - (0.729)\,(8.145) = 12.1823$

$UCL = \overline{\overline{X}} + A_2\,\overline{R} = 18.12 + (0.729)\,(8.145) = 24.0577$

(b) There are no sample ranges outside the control limits and there does not appear to be a pattern in the range chart. The sample mean on Day 15 is above the *UCL* and the sample mean on Day 16 is below the *LCL*, which is an indication there is evidence of special cause variation in the sample means.

19.28 (a) $\overline{R} = 0.3022$, R chart: $UCL = 0.6389$; LCL does not exist

$\overline{\overline{X}} = 90.1317$, $\overline{X}$ chart: $UCL = 90.3060$; $LCL = 89.9573$

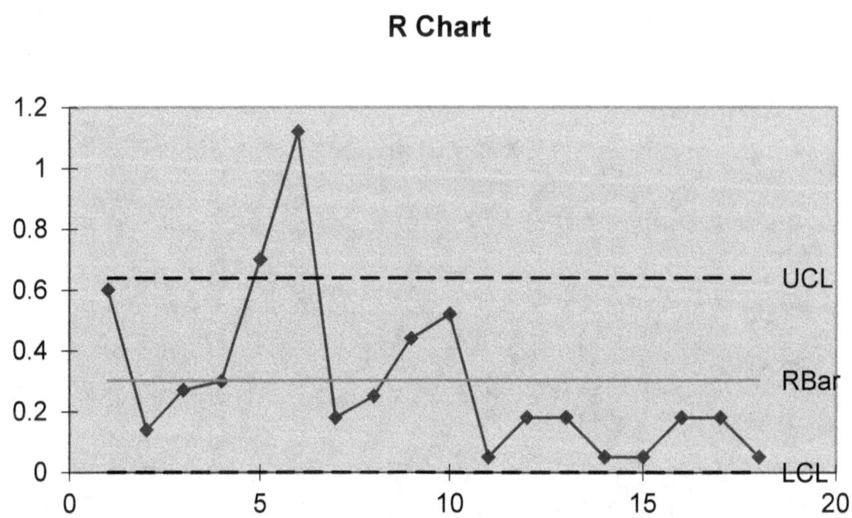

19.28 (a)
cont.

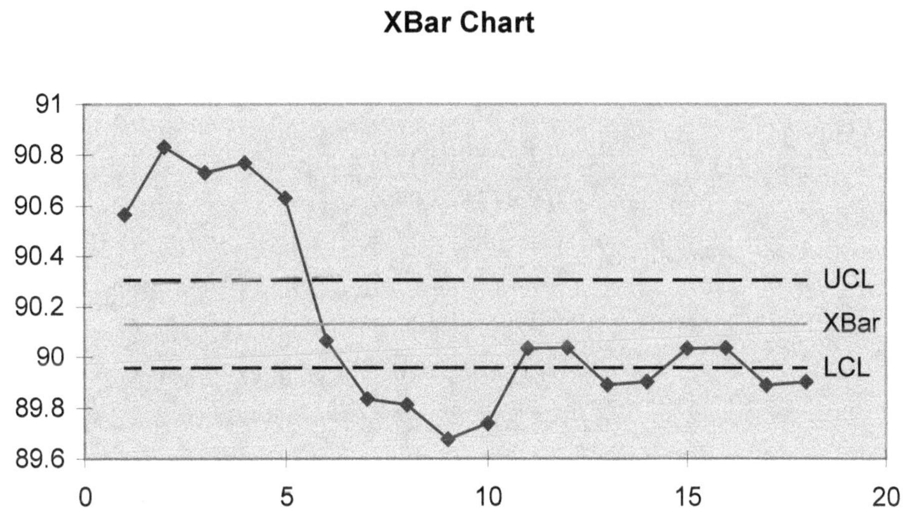

(b) The *R*-chart is out-of-control because the 5th and 6th data points fall above the upper control limit. There is also a downward trend in the right tail of the *R*-chart, which signifies that special causes of variation must be identified and corrected. Even though the *X*-bar chart also appears to be out-of-control because a majority of the data point fall above or below the control limit, any interpretation will be misleading because the *R*-chart has indicated the presence of out-of-control conditions. There is also a downward trend in both control charts. Special causes of variation should be investigated and eliminated.

19.30 (a) Estimate of the population mean = $\overline{\overline{X}} = 100$

Estimate of population standard deviation = $\overline{R}/d_2 = \dfrac{3.386}{1.693} = 2$

$$P(98 < X < 102) = P\left(\frac{98-100}{2} < Z < \frac{102-100}{2}\right) = 0.6827$$

(b) $$P(93 < X < 107.5) = P\left(\frac{93-100}{2} < Z < \frac{107.5-100}{2}\right) = .9997$$

(c) $$P(X > 93.8) = P\left(Z > \frac{93.8-100}{2}\right) = .9990$$

(d) $$P(X < 110) = P\left(Z < \frac{110-100}{2}\right) \cong 1$$

19.32 (a) $$P(18 < X < 22) = P\left(\frac{18-20.1065}{0.8794/2.059} < Z < \frac{22-20.1065}{0.8794/2.059}\right)$$

$$= P(-4.932 < Z < 4.4335) = 0.9999$$

19.32 (b) $C_p = \frac{(USL - LSL)}{6(\bar{R}/d_2)} = \frac{(22-18)}{6(0.8794/2.059)} = 1.56$

cont. $CPL = \frac{(\bar{\bar{X}} - LSL)}{3(\bar{R}/d_2)} = \frac{(20.1065-18)}{3(0.8794/2.059)} = 1.644$

$CPU = \frac{(USL - \bar{\bar{X}})}{3(\bar{R}/d_2)} = \frac{(22-20.1065)}{3(0.8794/2.059)} = 1.4778$

$C_{pk} = \min(CPL, CPU) = 1.4778$

19.34 (a) $P(5.2 < X < 5.8) = P\left(\frac{5.2-5.509}{0.2248/2.059} < Z < \frac{5.8-5.509}{0.2248/2.059}\right)$

$= P(-2.830 < Z < 2.665) = 0.9938$

(b) According to the estimate in (a), only 99.38% of the tea bags will have weight fall between 5.2 grams and 5.8 grams. The process is, therefore, incapable of meeting the 99.7% goal.

19.36 Chance or common causes of variation represent the inherent variability that exists in a system. These consist of the numerous small causes of variability that operate randomly or by chance. Special or assignable causes of variation represent large fluctuations or patterns in the data that are not inherent to a process. These fluctuations are often caused by changes in a system that represent either problems to be fixed or opportunities to exploit.

19.38 When only common causes of variation are present, it is up to management to change the system.

19.40 Attribute control charts are used for categorical or discrete data such as the number of nonconformances. Variables control charts are used for numerical variables and are based on statistics such as the mean and standard deviation.

19.42 From the red bead experiment you learned that variation is an inherent part of any process, that workers work within a system over which they have little control, that it is the system that primarily determines their performance, and that only management can change the system.

19.44 If a process has a $C_p = 1.5$ and a $C_{pk} = 0.8$, it indicates that the process has the potential of meeting production specification limits but fails to meet the specification limits in actual performance. The process should be investigated and adjusted to increase either the *CPU* or *CPL* or both.

19.46 (a) One the main reason that service quality is lower than product quality is because the former involves human interaction which is prone to variation. Also, the most critical aspects of a service are often timeliness and professionalism, and customers can always perceive that the service could be done quicker and with greater professionalism. For products, customers often cannot perceive a better or more ideal product than the one they are getting. For example, a new laptop is better and contains more interesting features than any laptop that he or she has ever imagined.

19.46 cont. (b) Both services and products are the results of processes. However, measuring services is often harder because of the dynamic variation due to the human interaction between the service provider and the customer. Product quality is often a straightforward measurement of a static physical characteristic like the amount of sugar in a can of soda. Categorical data are also more common in service quality.

(c) Yes.

(d) Yes.

19.48 (a) $\overline{R} = 0.1284$, R chart: $UCL = 0.33063$; LCL does not exist

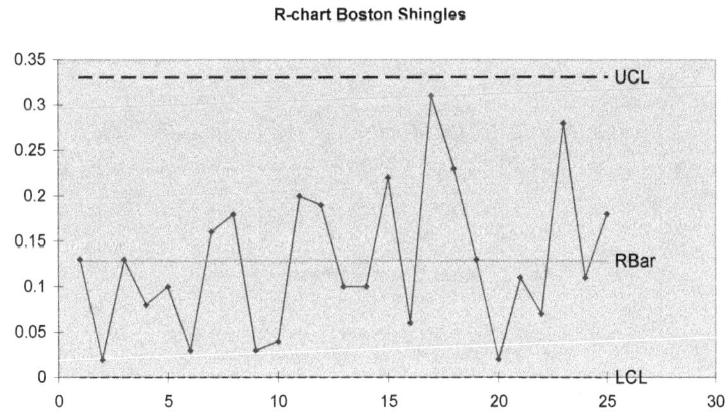

(b) $\overline{\overline{X}} = 1.2133$, $\overline{X}$ chart: $UCL = 1.3447$; $LCL = 1.0820$

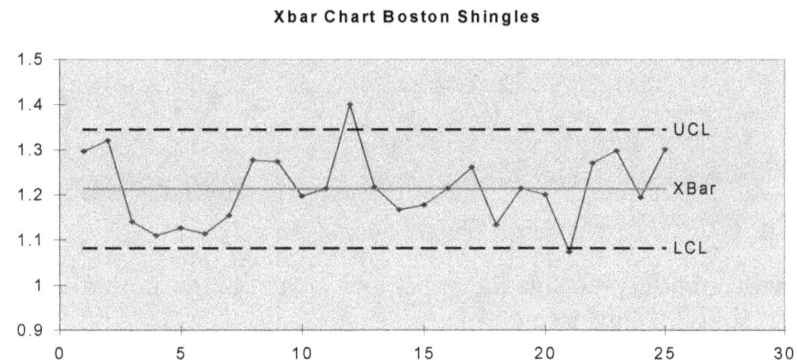

(c) There is one point above the UCL and one point below the LCL in the control chart for the mean sealant strength. So the process is out-of-control and the process should be investigated for special causes.

19.48 cont. (d) (a)

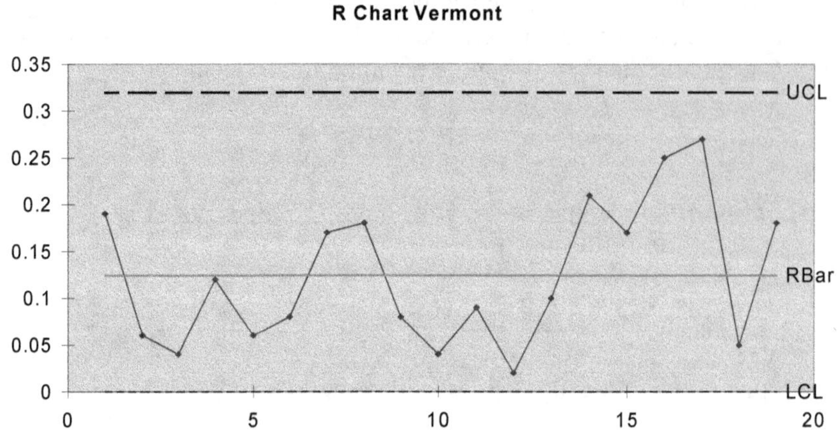

(b)

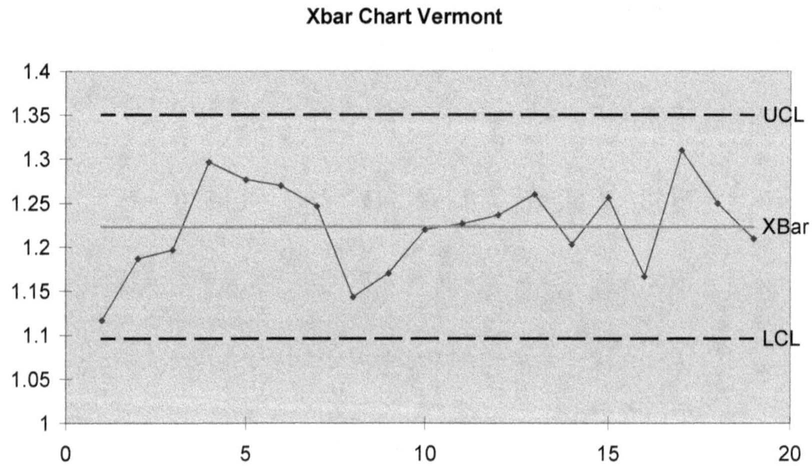

(c) Since no point falls outside the upper and lower control limit of either chart, the process appears to be in-control.

19.50 (a)

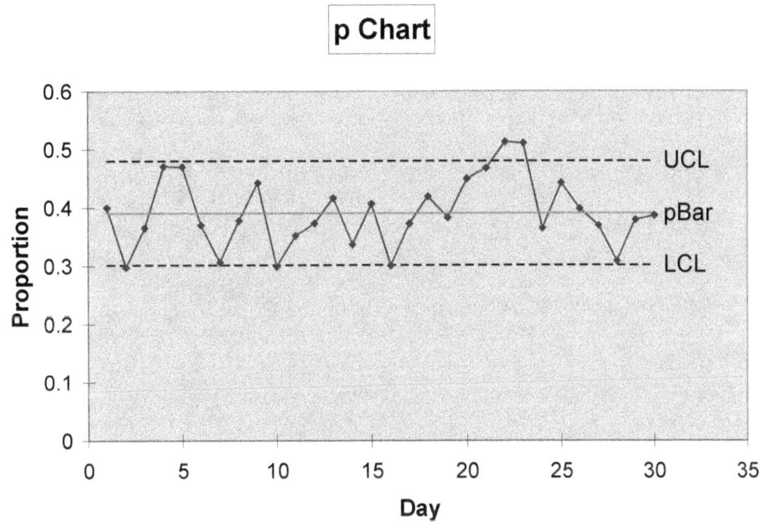

$\overline{p} = 0.391$, $LCL = 0.301$, $UCL = 0.480$.

(b) The process is out of statistical control. The proportion of investigations that are closed is below the *LCL* on Days 2 and 16 and are above the *UCL* on Days 22 and 23.

(c) Special causes of variation should be investigated and eliminated. Next, process knowledge should be improved to increase the proportion of investigations closed the same day. When the proportions are above the *UCL*, this is in the direction the process needs to go. Therefore, when investigating special causes for days 22 and 23, consideration of exploiting these special causes should be given.

19.52 Processing time:
Control chart for the range:

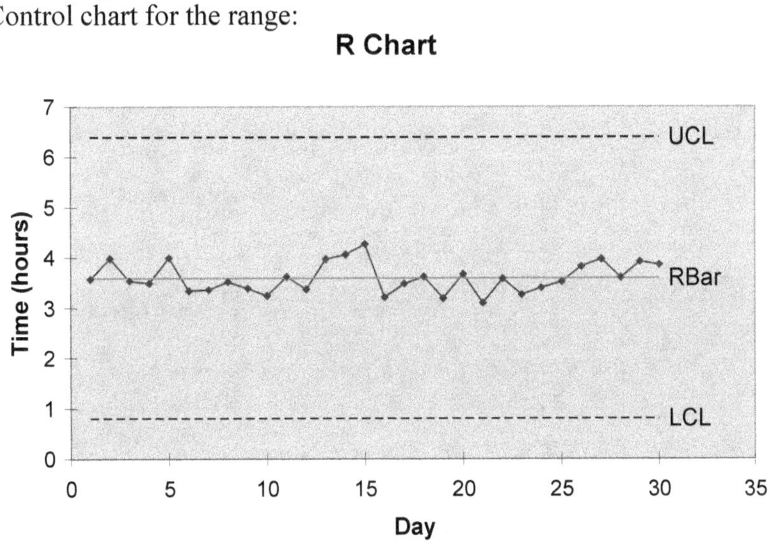

19.52 cont. $\overline{R} = 3.597$, $LCL = .802$, $UCL = 6.392$

Control chart for the mean:

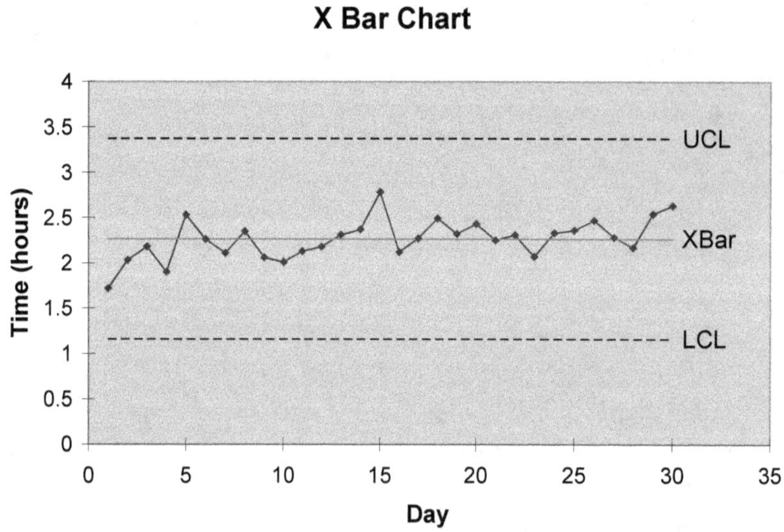

$\overline{\overline{X}} = 2.2653$, $LCL = 1.1575$, $UCL = 3.3732$

Processing time can be considered to be in control in terms of the mean and the range since there is no strong pattern in either chart and there are no points that are outside the control limits.

Proportion of rework in the laboratory:

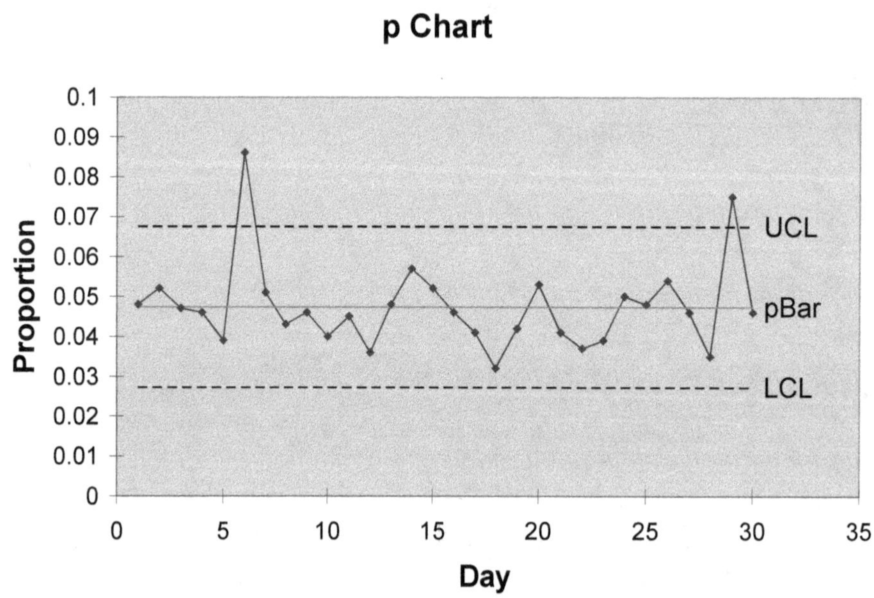

$\overline{p} = 0.04737$, $LCL = 0.02721$, $UCL = .06752$

Days 6 and 29 are above the *UCL*. Thus, the special causes that might be contributing to these values should be investigated before any change in the system of operation is contemplated. Then Deming's fourteen points can be applied to improve the system.

19.52 cont. Number of daily admissions:

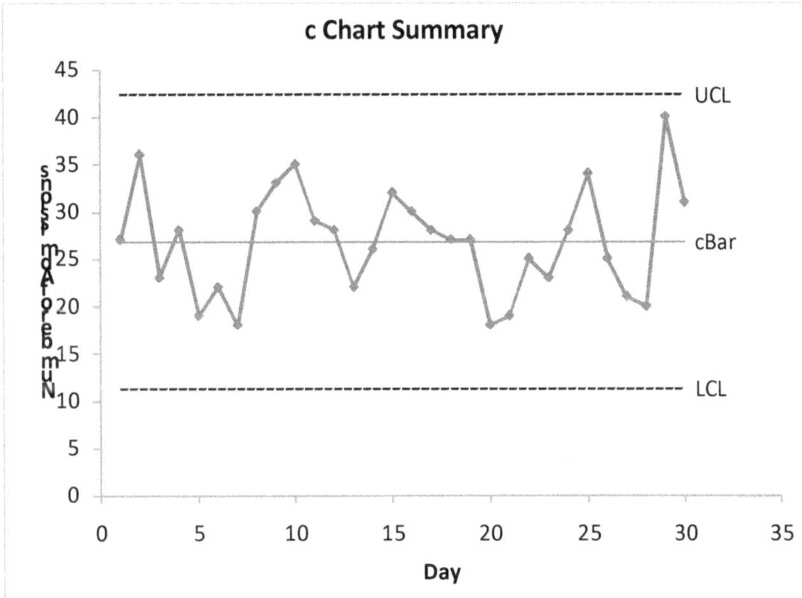

$\bar{c} = 26.8$, $LCL = 11.2694$, $UCL = 42.3306$

The number of daily admissions can be considered to be in control since there is no strong pattern in the chart and there are no points that are outside the control limits.

19.54 Shift 1 - Kidney

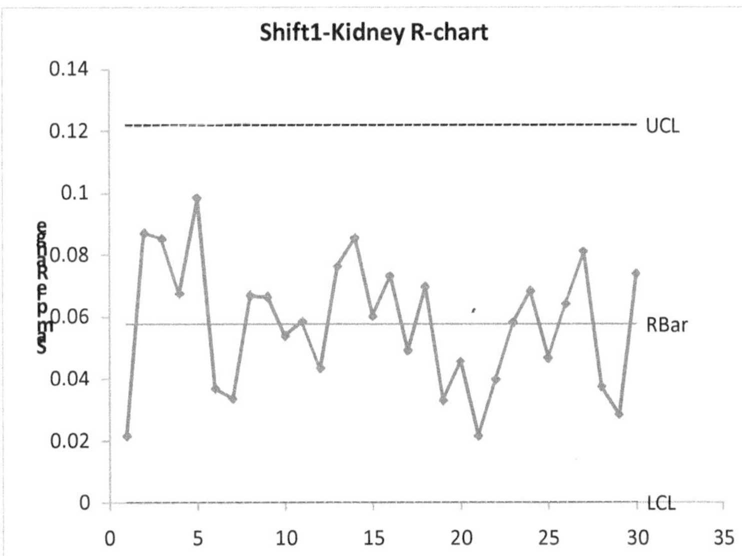

The *R*-chart shows a process in a state of statistical control, with the individual points distributed around the average range of weight without any pattern and all the points are within the control limits. Thus, any improvement in the process must come from the reduction of common cause variation. Such reductions require changes in the process. These changes are the responsibility of management since improvements in quality cannot occur until changes to the process itself are successfully implemented.

19.54
cont.

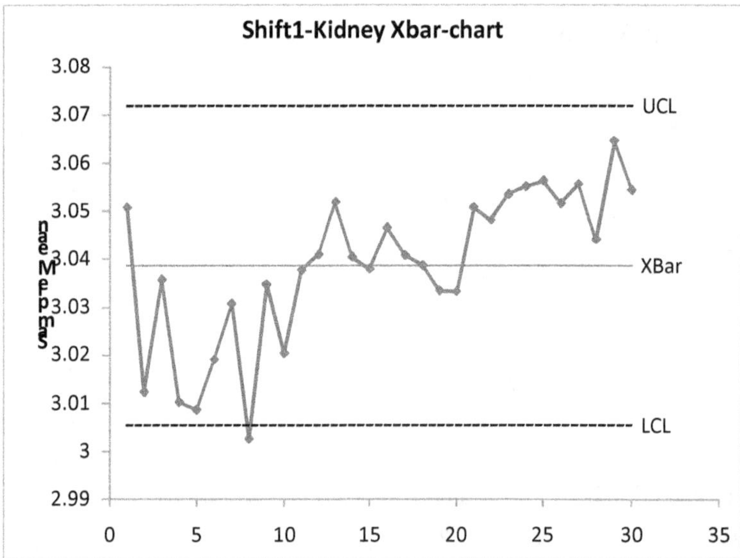

From the *X*bar-chart, you can see that the eighth interval is below the LCL. Management needs to determine the root cause for this special cause variation and take corrective action. Also, during the first half of the sequence almost all the 15-minute intervals had less than the mean subgroup average weight, and all the 15-minute intervals in the second half had more than the mean subgroup average weight. This is a degradation in the production capability which is due to some special cause of variation. So the special cause that produced this pattern needs to be determined. When identified, action will be needed to correct this special cause.

Shift 2 – Kidney

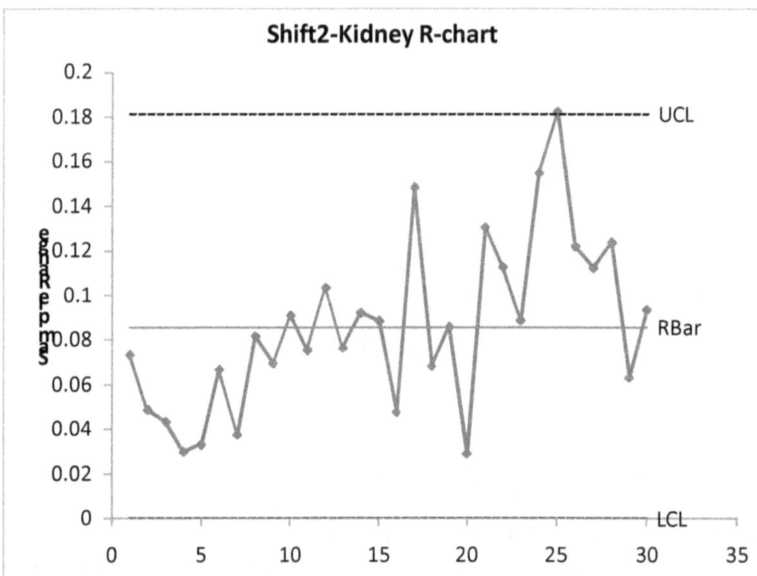

19.54 cont. The *R*-chart reveals that the 25th interval is above the UCL. Also, during the first half of the sequence almost all the 15-minute intervals had less than the mean subgroup weight range, and all the 15-minute intervals in the second half had more than the mean subgroup weight range. This is a degradation in the production capability which is due to some special cause of variation. So the special cause that produced this pattern needs to be determined. Management needs to determine the root cause for this special cause variation and take corrective action.

Since the *R*-chart indicates an out-of-control process, the interpretation of the chart for the mean will be misleading.

Shift 1 Shrimp

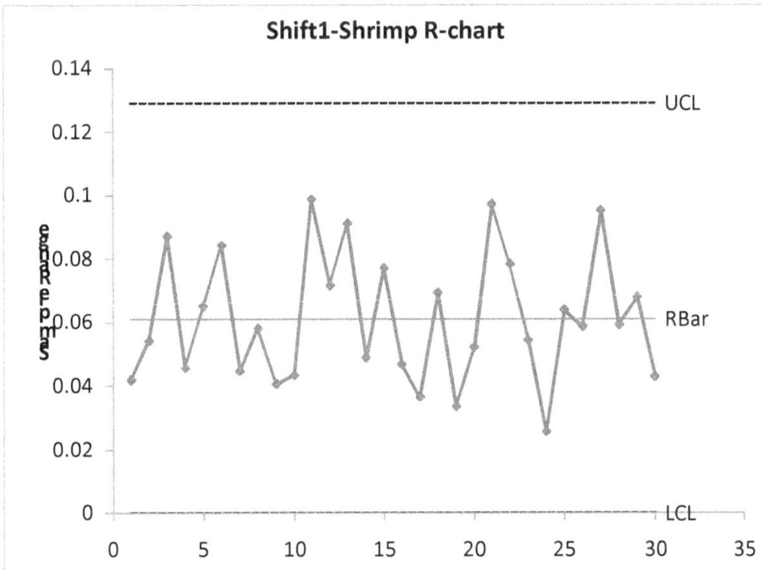

The *R*-chart shows a process in a state of statistical control, with the individual points distributed around the average range of weight without any pattern and all the points are within the control limits. Thus, any improvement in the process must come from the reduction of common cause variation. Such reductions require changes in the process. These changes are the responsibility of management since improvements in quality cannot occur until changes to the process itself are successfully implemented.

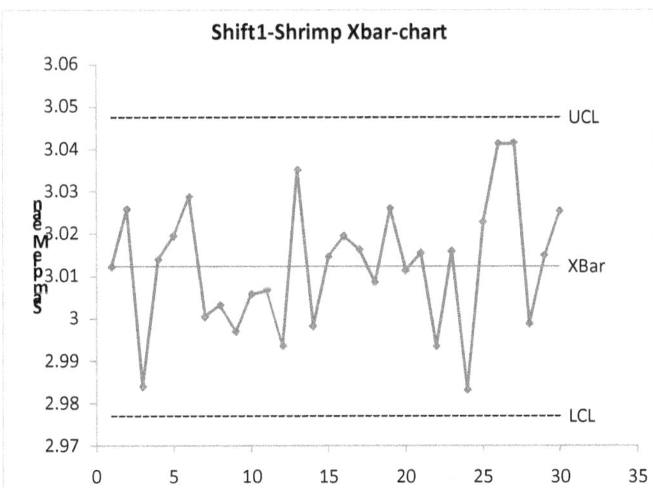

19.54 cont. The *X*bar-chart shows a process in a state of statistical control, with the individual points distributed around the average of the subgroup means without any pattern and all the points are within the control limits. Thus, any improvement in the process must come from the reduction of common cause variation. Such reductions require changes in the process. These changes are the responsibility of management since improvements in quality cannot occur until changes to the process itself are successfully implemented.

Shift 2 – Shrimp

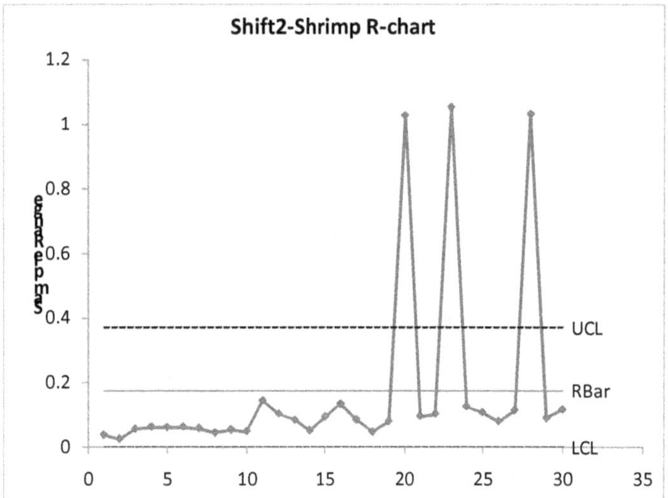

The *R*-chart reveals that the 20th, 23rd and 28th intervals are above the UCL. Also, there is an upward trend in the range. This is a degradation in the production capability which is due to some special cause of variation. So the special cause that produced this pattern needs to be determined. Management needs to determine the root cause for this special cause variation and take corrective action.
Since the *R*-chart indicates an out-of-control process, the interpretation of the chart for the mean will be misleading.

Chapter 20 (ONLINE)

20.2 (a)

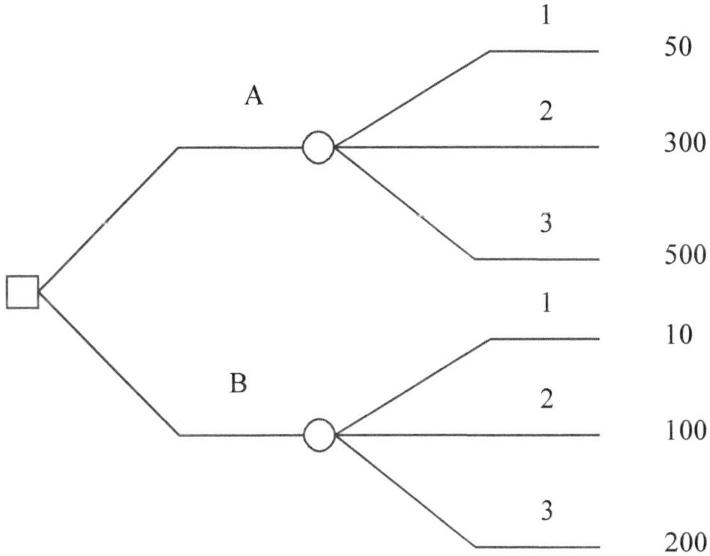

(b) Opportunity loss table:

Event	Optimum Action	Profit of Optimum Action	Alternative Courses of Action A	Alternative Courses of Action B
1	*A*	50	50 – 50 = 0	50 – 10 = 40
2	*A*	300	300 – 300 = 0	300 – 100 = 200
3	*A*	500	500 – 500 = 0	500 – 200 = 300

20.4 (a)-(b) Payoff table:

Event	Action: Company A		Action: Company B	
1	$10,000 + $2 · 1,000 =	$12,000	$2,000 + $4 · 1,000 =	$6,000
2	$10,000 + $2 · 2,000 =	$14,000	$2,000 + $4 · 2,000 =	$10,000
3	$10,000 + $2 · 5,000 =	$20,000	$2,000 + $4 · 5,000 =	$22,000
4	$10,000 + $2 · 10,000 =	$30,000	$2,000 + $4 · 10,000 =	$42,000
5	$10,000 + $2 · 50,000 =	$110,000	$2,000 + $4 · 50,000 =	$202,000

(c)

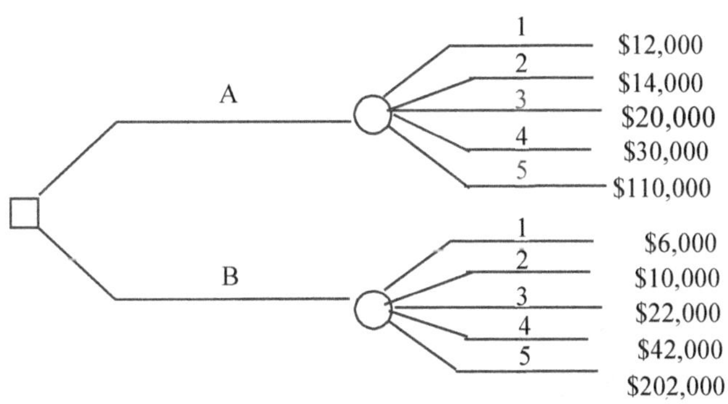

20.4 cont. (d) Opportunity loss table:

Event	Optimum Action	Profit of Optimum Action	Alternative Courses of Action *A*	*B*
1	*A*	12,000	0	6,000
2	*A*	14,000	0	4,000
3	*B*	22,000	2,000	0
4	*B*	42,000	12,000	0
5	*B*	202,000	92,000	0

20.6 Excel output:

Probabilities & Payoffs Table:				
	P	**A**	**B**	
E1	**0.5**	**50**	**100**	
E2	**0.5**	**200**	**125**	
Max		200	125	
Min		50	100	
Maximax		(a) 200		
maximin			(b) 100	
Statistics for:		**A**	**B**	
Expected Monetary Value		**(c) 125**	**(c) 112.5**	
Variance		**5625**	**156.25**	
Standard Deviation		**75**	**12.5**	
Coefficient of Variation		**0.6**	**0.111111**	
Return to Risk Ratio		**1.666667**	**9**	
Opportunity Loss Table:				
	Optimum	Optimum	Alternatives	
	Action	Profit	A	B
E1	B	100	50	0
E2	A	200	0	75
			A	**B**
Expected Opportunity Loss			**(d) 25**	**(d) 37.5**
			EVPI	

(a) The optimal action based on the maximax criterion is *Action A*.

(b) The optimal action based on the maximin criterion is *Action B*.

(c) $EMV_A = 50(0.5) + 200(0.5) = 125$ $\quad EMV_B = 100(0.5) + 125(0.5) = 112.50$

(d) $EOL_A = 50(0.5) + 0(0.5) = 25$ $\quad EOL_B = 0(0.5) + 75(0.5) = 37.50$

(e) Perfect information would correctly forecast which event, 1 or 2, will occur. The value of perfect information is the increase in the expected value if you knew which of the events 1 or 2 would occur prior to making a decision between actions. It allows us to select the optimum action given a correct forecast.

EMV with perfect information $= 100\ (0.5) + 200\ (0.5) = 150$
$EVPI = EMV$ with perfect information $- EMV_A = 150 - 125 = 25$

20.6 cont.

(f) Based on (c) and (d) above, select action *A* because it has a higher expected monetary value (a) and a lower opportunity loss (b) than action *B*.

(g) $\sigma_A{}^2 = (50 - 125)^2\,(0.5) + (200 - 125)^2\,(0.5) = 5625 \qquad \sigma_A = 75$

$$CV_A = \frac{75}{125} \cdot 100\% = 60\%$$

$\sigma_B{}^2 = (100 - 112.5)^2\,(0.5) + (125 - 112.5)^2\,(0.5) = 156.25 \qquad \sigma_B = 12.5$

$$CV_B = \frac{12.5}{112.5} \cdot 100\% = 11.11\%$$

(h) Return-to-risk ratio for $A = \dfrac{125}{75} - 1.667$

Return-to-risk ratio for $B = \dfrac{112.5}{12.5} = 9.0$

(i) Based on (g) and (h), select action *B* because it has a lower coefficient of variation and a higher return-to-risk ratio.

(j) The best decision depends on the decision criteria. In this case, expected monetary value leads to a different decision than the return-to-risk ratio.

20.8 (a) Rate of return $= \dfrac{\$100}{\$1,000} \cdot 100\% = 10\%$

(b) $CV = \dfrac{\$25}{\$100} \cdot 100\% = 25\%$

(c) Return-to-risk ratio $= \dfrac{\$100}{\$25} = 4.0$

20.10 Select stock *A* because it has a higher expected monetary value while it has the same standard deviation as stock *B*.

20.12 PHStat output:

Expected Monetary Value				
Probabilities & Payoffs Table:				
	P	Sell Soft Drinks	Sell Ice Cream	
Cool weather	0.4	50	30	
Warm weather	0.6	60	90	
max		60	90	
min		50	30	
Maximax			90	
Maximin		50		
Statistics for:		Sell Soft Drinks	Sell Ice Cream	
Expected Monetary Value		56	66	
Variance		24	864	
Standard Deviation		4.898979	29.39388	
Coefficient of Variation		0.087482	0.445362	
Return to Risk Ratio		11.43095	2.245366	
Opportunity Loss Table:				
	Optimum Action	Optimum Profit	Alternatives	
			Sell Soft Drinks	Sell Ice Cream
Cool weather	Sell Soft Drinks	50	0	20
Warm weather	Sell Ice Cream	90	30	0
			Sell Soft Drinks	Sell Ice Cream
Expected Opportunity Loss			18	8
				EVPI

(a) The optimal action based on the maximax criterion is to sell ice cream.

(b) The optimal action based on the maximin criterion is to sell soft drinks.

(c) $EMV(\text{Soft drinks}) = 50(0.4) + 60(0.6) = 56$

$EMV(\text{Ice cream}) = 30(0.4) + 90(0.6) = 66$

(d) $EOL(\text{Soft drinks}) = 0(0.4) + 30(0.6) = 18$

$EOL(\text{Ice cream}) = 20(0.4) + 0(0.6) = 8$

(e) *EVPI* is the maximum amount of money the vendor is willing to pay for the information about which event will occur.

(f) Based on (c) and (d), choose to sell ice cream because you will earn a higher expected monetary value and incur a lower opportunity loss than choosing to sell soft drinks.

(g) $CV(\text{Soft drinks}) = \frac{4.899}{56} \cdot 100\% = 8.748\%$

$CV(\text{Ice cream}) = \frac{29.394}{66} \cdot 100\% = 44.536\%$

(h) Return-to-risk ratio for soft drinks $= \frac{56}{4.899} = 11.431$

Return-to-risk ratio for ice cream $= \frac{66}{29.394} = 2.245$

(i) To maximize return and minimize risk, you will choose to sell soft drinks because it has the smaller coefficient of variation and the larger return-to-risk ratio.

20.12 cont. (j) Ignoring the variability of the payoff in (f), you will choose to sell ice cream. However, when risk, which is measured by standard deviation, is taken into consideration as in coefficient of variation or return-to-risk ratio, you will choose to sell soft drinks because it has the lower variability per unit of expected return or the higher expected return per unit of variability.

20.14 PHStat output:

Probabilities & Payoffs Table:				
	P	A	B	C
Economy declines	0.3	500	-2000	-7000
No change	0.5	1000	2000	-1000
Economy expands	0.2	2000	5000	20000
Max		2000	5000	20000
Min		500	-2000	-7000
Maximax				20000
Maximin		500		

Statistics for:	A	B	C
Expected Monetary Value	1050	1400	1400
Variance	272500	6240000	93240000
Standard Deviation	522.0153	2497.999	9656.086
Coefficient of Variation	0.497157	1.784285	6.897204
Return to Risk Ratio	2.011435	0.560449	0.144986

Opportunity Loss Table:					
	Optimum Action	Optimum Profit	Alternatives		
			A	B	C
Economy declines	A	500	0	2500	7500
No change	B	2000	1000	0	3000
Economy expands	C	20000	18000	15000	0
			A	B	C
Expected Opportunity Loss			4100	3750	3750
				EVPI	EVPI

(a) The optimal action based on the maximax criterion is to choose investment *C*.

(b) The optimal action based on the maximin criterion is to choose investment *A*.

(c) $EMV_A = 500(0.3) + 1{,}000(0.5) + 2{,}000(0.2) = 1{,}050$

$EMV_B = -2{,}000(0.3) + 2{,}000(0.5) + 5{,}000(0.2) = 1{,}400$

$EMV_C = -7{,}000(0.3) - 1{,}000(0.5) + 20{,}000(0.2) = 1{,}400$

(d) See the table above.

$EOL_A = 0(0.3) + 1{,}000(0.5) + 18{,}000(0.2) = 4{,}100$

$EOL_B = 2{,}500(0.3) + 0(0.5) + 15{,}000(0.2) = 3{,}750$

$EOL_C = 7{,}500(0.3) + 3{,}000(0.5) + 0(0.2) = 3{,}750$

(e) EMV with perfect information $= 500(0.3) + 2{,}000(0.5) + 20{,}000(0.2) = 5{,}150$

$EVPI = EMV$ with perfect information $- EMV_{B\ or\ C} = 5{,}150 - 1{,}400 = 3{,}750$

The investor should not be willing to pay more than \$3,750 for a perfect forecast.

(f) Action *B* and *C* maximize the expected monetary value and have the lower opportunity loss

(g) $\sigma_A^2 = (500 - 1{,}050)^2 (0.3) + (1{,}000 - 1{,}050)^2 (0.5) + (2{,}000 - 1{,}050)^2 (0.2)$

$= 272{,}500$

$\sigma_A = 522.02$

20.14 cont. (g)

$\sigma_B^{\ 2} = (-2{,}000 - 1{,}400)^2(0.3) + (2{,}000 - 1{,}400)^2(0.5) + (5{,}000 - 1{,}400)^2(0.2)$

$= 6{,}240{,}000$

$\sigma_B = 2{,}498.00$

$\sigma_C^{\ 2} = (-7{,}000 - 1{,}400)^2(0.3) + (-1{,}000 - 1{,}400)^2(0.5) + (20{,}000 - 1{,}400)^2(0.2)$

$= 93{,}240{,}000$

$\sigma_C = 9656.09$

$$CV_A = \frac{522.02}{1050}\cdot 100\% = 49.72\%$$

$$CV_B = \frac{2498.00}{1400}\cdot 100\% = 178.43\%$$

$$CV_C = \frac{9656.09}{1400}\cdot 100\% = 689.72\%$$

(h) Return-to-risk ratio for $A = \dfrac{1050}{522.02} = 2.01$

Return-to-risk ratio for $B = \dfrac{1400}{2498} = 0.56$

Return-to-risk ratio for $C = \dfrac{1400}{9656.09} = 0.14$

(i)-(j) Action *A* minimizes the coefficient of variation and maximizes the investor's return-to-risk.

(k)

	(1) 0.1, 0.6, 0.3	(2) 0.1, 0.3, 0.6	(3) 0.4, 0.4, 0.2	(4) 0.6, 0.3, 0.1
(c) Max *EMV*	*C*: 4,700	*C*: 11,000	*A* or *B*: 800	*A*: 800
σ Max *EMV*	σ_C: 10,169	σ_C: 11,145	σ_A: 548 σ_B: 2,683	σ_A: 458
(d) Min *EOL* & (e) *EVPI*	*C*: 2,550	*C*: 1,650	*A*: 4,000 or *B*: 4,000	*A*: 2,100
(g) Min *CV*	*A*: 40.99%	*A*: 36.64%	*A*: 54.77%	*A*: 57.28%
(h) Max Return-to-risk	*A*: 2.4398	*A*: 2.7294	*A*: 1.8257	*A*: 1.7457
(i) Choice on (g), (h)	Choose *A*	Choose *A*	Choose *A*	Choose *A*
(j) Compare (c) and (i)	Different: (c) *C* (j) *A*	Different: (c) *C* (j) *A*	Different: (c) *A* or *B* (j) *A*	Same: *A*

20.16 PHStat output:

Probabilities & Payoffs Table:				
	P	A	B	
Demand 1000	0.45	12000	6000	
Demand 2000	0.2	14000	10000	
Demand 5000	0.15	20000	22000	
Demand 10000	0.1	30000	42000	
Demand 50000	0.1	110000	202000	
Max		110000	202000	
Min		14000	10000	
Maximax			202000	
Maximin		14000		
Statistics for:		A	B	
Expected Monetary Value		25200	32400	
Variance		8.29E+08	3.32E+09	
Standard Deviation		28791.67	57583.33	
Coefficient of Variation		1.142526	1.777263	
Return to Risk Ratio		0.875253	0.562663	
Opportunity Loss Table:				
	Optimum	Optimum	Alternatives	
	Action	Profit	A	B
Demand 1000	A	12000	0	6000
Demand 2000	A	14000	0	4000
Demand 5000	B	22000	2000	0
Demand 10000	B	42000	12000	0
Demand 50000	B	202000	92000	0
			A	B
Expected Opportunity Loss			10700	3500
				EVPI

(a) The optimal action based on the maximax criterion is to sign with company *B*.

(b) The optimal action based on the maximin criterion is to sign with company *A*.

(c) $EMV_A = 12{,}000(0.45) + 14{,}000(0.2) + 20{,}000(0.15) + 30{,}000(0.1) + 110{,}000(0.1) = 25{,}200$

$EMV_B = 6{,}000(0.45) + 10{,}000(0.2) + 22{,}000(0.15) + 42{,}000(0.1) + 202{,}000(0.1) = 32{,}400$

(d) $EOL_A = 0(0.45) + 0(0.2) + 2{,}000(0.15) + 12{,}000(0.1) + 92{,}000(0.1) = 10{,}700$

$EOL_B = 6{,}000(0.45) + 4{,}000(0.2) + 0(0.15) + 0(0.1) + 0(0.1) = 3{,}500$

(e) EMV with perfect information $= 12{,}000(0.45) + 14{,}000(0.2) + 22{,}000(0.15) + 42{,}000(0.1) + 202{,}000(0.1) = 35{,}900$

$EVPI = EMV$, perfect information $- EMV_B = 35{,}900 - 32{,}400 = 3{,}500$

The author should not be willing to pay more than \$3,500 for a perfect forecast.

(f) Sign with company *B* to maximize the expected monetary value (\$32,400) and minimize the expected opportunity loss (\$3,500).

(g) $CV_A = \frac{28{,}792}{25{,}200} \cdot 100\% = 114.25\%$ $\quad CV_B = \frac{57{,}583}{32{,}400} \cdot 100\% = 177.73\%$

(h) Return-to-risk ratio for $A = \frac{25{,}200}{28{,}792} = 0.8752$

Return-to-risk ratio for $B = \frac{32{,}400}{57{,}583} = 0.5627$

(i) Signing with company *A* will minimize the author's risk and yield the higher return-to-risk.

20.16 cont. (j) Company *B* has a higher *EMV* than *A*, but choosing company *B* also entails more risk and has a lower return-to-risk ratio than *A*.

(k) (c)-(j) See the table below.

Probabilities & Payoffs Table:				
	P	A	B	
Demand 1000	0.3	12000	6000	
Demand 2000	0.2	14000	10000	
Demand 5000	0.2	20000	22000	
Demand 10000	0.1	30000	42000	
Demand 50000	0.2	110000	202000	
Max		110000	202000	
Min		14000	10000	
Maximax			202000	
Maximin		14000		
Statistics for:		A	B	
Expected Monetary Value		35400	52800	
Variance		1.42E+09	5.68E+09	
Standard Deviation		37672.8	75345.6	
Coefficient of Variation		1.064203	1.427	
Return to Risk Ratio		0.93967	0.700771	
Opportunity Loss Table:				
	Optimum	Optimum	Alternatives	
	Action	Profit	A	B
Demand 1000	A	12000	0	6000
Demand 2000	A	14000	0	4000
Demand 5000	B	22000	2000	0
Demand 10000	B	42000	12000	0
Demand 50000	B	202000	92000	0
			A	B
Expected Opportunity Loss			20000	2600
				EVPI

The author's decision is not affected by the changed probabilities.

20.18 (a) $$P(E_1 \mid F) = \frac{P(F \mid E_1)\cdot P(E_1)}{P(F \mid E_1)\cdot P(E_1) + P(F \mid E_2)\cdot P(E_2)} = \frac{0.6(0.5)}{0.6(0.5)+0.4(0.5)} = 0.6$$

$P(E_2 \mid F) = 1 - P(E_1 \mid F) = 1 - 0.6 = 0.4$

(b) $EMV_A = (0.6)(50) + (0.4)(200) = 110$

$EMV_B = (0.6)(100) + (0.4)(125) = 110$

(c) $EOL_A = (0.6)(50) + (0.4)(0) = 30$

$EOL_B = (0.6)(0) + (0.4)(75) = 30$

(d) $EVPI = (0.6)(100) + (0.4)(200) = 30$

You should not be willing to pay more than \$30 for a perfect forecast.

(e) Both have the same *EMV* and the same *EOL*.

(f) $\sigma_A^2 = (0.6)(-60)^2 + (0.4)(90)^2 = 5400 \qquad \sigma_A = 73.4847$

$\sigma_B^2 = (0.6)(-10)^2 + (0.4)(15)^2 = 150 \qquad \sigma_B = 12.2474$

$CV_A = \frac{73.4847}{110}\cdot 100\% = 66.8\% \quad CV_B = \frac{12.2474}{110}\cdot 100\% = 11.1\%$

20.18 (g) Return-to-risk ratio for $A = \frac{110}{73.4847} = 1.497$

cont. Return-to-risk ratio for $B = \frac{110}{12.2474} = 8.981$

(h) Action B has a better return-to-risk ratio.

(i) Both have the same EMV, but action B has a better return-to-risk ratio.

20.20 (a) $P(\text{forecast cool} \mid \text{cool weather}) = 0.80$

$P(\text{forecast warm} \mid \text{warm weather}) = 0.70$

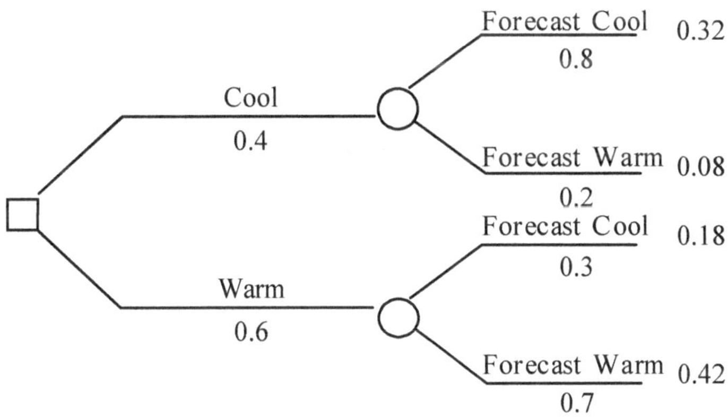

	Forecast Cool	Forecast Warm	Totals
Cool	0.32	0.08	0.4
Warm	0.18	0.42	0.6
Totals	0.5	0.5	

Revised probabilities: $P(\text{cool} \mid \text{forecast cool}) = \frac{0.32}{0.5} = 0.64$

$P(\text{warm} \mid \text{forecast cool}) = \frac{0.18}{0.5} = 0.36$

20.20 (a)
cont.

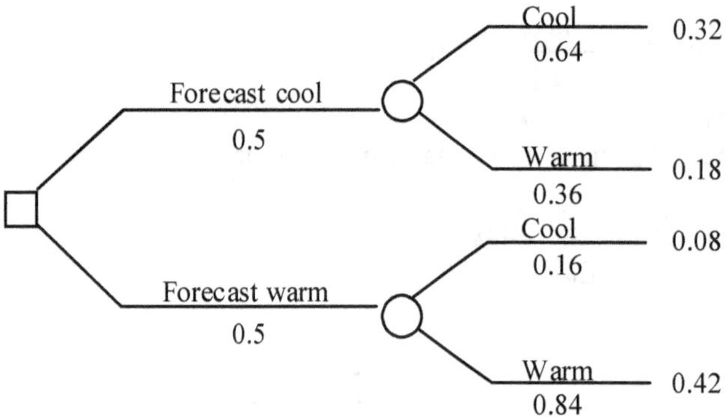

(b) *EMV*(Soft drinks) = 50(0.64) + 60(0.36) = 53.6
EMV(Ice cream) = 30(0.64) + 90(0.36) = 51.6
EOL(Soft drinks) = 0(0.64) + 30(0.36) = 10.8
EOL(Ice cream) = 20(0.64) + 0(0.36) = 12.8
EMV with perfect information = 50(0.64) + 90(0.36) = 64.4
$EVPI = EMV$, perfect information – EMV_A = 64.4 – 53.6 = 10.8
The vendor should not be willing to pay more than $10.80 for a perfect forecast of the weather.
The vendor should sell soft drinks to maximize value and minimize loss.

$$CV(\text{Soft drinks}) = \frac{4.8}{53.6} \cdot 100\% = 8.96\%$$

$$CV(\text{Ice cream}) = \frac{28.8}{51.6} \cdot 100\% = 55.81\%$$

$$\text{Return-to-risk ratio for soft drinks} = \frac{53.6}{4.8} = 11.1667$$

$$\text{Return-to-risk ratio for ice cream} = \frac{51.6}{28.8} = 1.7917$$

Based on these revised probabilities, the vendor's decision changes because of the increased likelihood of cool weather given a forecast for cool. Under these conditions, she should sell soft drinks to maximize the expected monetary value and also to minimize her expected opportunity loss, as well as minimizing risk and maximizing return.

20.22 (a) *P*(favorable | 1,000) = 0.01 *P*(favorable | 2,000) = 0.01
P(favorable | 5,000) = 0.25 *P*(favorable | 10,000) = 0.60
P(favorable | 50,000) = 0.99

P(favorable *and* 1,000) = 0.01(0.45) = 0.0045
P(favorable *and* 2,000) = 0.01(0.20) = 0.0020
P(favorable *and* 5,000) = 0.25(0.15) = 0.0375
P(favorable *and* 10,000)= 0.60(0.10) = 0.0600
P(favorable *and* 50,000)= 0.99(0.10) = 0.0990

20.22 cont. (a) Joint probability table:

	Favorable	Unfavorable	Totals
1,000	0.0045	0.4455	0.45
2,000	0.0020	0.1980	0.20
5,000	0.0375	0.1125	0.15
10,000	0.0600	0.0400	0.10
50,000	0.0990	0.0010	0.10
Totals	0.2030	0.7970	

Given an unfavorable review, the revised conditional probabilities are:

$P(1{,}000 \mid \text{unfavorable}) = 0.4455/0.7970 = 0.5590$

$P(2{,}000 \mid \text{unfavorable}) = 0.1980/0.7970 = 0.2484$

$P(5{,}000 \mid \text{unfavorable}) = 0.1125/0.7970 = 0.1412$

$P(10{,}000 \mid \text{unfavorable}) = 0.0400/0.7970 = 0.0502$

$P(50{,}000 \mid \text{unfavorable}) = 0.0010/0.7970 = 0.0013$

(b) Payoff table, given unfavorable review:

	Pr	*A*	*B*
1,000	0.5590	12,000	6,000
2,000	0.2484	14,000	10,000
5,000	0.1412	20,000	22,000
10,000	0.0502	30,000	42,000
50,000	0.0013	110,000	202,000
	EMV	14,658.60	11,315.4
	σ^2	31,719,333.50	126877326.67
	σ	5,631.99	11263.98
	CV	38.42%	99.55%
	Return-to-risk	2.6027	1.0046

Opportunity loss table:

	Pr	*A*	*B*
Event 1	0.5590	0	6,000
Event 2	0.2484	0	4,000
Event 3	0.1412	2,000	0
Event 4	0.0502	12,000	0
Event 5	0.0013	92,000	0
	EOL	1,004.40	4,347.60

(c) The author's decision is affected by the changed probabilities. Under the new circumstances, signing with company *A* maximizes the expected monetary value ($14,658.60), minimizes the expected opportunity loss ($1,004.40), minimizes risk with a smaller coefficient of variation and yields a higher return-to-risk than choosing company *B*.

20.26 A payoff table presents the alternatives in a tabular format, while the decision tree organizes the alternatives and events visually.

20.28 Since it is the difference between the *highest* possible profit for an event and the actual profit obtained for an action taken. It can never be negative.

20.30 The expected value of perfect information represents the maximum amount you would pay to obtain perfect information. It represents the alternative course of action with the smallest expected opportunity loss. It is also equal to the expected profit under certainty minus the expected monetary value of the best alternative course of action.

20.32 Expected monetary value measures the mean return or profit of an alternative course of action over the long run without regard for the variability in the payoffs under different events. The return-to-risk ratio considers the variability in the payoffs in evaluating which alternative course of action should be chosen.

20.34 A risk averter attempts to reduce risk, while a risk seeker looks for increased return usually associated with greater risk.

20.36 (a), (c), (g), (h) Payoff table:

Probabilities & Payoffs Table:

	P	Buy 6,000	Buy 8,000	Buy 10,000	Buy 12,000
Sell 6,000	0.1	6,840	6,340	5,840	5,340
Sell 8,000	0.5	6,840	9,120	8,620	8,120
Sell 10,000	0.3	6,840	9,120	11,400	10,900
Sell 12,000	0.1	6,840	9,120	11,400	13,680

Statistics for:	Buy 6,000	Buy 8,000	Buy 10,000	Buy 12,000
Expected Monetary Value	6840	8842	9454	9232
Variance	0	695556	3168644	4946176
Standard Deviation	0	834	1780.068538	2224
Coefficient of Variation	0	0.094322551	0.188287343	0.240901213
Return to Risk Ratio	#DIV/0!	10.60191847	5.311031456	4.151079137

(d) Opportunity loss table:

Opportunity Loss Table:

	Optimum Action	Optimum Profit	Alternatives			
			Buy 6,000	Buy 8,000	Buy 10,000	Buy 12,000
Sell 6,000	Buy 6,000	6840	0	500	1000	1500
Sell 8,000	Buy 8,000	9120	2280	0	500	1000
Sell 10,000	Buy 10,00(	11400	4560	2280	0	500
Sell 12,000	Buy 12,00(	13680	6840	4560	2280	0
			Buy 6,000	Buy 8,000	Buy 10,000	Buy 12,000
Expected Opportunity Loss			3192	1190	578	800
					EVPI	

20.36 (d)
cont.

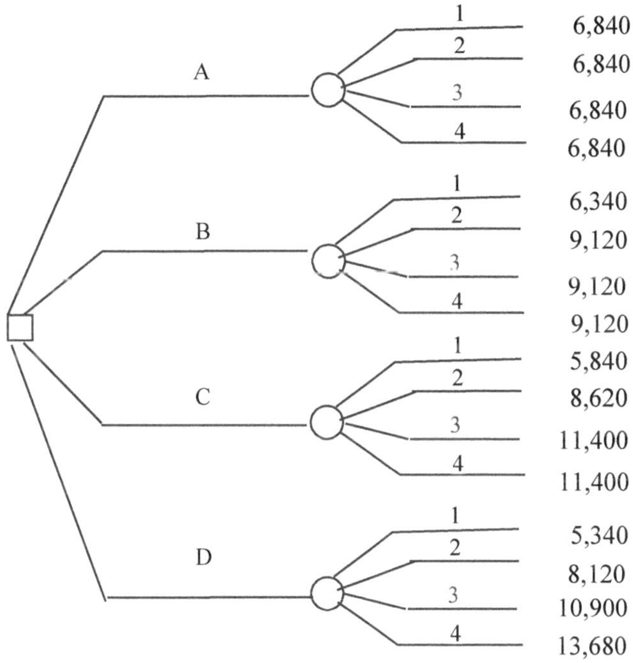

(e) *EVPI* = \$578. The management of Shop-Quick Supermarkets should not be willing to pay more than \$578 for a perfect forecast.

(f) To maximize the expected monetary value and minimize expected opportunity loss, the management should buy 10,000 loaves.

(i) Action *B* (buying 8,000 loaves) maximizes the return-to-risk and, while buying 6,000 loaves reduces the coefficient of variation to zero, action *B* has a smaller coefficient of variation than *C* or *D*.

(j) The results depend on what your objective is.

(k) (a), (c), (g), (h)
Payoff table:

Probabilities & Payoffs Table:

	P	Buy 6,000	Buy 8,000	Buy 10,000	Buy 12,000
Sell 6,000	0.3	6,840	6,340	5,840	5,340
Sell 8,000	0.4	6,840	9,120	8,620	8,120
Sell 10,000	0.2	6,840	9,120	11,400	10,900
Sell 12,000	0.1	6,840	9,120	11,400	13,680

Statistics for:	Buy 6,000	Buy 8,000	Buy 10,000	Buy 12,000
Expected Monetary Value	6840	8286	8620	8398
Variance	0	1622964	4637040	6878276
Standard Deviation	0	1273.956043	2153.37874	2622.646755
Coefficient of Variation	0	0.153748014	0.249811919	0.312294208
Return to Risk Ratio	#DIV/0!	6.504149059	4.003011564	3.202108704

20.6 (k) (d) Opportunity loss table:

Opportunity Loss Table:						
	Optimum	Optimum		Alternatives		
	Action	Profit	Buy 6,000	Buy 8,000	Buy 10,000	Buy 12,000
Sell 6,000	Buy 6,000	6840	0	500	1000	1500
Sell 8,000	Buy 8,000	9120	2280	0	500	1000
Sell 10,000	Buy 10,00(	11400	4560	2280	0	500
Sell 12,000	Buy 12,00(	13680	6840	4560	2280	0
			Buy 6,000	**Buy 8,000**	**Buy 10,000**	**Buy 12,000**
Expected Opportunity Loss			**2508**	**1062**	**728**	**950**
					EVPI	

(e) *EVPI* = \$728. The management of Shop-Quick Supermarkets should not be willing to pay more than \$728 for a perfect forecast.

(f) To maximize the expected monetary value and minimize expected opportunity loss, the management should buy 10,000 loaves.

(i) Action *B* (buying 8,000 loaves) maximizes the return-to-risk and, while buying 6,000 loaves reduces the coefficient of variation to zero, action *B* has a smaller coefficient of variation than *C* or *D*.

(j) The results depend on what your objective is.

20.38 (a)

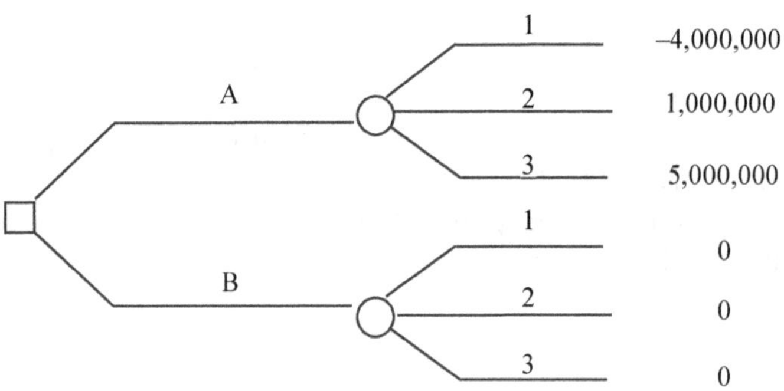

(c), (f) Payoff table:

Event		*Pr*	New	Old
1	Weak	0.3	– 4,000,000	0
2	Moderate	0.6	1,000,000	0
3	Strong	0.1	5,000,000	0
		EMV	– 100,000	0
		σ	2,808,914	0
		CV	– 2,808.94%	undefined
		Return-to-risk	– 0.0356	undefined

20.38 cont. (b), (d), (e) Opportunity loss table:

	Pr	New	Old
Weak	0.3	4,000,000	0
Moderate	0.6	0	1,000,000
Strong	0.1	0	5,000,000
	EOL	1,200,000	1,100,000

EVPI = \$1,100,000. The product manager should not be willing to pay more than \$1,100,000 for a perfect forecast.

(g) The product manager should continue to use the old packaging to maximize expected monetary value and to minimize expected opportunity loss and risk.

(h) (c), (f) Payoff table:

	Pr	New	Old
Weak	0.6	– 4,000,000	0
Moderate	0.3	1,000,000	0
Strong	0.1	5,000,000	0
	EMV	– 1,600,000	0
	σ	3,136,877	0
	CV	– 196.05%	undefined
	Return-to-risk	– 0.5101	undefined

(b), (d), (e) Opportunity loss table:

	Pr	New	Old
Weak	0.6	4,000,000	0
Moderate	0.3	0	1,000,000
Strong	0.1	0	5,000,000
	EOL	2,400,000	800,000

EVPI = \$800,000. The product manager should not be willing to pay more than \$800,000 for a perfect forecast.

(g) The product manager should continue to use the old packaging to maximize expected monetary value and to minimize expected opportunity loss and risk.

(i) (c), (f) Payoff table:

	Pr	New	Old
Weak	0.1	– 4,000,000	0
Moderate	0.3	1,000,000	0
Strong	0.6	5,000,000	0
	EMV	2,900,000	0
	σ	2,913,760.457	0
	CV	100.47%	undefined
	Return-to-risk	0.9953	undefined

(b), (d), (e) Opportunity loss table:

	Pr	New	Old
Weak	0.1	4,000,000	0
Moderate	0.3	0	1,000,000
Strong	0.6	0	5,000,000
	EOL	400,000	3,300,000

EVPI = \$400,000. The product manager should not be willing to pay more than \$400,000 for a perfect forecast.

20.38 cont. (i) (g) The product manager should use the new packaging to maximize expected monetary value and to minimize expected opportunity loss.

(j) P(Sales decreased | weak response) = 0.6
P(Sales stayed same | weak response) = 0.3
P(Sales increased | weak response) = 0.1
P(Sales decreased | moderate response) = 0.2
P(Sales stayed same | moderate response) = 0.4
P(Sales increased | moderate response) = 0.4
P(Sales decreased | strong response) = 0.05
P(Sales stayed same | strong response) = 0.35
P(Sales increased | strong response) = 0.6
P(Sales decreased *and* weak response) = 0.6(0.3) = 0.18
P(Sales stayed same *and* weak response) = 0.3(0.3) = 0.09
P(Sales increased *and* weak response) = 0.1(0.3) = 0.03
P(Sales decreased *and* moderate response) = 0.2(0.6) = 0.12
P(Sales stayed same *and* moderate response) = 0.4(0.6) = 0.24
P(Sales increased *and* moderate response) = 0.4(0.6) = 0.24
P(Sales decreased *and* strong response) = 0.05(0.1) = 0.005
P(Sales stayed same *and* strong response) = 0.35(0.1) = 0.035
P(Sales increased *and* strong response) = 0.6(0.1) = 0.06

Joint probability table:

	Pr	Sales Decrease	Sales Stay Same	Sales Increase
Weak	0.3	0.180	0.090	0.030
Moderate	0.6	0.120	0.240	0.240
Strong	0.1	0.005	0.035	0.060
	Total	0.305	0.365	0.330

(j) Given the sales stayed the same, the revised conditional probabilities are:

P(weak response | sales stayed same) = $\frac{.09}{.365} = 0.2466$

P(moderate response | sales stayed same) = $\frac{.24}{.365} = 0.6575$

P(strong response | sales stayed same) = $\frac{.035}{.365} = 0.0959$

(k) (c), (f) Payoff table:

	Pr	New	Old
Weak	0.2466	– 4,000,000	0
Moderate	0.6575	1,000,000	0
Strong	0.0959	5,000,000	0
	EMV	150,600	0
	σ	2,641,575.219	0
	CV	1,754.03%	undefined
	Return-to-risk	0.0570	undefined

20.38 cont. (k) (b), (d), (e) Opportunity loss table:

	Pr	New	Old
Weak	0.2466	4,000,000	0
Moderate	0.6575	0	1,000,000
Strong	0.0959	0	5,000,000
	EOL	986,400	1,137,000

EVPI = \$986,400. The product manager should not be willing to pay more than \$986,400 for a perfect forecast.

(g) The product manager should use the new packaging to maximize expected monetary value and to minimize expected opportunity loss.

(l) Given the sales decreased, the revised conditional probabilities are:

$$P(\text{weak response} \mid \text{sales decreased}) = \frac{.18}{.305} = 0.5902$$

$$P(\text{moderate response} \mid \text{sales decreased}) = \frac{.12}{.305} = 0.3934$$

$$P(\text{strong response} \mid \text{sales decreased}) = \frac{.005}{.305} = 0.0164$$

(m) (c), (f) Payoff table:

	Pr	New	Old
Weak	0.5902	– 4,000,000	0
Moderate	0.3934	1,000,000	0
Strong	0.0164	5,000,000	0
	EMV	– 1,885,400	0
	σ	2,586,864.287	0
	CV	– 137.21%	undefined
	Return-to-risk	– 0.7288	undefined

(b), (d), (e) Opportunity loss table:

	Pr	New	Old
Weak	0.5902	4,000,000	0
Moderate	0.3934	0	1,000,000
Strong	0.0164	0	5,000,000
	EOL	2,360,800	475,400

EVPI = \$475,400. The product manager should not be willing to pay more than \$475,400 for a perfect forecast.

(g) The product manager should continue to use the old packaging to maximize expected monetary value and minimize expected opportunity loss.

20.40 (a)

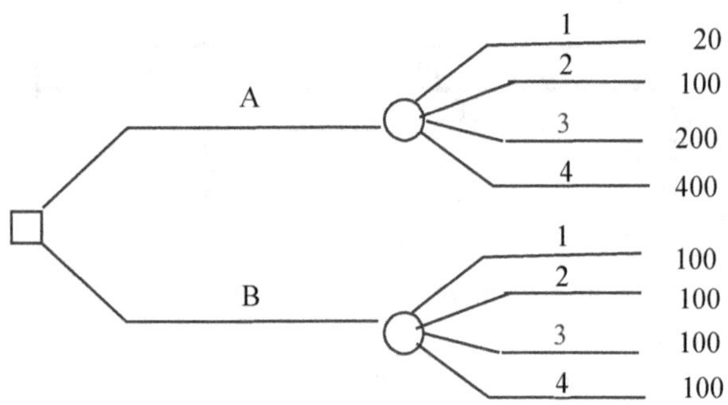

(c), (e), (f) Payoff table:*

Event		*Pr*	*A:* Do Not Call Mechanic	*B:* Call Mechanic
1	Very low	0.25	20	100
2	Low	0.25	100	100
3	Moderate	0.25	200	100
4	High	0.25	400	100
		EMV	180	100
		σ	142	0
		CV	78.96%	0
		Return-to-risk	1.2665	undefined

**Note:* The payoff here is cost and not profit. The opportunity cost is therefore calculated as the difference between the payoff and the minimum in the same row.

(b), (d) Opportunity loss table:

	Pr	*A:* Do Not Call Mechanic	*B:* Call Mechanic
Very low	0.25	80	0
Low	0.25	0	0
Moderate	0.25	0	100
High	0.25	0	300
	EOL	20	100

(e) *EVPI* = \$20. The manufacturer should not be willing to pay more than \$20 for the information about which event will occur.

(g) We want to minimize the expected monetary value because it is a cost. To minimize the expected monetary value, call the mechanic.

(h) Given 2 defectives out of 15, the binomial probabilities and their related revised conditional probabilities are:

	Pr	Binomial Probabilities	Revised Conditional Probabilities
Very low	0.01	0.0092	0.0092/0.6418 = 0.0143
Low	0.05	0.1348	0.1348/0.6418 = 0.2100
Moderate	0.10	0.2669	0.2669/0.6418 = 0.4159
High	0.20	0.2309	0.2309/0.6418 = 0.3598
		0.6418	

20.40 cont. (i) (c), (e), (f) Payoff table:

	Pr	*A:* Do Not Call Mechanic	*B:* Call Mechanic
Very low	0.0143	20	100
Low	0.2100	100	100
Moderate	0.4159	200	100
High	0.3598	400	100
	EMV	248.3860	100
	σ	121	0
	CV	48.68%	0
	Return-to-risk	2.0544	undefined

(b), (d) Opportunity loss table:

	Pr	*A:* Do Not Call Mechanic	*B:* Call Mechanic
Very low	0.0143	80	0
Low	0.2100	0	0
Moderate	0.4159	0	100
High	0.3598	0	300
	EOL	1.1440	149.53

(e) $EVPI = \$1.14$. The manufacturer should not be willing to pay more than \$1.14 for the information about which event will occur.

(g) We want to minimize the expected monetary value because it is a cost. To minimize the expected monetary value, call the mechanic.

ONLINE SECTIONS

Chapter 4

4.42 $P(B \mid A) = \dfrac{P(A \mid B) \cdot P(B)}{P(A \mid B) \cdot P(B) + P(A \mid B') \cdot P(B')}$

$= \dfrac{0.6 \cdot 0.3}{0.6 \cdot 0.3 + 0.5 \cdot 0.7} = \dfrac{0.18}{0.53} = 0.340$

4.44 (a) CT = complete trust MT = moderate trust NT = minimal or no trust

R = very likely to recommend NR = not very likely to recommend

$P(\text{CT} \mid \text{R}) = \dfrac{P(R \mid CT) \cdot P(CT)}{P(R \mid CT) \cdot P(CT) + P(R \mid MT) \cdot P(MT) + P(R \mid NT) \cdot P(NT)}$

$= \dfrac{0.68(.44)}{0.68(.44) + 0.2(0.49) + 0.03(0.07)} = \dfrac{0.2992}{0.3993} = 0.7493$

(b) $P(R) = 0.68(.44) + 0.2(0.49) + 0.03(0.07) = 0.2992 + 0.0980 + 0.0021 = 0.3993$

4.46 W = women M = men R = revenues of \$50,000 and above

$P(W) = 0.35$ $P(M) = .65$ $P(R \mid W) = 0.20$ $P(R \mid M) = 0.24$

(a) $P(W \mid R) = \dfrac{P(R \mid W) \cdot P(W)}{P(R \mid W) \cdot P(W) + P(R \mid M) \cdot P(M)} = \dfrac{0.20(0.35)}{0.20(0.35) + 0.24(0.65)} = \dfrac{0.07}{0.226} = 0.3097$

(b) $P(R) = P(R \mid W) \cdot P(W) + P(R \mid M) \cdot P(M) = 0.20(0.35) + 0.24(0.65) = 0.226$

4.48 (a) P(A rating | issued by city) = 0.35/0.56 = 0.625

(b) P(issued by city) = 0.5(0.7) + 0.6(0.2) + 0.9(0.1) = 0.56

(c) P(issued by suburb) = 0.4(0.7) + 0.2(0.2) + 0.05(0.1) = 0.325

4.52 (7)(3)(3) = 63

4.54 $n! = 4! = (4)(3)(2)(1) = 24$

4.56 $\dfrac{n!}{(n-X)!} = \dfrac{5!}{1!} = 120$

4.58 ${}_8C_2 = \dfrac{8!}{2!(6!)} = 28$

4.60 $\dfrac{n!}{X!(n-X)!} = \dfrac{7!}{4!(3!)} = \dfrac{(7)(6)(5)}{(3)(2)(1)} = 35$

4.62 ${}_{15}C_3 = \dfrac{n!}{X!(n-X)!} = \dfrac{15!}{3!(12!)} = \dfrac{(15)(14)(13)}{(3)(2)(1)} = 455$

Chapter 5

5.46 PHStat output:

Probabilities & Outcomes:	P	X	Y
	0.2	-100	50
	0.4	50	30
	0.3	200	20
	0.1	300	20
Weight Assigned to X	0.5		
Statistics			
E(X)	90		
E(Y)	30		
Variance(X)	15900		
Standard Deviation(X)	126.0952		
Variance(Y)	120		
Standard Deviation(Y)	10.95445		
Covariance(XY)	-1300		
Variance(X+Y)	13420		
Standard Deviation(X+Y)	115.8447		
Portfolio Management			
Weight Assigned to X	0.5		
Weight Assigned to Y	0.5		
Portfolio Expected Return	60		
Portfolio Risk	57.92236		

(a) $E(X) = (0.2)(\$-100) + (0.4)(\$50) + (0.3)(\$200) + (0.1)(\$300) = \$90$
$E(Y) = (0.2)(\$50) + (0.4)(\$30) + (0.3)(\$20) + (0.1)(\$20) = \$30$

(b) $\sigma_X = \sqrt{(0.2)(-100-90)^2 + (0.4)(50-90)^2 + (0.3)(200-90)^2 + (0.1)(300-90)^2}$
$= \sqrt{15900} = 126.10$

$\sigma_Y = \sqrt{(0.2)(50-30)^2 + (0.4)(30-30)^2 + (0.3)(20-30)^2 + (0.1)(20-30)^2}$
$= \sqrt{120} = 10.95$

(c) $\sigma_{XY} = (0.2)(-100-90)(50-30) + (0.4)(50-90)(30-30)$
$+ (0.3)(200-90)(20-30) + (0.1)(300-90)(20-30) = -1300$

(d) $E(X+Y) = E(X) + E(Y) = \$90 + \$30 = \$120$

5.48 (a) E(total time) = E(time waiting) + E(time served) = 4 + 5.5 = 9.5 minutes

(b) σ (total time) = $\sqrt{1.2^2 + 1.5^2} = 1.9209$ minutes

5.50 PHStat output for (a)-(c):

Covariance Analysis			
Probabilities & Outcomes:	**P**	**X**	**Y**
	0.1	**-100**	**50**
	0.3	**0**	**150**
	0.3	**80**	**-20**
	0.3	**150**	**-100**
Statistics			
E(X)	**59**		
E(Y)	**14**		
Variance(X)	**6189**		
Standard Deviation(X)	**78.6702**		
Variance(Y)	**9924**		
Standard Deviation(Y)	**99.61928**		
Covariance(XY)	**-6306**		
Variance(X+Y)	**3501**		
Standard Deviation(X+Y)	**59.16925**		

(a) $E(X) = \sum_{i=1}^{N} x_i P(x_i) = 59$

$E(Y) = \sum_{i=1}^{N} y_i P(y_i) = 14$

(b) $\sigma_X = \sqrt{\sum_{i=1}^{N}\left[x_i - E(X)\right]^2 P(x_i)} = 78.6702$

$\sigma_Y = \sqrt{\sum_{i=1}^{N}\left[y_i - E(Y)\right]^2 P(y_i)} = 99.62$

(c) $\sigma_{XY} = \sum_{i=1}^{N}\left[x_i - E(X)\right]\left[y_i - E(Y)\right]P(x_i, y_i) = -6306$

(d) Stock *X* gives the investor a lower standard deviation while yielding a higher expected return so the investor should select stock *X*.

5.52 PHStat output:

Probabilities & Outcomes:	P	X	Y
	0.1	-50	-100
	0.3	20	50
	0.4	100	130
	0.2	150	200

Statistics	
E(X)	71
E(Y)	97
Variance(X)	3829
Standard Deviation(X)	61.87891
Variance(Y)	7101
Standard Deviation(Y)	84.26743
Covariance(XY)	5113
Variance(X+Y)	21156
Standard Deviation(X+Y)	145.451

(a) $E(X) = \$71$ $E(Y) = \$97$

(b) $\sigma_X = 61.88$ $\sigma_Y = 84.27$

5.54 (a) PHStat output:

Covariance Analysis

Probabilities & Outcomes:	P	X	Y
	0.01	-200	-999
	0.09	-70	-300
	0.15	30	-100
	0.35	80	100
	0.3	100	150
	0.1	120	350

Weight Assigned to X	0.5

Statistics	
E(X)	66.2
E(Y)	63.01
Variance(X)	3273.56
Standard Deviation(X)	57.21503
Variance(Y)	38109.75
Standard Deviation(Y)	195.2172
Covariance(XY)	10766.74
Variance(X+Y)	62916.79
Standard Deviation(X+Y)	250.8322

Portfolio Management	
Weight Assigned to X	0.5
Weight Assigned to Y	0.5
Portfolio Expected Return	64.605
Portfolio Risk	125.4161

5.54 cont.

(a) Let X = corporate bond fund, Y = common stock fund.
$E(X)$ = \$66.2 $E(Y)$ = \$63.01.

(b) σ_X = \$57.2150 σ_Y = \$195.2172

(c) According to the probability of 0.01, it is highly unlikely that you will lose \$999 of every \$1,000 invested.

5.56 (a) PHStat output:

Hypergeometric Probabilities		
Data		
Sample size	4	
No. of successes in population	5	
Population size	10	
Hypergeometric Probabilities Table		
	X	P(X)
	3	0.238095

$$P(X=3)=\frac{\binom{5}{3}\binom{10-5}{4-3}}{\binom{10}{4}}=\frac{\frac{5\cdot4\cdot3!}{3!\cdot2\cdot1}\cdot\frac{5\cdot4!}{4!\cdot1!}}{\frac{10\cdot9\cdot8\cdot7\cdot6!}{6!\cdot4\cdot3\cdot2\cdot1}}=\frac{5}{3\cdot7}=0.2381$$

(b) PHStat output:

Hypergeometric Probabilities		
Data		
Sample size	4	
No. of successes in population	3	
Population size	6	
Hypergeometric Probabilities Table		
	X	P(X)
	1	0.2
	2	0.6
	3	0.2

$$P(X=1)=\frac{\binom{3}{1}\cdot\binom{6-3}{4-1}}{\binom{6}{4}}=\frac{\frac{3\cdot2!}{2!\cdot1}\cdot\frac{3!}{3!\cdot0!}}{\frac{6\cdot5\cdot4!}{4!\cdot2\cdot1}}=\frac{1}{5}=0.2$$

5.56 cont. (c) Partial PHStat output:

Hypergeometric Probabilities		
Data		
Sample size	5	
No. of successes in population	3	
Population size	12	
Hypergeometric Probabilities Table		
	X	P(X)
	0	0.159091

$$P(X=0)=\frac{\binom{3}{0}\cdot\binom{12-3}{5-0}}{\binom{12}{5}}=\frac{\dfrac{3!}{3!\cdot 0}\cdot\dfrac{9\cdot 8\cdot 7\cdot 6\cdot 5!}{5!\cdot 4\cdot 3\cdot 2\cdot 1}}{\dfrac{12\cdot 11\cdot 10\cdot 9\cdot 8\cdot 7!}{7!\,5\cdot 4\cdot 3\cdot 2\cdot 1}}=\frac{7}{44}=0.1591$$

(d) Partial PHStat output:

Hypergeometric Probabilities		
Data		
Sample size	**3**	
No. of successes in population	**3**	
Population size	**10**	
Hypergeometric Probabilities Table		
	X	**P(X)**
	3	**0.008333**

$$P(X=3)=\frac{\binom{3}{3}\cdot\binom{10-3}{3-3}}{\binom{10}{3}}=\frac{\dfrac{3!}{3!\cdot 0!}\cdot\dfrac{7!}{7!\cdot 0!}}{\dfrac{10\cdot 9\cdot 8\cdot 7!}{7!\cdot 3\cdot 2\cdot 1}}=\frac{1}{120}=0.0083$$

5.58 (a) Partial PHStat output:

Hypergeometric Probabilities		
Data		
Sample size	6	
No. of successes in population	25	
Population size	100	
Hypergeometric Probabilities Table		
	X	P(X)
	0	0.168918
	1	0.361968
	2	0.305888
	3	0.130286
	4	0.029448
	5	0.003343
	6	0.000149

If $n = 6$, $E = 25$, and $N = 100$,

$$P(X \geq 2) = 1 - [P(X = 0) + P(X = 1)] = 1 - \left[\frac{\binom{25}{0}\binom{100-25}{6-0}}{\binom{100}{6}} + \frac{\binom{25}{1}\binom{100-25}{6-1}}{\binom{100}{6}} \right]$$

$$= 1 - [0.1689 + 0.3620] = 0.4691$$

(b) Partial PHStat output:

Hypergeometric Probabilities		
Data		
Sample size	6	
No. of successes in population	30	
Population size	100	
Hypergeometric Probabilities Table		
	X	P(X)
	0	0.109992
	1	0.304593
	2	0.33459
	3	0.186438
	4	0.05552
	5	0.008368
	6	0.000498

If $n = 6$, $E = 30$, and $N = 100$,

$$P(X \geq 2) = 1 - [P(X = 0) + P(X = 1)] = 1 - \left[\frac{\binom{30}{0}\binom{100-30}{6-0}}{\binom{100}{6}} + \frac{\binom{30}{1}\binom{100-30}{6-1}}{\binom{100}{6}} \right]$$

$$= 1 - [0.1100 + 0.3046] = 0.5854$$

5.58 cont. (c) Partial PHStat output:

Hypergeometric Probabilities		
Data		
Sample size	6	
No. of successes in population	5	
Population size	100	
Hypergeometric Probabilities Table		
	X	P(X)
	0	0.729085
	1	0.243028
	2	0.026706
	3	0.001161
	4	1.87E-05
	5	7.97E-08

If $n = 6$, $E = 5$, and $N = 100$,

$$P(X \geq 2) = 1 - [P(X = 0) + P(X = 1)] = 1 - \left[\frac{\binom{5}{0}\binom{100-5}{6-0}}{\binom{100}{6}} + \frac{\binom{5}{1}\binom{100-5}{6-1}}{\binom{100}{6}} \right]$$

$$= 1 - [0.7291 + 0.2430] = 0.0279$$

(d) Partial PHStat output:

Hypergeometric Probabilities		
Data		
Sample size	6	
No. of successes in population	10	
Population size	100	
Hypergeometric Probabilities Table		
	X	P(X)
	0	0.522305
	1	0.368686
	2	0.096458
	3	0.011826
	4	0.000706
	5	1.9E-05
	6	1.76E-07

If $n = 6$, $E = 10$, and $N = 100$,

$$P(X \geq 2) = 1 - [P(X = 0) + P(X = 1)] = 1 - \left[\frac{\binom{10}{0}\binom{100-10}{6-0}}{\binom{100}{6}} + \frac{\binom{10}{1}\binom{100-10}{6-1}}{\binom{100}{6}} \right]$$

$$= 1 - [0.5223 + 0.3687] = 0.1090$$

5.58 cont. (e) The probability that the entire group will be audited is very sensitive to the true number of improper returns in the population. If the true number is very low ($E = 5$), the probability is very low (0.0279). When the true number is increased by a factor of six ($E = 30$), the probability the group will be audited increases by a factor of almost 21 (0.5854).

5.60 PHStat output:

Data		
Sample size	4	
No. of successes in population	4	
Population size	30	
Hypergeometric Probabilities Table		
	X	P(X)
	0	0.545521
	1	0.379493
	2	0.071155
	3	0.003795
	4	3.65E-05

(a) $P(X = 4) = 3.6490 \times 10^{-5}$
(b) $P(X = 0) = 0.5455$
(c) $P(X \geq 1) = 0.4545$
(d) $E = 6$
(a) $P(X = 4) = 0.0005$
(b) $P(X = 0) = 0.3877$
(c) $P(X \geq 1) = 0.6123$

5.62 Partial PHStat output:

Hypergeometric Probabilities

Data	
Sample size	4
No. of events of interest in population	6
Population size	12

Hypergeometric Probabilities Table

X	P(X)
0	0.030303
1	0.242424
2	0.454545
3	0.242424
4	0.030303

(a) $P(X = 1) - 0.2424$
(b) $P(X \geq 1) = 1 - P(X = 0) = 0.9697$
(c) $P(X = 3) = 0.2424$
(d) Because the number of events of interest in the population is a smaller fraction of the population size in (c), the probability in (c) is smaller than that in Example 5.7

Chapter 6

6.44 (a) PHStat output:

Exponential Probabilities

Data	
Mean	30
X Value	0.1

Results	
P(<=X)	0.9502

$P(\text{arrival time} < 0.1) = 1 - e^{-\lambda x} = 1 - e^{-(30)(0.1)} = 0.9502$

(b) $P(\text{arrival time} > 0.1) = 1 - P(\text{arrival time} \leq 0.1) = 1 - 0.9502 = 0.0498$

(c) PHStat output:

Exponential Probabilities

Data	
Mean	30
X Value	0.2

Results	
P(<=X)	0.9975

$P(0.1 < \text{arrival time} < 0.2) = P(\text{arrival time} < 0.2) - P(\text{arrival time} < 0.1)$
$= 0.9975 - 0.9502 = 0.0473$

(d) $P(\text{arrival time} < 0.1) + P(\text{arrival time} > 0.2) = 0.9502 + 0.0025 = 0.9527$

6.46 (a) PHStat output:

Exponential Probabilities

Data	
Mean	50
X Value	0.05

Results	
P(<=X)	0.9179

$P(\text{arrival time} \leq 0.05) = 1 - e^{-(50)(0.05)} = 0.9179$

6.46 cont. (b) PHStat output:

Exponential Probabilities

Data	
Mean	50
X Value	0.0167

Results	
P(<=X)	0.5661

$P(\text{arrival time} \leq 0.0167) = 1 - 0.4339 = 0.5661$

(c) PHStat output:

Exponential Probabilities

Data	
Mean	60
X Value	0.05

Results	
P(<=X)	0.9502

Exponential Probabilities

Data	
Mean	60
X Value	0.0167

Results	
P(<=X)	0.6329

If $\lambda = 60$, $P(\text{arrival time} \leq 0.05) = 0.9502$,
$P(\text{arrival time} \leq 0.0167) = 0.6329$

6.46 cont. (d) PHStat output:

Exponential Probabilities

Data	
Mean	30
X Value	0.05

Results	
P(<=X)	0.7769

Exponential Probabilities

Data	
Mean	30
X Value	0.0167

Results	
P(<=X)	0.3941

If $\lambda = 30$, $P(\text{arrival time} \le 0.05) = 0.7769$
$P(\text{arrival time} \le 0.0167) = 0.3941$

6.48 (a) PHStat output:

Exponential Probabilities

Data	
Mean	15
X Value	0.05

Results	
P(<=X)	0.5276

$P(\text{arrival time} \le 0.05) = 1 - e^{-(15)(0.05)} = 0.5276$

(b) PHStat output:

Exponential Probabilities

Data	
Mean	15
X Value	0.25

Results	
P(<=X)	0.9765

$P(\text{arrival time} \le 0.25) = 0.9765$

6.48 cont. (c) PHStat output:

Exponential Probabilities

Data	
Mean	25
X Value	0.05

Results	
P(<=X)	0.7135

Exponential Probabilities

Data	
Mean	25
X Value	0.25

Results	
P(<=X)	0.9981

If $\lambda = 25$, $P(\text{arrival time} \leq 0.05) = 0.7135$, $P(\text{arrival time} \leq 0.25) = 0.9981$

6.50 (a) PHStat output:

Exponential Probabilities

Data	
Mean	0.05
X Value	14

Results	
P(<=X)	0.5034

$P(X < 14) = = 1 - e^{-(1/20)(14)} = 0.5034$

(b) PHstat output:

Exponential Probabilities

Data	
Mean	0.05
X Value	21

Results	
P(<=X)	0.6501

$P(X > 21) = = 1 - \left(1 - e^{-(1/20)(21)}\right) = 0.3499$

6.50 cont. (c) PHStat output:

Exponential Probabilities

Data	
Mean	0.05
X Value	7

Results	
P(<=X)	0.2953

$P(X < 7) = = 1 - e^{-(1/20)(7)} = 0.2953$

6.52 (a) PHStat output:

Exponential Probabilities	
Data	
Mean	0.6944
X Value	1
Results	
P(<=X)	0.5006

$P(X < 1) = 1 - e^{-(0.6944)(1)} = 0.5006$

(b) PHStat output:

Exponential Probabilities	
Data	
Mean	0.6944
X Value	2
Results	
P(<=X)	0.7506

$P(X < 2) = 1 - e^{-(0.6944)(2)} = 0.7506$

(c) PHStat output:

Exponential Probabilities	
Data	
Mean	0.6944
X Value	3
Results	
P(<=X)	0.8755

$P(X > 3) = 1 - \left(1 - e^{-(0.6944)(3)}\right) = 0.1245$

(d) The time between visitors is similar to waiting line (queuing) where the exponential distribution is most appropriate.

6.54 $n = 100, p = 0.40.$ $n\pi = 40 \geq 5$ and $n(1-\pi) = 60 \geq 5$

$\mu = n\pi = 40$ $\sigma = \sqrt{n\pi(1-\pi)} = 4.8990$

(a)

Probability for a Range	
From X Value	39.5
To X Value	40.5
Z Value for 39.5	-0.102062
Z Value for 40.5	0.102062
P(X<=39.5)	0.4594
P(X<=40.5)	0.5406
P(39.5<=X<=40.5)	0.0813

$P(X = 40) \cong P(39.5 \leq X \leq 40.5) = P(-0.1021 \leq Z \leq 0.1021) = 0.0813$

(b)

Probability for X >	
X Value	40.5
Z Value	0.1020616
P(X>40.5)	0.4594

$P(X > 40) = P(X \geq 41) \cong P(X \geq 40.5) = P(Z \geq 0.1021) = 0.4594$

(c)

Probability for X <=	
X Value	40.5
Z Value	0.1020616
P(X<=40.5)	0.5406461

$P(X \leq 40) \cong P(X \leq 40.5) = P(Z \leq 0.1021) = 0.5406$

(d)

Probability for X <=	
X Value	39.5
Z Value	-0.102062
P(X<=39.5)	0.4593539

$P(X < 40) = P(X \leq 39) \cong P(X \leq 39.5) = P(Z \leq -0.1021) = 0.4594$

6.56 $\pi = \frac{1}{3} = 0.3333$, $n = 150$, $n\pi = 50 > 5$, $n(1-\pi) = 100 > 5$

(a) $P(X \leq 60) = P\left(\frac{X - n\pi}{\sqrt{n\pi(1-\pi)}} = \frac{59.5 - 150(0.3333)}{\sqrt{150(0.3333)(1-0.3333)}}\right)$

$= P(Z > 1.6454) = 0.0499$

(b) $P(X = 60) = P(59.5 \leq X_a \leq 60.5) = P(1.6454 \leq Z \leq 1.8187) = 0.0155$

(c) $P(X < 60) = P(X_a \leq 59.5) = P(Z \leq 1.6454) = 0.9501$

(d) $P(X = 71) = P(70.5 \leq X_a \leq 71.5) = P(3.5507 \leq Z \leq 3.7239) = 0.0001$

Chapter 8

8.70 $$N \cdot \bar{X} \pm N \cdot t \cdot \frac{S}{\sqrt{n}} \sqrt{\frac{N-n}{N-1}} = 500 \cdot 25.7 \pm 500 \cdot 2.7969 \cdot \frac{7.8}{\sqrt{25}} \cdot \sqrt{\frac{500-25}{500-1}}$$

$10,721.53 ≤ Population Total ≤ $14,978.47

8.72 (a) $$p + Z \cdot \sqrt{\frac{p(1-p)}{n}} \sqrt{\frac{(N-n)}{(N-1)}} = 0.04 + 1.2816 \cdot \sqrt{\frac{0.04(1-0.04)}{300}} \sqrt{\frac{(5000-300)}{(5000-1)}}$$

$\pi < 0.05406$

(b) $$p + Z \cdot \sqrt{\frac{p(1-p)}{n}} \sqrt{\frac{(N-n)}{(N-1)}} = 0.04 + 1.645 \cdot \sqrt{\frac{0.04(1-0.04)}{300}} \sqrt{\frac{(5000-300)}{(5000-1)}}$$

$\pi < 0.05804$

(c) $$p + Z \cdot \sqrt{\frac{p(1-p)}{n}} \sqrt{\frac{(N-n)}{(N-1)}} = 0.04 + 2.3263 \cdot \sqrt{\frac{0.04(1-0.04)}{300}} \sqrt{\frac{(5000-300)}{(5000-1)}}$$

$\pi < 0.06552$

8.74 $$N \cdot \bar{X} \pm N \cdot t \cdot \frac{S}{\sqrt{n}} \sqrt{\frac{N-n}{N-1}} = 3000 \cdot \$261.40 \pm 3000 \cdot 1.8331 \cdot \frac{\$138.8046}{\sqrt{10}} \cdot \sqrt{\frac{3000-10}{3000-1}}$$

$543,176.96 ≤ Population Total ≤ $1,025,223.04

8.76 $$N \cdot \bar{D} \pm N \cdot t \cdot \frac{S_D}{\sqrt{n}} \sqrt{\frac{N-n}{N-1}} = 4000 \cdot \$7.45907 \pm 4000 \cdot 2.6092 \cdot \frac{\$29.5523}{\sqrt{150}} \cdot \sqrt{\frac{4000-150}{4000-1}}$$

$ 5,126.26 ≤ Total Difference in the Population ≤ $54,546.28

Note: The t-value of 2.6092 for 99% confidence and d.f. = 149 was derived on Excel.

8.78 (a) $$p + Z \cdot \sqrt{\frac{p(1-p)}{n}} \sqrt{\frac{N-n}{N-1}} = 0.0367 + 1.645 \cdot \sqrt{\frac{0.0367(1-0.0367)}{300}} \sqrt{\frac{10000-300}{10000-1}}$$

$\pi < 0.0542$

(b) Since the upper bound is higher than the tolerable exception rate of 0.04, the auditor should request a larger sample.

8.80 $$\bar{X} \pm t_{n-1} \frac{S}{\sqrt{n}} \sqrt{\frac{N-n}{N-1}} = 75 \pm 2.0301 \frac{24}{\sqrt{36}} \sqrt{\frac{200-36}{200-1}}$$ $67.63 \le \mu \le 82.37$

8.82 (a) $$\bar{X} \pm Z \frac{\sigma}{\sqrt{n}} \sqrt{\frac{N-n}{N-1}} = 350 \pm 1.96 \frac{100}{\sqrt{50}} \sqrt{\frac{2000-50}{2000-1}}$$ $322.6238 \le \mu \le 377.3762$

(b) $$n_0 = \frac{Z^2 \sigma^2}{e^2} = \frac{1.96^2 (100)^2}{20^2} = 96.0364$$

$$n = \frac{n_0 N}{n_0 + (N-1)} = \frac{96.0364(2000)}{96.0364 + (2000-1)} = 91.6799$$ Use $n = 92$

8.82 (c) (a) $\bar{X} \pm Z\frac{\sigma}{\sqrt{n}}\sqrt{\frac{N-n}{N-1}} = 350 \pm 1.96\frac{100}{\sqrt{50}}\sqrt{\frac{1000-50}{1000-1}}$

cont. $322.9703 \le \mu \le 377.0297$

(b) $n_0 = \frac{Z^2\sigma^2}{e^2} = \frac{1.96^2(100)^2}{20^2} = 96.0364$

$n = \frac{n_0 N}{n_0 + (N-1)} = \frac{96.0364(1000)}{96.0364 + (1000-1)} = 87.7015$ Use $n = 88$

8.84 (a) $p \pm Z\sqrt{\frac{p(1-p)}{n}}\sqrt{\frac{N-n}{N-1}} = 0.3 \pm 1.6449\sqrt{\frac{0.3(1-0.3)}{100}}\sqrt{\frac{1000-100}{1000-1}}$

$0.2285 \le \pi \le 0.3715$

(b) $n_0 = \frac{Z^2 p(1-p)}{e^2} = \frac{1.6449^2(0.3)(1-0.3)}{0.05^2} = 227.2656$

$n = \frac{n_0 N}{n_0 + (N-1)} = \frac{227.2656(1000)}{227.2656 + (1000-1)} = 185.3315$ Use $n = 186$

(c) (a) $p \pm Z\sqrt{\frac{p(1-p)}{n}}\sqrt{\frac{N-n}{N-1}} = 0.3 \pm 1.6449\sqrt{\frac{0.3(1-0.3)}{100}}\sqrt{\frac{2000-100}{2000-1}}$

$0.2265 \le \pi \le 0.3735$

(b) $n_0 = \frac{Z^2 p(1-p)}{e^2} = \frac{1.6449^2(0.3)(1-0.3)}{0.05^2} = 227.2656$

$n = \frac{n_0 N}{n_0 + (N-1)} = \frac{227.2656(2000)}{227.2656 + (2000-1)} = 204.1676$ Use $n = 205$

8.86 (a) $\bar{X} \pm Z\frac{\sigma}{\sqrt{n}}\sqrt{\frac{N-n}{N-1}} = 1.99 \pm 1.96\frac{0.05}{\sqrt{100}}\sqrt{\frac{2000-100}{2000-1}}$ $1.9804 \le \mu \le 2.0000$

(b) $n_0 = \frac{Z^2\sigma^2}{e^2} = \frac{1.96^2(0.05)^2}{0.01^2} = 96.0364$

$n = \frac{n_0 N}{n_0 + (N-1)} = \frac{96.0364(2000)}{96.0364 + (2000-1)} = 91.6799$ Use $n = 92$

(c) (a) $\bar{X} \pm Z\frac{\sigma}{\sqrt{n}}\sqrt{\frac{N-n}{N-1}} = 1.99 \pm 1.96\frac{0.05}{\sqrt{100}}\sqrt{\frac{1000-100}{1000-1}}$

$1.9807 \le \mu \le 1.9993$

(b) $n_0 = \frac{Z^2\sigma^2}{e^2} = \frac{1.96^2(0.05)^2}{0.01^2} = 96.0364$

$n = \frac{n_0 N}{n_0 + (N-1)} = \frac{96.0364(1000)}{96.0364 + (1000-1)} = 87.7015$ Use $n = 88$

Chapter 9

9.80 $H_0: \mu \geq 7$, $H_1: \mu < 7$, $\alpha = 0.05$, $n = 16$, $\sigma = 0.2$

Lower critical value: $Z_L = -1.6449$, $\bar{X}_L = \mu + Z_L\left(\frac{\sigma}{\sqrt{n}}\right) = 7 - 1.6449\left(\frac{.2}{\sqrt{16}}\right) = 6.9178$

(a) $$Z_{STAT} = \frac{\bar{X}_L - \mu_1}{\frac{\sigma}{\sqrt{n}}} = \frac{6.9178 - 6.9}{\frac{.2}{\sqrt{16}}} = 0.3551$$

$\text{power} = 1 - \beta = P(\bar{X} < \bar{X}_L) = P(Z < 0.3551) = 0.6388$

$\beta = 1 - 0.6388 = 0.3612$

(b) $$Z_{STAT} = \frac{\bar{X}_L - \mu_1}{\frac{\sigma}{\sqrt{n}}} = \frac{6.9178 - 6.8}{\frac{.2}{\sqrt{16}}} = 2.3551$$

$\text{power} = 1 - \beta = P(\bar{X} < \bar{X}_L) = P(Z < 2.3551) = 0.9907$

$\beta = 1 - 0.9907 = 0.0093$

9.82 $H_0: \mu \geq 7$, $H_1: \mu < 7$, $\alpha = 0.05$, $n = 25$, $\sigma = 0.2$

Lower critical value: $Z_L = -1.6449$, $\bar{X}_L = \mu + Z_L\left(\frac{\sigma}{\sqrt{n}}\right) = 7 - 1.6449\left(\frac{.2}{\sqrt{25}}\right) = 6.9342$

(a) $$Z_{STAT} = \frac{\bar{X}_L - \mu_1}{\frac{\sigma}{\sqrt{n}}} = \frac{6.9342 - 6.9}{\frac{.2}{\sqrt{25}}} = 0.8551$$

$\text{power} = 1 - \beta = P(\bar{X} < \bar{X}_L) = P(Z < 0.8551) = 0.8038$

$\beta = 1 - 0.8038 = 0.1962$

(b) $$Z_{STAT} = \frac{\bar{X}_L - \mu_1}{\frac{\sigma}{\sqrt{n}}} = \frac{6.9342 - 6.8}{\frac{.2}{\sqrt{25}}} = 3.3551$$

$\text{power} = 1 - \beta = P(\bar{X} < \bar{X}_L) = P(Z < 3.3551) = 0.9996$

$\beta = 1 - 0.9996 = 0.0004$

(c) Holding everything else constant, the larger the sample size, the higher the power of the test will be and the lower the probability of committing a Type II error will be.

9.84 $H_0: \mu \geq 25{,}000$ vs. $H_1: \mu < 25{,}000$, $\alpha = 0.01$, $n = 100$, $\sigma = 3500$

Lower critical value: $Z_L = -2.3263$,

$$\bar{X}_L = \mu + Z_L\left(\frac{\sigma}{\sqrt{n}}\right) = 25{,}000 - 2.3263\left(\frac{3{,}500}{\sqrt{100}}\right) = 24{,}185.7786$$

9.84 (a) $$Z_{STAT} = \frac{\bar{X}_L - \mu_1}{\frac{\sigma}{\sqrt{n}}} = \frac{24{,}185.7786 - 24{,}000}{\frac{3500}{\sqrt{100}}} = 0.5308$$

cont. power $= 1-\beta = P(\bar{X} < \bar{X}_L) = P(Z < 0.5308) = 0.7022$

$\beta = 1 - 0.7022 = 0.2978$

(b) $$Z_{STAT} = \frac{\bar{X}_L - \mu_1}{\frac{\sigma}{\sqrt{n}}} = \frac{24{,}185.7786 - 24{,}900}{\frac{3500}{\sqrt{100}}} = -2.0406$$

power $= 1-\beta = P(\bar{X} < \bar{X}_L) = P(Z < -2.0406) = 0.0206$

$\beta = 1 - 0.0206 = 0.9794$

(c) Holding everything else constant, the greater the distance between the true mean and the hypothesized mean, the higher the power of the test will be and the lower the probability of committing a Type II error will be. Holding everything else constant, the smaller the level of significance, the lower the power of the test will be and the higher the probability of committing a Type II error will be.

9.86 $H_0: \mu = 25{,}000$, $H_1: \mu \neq 25{,}000$, $\alpha = 0.05$, $n = 100$, $\sigma = 3500$

Critical values: $Z_L = -1.960$, $Z_U = 1.960$

$$\bar{X}_L = \mu + Z_L\left(\frac{\sigma}{\sqrt{n}}\right) = 25{,}000 - 1.960\left(\frac{3{,}500}{\sqrt{100}}\right) = 24{,}314.0130$$

$$\bar{X}_U = \mu + Z_U\left(\frac{\sigma}{\sqrt{n}}\right) = 25{,}000 + 1.960\left(\frac{3{,}500}{\sqrt{100}}\right) = 25{,}685.9870$$

(a) $\beta = P(\bar{X}_L < \bar{X} < \bar{X}_U) = P(0.8972 < Z < 4.8171) = 0.1848$

power $= 1 - \beta = 1 - 0.1848 = 0.8152$

(b) $\beta = P(\bar{X}_L < \bar{X} < \bar{X}_U) = P(-1.6742 < Z < 2.2457) = 0.9406$

power $= 1 - \beta = 1 - 0.9406 = 0.0594$

(c) A one-tail test is more powerful than a two-tail test, holding everything else constant.

Chapter 11

11.44 (a) $df\,A = c - 1 = 5 - 1 = 4$
(b) $df\,BL = r - 1 = 7 - 1 = 6$
(c) $df\,E = (r - 1)(c - 1) = (7 - 1)(5 - 1) = 24$
(d) $df\,T = rc - 1 = 7 \times 5 - 1 = 34$

11.46 (a)

Source	Df	SS	MS	F
Among groups	4	60	15	4.80
Among blocks	6	75	12.5	4.00
Error	24	75	3.125	
Total	34	210		

For testing the treatment means:
(b) Decision rule: If $F_{STAT} > 2.78$, reject H_0.
Decision: Since $F_{STAT} = 4.80$ is greater than the upper critical bound of 2.78, reject H_0.
For testing the block means:
(c) Decision rule: If $F_{STAT} > 2.51$, reject H_0.
Decision: Since $F_{STAT} = 4.00 > 2.51$, reject H_0. There is enough evidence of a difference due to blocks.

11.48 (a) $df\,A = c - 1 = 3 - 1 = 2$ (b) $df\,BL = r - 1 = 7 - 1 = 6$
(c) $df\,E = (r - 1)(c - 1) = (7 - 1)(3 - 1) = 12$
(d) $df\,T = rc - 1 = 7 \times 3 - 1 = 20$

11.50

Source	df	SS	MS	F
Among groups	4 – 1 = 3	3 x 80 = 240	80	80÷ 15.4286 = 5.185
Among blocks	8 – 1 = 7	540	540 ÷ 7 = 77.1429	5.000
Error	3 x 7 = 21	15.4286 x 21= 324	77.1429 ÷ 5 = 15.4286	
Total	32 – 1 = 31	240 + 540 + 324 = 1104		

11.52 H_0: $\mu_A = \mu_B = \mu_C = \mu_D$ H_1: At least one mean differs.
Decision rule: If $F_{STAT} > 4.718$, reject H_0.

Anova: Two-Factor Without Replication

Source of Variation	SS	df	MS	F	P-value	F crit
Rows	153.2222	8	19.15278	19.06452	1.21E-08	3.362857
Columns	79.63889	3	26.5463	26.42396	8.86E-08	4.718061
Error	24.11111	24	1.00463			
Total	256.9722	35				

Test statistic: $F_{STAT} = 26.42$
Decision: Since $F_{STAT} = 26.42$ is greater than the critical bound 4.718, reject H_0. There is adequate evidence to conclude that there is a difference in the mean summed ratings of the four brands of Colombian coffee.

11.52 From Table E.10, $Q_\alpha = 3.9$. Critical range = $Q_\alpha \sqrt{\frac{MSE}{r}} = 3.9\sqrt{\frac{1.0046}{9}} = 1.303$

cont. Pairs of means that differ at the 0.05 level are marked with * below.

$|\bar{X}_A - \bar{X}_B| = 1.56*$ $|\bar{X}_A - \bar{X}_C| = 0.89$ $|\bar{X}_A - \bar{X}_D| = 2.56*$

$|\bar{X}_B - \bar{X}_C| = 2.45*$ $|\bar{X}_B - \bar{X}_D| = 4.12*$ $|\bar{X}_C - \bar{X}_D| = 1.67*$

Brand B is rated highest with a sample mean rating of 25.56.

11.54 (a) H_0: $\mu_{.1} = \mu_{.2} = \mu_{.3} = \mu_{.4}$

where *1* = Publix, *2* = Winn-Dixie, *3* = Target, *4* = Walmart

H_1: Not all $\mu_{.j}$ are equal where j = 1, 2, 3, 4

Excel Output:

ANOVA

ce of Varic	SS	df	MS	F	P-value	F crit
Rows	157.4235	32	4.919485	18.57225	1.02E-28	1.564048
Columns	2.926748	3	0.975583	3.683061	0.01468	2.699393
Error	25.42883	96	0.264884			
Total	185.7791	131				

$F_{STAT} = 3.6831$. Since p-value = 0.0147 < 0.05, reject H_0. There is evidence of a difference between the mean price of these items at the four supermarkets.

(b) The assumptions needed are: (i) samples are randomly and independently drawn, (ii) populations are normally distributed, (iii) populations have equal variances and (iv) no interaction effect between treatments and blocks.

(c) Excel output for the Tukey procedure:

Tukey-Kramer Multiple Comparisons

Group	Sample Mean	Sample Size
1: Publix	2.685455	33
2: Winn-Dixie	2.803636	33
3: Target	2.553636	33
4: Walmart	2.404242	33

Comparison	Absolute Difference	Std. Error of Difference	Critical Range	Results
Group 1 to Group 2	0.1181818	0.089592278	0.3306	Means are not different
Group 1 to Group 3	0.1318182	0.089592278	0.3306	Means are not different
Group 1 to Group 4	0.2812121	0.089592278	0.3306	Means are not different
Group 2 to Group 3	0.25	0.089592278	0.3306	Means are not different
Group 2 to Group 4	0.3993939	0.089592278	0.3306	Means are different
Group 3 to Group 4	0.1493939	0.089592278	0.3306	Means are not different

Other Data	
Level of significance	0.05
Numerator d.f.	4
Denominator d.f.	96
MSW	0.264884
Q Statistic	3.69

Using $Q_\alpha = 3.69$ for numerator d.f. = 4 and denominator d.f. = 120, the mean price of items at Walmart differs from that of Winn-Dixie at 5% level of significance.

(d) $H_0: \mu_{1.} = \mu_{2.} = \cdots = \mu_{33.}$

H_1: Not all $\mu_{i.}$ are equal where i = 1, 2, …, 33

F_{STAT} =18.5723 and p-value is essentially 0. Reject H_0. There is evidence of a significant block effect in this experiment. The blocking has been advantageous in reducing the experimental error.

11.56 To test at the 0.01 level of significance whether there is any difference in the mean thickness of the wafers for the five positions, you conduct an F test:

H_0: $\mu_1 = \mu_2 = \mu_3 = \mu_4 = \mu_5$ where 1 = position 1, 2 = position 2, 3 = position 18, 4 = position 19, 5 = position 28

H_1: At least one mean is different.

Decision rule: *df*: 4, 116. If $F_{STAT} > 3.4852$, reject H_0.

ANOVA

Source of Variation	*SS*	*df*	*MS*	*F*	*P-value*	*F crit*
Rows	601.5	29	20.74138	5.922219	1.93E-12	1.878497
Columns	1417.733	4	354.4333	101.2002	6.84E-37	3.485212
Error	406.2667	116	3.502299			
Total	2425.5	149				

Test statistic: $F_{STAT} = 101.2$

Decision: Since $F_{STAT} = 101.2$ is greater than the critical bound of 3.4852, reject H_0. There is enough evidence to conclude that the means of the thickness of the wafers are different across the five positions.

To determine which of the means are significantly different from one another, you use the Tukey-Kramer procedure to establish the critical range:

$Q_\alpha = 4.71$

$$\text{critical range} = Q_\alpha\sqrt{\frac{MSE}{r}} = 4.71\sqrt{\frac{3.5023}{30}} = 1.609$$

Pairs of means that differ at the 0.01 level are marked with * below.

$|\bar{X}_1 - \bar{X}_2| = 2.2^*$ $|\bar{X}_1 - \bar{X}_3| = 5.533^*$ $|\bar{X}_1 - \bar{X}_4| = 8.567^*$

$|\bar{X}_1 - \bar{X}_5| = 6.533^*$ $|\bar{X}_2 - \bar{X}_3| = 3.333^*$ $|\bar{X}_2 - \bar{X}_4| = 6.367^*$

$|\bar{X}_2 - \bar{X}_5| = 4.333^*$ $|\bar{X}_3 - \bar{X}_4| = 3.033^*$ $|\bar{X}_3 - \bar{X}_5| = 1$

$|\bar{X}_4 - \bar{X}_5| = 2.033^*$

At 1% level of significance, the *F* test concludes that there are significant differences in the mean thickness of the wafers among the 5 positions. The Tukey-Kramer multiple comparison test reveals that the mean thickness between all the pairs are significantly different with only the exception of the pair between position 18 and position 28.

Chapter 12

12.60 (a) $H_0: \pi_1 = \pi_2$ $H_1: \pi_1 \neq \pi_2$ where 1 = group1, 2 = group2

Decision rule: If $Z_{STAT} < -1.96$ or $Z_{STAT} > 1.96$, reject H_0.

Test statistic: $Z_{STAT} = \frac{B-C}{\sqrt{B+C}} = \frac{25-16}{\sqrt{25+16}} = 1.4056$

Decision: Since $Z_{STAT} = 1.4056$ is between the critical bounds of – 1.96 and the upper critical bound of 1.96, do not reject H_0. There is not enough evidence of a difference between group 1 and group 2.

12.62 (a) $H_0: \pi_1 = \pi_2$ $H_1: \pi_1 \neq \pi_2$ where 1 = prior, 2 = after

Decision rule: If $Z < -2.5758$ or $Z > 2.5758$, reject H_0.

Test statistic: $Z_{STAT} = \frac{B-C}{\sqrt{B+C}} = \frac{21-36}{\sqrt{21+36}} = -1.9868$

Decision: Since $Z_{STAT} = -1.9868$ is in between the two critical bounds, do not reject H_0. There is not enough evidence to conclude there is a difference in the proportion of voters who favored Candidate *A* prior to and after the debate.

(b) *p*-value = 0.0469. The probability of obtaining a sample which gives rise to a test statistic that differs from 0 by – 1.9868 or more in either direction is 0.0469 if there is not a difference in the proportion of voters who favor Candidate *A* prior to and after the debate.

12.64 (a) $H_0: \pi_1 \geq \pi_2$ $H_1: \pi_1 < \pi_2$ where 1 = last year, 2 = now

Decision rule: If $Z_{STAT} < -1.645$, reject H_0.

(a) Test statistic: $Z_{STAT} = \frac{B-C}{\sqrt{B+C}} = \frac{5-20}{\sqrt{5+20}} = -3$

Decision: Since $Z_{STAT} = -3 < -1.645$, reject H_0. There is enough evidence to conclude that satisfaction was lower last year prior to introduction of Six Sigma management.

(b) *p*-value = 0.0014. The probability of obtaining a data set which gives rise to a test statistic smaller than – 3 is 0.0014 if the satisfaction was not lower last year prior to introduction of Six Sigma management.

12.66 (a) For *df* = 25 and $\alpha = 0.01$, $\chi^2_{\alpha/2} = 10.520$ and $\chi^2_{1-\alpha/2} = 46.928$.

(b) For *df* = 16 and $\alpha = 0.05$, $\chi^2_{\alpha/2} = 6.908$ and $\chi^2_{1-\alpha/2} = 28.845$.

(c) For *df* = 13 and $\alpha = 0.10$, $\chi^2_{\alpha/2} = 5.892$ and $\chi^2_{1-\alpha/2} = 22.362$.

12.68 $\chi^2_{STAT} = \frac{(n-1)\cdot S^2}{\sigma^2} = \frac{24\cdot 150^2}{100^2} = 54$

12.70 $df = n - 1 = 16 - 1 = 15$

12.72 (a) If $H_1: \sigma \neq 12$, do not reject H_0 since the test statistic $\chi^2 = 10.417$ falls between the two critical bounds, $\chi^2_{\alpha/2} = 6.262$ and $\chi^2_{1-\alpha/2} = 27.488$.

(b) If $H_1: \sigma < 12$, do not reject H_0 since the test statistic $\chi^2 = 10.417$ is greater than the critical bound 7.261.

12.74 (a) H_0: $\sigma \le 1.2^\circ$F. The standard deviation of the oven temperature has not increased above 1.2°F.

H_1: $\sigma > 1.2^\circ$F. The standard deviation of the oven temperature has increased above 1.2°F.

Decision rule: $df = 29$. If $\chi^2_{STAT} > 42.557$, reject H_0.

Test statistic: $\chi^2_{STAT} = \dfrac{(n-1)\cdot S^2}{\sigma^2} = \dfrac{29 \cdot 2.1^2}{1.2^2} = 88.813$

Decision: Since the test statistic of $\chi^2_{STAT} = 88.813$ is greater than the critical boundary of 42.557, reject H_0. There is sufficient evidence to conclude that the standard deviation of the oven temperature has increased above 1.2°F.

(b) You must assume that the data in the population are normally distributed to be able to use the chi-square test of a population variance or standard deviation.

(c) p-value = 5.53×10^{-8} or 0.00000005. The probability that a sample is obtained whose standard deviation is equal to or larger than 2.1°F when the null hypothesis is true is 5.53×10^{-8}, a very small probability.

Note: The p-value was found using Excel.

12.76 (a) H_0: $\sigma = 12$.

H_1: $\sigma \neq 12$.

Decision rule: $df = 14$. If $\chi^2_{STAT} < 6.571$ or $\chi^2_{STAT} > 23.685$, reject H_0.

Test statistic: $\chi^2_{STAT} = \dfrac{(n-1)\cdot S^2}{\sigma^2} = \dfrac{14 \cdot 9.25^2}{12^2} = 8.319$

Decision: Since the test statistic of $\chi^2_{STAT} = 8.319$ is between the critical boundaries of 6.571 and 23.685, do not reject H_0. There is insufficient evidence that the population standard deviation is different from 12.

(b) You must assume that the data in the population are normally distributed to be able to use the chi-square test of a population variance or standard deviation.

(c) p-value = 2(1 – 0.8721) = 0.2558. The probability of obtaining a test statistic equal to or more extreme than the result obtained from this sample data is 0.2558 if the standard deviation is 12.

Note: Excel returns an upper-tail area of 0.8721 for $\chi^2_{STAT} = 8.319$. But since the sample standard deviation is smaller than the hypothesized value, the amount of area in the lower tail is (1 – 0.8721). That value is doubled to accommodate the two-tail hypotheses.

Chapter 16

16.66 (a) 2013 as the base year:

$$I_{2013} = \frac{P_{2013}}{P_{2013}}(100) = \frac{\$5}{\$5}(100) = 100$$

$$I_{2014} = \frac{P_{2014}}{P_{2013}}(100) = \frac{\$8}{\$5}(100) = 160$$

$$I_{2015} = \frac{P_{2015}}{P_{2013}}(100) = \frac{\$7}{\$5}(100) = 140$$

(b) 2014 as the base year:

$$I_{2013} = \frac{P_{2013}}{P_{2014}}(100) = \frac{\$5}{\$8}(100) = 62.5$$

$$I_{2014} = \frac{P_{2014}}{P_{2014}}(100) = \frac{\$8}{\$8}(100) = 100$$

$$I_{2015} = \frac{P_{2015}}{P_{2014}}(100) = \frac{\$7}{\$8}(100) = 87.5$$

16.68 (a),(b)

Year	DJIA	Price Index (base = 1979)	Price Index (base = 2000)
1979	838.7	100	7.77437894
1980	964.0	114.9397878	8.935854653
1981	875.0	104.3281269	8.110863923
1982	1046.5	124.7764397	9.700593252
1983	1258.6	150.0655777	11.66666667
1984	1211.6	144.4616669	11.2309974
1985	1546.7	184.4163587	14.33722655
1986	1896.0	226.0641469	17.57508343
1987	1938.8	231.1672827	17.97182054
1988	2168.6	258.5668296	20.10196515
1989	2753.2	328.2699416	25.5209492
1990	2633.7	314.0217003	24.41323693
1991	3168.8	377.822821	29.37337783
1992	3301.1	393.5972338	30.59974045
1993	3754.1	447.6093955	34.79885057
1994	3834.4	457.1837367	35.54319614
1995	5117.1	610.1228091	47.43325918
1996	6448.3	768.8446405	59.77289581
1997	7908.3	942.9235722	73.30645161
1998	9181.4	1094.718016	85.10752688
1999	11497.1	1370.823894	106.5730441
2000	10788.0	1286.27638	100
2001	10021.5	1194.884941	92.8948832
2002	8341.6	994.5868606	77.32295143
2003	10453.9	1246.44092	96.90304042
2004	10788.0	1286.27638	100
2005	10717.5	1277.870514	99.34649611
2006	12463.2	1486.014069	115.5283648
2007	13264.8	1581.590557	122.9588432
2008	8772.3	1045.934184	81.31488691
2009	10430.7	1243.673542	96.68789396
2010	11577.4	1380.398235	107.3173897
2011	12221.2	1457.15989	113.2851316
2012	13104.1	1562.429951	121.4692251
2013	16576.5	1976.451651	153.6568409
2014	17823.1	2125.086443	165.2122729

(c) The price index using 2000 as the base year is more useful because it is closer to the present and the DJIA has grown more than 1500% over the period.

16.70 (a), (c)

Year	Price	Price Index (base = 1980)	Price Index (base = 1990)
1980	0.70	100	40.51873199
1981	0.79	112.6600284	45.64841499
1982	0.76	108.5348506	43.97694524
1983	0.73	103.2716927	41.8443804
1984	0.85	121.4793741	49.22190202
1985	0.70	99.14651494	40.17291066
1986	1.10	157.0412518	63.63112392
1987	0.94	134.1394026	54.35158501
1988	0.87	123.8975818	50.20172911
1989	0.80	113.371266	45.93659942
1990	1.74	246.799431	100
1991	0.91	129.7297297	52.5648415
1992	0.94	133.14367	53.9481268
1993	1.14	162.3044097	65.76368876
1994	1.60	228.1650071	92.44956772
1995	1.32	188.1934566	76.25360231
1996	1.10	156.8990043	63.57348703
1997	1.21	172.5462304	69.91354467
1998	1.45	206.5433855	83.68876081
1999	1.90	270.8392603	109.740634
2000	1.44	205.2631579	83.17002882
2001	1.41	201.1379801	81.49855908
2002	1.45	206.401138	83.63112392
2003	1.71	243.3854908	98.6167147
2004	1.47	209.3883357	84.84149856
2005	1.66	236.1308677	95.67723343
2006	2.16	307.5391181	124.610951
2007	1.65	234.2816501	94.92795389
2008	1.73	246.6571835	99.94236311
2009	1.96	278.9473684	113.0259366
2010	1.59	226.3157895	91.70028818
2011	1.53	217.7809388	88.24207493
2012	1.60	228.1650071	92.44956772
2013	1.73	246.0881935	99.71181556
2014	2.19	311.5220484	126.2247839

(b) The average price per pound of fresh tomatoes in 2014 in the U.S. is 311.52% higher than it was in 1980.

(d) The average price per pound of fresh tomatoes in 2014 in the U.S. is 26.22% higher than it was in 1990.

16.70 (e)
cont.

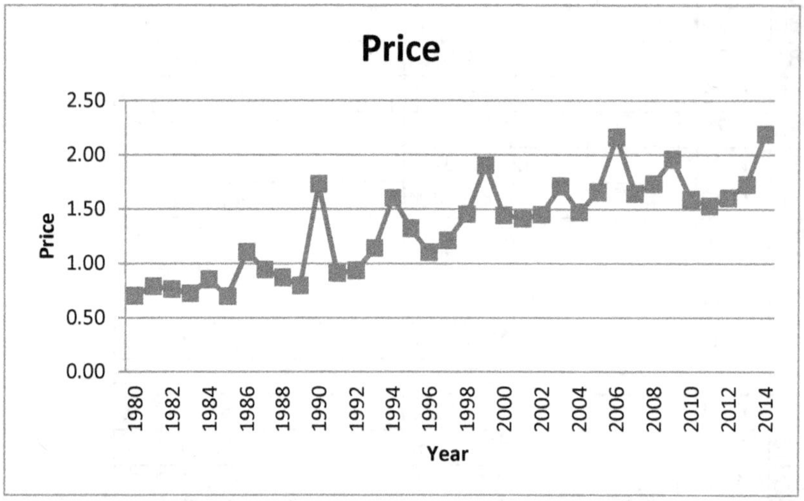

There is an upward trend in the cost of fresh tomatoes from 1980 to 2014 with a prominent cyclical component.

www.ingramcontent.com/pod-product-compliance
Lightning Source LLC
LaVergne TN
LVHW080010210926
848481LV00011B/2983
* 9 7 8 0 1 3 5 9 7 0 0 2 7 *